Amsterdam

THE ROUGH GUIDE

There are more than one hundred Rough Guide titles
covering destinations from Amsterdam to Zimbabwe

Forthcoming titles include
Bangkok • Barbados • Edinburgh
Japan • Jordan • Syria

Rough Guide Reference Series
Classical Music • European Football • The Internet • Jazz • Opera
Reggae • Rock Music • World Music

Rough Guide Phrasebooks
Czech • French • German • Greek • Hindi & Urdu • Indonesian • Italian
Mandarin Chinese • Mexican Spanish • Polish • Portuguese • Russian
Spanish • Thai • Turkish • Vietnamese

Rough Guides on the Internet
http://www.roughguides.com
http://www.hotwired.com/rough

Rough Guide Credits

Editor:	Kate Berens
Series Editor:	Mark Ellingham
Editorial:	Martin Dunford, Jonathan Buckley, Samantha Cook, Jo Mead, Amanda Tomlin, Ann-Marie Shaw, Paul Gray, Sarah Dallas, Chris Schüler, Julia Kelly, Helena Smith, Caroline Osborne, Kieran Falconer, Judith Bamber, Olivia Eccleshall (UK); Andrew Rosenberg (US)
Online Editors:	Alan Spicer (UK); Geronimo Madrid (US)
Production:	Susanne Hillen, Andy Hilliard, Judy Pang, Link Hall, Nicola Williamson, Helen Ostick
Cartography:	Melissa Flack, David Callier, Maxine Burke
Finance:	John Fisher, Celia Crowley, Catherine Gillespie
Marketing & Publicity:	Richard Trillo, Simon Carloss, Niki Smith (UK); Jean-Marie Kelly, SoRelle Braun (US)
Administration:	Tania Hummel, Alexander Mark Rogers

Acknowledgements

Many thanks for help with this edition to Ann Carmody, Malijn Maat, Mariska Majoor and the PIC, Petra van Arum at the Amsterdam VVV and the Netherlands Board of Tourism (Els Wamsteeker in Amsterdam and Madeleine Tuinstra-Ralston in London); Alison Cowan for getting the project underway; Jane Bainbridge for proofreading; Stratigraphics for mapping; most of all, though, to Kate Berens for her enthusiasm and her skilful editing and Matthew Teller for writing and researarch beyond the call of duty.

The publishers and authors have done their best to ensure the accuracy and currency of all information in *The Rough Guide to Amsterdam*; however, they can accept no responsibility for any loss, injury, or inconvenience sustained by any traveller as a result of information or advice contained in the guide.

This fifth edition published April 1997, reprinted November 1997 by Rough Guides Ltd, 1 Mercer Street, London WC2H 9QJ.
Distributed by the Penguin Group:
Penguin Books Ltd, 27 Wrights Lane, London W8 5TZ.
Penguin Books USA Inc, 375 Hudson Street, New York 10014, USA.
Penguin Books Australia Ltd, 487 Maroondah Highway, PO Box 257, Ringwood, Victoria 3134, Australia.
Penguin Books Canada Ltd, 10 Alcorn Avenue, Toronto, Ontario, Canada M4V 1E4.
Penguin Books (NZ) Ltd, 182–190 Wairau Road, Auckland 10, New Zealand.

Printed in England by Clays Ltd, St Ives PLC.
Typography and **original design** by Jonathan Dear and The Crowd Roars.
Illustrations throughout by Edward Briant.

A catalogue record for this book is available from the British Library.
ISBN 1-85828-218-7

Amsterdam

THE ROUGH GUIDE

Written and researched by
Martin Dunford and Jack Holland

With additional accounts and research by
Matthew Teller

THE ROUGH GUIDES

Help us update

We've gone to a lot of trouble to ensure that this fifth edition of the *Rough Guide to Amsterdam* is accurate and up-to-date. However, things inevitably change, and if you feel we've got it wrong or left something out, we'd like to know: any suggestions, comments or corrections would be much appreciated. We'll credit all contributions and send a copy of the next edition – or any other *Rough Guide* if you prefer – for the best correspondence.

Please mark letters "Rough Guide to Amsterdam" and send to:
Rough Guides, 1 Mercer St, London WC2H 9QJ or
Rough Guides, 375 Hudson St, 9th floor, New York, NY 10014.

E-mail should be sent to:
amsterdam@roughtravl.co.uk

Online updates about Rough Guide titles can be found on our website at http://www.roughguides.com/

Readers thanks

We'd like to thank all the readers who wrote in with comments and updates to the previous edition: Mr S.J. Harmsworth, Roberta Gregory, Chrystalla Philalithes, Mrs S.A. Frackiewicz, Ms Joanna C. Huxley, Laura Edwards, Stuart & Lynne Stagg, Jayne Scotney, Ann Peskett, A. Mahmood, Graham Perkins, Marc Wilson, Paul & Siobhan Harrison, Cathy Leeney, Kate Bull, Mary Byrne, Chris Keane, V.S. Howell, Mark Englebert, Ellen Grande, Leanda Morrison, Amy & Ross Bannatyne, Claire Goodenough, R.Brock, Krish Sakhamuru, Steve McMullen, Mrs Susan Evans, W.T. Blunt, Susan Gregory, Ms Carolyn Bray, Leland R. Sisk, Ms K.E. Peel, Brian Espiner, Tim Noble, Adrian Lewis, Sue & Colin Smith, Alan McCormick, Miss Susanna Hardy, Zora O'Neill, D.J. Greenslade, Paul Hubers, Catherine Crawford-O'Neill, Sheila Ryall, Elaine Forrest, Hazel McCall, I.F.M. Walker, David Menzies, Adrian Gosbell, Keren Bellringer-Jones, Peter Schouten, Mrs Jayne Townsend, Catherine Ford, A. Gunn, Neil & Ian Wright, Angela Morton, Clare Havard, Simon Skerritt, Anna M. Rasmussen, Mark West, Rachel Thompson, Gordon Elliot & Brian Gibbs, E.G. Moloney.

Rough Guides

Travel Guides • Phrasebooks • Music and Reference Guides

We set out to do something different when the first Rough Guide was published in 1982. Mark Ellingham, just out of University, was travelling in Greece. He brought along the popular guides of the day, but found they were all lacking in some way. They were either strong on ruins and museums but went on for pages without mentioning a beach or taverna. Or they were so conscious of the need to save money that they lost sight of Greece's cultural and historical significance. Also, none of the books told him anything about Greece's contemporary life – its politics, its culture, its people, and how they lived.

So with no job in prospect, Mark decided to write his own guidebook, one which aimed to provide practical information that was second to none, detailing the best beaches and the hottest clubs and restaurants, while also giving hard hitting accounts of every sight, both famous and obscure, and providing up-to-the-minute information on contemporary culture. It was a guide that encouraged independent travellers to find the best of Greece, and was a great success, getting shortlisted for the Thomas Cook travel guide award, and encouraging Mark, along with three friends, to expand the series.

The Rough Guide list grew rapidly and the letters flooded in, indicating a much broader readership than had been anticipated, but one which uniformly appreciated the Rough Guides' mix of practical detail and humour, irreverence and enthusiasm. Things haven't changed. The same four friends who began the series are still the caretakers of the Rough Guide mission today: to provide the most reliable, up-to-date and entertaining information to independent-minded travellers of all ages, on all budgets.

We now publish 100 titles and have offices in London and New York. The travel guides are written and researched by a dedicated team of more than 100 authors, based in Britain, Europe, the USA and Australia. We have also created a unique series of phrasebooks to accompany the travel series, along with the acclaimed series of music guides, and a best-selling pocket guide to the Internet and World Wide Web. We also publish comprehensive travel information on our two websites: http://www.hotwired.com/rough and http://www.roughguides.com/

The Authors

Martin Dunford and **Jack Holland** first met at the University of Kent at Canterbury. Following jobs as diverse as insurance collection, beer-barrel rolling and EFL teaching in Greece they co-founded the Rough Guides in the mid-1980s. After co-authoring several other titles, Martin is now editorial director of Rough Guides while Jack recently escaped from Berlin, where he lived for four years.

Contents

List of Maps

MAP SYMBOLS

——	Road	*(i)*	Tourist office
	Waterway	⊠	Post office
—•—	Railway	➕	Church
- - - -	Chapter division boundary	✡	Synagogue
—••—	International Boundary	†₊†	Cemetery
✈	Airport	▨	Park

Introduction

Amsterdam is a compact, instantly likeable capital. It's appealing to look at and pleasant to walk around, an intriguing mix of the parochial and the international; it also has a welcoming attitude towards visitors and a uniquely youthful orientation, shaped by the liberal counterculture of the last three decades. It's hard not to feel drawn in by the buzz of open-air summer events, by the intimacy of the clubs and bars, or by the Dutch facility with languages: just about everyone you meet in Amsterdam will be able to speak near-perfect English, on top of their own native Dutch and fluent German and French.

The city's layout is determined by a web of **canals** radiating out from a historical core to loop right around the centre: these planned, seventeenth-century extensions to the medieval town make for a uniquely elegant urban environment, with tall, gabled houses reflected in their still, green water. With its tree-lined canals, cobbled streets, tinkling bicycle bells and stately architecture, Amsterdam is a world away from the traffic and noise of other European city centres – clean, modern and quiet, while still retaining a perfectly preserved 400-year-old centre.

The conventional sights are for the most part low-key – the **Anne Frank House** being a notable exception – but, thanks to an active and continuing government policy of supporting the arts, Amsterdam has developed a world-class group of museums and galleries. The **Van Gogh Museum** is, for many people, reason enough to visit the city; add to it the **Rijksmuseum**, with its collections of medieval and seventeenth-century Dutch paintings, the contemporary and experimental **Stedelijk Museum**, and hundreds of smaller galleries, and the quality and range of art on display is evident.

However, it's Amsterdam's **population and politics** that constitute its most enduring characteristics. Notorious during the 1960s and 1970s for its radical permissiveness, the city mellowed only marginally during the 1980s, and, despite the inevitable gentrification of the last decade, it retains a laid-back feel. It is, however, far from being as cosmopolitan a city as London or Paris: despite the huge

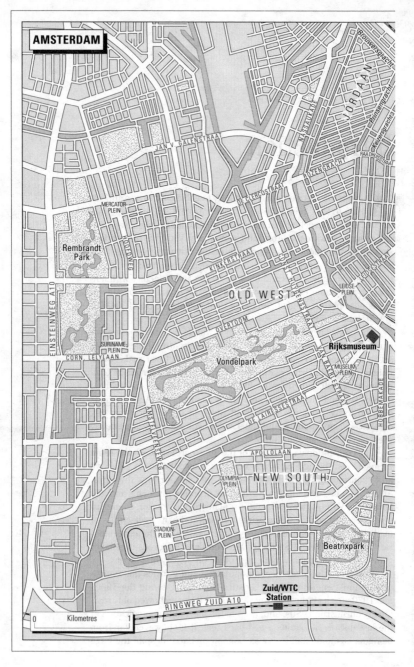

AMSTERDAM

JORDAN

Brouwersgracht

Prinsengracht

Keizersgracht

RAADH VESSTRAAT

NASSAUKADE

ROZENGRACHT

JAN V. GALENSTRAAT

DE CLERCQSTRAAT

MERCATOR-
PLEIN

Rembrandt
Park

HOOFDWEG

KINKERSTRAAT

LEIDSE-
PLEIN

OLD WEST

HUGO DE GROOTSTRAAT

OVERTOOM

EINSTEINWEG A10

SURINAME-
PLEIN

CORN. LELYLAAN

Vondelpark

Rijksmuseum

MUSEUM-
PLEIN

DE LAIRESSESTRAAT

HOBBEMAKADE

VAN BAERLESTRAAT

APOLLOLAAN

AMSTELVEENSEWEG

OLYMPIA-
PLEIN

NEW SOUTH

STADION-
PLEIN

Beatrixpark

Zuid/WTC
Station

RINGWEG ZUID A10

0   Kilometres   1

A MAP OF AMSTERDAM

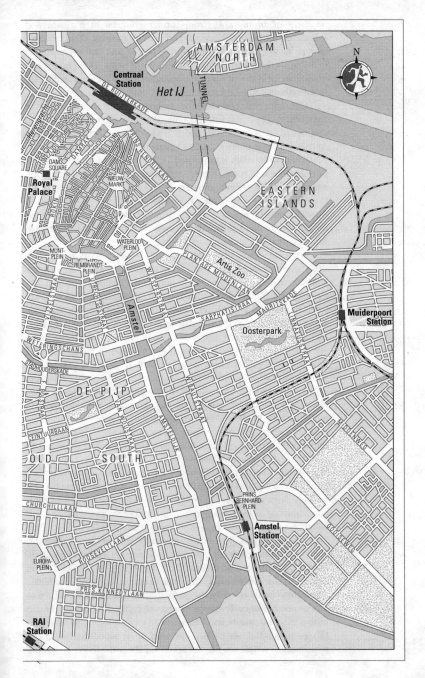

A MAP OF AMSTERDAM

numbers of **immigrants** from former colonies in Surinam and Indonesia, as well as Morocco and Turkey (among other places), almost all live and work outside the centre and can seem almost invisible to the casual visitor. Indeed there is an ethnic and social homogeneity in the city-centre population that seems to run counter to everything you might have heard of Dutch integration.

This apparent contradiction embodies much of the spirit of Amsterdam. The city is world famous as a place where the possession and sale of cannabis are effectively legal – and yet, for the most part, Amsterdammers themselves can't really be bothered with the stuff. And while Amsterdam is renowned for its tolerance towards all styles of behaviour and dress, a more prim, correct-thinking capital city, with a more mainstream dress sense, would be hard to find. Behind the cosy cafés and dreamy canals lurks the suspicion that Amsterdammers' hearts lie squarely in their wallets. And while new-comers might see the city as a haven of liberalism and tolerance, Amsterdammers can seem just as indifferent to this as well.

In recent years, increasingly hard-line city mayors have taken this conservatism on board and seem to have embarked on a gener-ally successful – if unspoken – policy of quashing Amsterdam's image as a counterculture icon and depicting it instead as a centre for business and international high finance. Most of the inner-city squats – which once defined Amsterdam's people-power for locals and visitors alike – are now either empty or legalized. Coffeeshops are now forced to choose between selling dope or alcohol, and, if only for economic reasons, many are switching to the latter. Such shifts in attitude, combined with alterations to the city's landscape, in the form of large-scale urban development projects on the out-skirts and an almost continuous modernization of buildings and infrastructure in the historic centre, together generate an unmis-takeable feeling that Amsterdam and its people are busy reinventing themselves, writing off their hippyish adventures and returning to earlier, more respectable days.

Perhaps mercifully, this hasn't happened yet, and Amsterdam remains a casual and intimate place, modern and innovative yet com-fortably familiar. Amsterdammers themselves make much of their city and its attractions being *gezellig*, a rather overused Dutch word roughly corresponding to a combination of "cosy", "lived-in" and "warmly convivial". The city's unparalleled selection of *gezellig* drinking places is a delight, whether you choose a traditional, bare-floored **brown café** or one of the many designer bars or "grand cafés". Amsterdam's unique approach to combating hard-drug abuse – embodied in the effective decriminalization of cannabis – has led to a large number of **coffeeshops**, which sell coffee only as a sideline to high-quality marijuana and hashish. The city's wide range of **enter-tainment** possibilities means you need never wonder what to do: **multimedia complexes** like the *Melkweg* are at the forefront of contemporary European film, dance, drama and music, while dozens of other venues present **live music** from all genres (the Dutch have a particular soft spot for jazz), and, resident in the world-famous Concertgebouw concert hall, Amsterdam has one of the world's leading classical **orchestras**. The **club** scene, on the other hand, is subdued by the standards of other capital cities, dominated by more or less mainstream house music, and with the emphasis far more on dancing than on posing. **Gay** men, however, will discover that Amsterdam has Europe's most active nightlife network, although women might be disappointed at the exclusivity of the proclaimed "Gay Capital of Europe".

Though it's by no means a cheap city, careful **spending** can make a visit to Amsterdam possible on the tightest of budgets. Overall, reckon on getting by on £20 ($31) a day as an absolute minimum; if you want to actually enjoy yourself, and sleep in a hotel, £45 ($70) a day is a more realistic figure; £75 ($115) a day would allow you to live in some style. See "Banks, Money and Costs" in *Basics* for a full rundown on Amsterdam expenses.

When to go

Whether you're coming for canals and architecture, or sex and drugs, Amsterdam is a delight at any time of year. In high **summer**, the city parks are packed and every pavement, doorway and stretch of canalside becomes a choice spot for lazy hanging-out. **Spring** and **autumn** are particularly beautiful, with mist hanging over the canals until late morning and low sunlight piercing through the cloud cover. The flatness of the surrounding countryside means that the weather is always changeable, and it's common at any time of year for heavy morning clouds to be blown away to reveal a sunny afternoon. It's never too hot, though, and, save for **January** and **February**, when icy winds blow off the canals, the weather is never so relentlessly miserable as to ruin a visit – the persistent winter rain can give the city a romantic cast, with wet cobbles glistening under the street-lights and the canals rippled by falling raindrops. But whatever the time of year, you should bear two things in mind: firstly, there are plenty of remarkably hardy mosquitoes living on the canals, at their friskiest in the hot summer evenings, although still a nuisance as late as October; and secondly, the few square kilometres of central Amsterdam comprise one of the most densely populated urban areas in the world – space is at a premium, and you should *always* book accommodation before leaving home.

Getting out of Amsterdam

Finally, don't fall into the trap of thinking that there's nothing to the Netherlands beyond Amsterdam. Although Amsterdam utterly disproves the theory that a capital city is a microcosm of the nation, there is plenty to see and do outside the city. In spring and early summer the famous **bulbfields** are in full bloom, and the **Randstad cities** to the south of Amsterdam, such as Haarlem, Leiden and Utrecht, are worth a visit at any time of the year, not to mention the **harbourside towns** of Hoorn and Enkhuizen to the north. Although there isn't much wild nature to be found in the Netherlands, there is some pleasant hiking to be had in the dunes to the northwest of Amsterdam, and there are popular **beach resorts** and deserted little spots all the way up the coast from Scheveningen to Camperduin. Just about everywhere can be reached quickly and painlessly by public transport – for full details see Part Four, "Out of the City".

Average Maximum Temperatures

	Jan	Feb	Mar	April	May	June	July	Aug	Sept	Oct	Nov	Dec
Min °C	-0.2	-0.5	1.5	3.8	7.5	10.5	12.5	12.5	10.5	7.3	3.8	1.1
Min °F	32	31	35	39	46	51	55	55	51	45	39	34
Max °C	4.3	4.9	8.1	11.6	16.0	19.1	20.5	20.5	18.3	14.0	8.8	5.7
Max °F	40	41	47	53	61	66	69	69	65	57	48	42

The Basics

Getting There from Britain

There are many ways to reach Amsterdam, but it basically comes down to deciding between a low-cost but time-consuming bus or train and ferry journey, and a swift but more expensive flight; travelling by train through the Channel Tunnel is an attractive alternative, little cheaper than a flight, but taking you directly from city centre to city centre. Whichever method you opt for, you'll find a variety of competitive fares.

By Air

The flight to **Amsterdam Schiphol** (*skip-oll*) from London takes just 45 minutes – representing a huge saving in time compared with the ferries. The large number of flights to Schiphol has led to a mass of cheap tickets, and it's reasonably

easy to find a return fare from London for £90–130. To find the best bargains, study the ads in the weekend travel sections of the quality newspapers, or, if you live in London, the back pages of the listings magazine *Time Out* or the *Evening Standard*. Alternatively, contact a **discount flight agent** such as *STA Travel, Campus Travel, Council Travel* or *Trailfinders* (see below), who specialize in youth flights and, if you're under 26 (or a student under 32), can offer substantial savings; they also sell ordinary discounted tickets to non-students.

Approaching the airlines direct, the **smaller operators**, such as *British Midland, Air UK* and *Transavia*, can sometimes work out cheaper, but it's also worth trying the **national airlines** – *British Airways* and *KLM*. The best deal you'll get with a scheduled airline is an APEX (Advance Purchase Excursion) or Super Pex return ticket: these cost around £120 (a little more if you travel at the weekend) and usually have to be booked fourteen days in advance; you have to spend one Saturday night abroad, and can't make any changes to the flight. To gain more flexibility you'll need to buy a standard return, which is likely to prove more expensive.

You could alternatively try one of the **long-haul airlines**, some of which make a short London–Amsterdam hop on their way to more distant destinations. For example, among the many long-haul carriers with representation in

---

Airlines and Routes

Air UK ☎ 0345/666777
London (City and Stansted), Aberdeen, Edinburgh, Glasgow, Humberside, Leeds/Bradford, Manchester, Newcastle, Norwich and Teesside to Schiphol.

British Airways ☎ 0345/222111
London (Gatwick and Heathrow), Birmingham and Manchester to Schiphol.

British Midland ☎ 0345/554554
London (Heathrow) and East Midlands to Schiphol.

KLM ☎ 0181/750 9000
London (Heathrow), Birmingham, Bristol, Cardiff, Guernsey, Jersey and Southampton to Schiphol.

Suckling Airways ☎ 01223/293393
Cambridge, Luton and Manchester to Schiphol.

Transavia ☎ 01293/538181
London (Gatwick) to Schiphol.

Discount Flight Agents

Alpha Flights ☎ 0171/579 8444	**Nouvelles Frontières** ☎ 0171/629 7772

APA Travel
☎ 0171/387 5337

STA Travel

London	☎ 0171/361 6161
Bristol	☎ 0117/929 4399
Cambridge	☎ 01223/366966
Manchester	☎ 0161/834 0668
Leeds	☎ 0113/244 9212
Oxford	☎ 01865/792800

Plus other branches nationwide.

Campus Travel

London	☎ 0171/730 3402
Birmingham	☎ 0121/414 1848
Brighton	☎ 01273/570226
Bristol	☎ 0117/929 2494
Cambridge	☎ 01223/324283
Edinburgh	☎ 0131/668 3303
Manchester	☎ 0161/833 2046
Oxford	☎ 01865/242067

Plus other branches on university campuses.

Trailfinders

London	☎ 0171/937 5400
Birmingham	☎ 0121/236 1234
Bristol	☎ 0117/929 9000
Glasgow	☎ 0141/353 2224
Manchester	☎ 0161/839 6969

Council Travel
☎ 0171/287 3337

Travel Bug
☎ 0161/721 4000

Destination Group
☎ 0171/253 9000

Travel Cuts
☎ 0171/255 1944

Masterfare
☎ 0171/259 2000

Union Travel
☎ 0171/493 4343

both Amsterdam and London, *Air Lanka* currently flies twice a week between Heathrow and Schiphol before heading on to Sri Lanka. Be prepared for a greater likelihood of delays, and a limited choice of when to fly, but on the plus side some of these fares have no maximum stay and allow free date-changes. A good travel agent should be able to tailor a fare to suit you.

For those wanting to reach Amsterdam from central London with the minimum of hassle, *Air UK* run a regular service between **London City Airport** and Schiphol. There are three flights daily during the week, plus a morning flight on Saturday and one on Sunday evening. Fares start at around £90 for midweek departures that include at least one Saturday night away, but special offers can bring return fares down as low as £59 – check with the airline and with flight agents. Check-in time at London City has been cut to a minimum (10min before departure) and tickets can be collected at the check-in desk. Shuttle buses for the airport leave every 20min from Liverpool Street Station (Bus Stand A; £4; 30min) and every 15min from Canary Wharf Station (North Colonnade; £2; 10min).

There are plenty of flights to Amsterdam direct from various **UK regional airports**, which can turn out to be very good value, particularly if you use the smaller operators (see box). As a broad guide, APEX fares work out at £130–185, depending on where you travel from. If there are no direct flights from an airport near you, changing planes (most often in London) is relatively easy, and often no more expensive than flying nonstop. Carriers such as *Air UK* and *British Midland* have a wide network of domestic routes to connect with flights to Schiphol, and most discount flight agents can devise specific routings from almost any airport in the UK. It's also worth considering a **package deal** if you don't mind having your accommodation organized beforehand; these can be surprisingly good value (see pp9–10 for more details).

By Train

All international trains arrive in Amsterdam at Centraal Station. *International Rail* (formerly *British Rail International*) acts as an agent for the combined **boat-train services** of *South Eastern International* and *Anglia International* between

London and Amsterdam; it also sells its own InterRail and Euro Domino ("Freedom") rail passes, which offer greater flexibility. However, **Eurostar**'s passenger services through the **Channel Tunnel** to Amsterdam (via Brussels) have cut boat-train travelling times in half, and, unless you're on the tightest of budgets, the good night's sleep you'll gain is worth the extra spent on a Eurostar ticket. Beware, though, that if you need a visa to visit France, you'll have to get one in order to use the Eurostar service.

Eurostar: the Channel Tunnel route

Eurostar's rapid passenger service from **London Waterloo** through the Channel Tunnel can cut journey times down to a manageable 6hr 30min, but the closest trains get to Amsterdam is Brussels Midi station (Brussel-Zuid in Dutch); you must change trains there for the last leg to Amsterdam. Currently Eurostar are running seven trains a day from Monday to Saturday, with five on Sunday, though there are no overnight services; the most convenient departures are the 10.30am and 12.30pm, which get you to Amsterdam by 6pm and 8pm respectively. Travel is simple: you check in twenty minutes before departure, passports are checked on the train, and in Brussels you disembark with no further complications; the onward connection to Amsterdam entails about half an hour's wait. If you're coming from the **south of England,** you don't necessarily have to go into London, since many Eurostar trains stop at Ashford International station; Ashford has easy access from the motorway network with parking space for 11,000 cars in and around the station.

There is a range of **fares** on Eurostar, offering varying degrees of flexibility, although none is valid for more than three months. The standard adult return fare from London to any station in the Netherlands is £105, bookable fourteen days in advance with no date changes permitted; the "leisure return" fare of £135 must include either a Saturday or three other nights away, and does allow date changes; there is also a fully flexible £165 fare, plus business and first-class options. **Under-26s** pay a flat £77 return, but this fare has a number of restrictions. One-way tickets are available only to under-26s and cost £38.50. However, all these fares can be significantly reduced by Eurostar's frequent **special offers** – call them for details, and also call Trailfinders,

who offer a return on Eurostar from London to Brussels for a remarkable £59. Eurostar is planning to start a night-sleeper service direct from London to Amsterdam, though at the time of writing the service had not materialized.

Proposed services on Eurostar through from **Scotland** and the **north of England** direct to Paris and Brussels (bypassing London) have also been postponed, and are planned to begin late in 1997. Until then, Eurostar are subsidizing two link-trains, one from **Glasgow** along the East Coast Line (via Edinburgh, Newcastle and York), the other from **Manchester** (via Birmingham), both of which arrive at London Waterloo to connect with onward services to Paris and Brussels. The first departs Glasgow daily at 6.55am, which should get you to Amsterdam by 10.06pm. The second departs Manchester Piccadilly daily at 7.37am, aiming to get you to Amsterdam by 8.08pm. Eurostar's **subsidies** on these two services mean that fares are drastically reduced: as an example, if you book a ticket through from Edinburgh to Amsterdam (currently £125 APEX return for the 14-hr journey), the Edinburgh–London leg costs just £20 return. Contact any travel agent, or Eurostar direct, for full details of these tickets and of any special promotions.

Boat-train routes

There are two routes used by the boat-trains to get to Amsterdam. From **London Liverpool Street** there are two daily departures via **Harwich** and the **Hook of Holland** to Amsterdam, one of them overnight, with a total journey time of eleven hours; fares are £69 for an ordinary return valid for two months, £55 for a one-way ticket. There is also an APEX one-month return fare costing £49, which has to be booked fourteen days in advance.

Alternatively, there are four daily departures from **London Victoria** via **Ramsgate** and **Oostende** in Belgium: two morning trains connect with both the ferry and the faster jetfoil, the afternoon service is via jetfoil only, and the overnight train uses the ferry. **Fares** are £75 for a two-month return, £49 one-way. Five-day excursion tickets cost £63. The jetfoil costs an extra £4.50 each way but knocks four hours off the journey time (13hr by ferry, 9hr by jetfoil).

Travelling at night on either route, you should add on the price of (obligatory) accommodation on the ferry – a minimum of £6 for a reclining seat, £9 upwards for a berth in a cabin. Tickets for either boat-train service can be bought from any large train station, many high street travel agents, or direct from *International Rail*. Bear in mind that all these tickets allow the option of stopping off en route as many times as you wish, and that you can travel out by one route and back by the other.

For those **under 26**, fares can be cut by way of *BIJ* youth tickets, which currently cost £64 return on the Harwich–Hook route, or £62 via Ramsgate–Oostende – though special APEX offers can undercut even these prices. *Campus Travel's Eurotrain* tickets can be cheaper still, and check also for deals with *Wasteels*.

Rail passes

If Amsterdam is only part of your travel plans, and you plan to go further afield in the Benelux countries or beyond, there are a number of different **rail passes** available.

For those **under 26** (and resident in Europe for six months) the **InterRail** pass works on a zonal basis: the Netherlands falls into Zone E (along with France, Belgium and Luxembourg). A pass to travel in this zone for 15 days currently costs £185, and can be bought from *International Rail*, larger train stations or student/youth travel agents. *InterRail* passes also give discounts on certain ferry routes and on *Eurostar's* service to Paris and Brussels; check for specific details. Those **over 26** are poorly served by *InterRail* passes, as the over-26 version cost £215 for fifteen days' travel, or £275 for a month, but is not valid for travel in France, Belgium, Switzerland, Italy, Spain, Portugal or Morocco. Stringing together combinations of *Euro Domino* passes (see below) is a better option.

A convenient alternative to *InterRail* is the **Euro Domino** pass (also called the "Freedom" pass), which is valid for unlimited travel within a single country, though you can buy several to run concurrently in different countries. There is no residence requirement for these tickets (very useful for non-EU visitors), and also no age restrictions, and they are remarkably good value. *Euro Dominos* are valid for either three, five or ten days' travel within an overall period of one month, and prices for Holland are, for under-26s, £29, £49 and £79; for over-26s £39, £69 and £109. The Netherlands is also unique in having a **Euro Domino Plus** pass, which covers travel on any form of public transport in the country (trains, buses, trams and the metro) for the same time periods. Prices are slightly higher, but if Amsterdam is only one of your destinations in the country, they can be extremely good value: under-26s pay £39, £59 or £99; over-26s pay £49, £79 or £129. As a guide, combining two *Euro Dominos* into a month-long pass giving ten days on all Dutch public transport and five days on Belgian trains costs £138 for under-26s, £188 for over-26s. Although you can't use an *InterRail* ticket for travel in the country in which you bought it, you *can* buy a *Euro Domino* ticket for Holland after you've arrived (you just need to show your passport); Dutch prices are even slightly lower than British ones.

Train Information

International Rail
Platform 2, Victoria Station ☎0171/834 2345

Eurostar
☎0345/881881

Campus Travel
52 Grosvenor Gardens,
London SW1W 0AG ☎0171/730 3402
Main London office; their under-26 discounted *Eurotrain* tickets can only be bought in person.

Holland Rail
Chase House
Gilbert St
Ropley
Hants SO24 0BY
☎01962/773646
fax 01962/773625

Wasteels
Platform 2, Victoria Station
☎0171/834 7066

Bus Information

Hoverspeed ☎01304/240241

National Express/Eurolines ☎0990/808080

Lastly, for students and those under 26, *Campus Travel* has a great variety of **Eurotrain Explorer passes**, some covering just one country, others a combination. Call them for details; they are also agents for *InterRail* and *Eurostar*, and sell *Euro Domino* passes as well.

By Bus

Travelling by long-distance **bus** can be one of the cheapest ways of reaching Amsterdam. A major advantage is that you don't need to worry about looking after your bags: the storage compartment under the bus is locked in London and remains locked until arrival in Amsterdam. Two companies operate between London and Amsterdam, giving a choice of Channel crossings and arrival points in Amsterdam.

There are three Channel crossing options, all costing the same: from **Dover to Calais** by hovercraft (35min) or **ferry** (1hr 30min), or by ferry from **Ramsgate to Oostende** by ferry only (5hr 30min). Total journey times from London to Amsterdam clock in at approximately ten, eleven and twelve hours respectively. **Eurolines**, operated by *National Express*, uses only the ferries, with three daily departures year-round from London's Victoria Coach Station: one in the morning via Dover–Calais, one overnight via Dover–Calais, and a longer overnight routing via Ramsgate–Oostende (useful if you'd otherwise need to get a French visa). In July and August there's an additional, slightly faster daytime service via Dover–Calais. Prices are £36 one-way, £44 return (slightly reduced for under-26s), with an exceptionally good-value APEX-type advance ticket at £25 return.

Eurolines act as agents for the other bus operator, **Hoverspeed**, which provides a relatively fast daytime service via the Dover–Calais hovercraft and an overnight service using the ferry. In July and August, *Hoverspeed*, too, put on an extra daytime bus. Their prices are identical.

As far as **arrival points** go, all *Eurolines* buses arrive at Amstel Station, out in the southeast of Amsterdam; to reach the centre you have to take a tram, taxi or the metro (see pp.33–35). *Hoverspeed* services, however, stop first at the Olympic Stadium in the south of the city, but then go on to Leidseplein, which is right in the heart of the city centre, close to numerous hostels and hotels.

Tickets for all services can be bought through travel agents or from the operators direct.

By Car: the Ferries and Channel Tunnel

There are two ways to take a car or caravan to the Netherlands: by **ferry** to one of the coastal ports, or by **train** through the Channel Tunnel. In terms both of cost and convenience, though, the ferry is preferable by far.

The most direct ferry **crossings** into Holland from the southeast of England are from **Harwich to the Hook of Holland**, and from **Sheerness to Vlissingen**. It takes approximately one hour to drive from the Hook to Amsterdam; from Vlissingen it's roughly two and a half hours. If you want to spend less time crossing the water, consider sailing instead from **Ramsgate to Oostende** in Belgium. From the northeast of England there are overnight services from **Hull to Zeebrugge** (Belgium) **and Rotterdam**; after a full night's sleep on the ferry, the latter leaves you just an hour or so's drive from Amsterdam. Even more convenient is the overnight ferry from **Newcastle-upon-Tyne** (actually departing from North Shields), which docks in **IJmuiden** (pronounced "EYE-mao-dn") port, just twenty minutes from Amsterdam city centre.

Numerous brochures detailing the various fares can be found in high-street travel agents; it's worth shopping around for the most competitive deals. Booking fourteen days or more ahead can often turn up extremely good fares, cheaper than the "standard return" prices quoted in our table; in any case, booking is strongly recommended for motorists (and essential at peak times). Foot passengers and cyclists can normally just turn up and board, although in the summer it's often advisable to reserve some kind of accommodation on the ferry, even if just a reclining seat. Bear in mind that some sort of accommodation is obligatory on all night sailings, and should be added on to the price of an ordinary ticket. Prices vary with the month, day and even hour that you're sailing, how long you're staying, the size of your car – and the ferry companies are always offering special fares to outdo their competitors. On most fares, operators don't insist that you cross over and back using the same port. If you're just going for a weekend break, check out the short-period excursion fares on offer – usually 53-hour or

Ferry Routes and Prices

	Operator	Frequency	Duration	Standard rtn	Foot Passenger
Harwich–Hook of Holland	*Stena*	2 daily	6–9hr	£228–312	£68
Hull–Rotterdam	*North Sea*	1 daily	14hr	£286	£80
Hull–Zeebrugge	*North Sea*	1 daily	15hr	£286	£80
Newcastle–IJmuiden	*Scandinavian*	3 weekly	16hr	£352	£79
Ramsgate–Oostende	*Sally*	6 daily	4hr	£128–221	£44
Sheerness–Vlissingen	*Eurolink*	2 daily	8–9hr	£75	£28

Fares and frequencies are for travel during the peak June–August period; "standard return" indicates an average price for two people plus a small car.

five-day returns – which can cut costs dramatically. All the operators have slightly different price deals for kids: you'll need to call around for the latest quotes.

Le Shuttle operate the car service through the **Channel Tunnel** (the equivalent of the *Eurostar* passenger train service). It's important to remember that all you're paying for is the 35-minute tunnel crossing and that the drive up from Calais to Amsterdam could take the best part of a day. Trains run through the tunnel 24 hours a day; from 7am to midnight there are trains every 20 minutes or so, dropping to every 75 minutes at

other times. All kinds of vehicle (including minibuses carrying up to 16 people) can use the service for the same price: £266 return at peak times of the day, £218 off-peak. There are no booking restrictions; indeed, you can just turn up, pay and board (though the process may take as long as 45 minutes). The **tunnel entrance** on the English side is near Folkestone, at junction 11a on the M20; on the French side, you emerge on the A16 motorway at junction 14, 4km south of Calais (and about 500km south of Amsterdam). *Le Shuttle* can also transport **bicycles** for £10 each way, but you need to book ahead.

Ferry Company Addresses

Eurolink Ferries
Ferry Terminal
Sheerness Docks
Kent ME12 1RX ☎01795/581000

North Sea Ferries
King George Dock
Hedon Rd
Hull HU9 5QA ☎01482/377177

Sally Line
Argyle Centre
York St
Ramsgate
Kent CT11 9DS ☎01843/595566
and London ☎0181/858 1127

Scandinavian Seaways
Head Office – Scandinavia House
Harwich International Port
Harwich
Essex CO12 4QG ☎0191/293 6262

Stena Line
Charter House
Park St
Ashford
Kent TN24 8EX ☎01233/647047
24hr information ☎01304/240028

Le Shuttle
PO Box 300
Cheriton Park
Folkestone
Kent CT19 4QD ☎0990/353535

Taking your bike

Most people who take their bikes to Holland go by **train**. In order to do this, you must take your bike with you to the station at least an hour before departure and register it with *International Rail*. It's then loaded onto the train for you and delivered at your destination station. There's no guarantee it will turn up when you do. In practice, bikes can arrive anything up to 48 hours later – and you should plan accordingly. Taking your bike on the **ferry** presents few problems. Bicycles are carried free on all the ferry operators listed opposite (except for a £5 charge on *Eurolink*'s night ferry between Sheerness and Vlissingen). Simply turn up with your bike and secure it in the designated area. Travelling by **plane** with your bike is equally straightforward, provided you let the airline know at least a week

in advance. Contact them directly to make a cargo booking for your bike, then take your machine with you when you travel. At the airport you'll need to detach the wheels and fold down the handlebars. The bike will be included in your luggage allowance (usually 20kg); if the total exceeds that, you'll need to pay for the difference. Once you're in Holland, you can take your bike on Dutch trains for a smallish fee: ƒ10 one-way and ƒ17.50 return up to 80km; ƒ15 one-way over 80km and ƒ25 for a nationwide day ticket, which covers return journeys over 80km. However, you're not allowed to take your bike on Dutch trains during the weekday morning or evening rush hours; the only exception to this is if you're travelling in either direction on the Hook–Amsterdam boat train. For more on cycling, see p.37.

Hitching and lift-sharing

In much of northern Europe, **hitching** is a genuinely viable means of getting around – the locals are much more favourably inclined towards the whole practice than in Britain or America (as long as you don't look *too* outlandish on the roadside), and, although there are certain notorious blackspots for hitching (Oostende port is one of them), in general it's relatively easy to get lifts. As anywhere, though, hitching alone is inadvisable, and hitching after dark doubly so. Bear in mind also that since drivers have been made to account for unauthorized passengers, it's no longer possible to travel over on the ferry for free in a truck driver's cab.

However, the Channel Tunnel – and, more specifically, the fare structure on *Le Shuttle* – has significantly opened up the possibilities for reaching Europe for no money. All cars, vans and minibuses pay a flat fare to use the Folkestone–Calais shuttle train, regardless of the number of passengers they carry: if you can persuade someone to give you a lift through the formalities and onto the train, it'll cost them nothing (or nothing more than they were already going to pay), and it means you can be in France in half an hour, with as much money in your pocket as when you left England. If you're lucky, too, your lift might be moving on in the right direction; otherwise, use the half-hour crossing to find someone in your carriage who is driving north into

Belgium, and try and cajole them into taking you along too. With an early start, luck, and a fast car, you could beat the boat-train to Amsterdam. On the other hand, you could just as easily spend the day on the hard shoulder, watching all those fast, half-empty cars whizzing by without you.

If the uncertainties of hitching put you off, you might prefer to arrange a lift beforehand. *Freewheelers*, at 25 Low Friar St, Newcastle-upon-Tyne, NE1 5UE ☎0191/222 0090, matches passengers and drivers for lifts across the UK and to Europe. Membership costs £10 for one year; £22 for three years.

Inclusive holidays

Don't dismiss the idea of going on a **package holiday**: most consist of no more than travel and accommodation (from two nights to two weeks or more) and can work out an easy way of cutting costs and hassle – especially if you live some distance from London, since many operators provide a range of good-value regional departures. In such a competitive market, too, many operators throw in free extras to entice customers – these can range from a glass of Dutch gin or a canal cruise up to a night's accommodation. Depending on the type of accommodation you opt for (anything from budget to five-star hotels are available with most companies), short breaks in Amsterdam start at around £130 per person for return bus or train travel (crossing the Channel via ferry or hovercraft) plus two nights' accommodation with breakfast in a one-star hotel. The same package with return flights from a London airport works out around £180 – a little more from regional airports – and travelling by *Eurostar* through the Channel Tunnel costs about the same as flying. Many operators can also do accommodation plus ferry tickets if you want to design your own self-drive package. There are even day trips to Amsterdam available through some companies, from around £110 per person from London. Before you book, check carefully exactly what your money buys you – although train travel from Schiphol Airport to Centraal Station is always included, few operators provide any means of transport on from the station to your hotel. Low- and high-season dates can also vary from operator to operator, and price differences between the two can be astonishing. Any good travel agent can advise further on the best deals available, or contact one of the operators listed below.

Selected Tour Operators

Amsterdam Travel Service
Bridge House
55–59 High Rd
Broxbourne
Herts EN10 7DT ☎01992/456056

British Airways Holidays
Astral Towers
Betts Way
London Rd
Crawley
W. Sussex RH10 2XA ☎01293/723100

Cresta
Tabley Court
Victoria St
Altrincham
Cheshire WA14 1EZ ☎0161/927 7000

Crystal Holidays
Crystal House
The Courtyard
Arlington Rd
Surbiton
Surrey KT6 6BW ☎0181/390 9900

Eurobreak
10–18 Putney Hill,
London SW15 6AX ☎0181/780 7700

Time Off
Chester Close ☎0345/336622
London SW1X 7BQ or
☎0171/235 8070

Travelscene
11–15 St Anne's Rd
Harrow
Middx HA1 1AS ☎0181/427 8800

Getting There from Ireland

Taking into account the time and inconvenience of crossing the UK and then the Channel, travelling by air is by far the simplest way to reach Amsterdam from Ireland. Unless you're on the tightest of budgets, the extra money spent on a flight is worth it for the savings in time and hassle.

By Air

Only *Aer Lingus* flies direct from Ireland to Amsterdam, with a daily flight from Dublin plus one from Cork on Saturday; there are connections to Dublin from Cork, Galway, Kerry, Shannon and Sligo. Ordinary scheduled APEX fares in peak season work out at about IR£180 from Dublin, a little more from regional airports. *USIT* (see below) quotes peak-season **under-26** and student fares from Dublin of IR£145 return, IR£180 out of regional airports; these student tickets are mostly open for a year.

Other flight options involve **transfers** in the UK. These tickets almost always mean switching carriers from the Ireland–UK leg to the UK–Amsterdam leg. Flying with *Aer Lingus* to London Stansted, then with *Air UK* to Amsterdam works out around the same price as a direct *Aer Lingus* flight. Flying with various combinations of *Aer Lingus*, *British Midland* and *British Airways* via London Heathrow, Birmingham or Manchester costs around IR£210, IR£170 for under-26s. *USIT*, or any of the discount agents listed in the box, can advise you on the best deals to be had.

By Train

The train journey between Dublin and Amsterdam is a real endurance test. There are two daily departures, both taking around 24 hours in total. The favoured route is Dun Laoghaire to Holyhead on the ferry; then a train from Holyhead to London Euston (changing at Crewe). In London you must make your own way across the city to Liverpool Street station, then catch the train to Harwich, the ferry to the Hook of Holland, and the connecting train to

---

Airlines, Bus, Train and Ferry Companies

Aer Lingus
40 O'Connell St
Dublin 1   ☎ 01/844 4777
Dublin and Cork to Schiphol direct; Cork,
Galway, Kerry, Shannon and Sligo to
Schiphol via Dublin.

KLM
58 Mulgrave St
Dun Laoghaire   ☎ 01/284 2740

Bus Éireann
Busaras
Store St
Dublin 1   ☎ 01/836 6111

Iarnród Éireann
Travel Centre
35 Lower Abbey St
Dublin 1   ☎ 01/703 4095

Irish Ferries
2–4 Merrion Row
Dublin 2   ☎ 01/661 0511

Discount Travel Agents

Aran Travel
52 Dominick St
Galway ☎ 091/62595

Discount Travel
4 South Great Georges St
Dublin 2 ☎ 01/679 5888

Fahy Travel
3 Bridge St
Galway ☎ 091/563055

Flight Finders International
13 Baggot St Lower
Dublin 2 ☎ 01/676 8326

Joe Walsh Tours
8–11 Baggot St
Dublin 2 ☎ 01/676 3053

Lee Travel
23 Princes St
Cork ☎ 021/277111

McCarthy Travel
56 Patrick St
Cork ☎ 021/270127

Specialised Travel Services
32 Bachelor's Walk
Dublin 1 ☎ 01/873 1066

Student & Group Travel
71 Dame St
Dublin 2 ☎ 01/677 7834

Travel Shop
35 Belmont Rd
Belfast 4 ☎ 01232/471717

USIT
Fountain Centre
Belfast BT1 6ET ☎ 01232/324073

19–21 Aston Quay,
O'Connell Bridge, ☎ 01/679 8833
Dublin 2 or ☎ 01/677 8117

10–11 Market Parade
Cork ☎ 021/270900

Victoria Place
Eyre Square
Galway ☎ 091/565177

Central Buildings
O'Connell St
Limerick ☎ 061/415064

36–37 Georges St
Waterford ☎ 051/72601

Amsterdam. The standard return fare quoted by *Iarnród Éireann* (formerly *Irish Rail*), which is valid for a month and includes all ferry costs, is a non-competitive IR£180.

There's a great variety of **InterRail passes** on offer, but bear in mind that to travel from Ireland you must buy a pass for two zones in order to cover travel across the UK. For under-26s resident in Ireland who buy the pass before they leave, an *InterRail* giving a month's unlimited travel throughout Zone A (UK) and Zone E (France, Belgium, Luxembourg and the Netherlands) costs IR£210; this also gives reductions on the ferries. Those **over 26** cannot use an *InterRail* pass in Belgium, France, Switzerland, Italy, Spain, Portugal or Morocco; this means that the only crossing from the UK that you can make is the Harwich–Hook ferry directly into Holland. A 15-day pass costs IR£200; a month-long pass IR£260.

A more flexible option, infinitely more convenient if you're over 26, is a **Euro Domino** pass to cover train travel within the Netherlands only. These tickets cover either three, five or ten days'

unlimited travel within a period of a month; prices for under-26s are IR£28, IR£42 and IR£73 respectively, and for over-26s IR£37, IR£59 and IR£105. *Euro Domino* pass-holders are also entitled to fifty percent reductions on the ferries between Ireland and the UK, and between the UK and the Netherlands, as well as a 25 percent discount on the train journey across the UK to Harwich. Prices for a **Euro Domino Plus** pass for the Netherlands, which covers all train, bus, tram and metro travel throughout the country, are: for under-26s IR£36 (three days in a month), IR£55 (five days) and IR£94 (ten days); for over-26s IR£46, IR£72 and IR£125.

By Bus

Despite the fact that the bus journey from Ireland to Amsterdam can take about the same time as the train, prices are low enough for this option to appeal to those watching every punt. The only way to get to Amsterdam by bus is to go via London, where you pick up a *Eurolines* bus for Amsterdam (although you can buy through

Package Tour Specialists			
CIE Tours International		13 Lower Liffey St	
35 Lower Abbey St		Dublin 1	☎01/873 4900
Dublin 1	☎01/703 1888	**Neenan Travel**	
JWT Holidays		12 South Leinster St	
34 Grafton St		Dublin 2	☎01/676 5181
Dublin 1	☎01/671 8751	**Thomas Cook**	
69 Upper O'Connell St		11 Donegal Place	
Dublin 2	☎01/872 2555	Belfast	☎01232/240833
Liffey Travel		118 Grafton St	
Abbey Mall		Dublin	☎01/677 1721

tickets in Ireland before you go) – see p.7 for details. *Bus Éireann* operate two daily services from Dublin to London, and they also act as agents for *Irish Ferries'* services; return prices can be as low as IR£44 for the twelve-hour trek. Add to this the cost of the London–Amsterdam leg (IR£39 return), and it becomes possible to reach Amsterdam within 24 hours for IR£83 return (or a rock-bottom IR£54 one-way). Fares do fluctuate, though, depending upon departure time, and on whether the Irish Sea crossing is via the fast Dublin–Holyhead route or the slower crossing from Dun Laoghaire, where you must get off the bus and board the ferry on foot. Check with *Bus Éireann* for exact details, and also for their connections and prices from other Irish cities. Bear in mind, though, that they do not take bookings over the phone: you must pay in person.

By Ferry

There are no ferries direct from Ireland to either Belgium or the Netherlands. The nearest ferries get to Holland is the northwest of France, and, with the fare for a car plus two students on the Cork–Le Havre route currently at IR£464 in the peak season, this is a long way from being a competitive option.

Inclusive holidays

Package holidays – which can simply mean flights plus accommodation – are a feasible and sensible method of eliminating snags, and can easily cut costs as well. *USIT* (see below) do packages for a minimum of two nights, with prices ranging from IR£27 to IR£45 per person per night (sharing a double room), depending on the type of hotel you choose. Both *KLM* and *Aer Lingus* also offer several different "weekend break" packages to suit various budgets and styles; travel agents should have the relevant brochures, or you can call the airlines direct for information. Many travel agents can also give deals on city breaks in Amsterdam (see box).

Getting There from the USA and Canada

Amsterdam is among the most popular and least expensive gateways to Europe from North America, and getting a convenient and good-value flight is rarely a problem. Virtually every region of the United States and Canada is well served by the major airlines, though only two scheduled carriers offer nonstop flights – *KLM/Northwest Airlines* and *Delta*. The rest fly via London and other European centres. Look out, too, for deals offered by the Dutch charter company *Martinair*, which offers mid-priced seats on nonstop flights from a number of cities in the USA and Canada.

Shopping for tickets

Barring special offers, the cheapest fare is usually an **APEX** ticket, although this will carry certain restrictions: you have to book – and pay – at least 21 days before departure, spend at least seven days abroad (maximum stay 3 months), and you tend to get penalized if you change your schedule. Some airlines also issue **Special APEX** tickets to people younger than 24, often extending the maximum stay to a year. Many airlines offer youth or student fares to **under-25s**; a passport or drivers licence is sufficient proof of age, though these tickets are subject to availabil-

ity and can have eccentric booking conditions. It's worth remembering that most cheap round-trip fares will only give a percentage refund if you need to cancel or alter your journey, so make sure you check the restrictions carefully before buying.

You can normally cut costs further by going through a **specialist flight agent** – either a **consolidator**, who buys up blocks of tickets from the airlines and sells them at a discount, or a **discount agent**, who wheels and deals in tickets offloaded by the airlines, and often offers special student and youth fares and a range of other travel-related services, such as travel insurance, car rental and tours. Bear in mind, though, that the penalties for changing your plans can be stiff. Remember too that these companies make their money by dealing in bulk, so don't expect them to answer lots of questions. Some agents specialize in **charter flights**, which may be cheaper than any scheduled flight available, but again departure dates are fixed and withdrawal penalties are high (check the refund policy). If you travel a lot, **discount travel clubs** are another option – the annual membership fee may be worth it for benefits such as cut-price air tickets and car rental.

A further possibility is to see if you can arrange a **courier flight**, although the hit-and-miss nature of these makes them most suitable for the single traveller who travels light and has a very flexible schedule. In return for shepherding a package through customs and possibly giving up your baggage allowance, you can expect you get a heavily discounted ticket. See below or, for more options, consult *A Simple Guide to Courier Travel* (Pacific Data Sales Publishing).

Regardless of where you buy your ticket, the fare will depend on the **season**. Fares are highest in December, June, July and August, and fares during these months can cost between $100 and $300 more, depending on the airline. Flying at weekends can add $100 to the cost of a round-trip ticket: prices quoted below assume midweek travel.

Airlines

British Airways
☎ 1-800-247-9297 (USA)
☎ 1-800-668-1069 (Canada)
Daily nonstop to London from 18 US gateway cities, Montréal, Toronto and Vancouver, with connections to Amsterdam.

Delta Airlines
☎ 1-800-241-4141
Daily nonstop to Amsterdam from New York and Atlanta.

KLM/Northwest Airlines
☎ 1-800-374-7747 and 1-800-447-4747 (USA)
☎ 1-800-361-5073 (Canada)
Daily nonstop or direct services to Amsterdam from New York (JFK), Boston, Washington DC, Atlanta, Detroit, Chicago, Minneapolis, San Francisco, Los Angeles, Houston, Memphis, Montréal, Calgary, Québec, Toronto, Halifax and Vancouver.

Martinair
☎ 1-800-627-8462
Nonstop to Amsterdam from Newark (May–Sept 2 weekly), Denver (Dec–March & May–Sept weekly), Oakland (April–Oct 2 weekly), Los Angeles (April–Oct 3 weekly), Seattle (May–Oct 2 weekly), Miami and Tampa (year-round 2 weekly), Orlando (year-round 4 weekly) and Toronto (April–Oct 2 weekly).

United Airlines
☎ 1-800-538-2929
Daily nonstop to Amsterdam from Washington DC.

Virgin Atlantic Airways
☎ 1-800-862-8621
Daily nonstop to London from New York, with connections to Amsterdam.

Flights from the USA

KLM and Northwest Airlines, which operate a joint service from the United States and Canada to Amsterdam, offer the widest range of flights, with nonstop or direct services from eleven US cities and connections from dozens more via *Northwest.* Their APEX fares are usually identical to those offered by other carriers, so for convenience at least, *KLM/Northwest* is your best bet. It's also worth looking into deals offered by the Dutch charter carrier, **Martinair**, which flies nonstop from eight US cities.

One-way fares are rarely good value, but if you're set on one, the best source is the seat consolidators that advertise in the back pages of the travel sections of the major Sunday newspapers – or see the box below. Note that the **APEX fares** quoted are for midweek travel with a maximum stay of thirty days, and tickets must be bought at least fourteen days in advance.

Travelling from the **East Coast**, *KLM's* nonstop flights out of New York JFK start at around $570 in low season, rising to $716 in May and peaking at around $870 in July and August. Nonstop fares out of Washington DC, Atlanta, Detroit, Chicago and Minneapolis cost $50–100 more; connecting flights from other major cities are usually thrown in for free. *Delta* has similar fares on its nonstop flights out of New York and Atlanta,

as does *United* from Washington DC, and most carriers match these prices on their flights via London Heathrow. Especially during winter, many airlines have special offers that can reduce fares to well under $500 round-trip, and discount travel agents and consolidators can often find you fares as low as $350 (low season) or $650 (high season). *Martinair* operates twice-weekly **charter flights** out of Newark from May through September, costing $698–878, and a year-round service from Miami and Tampa (both twice-weekly) and Orlando (4 weekly).

As for the **West Coast**, *KLM/Northwest Airlines'* round-trip APEX fares on nonstop flights out of Los Angeles start at around $816 in low season, rising to $956 in May and $1100 in July and August. Consolidators can probably get you a seat for as little as $572 (low season) or $795 (high season). Fares from San Francisco or Seattle usually cost $50–100 more and most international carriers charge similar prices. Special offers sometimes bring the fares down to under $500, though these are usually only available during winter.

Martinair's round-trip charter fares out of Los Angeles (3 weekly), Oakland (2 weekly), Seattle (2 weekly) and Denver (weekly), start at around $668 for departures in April and May and climb to $828 in the summer peak season. On winter flights out of Denver, fares drop as low as $498.

Round-the-world tickets and courier flights

If you plan to visit Amsterdam as part of a major world trip, then you might want to think about getting a **round-the-world** ticket that includes the city as one of its stops. A sample route from the West Coast, using a combination of airlines, might be San Francisco/Los Angeles/Portland/Seattle–Taipei/Hong Kong–Bangkok–Cairo–Amsterdam–New York–Los Angeles, which costs $1297. From the East Coast, a ticket covering New York–Hong Kong–Bangkok–Cairo–Amsterdam–New York costs $1384. See the box below for details of agents specializing in round-the-world tickets.

Round-trip **courier flights** to Amsterdam from major US cities are available for around $200–250, with last-minute specials, booked within three days of departure, going for as little as $100. For more information about courier flights, contact *The Air Courier Association*, 191 University Blvd, Suite 300, Denver, CO 80206 ☎303/279-3600; *Discount Travel International*, 169 W 81st St, New York, NY 10024 ☎212/362-3636, fax 212/362-3236; or *Now Voyager*, 74 Varick St, Suite 307, New York, NY 10013 ☎212/431-1616, fax 212/334-5243.

Flights from Canada

Again, **KLM/Northwest Airlines** has the best range of routes, with nonstop flights from all major Canadian airports, and fares approximately the same as they are from the USA. Round-trip tickets out of **Toronto** start at around CDN$668 in the low season, stepping up to CDN$888 in May and CDN$1048 in July and August. Fares from **Vancouver** start at around CDN$629, climbing to CDN$1158 and CDN$1368.

Canadian **charter** operations, such as *Air Transat* and *Fiesta West/Canada 3000* (see the box on p.18 for addresses) offer some of the best deals on spring through fall travel, with fares as low as CDN$569 round-trip from Halifax, CDN$539 from Toronto and CDN$738 from Vancouver and Calgary. Neither *Air Canada* nor *Canadian Airlines* serves Amsterdam, though *Martinair* flies twice-weekly nonstop out of Toronto (April–Oct): low-season fares start at CDN$599, rising to CDN$759 in high season.

Canadian departures for **round-the-world** tickets can usually be arranged for around CDN$150 more than the US fare (see above).

Travelling via Europe

Even though many flights from North America to Amsterdam are routed via London, because of the various special fares it's often cheaper to stay on the plane all the way to Amsterdam. In general you can't stop over and continue on a later flight, as US and Canadian airlines are not allowed to provide services between European cities.

However, if you want to combine a trip to Amsterdam with visits to other European cities, **London** makes the best starting point, as onward flights are relatively inexpensive. Besides having the best range of good-value transatlantic flights (New York to London is the busiest and cheapest route), London also has excellent connections on to Amsterdam. **Paris**, too, is becoming a popular gateway to Europe. *United* and *American Airlines*, as well as *British Airways* and the British carrier *Virgin Atlantic*, all have frequent flights to London from various parts of the US, *BA* flying from Canada too; *Air France*, *United* and *American* fly daily to Paris. See "Getting There from Britain", p.3, for details on travel from Britain to Amsterdam.

Rail passes

If you intend Amsterdam to form just part of your European travels, or envisage using the European rail network extensively, then you should consider investing in a **Eurail train pass**. These are good for unlimited travel within 17 European countries, including Holland, and they should be purchased before you leave, as they cost ten percent more in Europe: you can get them from most travel agents in the USA and Canada or from *Rail Pass Express* (☎1-800/722-7151). The standard **Eurail** pass is valid for unlimited first-class travel for periods of 15 days ($498), 21 days ($648), 1 month ($798) or 2 months ($1098). For those under 26, the **Eurail Youthpass** allows second-class rail travel for 15 days ($398), 1 month ($578), 2 months ($768) or 3 months ($1398). There's also the **Eurail Flexipass**, which comes in three versions. One covers travel on any 5 days within a 2-month period and costs $348 for adults travelling first-class, $255 for under-26s travelling second-class; a second is valid for travel on any 10 days in 2 months ($560 and $398 respectively); the third version allows travel on 15 days within 2 months ($740 and $540).

Discount Flight Agents, Travel Clubs and Consolidators

Access International
101 W 31st St, Suite 104,
New York, NY 10001
☎ 1-800/TAKE-OFF
Consolidator with good East Coast and central US deals.

Air Brokers International
323 Geary St, San Francisco, CA 94102
☎ 1-800/883-3273
Consolidator selling round-the-world tickets.

Airkit
1125 W 6th St, Los Angeles, CA 90017
☎ 213/957-9304
Consolidator with seats from San Francisco and LA.

Council Travel
205 E 42nd St, New York, NY 10017
☎ 1-800/226-8624 e-mail cts@ciee.org
Agent specializing in student discounts; branches in 40 US cities.

Encore Short Notice
4501 Forbes Blvd, Lanham, MD 20706
☎ 301/459-8020
East Coast travel club.

Flight Centre
3030 S Granville St, Vancouver, BC V6H 3J9
☎ 604/739-9539
Discount air fares from Canadian cities.

High Adventure Travel Inc.
253 Sacramento St, Suite 600, San Francisco,
CA 94111
☎ 1-800/428-8735
Web site: http://www.highadv.com
Round-the-world tickets.

Interworld
3400 Coral Way, Miami, FL 33145
☎ 305/443-4929 or 1-800/468-3796
Southeastern US consolidator.

Last-Minute Travel Club
132 Brookline Ave, Boston, MA 02215
☎ 617/267-9800 or 1-800/LAST-MIN

Nouvelles Frontières
12 E 33rd St, New York, NY 10016
☎ 212/779-0600
800 blvd de Maisonneuve Est, Montréal, PQ
H2L 4L8
☎ 514/288-9942

Main US and Canadian branches of the French discount travel outfit. Other branches in LA, San Francisco and Québec City.

Overseas Tours
475 El Camino Real, Room 206, Millbrae, CA
94030
☎ 1-800/323-8777
Discount agent.

Rebel Tours
25050 Avenue Kearny, Valencia, CA
☎ 805/294-0900 or 1-800/227-3235
Good source of deals with Martinair.

STA Travel
10 Downing St, New York, NY 10014
☎ 212/627-3111 or 1-800/777-0112
Other branches in the Los Angeles, San
Francisco and Boston areas.
Worldwide discount firm specializing in student/youth fares.

TFI Tours
34 W 32nd St, New York, NY 10001
☎ 212/736-1140 or 1-800/825-3834
The very best East Coast deals, especially worth looking into if you only want to fly one-way.

Travac
1177 N Warson Rd, St Louis, MO 63132
☎ 1-800/872-8800
Good central US consolidator.

Travel Cuts
187 College St, Toronto, ON M5T 1P7
☎ 416/979-2406
Main office of the Canadian student travel organization. Many other offices nationwide.

Travelers Advantage
49 Music Square, Nashville, TN 37203
☎ 1-800/548-1116
Reliable travel club.

Travel Avenue
180 N Jefferson St, Chicago, IL 60606
☎ 312/876-1116 or 1-800/333-3335
Discount travel agent.

Unitravel
1177 N Warson Rd, St Louis, MO 63132
☎ 1-800/325-2222
Reliable consolidator.

A convenient alternative if your travels are going to be restricted to the Netherlands is the **Holland Rail** pass, which is valid for unlimited travel for either three, five or ten days within a period of one month. Prices are, for under-26s, $56, $79 and $130; for over-26s $68/88, $104/140 and $184/260, depending on whether you travel second- or first-class. You can also buy the pass once in Holland.

For more **information** on European rail travel, call *Rail Europe*: ☎1-800/4EURAIL in the USA and ☎1-800/361-RAIL in Canada.

Inclusive tours

There are any number of **packages and organized tours** from North America to Amsterdam and elsewhere in Holland. Prices vary, with some operators including the air fare,

---

Specialist Operators

Abercrombie & Kent
☎1-800/323-7308
Six-night river and canal cruising tours from Amsterdam to Bruges starting at $990. Airfare extra.

AESU Travel
☎1-800/3638-7640
Tours, independent city stays, discount air fares. 31-day Classic Europe tour includes wind surfing, biking and canoeing in Holland, 2 days in Amsterdam and a stop in Brussels; $3100 including airfare.

Air Transat Holidays
☎604/688-3350
Canadian charter company offering discount fares from major Canadian cities, tours and fly-drive trips. Contact travel agents for brochures.

American Airlines Fly Away Vacations
☎1-800/433-7300
Package tours and fly-drive programmes. A 7-day, 6-night London and Amsterdam tour costs $919 including airfare, accommodation and sightseeing.

Back Door Travel
☎206/771-8303
Off-the-beaten-path, small-group travel with budget travel guru Rick Steves and his enthusiastic guides. 21-day "Best of Europe" Tour, including stops in Haarlem and Amsterdam, costs $2900. Write or call for a free newsletter.

British Airways Holidays
☎1-800/359-8722
Package tours and fly-drives. A 7-day, 6-night London and Amsterdam package including airfare costs from $919.

Canada 3000/FiestaWest
Discount charter flights, car rental, accommodation and package tours. Book through travel agents or by calling BCAA TeleCentre in Canada: ☎1-800/663-1956.

CBT Bicycle Tours
Affordable tours in Holland, Belgium and Luxembourg. 16-day Amsterdam to Luxembourg tour starts at $1570. Airfare extra. Available through travel agents.

Contiki Tours
☎1-800/CONTIKI
Budget tours to Europe. A 12-day tour of seven countries, including 2 days in Amsterdam, starts at $1299 including air fare from the USA.

Euro Bike Tours
☎1-800/321-6060
Upscale cycling tours and "bicycling and barging" tours in Holland, Belgium and Luxembourg – with one day in Amsterdam – starting at $1795. Airfare extra.

Saga International Holidays
☎1-800/952-9590
19-day Dutch waterways tours covering Amsterdam, North and South Holland and Belgium, starting at $1899 including airfare.

KLM/Northwest World Vacations
☎1-800/447-4747
Hotel and sightseeing packages and escorted tours. Two-night Amsterdam package from $114. Contact travel agents.

United Vacations
☎1-800/538-2929
Six nights in Amsterdam, starting at $389 including hotels and breakfast. Airfare extra. Contact travel agents.

while others cover just accommodation, sight-seeing, and activities such as cycling or hiking. In addition, many airlines offer fly-drive deals that include a week's hotel accommodation. As an example, *United Vacations* offers a six-night Amsterdam bed and breakfast package starting at $389, excluding airfare; a city sightseeing tour costs an extra $27 and day trips to Volendam, Marken and Edam (see p.318) are available for the same sort of price. *KLM/Northwest World* *Vacations* do a two-night Amsterdam package from $114, including accommodation, breakfast and a diamond factory tour – sightseeing tours cost extra.

You'll find that most European tours include Amsterdam on their itineraries, too. Among the best of the Europe-wide operators are *Back Door Travel*, a specialist in independent budget travel, with the emphasis on simple accommodation and meeting local people.

Getting There from Australia and New Zealand

There is no shortage of flights to Amsterdam from Australia and New Zealand, though all of them involve at least one stop. When buying a ticket, as well as the price you might want to take into account the airline's route – whether, for example, you'd rather stop in Moscow or Bali. Some of the airlines allow free stopovers (see the box below).

The cheapest option is to fly with *Britannia* during their charter season, which runs from November to March; a round-trip ticket via Singapore and Abu Dhabi costs between A$1200/NZ$1420 and A$1800/NZ$2130, depending on the date of departure. *Garuda* offers the next cheapest flights, stopping in Bali or Jakarta for around A$1700/NZ$1999 (high season) or A$2100/NZ$2450 (low season). For the same price *Aeroflot* fly twice a week from Sydney via Bangkok and Moscow. *Malaysia Airlines* (via Kuala Lumpur), *Olympic* (via Athens), *Alitalia* (via Rome), *Thai* (via Bangkok) and *Cathay Pacific* (via Hong Kong) have flights from all the major cities for around A$1990/NZ$2199 to A$2490/NZ$2899. Fares are the same with the Dutch national airline, *KLM*, on its flights from Sydney, via Singapore. For a little more – around A$2399 to A$2999/NZ$2699 to NZ$3399 – you can fly with *BA*, *Qantas*, *Air New Zealand* and *Singapore*

Airlines: with these airlines you can expect to get some good deals on European side trips, fly-drive/accommodation packages and free stopovers en route; check out, too, the offers provided by *Cathay Pacific*, *Alitalia* and *Thai Airways*. If you want to combine Amsterdam with a stay in another European centre, probably your best bet is to get a cheap fare to London, which usually offers the best-value onward flights to Amsterdam (see "Getting There from Britain", p.3).

As a general rule, **travel agents** can get you a better deal than buying direct from the airlines; they also have the latest information on limited special offers and can give advice on visa regulations. See the box below for the addresses of specialist agents.

Round-the-world tickets and air passes

If your visit to Amsterdam is just one stop on a worldwide trip, then you might want to buy a **round-the-world** ticket that includes the city as one of its stops. RTW tickets usually give six free stopovers, with limited backtracking and side trips, with additional stopovers charged at around $100 each. Fares start at A$2399/NZ$2699. *Cathay Pacific-UA*'s "Globetrotter" and *Air New Zealand-KLM-Northwest*'s "World Navigator" both take in Amsterdam. *Qantas-BA*'s "Global Explorer" is more restrictive, allowing six stopovers but no backtracking within the US. *Thai* and *Malaysia* also combine with other carriers to provide a variety of routes at similar prices. **Air passes** are available if your journey from Australia or New Zealand is made entirely on *British Airways*, *KLM* or *Alitalia-Qantas*, starting at A$100/NZ$115 per flight.

Rail passes

If you're planning to travel around the Netherlands or the rest of Europe by train, then it's best to get hold of a rail pass before you go. **Eurail passes** (see p.16 for details on the full

Airlines

Aeroflot

388 George St, Sydney ☎02/9233 7911
No New Zealand office.
Twice-weekly flights to Amsterdam from Sydney via Bangkok and Moscow.

Air New Zealand

5 Elizabeth St, Sydney ☎02/9223 4666
17th floor Quay Tower, Customs St, Auckland
☎09/366 2803
Several flights a week to Amsterdam from major New Zealand cities via LA and London

Alitalia

Orient Overseas Building, 32 Bridge St, Sydney
☎02/9247 1308
6th Floor, Trustbank Building, 229 Queen St,
Auckland ☎09/379 4457
Three flights weekly to Amsterdam from Brisbane, Sydney, Melbourne and Auckland via Rome.

Britannia Airways

Aus-Extras Level 6, 210 George St, Sydney
☎02/9251 1299
No New Zealand office.
Several charter flights to Amsterdam per month during their charter season (Nov–March) from Cairns, Brisbane, Sydney, Melbourne, Adelaide, Perth and Auckland, via Singapore and Abu Dhabi.

British Airways

Level 26, 201 Kent St, Sydney ☎02/9258 3300
154 Queen St, Auckland ☎09/356 8690
Several flights weekly to Amsterdam from major Australian cities via Bangkok/Singapore and London, and from Auckland via LA and London.

Cathay Pacific

Level 12, 8 Spring St, Sydney ☎02/9931 5500,
local-call rate 13 1747
11f Arthur Andersen Tower, 205–209 Queen St,
Auckland ☎09/379 0861
Several flights a week to Amsterdam from major Australian cities with a transfer or stopover in Hong Kong.

Garuda Indonesia

55 Hunter St, Sydney ☎02/9334 9944
120 Albert St, Auckland ☎09/366 1855
Several flights weekly to Amsterdam from major Australian and New Zealand cities with a transfer or stopover in Bali/Jakarta.

KLM

5 Elizabeth St, Sydney ☎02/9231 6333, toll-free
1800/505 747
No New Zealand office.
Three flights weekly to Amsterdam from Sydney via Singapore.

Malaysia Airlines

16 Spring St, Sydney, local-call rate ☎13 2627
Floor 12, Swanson Centre, 12–26 Swanson St,
Auckland ☎09/373 2741
Several flights weekly to Amsterdam from major Australian and New Zealand cities with a transfer or stopover in Kuala Lumpur.

Olympic Airways S.A.

Floor 3, 37–49 Pitt St, Sydney ☎02/9251 2044
No New Zealand office.
Twice-weekly service to Amsterdam from Sydney, Melbourne and Auckland, with a transfer or stopover in Athens.

Qantas

Chifley Square, cnr Hunter and Phillip streets,
Sydney ☎02/9957 0111
Qantas House, 154 Queen St, Auckland
☎09/357 8900
Several flights weekly to Amsterdam from Australian cities and Auckland via Singapore/Bangkok and London.

Singapore Airlines

17–19 Bridge St, Sydney, local-call rate ☎13
1011
Lower Ground Floor, West Plaza Building, cnr
Customs and Albert streets, Auckland ☎09/379
3209
Several flights weekly to Amsterdam from major Australian and New Zealand cities with a transfer or stopover in Singapore.

Thai Airways

75–77 Pitt St, Sydney ☎02/9844 0999, toll-free
1800/422 020
Kensington Swan Building, 22 Fanshawe St,
Auckland ☎09/377 3886
Several flights weekly to Amsterdam from eastern Australian cities and Auckland via Bangkok.

Discount Travel Agents

Anywhere Travel
345 Anzac Parade, Kingsford, Sydney
☎ 02/9663 0411

Brisbane Discount Travel
260 Queen St, Brisbane ☎ 07/3229 9211

Budget Travel
16 Fort St, Auckland
other branches around the city
☎ 09/366 0061, toll-free 1800/808 040

Destinations Unlimited
3 Milford Rd, Milford, Auckland
☎ 09/373 4033

Flight Centres
Australia: Level 11, 33 Berry St, North Sydney
☎ 02/9241 2422; Bourke St, Melbourne
☎ 03/9650 2899; plus other branches nationwide. New Zealand: National Bank Towers,
205–225 Queen St, Auckland ☎ 09/209 6171;
Shop 1M, National Mutual Arcade, 152 Hereford
St, Christchurch ☎ 03/379 7145; 50–52 Willis
St, Wellington ☎ 04/472 8101; other branches
countrywide.

Northern Gateway
22 Cavenagh St, Darwin ☎ 08/8941 1394

Passport Travel
320b Glenferrie Rd, Malvern ☎ 03/9824 7183

STA Travel
Australia: 702–730 Harris St, Ultimo, Sydney
☎ 02/9212 1255, toll-free 1800/637 444; 256
Flinders St, Melbourne ☎ 03/9654 7266; other
offices in state capitals and major universities. New
Zealand: Travellers' Centre, 10 High St, Auckland
☎ 09/309 0458; 233 Cuba St, Wellington ☎ 04/385
0561; 90 Cashel St, Christchurch ☎ 03/379 9098;
other offices in Dunedin, Palmerston North,
Hamilton and major universities.

Thomas Cook
Australia: 321 Kent St, Sydney ☎ 02/9248 6100;
257 Collins St, Melbourne ☎ 03/9650 2442; branches in other state capitals. New Zealand: Shop 250a
St Luke's Square, Auckland ☎ 09/849 2071

Topdeck Travel
65 Glenfell St, Adelaide ☎ 08/8232 7222

Tymtro Travel
428 George St, Sydney ☎ 02/9223 2211

YHA Travel Centres
422 Kent St, Sydney ☎ 02/9261 1111
205 King St, Melbourne ☎ 03/9670 9611
38 Stuart St, Adelaide ☎ 08/8231 5583
154 Roma St, Brisbane ☎ 07/3236 1680
236 William St, Perth ☎ 08/9227 5122
69a Mitchell St, Darwin ☎ 08/8981 2560
28 Criterion St, Hobart ☎ 03/6234 9617

range of passes) are available through most trav-
el agents or from *CIT*, 123 Clarence St, Sydney
(☎ 02/9267 1255; offices in Melbourne,
Brisbane, Adelaide and Perth), or from *Thomas*
Cook World Rail (Australia ☎ 1800/422 747; New
Zealand ☎ 09/263 7260). Once you get to the
Netherlands, you can also buy a Euro-Domino
pass – see p.6.

Specialist Operators

All the following can arrange city sight-seeing
tours, car rental, and accommodation in
Amsterdam from $70 twin share.

Adventure World
73 Walker St, North Sydney ☎ 02/9956 7766,
toll-free 1800/221 931; level 3, 33 Adelaide St,
Brisbane ☎ 07/3229 0599; 8 Victoria Ave, Perth
☎ 08/9221 2300; 101 Great South Rd, Remuera,
Auckland ☎ 09/524 5118

CIT
123 Clarence St, Sydney ☎ 02/9267 1255.
Offices in Melbourne, Brisbane, Adelaide and
Perth. *Also handles Eurail passes.*

Creative Tours
Level 3, 55 Grafton St, Sydney ☎ 02/9386 2111

Eurolynx
3rd Floor, 20 Fort St, Auckland ☎ 09/379 9716

European Travel Office
122 Rosslyn St, West Melbourne ☎ 03/9329
8844; Level 20, 133 Castlereagh St, Sydney
☎ 02/9267 7727; 407 Great South Rd, Penrose,
Auckland ☎ 09/525 3074

KLM Vacations
Level 17, 456 Kent St, Sydney ☎ 02/9264 8300,
toll-free 1800 505 074; 199 Ponsonby Rd,
Auckland ☎ 09/376 7029

Visas and Red Tape

Citizens of Britain, Ireland, Australia, New Zealand, Canada and the USA need only a valid passport to stay for three months in the Netherlands. On arrival, be sure to have enough money to convince officials you can stay alive. Poorer-looking visitors are often checked out, and if you come from outside the EU and can't flash a credit card, or a few travellers' cheques or notes, you may not be allowed in.

If you want to stay longer than three months, officially you need a *verblijfsvergunning* or residence permit from the Aliens' Police. Even for **EU citizens**, however, this is far from easy to obtain

Dutch Embassies and Consulates
Australia
19th floor, 500 Oxford St, Bondi Junction
☎ 02/9387 6644 (Mon–Fri 9am–2pm)
Britain
38 Hyde Park Gate,
London SW7 5DP ☎ 0171/584 5040
Canada
350 Albert St, Ottawa, Canada
☎ 613/237-5030
New Zealand
Investment House, 10th Floor, cnr Balance and Featherston streets, Wellington ☎ 04/473 8652
USA
4200 Linnean Ave NW, Washington DC 20008 ☎ 202/244-5300

(impossible if you can't show means of support), and the bureaucracy involved is byzantine to say the least.

For **non-EU nationals**, the chance of gaining legal resident's status in the Netherlands without pre-arranged work is extremely slim. To work legally, non-EU nationals need a work permit (*werkvergunning*), and these are even harder to get than a residence permit: cruelly, every single

Foreign Embassies in the Netherlands

Australia		**New Zealand**	
Carnegielaan 10–14		Carnegielaan 10	
2517 KH The Hague	☎ 070/310 8200	2517 KH The Hague	☎ 070/346 9324
Britain		**Republic of Ireland**	
Embassy:		Dr Kuyperstraat 9	
Lange Voorhout 10		2514 BA The Hague	☎ 070/363 0993
2514 ED The Hague	☎ 070/364 5800	**USA**	
Consulate-General:		*Embassy:*	
Koningslaan 44		Lange Voorhout 102	
1075 AE Amsterdam	☎ 020/676 4343	2514 EJ The Hague	☎ 070/310 9209
Canada		*Consulate-General:*	
Sophialaan 7		Museumplein 19	
2514 JP The Hague	☎ 070/361 4111	1071 DJ Amsterdam	☎ 020/664 5661

EU citizen has preference in the job market over a non-EU citizen with the same skills. The only exceptions to this rule are Australians aged 18 to 25, who are eligible to apply for a year-long Working Holiday Visa.

The process of applying for residency and work permits is described in "Long-Term Stays", p.61, along with tips on finding jobs and rented accommodation, plus lots of useful addresses.

Information and Maps

Before you leave it's worth contacting the Netherlands Board of Tourism, which puts out a variety of glossy, informative (and free) booklets. Most of these cover Holland in its entirety, but some are specifically devoted to Amsterdam, with useful – if sketchy – introductory maps of the city and brief details of hotels, principal tourist attractions and annual events.

Once in Amsterdam, the place to head for is the **VVV** (pronounced "fay-fay-fay"), the nation-wide tourist organization – actually a private, non-profit company, though many VVV offices receive funding from local councils. There are four branches: one inside Centraal Station (Mon–Sat 8am–7.30pm, Sun 9am–4.30pm); one immediately outside Centraal Station (daily 9am–5pm); another on Leidsestraat, on the corner with Leidseplein (Mon–Sat 9am–7pm, Sun 9am–5pm); and one at Stadionplein (Mon–Sat 9am–5pm) – only really useful if you're arriving via *Hoverspeed*. The main VVV telephone **information line** is ☎06/340 34066 (Mon–Fri 9am–5pm; 50c/min). Any of the offices can sell you a map, reserve accommodation for a ƒ5 fee (plus a ƒ5 "deposit" which you reclaim from the hotel), book theatre and concert tickets and provide informed answers to most other enquiries. In spring and summer all the city centre offices get very crowded, and you may have to queue for some time before reaching the counter. Keep an

Netherlands Board of Tourism Offices

World Wide Web
http://www.nbt.nl/holland

Britain
25–28 Buckingham Gate,
London SW1E 6LD   ☎0891/200277

Canada
25 Adelaide St East, Suite 710, Toronto,
Ont M5C 1Y2   ☎416/363-1577
fax 416/363-1470

USA
225 N Michigan Ave #326, Chicago,
IL 60601   ☎312/819-0300
fax 312/819-1740

355 Lexington Ave, 21st floor, New York, NY
10017   ☎212/370-7367
fax 212/370-9507

There are no offices in Australia or New Zealand.

eye on your belongings and try to be as concise as possible. A recently opened private alternative to the VVV, worth a visit if the queues are too long, is the **Dutch Tourist Information Office** at Damrak 35 (Mon–Sat 8.30am–10pm, Sun 9am–10pm; ☎638 2800).

For tickets to all kinds of **cultural events** in Amsterdam, the *Amsterdam Uitburo*, or AUB – the cultural office of the city council – has a walk-in booking centre and café tucked away on one corner of Leidseplein. For a ƒ2 fee they can book tickets for practically any event in the city (ƒ5 for phone bookings – call ☎621 1211). If you're under 26, you can also buy the CJP (*Cultureel Jongeren Passport*) here, which costs ƒ20 and gives discounts on entry to all sorts of museums and events across the country. Needless to say, you can also browse at leisure through stacks of flyers and brochures for every conceivable cultural event.

Our **maps** are adequate for most purposes, but if you need one on a larger scale, or with a street index, there are any number of maps of Amsterdam you can buy before you leave (see the box below for outlets). If you wait until you arrive, the best and clearest maps of the city are the light blue *Cito-plan* series, only distributed in Holland. They have a detailed map of the centre (titled *"Uitgebreide Centrumkaart"*) for ƒ3.95, a map of the whole city (*"Plattegrond"*) for ƒ7.50 and, perhaps most convenient of all, a spiral-bound street atlas (*"Stratengids"*) for ƒ11.50.

MAP OUTLETS

Britain and Ireland

Belfast
Waterstone's, Queens Building, 8 Royal Ave, BT1   ☎ 01232/247355

Dublin
Easons Bookshop, 40 O'Connell St, 1 ☎ 01/873 3811; *Fred Hanna's Bookshop*, 27–29 Nassau St, 2 ☎ 01/677 1255; *Hodges Figgis Bookshop*, 56–58 Dawson St, 2 ☎ 01/677 4754

Edinburgh
Thomas Nelson and Sons Ltd, 51 York Place, EH1   ☎ 0131/557 3011

Glasgow
John Smith and Sons, 57–61 St Vincent St, G2
                    ☎ 0141/221 7472

London
Daunt Books, 83 Marylebone High St, W1
☎ 0171/224 2295; *National Map Centre*, 22–24 Caxton St, SW1 ☎ 0171/222 4945; *Stanfords*, 12–14 Long Acre, WC2 ☎ 0171/836 1321, also 52 Grosvenor Gardens and 156 Regent St; *The Travel Bookshop*, 13–15 Blenheim Crescent, W11   ☎ 0171/229 5260

Maps by **mail** or **phone order** are available from *Stanfords* on   ☎ 0171/836 1321

USA and Canada

Chicago
Rand McNally, 444 N Michigan Ave, IL 60611
                    ☎ 312/321-1751

Montréal
Ulysses Travel Bookshop, 4176 St-Denis
                    ☎ 514/289-0993

New York
The Complete Traveler Bookstore, 199 Madison Ave, NY 10016 ☎ 212/685-9007; *Rand McNally*, 150 E 52nd St, NY 10022 ☎ 212/758-7488; *Traveler's Bookstore*, 22 W 52nd St, NY 10019   ☎ 212/664-0995

San Francisco
The Complete Traveler Bookstore, 3207 Fillmore St, CA 94123 ☎ 415/923-1511; *Rand McNally*, 595 Market St, CA 94105
                    ☎ 415/777-3131

Santa Barbara
Map Link Inc., 30 S La Patera Lane, Unit 5, CA 93117   ☎ 805/692-6777

Seattle
Elliot Bay Book Company, 101 S Main St, WA 98104   ☎ 206/624-6600

Toronto
Open Air Books and Maps, 25 Toronto St, M5R 2C1   ☎ 416/363-0719

Vancouver
World Wide Books and Maps, 1247 Granville St
                    ☎ 604/687-3320

Rand McNally *has stores all across the US; call* ☎ *1-800/333-0136, ext 2111, for the address of your nearest store, or for maps by* **mail**.

Australia and New Zealand

Adelaide
The Map Shop, 16a Peel St, SA 5000
                    ☎ 08/8231 2033

Auckland
Specialty Maps, 58 Albert St ☎ 09/307 2217

Melbourne
Bowyangs, 372 Little Bourke St, VIC 3000
                    ☎ 03/9670 4383

Perth
Perth Map Centre, 891 Hay St, WA 6000
                    ☎ 09/9322 5733

Sydney
Travel Bookshop, 20 Bridge St, NSW 2000
                    ☎ 02/9241 3554

Health and Insurance

As fellow members of the European Union, both Britain and Ireland have reciprocal health agreements with the Netherlands. In theory, this allows free medical advice and treatment on presentation of certificate E111. In practice, many doctors and pharmacists charge, and it's up to you to arrange reimbursement from the Department of Health once you're home. To get an E111, fill in a form at any post office and you'll be issued with one immediately; read the small print on the back to find out how to get reduced-price treatment (you'll probably have to explain things to the doctor who treats you). Also photocopy your E111 a few times, as you'll need to leave copies with any hospital that treats you. Without an E111 you won't be turned away but will almost certainly have to pay towards treatment. Australians are able to receive treatment through a reciprocal arrangement with Medicare (check with your local office for details) but citizens from all other countries should be sure to take out their own private medical insurance before they leave home.

Minor ailments can be remedied at a **drugstore** (*drogist*), which sells toiletries, non-prescription drugs, tampons, condoms and the like. A **pharmacy** or *apotheek* (open Mon–Fri 9.30am–6pm; often closed Mon mornings) is where you go to get a prescription filled. No pharmacy is open 24 hours, but the **Central Medical Service** (*Centrale Doktersdienst*; ☎06/350 32042

In emergencies dial ☎ 112 for an ambulance

– 50c/min) will give the details of duty doctors and dentists, and can supply addresses for late-opening pharmacies. To get a prescription or **consult a doctor**, again phone the Central Medical Service – something the VVV tourist office will do for you if you need help (address on p.25). **Minor accidents** can be treated at the out-patients department of most **hospitals** (*ziekenhuis*); the most central one is the Onze Lieve Vrouwe Gasthuis, east of the city centre at Eerste Oosterparkstraat 179 (open 24hr; ☎599 9111; tram #3, #6, #10 or metro Wibautstraat). The VVV can also advise on outpatient clinics.

For urgent **dental treatment**, ring the Dentist Administration Bureau on ☎06/821 2230. This costs about *f*1 a minute, but they can find a dentist (*tandarts*) for you 24 hours a day. Try also *AOC Dentist Practice*, Wilhelmina Gasthuisplein 167 (Mon–Fri 8.30am–8pm, Sat 8am–7pm, Sun noon–5pm; ☎616 1234), who will sort out an appointment for you; without insurance the cost can be high, but they do take credit cards.

Information and anonymous testing for **sexually transmitted diseases** is available at the GG&GD (Municipal Health Department) clinic at Groenburgwal 44, near Waterlooplein; a walk-in service operates (Mon–Fri 8–11.30am & 1.30–3.30pm), but it's better to call ☎555 5822 first to make an appointment. The SAD Schorerstichting runs a clinic offering STD and HIV testing for gay men at the same address (Fri 7–9pm only; for more information, see "Gay and Lesbian Amsterdam", p.54). The free national AIDS helpline is open Mon–Fri 2–10pm on ☎06/022 2220. For details of how to get contraceptives or the morning-after pill, see p.60.

If you're travelling on from Amsterdam and need **immunizations**, the GG&GD also has a travellers' walk-in consultation service and clinic at Nieuwe Achtergracht 100 (Mon–Fri 8–10am; ☎555 5370); currently, a typhoid shot costs *f*45, diphtheria/tetanus/polio *f*25 and the Havrix vaccine against hepatitis A *f*100.

Insurance

Taking out a **travel insurance** policy is a good idea for anyone travelling abroad. Although British and Irish citizens are covered for any medical treatment in Amsterdam with form E111 (see above), a policy is still worth taking out, since it covers loss of possessions and money, plus eventualities such as cancelled flights. It's worth noting that bank and credit cards often have certain levels of medical or other insurance included, especially if you use them to pay for your trip. This can be quite comprehensive, anticipating anything from lost or stolen baggage and missed connections to charter companies going bankrupt; however, certain policies (notably in North America) only cover medical costs.

Medical services in Amsterdam are good, but even if you hold form E111 you'll generally have to pay for all your treatments on the spot – and it can be expensive. Make sure that your medical cover is high enough – ie sufficient to get you home under supervision if you fall really ill – and that there is a 24-hour emergency contact number.

For medical treatment and drugs, keep all the **receipts** so that you can claim the money back later. If you have anything **stolen**, register the loss immediately with the police, since without their report, you won't be able to claim. See p.46 for the locations of police stations in Amsterdam.

British and Irish cover

Most travel agents and tour operators will offer you insurance when you book your flight or holiday, and some will insist you take it. These policies are usually reasonable value, though as ever you should check the small print. If you feel the cover is inadequate, or you want to compare prices, any travel agent, insurance broker or bank should be able to help. If you have a good "all risks" home insurance policy it may well cover your possessions against loss or theft even when overseas, and many private medical schemes also cover you when abroad – make sure you know the procedure and the helpline number.

In **Britain and Ireland**, travel insurance schemes are also sold by various specialist companies – see the box below for addresses. Cover anywhere in Europe currently costs from around £10 for 1–4 days, £17 for 12–17 days, £24 for up to a month, and £60 for three months. Irish policies cost from IR£20 for 6–10 days, or IR£30 for a month, though students and those under 26 may be eligible for discounts.

North American cover

Before buying an insurance policy, check that you're not already covered. **Canadians** are usually covered for medical mishaps overseas by their provincial health plans. Holders of official **student/teacher/youth cards** are entitled to accident coverage and hospital in-patient benefits. **Students** will often find that their student health coverage extends during the vacations and for one term beyond the date of last enrollment. **Homeowners' or renters'** insurance often covers theft or loss of documents, money and valuables

---

Travel insurance companies

Britain and Ireland

Columbus Travel Insurance, 17 Devonshire Square, London EC2M 4SQ ☎0171/375 0011; *Endsleigh Insurance*, 97–107 Southampton Row, London WC1B 4AG ☎0171/436 4451; *Frizzell Insurance*, Frizzell House, County Gates, Bournemouth, Dorset BH1 2NF ☎01202/292 333

Note: *Good-value policies are also available through* Campus *and* STA *(see p.4 for telephone numbers).*

USA and Canada

Access America, PO Box 90310, Richmond, VA 23230 ☎1-800/284-8300; *Carefree Travel Insurance*, The Berkeley Group, 120 Mineola Blvd, PO Box 310, Mineola, NY 11501 ☎1-800/645-2424; *Travel Guard International*, 1145 Clark St, Stevens Point, WI 54481 ☎1-800/782-5151; *TravMed*, PO Box 10623, Baltimore, MD 21385 ☎1-800/732-5309

Australia and New Zealand

Cover More, Level 9, 32 Walker St, North Sydney, NSW ☎02/9202 8000 or 1800/251 881; *Ready Plan*, 141–147 Walker St, Dandenong, VIC ☎1800/337 462 and 10th Floor, 63 Albert St, Auckland ☎09/379 3208

---

while overseas, though conditions and maximum amounts vary from company to company.

After exhausting the possibilities above, you might want to contact a specialist **travel insurance** company; your travel agent can usually recommend one, or see the box below. Policies are comprehensive (accidents, illnesses, delayed or lost luggage, cancelled flights, etc) but maximum payouts tend to be meagre. Premiums vary, so shop around. The best deals are usually to be had through student/youth travel agencies and start at around $65 for a two-week trip and $85 for three weeks to a month.

Most North American travel policies apply only to items lost, stolen or damaged while in the custody of an identifiable, responsible third party – hotel porter, airline, luggage consign-

ment, etc. Even in these cases you will have to contact the local police within a certain time limit to have a complete report made out so that your insurer can process the claim. Note also that very few insurers will arrange on-the-spot payments in the event of a major expense or loss; you will usually be reimbursed only after going home.

Cover in Australia and New Zealand

Travel insurance is put together by the airlines and travel agent groups in conjunction with insurance companies. They are all comparable in premiums and coverage; you can expect to pay around A$190/NZ$220 for one month, A$270/NZ$320 for two and A$330/NZ$400 for three months.

Money, Banks and Costs

The Netherlands is a cash society; people prefer to pay for most things with notes and coins. Quite a lot of smaller shops still refuse all other forms of payment (except Eurocheques, which are widely accepted), although larger hotels, shops and most restaurants will take one or other of the major credit cards for a minimum purchase of around ƒ50.

The Dutch **currency** is the **guilder**, generally indicated by "ƒ" or "ﬂ" ("guilders" were originally "florins"); other abbreviations include "Hfl", "Dfl" and "NLG". Each guilder is divided into 100 cents. There are notes of ƒ1000, ƒ250, ƒ100, ƒ50, ƒ25 and ƒ10; coins come as ƒ5 (thick bronze), ƒ2.50, ƒ1, 25c, 10c (all silver) and 5c (thin bronze). As in the rest of Europe, decimal points are indicated by a comma, thousands by a full stop. Thus "ƒ2,50" means two guilders and fifty cents; "ƒ2.500" means two thousand five hundred guilders. Round figures are often indicated with a little dash: "ƒ3,-" means three guilders exactly. Although some prices (mostly in supermarkets) are still marked in individual cents, these are always rounded up or down to the nearest 5c.

Guilders are available in advance from any high street bank: current exchange rates are around ƒ2.80 to £1, ƒ1.80 to US$1, and there are no restrictions on bringing currency into the country. The safest way of carrying your money is in **travellers' cheques**, available from most high street banks for a fee of around one percent of the amount ordered, although your own bank

may provide them free of charge. For EU citizens, an alternative is the **Eurocheque** book and card, issued on request by most banks, which can be used both to get cash in Dutch banks and bureaux de change, and to pay for goods and services like a normal cheque. This works out slightly more expensive than travellers' cheques but can be more convenient. Bear in mind that you'll need your passport as well as your Eurocheque card to get cash in a bank.

However, the easiest way of getting guilders is simply to withdraw them as you need them from a **cash machine** or ATM (*geldautomaat*) in Amsterdam, using your bank card, Eurocheque card or credit card. There are a number of ATMs dotted around the city in which you can use foreign cards, notably *Rabobank*, *VSB* and *ABN-Amro* machines, but the most common *Giromaat* machines won't accept them. Although this method doesn't avoid normal commission charges (they pop up later on your statement), and getting cash on credit cards can incur interest charges, you do avoid the hassle of changing money and have much more control over your cash.

Changing money

If you do need to change money, Amsterdam's **banks** usually offer the best deals. Hours are Monday to Friday 9am to 4pm, with a few banks also open Thursday until 9pm or on Saturday morning; all are closed on public holidays (see p.48). Outside these times you'll need to go to one of the many **bureaux de change** scattered around town. The best of these are the *GWK* (main branches at Centraal Station and Schiphol Airport, open 24hr), which tend to give the best rates; others include *Change Express* and *Thomas Cook*. Beware of places such as *Chequepoint* that offer seemingly good rates but then charge very high commissions (see box opposite), or, conversely, charge no commission but give bad rates. You can also change money at post offices, major department stores like *Vroom & Dreesman* and *De Bijenkorf*, and VVV counters, though you won't get as good a deal. Hotels, hostels and campsites nearly always give poor rates of exchange.

Where not to change your money

A huge rip-off now prevalent throughout the city is the existence of **private bureaux de change** that mimic the names and appearance of the "official" change places so as to lure in unsuspecting travellers. Although they appear to offer decent exchange rates, they charge extortionate commissions (nine percent or more) – far more than the banks or *GWK*. Stick to the official places mentioned below whenever possible – but, if you have to go elsewhere, always ascertain all the charges before you let go of your money.

spending. In addition, *Visa, Access/Mastercard/ Eurocard, Diners Club* and *American Express* cards can be used to get cash over the counter in most Dutch banks and bureaux de change, if you're prepared to withdraw a minimum amount (between ƒ200 and ƒ500). **American Express** card holders can also withdraw cash or replace lost travellers' cheques by using the machine and office at Damrak 66. Holders of *Amex* cards or cheques can pick up mail sent to this office; letters should be addressed to you by name, and sent to Client Mail Service, *American Express,* Damrak 66, 1012 LM Amsterdam, Netherlands. You need your card or cheques and some form of ID to pick up mail.

Credit and charge cards

Credit cards are less popular in Amsterdam than would be expected, although most mainstream shops, hotels and restaurants will take at least one brand. Check before you commit yourself to

Costs

Despite the fact that eating out can be inexpensive, and getting around the city needn't cost anything at all, visiting Amsterdam can still significantly drain your finances. If you're one person

Banks and bureaux de change

These are the most conveniently placed branches: for full listings, look in the Yellow Pages.

ABN-Amro Vijzelstraat 32 (corner Kerkstraat); Dam Square; Damrak 33; Leideseplein; Leidsestraat 1; Rozengracht 88; Rokin 80

Rabobank Dam Square; Nieuwmarkt 20

ING Bank Damrak 80; Herengracht 580 (near Amstel); Rozengracht 8

VSB Bank Singel 548, near Muntplein

Change Express
Damrak 86 (daily 8am–midnight; ☎624 6682)
Leidsestraat 106 (daily 8am–midnight; ☎622 1425)
Kalverstraat 150 (daily 8am–8pm; ☎627 8087)

GWK
nationwide toll-free number ☎06/0566
Centraal Station (24hr; ☎627 2731)
Schiphol Plaza (24hr; ☎653 5121)
Leidseplein (daily 8am–11pm; ☎627 3102)
Amstel Station (Mon–Sat 8am–8pm; ☎693 4545)
Sloterdijk Station (daily 8am–8pm; ☎688 1213)

Thomas Cook
Dam Square (daily 9am–6pm; ☎625 0922)
Damrak 1–5 (daily 8am–8pm; ☎620 3236)
Leidseplein (daily 9am–6pm; ☎626 7000)

American Express
Damrak 66 (Mon–Fri 9am–5pm, Sat 9am–noon; ☎520 7777)

Emergency numbers for lost and stolen cards and cheques

Access/Mastercard/Eurocard		**Thomas Cook**	
cards	☎030/283 5555	travellers' cheques	☎06/022 8630
travellers' cheques	☎06/022 5821	**Visa**	
American Express		cards	☎06/022 4176
cards	☎504 8666	travellers' cheques	☎06/022 5484
travellers' cheques	☎06/022 0100		
Diners Club		**Note:** *calls to ☎06/0 numbers are free.*	
cards	☎557 3407		

sharing a double room in a reasonably comfortable hotel, eating in moderately priced restaurants and taking in a few museums along with the occasional café stop and canal ride, you would probably be looking at spending around ƒ170–190 a day (£70–80/$105–120). By watching every cent, staying in the cheapest hostels and hanging out on the canal-side with supermarket sustenance, you could scrape by on ƒ50 a day (£20/$35), ƒ60 if you include one meal at a student cafeteria.

As a guide, Amsterdam's **accommodation** runs from ƒ20 (£8/$12) for a bed in a single-sex dorm up to ƒ4,250 for the Royal Suite at the *Amstel Intercontinental Hotel*. A more average double room costs around ƒ180 (£75/$115). **Food** can cost as much or (almost) as little as you like. Many restaurants serve good, simple, unremarkable fare for ƒ20–40 a head (£8–17/$13–25). Snacks on the street – *frites* (chips/french fries), falafel (Middle Eastern-style fast food), pizza and the ubiquitous *broodje* (sandwich) – are mostly ƒ5 or less. Supermarket food, especially fresh vegetables, can often cost more than you'd expect, so it pays to explore the

street markets too. **City transport** is incredibly good value. If you buy a 15-strip *strippenkaart* for ƒ11.25 (£4.00/$6.25) on your first day, you can make seven separate tram, bus or metro journeys (or seven people can make one journey) before you need to buy another one. And bear in mind that in central Amsterdam no attraction is more than a half-hour's stroll away in any case. **Museums**, though, can easily eat away at your wallet: average admission prices hover around the ƒ7.50–10 mark (around £4/$6). If you intend to visit more than four museums during your stay, the *museumjaarkaart* ("museum year-card") will turn out worthwhile: at ƒ45 it gives free entry to most museums in the country (although not, significantly, the Anne Frank House).

As for **incidental expenses**, ƒ2.50 buys a cup of coffee or a small glass of beer (with a large head); no Dutch person would drink a pint of beer, but if you ask for one you'll get charged about ƒ7. A wedge of apple cake is ƒ2.75, today's English newspaper ƒ5, developing a roll of film an outrageous ƒ35. And just so you know, hashish and marijuana both come in ƒ10 and ƒ25 bags; the more powerful it is, the less you get.

Points of arrival

Points of arrival in Amsterdam are fairly central, with the exception of Schiphol Airport, which has, in any case, quick and efficient connections with the city. The hub for most travel is Centraal Station, in the heart of the city and connected by tram, bus and metro with all parts of Amsterdam.

By Air

Amsterdam has only one international airport, **Schiphol**. This is connected by **train** with Amsterdam's Centraal Station (often abbreviated to C.S.) – a fast service leaving every fifteen minutes during the day, and every hour at night

(1am–6am); the journey takes twenty minutes and costs *f*6. There are trains from Schiphol to almost all of the suburban stations around Amsterdam, should you need them, though bear in mind that not all trains from Schiphol to Amsterdam stop at Centraal Station – check the signs on the platforms.

Getting into the city by **taxi** is quick and easy but will set you back well over *f*50. More affordable is *KLM*'s "Hotel Bus Service" (☎649 1393), which runs daily from Schiphol direct to several useful points in the centre of Amsterdam – the service is open to anyone and you don't have to be staying at one of the five-star hotels on the route. Buses leave Schiphol main entrance every

---

TRAVEL INFORMATION

Schiphol Airport General information ☎601 9111. Flight and arrivals information ☎06/350 34050 (50c/min; touch-tone operation; English option).

Train Information International ☎06/9296; domestic ☎06/9292 (both 50c/min).

Travel agents (reisburo's)

NBBS
Central booking line ☎620 5071
Branches at Rokin 38 and Utrechtsestraat 48. The nationwide student/youth travel organization, and the best source (for everyone) of discount train tickets and flights.

Eurolines
Rokin 10 ☎627 5151
Long-distance buses all over Europe.

Budget Air
Rokin 34 ☎627 1251

Nouvelles Frontières
Van Baerlestraat 3 ☎664 4131
P.C. Hooftstraat 116 (3rd floor) ☎664 4131
See also the Gouden Gids (Yellow Pages) for small high-street agents dealing in specific destinations.

Airlines (luchtvaartmaatschappijen)

Aer Lingus			**KLM**	
Heiligeweg 14	☎623 8620		G. Metsustraat 2–6	☎474 7747
Air France			**Martinair**	
Schiphol Airport	☎446 8800		Schiphol Airport	☎601 1222
Air UK			**Northwest Airlines**	
Schiphol Airport	☎601 0633		Weteringschans 85c	☎627 7141
British Airways			**Sabena**	
Schiphol Airport	☎601 5413		Weteringschans 26	☎626 2966
British Midland			**Transavia**	
Strawinskylaan 721	☎662 2211		Schiphol Airport	☎604 6555

---

half-hour from 6.30am to 3pm, then every hour from 3pm until 8pm, and stop at Leidseplein, Westermarkt, Dam Square, Nieuwezijds Voorburgwal and Prins Hendrikkade, before returning to Schiphol. A one-way ticket costs ƒ17.50.

As for Schiphol itself, its claim to be the businessperson's favourite airport is well founded: it's compact enough to keep walking to a minimum, directional signs are clear and plentiful, and the duty-free shop is the cheapest in Europe. There are **bureaux de change** in the arrivals hall, plus a *GWK* exchange office in Schiphol's train station (open 24hr) and a **post office** in the departures lounge (daily 6am–10pm). **Left-luggage** is open daily from 7am to 11pm and costs ƒ8 per item per day; there are also lockers, starting at ƒ8 per day, with a maximum of five days. The **lost and found** enquiry number is ☎601 2325 (Mon–Fri 9am–4pm).

By Train

Amsterdam has a number of suburban **train stations**, but all major domestic and international traffic comes through Amsterdam Centraal Station (C.S.).

Arriving here, you are at the end of the metro line, at the hub of most bus and tram routes, and Dam Square is just five minutes' walk away. The station's facilities include a **porter** service (24hr; ƒ2.50 per item), a 24-hour *GWK* **bank and money-changing office**, a *VVV* tourist information office (Mon–Sat 8am–7.30pm, Sun 9am–4.30pm), self-service **lockers** (24hr access, but you can only open and close the locker once; ƒ4 or ƒ6 for 24hr, depending on size; maximum period 72hr), a staffed **left-luggage** office (24hr access; ƒ10 per item; maximum period 10 days, after which ƒ50 per item per week), a **cashpoint machine** (which accepts *Eurocheque* cards, *Cirrus*, *Visa*, *Eurocard* and *Mastercard*), as well as the usual array of shops, newsstands and restaurants, including a deeply atmospheric café on Platform 2b, which doubles as a top-class French restaurant – see p.217 for details. It's worth mentioning that not only is it forbidden to **sleep** anywhere in the station (and the police will move you on if you try), but with the number of shady characters hanging around after midnight, it's also inadvisable.

Leaving the station, taxis queue for custom to your right (call ☎677 7777 24hr). Two ranks of trams converge here: on your left are trams #4,

#9, #16, #24 and #25; on your right are trams #1, #2, #5, #11, #13 and #17. For details of the ticketing system, see p.36–37. The *GVB* public transport office is in the small, squat building with a revolving sign in English, to your left over the tram tracks; the *VVV* tourist information office is close by, in the same building as *Smits Koffiehuis*. If you know where you're heading for in the city, and need other tram lines, take the #1 from Centraal Station to connect with the #14 at Dam Square, the #6, #7 and #10 at Leidseplein, or the #3 and #12 at 1e Constantijn Huygensstraat.

The metro can be reached down the stairs to the left; all the city buses leave from further over behind the trams to the left.

By Bus

Eurolines long-distance buses arrive at **Amstel Station**, out to the southeast of the city. The station concourse has a *GWK* bank and money-changing office (open Mon–Sat 7.30am–9pm, Sun 10am–6pm), and a *GVB* municipal transport office; **taxis** are generally available (if not call ☎677 7777). If you're going to take any form of public transport from here, you need a *strippenkaart* (see p.361). The metro journey to Centraal Station takes about ten minutes; if you know you're staying in or around the Red Light District, get off at Nieuwmarkt instead. From Amstel Station there is only one tram line, the #12, which leaves from across the road and down the steep grassy bank. The route skirts the centre of the city, but it does run close to the museums. To reach the centre, take it to Museumplein (tenth stop), then wait on the same side of the street for a tram #5, which runs up to Centraal Station. The buses from Amstel Station don't go anywhere useful at all.

Hoverspeed's buses stop at two places in Amsterdam. The first stop is at **Stadionplein**, near the old Olympic Stadium out in the south of the city, from where you can take tram #6 to Leidseplein or tram #16 to Dam Square and Centraal Station; but it's far better to wait until the end of the line at **Leidseplein**, one of Amsterdam's main central squares. From here you can take trams #1, #2, #5 or #11 north to Dam Square and Centraal Station; tram #5 south to the museums; tram #6 east to the *Arena* hostel; or tram #10 west to the Jordaan. There is a cashpoint machine just next to *Häagen-Dazs* that accepts *Eurocheque* cards, *Cirrus*, *Visa*, *Master-card* and *Eurocard*; and just round the corner is a VVV information office (Mon–Sat 9am–7pm, Sun 9am–5pm), where you can book a hotel, buy a map or get a *strippenkaart*.

By Car

Coming in on either the **A4 (E19)** from The Hague or the **A2 (E35)** from Utrecht, you should experience few traffic problems, and the city centre is clearly signposted as soon as you approach Amsterdam's southern reaches. For the western and central portions of the city, follow the A10

Einsteinweg and come off at either the Osdorp or Geuzenveld exits; for the south, follow the A10 Ringweg-Zuid ("Orbital-South") and come off at either the Amstelveen or the RAI Exhibition Centre exits.

Be advised, though, that in the central portion of the city – the area bounded by the canals – tortuous **one-way systems** have been set up deliberately to discourage people from using cars; **street parking**, as well as being limited, is very expensive, and there are teams of wheel-clampers who take their job very seriously. For more on the hazards of driving in Amsterdam, see p.38.

City Transport

Amsterdam is small by European capital standards, its public transport is excellent, and most of the things you might conceivably want to see can be found in the city's compact centre. Getting around couldn't be easier.

Walking

The best way to get around is to **walk**: virtually everything of interest is within walking distance and you'll also see more (remember, this is a city built around canals). As a broad reference, it takes at most three-quarters of an hour to stroll from Centraal Station to the Rijksmuseum, which is about the longest walk you'd ever need to do. Bear in mind, however, that it takes a while to get used to the traffic, a combination of cars, trams, buses and bicycles that can make crossing the road a hazardous business.

Trams, buses and the metro

Apart from walking, **trams** are the easiest way to get around, with a network that's comprehensive and inexpensive. Apart from a couple of stops in the eastern section of the centre, most of the city's **metro** stations are in the suburbs and used mainly by commuters: starting at Centraal Station, the routes connect with the building complexes of Bijlmermeer to the southeast, and the *sneltram* ("rapid-tram") running down to Amstelveen. The system is clean, modern and punctual, but can be a bit frightening at night.

Similarly, **buses** are only really useful for going to the outskirts.

Your first stop should be the **GVB** public transport office (Mon–Fri 7am–9pm, Sat & Sun 8am–9pm) in front of Centraal Station, where you'll find a free **route map** and an English guide to the ticketing system. Failing that, for details of all public transport nationwide, phone ☎06/ 9292 (Mon–Fri 7am–11pm, Sat & Sun 8am–11pm; 50c/min). All tram and bus stops have a detailed map of the network. The entire system runs at approximately the same **times** (Mon–Fri 6am–12.15am, Sat 6.30am–12.15am, Sun 7.30am–12.15am). After midnight seven hourly **night bus** routes come into operation, with those numbered #73–76 serving the centre. Be warned, though, that for some reason there is a city-wide gap in the night bus service between 2am and 4am; the *GVB* has a leaflet detailing all the routes.

As a general rule, **get on trams** by the rear doors (push the button). If the doors start to close before you've got on, put your foot on the bottom step, which will keep them open. To signal to the driver that you want to get off, push one of the buttons dotted at regular intervals down the length of the cars. This is especially important out in the suburbs or after dark, when drivers will blithely keep driving until someone tells them to stop. To get on a tram after dark, hold out your hand.

Tickets

The most common type of ticket, used on all forms of transport, is the **strippenkaart**. These are valid all over the country and work on a zonal basis: you stamp a number of strips for your journey, with each zone you cross counting as one strip. However, in addition to counting the zones, you must also stamp a strip for yourself: a journey across one zone requires two strips to be stamped, a journey across two zones requires three strips, and so on. Most journeys in the centre of the city only cross one zone (and therefore need two strips). More than one person can use a *strippenkaart*, as long as the requisite number of strips is stamped.

Some **trams** have a conductor sitting in the back, in which case offer him/her your *strippenkaart* and ask for "one zone". On other trams you're trusted to do it yourself. Fold your *strippenkaart* over to expose only the last of the strips your journey requires, and feed it into the little yellow box near the tram doors. On **buses**, get on at the front and ask the driver to stamp your *strippenkaart*. Once stamped, *strippenkaarts* can be used to transfer between trams, buses and the metro for up to an hour.

The most economical *strippenkaart* has fifteen strips (currently ƒ11.25); they can be picked up all over the city at many postcard shops and tobacconists, *GVB* offices (at Centraal Station, Prins Hendrikkade 108 and Amstel Station), VVV offices, post offices, and in all train stations at the ticket counters and from the yellow ticket machines (punch in code "2222" and pay in coins only). There's also a 45-strip card available for ƒ33.00 – useful if you intend to stay a little longer, or travel further afield. Two-, three- and eight-strip tickets can be bought on board trams, but these work out considerably more expensive.

If you don't want to be bothered with stamping a *strippenkaart*, you can buy a **dagkaart** or day ticket – valid for as many days as you need, up to a maximum of nine: prices start at a steep ƒ8 for one day, going up to ƒ23.50 for four days, with each additional day charged at ƒ3.75. Those planning to stay for some time might consider investing in longer-term tickets. The first possibility is a *sterabonnement* or **season ticket**, valid for a week, month or year and available from the same outlets as a *strippenkaart*. A one-star weekly pass, valid for one zone only, currently costs ƒ16.25, and you'll need a photograph and your passport to buy one. There is also a season ticket particularly aimed at part-time workers, who might use the transport system only three days a week. The **twaalf-reizenkaart** ("12-journeys card") costs ƒ16.25 and is valid for a maximum of 14 days; you use it like a *strippenkaart*, except you only stamp one strip for each journey, not two.

The whole transport network is remarkably inexpensive, well-maintained and efficient, and certainly worth paying for; unfortunately, the ticketing system is also wide open to abuse. But the city has been cracking down recently on those who don't pay (known as **zwartrijders** – "black riders"), and wherever you're travelling, and at whatever time of day, there's a reasonable

chance you'll have your ticket checked. If caught riding "black", you're liable for a ƒ60 fine (plus the price of the ticket you should have bought), due on the spot; claims of "I didn't know" or "No Nederlands speaking" simply don't wash. In a typically pragmatic Amsterdam move, the *GVB* has also recently begun converting many tram lines back to two-person operation: paying to have more conductors on the trams means losing less money in the end to the *zwartrijders*, since it's quite literally impossible for a potential fare-dodger to avoid a conductor's eye.

Bikes

Another possibility, and a practical one, is to go native and opt for a **bicycle**: the city's well-defined network of bicycle lanes (*fietspaden*) makes this a very safe and pleasurable way of getting around. If you haven't brought your own, it's possible to **rent a bike** from the *Take-A-Bike* cycle store at Centraal Station (turn left when you come out of the station; about 75m), or from a number of bike rental firms scattered around town (see box on p.38); if you're camping, it's usually possible to rent bikes from the campsite. Before renting, check out the time you have to bring the bike back (Centraal Station is currently

Cycling Terms	
Tyre	*Band*
Puncture	*Lek*
Brake	*Rern*
Chain	*Keting*
Wheel	*Wiel*
Pedal	*Trapper*
Pump	*Pomp*
Handlebars	*Stuur*
Broken	*Kapot*

Bike rental firms (fietsen-verhuur)

Bike City			**Sint Nicolaas Rent-a-Bike**	
Bloemgracht 70	☎ 626 3721		Sint Nicolaasstraat 14	☎ 623 9715
Bulldog Rent-a-Bike			**Take-A-Bike**	
Oudezijds Voorburgwa 1220	☎ 624 8248		Stationsplein 12	☎ 624 8391
Damstraat Rent-a-Bike			Stationsplein 33	☎ 625 3845
just off Damstraat	☎ 625 5029		**Truus Rent-A-Mountainbike**	
Frédéric Rent-a-Bike			Leidsekruisstraat 23	☎ 638 9481
Brouwersgracht 78	☎ 624 5509		**Zijwind**	
Koenders			Ferdinand Bolstraat 168	☎ 673 7026
Utrechtsedwarsstraat 105	☎ 623 4657			
Macbike			**Moped Rental Service**	
Houtkopersburgwal 16	☎ 620 0985		Marnixstraat 208	☎ 422 0266
Marnixstraat 220	☎ 626 6964			

open latest), any discounts for longer rental periods, the age of the bikes, and so on. All firms ask for some type of security, in the form of a cash deposit (some will take credit card imprints) and/or passport. Some rent out tandems and mountain-bikes.

As for the **rules of the road**, remember that you are legally obliged to have reflector bands on both wheels. Bike lanes are denoted by a white bicycle on a blue background, or a small black oblong sign saying "Fietspad".

A **word of warning**: lock up your bike at *all times*. Bike theft is rife in Amsterdam, and it's common to see the dismembered parts of bicycles still chained to railings, victims of organized gangs armed with bolt cutters – bikes from Amsterdam regularly turn up for sale in Switzerland – or of junkies hoping that someone will buy the bike off them for the price of a fix. Needless to say, if you buy one of these bikes, you're perpetuating a vicious circle of reliance on crime and drugs. If you want to buy a bike from a legal outlet, a clapped-out boneshaker can be had for ƒ40 or so (and sold back when you leave); ƒ100 should get you quite a decent machine. A necessary expense, if you have a bike worth stealing, is a **lock** – plenty of stalls at the Waterlooplein flea market sell bike-locks, though anything flimsier than a ƒ100 reinforced steel loop isn't worth considering. See "Shops and Markets" (p.249) for a list of bike shops.

Taxis

Taxis are plentiful in Amsterdam. They can be found in ranks on the main squares or by phon-

ing the 24-hour radio-controlled central office on ☎677 7777 – you can't hail taxis in the street. Most drivers know their way around fairly well, though rates are pricey by any standards – a ƒ5.60 flat fee, plus ƒ2.80 per kilometre during the day, ƒ3.25 between midnight and 6am. You are legally entitled to see a receipt before handing over any money.

Cars

Amsterdam is a tram and bicycle city. It's generally a bad idea to bring your **car**: the whole of the city centre has a network of convoluted **one-way systems** that will, quite literally, send you round in circles; the official policy of the city government is to limit parking spaces in favour of more bicycle racks; and there are zealous, fast-acting teams of **traffic police** roaming the city (information ☎523 3111), who will clamp or tow away your car whatever the registration plate state. It is also far from unusual, on the narrow canal-side streets, to find yourself stuck behind a motionless lorry, with no way to pass or turn back. What **parking** there is there is expensive, as the entire city is metered: Mon–Sat 9am–7pm you pay ƒ4.25 an hour, Mon–Sat 7–11pm and Sun noon–11pm this drops to ƒ2.25 an hour; during the night metered spaces are free. Meters are not set beside each parking space, though – look for the "pay-and-display"-type machine somewhere nearby, with a luminous yellow "P" sign. A number of hotels offer a special three-day **parking permit** for ƒ60, which, when stuck inside the rear window, means you can park in metered spaces

Car parks

De Bijenkorf
Beursplein, off Damrak

Byzantium
near Leidseplein

Centraal
Prins Hendrikkade 20

Europarking
Marnixstraat 250

De Kolk
N.Z. Voorburgwal

Kroon & Zn
Waterlooplein (under City Hall)

Museumplein
Museumplein

Parking Prinsengracht
Prinsengracht 540–542

*The main 24-hour petrol stations are at
Gooiseweg 10, Sarphatistraat 225,
Marnixstraat 250 and Spaarndammerdijk 218.*

Parking Management Offices (Dienst·Parkeerbeheer)

Bakkerstraat 13 – Rembrandtplein
(Mon–Sat 8am–8pm; ☎ 639 2469)

Korte Leidsedwarsstraat 2 – Leidseplein
(open 24hr; closed from 11pm on Sat to 7.30am
on Mon; ☎ 523 3120)

Prins Hendrikkade 108 – Centraal Station
(Mon–Fri 8.30am–4.30pm; ☎ 555 9849)

Korte Prinsengracht 91 – Jordaan
(Mon–Sat 8am–8pm; ☎ 638 0088)

Cruquiuskade 25 – Eastern Islands
(24hr; ☎ 555 9833)

Car rental agencies

Britain

Avis	☎ 0181/848 8733
Budget	☎ 0800/181181
Eurodollar	☎ 0990/565656
Europcar	☎ 0345/222525
Hertz	☎ 0345/555888
Holiday Autos	☎ 0990/300400

Ireland

Avis	
Belfast	☎ 01232/240404
Budget	
Belfast	☎ 01232/230700
Europcar	
Belfast	☎ 01232/450904
or	☎ 01232/423444
Hertz	
Dublin	☎ 01/660 2255
Holiday Autos	
Dublin	☎ 01/454 9090

Australia and New Zealand

Avis Australia	☎ 1800/225 533
New Zealand	☎ 09/579 5231
Budget Australia	☎ 13 2848
New Zealand	☎ 09/375 2220.
Fly and Drive Holidays	
New Zealand	☎ 09/529 3790
Hertz Australia	☎ 13 3039
New Zealand	☎ 09/309 0989.

North America

Avis	☎ 1-800/331-1084
Budget	☎ 1-800/527-0700
Dollar	☎ 1-800/421-6868
Hertz USA	☎ 1-800/654-3001
Canada	☎ 1-800/263-0600

Car rental agencies (*auto-verhuur*) in Amsterdam

Adams		
Nassaukade	344	☎ 685 0111
Avis		
Nassaukade 380		☎ 683 6061
Bakker		
Hoofdweg 133		☎ 612 4047
Budget		
Overtoom 121		☎ 612 6066
Diks		
van Ostadestraat 278		☎ 662 3366
Eurodollar		
Overtoom 184		☎ 616 2466
Europcar		
Overtoom 51		☎ 683 2123
Hertz		
Overtoom 333		☎ 612 2441
Ouke Baas		
van Ostadestraat 362		☎ 679 4842

without paying any more money. Otherwise, parking permits can be bought in person from any of the Parking Management Offices (see box below) for ƒ25.50 per day, or ƒ127.50 for a week. For answers to any enquiries about parking in Amsterdam, call ☎553 0300.

If you've been **clamped**, a sticker on your windscreen tells you where to pay the ƒ130 fine (information ☎553 0333); once you've done this, return to your car and the police will come and remove the clamp. Or, if you prefer, you can pay ƒ29 extra for a courier from *Klem Hulp* (☎620 3750) to go and pay for you. If you cause an obstruction, park in an illegal place or don't pay your fine within 24 hours, your car will be **towed away**. Reclaiming a car from the pound costs a further ƒ350 or so if you do it within 24 hours; if you leave it any longer you pay another ƒ55 for every six hours. The car pound is way out in the northeast of the city at Cruquiuskade 25 (☎555 9800; open 24hr; bus #22 or #28 from Centraal Station), and they don't accept credit cards.

Even when you're mobile, the abundance of trams and bikes makes driving hazardous, to say the least: bikes and pedestrians generally take precedence, trams hardly ever give way to cars, and private cars are not permitted to drive on the tram tracks. And in situations involving injury to a pedestrian or cyclist, at least fifty percent of the blame lies automatically with the car driver, even if the vehicle was stationary at the time. If you do **bring your own car**, an ordinary driver's licence is acceptable, and the Dutch automobile organization, *ANWB* (pronounced "ah-en-vay-bay"), offers reciprocal repair/breakdown services to members of most foreign motoring organizations, as long as they hold a Letter of International Assistance – available from your home organization. Their office in Amsterdam is at Museumplein 5 (Mon–Fri 9am–5.30pm, Sat 9am–4pm; ☎673 0844). Their repair service – **De Wegenwacht** – can be called for free nationwide on ☎06/0888. If you're not a member of your home motoring organization, you can either pay for breakdown service (although they may not take cheques or credit cards on the spot), or, for ƒ150, become a member of the *ANWB* (much the cheaper option).

For getting out of town, it's better to **rent a car** by the day or week. All the major agencies are represented in Amsterdam, although the best deals are often with the local operators, whose prices start at around ƒ50–70 a day plus around

40c per kilometre over 100km. For long journeys out of Amsterdam, the major firms' unlimited mileage rates can prove cheaper; phone around for special weekend rates as well. Another option is to book a car in advance through a specialist agent like *Holiday Autos* (see p.39 for phone number), whose rates can sometimes undercut all the competition. *Ouke Baas*, on Van Ostadestraat (☎679 4842), offer a discount to students. Briefly, the **rules of the road** include a maximum speed limit within the city of 50kph (31mph), and seatbelts must be worn by all drivers and front-seat passengers.

Water transport

More for fun than for serious transport are the **canal bikes**, pedalboats that take up to four people and can be rented by the hour. From July to September they can be rented daily between 10am and 9.30pm (last pick-up 8.30pm) at any of four central locations – outside the *American Hotel* near Leidseplein, on the Singelgracht opposite the Rijksmuseum, the Prinsengracht outside the Westerkerk, and Keizersgracht near Leidsestraat. In spring and autumn opening times are limited (10am–5pm, 10am–8.30pm & Fri–Sat) and between November and March only the Rijksmuseum pick-up point is in use (daily 10am–5pm, ice permitting). Rental costs ƒ12.50 an hour for the first person, ƒ12.50 for the second person, and ƒ8 each for the third and fourth. There is a deposit of ƒ50, and a map is available for ƒ3.50 showing five possible routes between the pick-up/drop-off points. For further information phone ☎626 5574.

In addition, *Roell Watersport* on Mauritskade, behind the *Amstel Hotel*, is open all year from 8am to sunset, with a jetty on the Prinsengracht at Leidsestraat open in summer only (☎692 9124). They rent pedalboats (two people ƒ18; four people ƒ30) and **rowing boats** (up to four people ƒ30) by the hour, with a ƒ50 deposit. They also rent small **motorboats**, at ƒ80 for an hour and a half (ƒ150 deposit plus ID), and an entire wood-and-brass **lounge boat** (with skipper) for up to 35 people at ƒ400 per hour and a half.

If you want to combine a canal tour (see below) with genuine transport, there is a **canal bus** service that operates on two circular routes beginning and ending on the Singelgracht opposite the Rijksmuseum; stopping points are Leidseplein, Keizersgracht (corner Raadhuisstraat), Prinsengracht (Westerkerk), Centraal Station and Waterlooplein. The whole journey takes about an hour and boats leave the Rijksmuseum every twenty minutes – you can pick them up at any stop. A day ticket (10am–8pm) allowing you to hop on and off as many times as you like costs ƒ19.50; for ƒ27.50 you get admission to the Rijksmuseum as well. They also run candlelight cruises after dark; for more details call ☎623 9886.

Another combination of canal trip and real transport is the **Museumboat**. This runs once every half-hour (45min in winter) calling at seven jetties located at or near eighteen of the city's major museums. A day ticket will cost you ƒ22; a day ticket including a canal cruise and free entrance to *Madame Tussaud's* (if you can pack it all in with the museums) is ƒ27.50. Their office and main boarding point is in front of Centraal Station; for more details call ☎625 6464.

For the seriously moneyed, there are also private **canal taxi** services. For an eight-person skippered boat, *Water Taxi*, outside Centraal Station (daily 11am–10pm; ☎622 2181), charges a steep ƒ90 for thirty minutes; larger boats cost more. You can order a canal taxi for any time of the day or night, although prices rise after midnight.

Organized tours

One way of getting oriented is to take a **canal trip** on one of the ubiquitous glass-topped boats that jam the major canals during the summer season. While not exactly riveting, these trips are the best way to see the canal houses, and have a soporific charm if you're feeling lazy. There are many to choose from, dotted all over the city centre (*Amstel* and *P. Kooij* are two of the better ones, with refreshingly uncanned commentaries); prices for a one-hour tour are around ƒ15 for adults, ƒ7.50 for kids. However, they are so popular you may well find you have to queue for a place in summer – see box for a list of operators.

An appealing **alternative** is to hang out on the "Smoke Boat Cruises" run by the American comedy company *Boom Chicago* (information ☎639 2707). Their open boat is tiny (a maximum of 12 people) and leaves at 3pm and 10.30pm daily from *Boom Chicago's* theatre at Lijnbaansgracht 238, near Leidseplein, for a ninety-minute tour through the tiny canals of the Red Light District (inaccessible to the larger boats). A ticket costs ƒ15 and includes a free drink, but on the night boat priority is given to members of *Boom Chicago's* audience that night. An indication of the mood of the "cruise" is that there are no restrictions on smoking cannabis while on board.

For a more mainstream experience, the GVB offers a two-hour tour of the "nostalgic side of Amsterdam" by **ferry** (mid-April to mid-Oct Sun & hols except April 30 11am, 12.45pm, 2.30pm & 4.15pm); tickets are a very reasonable ƒ9 (children ƒ6), with a buffet on board. Starting from Pier 8 on De Ruyterkade, behind Centraal Station, the ferry follows a circuitous route along the River IJ eastwards, skirting the KNSM island and the eastern harbours, as well as winding into Nieuwendam, a quiet and picturesque old district of Amsterdam North, before returning to Centraal Station.

As far as land-based **city tours** go, the GVB runs a ninety-minute tour by **tourist tram** (June–Sept Sun & hols every half-hour noon–4pm) from the *Victoria Hotel* near Centraal Station, which takes in the main sights of the immediate city centre for just ƒ10 (children ƒ7.50) – tickets allow you to hop on and off all afternoon. As for **bus** tours, operators like *Lindbergh* (the cheapest – Damrak 26, ☎622 2766), *Keytours* (Dam 19, ☎623 5051) and *Holland International* (Damrak 90, ☎625 3035) run three-hour tours with stopoffs and live commentary; tickets start at around ƒ30, with pricier options often including a visit to a diamond factory, a canal cruise or entry to the Rijksmuseum. The same organizations also run a range of **excursions** into the outlying regions of Holland – pick up leaflets for details.

If you fancy a **cycle tour**, contact *Yellow Bike*, Nieuwezijds Kolk 29 (April–Oct daily 9.30am & 1pm; ☎620 6940), which organizes three-hour guided tours around the city, taking in all the major sights (and a few minor ones). Tours cost ƒ29, which includes the bike. They also do a full-day bike tour of the countryside to the north of Amsterdam; reserving ahead is advisable.

Yellow Bike are also among the number of companies and individuals that lead **walking tours** of the city. In their *What's On* magazine, the VVV publishes an extensive list of recommended guides; the sample we list here covers those with a particular specialist angle. It makes sense to call around for prices and full information before booking any guided tour.

Canal trips

Amstel

Stadhouderskade, opposite Heineken Brewery
☎ 626 5636. Daily every 30min 9am–6pm. Live commentary.

Holland International

Stationsplein ☎ 622 7788. April–Oct daily every 15min 9am–6pm, every 45min 6–10pm; Nov–March daily every 30min 10am–6pm. Taped commentary.

P. Kooij

Opposite Rokin 125 ☎ 623 3810. April–Oct daily every 30min 9.30am–10pm; Nov–March daily every 30min 10am–5pm. Live commentary.

Lovers

Opposite Prins Hendrikkade 25 ☎ 622 2181. April–Oct daily every 15min 9am–6pm; Nov–March daily every 30min 9am–6pm. Video commentary.

Meyers

Damrak, Jetties 4 & 5 ☎ 623 4208. April–Oct daily every 20min 9am–6pm; Nov–March daily every 30min 9am–5pm. Taped commentary.

Guides

Walter M.G. Altena
national guide ☎ 662 9784

Amsterdam Walking Tours
cultural and historic tours ☎ 640 9072

Archivisie
architecture ☎ 625 8908

Artifex
art history ☎ 620 8112

Camille's Pleasure Tours
Red Light District ☎ 675 2822

Van Garderen
history and architecture ☎ 627 5822

Guidor Netherlands
nationwide ☎ 070/320 2558

Post and Phones

City centre post offices

Singel 250, corner with Raadhuisstraat

Oosterdokskade, 5min east of Centraal Station (closes 9pm)

St Antoniebreestraat 16, near Nieuwmarkt

Keizersgracht 757, corner with Amstel

Kerkstraat 167, corner with Nieuwe Spiegelstraat

Waterlooplein, in the Stadhuis

Plantage Middenlaan 167, corner with Pl. Kerklaan

Haarlemmerdijk 99

Bloemgracht 300, corner with Lijnbaansgracht

For further locations, and information on the postal service, call free ☎ 06/0417.

Amsterdam's main **post office** is at Singel 250, on the corner with Raadhuisstraat, and is open Monday to Friday 9am to 6pm (until 8pm on Thurs) and on Saturday from 10am to 1.30pm (☎ 556 3311). Turn left at the top of the stairs for the postal services section, and take a queue number. Other facilities include phones, phone directories, phonecard vending machines, photocopiers (25c), passport-photo booths, a philatelic counter, a stationery department for parcel-packing, string and envelopes, as well as a bank, a travel agency and a temp agency. For the record, **postal charges** right now are: ƒ1 for an airmail letter (up to 20g) to anywhere in Europe; ƒ1.60 airmail to the rest of the world (ƒ1.20 by surface mail). Postcards to all destinations cost ƒ1 and aerogrammes ƒ1.30. **Postboxes** are everywhere, but be sure to use the correct slot – labelled *overige* for destinations other than Amsterdam. To receive mail **poste restante**, letters should be addressed to you at "Poste Restante, Hoofdpostkantoor PTT, Singel 250, 1012 SJ Amsterdam, Netherlands". The poste restante section, along with the postboxes, has a separate street entrance from the main office, to the left and down the stairs (open Mon–Fri 7am–7pm, Sat 9am–noon). To pick up mail you'll need your passport.

You can send and receive **e-mail** at the *Freeworld Internet Café*, Korte Nieuwendijk 30 (Mon–Thurs & Sun 9am–1am, Fri & Sat 9am–2am; ☎ 620 0902; Mac or PC access costs ƒ2.50 for 20min; addresses <visitor1@cafe.euronet.nl> and <visitor2...>). You can also send e-mail from *Internet Café Tops*, Prinsengracht 480, near the Leidsestraat (Mon–Thurs & Sun 10am–1am, Fri & Sat 10am–2am; ☎ 638 4108). They charge ƒ2.50 per 15min; or, for ƒ50 you get 7 hours' access plus a personal e-mail address. To send a **telegram**, call ☎ 06/0409.

Telephones

Although there are some coin-phones left (most requiring 50c as a minimum), most **public phones** in the street now take **phonecards** only – these can be bought at post offices and VVV offices in denominations of ƒ5, ƒ10 and ƒ25, and are valid in Germany as well as the Netherlands. The green-trim phone-booths are similar to modern British kiosks and most others in Europe, with a digital display indicating the amount of credit remaining when you insert your card. Although the display starts out in Dutch with *"neem hoorn op"* ("pick up the receiver"), pressing the button marked "English Français Deutsch" makes it switch languages. It's possible to dial direct to anywhere in the world, and all these phones have an inbuilt

Addresses are written as, for example, "Kerkstr. 79 II", which means the second-floor apartment at number 79, Kerkstraat. The ground floor is indicated by **hs** (*huis*, "house") after the number; the basement is **sous** (*sousterrain*).

For some reason, the Dutch ran out of ideas for street names, and many streets share the same name. To differentiate between them, **1e** or **2e** is placed in front: these are abbreviations for *Eerste* ("first") and *Tweede* ("second") – first and second streets of the same name. Thus, "1e Vogelstraat 10" is a completely different address from "2e Vogelstraat 10". There are plenty of **3e** (*Derde*, or "third"), and occasionally **4e** (*Vierde*, "fourth") streets too.

To confuse matters even more, many **side streets** take the name of the main street they

run off, with the addition of the word *dwars*, meaning "crossing": Palmdwarsstraat is a side street off Palmstraat.

T/O (*tegenover*, or "opposite") in an address shows that the address is a boat: hence "Prinsengracht T/O 26" would indicate a boat to be found opposite building no. 26 on Prinsengracht.

The main canals begin their **numbering** from the top left at Brouwersgracht and increase as they progress counterclockwise. By the time they reach the Amstel, Herengracht's house numbers are in the 600s, Keizersgracht's in the 800s and Prinsengracht's in the 1100s.

Dutch **post codes** – made up of four figures and two letters – can be found in the directory kept at post offices.

memory of "Home Country Direct" numbers: see "Collect calls" below. The cheap rate period for international calls is between 8pm and 8am during the week and all day at weekends. Most hotels will allow you to make international calls, but check prices first as charges are considerably higher than from a public phone. There are also a few commercial **phone centres** dotted around town, which offer phone service, fax and photocopying facilities, but most are targeted at businesspeople and consequently very expensive.

Since 1996, the PTT has started charging a ƒ1 fee for **International Directory Enquiries** (☎06/8418); you can get around this by calling from a public phone, but you still have to insert a phonecard first. The **International Operator** remains free (☎06/0410). For further assistance, the **Amsterdam Yellow Pages** (*Gouden Gids*) can be found in most bars and cafés and includes a "Tourist Page" in English; many hotels stock the free "Visitors Guide", a mini-Yellow Pages in English. To obtain your own copy, contact customer services on ☎567 6767.

All **Amsterdam phone numbers** are made up of seven digits; despite the fact that the switch from six digits was made in 1991, some businesses have yet to update. If the number you want to call has only six digits, adding a "6" to the front is pretty reliable. Amsterdam's **area code**, which you use when dialling the city from anywhere else in Holland, is ☎020 (Schiphol Airport falls within Amsterdam's boundaries).

Calling from abroad, dial your international access number (☎00 in the UK, ☎011 in the US), followed by ☎3120, then the seven-digit number. Where applicable, area codes for other cities are given in the text.

In 1995, the Netherlands underwent a complete phone renumbering scheme; every single number in the country apart from those in Amsterdam, The Hague and Rotterdam changed. If you need to contact someone in another part of the country and can't get through, try the operator or national directory enquiries.

The ubiquitous and confusing ☎**06 numbers** are the Dutch equivalent of the British ☎0800 and ☎0891 numbers (US ☎1-800 and ☎1-900) combined into one. Although they can be anything between four and seven digits long, any number beginning ☎06/0 or ☎06/4 is **toll-free**. ☎06 followed by anything else is generally an information line or mobile phone and more

PTT Telecom are currently planning to change the ☎**06 system** and from January 1998 the ☎06 code will no longer exist. Precise information wasn't available at the time of writing but it seems likely that 06 toll-free numbers will be prefaced with ☎0800 and information lines numbers will have the code ☎0900. If you can't get through on one of the numbers we've listed, check with your hotel, or look in a phone booth, where the new codes should be displayed.

Home Country Direct access numbers

UK Direct (BT)	☎ 06/022 9944
Call UK (Mercury)	☎ 06/022 4405
USA Direct (AT&T)	☎ 06/022 9111
Call USA (MCI)	☎ 06/022 9122
Sprint Express	☎ 06/022 9119
Australia Direct	☎ 06/022 0061
Canada Direct	☎ 06/022 9116
Ireland Direct	☎ 06/022 0353
NZ Direct	☎ 06/022 4464

expensive than usual; occasionally, though, it's a little cheaper – the rate should be stated wherever you find the number listed, but a voice will warn you (in Dutch) how much the call will cost before you're connected.

Collect calls

The multilingual **international operator** (see box) is able to place collect calls. Alternatively, you can use the **"Home Country Direct"** numbers – all toll-free – that connect you to the operator in your own country for making collect calls, calling-card calls or credit-card calls; this can be a cheaper method. Access numbers are listed in the box below. All public callboxes, however, have an inbuilt **memory** of these access numbers. Lift up the receiver, press "English Français Deutsch" to get English information, then press "Special Functions". Press the button next to the "Home Country Direct" option and an alphabetical list of countries will appear, which you can scroll through using the "More" button. When you've found the one you want, press the adjacent button and the phone will dial the number automatically.

International Dialling Codes

(plus cost of off-peak direct-dialled calls)

Britain and Northern Ireland ☎ 00 44
(ƒ0.82/min)

Republic of Ireland ☎ 00 353
(ƒ1.10/min)

Australia ☎ 00 61
(ƒ3.30/min)

New Zealand ☎ 00 64
(ƒ3.30/min)

South Africa ☎ 00 27
(ƒ3.85/min)

USA and **Canada** ☎ 00 1
(ƒ1.37/min)

Useful Numbers

Operator (domestic and international)
☎ 06/0410
24hr; free

Domestic directory enquiries ☎ 06/8008
7am–2am; 60c per call

International directory enquiries ☎ 06/8418
24hr; ƒ1 per call

Emergency numbers

In an emergency, dial	☎ 112
Police (*politie*)	☎ 622 2222
Fire (*brandweer*)	☎ 621 2121
Ambulance (*ambulance*)	☎ 555 5555
Rape/sexual assault	☎ 612 7576

Mon–Fri 10.30am–11.30pm, Sat & Sun 3.30pm–11.30pm

The Police and Drugs

Emergencies ☎ 112

City-centre police stations
HQ/JordaanElandsgracht 117 ☎ 559 9111

Red Light District Warmoesstraat 44
☎ 559 2210

Dam SquareN.Z. Voorburgwal 104
NieuwmarktKloveniersburgwal T/O 26
☎ 559 3260

Flower MarketSingel 455 ☎ 559 3295

UtrechtsestraatPrinsengracht 1109
☎ 559 4320

WeteringcircuitLijnbaansgracht 219
☎ 559 2310

You're unlikely to come into much contact with Amsterdam's police force (*politie*), a laid-back bunch in dodgem-sized patrol cars. Few operate on the beat, and in any case Amsterdam is one of the safest cities in Europe: bar-room brawls are highly unusual, muggings uncommon, and street crime much less conspicuous than in many other capitals.

Nonetheless, it's always worth taking precautions against **petty crime**: secure your things in a locker when staying in a dorm; never leave any valuables in a tent; and if you're in a car, take with you everything you don't want to lose, especially the radio, and park in a well-lit public place if you can't find a car park. As far as **personal safety** goes, it's possible to walk anywhere in the city centre at any time of the day or night – though women might get tired of being hassled if they walk through the red-light areas alone. However, the area known as "De Pijp" – specifically the area south of the Sarphatipark – is slowly gaining a minor reputation for crime: there has been the occasional stabbing or shooting on the quieter backstreets late at night. During the day, the area is as safe as anywhere else in Amsterdam; after dark, stick to the main streets.

If you're unlucky enough to have something **stolen**, you'll need to report it to a police station immediately and get them to write out a statement for your insurance company; see "Health and Insurance", p.2.8

If you're **detained** by the police, you don't automatically have the right to a phone call, although in practice they'll probably phone your consulate for you. If your alleged offence is a minor matter, you can be held for up to six hours without questioning; if it is more serious, you can be detained for up to 24 hours.

Drugs

Some residents claim that the liberal municipal attitude to the sale of **drugs** has attracted all sorts of undesirables to the city. This is partly true, but the "cleaning up" of the Zeedijk, once Amsterdam's heroin-dealing quarter, seems to have made open trafficking less frequent and the city a safer place.

Amsterdam has sanctioned the sale of **cannabis** at the *Melkweg* and *Paradiso* nightspots, and at many coffeeshops, since the 1960s. However, bowing to pressure from France and Germany to bring Dutch drugs policy more into line with the rest of Europe, Amsterdam is attempting to force coffeeshops to choose between selling either drugs or alcohol but not both, and limit over-the-counter sales of cannabis to 5g per purchase, down from 30. Accepted practice and the muddiness of existing legislation mean that the police continue to maintain a low public profile and the five-gramme law remains as unenforceable within the city as the old 30-gramme law used to be.

While busts are rare, people over the age of eighteen are now legally allowed to buy just 5g of hashish or marijuana (under one-fifth of an ounce) for personal use at any one time. Possession of amounts up to 30g (1oz) is ignored by the police. Even if you have less on you, the police are still technically entitled to confiscate any quantity they find. In practice, though, you'll probably never even see a policeman from one day to the next, and you'll certainly never be arrested for discreet personal use. It's acceptable to smoke in some bars, but many are strongly against it so don't make any automatic assumptions. If in doubt, ask the barperson. **"Space cakes"** (cakes baked with hashish and sold by the slice), although widely available, count as hard drugs and are illegal; if you choose to indulge, spend a few days working your way up to them, since the effect can be exceptionally powerful and long-lasting (and you can never be sure what's in them anyway). And a word of warning: since all kinds of cannabis are so widely available in coffeeshops, there's no need to buy any on the street – if you do, you're asking to be ripped off.

Dutch drug law is the same throughout the **rest of the country**, as is the attitude, at least in the cities of the Randstad, although the legal niceties are perhaps more strictly interpreted outside central Amsterdam. Needless to say, the one thing you shouldn't do is attempt to take cannabis products out of the country, even across the unmarked land borders. Sniffer dogs regularly meet incoming flights and ferries from the Netherlands, and customs officials around the world are well aware of the attractions of Amsterdam's liberal drug policy.

As far as **other drugs** go, the law surrounding magic mushrooms is that you can legally buy and possess any amount so long as they are fresh, but as soon as you tamper with them in any way (dry or process them, boil or cook them), they become as illegal as crack. *Conscious Dreams*, at Kerkstraat 117 (among other shops), has sold mushrooms openly for years, and continues to do so – see box on p.259. Despite the existence of a lively and growing trade in cocaine and heroin, possession of either could mean a stay in one of the Netherlands' lively and growing jails. And Ecstasy, acid and speed are as illegal in the Netherlands as they are anywhere else.

For **drug-related problems**, *Jellinek Prevention and Consultancy* (office ☎570 2355) operates a Drugs Prevention Centre (Mon–Fri 1–5pm; ☎626 7176) that can provide advice and help in English.

Business Hours and Public Holidays

Holland's reputation for peacefulness and domesticity, as well as its left-leaning labour laws, are borne out by the attitude to shopping – Amsterdam is a long way from being a consumer paradise. Sundays are still valued as a time for relaxation, and the attitude prevails that shopworkers should be allowed Sundays off along with everybody else. Under the law, shops are only allowed to open between certain specific times and for a maximum number of hours in the week. As a consequence, it can be hard (and expensive) to do any shopping outside of normal working hours.

The Dutch weekend fades painlessly into the working week with many smaller shops, even in the centre, staying closed either all day Monday, or on Monday mornings until noon or 1pm. Normal **opening hours** are usually from 9am to 6pm; on Thursday evenings – *koopavond* or "shopping night" in Amsterdam – most places stay open until 9pm. Things shut down a little earlier on Saturday (5 or 5.30pm), and only specifically licensed shopkeepers are supposed to open up on Sunday, although for the big chains on the major shopping streets – Leidsestraat and Kalverstraat – it's pretty much business as usual. A handful of **night shops** – *avondwinkels* – open during the evenings – most of them between about 4pm and 1am; see p.257 for a list.

Museums, especially those that are state-run, tend to follow a pattern: closed on Monday, open Tuesday to Saturday from 10am to 5pm, and from 1 to 5pm on Sunday and public holi-days, though things are slowly changing in favour of seven-day opening. Though closed on December 25 and 26 and January 1, the state-run museums adopt Sunday hours on the remaining **public holidays**, when most shops and banks are closed. For a full list of museums and galleries, and precise details of their opening hours, see the *Museums and Galleries* chapter.

Most **restaurants** are open for dinner from about 5 or 6pm, and though many close as early as 9pm, a few stay open past 11pm. **Bars**, cafés and coffeeshops are either open all day from around 10am or don't open until about 5pm; both varieties close at 1am during the week and 2am at weekends. **Nightclubs** generally function from 11pm to 4am during the week, staying open until 5am at weekends.

Public Holidays (Nationale Feestdagen)

Jan 1, New Year's Day

Good Friday (many shops open)

Easter Sunday and Monday

April 30, the Queen's Birthday

May 5, Liberation Day

Ascension Day – around the end of May

Whit Sunday and Monday – early June

Dec 5, St Nicholas's Birthday (early closing)

Dec 25, Christmas Day (many shops and services run)

Dec 26

Festivals and Events

Most of Amsterdam's **festivals** aren't so much street happenings as music and arts events, in addition to which there are a sprinkling of religious celebrations. Most, as you'd expect, take place in the summer; the Queen's Birthday celebration at the end of April is rapidly becoming the city's most touted and most exciting annual event, with most of the city given over to an impromptu flea market. On a more cultural level, the Holland Festival, held throughout June, attracts a handful of big names. Check with the VVV for further details, and remember that many other interesting events, such as the Easter performance of Bach's *St Matthew Passion* in Naarden and the North Sea Jazz Festival in The Hague, are only a short train ride away.

Diary of Events – February to May

February

• February is normally *Carnaval* month – basically six weeks before Easter – though the three-day celebrations are confined to the south of the Netherlands, centring on Breda, 's-Hertogenbosch and Maastricht. There is, however, also a parade through Amsterdam itself (info on ☎ 623 2568).

• Feb 25: *Commemoration of the February Strike*, around the Docker Statue on J.D. Meijerplein (see p.130).

March

• Sunday closest to March 15: *Stille Omgang* "silent procession" by local Catholics through the Red Light District to the Sint Nicolaaskerk (info on ☎ 023/524 5415; and see p.79).

• Third week: *Blues Festival* at the Meervaart Theatre.

• Last week: *Head of the River* rowing competition on the River Amstel.

April

• April–Aug: *Vondelpark Open Air Theatre* – free theatre, dance and music performances throughout the summer.

• Second or third week: *Paasopenstelling* – the Royal Palace open day.

• Second week: *Nationaal Museumweekend* – free entrance to all the museums in the Netherlands.

• April 30: *Koninginnedag*, the Queen's Birthday, celebrated by a fair on Dam Square, street markets throughout the city, and fireworks in the evening. A street event *par excellence*, which seems to grow annually and is almost worth planning a visit around, though some people claim it has become too commercialized over recent years.

May

• Throughout May: *World Press Photo Exhibition* in the Nieuwe Kerk.

• May 4: *Herdenkingsdag* (Remembrance Day). There's a wreath-laying ceremony and two-minute silence at the National Monument in Dam Square, commemorating the Dutch dead of World War II, as well as a smaller event at the Homomonument in Westermarkt.

• May 5: *Bevrijdingsdag* (Liberation Day). The country celebrates the 1945 liberation from Nazi occupation with bands, speeches and impromptu markets around the city.

Diary of Events – May to December

• First week: *Oosterparkfestival*, held in the large park near the Tropenmuseum. This free festival celebrates the mix of cultures living in the area, with live music and numerous food stands.

• Third week: *KunstRAI*, the annual mainstream contemporary arts fair, held in the RAI conference centre.

June

• Throughout June: the *Holland Festival*, the largest music, dance and drama event in the Low Countries; see the *Entertainment and Nightlife* chapter (p.223) for details.

July

• Last week: *Zomerfestijn*, an informal international festival of modern theatre, music, dance and mime.

August

• First or second week: *Amsterdam 700*, a weekend-long football tournament featuring Ajax Amsterdam and top European clubs.

• Last week: *Uitmarkt*, a weekend where every cultural organization in the city advertises itself with performances either on Museumplein or by the Amstel.

• Last week: *Prinsengrachtconcert*, an evening of classical music on Prinsengracht outside the *Pulitzer Hotel*.

September

• Throughout Sept: *Open Monumentendag* – most of the state-owned monuments have an open day.

• First week: *Bloemencorso*, the Aalsmeer–Amsterdam flower pageant in the city centre, celebrating every kind of flower except tulips, which are out of season. Vijzelstraat is the best place to see things, since the events in Dam Square are normally packed solid.

• Second week: *Hiswa te Water*, state-of-the-art boat show at the Oosterdok. Illuminated canoe-row at night.

• Second or third week: the *Jordaan Festival*, a street festival in a friendly neighbourhood. There's a commercial fair on Palmgracht, talent contests on Elandsgracht and a few street parties.

• Last week: *Amsterdam City Marathon*.

November

• Second or third week: *Parade of Sint Nicolaas*, with the traditional arrival of *Sinterklaas* (Santa Claus) behind Centraal Station; he then parades through the city on his white horse, with his helpers (called *Zwarte Pieten*, "Black Peters" – a bizarrely maintained tradition of white Dutch men blacking-up their faces) handing out sweets and little presents.

December

• Dec 5: Though it tends to be a private affair, *Pakjesavond*, rather than Christmas Day, is when Dutch kids receive their Christmas presents. If you're here on that day and have Dutch friends, it's worth knowing that it's traditional to give a present together with an amusing poem you have written caricaturing the recipient.

• Dec 31: New Year's Eve is big in Amsterdam, with fireworks and crazy celebration everywhere. Most bars and discos stay open until morning. A word of warning, though: Amsterdammers seem to love the idea of throwing lit fireworks around and won't hesitate to chuck one at you: in 1995 two people died and over 800 were injured because of it, half of them bystanders. To preserve your sanity (and looks), stay away, but this might qualify as the wildest and most reckless street partying in Europe.

The Media

There's no difficulty in finding British newspapers – they are on sale almost everywhere in the city on the day of publication, as is the *International Herald Tribune*. Places with a good selection of international publications include the Centraal Station shop, the *Athenaeum Nieuwscentrum* and the *American Book Center* (see p.249).

For those wanting to practise their Dutch, *NRC Handelsblad* is a right-of-centre paper that has perhaps the best news coverage and a liberal stance on the arts; it is the one favoured by the city's intellectuals. *De Volkskrant* is a progressive, leftish daily. *De Telegraaf* was the one paper permitted to continue publication throughout the Nazi occupation; today it is a right-wing popular paper with a well-regarded financial section, and boasts the highest circulation figures in the country. *Algemeen Dagblad* is a right-wing broadsheet, while the middle-of-the-road *Het Parool* ('The Password') and the news magazine *Vrij Nederland* ('Free Netherlands') are the successors of underground resistance newspapers printed during wartime occupation. The Protestant *Trouw* ('Trust'), another former underground paper, is centre-left in orientation with a focus on religion. Bundled in with the weekend *International Herald Tribune* is *The Netherlander*, a small but useful business-oriented review of Dutch affairs in English.

For information about **what's on**, non-Dutch readers have to grapple with the hole left by *Time Out Amsterdam*'s 1996 decision to switch to Internet publication – which has left the city without a single English-language magazine in print. *Time Out* is now to be found at <http://www.time-out.nl>, where its listings are updated weekly. There are some listings sources available, but they're all published by various interested parties, and so none of them can provide objective information. The *Amsterdam Uitburo* (AUB), the cultural office of Amsterdam's city council, publishes the *Uitkrant,* a monthly newspaper in Dutch (free from cafés, bars, libraries, etc) which gives interpretable listings of places and events, though with little or no information attached. The VVV tourist office issues the blandest, most basic listings guide imaginable, *What's On In Amsterdam* monthly, which you can either pick up directly from their offices for ƒ3.50, or free from selected hotels, hostels and restaurants.

TV and Radio

Dutch **TV** isn't up to much, although the quantity of English-language programmes broadcast is high. If you're staying somewhere with cable TV (which covers almost 90 percent of Dutch households), it's also possible to find many foreign TV channels: Britain's BBC1 and BBC2 are available everywhere, along with TV10 Gold, which shows reruns of old British sitcoms and dramas. There's also a host of German, French, Spanish, Italian, Turkish and Arabic stations, some of which occasionally show undubbed British and American movies. Most hotels also pick up some European-wide cable and satellite stations, such as MTV Europe and CNN International. Other Dutch and Belgian TV channels, cable and non-cable, regularly run English-language movies with Dutch subtitles.

As for **Dutch radio**, Radio Honderd at 98.3FM is a stalwart of the squat movement and has an eclectic programming style – world music and dance rubbing shoulders with hardcore noise and long sessions of beat-free bleeps. Radio London (90.4FM) has no discernible English connection, but does have a play-list covering Latin, reggae and African music. Jazz Radio, at 99.8FM, speaks for itself. The Dutch Classic FM, at 101.2FM, like the British version, has bits of well-known classical music jumbled together, with jazz after 10pm. Also, there are a few run-of-the-mill local and national stations – Top 40, easy listening, talk – but surprisingly little music catering to Amsterdam's sizeable immigrant communities, and surprisingly little music of lasting interest in general. There's next to no English-language programming. However, the **BBC** World Service broadcasts practically all day in English on 648kHz (medium wave), with occasional news in German; between 2am and 7am it also occupies 198kHz (long wave). The rest of the time, the BBC's domestic Radio 4 is very clear on 198kHz, though remember that the Six O'Clock News is at 7pm over here. Other domestic British stations that can be picked up include the sports station BBC Radio 5 Live on 693 and 909kHz (MW) and Talk Radio UK on 1053 and 1089kHz (MW).

Travellers with Disabilities

Despite its social progressiveness in other ways, Amsterdam is far from well equipped to deal with the particular requirements of people with mobility problems. The most obvious difficulty you'll face is in negotiating the cobbled streets and narrow, often broken pavements of the central part of the city. Provision on the city's public transport for people with disabilities is practically nonexistent, although, in contrast, the national train network is very well geared up. And yet, while it can be difficult simply getting around, practically all museums and public buildings, including theatres, cinemas, concert halls and hotels, have generally good access.

It's possible to visit Amsterdam on an organized tour specifically designed for people with disabilities – the contacts in the box opposite will be able to put you in touch with specialists. If you prefer to be more independent, it's important to become an authority on where you must be self-reliant and where you may expect help, especially regarding transport and accommodation. It is also vital to be honest – with travel agencies, insurance companies and travel companions. Know your limitations and make sure others know them. If you use a wheelchair (*rolstoel*), have it serviced before you go and carry a repair kit.

Before you go, check your travel insurance small print carefully to make sure that people with a pre-existing medical condition are not excluded. And use your travel agent to make your journey simpler: airlines and bus and train companies can cope better if they are expecting you. A doctor's medical certificate stating your fitness to travel is also extremely useful; some airlines or insurance companies may insist on it. Make sure that you have extra supplies of drugs – carried with you if you fly – and a prescription including the generic name in case of emergency. Carry spares of any clothing or equipment that might be hard to find; if there's an association representing people with your disability, contact them early in the planning process.

If you're **flying**, your airline should automatically notify both your departure and arrival airports (and any transfer airports in between) of any special needs you have. At Schiphol, the national carrier *KLM* has its own team of paramedics to help people with disabilities through the airport; all other airlines use the services of *International Help for the Disabled (IHD)*, who can assist you in all stages of both arrival and departure. They can also be contacted directly on ☎316 1417, 24 hours a day.

If you're planning to use the Dutch **train** network at all during your stay, it is well worth calling the Head Office of *Netherlands Railways* in Utrecht at least 24 hours beforehand (☎030/235 5555). As well as producing informative leaflets on train travel for people with disabilities, they can provide practical help during your journey.

Access in the City

Once in Amsterdam, you'll find the **metro** is accessible, with lifts at every station; you have to press a button to open the train doors. Each stop is normally announced over the PA by the conductor. However, it's the **trams** that are most useful for getting around, and it's the trams that are all but inaccessible to wheelchairs – with their high steps, they may cause problems for those with limited mobility as well. Some more modern trams, mostly to be found on line #5, although also occasionally on lines #1, #2, #11, #13 and #17, have their central doors positioned at pavement level. Outside the rush hour, and with a little help to negotiate the gap between kerb and tram, you might just be able to squeeze your wheelchair on board. One thing you can probably count on if you attempt this is a reasonably enlightened attitude from fellow travellers.

If you can't get around without your **car**, bear in mind all the expense and hassle parking in Amsterdam can involve – see "City Transport" (p.38) for details. Regular **taxis** can only take wheelchairs if they are folded. If you need to travel in your wheelchair, contact the private taxi company *Boonstra* (Koningsbergerstraat 79 ☎613 4134), which has specially designed wheelchair taxis that cost around the same as normal taxis –

a relatively steep ƒ3 or so per kilometre within the city. You need to book at least a day ahead.

Where possible, our listings of **museums** and **accommodation** give an indication of wheelchair access, although you should always call ahead to make sure of the facilities available. One hazard particular to the city are the thousands of *Amsterdammertjes* lining every street – small bollards set into both sides of the roadway, which do a double job of keeping cars off the pavements and out of the canals. Unfortunately, streets in the touristed part of central Amsterdam are narrow enough that sometimes you'll find the *Amsterdammertjes* positioned uncomfortably close to the house-fronts; if someone has chosen to chain up their bicycle in the narrow gap, the pavement may well become impassable to a wheelchair. Again, one thing to take comfort from is the fact that the generally calm local drivers are well used to dealing with bicycles on narrow streets, and should certainly be able to take a slow-moving wheelchair in their stride.

USEFUL CONTACTS

Britain and Europe

Holiday Care Service
2nd floor, Imperial Building
Victoria Rd
Horley
Surrey RH6 9HW   ☎01293 774535
Information on all aspects of travel.

Mobility International
25 rue de Manchester
1070 Brussels
Belgium from UK   ☎00322/410 6297
or   ☎00322/410 6874
Information, guides, tours and exchange programmes.

RADAR
(Royal Association for Disability & Rehabilitation)
12 City Forum
250 City Rd
London EC1V 8AS   ☎0171/250 3222
Minicom   ☎0171/250 4119
A good source of advice on travel abroad.

Tripscope
The Courtyard
Evelyn Rd
London W4 5JL   ☎0181/994 9294
National telephone service offering travel advice.

Ireland

Disability Action Group
2 Annadale Ave
Belfast BT7 3JH   ☎01232/91011

Irish Wheelchair Association
Blackheath Drive

Clontarf
Dublin 3   ☎01/833 8241

North America

Kéroual
4545 av. Pierre de Coubertin
CP 1000
Montréal
PQ, H1V 3R2
Canada   ☎514/252 3104
Specialists in travel for people with limited mobility.

Mobility International USA
PO Box 3551
Eugene, OR 97403   ☎503/343 1248

Travel Information Center
Moss Rehabilitation Hospital
1200 W Tabor Rd
Philadelphia
PA 19141   ☎215/329 5715
ext 2233
Write for access information.

Australia

ACROD
P O Box 69
Curtin
ACT 2605   ☎06/682 4333

New Zealand

Disabled Persons Assembly
P O Box 10
138 The Terrace
Wellington   ☎04/472 2626

Gay and Lesbian Amsterdam

In keeping with the Dutch reputation for tolerance, no other city in Europe accepts **gay people** as readily as Amsterdam. Here, more than anywhere, it's possible to be openly gay and accepted by the straight community. Gays are prominent in business and the arts, the age of consent is sixteen, and, with the Dutch willingness to speak English, French and just about any other language, Amsterdam has become a magnet for the international gay scene – a city with a dense sprinkling of advice centres, bars, clubs and cinemas. The COC (pronounced "say-oh-say"), the national gay and lesbian pressure group, celebrated its fiftieth birthday in 1996 – one of the longest-lived, and largest, groups of its kind in the world.

The practice of homosexuality was decriminalized in the Netherlands as long ago as 1811; a century later – still sixty years ahead of the UK – the gay **age of consent** was reduced to 21, and in 1971 it was brought into line with that of heterosexuals at 16. The most recent legal development has been the Dutch parliament's 1996 resolution calling for a bill to allow **same-sex marriages**, though the legislation probably won't be enacted for sevral years.

Otherwise, gay couples have full legal rights these days, and it is maybe a mark of the level of acceptance of gay lifestyles in mainstream Dutch society that every year there is a party in Amsterdam for Holland's gay and lesbian civil servants. It also says much for the strength of the gay community that the arrival of **AIDS** was not accompanied by the homophobia seen in many other places. Rather than close down clubs and saunas, the city council funded education programmes, encouraged the use of condoms, and has generally conducted an open policy on the issue; today there are a number of well-established organizations and foundations devoted to HIV prevention and support for HIV/AIDS sufferers.

However, gay men in Amsterdam are much better catered for than **lesbians**. Although there is a sizeable lesbian community in Amsterdam, there is only one women-only café – the *Saarein* – and just one or two lesbian-only clubs that are constantly changing venue; in many ways,

London, New York or San Francisco have livelier scenes for gay women than Amsterdam. With the strength and achievements of the mainstream Dutch feminist movement, many of the battles currently being fought by women around the world have already been won in the Netherlands: women are fully integrated into policy-making at national and local levels, the degree of sexism in society is low, gay and lesbian lifestyles are openly presented and discussed in schools, and so on. In the last ten or fifteen years, there seems to have been less and less general need for exclusively women-only activities in Amsterdam, and exclusively lesbian entertainment has also largely been subsumed into the mainstream. Although there are a number of lesbian-owned businesses in the city, many lesbian support organizations have been forced to close for economic reasons. Amsterdam's politically active lesbians tend to move within tight circles, and it can take time to find out what's happening.

The city has four recognized **gay areas**: the most famous and most lively centres, populated as much by locals as visitors, are **Kerkstraat** and **Reguliersdwarsstraat**, the latter with a more outgoing, international scene. The streets just north of **Rembrandtplein** are a camp focus, as well as being home to a number of rent-boy bars, while **Warmoesstraat**, in the heart of the Red Light District, is cruisy and mainly leather- and denim-oriented.

As far as the attitude of the general public goes, the bottom line is that, if you're **discreet** about it, you can do what you like. Same-sex couples holding hands and kissing in the streets are no more worthy of comment than straight couples. **Cruising** is generally tolerated in places where it's not likely to cause offence; if you're new to the city, take some time to get acquainted with what's what. Many bars and clubs have **darkrooms**, which are legally obliged to provide safe sex information and condoms.

You'll find descriptions of gay **bars and nightclubs** scattered throughout Chapter 9, while recommended **gay hotels** are reviewed in Chapter 8. If you want more information, get hold of a copy of the widely available **Gay Tourist Map** of

Amsterdam produced by the *SAD-Schorerstichting* (see below). You could also invest in a copy of the *Best Guide to Amsterdam* (*f*24.95), a comprehensive gay **guidebook** (in English) available from any of the shops listed below and most gay bookshops around the world. Britain's *Gay Times* carries **listings** for Amsterdam; among the many local gay newspapers and magazines, the fortnightly *Gay Krant* has all the details you could conceivably need, including up-to-the-minute listings, though it is in Dutch only. *De Regenbooggids* is a gay/gay-friendly version of the Yellow Pages. You can find the **Pink Pages** on the World Wide Web at <http://clix.net/clix/pinkpages>.

Resources and contacts

COC, Rozenstraat 14; office open Mon–Fri 9am–5pm ☎626 3087; information on ☎623 4079. Amsterdam branch of the national gay and lesbian organization, offering advice, contacts and social activities (including an English-speaking group; info ☎420 3068), plus a coffeeshop (Mon–Sat 1–5pm) and a large noticeboard. The general COC café is open Wed 8pm–midnight, Fri 8pm–3am. HIV café open Mon & Thurs 8pm–midnight. One of the most popular women-only nights in Amsterdam is held regularly on Saturday in both the café (8pm–3am) and the nightclub (10pm–3am; *f*5).

Gay and Lesbian Switchboard ☎623 6565; daily 10am–10pm. An English-speaking service providing information on the gay and lesbian scenes. Also a good source of help and advice.

SAD Schorerstichting, P.C. Hooftstraat 5 ☎662 4206; Mon–Fri 9am–5.30pm. Gay and lesbian counselling centre offering professional and politically conscious advice on identity, sexuality and lifestyle.

Vrouwen Bellen Vrouwen ("Women Call Women"), ☎625 0150; Tues–Thurs 9.30am–12.30pm & 7.30–10.30pm. Women's advice line; not specifically lesbian.

Homodok (The Documentation Centre for Lesbian and Gay Studies), Oudezijds Achterburgwal 185, 1012 DK Amsterdam ☎525 2601, fax 525 3010, e-mail <homodok@sara.nl>; open to visitors Wed–Fri 10.30am–4.30pm. A major archive of all forms of literature relating to lesbian and gay studies, contemporary and historical. It's recommended that prospective visitors

write several weeks ahead detailing areas of interest: they'll write back to tell you what they can offer. Visit their web site at <http://www.adamnet.nl>.

Lesbisch Archief, 1e Helmersstraat 17 ☎618 5879; open to visitors Mon–Fri 1–4.30pm. Reference centre for contemporary lesbian culture and history, including books, videos and photographs, mostly in Dutch; they also run monthly tours of lesbian Amsterdam, on foot or by boat – call or visit for details. See also *IIAV archive* in the "Women's Amsterdam" section.

MVS Radio. Amsterdam's gay and lesbian radio station (office ☎620 0247) broadcasts daily 6–9pm on 106.8FM (or 103.8 via cable). Try and catch the English-language talk show *Aliens*, on Sunday. National Radio 5 (1008kHz MW) broadcasts *Het Roze Rijk* ("The Pink Empire") on Saturday from 6–7pm.

Sjalhomo ("Shalom-o"), Postbus 2536, 1000 CM Amsterdam ☎023/531 2318 (evenings only). National organization for Jewish gays and lesbians.

Beit Ha-Chidush A new gay- and lesbian-friendly Jewish congregation in Amsterdam; e-mail to <chidush@dds.nl> for information.

The Long Yang Club, Postbus 58253, 1040 HG Amsterdam. International organization for Asian gays, which holds regular parties in Amsterdam.

Wildside is a lesbian SM group which has regular open meetings at the COC (see above).

Stichting Tijgertje ☎673 2458, e-mail <tijgertj@xs4all.nl>. Gay and lesbian sports club.

ACT UP!, Houtkopersburgwal 14–15 ☎639 2522. Local branch of the radical direct action group, with fortnightly meetings.

Sissy. Ask around at squat cafés or nightclubs about this group of gay and lesbian squatters which, through various activities and events, aims to raise awareness and acceptance of alternative lifestyles.

Bookstores

American Book Centre, Kalverstraat 185 ☎625 5537. Large general bookstore, with a fine gay and lesbian section.

Intermale, Spuistraat 251 ☎625 0009. Well-stocked gay bookshop, with a wide selection of English, French, German and Dutch literature, as

Condoms specifically designed for gay sex are available in a large number of bars and sex shops, specifically those geared towards gay men. Brand-names include: *Duo*, *Gay Safe*, *Hot Rubber* and *Mondos Yantra*.

well as cards, newspapers and magazines. They have a worldwide mail order service.

Vrolijk, Paleisstraat 135 ☎623 5142. "The largest gay and lesbian bookstore on the continent", with a vast stock of new and second-hand books and magazines, as well as music and videos.

Xantippe, Prinsengracht 290 ☎623 5854. An impressively wide range of books and resources by, for and about women, with a large lesbian section.

Health

See also "Health and Insurance", p.27.

AIDS Helpline ☎06/022 2220 (free); Mon–Fri 2–10pm.

SAD Schorerstichting (see above) runs a weekly clinic for gay men, offering STD (including HIV) tests and treatment; at the GG&GD, Groenburgwal 44 (Fri 7–9pm).

HIV Vereniging, 1e Helmersstraat 17 ☎616 0160. STD clinic for gay men; call first to make an appointment. Clinic open Mon & Wed 1–3pm.

Women's Healthcentre, Obiplein 4 ☎693 4358. Information and advice for women – given by

women – on all health matters. Can recommend non-sexist, non-homophobic doctors, dentists and therapists. Call for opening times.

NVSH, Blauwburgwal 7–9 ☎623 9359; Mon–Fri 11am–6pm, Sat 11am–4pm. The Amsterdam branch of the *Netherlands Society for Sexual Reform*, with booklets on safe sex and general health information, as well as leather accessories and sex toys. Adjacent bar often has nights exclusively for transsexuals or bisexual men; call or visit for details.

HIV Plus Line ☎685 0055; Mon, Wed & Fri 1–4pm, Tues & Thurs 8–10.30pm. Confidential help and information for those who are HIV-positive.

Nightlife and entertainment

The main gay areas in the Old Centre and Grachtengordel South are dotted with numerous **gay bars**, reviewed in detail in *Eating and Drinking* – see pp.197 and 204. Of the late-night bars in and around Kerkstraat and Warmoesstraat, *Cockring* (p.235), *Spijker* (p.204) and many others are exclusively **male**; watch also for posters for Wasteland and Club Trash once a month. *Havana* (p.235), *iT* (Sat; p.235), *RoXY* (Wed; p.235), *Seymour Likely Too* (Wed; p.235) and *De Trut* (Sun; p.236) have mixed gay nights. There are currently no clubs exclusively for **lesbians** in Amsterdam. The famed Clit Club, after its demise in 1994, still has occasional one-off parties – watch for fliers or call its organizer, Ann,

---

Gay and Lesbian Accommodation

Listed below are the city's gay-friendly hotels, in ascending price order, and cross-referenced to the reviews in the *Accommodation* chapter. There are no women-only hotels, although two unofficial, privately run bed-and-breakfasts – *Johanna's* (p.177) and *Liliane's Home* (p.180) – cater for gay women

while also welcoming their gay male travelling companions. Hotels *Quentin* and *Granada* are particularly popular with lesbians, though all the hotels listed below are lesbian-friendly. Note that it's illegal for a hotel to refuse entry to anyone on the grounds of sexual orientation.

Monopole (p.176)
Greenwich Village (p.176)
West End (p.177)
Quentin (p.177)
Orfeo (p.177)
Aero (p.176)
Unique (p.177)
Granada (p.176)

Anco (p.171)
Stablemaster (p.171)
ITC (p.176)
Centre Apartments (p.171)
Waterfront (p.177)
New York (p.173)
Sander (p.183)

---

for details (☎364 0454). She can tell you what's currently hot and what's not; also try the Gay and Lesbian Switchboard. The most popular women-only night at present is Saturday at the COC (see above); *De Trut's* mixed gay and lesbian parties on Sunday nights (p.236) have people queuing round the block; and the *RoXY's* Wednesday night gay and lesbian parties (p.235) are popular. At a pinch, check out *Havana*, the *iT* or *Vive la Vie*. The Vrouwenhuis (see "Women's Amsterdam") organizes occasional women-only nights at different venues.

Several cinemas in Amsterdam show **gay films**: the *Filmtheater Desmet* (☎627 3434) has fortnightly screenings on Saturday at midnight and Sunday at 4.15pm – call them or check listings schedules for details. The *Filmhuis Cavia* (☎681 1419) often has gay programmes, too; *De Roze Filmdagen* ("The Pink Film Days") is a mini-season of gay and lesbian movies that takes place at the end of June. The *Cavia's* first Lesbian Film Festival ran over a weekend in March 1996, and may turn into a regular event. Call them, or the Gay and Lesbian Switchboard (see above), for details of gay movies showing around town.

Events

The three long-standing major events in Amsterdam's gay calendar are **Coming Out Day** (Sept 5), **World AIDS Day** (Dec 1) and **Remembrance Day** (May 4), all of which occasion ceremonies and happenings around the Homo-monument, the symbolic focus of the city's gay community (see p.99). Other events occur on a less regular basis.

The first **Amsterdam Pride** took place in 1996, organized by the Gay Business Association (☎620 8807), with street parties and performances, as well as a "Canal Pride" flotilla of boats parading along the Prinsengracht. If you're in the city in August, keep an eye out for flyers, as it may well turn out to be a regular annual event.

Amsterdam has been selected to host the fifth **Gay and Lesbian Games** from August 1–8, 1998 – the first time the Games have been held outside North America. A Cultural Festival is planned to run concurrently with the sporting activities. For more information, call ☎620 1998, or e-mail <info@gaygames.nl>; they also have a site on the World Wide Web at <http://www.dds.nl/~gaygames>.

Finally, the old Amsterdam tradition of **Hartjesdag** (Day of the Hearts), which ceased to be observed just before World War II, was recently uncovered during research by a lecturer in Gay and Lesbian Studies at the University of Amsterdam. Apparently, at some time in August, people who so desired would spend the day in the clothes of the opposite sex. Unfortunately, the tradition seems to have vanished as far as the general public goes, but Amsterdam's nightclubs often have themed drag weekends in August to keep the old values alive.

Shops and services

Beach Boy Holidays, W.G. Plein 104 ☎616 4747. Gay travel agent.

Black Body, Lijnbaansgracht 292 ☎626 2553. Huge selection of rubber and leather, new and second-hand.

Bronx, Kerkstraat 55 ☎623 1548. Strictly porno books, magazines and videos for men.

Demask, Zeedijk 64 ☎492 1323. Expensive rubber and leather fetish store for men and women.

Drake's, Damrak 61 ☎627 9544. Gay porn cinema.

Expectations, Warmoesstraat 32 ☎624 5573. Rubber, leather and latex wear – made on the premises.

Female and Partners, Spuistraat 100 ☎620 9152. New premises to accommodate a growing stock of plain and kinky sex toys for women, with probably the widest variety of vibrators in the city.

Fenomeen, 1e Schinkelstraat 14 ☎671 6780. Laid-back, inexpensive sauna in an open-plan setting, with café and chill-out room, attracting a faithful lesbian clientele on Monday 1–11pm.

De Leertent, Sarphatistraat 61 ☎627 8090. Huge collection of denim wear.

Mail and Female, Prinsengracht 489 ☎623 3916. A wide range of erotica for women in a classy scarlet environment, with helpful (female) staff.

Mandate, Prinsengracht 715 ☎625 4100. Exclusively gay male gym, open daily.

Manstore, Max Euweplein 52 ☎626 9802. Designer underwear, swimwear and nightclothes.

Mister B, Warmoesstraat 89 ☎422 0003. Rubber and leather clothing and sex toys, spread over three floors. Piercing by appointment. Web site at <http://www.neturl.nl/mrb>.

RoB gallery, Weteringschans 253 ☎625 4686. Top-quality made-to-measure leather wear, with a worldwide mail order service. Also in London and San Francisco.

Robin and Rik, Runstraat 30 ☎627 8924. Handmade leather clothes and accessories.

Splash, Looiersgracht 26 ☎624 8404. Gay-friendly gym.

Thermos Day Sauna, Raamstraat 33 ☎623 9158. Gay men's sauna, with steam room, whirlpool, cinema and coffee bar. (Mon–Fri noon–11pm, Sat & Sun noon–10pm. *f27.50*).

Thermos Night Sauna, Kerkstraat 58–60 ☎623 4936. Much the same facilities as the day sauna, with the addition of a jacuzzi and darkroom. Daily 11pm–8am. *f27.50*.

Women's Amsterdam

Just over a century ago, the only women out at night in Amsterdam were prostitutes, and a respectable woman's place was firmly in the home; after voting rights were extended to women in 1919, Dutch feminism largely faded out of sight until the radical upheavals of the late 1960s. During the 1970s, though, while in many other countries feminist movements were struggling for recognition, in the Netherlands assimilation of feminist values into the mainstream came by leaps and bounds. A law was passed on abortion in 1981, and four years later abortions became available through the national health service. The controversial morning-after pill is now also available, and every town in the country has a Commissioner for Women's Affairs taking part in policy decisions. Today, Amsterdam has an impressive **feminist infrastructure**: support groups, health centres and businesses run by and for women, and there's a good range of bars and discos too. Unless you're here for an extended stay, however, or are positively seeking out information, much of this can remain invisible: feminist circles are generally indifferent to travellers, and most of the contacts you'll make will be with other visitors to the city.

As far as **safety** on the streets is concerned, Amsterdam is relatively problem-free for women travellers. As always, when exploring by yourself, it helps to project a confident attitude. The brashness of the main **Red Light District** around Oudezijds Achterburgwal can be initially intimidating, and walking with a friend is a good idea here, if only to ward off unwelcome leers. However, the smaller backstreet red-light areas, such as those around the northern end of Spuistraat, are best avoided altogether, as is the southern district of "De Pijp" after dark.

General contacts and resources

Antiquariaat Lorelei, Prinsengracht 495 ☎623 4308. A huge second-hand bookstore with a lesbian-feminist stock and clientele; they also have

For specifically lesbian information, see the previous section, "Gay and Lesbian Amsterdam".

Emergency phone numbers

Police, ambulance, fire ☎112

Meldpunt Vrouwen Opvang Amsterdam ☎611 6022 (daily 9am–5pm; leave a message outside these times). Central umbrella organization for a number of different women's groups; they have an emergency refuge for battered women.

TOSG ☎612 7576 (Mon–Fri 10.30am–11.30pm, Sat & Sun 3.30–11.30pm). Hotline for victims of rape or sexual assault.

a noticeboard for general contacts. (Open Wed–Fri noon–6pm, Sat noon–5pm).

Het Vrouwenhuis, Nieuwe Herengracht 95 ☎625 2066. Information by phone (Mon–Fri 11am–4pm); call for other services. The "Women's House" is an organizing centre for women's activities and cultural events. There's a well-stocked library of books by and about women, a bar open weekday evenings, and a whole range of classes.

IIAV, Obiplein 4 ☎665 0820. (Mon noon–5pm, Tues 10am–7pm, Wed–Fri 10am–5pm). The International Archives of the Women's and Lesbian Movement has a wealth of literature of all kinds detailing the history of the feminist movement in the Netherlands, and information regarding the current status of women in Dutch society. There is also an elaborate historical collection from international sources, and a referral service for Women's Studies.

Vrouwen Bellen Vrouwen ☎625 0150. (Tues–Thurs 9.30am–12.30pm & 7.30–10.30pm). "Women Call Women": advice and support line.

Vrouwen in Druk, Westermarkt 5 ☎624 5003. "Women in Print" stocks second-hand books by female authors, with a large English selection. (Open Wed–Fri 1–6pm).

Xantippe, Prinsengracht 290 ☎623 5854. Amsterdam's foremost women's bookshop, with a wide selection of feminist titles in English.

Health

AIDS Helpline ☎06/022 2220. (Mon–Fri 2–10pm).

Aletta Jacobshuis, Overtoom 323 ☎616 6222. (Mon–Fri 9am–4.30pm, Tues & Thurs also 7.30–9pm, Sat emergencies only). Named after the country's first female doctor, the Jacobshuis offers sympathetic information and help on sexual problems and birth control. It's possible to get condoms here, as well as prescriptions for contraceptive pills and the morning-after pill, IUD fitting and cervical smear tests.

GG&GD clinic, Groenburgwal 44 ☎555 5822. Municipal Health Department STD clinic; they have women-only days – phone for details and an appointment.

MR '70, Sarphatistraat 620–626 ☎624 5426. Independent abortion clinic, offering help and advice. Call first for an appointment.

Polikliniek Oosterpark, Oosterpark 59 ☎693 2151. Sympathetic information and advice on contraception and abortion (the procedure itself costs upwards of ƒ500).

Women's Healthcentre, Obiplein 4 ☎693 4358. Information and advice for women – given by women – on all health matters. Can recommend non-sexist, non-homophobic doctors, dentists and therapists. Call for opening times.

Women's centres and groups

Amazone, Singel 120 ☎420 5061. (Tues–Fri 10am–5pm, Sat & Sun 1–5pm.) Women's art gallery and exhibition centre focusing on cultural and social topics affecting women.

Avalon, Roerstraat 79 ☎664 6530. Feminist spirituality centre offering a wide range of workshops and weekend courses.

Clara Wichmann Institute ☎668 4069. Foundation providing advice and guidance for lawyers and journalists on points of law involving women. They have a nationwide list of legal practices specializing in womens' rights, and a library that's open to the public by appointment only.

Eastern Bathhouse Hammam, Zaanstraat 88 ☎681 4818. (Mon, Wed & Fri 1–9pm, Tues & Thurs 5.30–9.30pm, Sun noon–5pm; evenings only during July; closed Aug. Admission ƒ12.50.) A unique and wonderful women-only institution, comprising hot and cold rooms and top to toe washing; full body scrub and massage costs a little more. Emerge feeling cleaner and more alive than you ever thought possible.

De Hippe Heks, Confuciusplein 10 ☎611 2268. Mon–Fri 9.30am–4.30pm. Women's meeting place, running, amongst others, Dutch-language courses.

Kenau, Overtoom 270 ☎616 2913. Self-defence centre with summer weekend courses on oriental defence techniques for women.

Prostitution Information Centre, Enge Kerksteeg 3 ☎420 7328. For a slightly more enlightening visit to the Red Light District, find out how the women in the windows are improving their working conditions and campaigning for greater legal and social provisions. See also the box on p.77, and the website <http://fun2.fun.nl/pic>.

Rechtshulp voor Vrouwen, Willemstraat 24 ☎624 0323. Legal help for women (but not over the phone), especially in cases involving women's rights.

De Rode Draad, Kloveniersburgwal 47 ☎06/320 23060 (ƒ1/min). Prostitutes' trade union.

Sauna Aquafit, Van 't Hofflaan 4 ☎694 5211. Phone to check times. Women-only sauna, with full facilities. Out to the east of the centre.

Vrouwen in de Beeldende Kunst, Entrepotdok 66 ☎626 6589. A foundation for women artists.

Xenia Intercultural Women's Centre, Klaas Katerstraat 2 ☎619 8765. Mon–Fri 9am–10pm, Sun 4–8pm. Classes and courses of all kinds for women from all backgrounds. Sunday evening is a communal dinner and hang-out; call to reserve beforehand – it's a long trek out (on the southwest edge of the city).

Feminist businesses

Freewheel, Akoleienstraat 7 ☎627 7252. Bike repairs and sales.

Het Lokaal, Amstelveenseweg 758 ☎644 8164. (Tues & Fri 9.30am–noon & 1.30–4pm, Wed 9.30am–noon, Thurs 9.30am–noon & 7.30–10pm.) Price ƒ10 per session; call first to make a reservation. Fully equipped workshop for women, with tools and materials for working in wood, glass, clay, plaster, paint or linoleum. No previous experience necessary.

Knalpot ☎665 3218. Garage where women teach you how to fix your car.

Vrouwenfietsenmakerij, Palembangstraat 67 ☎665 3218. (Tues, Wed & Fri 9am–5.30pm, Thurs 1–5.30pm, Sat 9am–5pm.) Bicycle repair shop run by the *Knalpot* women; also sells second-hand bikes.

Zijwind, Ferdinand Bolstraat 168 ☎673 7026. Another bicycle repair shop run by women; they also rent bikes.

Long-term Stays

Many people come to Amsterdam for a visit and decide to stay. This isn't particularly advised, and in any case only EU and US citizens are eligible to look for work once in the Netherlands. However, if you are keen to stay in the city for a prolonged period of time, the following should provide you with a few basic pointers to how to go about it.

Residency and work permits

The first thing that both EU and non-EU nationals should know is that the **law** on foreigners working in the Netherlands has been significantly tightened up. On September 1, 1995, the *Wet Arbeid Vreemdelingen* (Employment of Foreigners Act) came into force, with the explicit aim of bringing about a decrease in the number of foreigners coming to the Netherlands to work. Work permits and residence permits are now issued with even less willingness than before.

Anyone who wants to stay in the Netherlands for more than three months must apply for **residency**. To do this, you need four things: a full passport, evidence of health insurance, your original birth certificate, and proof of a regular income that the Aliens' Police think sufficient to support you. The Dutch authorities require that birth certificates issued by both the UK and the US (check with the Population Registry for other nationalities; ☎551 9911) be authenticated by means of an apostille, or seal. In the UK this can

be done by the Legalisation Office, Foreign and Commonwealth Office, 20 Victoria St, London, SW1H 0NZ (☎0171/210 2521); an apostille costs £10. In the US, apply to the Secretary of State's office in your home state. UK citizens should also bear in mind that the short version of your birth certificate, even though original, is not acceptable – you need the full version.

One characteristic liberality in the Dutch laws surrounding residency is that anyone – EU or non-EU – who is in a permanent **relationship** with someone who already has Dutch resident status can apply for residency while in the Netherlands – no marriage certificate is needed (in fact, an "affirmation of single status" is), and the only requirement is that the Dutch resident be able to support both partners. This puts unmarried couples and same-sex couples on the same footing as married couples in the eyes of the Aliens' Police. At heart, the single most important criterion for gaining residency in the Netherlands is that you be financially self-supporting.

For help and advice, the **Information Centre** and **Municipal Service Centre** in the Stadhuis on Waterlooplein (Mon–Fri 9am–5pm; ☎624 1111) provides information on all municipal policies and answers general questions about living in Amsterdam. You can also pick up various helpful brochures and leaflets from them, including *Amsterdam Information*, which has details on the job market, social security, housing, health care, education and the like, though it hasn't been revised since 1991. *What Every Amsterdammer Should Know* lists the functions and phone numbers of every conceivable municipal department in the city, from the Mayor's Office to the City Pawn Shop. If still in doubt, the **Sociaal Raadslieden** (Citizens' Advice Bureau – see address p.65) at the Stadhuis offers free personal – and confidential – advice on a wide range of issues. If you can't or don't want to go into the office they also give advice on the phone (Mon, Tues, Thurs & Fri 2–4pm; ☎625 8347).

EU nationals

EU nationals do not require a **work permit** – a *werkvergunning* – in order to work legally in the

Netherlands; however, if you want to stay for more than three months, you must have a **residence permit** – a *verblijfsvergunning* – and you won't get a residence permit without a job or some other means of support. However, with the approach of European integration, and since EU passports are never stamped on arrival at Schiphol or at land borders, officials are generally relaxed about the three-month stipulation. If you do arrive with the intention of staying, though, it's best to begin the whole tortuous process as soon as possible.

First of all, you need to report to the **Aliens' Police** (*Vreemdelingenpolitie* – address on p.65). Here you should get a stamp in your passport to prove you've been given your automatic three months' legal residency, pick up the so-called *EEG brief* ("EU letter"), which states that you have the right to look for work, and collect a yellow form to apply for a residence permit (entitled "We Will Help You"). Then take your passport and *EEG brief* to the **Tax Office** (*Belastingdienst* – address on p.65), who will issue you with a **social-fiscal (SOFI) number**, without which you cannot work legally. Once you've found work (see the section below), fill in the yellow residency form and send it back to the Aliens' Police, together with photocopies of your health insurance details, your apostilled birth certificate, the pages of your passport with the Aliens' Police stamp and your personal details, two identical photos (they say ones from a machine aren't suitable), and a *werkgeversverklaring* or written statement from your employer. The Aliens' Police will make an appointment to see you (with your original documents) in five or six weeks' time. At this appointment, after you've paid a processing fee of *f*35, and assuming they're satisfied, they'll grant you a residence permit either for the duration of your job or for five years, if your job contract is for more than a year. At the same time, you'll also have to visit the aliens' department of the **Population Registry** (*Bevolkingsregister*), in the same building: almost all employers require you to have a **bank account**, and you need to be registered at the *Bevolkingsregister* before you can get one. All your details will be entered on their computer, which is linked to City Hall and the Tax Office; a week or so later, you have to go to City Hall (the Stadhuis) at Waterlooplein (☎551 9052) and pay *f*9.75 for a computer-printed extract (*uittreksel*) of your details, which you then send off to the bank to open an account.

In previous years, new recipients of residence permits were eligible for a number of benefits, not least of which were subsidized **Dutch lessons**. However, this practice now seems to have been curtailed – check with the Stadhuis for the current situation. Otherwise, the cheapest place to study Dutch is the *Volksuniversiteit*, Rapenburgerstraat 73 (☎626 1626), which does full- and part-time courses in all sorts of other subjects, too; call or drop in for their prospectus, published twice a year. *RBO Scholingsburo* on Frederiksplein (☎627 9360) also runs inexpensive and very popular Dutch-language courses twice a year.

Other nationalities

US citizens, uniquely among non-EU nationals, are legally permitted to arrive in the Netherlands as tourists, and then look for work while they're here. However, there's a catch to this. Nobody can work legally in the Netherlands without a social-fiscal (SOFI) number, but the Tax Office won't issue a SOFI number to non-EU nationals without a residence permit, and the Aliens' Police won't issue a residence permit to anyone without a SOFI number. These regulations are designed to make things difficult, but there do seem to be two ways around them. The first relies on the slim chance that you can find an employer in the first three months of your stay who is prepared to give a written statement to both the Aliens' Police and Immigration Department that you alone are the right person for the job (see below); if an employer will do this, and you apply for residency at the same time that your work permit is being processed, then – assuming you're granted the work permit – you'll be given residency and a SOFI number to start work with. The second way around the catch is that if you live with either a Dutch citizen or an EU national, you can gain residency (and thus a SOFI number) without having a job on the grounds of "setting up a family with a partner", as long as the Aliens' Police are satisfied that your partner is earning enough to support both of you. Bear in mind that the processing fee for a residence permit for US nationals is *f*130. Once this is all done, you can look for work, but once you've found an employer you still need to go through the process of getting a work permit before you can begin earning legally.

For all **other nationals**, the whole situation is more fraught still. If you want to work in the Netherlands, or stay more than three months, you need to have an official work permit before you arrive. Except for certain very specialized jobs, you're only granted this, along with the resulting MVV (*Machtiging tot Voorlopig Verblijf*, "Authorization for Temporary Residence") once you have a job already set up with a Dutch employer. However, for all non-EU nationals (US included), the new Employment of Foreigners Act means that work permits are granted only on certain stringent conditions. Any job must be **advertised** first throughout the country, then throughout Europe, and only if no EU citizen who applies for it turns out to be suitable can the employer then ask for a work permit on your behalf – so you'll only get one if nobody in Europe can do what you can do. If you do manage to find someone who is willing to employ you, they must apply for the work permit for you before you arrive in the Netherlands, while you must also start your own application to the Dutch embassy or consulate in your home country. Needless to say, even if an employer is willing to go through with the whole process, it can take months, and at the end of it all a work permit is far from even a probability.

Finding work in Amsterdam

On top of all this, actually **finding a legal job** is hard and getting harder. Bear in mind that, before you begin, you need the *EEG brief* described above, a SOFI number and a bank account. In previous years **temp agencies** (*uitzendburos*) were the main source of casual, quasi-legal work for EU nationals, but nowadays most of them won't even register you unless you speak some Dutch. If you do, or if you find an agency with less strict conditions – and you're prepared to tramp around to their offices twice a day and to take any job they give you – you may come up with something, especially if you're under 23 (by law, employers have to pay substantially more to older individuals). The sort of jobs you'll find in this way vary enormously: in the summer there's some demand in the hotel and catering industry – though you may do better applying directly to tourist establishments; it's rare, though, for people to pick up secretarial jobs without some Dutch. You could try scanning the newspapers, though this isn't much use save for irregular adverts from *uitzendburo's* and cleaning agencies. A slightly

better bet is to head for the main *Arbeidsburo* (Job Centre – address on p.65); they'll register you on their books and talk through job possibilities with you. They have a large file of continuously updated job openings, but you can always just wander in and scan the boards without registering if you prefer. They have been known to find work for non-Dutch speakers, mainly as skilled manual workers – although this, too, seems to have dried up considerably.

As for **working illegally**, there's no greater chance of finding work in Amsterdam than in any other European city; less, in fact, since most Amsterdammers speak near-perfect English and there is practically no chance of work in language teaching. Places such as coffeeshops, bars, cafés and hostels are obvious choices, the closer in to the centre the better; foot-slogging and luck'll be your only hope, though if you're aiming to spend the summer in Amsterdam, be warned that whatever jobs there are will probably have been taken by May. Summer work in the glasshouses and bulbfields outside Amsterdam can occasionally be found; the best way of doing so is to head down to Aalsmeer and the bulb areas around Haarlem, although bear in mind that these kinds of jobs are generally low-paid and exploitative.

It's worth being aware that, even once you're working, an alarmingly large chunk of your wages will vanish into the highly supportive Dutch welfare system: the basic rate of **income tax** in the Netherlands is 37.5 percent, and compulsory **health insurance**, either through a local *ziekenfonds* (state-controlled fund) or through a private company, can be several dozen guilders a month on top.

Finding accommodation

Reasonably priced **rented accommodation** in Amsterdam is in desperately short supply, and flat-hunting requires a determined effort. Before you begin you'll need to have access to enough money to cover the first month's rent, a deposit of a similar amount, and any possible *overname* (see below) – a realistic sum would be upwards of ƒ2000. With the exception of tiny apartments, and places in Amsterdam Zuid-Oost (Southeast), most of the housing with a monthly rent of under ƒ700 is controlled by the **council**, and can only be rented with a Housing Permit (*woonruimteverklaring*), and in most cases a Certificate of Urgency (*urgentiebewijs*) too. These documents are issued by the **Municipal Housing Office** (*Stedelijke*

Woningdienst – address on p.65), where you'll find all kinds of information on housing in Amsterdam, including the addresses of non-commercial letting agencies. However, you will only be issued a housing permit or *urgentiebewijs* if you have been registered as living in Amsterdam for four years. Anyone planning to stay a while should therefore register at the **Bevolkings-register** (see above; address on p.65) as quickly as possible after arriving, since it's this date that counts as the official beginning of your stay in Amsterdam. You should only do this, however, once you've registered with the Aliens' Police, and you must remember to keep both places informed of any change of address during the four-year period, or they'll lose track of you.

In the meantime, though, you're forced to seek accommodation in other ways, which can prove difficult and expensive. One way of cutting costs is to look for a place in **Amsterdam Zuid-Oost**, an unpopular and somewhat notorious concrete extension to the city that is a great deal cheaper than any other neighbourhood. That said, the apartments are spacious and generally in good condition, with rents of ƒ500–600 a month; and although you're a long way out of the centre, there is a fast metro link. The Housing Office can give you details of letting agencies down here, or try contacting the **Nieuw Amsterdam** agency (☎567 5100), which handles accommodation exclusively in Bijlmermeer, a particularly unpopular high-rise corner of Amsterdam Zuid-Oost (look in the phone book under "*woning*" for other agencies). The rents in **Amsterdam Noord** (North), across the River IJ, are also cheaper than in central Amsterdam; this is more brick-and-concrete territory, with sparse public transport and only the ferry (or car tunnel) to link you to the city.

Otherwise, in the **private sector**, the cardinal rules to remember are that Amsterdam is a land-lord's market (although the law is definitely pro-tenant), and that the city runs very much on word-of-mouth. If you're looking for a place to live, tell absolutely *everybody* you meet. An easily legible notice pinned up on a noticeboard, with a contact phone number, is a worthwhile investment – good noticeboards to use and scan can be found at the main library, all *Albert Heijn* supermarkets, small neighbourhood cafés such as *Gary's Muffins* and the *Vliegende Schotel*, and other English-speaking outlets such as the *American Book Center*; the student mensas can also be a good way of finding cheap accommodation in student dorms.

Be aware that, if you're looking for a permanent, contracted apartment, there's little chance of finding anything for much under ƒ850 a month, higher the closer in you get. However, if you're prepared (and you may have to be) to settle for a temporary **sublet** of someone else's apartment while they're away – this is legal in Amsterdam – you can cut costs and improve your chances no end, although you will lose out on a contract, and thus legimita-cy of residence. Again, word-of-mouth is the key: the waitress who just served you that coffee might have a friend whose next-door neighbours might be looking for someone trustworthy to take care of the cat while they're on their dream holiday. Far and away your next best bet is to buy a pocket Dutch dictionary to decipher the *Via Via*, Amsterdam's free-ads paper, which is packed with hundreds of ads for contract apartments, sublets and the occasional flatshare, along with computers, old Osmonds' LPs and everything else. It's published every Thursday for ƒ3.95, but anything remotely interesting will have gone by 10am – you'll need to get the first one off the pile at Centraal Station when the kiosk opens at 6.30am to stand a chance. A recent innovation is for peo-ple to avoid advertising their phone number in the *Via Via*: instead they rent a ☎06 number from the paper, which means that every call you make will cost you 50c a minute – galling, but unavoidable.

Otherwise, the **newspapers** De Telegraaf and De Volkskrant are a must, with large "For Rent" (*Te Huur*) sections, particularly on Friday and Saturday – though it's well worth buying them every morning (again at the crack of dawn for any sort of chance; look out in bars for roving sellers of the Saturday edition on Friday night).

A slim possibility lies in the fact that some of the old warehouse buildings around the central harbour area have been converted into small stu-dios and rooming houses, which are compara-tively cheap, if a little tacky; ask in 't Anker bar, behind Centraal Station at De Ruyterkade 100 (☎622 9560), for more information.

Apartment-finding **agencies** advertise regularly in the newspapers and the *Via Via*, and are anoth-er useful source if you can afford the fee – nor-mally one or two months' rent for finding a place – but beware of agencies that ask for money before they hand out an address, since fly-by-night operators are common. If you're really des-perate, try some of the agencies advertising short-term holiday rentals for tourists – many of them are located on or near the Damrak – although the places they show you won't be cheap. Bear in mind, too, that whether you rent through an agency or direct from the paper, many people will slap an *overname* (pronounced "oh-fer-nah-meh") charge on you – this is key-money which they paid to the previous tenant to cover fixtures and fittings, and which they in turn charge you. These vary tremendously and can be exorbitant (four figures is common), but they're usually unavoidable and can only be recovered by continuing the vicious circle and charging them to the next tenant when you move out. Landlords also often ask for a *borgsom* – a refundable security deposit – of one, two or three months' rent up front.

Squatting

From the heady days of the early 1980s, when the squatting movement in Amsterdam was at its zenith, things have changed dramatically, and what squats are left survive only by the skin of their teeth and in the face of a sea-change in pub-

lic perception and governmental policy. Successive administrations in the city council – and the national government – have taken an ever-stronger line with surviving squats, with a less and less impassioned response from Amsterdammers themselves. Public policy in Amsterdam has slowly been changing the city (and its self-image) away from the freewheeling bastion of anarchistic hippiedom that it still was in the late 1970s towards the image of an ambitious, dynamic centre for international business that it hankers after today. One consequence of this has been a fading in the significance and popularity of overt signs of "people power", such as the values borne out in the few remaining big community squats. For established and committed Dutch political activists, for whom squatting is part of a way of life, times are hard enough; a foreign visitor looking to solve a short-term housing problem by squatting can expect little sympathy from locals and extremely short shrift from the Dutch authorities.

Useful addresses

Aliens' Police (*Vreemdelingenpolitie*)
Johan Huizingalaan 757 (tram #2, stop Aletta Jacobslaan) ☎559 6300. Mon–Fri 8am–4pm – arrive early and expect to wait, the queues can be enormous.

Citizens' Advice Bureau (*Sociaal Raadslieden*)
Stadhuis, Waterlooplein ☎552 2537. Mon & Tues 9am–noon & 1–4pm, Wed & Fri 9am–noon, Thurs 9am–noon, 1–4pm & 5–7pm. Phone consultations Mon, Tues, Thurs & Fri 2–4pm: ☎625 8347. Free advice on all subjects.

Information Centre (*Voorlichtingscentrum*)
Stadhuis, Waterlooplein ☎624 1111. Mon–Fri 9am–5pm. Can't solve your problems, but can tell you the phone number of the person who can.

Job Centre (*Arbeidsburo*)
Westeinde 26 (near Frederiksplein) ☎553 3444. Mon–Fri 9am–5pm. Anyone is free to walk in and scan the boards.

Legal Aid Office (*Bureau voor Rechtshulp*)
Spuistraat 10 ☎626 4477. Free 30min of legal advice on housing, unemployment, social security, welfare, immigration and consumer rights – either on the phone, at a walk-in consultation or a pre-arranged appointment. Mon

12.30–4pm, Wed & Fri 9am–12.30pm, Thurs appointments only 5–7pm.

Main Public Library (*Openbare Bibliotheek*)
Prinsengracht 587 ☎523 0900. Mon 1–9pm, Tues–Thurs 10am–9pm, Fri & Sat 10am–5pm; Oct–March also open Sun 1–5pm.

Municipal Housing Office (*Stedelijke Woningdienst*)
Stadhuis, Waterlooplein ☎581 0800. Mon–Wed 1.30–4pm, Thurs 1.30–4pm & 5–7pm.

Nieuw Amsterdam
Letting office for Bijlmermeer ☎567 5100. Mon–Fri 9am–4pm.

Population Registry (*Bevolkingsregister*)
Aliens Department: Johan Huizingalaan 757 (tram #2, stop Aletta Jacobslaan) ☎559 6300. Mon–Fri 8am–4pm. Main office: Herengracht 531–537 ☎551 9911. Mon–Fri 8.30am–3pm. Also in the Stadhuis, Waterlooplein ☎551 9911. Mon–Wed & Fri 8.30am–3.30pm, Thurs 8.30am–3.30pm & 5–7pm.

Tax Office (*Belastingdienst*)
Kingsfordweg 1, near Sloterdijk Station (second-to-last stop on tram #12) ☎687 7777. Mon–Fri 8.30am–4pm.

Directory

BABIES Some hotels don't accommodate babies, or will do so only during the low season, so you'll need to check when booking rooms. For details of babysitting services, see *Kids' Amsterdam* (p.264).

BBC WORLD SERVICE On 648kHz medium wave 24 hours a day.

BRING . . . Toiletries, film and English-language books, all of which are expensive in Amsterdam.

CONTRACEPTIVES Condoms are widely available from *drogists* or the *Condomerie* (see p.260) – generally they're on view but behind the counter, so you have to point to what you want. To get the pill you need a prescription – see "Women's Amsterdam", p.60.

CUSTOMS With the advent of the Single European Market, EU nationals over the age of 17 can bring in and take out most things, as long as they've paid tax on them in an EU country, and they are for personal consumption. For non-EU nationals, and for all goods bought duty-free, the following limits apply: 200 cigarettes or 250g tobacco or 50 cigars; 1 litre spirits or 2 litres fortified wine or 2 litres sparkling wine; 60ml perfume. Non-EU nationals who spend more than ƒ300 in one shop in one day, and then export the goods within 3 months of purchase, can reclaim the VAT (sales tax). Shops displaying the "Tax Free for Tourists" logo will help with the formalities.

DIAMONDS The industry was founded here in the late sixteenth century by refugee diamond workers from Antwerp, but since World War II it has depended on tourists for a livelihood. Currently around twenty diamond firms operate in Amsterdam. All are working factories, but many open their doors to the public for viewing the cutting, polishing and sorting practices, and (most importantly) for buying. City tours often include diamond factories (see p.41), but a few can be visited individually. Among them are *Coster*, Paulus Potterstraat 2–4 ☎676 2222, *Van Moppes*, Albert Cuypstraat 2–6 ☎676 1242, the *Amsterdam Diamond Centre*, Rokin 1 ☎624 5787, *Stoeltie*, Wagenstraat 13–17 ☎623 7601, and the famous *Gassan*, Nieuwe Uilenburgerstraat 173–175 ☎622 5333. Admission is free.

DOG SHIT With so little green space in the centre of Amsterdam, this is a major problem. Unfortunately, dog-owners seem unwilling or unable either to train their animals to use the gutter or to clear up after them. Every time some form of legislation is proposed, the dog lobby shouts it down. Until something gets done, keep one eye where you're walking.

ELECTRIC CURRENT 220v AC – effectively the same as British, although with round two- (or occasionally three-) pin plugs. British equipment will need either an adaptor or a new plug; American requires both a transformer and a new plug.

FREE AMSTERDAM Larger branches of *Albert Heijn* supermarkets often have free **coffee** for shoppers (and occasionally nibbles of this and that too), and many bakeries around town offer bite-sized bits of fresh gourmet **bread** or pastries (although generally as an incentive to buy at least something). The **markets** on Albert Cuypstraat and Dapperstraat close at 5pm, when over-juicy tomatoes and bruised apples go begging. Fine wines and cheeses can be found on offer at the opening of a new exhibition at one of Amsterdam's many **galleries**; just try and look interested in the art as well. There are no restrictions on listening to your favourite **CDs** all day long on the top floor of *Vroom and Dreesman*

(Kalverstraat) or in the *Virgin Megastore*, where you can also play the latest **video games** to your heart's content. Many larger cafés trust you with today's English **newspapers**, so long as you leave them behind for the next freeloader. The café in *De Bijenkorf* is next to their magazine department; they allow you to pick any magazine off the shelf, peruse it at your leisure over a (paid-for) cup of coffee, then put it back. There is also free **art** (the Schuttersgallerij outside the Amsterdam Historical Museum on Kalverstraat), a free **boat-ride** across the IJ to Amsterdam North and back (the "IJveer" boats leave Pier 8 behind Centraal Station roughly every 10min), free lunchtime **concerts** at the Concertgebouw (October to June only), free **jazz** nightly at *Bourbon Street*, *Café Alto* and the *Bamboo Bar* (all near Leidseplein), even free **postcards** in café racks that are sometimes worth sending.

INTERNET One area where the Dutch lead Europe is in computer literacy: from the earliest days of the Internet Amsterdam has been a node for transatlantic data interchange and today computers are omnipresent. Many official bodies and private businesses advertise themselves on the World Wide Web, and if you're online you can check some out before you arrive. In 1994 the city council funded a group of hackers to form The Digital City (*De Digitale Stad*), at <http://www.dds.nl>, a kind of virtual neighbourhood of Amsterdam with some information in English. Other English-language sites include the city council's own web server at <www.amsterdam.nl>, the Dutch tourist office at <www.nbt.nl> and *Time Out's* listings for what's on in Amsterdam at <www.timeout.nl>. The address <www.drugspeace.nl> speaks for itself. The Dutch home page contains links for everything to do with Holland and Amsterdam – find it at <www.dhp.nl/uk>.

ISIC CARDS Student ID won't help gain reduced admission to anything in the city – for this you need a museumcard, a "culture and leisure pass" or a *CJP* (see p.241).

LAUNDRY (wassalons) The Clean Brothers, Kerkstraat 56 (daily 7am–9pm) is the best self-service launderette, with a sizeable load currently ƒ8 to wash, 25c per five minutes in the drier; they also do service-washes, dry-cleaning, ironing, etc; branches at Jacob van Lennepkade 179 and Westerstraat 26. Other launderettes are to be

found at: Oudebrugsteeg 22 (off Damrak), Elandsgracht 59 (Jordaan), Warmoesstraat 30, Monnikenstraat 8 and Oude Doelenstraat 12 (Red Light District) and Herenstraat 24.

LIBRARIES No one will stop you from using any of the public libraries, or *Openbare Bibliotheken*, for reference purposes, but to borrow books you'll need to show proof of residence and pay around ƒ34 for a year's membership (less for under-18s). The main branch at Prinsengracht 587 (Mon 1–9pm, Tues–Thurs 10am–9pm, Fri & Sat 10am–5pm; Oct–March also Sun 1–5pm; ☎523 0900) has English newspapers and magazines and a cheap snack bar; there's also a CD library and a piano for rent (ƒ2.50/hr, no library card needed). The American Institute Library is at Plantage Muiderstraat 12 (☎525 4380); the British Council Library is at Keizersgracht 343 (☎622 3644).

LOST PROPERTY For items lost on the trams, buses or metro, contact *GVB* Head Office, Prins Hendrikkade 108–114 ☎551 4911. For property lost on a train, go to the *Gevonden Voorwerpen* office at the nearest station; Amsterdam's is at Centraal Station ☎557 8544. If you collect your property within two days there is no charge, but after two days each item costs ƒ5, and after four days all unclaimed property goes to the Central Lost Property Office at 2e Daalsedijk 4, Utrecht ☎030/235 3923, and costs ƒ7.50 per item to pick up; the leaflet *Verloren Voorwerpen* has a map showing the location of the office. If you lose something in the street or a park, try the police lost property at Stephensonstraat 18 (Mon–Fri noon–3.30pm ☎559 3005). Schiphol Airport's lost and found number is ☎601 2325. The Hook of Holland ferry terminal has no central lost property office: if you lose something here, try contacting the ferry company.

MOSQUITOES These thrive in Holland's watery environment, and bite their worst in the canal-filled city centre and at the campsites. *Muggenmelk*, with DEET, is very powerful: a little smear will keep the critters well away for a good night's sleep. Other popular brands include the *Autan* range. For more sensitive skins, *Prrrikweg* (honestly) contains pungent citronella oil. After the event, an antihistamine cream such as *Phenergan* helps. All these and more are available all over Amsterdam.

NOTICEBOARDS Most "brown cafés" have noticeboards with details of concerts, events and the like, occasionally displaying personal notices too. The main library (see above) and all *Albert Heijn* supermarkets have noticeboards useful for apartment- and job-hunting, sharing lifts, and the like. Small neighbourhood cafés or restaurants often have thriving boards; try *Gary's Muffins* or the *Vliegende Schotel*; also the *American Book Centre*. There's a travellers' noticeboard in the Tropen Museum if you're looking for companions or rides to other parts of the world.

NUCLEAR ALERT On the first Monday of every month, at exactly noon, wailing klaxons start up all over the city as Amsterdam's nuclear early-warning system is tested. Amsterdammers make a show of ignoring the noise, but it is deeply sinister and unsettling. If klaxons start up at any other time, you'd be well advised to run with everybody else.

PHOTO BOOTHS Scattered around town, but most reliably on the stairway at *Vroom & Dreesmann* on Kalverstraat, or at Centraal Station. You'll pay around ƒ5 for four black and white pictures.

PHOTOCOPYING Places like the central library and main post office have clunky old machines that cost 25c per page to use. Specialist copy shops, whose prices mostly start at around 6c, are cheaper and better, and have all kinds of fancy paper and colour copying as well. The most people-friendly place is *Copy-Copy*, at Keizersgracht 306; also try *Printerette* (Spuistraat 128, Vijzelstraat 76). *Kinko's* (Overtoom 62) is open 24 hours daily, but has higher prices and a corporate attitude to match. All these places also let you use computers running everything from simple wordprocessors to desktop publishing packages; all do laser-printing too.

PROSTITUTES The women in the windows set their own prices; some pay income tax and so charge more to their customers. Expect to pay a minimum of ƒ50 for either oral sex or intercourse, always with a condom. It won't take more than fifteen minutes.

RELIGIOUS SERVICES Christian in English: Sun 12.15pm, at St John and St Ursula (Catholic),

Begijnhof 30 ☎622 1918; Sun 10.30am, at the Anglican Church, Groenburgwal 42 ☎624 8877; Sun 10.30am, at the English Reformed Church, Begijnhof 48 ☎624 9665. High Mass in Latin: Sun 9.30am and 11am, at De Krijtberg, Singel 448 ☎623 1923. **Jewish** Liberal, Jacob Soetendorpstraat 8 ☎642 3562; Orthodox, Van der Boechorststraat 26 ☎646 0046. **Muslim** THAIBA Islamic Cultural Centre, Kraaiennest 125 ☎698 2526.

TELEPHONE HELPLINES AND SERVICES Samaritans/Lifeline/Crisis Helpline ☎675 7575; Legal Advice Centre ☎626 4477, also free legal advice from student lawyers ☎548 2611; ACCESS (Administrative Committee to Co-ordinate English Speaking Services) ☎070/383 6161; public transport information ☎06/9292; wake-up service ☎06/9655.

TIME One hour ahead of Britain, six hours ahead of New York, nine hours ahead of Los Angeles. Daylight-saving operates from the end of March to the end of October.

TIPPING Don't bother, since restaurants, hotels, taxis, etc, must include a fifteen percent service charge by law. Only if you're somewhere really upmarket is it considered proper to round up the bill to the nearest five guilders.

TOILETS are invariably spotlessly clean and well maintained, and equally invariably cost 25c or 50c. For men, there are evil-smelling pissoirs located all over the city.

WEATHER Changeable, with a good chance of rain later in the day. Recorded information in Dutch on ☎06/8003.

WINDMILLS The most central windmill in Amsterdam is De Gooyer in the Eastern Islands district (see p.136), and the best preserved one is in the south of Amstel Park (see p.150)). But the best place to see windmills is Kinderdijk near Rotterdam; they're also very much part of the landscape in the polderlands north of Amsterdam. Some have been moved and reassembled in the open-air museums at Zaanse Schans, near Zaandam (see p.319), and just outside Arnhem.

The City

Chapter 1

Introducing the City

A   msterdam is an easy city to find your way around. Centraal
      Station, where you're likely to arrive, lies on the northern
      edge of the city centre, its back to the River IJ: from the sta-
tion, the city fans south in a web of concentric canals, surrounded
by expanding suburbs. The city is small enough not to have any really distinct neighbourhoods: it's easier just to distinguish between
the Old Centre and the ring of canals that encircle it. The neighbourhoods outside this broad half-circle are residential for the most
part, although they do hold a number of attractions, not least the
city's major museums and its largest central open space, the
Vondelpark; as such, they're often near the top of most people's

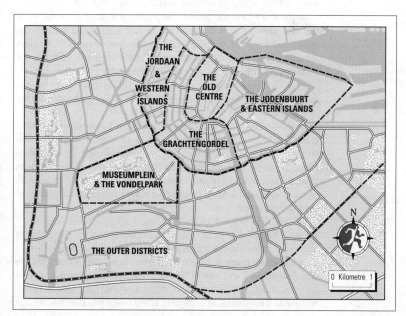

travel agendas and, with the city's compactness, they're very easy to get to.

We've divided Amsterdam according to the chapter headings·that follow for ease of reference; because of the nature of the city they don't always refer to uniform areas and certainly don't indicate itineraries to be followed slavishly. Amsterdam is a city of low-key attractions and charms, and wandering its streets and canals is as good a way as any to explore.

At the centre of Amsterdam is the medieval town or **Old Centre** (Chapter 2), which fans south from Centraal Station, revolving around the main streets of Damrak and Rokin, which lead into and out of Dam Square at the city's core. This area is Amsterdam's commercial heart, with the best of its bustling street life, home to shops, many bars and restaurants and, not least, the infamous **Red Light District** on one side of Damrak. The Old Centre is bordered by the first of the major **canals**, the Singel, followed closely by the Herengracht, Keizersgracht and Prinsengracht: all four are collectively referred to as the **Grachtengordel**, or "Girdle of Canals" (Chapter 3). These canals are part of a major seventeenth-century urban extension and, with the radial streets of Raadhuisstraat, Leidsestraat, Vijzelstraat and Weesperstraat, create Amsterdam's distinctive web shape. This is the Amsterdam you see in the brochures: still, dreamy canals, crisp reflections of seventeenth-century town houses, cobbled streets, railings with chained bicycles – an image which, although cloying, is still utterly authentic.

Beyond the Grachtengordel, the **Jordaan** district (Chapter 4) to the west grew up as a slum and immigrant quarter and remains the traditional heart of working-class Amsterdam, though these days there is a gentrified edge to the area. On the other side of town, the **Jodenbuurt** (Chapter 5) was once home to the city's Jewish community. Since the construction of the City Hall complex here, as well as the digging of the metro beneath the area, it's probably the district that's changed most visibly since World War II.

In its Golden Age, the city's riches were founded on maritime trade, and the Amsterdam docks used to stretch along the full frontage of the IJ. These days the shipping industry has long since gone, but the old merchant and shipbuilding quarters – the **Western Islands** district north of the Jordaan and the **Eastern Islands** north of the Jodenbuurt – are now experiencing something of a revival as desirable riverside residential areas.

The districts beyond the meandering Singelgracht are largely residential, though one of the city's highlights lies just to the south of this canal: the cluster of world-class museums around **Museumplein and the Vondelpark** (Chapter 6). Beyond here, the **Outer Districts** to the south, east and west (Chapter 7) are in themselves not of great interest, though there are a few attractions – street markets, architecture and a museum or two – that could tempt you out. Amsterdam

North, on the other hand, across the River IJ, remains a quite distinct and thoroughly nondescript entity; it's good cycling country, but otherwise there's little reason to venture out this way.

Getting around the city couldn't be easier. With its narrow streets and canals, by far the best way is to **walk**: you could stroll from Centraal Station out to the Rijksmuseum in about 45 minutes, and see the whole of the centre on the way. Alternatively, there is a comprehensive network of **trams** running all over the city, with each stop carrying a detailed route map, or there are myriad outlets where you can copy the locals and **rent a bike**. The buses and metro are only really useful for commuters, and driving your own car is a fringe activity that is generally frowned upon.

Chapter 2

The Old Centre

Amsterdam's **OLD CENTRE**, poking south into the elegant girdle of the major canals, is by far the city's busiest and most vigorous district, lacking the gracious uniformity of much of the rest of the city centre but making up for it in excitement. Given the dominance of Centraal Station on most transport routes, the old centre is where you'll almost certainly arrive. It's a small but varied area, ranging from the vigour of Stationsplein – international buskers' meeting point and home of the VVV tourist office – to the strategic tourist trap of Damrak, and the studied sleaze of the Red Light District, which is not surprisingly one of Amsterdam's biggest attractions, and also home to a couple of its most beautiful canals.

Historically, the Old Centre divides into a new side and an old side. The **"New Side"** was the western half of the medieval city, bordered by the streets of Nieuwezijds Voorburgwal (literally, "In Front of the Town Wall on the New Side") and Damrak. On the other side of Damrak is the **"Old Side"**, much of it dating back to the fifteenth century: Warmoesstraat, running parallel to Damrak, is the city's oldest street, connecting the Dam with the River IJ. Unlike the New Side, whose waterways were filled in around the turn of this century, the Old Side has largely kept the beauty of its canals intact. Of these, the Oudezijds Voorburgwal (often abbreviated to O.Z. Voorburgwal) used to run in front of (*voor*) the city wall, while the O.Z. Achterburgwal ran behind (*achter*).

A map of the Old Centre appears in the colour insert in the central section of the book.

Centraal Station and Damrak

The neo-Gothic **Centraal Station** is an imposing prelude to the city. When built on an artificial island late in the last century, it aroused controversy because it obscured the views of the port that brought

Amsterdam its wealth. Since then, however, shipping has moved out to more spacious dock areas to the west, and the station, embellished with all manner of Victorian ornament by its architect P.J.H. Cuypers (who also designed the very similar Rijksmuseum), is now one of Amsterdam's most resonant landmarks, and a natural focal point for urban life. Stand here and all of Amsterdam, with its faintly oriental skyline of spires and cupolas, lies before you.

Centraal
Station and
Damrak

Stationsplein, immediately outside, is a messy open space, fragmented by ovals of water and dotted with barrel organs, chip stands, and "M" signs indicating the city's rapidly ageing metro. Come summer, there's no livelier part of the city, as street performers compete for attention with the careening trams that converge dangerously from all sides. It's without doubt a promising place to arrive, and with that in mind the municipal authorities have been cleaning up the area's image, notably along its southeastern edge, where there's a luxury hotel and other new development slowly creeping down the once-notorious Zeedijk (see p.80).

Close by here, the dome of the **St Nicolaaskerk** catches the eye. Despite a dilapidated exterior, currently under renovation, it's the city's foremost Catholic church, having replaced the clandestine Amstelkring (see p.79) in 1887. St Nicholas is the patron saint of sailors, which explains the church's proximity to the harbour. If you're here at the right time to enter the lavishly gloomy interior (Easter to mid-Oct Mon 1.30–4pm, Tues–Sat 11am–4pm), on the high altar you'll find the crown of the Austro-Hungarian Emperor Maximilian, very much a symbol of the city and one you'll see again and again (on top of the Westerkerk and in much of the city's official literature). Amsterdam had close ties with Maximilian: in the late fifteenth century he came here as a pilgrim and stayed on to recover from an illness. The burghers funded many of his military expeditions; in return, he let the city use his crown in its coat of arms, which gave the upstart port immediate prestige in the eyes of the rest of the world.

While searching for a hotel, you can leave heavy bags in the 24-hour lockers at Centraal Station; or try Rent-a-Safe, at Warmoesstraat 47, just behind the Beurs.

Along Damrak

Above all, Stationsplein acts as a filter for Amsterdam's newcomers, and from here **Damrak**, an unenticing avenue lined with tacky restaurants, bureaux de change, and the bobbing canal boats of Amsterdam's considerable tourist industry, storms south into the heart of the city. Just past the boats is the Stock Exchange, or **Beurs** – known as the "Beurs van Berlage" – designed at the turn of the century by the leading light of the Dutch Modern movement, H.P. Berlage, and something of a seminal work, with its various styles from Romanesque to neo-Renaissance interwoven with a minimum of ornamentation. These days it's no longer used as an exchange, but often hosts visiting theatre groups, concerts and exhibitions. If you get the chance, look into the main hall, where

Centraal
Station and
Damrak

exposed ironwork and shallow-arched arcades combine to give a real sense of space. The much duller **Effectenbeurs**, flanking the eastern side of Beursplein, is the home of such stock trading as goes on these days – phone for an appointment (☎523 4257) to view the proceedings from the visitors' gallery. Should such things grab you, options are traded in the Optiebeurs at Rokin 65 (☎550 4550).

On the other side of the street, two of Amsterdam's tackier museums are within steps of each other. At Damrak 18, the **Sex Museum** (daily 10am–11.30pm; ƒ3.95) is frankly more of a commercial enterprise than a museum, although it does display some erotic pictures, statues, cartoons and examples of early pornographic films. Seconds away, at no. 22, is the **Torture Museum** (daily 10am–11pm; ƒ7.50), a collection of original medieval instruments of torture assembled from the dungeons of Europe and presented with suitably dramatic music (and English explanations). Old favourites like the chair of nails, the pillory and the iron maiden are on display, as well as a grill for roasting heretics and a wheel for spinning them on, although perhaps the most horrific item is the one that simply manacles the victim into a crouching position until they go mad with muscle cramps – a device apparently used on Guy Fawkes.

Further up on the same side, one of Amsterdam's best bookshops, **Allert de Lange**, is the contemporary outlet of a pioneering Jewish publisher who, in the 1930s, made available much of the work of refugee authors from Nazi Germany, such as Bertholt Brecht and Max Brod. Crossing over the street again, the **De Bijenkorf** – literally "beehive" – department store building, facing the Beurs and extending south as far as Dam Square, was another successful Jewish concern – so much so that during the Nazi occupation the authorities, fearing altercations with the Jewish staff, forbade German soldiers to shop on the ground floor. Today *De Bijenkorf* is a nationwide chain.

For more on De Bijenkorf, and Amsterdam's other department stores, see Shops and Markets, p.254.

The Red Light District

The whole area to the left off Damrak, between Warmoesstraat and Nieuwmarkt, is the **Red Light District**, known locally as the "Walletjes" (since this was where the old city walls ran); it stretches across the two canals that marked the edge of medieval Amsterdam, **Oudezijds Voorburgwal** and **Oudezijds Achterburgwal**, though the action peters out south of Damrak. The prostitution here is world-renowned and sadly, but perhaps inevitably, it's one of the real sights of the city and one of its most distinctive draws; the two canals with their narrow connecting passages are on most evenings of the year thronged with people here to discover just how shocking it all is. The atmosphere is a festive one, with entertainment for all, as entire families titter and blush at the invitations to various kinds of illicit thrills. Groups of men line the streets hawking the peep shows and "live sex" within (and, unlike in London or New York, there actually is live sex within), while lingerie-clad women sit looking bored behind glass, in red-lit shop windows that take their place among more conventional businesses on the same streets. There's a nasty edge to the district too, oddly enough sharper during the daytime, when the pimps hang out in shifty gangs and drug addicts wait anxiously, assessing the chances of scoring their next hit.

Commercial sex in Amsterdam

Since the 1960s, Amsterdam's liberal approach to social policy has result-ed in the city's gaining worldwide notoriety as a major international centre for both drugs (see p.82) and the commercial sex industry. However, the tackiness of the Red Light District is just the surface sheen on what is a serious attempt to address the reality of sex-for-sale, and to allow it to take its place in a normal, ordered society. In Dutch law, prostitutes are seen as victims; prostituting oneself is legal here, although organizing prostitution currently isn't – the last attempt to legalize brothel-keeping foundered in 1993, but there remains a significant lobby in its favour, led by the prosti-tutes' trade union, De Rode Draad ("The Red Thread"), and backed by Cabinet support. The commercial sex industry is becoming increasingly dynamic: prostitutes are now liable for income tax on their earnings, De Rode Draad has a number of offshoot support networks currently setting up health insurance and pension schemes for prostitutes, and recently the VER, the Organization of Entrepreneurs in Prostitution, established a code of self-regulation in an attempt to discourage customers from using exploitative establishments.

One of the strongest features of the Dutch approach is its lack of prud-ery in addressing the issues. The Prostitution Information Centre, at Enge Kerksteeg 3 (between Warmoesstraat and the Oude Kerk; Tues–Sat noon–9pm; ☎ 420 7328), is a legally recognized *stichting*, or charitable foundation, set up to provide prostitutes, their clients and general visitors with clear, dispassionate information about prostitution. In addition to selling books and pamphlets (as well as lingerie, tasteful postcards and a range of condoms), the PIC runs courses in prostitution at beginner and advanced level, provides support groups for clients and their partners, and publishes the *Pleasure Guide* in Dutch and English, which bills itself as "an informative magazine about having a paid love-life". It also has a site on the World Wide Web at <http://fun2.fun.nl/pic>. By positioning itself on the commercial interface between the Red Light District and the rest of the city – and devoting itself to aiding communication between the two – the PIC and its owner Mariska Majoor have done much to subvert the old exploitative dominance of underworld pimps and have helped bring the living and working conditions of women who choose to be prostitutes out into the light of day.

More information is available via the Internet: you can read about the city government's regulations and attitude towards prostitution at <http://www.amsterdam.nl>, while businesses in the Red Light District operate an information server at <http://www.fun.nl>.

Warmoesstraat

Soliciting hasn't always gone on here, and the rich facades of Oudezijds Voorburgwal – known in the sixteenth century as the "Velvet Canal" because it was home to so many wealthy people – point to a more venerable past. As the city prospered, and the then nearby docks grew busier, the area grew sleazier as more and more prostitutes were required to service the growing population of itinerant seamen. Today narrow **Warmoesstraat** is seedy and uninviting, but it was once one of the city's most fashionable streets, and home of Holland's foremost poet, **Joost van der Vondel**, who ran his seventeenth-century hosiery business from no. 110, in between writing and hobnobbing with the Amsterdam elite.

One of the highlights of Warmoesstraat is the Condomerie, at no. 141, which specializes in every imaginable design of condom for all budgets.

Vondel is a kind of Dutch Shakespeare: his *Gijsbrecht van Amstel*, a celebration of Amsterdam during its Golden Age, is one of the classics of Dutch literature, and he wrote regular, if ponderous, official verses, including well over a thousand lines on the inauguration of the new town hall. His house no longer stands, but a little way down on the right, by the wall of the city's Stock Exchange, a statue of the poet marks its site. After his son had frittered away the modest family fortune, Vondel lived out his last few years as doorkeeper of the pawn shop on Oudezijds Voorburgwal (see p.83), dying at the age of 92 of hypothermia brought on by his advanced years. Unassuming to the end, his own suggested epitaph ran:

> *Here lies Vondel, still and old*
> *Who died – because he was cold.*

Close to the junction with Oude Brugsteeg, at Warmoesstraat 67, the **Geels & Co. Museum** (Tues 2–4pm, Fri & Sat 2–4.30pm; ☎624 0683; free), above the wonderful old shop of the same name, displays mills, machinery and assorted paraphernalia related to the consumption of coffee and tea.

The Oude Kerk

Just off Warmoesstraat, the precincts of the **Oude Kerk** (Mon–Sat 11am–5pm, Sun 1–5pm; f5; tower open mid-June to Sept Wed–Sat 2–4pm; f3) provide a reverential peace after the excesses of the Red Light District. Even around here, though, many of the houses have the familiar *Kamer te Huur* ("Room for Rent") sign and window seat; away from the bustle of the canals, this is known as "Dutch Alley", much more the territory of local clients, and single men will have to run the gauntlet of insistent taps from each window as they walk by.

There's been a church on this site since the late thirteenth century, even before the Dam was built, but most of the present building dates from the fourteenth century. In the Middle Ages, pilgrims flocked to Amsterdam – and specifically to this church – thanks to a mid-fourteenth-century miracle in which a dying man regurgitated the Host he had received at Communion, which was then thrown on a fire yet did not burn. The Host was placed in a chest (now in the Amsterdam Historical Museum) and installed in a chapel somewhere between Nieuwezijds Voorburgwal and Kalverstraat, close to where the miracle happened. When the chapel burnt down but the Host still didn't burn, a plaque was put up in the Oude Kerk to commemorate the event. In the manner of such tales, the Host began to turn up in different spots all over town, attracting pilgrims in droves. To this day, the faithful still come to take part in the annual commemorative *Stille Omgang*, a silent nocturnal procession terminating at the Oude Kerk on the Sunday closest to March 15, which is normally joined by some ten thousand people.

Having been stripped bare during the Reformation and recently very thoroughly restored, the Oude Kerk is nowadays a survivor rather than any sort of architectural masterpiece. Apart from a few faded vault paintings, its handful of interesting features include some beautifully carved misericords in the choir and elegant stained-glass windows dating from the sixteenth century. The church also contains the tomb of one of seventeenth-century Holland's naval heroes, Admiral J. van Heemskerk, and the memorial tablet of Rembrandt's wife, Saskia van Uylenburg, who is also buried here. Her tomb was apparently sold by the bankrupt Rembrandt to pay for the burial of his second wife.

During the summer, the Oude Kerk holds a series of "walking" concert evenings; see Entertainment and Nightlife, p.229.

The Amstelkring

Towards the northern end of Oudezijds Voorburgwal, the clandestine **Amstelkring** (Mon–Sat 10am–5pm, Sun 1–5pm; ☎624 6604; ƒ7.50), once the principal Catholic place of worship in the city, is now one of the city's best and least demanding small museums, and a still relatively undiscovered escape from the surrounding sleaze.

Seventeenth-century Holland was, by the standards of its contemporaries, a remarkably tolerant society: in Amsterdam many religions were accepted if not exactly encouraged, and most freedoms could be bought, either with hard cash or a proven popularity. Catholics, however, had to confine their worship to the privacy of their own homes – an arrangement that led to the growth of so-called clandestine Catholic churches throughout the city. This one, known as "Ons Lieve Heer Op Solder" – or "Our Dear Lord in the Attic" – is the only one left; it occupies the loft of a wealthy merchant's house, together with those of two smaller houses behind it. The **church** is delightful, three balconied storeys high, with a massive organ at one end (which must have been heard all over the neighbourhood) and a mock marble altar decorated with a chubby *Baptism of Christ* by Jacob de Wit – one of three painted for the purpose. In addition, the **house** itself has been left beautifully untouched, its original furnishings reminiscent of interiors by Vermeer or De Hooch. "Amstelkring", meaning "Amstel Circle", was the name of the group of nineteenth-century historians that saved the building from destruction.

Zeedijk

Running behind Oudezijds Achterburgwal from Centraal Station
down to Nieuwmarkt, **Zeedijk** was originally just that – a dike to hold
back the sea – and the wooden house at no. 1 is one of the oldest in
the city. It was built as a sailors' dosshouse around 1550, and
became known as the place where a sailor who had drunk, whored or
gambled away his money away could still get a bed – as long as he
gave the owner his pet monkey in exchange. It didn't take long for
the place to be completely overrun with the creatures, earning the
hostel the name of *In't Aepjen* ("In the Monkeys"); the café that
occupies the house today has kept the name.

Zeedijk itself is much cleaned up now but was a pretty lurid spot in
the mid-1980s, when you had to run the gauntlet of Surinamese heroin dealers trying to fast-talk you into a quick sale while idle groups of
policemen looked on. However, with the city-wide push to polish up
Amsterdam's tarnished reputation, Zeedijk's bad old days seem to
have gone for ever. The luxury *Barbizon Plaza Hotel* has been
planted at the northern end of the street, and many new bars and

*One of the best
of the Chinese
restaurants in
the area is Hoi
Tin, at Zeedijk
122; see p.214.*

restaurants have moved into the area. A sign on the wall lets everyone know where the priorities are these days: "Zeedijk: the oldest and
newest street in Amsterdam". But there's still some way to go before
the area becomes as swish as the developers would like to have us
think: the dealers may have moved on, but junkies still hang out in
ramshackle doorways, and the southern end of the street, with its
empty houses, peeling restaurants and rubble-filled wasteground,
still retains a hard-edged tension, enough to make you hurry on
through to the open spaces of Nieuwmarkt.

Nieuwmarkt and south

Zeedijk opens out onto **Nieuwmarkt** and the bottom end of
Geldersekade, which together form the hub of Amsterdam's tiny
Chinese quarter, consisting of a handful of oriental supermarkets
and a couple of bookshops. Nieuwmarkt has always been one of
Amsterdam's most important markets, first for fish, later for the
cloth traders from the adjacent Jewish quarter; however, during the
last war, after increasingly random arrests by the occupying Nazis in
and around the once bustling market, the whole area was cordoned

*Café 't Loosje,
with a
terrace on
Nieuwmarkt,
is a fine place
to while away
a sunny after-
noon.*

off with barbed wire and turned into a holding pen for the city's Jews
awaiting deportation. The old exuberance never returned, and these
days the market has all but vanished: there is a small market for
organic food on Saturdays and one for antiques on Sundays, with a
few stalls selling fish, fruit and vegetables during the week.

The main focus of the square, the turreted **Waag** or old **Sint
Antoniespoort**, has played a variety of roles over the years.
Originally part of the fortifications that encircled Amsterdam before

the seventeenth-century expansion, it later became the civic weighing house, and for more than two centuries housed the Surgeons' Guild; in a specially designed theatre, constructed in the octagonal tower in 1691, the guild held lectures on anatomy and public dissections – the young Rembrandt's *Anatomy Lesson of Dr Tulp* was based on the activities here. In this century, the Waag was for a time the home of the Amsterdam Jewish Museum, but it fell into disuse after the Jewish collection moved to new premises in 1987. Plans to turn it into a children's book museum fell through, but the building has now been bought by the Society for Old and New Media (☎557 9898) and renovated from top to bottom: in addition to a café and restaurant (with a "Digital Reading Table" allowing you to browse the World Wide Web), there are changing exhibitions, lectures and readings in the old anatomy theatre upstairs. You can find out more about the Society from its Web page at <http://www.waag.org>.

Kloveniersburgwal

Leading south from Nieuwmarkt, **Kloveniersburgwal** was the outer of the three eastern canals of sixteenth-century Amsterdam. A long, dead-straight waterway, with dignified facades jostling each other the whole way down, it boasts, on the left at no. 29, one of the city's most impressive canal houses.

The Engelbe-waarder at Kloveniers-burgwal 59 is an attractive brown café, with live jazz on Sundays.

Built for the Trip family in 1662, and large enough to house the Rijksmuseum collection for most of the nineteenth century, the **Trippenhuis** is a huge overblown mansion, its Corinthian pilasters and grand frieze providing a suitable reflection of the owners' importance among the Amsterdam *Magnificat* – the name given to the clique of families (Six, Trip, Hooft and Pauw) who shared power during the Golden Age. The Trips, incidentally, made their fortune from arms dealing; today their house contains the Dutch Academy of Sciences.

Directly opposite, on the right bank of the canal, there's a quite different house that gives an idea of the sort of resentment such ostentatious displays of wealth engendered. Mr Trip's coachman was so taken aback by the size of the new family residence that he exclaimed he would be happy with a home no wider than the Trips' front door – which is exactly what he got, and Kloveniersburgwal 26 is known as the **House of Mr Trip's Coachman**. Not surprisingly, at a metre or so across, it is the narrowest house in Amsterdam.

Further along the canal, on the corner of Oude Hoogstraat, is the former headquarters of the **Dutch East India Company**, a monumental red-brick structure, built in 1605 shortly after the founding of the company. It was from here that the Dutch organized and regulated their trading interests in the Far East, which made the country so profitable in the seventeenth century. Under the greedy auspices of the East India Company, the Netherlands (especially its most prosperous provinces, Holland and Zeeland) exploited the natural

*De Hoogte, on
Nieuwe
Hoogstraat, is
a small,
friendly bar
open all day
playing loud,
alternative
music.*

resources of the group of islands now known as Indonesia for several centuries, satisfying the whims of Amsterdam's burghers with shiploads of spices, textiles and exotic woods. However, for all that, the building itself is of little interest, being occupied these days by offices and the university: enter by the small gate in Oude Hoogstraat for a quick look.

The Hash Museum and the Spinhuis

At the other end of the tiny Oude Hoogstraat, at Oudezijds Achterburgwal 148, the **Hash Marihuana Hemp Museum** (daily 11am–10pm; ☎623 5961; ƒ6) is still going strong amid intermittent

---

Drugs in Amsterdam

Amsterdam's liberal policies on commercial sex (see p.77) are similarly extended to soft **drugs**, and the city's reputation among dope-smokers worldwide as a unique place to legally buy and smoke hashish and marijuana is legendary. New York's *High Times* magazine regularly holds its annual Cannabis Cup in Amsterdam each November – no doubt the event would be much harder to put on in Manhattan. Technically, all drugs are illegal in Amsterdam; however, since 1976 the possession of small amounts of cannabis (up to 28g/1oz; see p.46) has been ignored by the police, a situation that has led to the rise of "smoking" coffeeshops, selling bags of dope much as bars sell glasses of beer.

With the move towards European integration, the Netherlands has come under increasing pressure, particularly from the neighbouring French and Germans, to bring its drug policy into line with that of the rest of Europe; one recent concession made by the mayor of Amsterdam, Schelto Patijn, was to force coffeeshops to choose between selling dope or alcohol. As a result, many coffeeshops are sticking with alcohol, mostly because of higher sales; some, such as the famous *Bulldog* (see p.205), now have two separate entrances, one for drinkers and one for smokers.

However, the Dutch are still largely sticking to their guns, citing a lack of evidence to link recreational drugs with hard drugs: the country's figures for hard-drug addiction are actually among the lowest in Europe. Indeed, Amsterdam's authorities are often at the cutting edge of movements to limit social damage from drugs. For instance, in many nightclubs, the city's drug research unit has set up tables where, for ƒ5, you can have your (illegal) tab of Ecstasy chemically tested to ascertain purity; stories abound of disgruntled buyers returning to confront the dealers who've sold them low-quality drugs.

As far as hard drugs are concerned, areas such as the Zeedijk and Nieuwmarkt used to be notorious; the canal bridge at Oude Hoogstraat was even nicknamed the "Pillenbrug", or "Pill Bridge", for the amount of dealing that went on there. But since the 1980s cleanup, the city government has adopted a characteristically enlightened approach to the problem, with emphasis on the health and social wellbeing of addicts rather than law enforcement: needle exchanges and free methadone are common, as is the acquittal of addicts on criminal charges in exchange for their registration on municipal rehabilitation programmes.

---

battles with the police, with displays on various types of dope and numerous ways to smoke it. Pipes, books, videos and plenty of souvenirs are also on show, along with a live indoor marijuana garden, and there are pamphlets on the medicinal properties of cannabis as well as samples of textiles and paper made with hemp.

.While you're on Oudezijds Achterburgwal, stop off at the **Spinhuis**, at no. 28. This used to be a house of correction for "fallen women", who would work at looms and spinning wheels to atone for their wayward ways – ironic given its proximity to today's Red Light District. Oddly enough, places like this used to figure on tourist itineraries: for a small fee the public were allowed to watch the women at work, and at carnival times admission was free and large crowds came to jeer and mock. Shame was supposed to be part of the reforming process, although it's undoubtedly true that the city fathers also made a nice return on their unfortunate inmates. You can't go in now – the building is given over to municipal offices – but the facade remains pretty much intact, with an inscription by the seventeenth-century Dutch poet Pieter Cornelisz Hooft: "Cry not, for I exact no vengeance for wrong but to force you to be good. My hand is stern but my heart is kind."

*The Cul De Sac
bar, down an
alleyway at
O.Z.
Achterburgwal
99, is a good
place to stop
for a drink.*

Around the University

At the southern end of Oudezijds Achterburgwal, **Oudemanhuispoort** leads through to Kloveniersburgwal. This passage was once part of an almshouse for elderly men (hence the strange name), but is now filled with second-hand bookstalls and a group of buildings serving the University of Amsterdam.

From Oudezijds Achterburgwal you can see across to the pretty **Huis op de Drie Grachten**, the "House on the Three Canals", on the corner of Grimburgwal, which runs alongside more university buildings. A little way down Oudezijds Voorburgwal on the right, through an ornate gateway, is the fifteenth-century **Agnietenkapel** (Mon–Fri 9am–5pm; ☎525 3339; ƒ2.50), also owned by the university and containing its so-called **Historical Collection**, made up of collections of books, prints, letters and suchlike, all related to the history of the city's university – real specialist stuff on the whole. Roughly opposite, the building at Oudezijds Voorburgwal 300 has been known for years as **"ome Jan"** (Uncle John's) for its function as central Amsterdam's pawn shop, established 350 years ago in a typically enlightened attempt to put a stop to the crippling activities of moneylenders who were making a killing among the city's poor. The poet Vondel ended his days working here, and a short verse above the entrance extols the virtues of the pawn shop and the evils of usury.

*Gasthuis,
Grimburgwal
7, is a cosy bar
popular with
students, with
canalside seating in summer.*

At the corner a passage cuts through to **Nes**, a long, narrow street leading to the Dam, which was once home to the philosopher Spinoza and is now filled with theatres; or you can make your way back down the canal past the **Galerie Mokum**, named for the old Jewish nickname for the city, which has now passed into general use. From here it's just a few yards to the trams and traffic of **Rokin**. This broad street, which follows the old course of the River Amstel, is lined with grandiose nineteenth-century mansions – Amsterdam's *Sotheby's* is here, and, further down, the elaborate *fin-de-siècle* interior of the *Maison de Bonneterie* clothes store.

The Allard Pierson Museum

Along Rokin, just beyond the corner with Lange Brugsteeg, the **Allard Pierson Museum** at Oude Turfmarkt 127 (Tues–Fri 10am–5pm, Sat & Sun 1–5pm; ☎525 2556; *f*6) holds Amsterdam's archeological collection. It's a small and excellent museum, managing to avoid the fatigue often induced by such places by arranging its high-quality exhibits in intimate galleries that encourage you to explore. Clear background information personalizes what might otherwise be meaningless objects. The museum's highlights include a life-size model of a Greek chariot, a remarkably well-preserved collection of Coptic clothes and artefacts from the sixth century, Greek pottery and jewellery, and fine gold and precious stones from all periods.

Muntplein and the Flower Market

The elegant wide sweep of Rokin curls southeast down to **Muntplein**, from where garish Reguliersbreestraat turns left towards the gay bars and noisy restaurants of Rembrandtplein, while the more sedate Vijzelstraat heads straight out across the canals to the south of the city.

Originally a mint and part of the old city walls, the **Munttoren** here was topped with a spire by Hendrik de Keyser in 1620 and is possibly the most famous of the towers dotting the city, a landmark perfectly designed for postcards, especially when framed by the flowers of the nearby floating **Flower market**, or Bloemenmarkt (Mon–Sat 9am–6pm), which extends along the southern bank of the Singel west as far as Koningsplein. It's nearly always packed with visitors, but there are still many genuine bargains to be found among the clogs-and-Delft tat, including bulbs for export. Even if you're not buying, just to walk around savouring the sight and smell of so many flowers and plants is a lovely experience, especially in spring, when tulips of all shades sell by the thousand.

After walking around the Bloemenmark, stop at Gary's Muffins for coffee and bagels, one street south at Reguliersdwarsstraat 53.

From Koningsplein, at the far end of the market, the main Leidsestraat artery leads south to your left; ahead, the Singel canal curls round to the Spui (see below); while to your right, the cramped Heiligeweg leads back into the heart of the shopping district.

The New Side: west of Damrak

Even before Amsterdam's seventeenth-century expansion, the town could be divided into old and new sectors: the outer boundaries were marked by a defensive wall, and it's this that gives **Nieuwezijds Voorburgwal** ("In Front of the Town Wall on the New Side") its name. The wall itself disappeared as the city grew, and at the end of the nineteenth century the canal that ran through the middle of the street was filled in, leaving the unusually wide swathe that runs from just below Prins Hendrikkade all the way down to the little square at the Spui (pronounced to rhyme with "cow"). The street used to be the home of most of the capital's newspaper offices, but rising costs have forced the majority out to the suburbs; you can still see the papers' names on some of the buildings, and the old journos' watering hole, *Scheltema*, halfway down at Nieuwezijds Voorburgwal 242, remains a good place for a drink.

The Koepelkwartier

Nieuwezijds Voorburgwal begins with a bottleneck of trams swinging down from Centraal Station, and one of the first buildings you see is the **Holiday Inn**, built on the site of an old tenement building called **Wyers**.

The 1985 clearance of squatters from Wyers ranks among the most infamous of the decade's anti-squatting campaigns, involving a great deal of protest (and some violence) throughout the city. The squatters had occupied the building in an attempt to prevent yet another slice of the city being converted from residential use and handed over to a profit-hungry multinational. Although widely supported by the people of Amsterdam, they were no match for the economic muscle of the American hotel company, however, and it wasn't long before the riot police were sent in; construction of the hotel soon followed.

The **Luthersekerk**, directly west from here on Kattengat, hasn't fared much better. Its copper-green dome gives this area its label of **Koepelkwartier** or "Dome Neighbourhood", but the church itself was deconsecrated in the 1930s due to falling attendances, and after many years of disuse it was acquired by the nearby *Renaissance Hotel* as a conference centre. In 1993 a major fire gutted the church and, though restoration work is now complete, it remains the property of the hotel and is closed to the public.

Barely fifty metres away, **Spuistraat** (pronounced "spow-straat") – the main north–south cycle route between Centraal Station and the Dam – begins at a fork in Nieuwezijds Voorburgwal. A little way south, around the St Dominicus Kerk and the Oude Nieuwstraat, a small red-light district sits uneasily in the alleyways between the canal and the trams. Little here is for show – these are the red lights the tourists miss – and the business that goes on is serious and seamy.

The Flying Dutchman, close to the Holiday Inn at Martelaarsgracht 13, is the city's best-known English pub.

For more on the history of Amsterdam's squatting movement, see p.65.

South to the Dam

Back on Nieuwezijds Voorburgwal, the new building at the junction
with Nieuwezijds Kolk is testament to the recent large-scale construction work in the area. While the underground car park was
being dug, workers discovered archeological remains dating back to
the thirteenth century; this turned out to be the **castle** of the "Lords
of Aemstel", which, it is thought, had occupied the site when it was
open marshland, even before the Amstel was dammed. However, the
owners of the site, *ABN-AMRO Bank* (see also p.104), decided that
putting the remains on show to the public was incompatible with
their plans for the area; a brand-new glass office building, paved
plaza and luxury hotel now occupy the site. The razing of old buildings to make way for this new complex – and the presence of the
complex itself – has resulted in much of the area's character being
erased. The intricate alleys of the New Side, once filled with quirky
shops, small bars and homes, are now largely given over to more
generic hotels and businesses, and most of the residents have been
forced to move elsewhere. One significant casualty in the area was
the famous *Egg Cream*, one of the city's best vegetarian restaurants,
which closed for good in 1996 after 26 years of business.

The trees that fringe Nieuwezijds Voorburgwal conceal some
impressive canal houses, and the specialized shops and private galleries hereabouts try hard to preserve the refinement the street must
have had before canal traffic gave way to trams. You need only compare the street to the parallel **Nieuwendijk** to see that it has retained
some of its character. Nieuwendijk, in contrast, is a shabby, uninviting stretch of cheap shops and not-so-cheap restaurants, and the dark
side alleys give off a frightening sense of illicit dealings that hurries
you back to the main roads. Things improve as you approach the
Dam: there's a medieval eccentricity to the streets here, and all seediness vanishes as designer clothes shops appear in the old workshops
clustered in the cobbled back lanes. Walk down the wonderfully
named Zwarte Handsteeg (Black Hand Alley) and you're back on
Nieuwezijds Voorburgwal. Just across the road, the huge building
now labelled **Magna Plaza** – an indoor shopping mall, complete with
Virgin Megastore and fashion chains – used to be the old post office,
and it still manages to hold its own against the Nieuwe Kerk and Royal
Palace opposite. Built in 1899, its whimsical embellishments continue the town's tradition of sticking towers on things – here, as everywhere, purely for the hell of it. Amsterdam's central post office has
since moved a short way to the corner of Singel and Raadhuisstraat.

*De Drie
Fleschjes,
opposite
Magna
Plaza at
Gravenstraat
16, is a stand-
up, knock-it-
back tasting
house for spir-
its and
liqueurs; if
you're not
sure what to
try, ask for the
barman's
choice.*

Dam Square

Situated at the heart of the city, **Dam Square** gives Amsterdam its
name: in the thirteenth century the River Amstel was dammed here,

and the small fishing village that grew around it became known as "Amstelredam". Boats could sail right into the square down the Damrak and unload their imported grain in the middle of the rapidly growing town; later, the building of Amsterdam's principal church, the Nieuwe Kerk, along with the town hall (now the Royal Palace), formally marked Dam Square as Amsterdam's centre.

Though robbed a little of its dignity by the trams that scuttle across it, the square is still the hub of the city, with all the main streets zeroing in on the maelstrom of buskers, artists and ice-cream vans, who find an instant and captive clientele in the passers-by. On the far side there's a **War Memorial**, an unsightly stone tusk designed by J.J.P. Oud that's filled with soil from each of the Netherlands' eleven provinces plus Indonesia; this serves as a gathering place for the square's milling tourists, and for dubious looking characters selling dope to gullible teenagers. The square's single commercial tourist pull is the Amsterdam branch of **Madame Tussaud's** waxworks at Dam 20 (daily 10am–5.30pm; ☎622 9949; ƒ17.50, children ƒ10).

The Royal Palace

The main feature of the square is the **Royal Palace** (June–Aug daily 12.30–5pm; Sept–May Tues–Thurs 1–4pm; ☎624 8698; ƒ5, no museumcards), which seems neither Dutch nor palatial – understandably so, since it was originally built as the city's town hall, using imported stone. The authorities of Europe's mercantile capital wanted a grandiose declaration of civic power, a building that would push even the Nieuwe Kerk (see below) into second place, and Jacob van Campen's then startlingly progressive design, a Dutch rendering of the classical principles revived in Renaissance Italy, did exactly that. At the time of its construction in the mid-seventeenth century, it was the largest town hall in Europe, supported by 13,659 wooden piles driven into the Dam's sandy soil (a number every Dutch schoolchild remembers by adding a "1" and a "9" to the number of days in the year). The poet Constantijn Huygens called the new building "the world's Eighth Wonder / With so much stone raised high and so much timber under". It's the magisterial interior that really deserves this praise, though: the Citizen's Hall proclaims the pride and confidence of the Golden Age, with the enthroned figure of Amsterdam looking down on the world and heavens laid out at her feet, the whole sumptuously inlaid in brass and marble. A good-natured and witty symbolism pervades the building: cocks fight above the entrance to the Court of Petty Affairs, while Apollo, god of the sun and the arts, brings harmony to the disputes; and a plaque above the door of the Bankruptcy Chamber aptly shows the Fall of Icarus, who flew too close to the sun, surrounded by marble carvings depicting an empty chest and unpaid bills, around which scurry hungry rats. On a more sober note, death sentences were pronounced at the High Court of

Justice at the front of the building, and the condemned were executed on a scaffold outside.

Otherwise, the palace's interior is dull, darkened with the grand but uninspired paintings of the period. Rembrandt, whose career was waning, had his sketches for the walls rejected by the city fathers; today's city council must bemoan their predecessors' lack of judgement, since there's a good chance they'd now be sitting on one of Europe's major art treasures. The building received its royal designation in 1808, when Napoleon's brother Louis commandeered it as the one building fit for a king. Lonely and isolated, Louis briefly ruled from here until he was forced to acquiesce to Napoleon's autocratic demands. On his abdication in 1810 he left behind a sizeable amount of Empire furniture, most of which is exhibited in the rooms he converted.

The Nieuwe Kerk

Vying for importance with the palace is the **Nieuwe Kerk** (hours and admission prices vary; ☎ 638 6909), which, despite its name, is a fifteenth-century structure rebuilt several times following fires. Though impressive from the outside, the Nieuwe Kerk has long since lost out in rivalries with the Oude Kerk and the Royal Palace (it was forbidden a tower in case it outshone the new town hall), and is now used only for exhibitions, organ concerts and state occasions: Queen Beatrix was crowned here in 1980. The interior is neat and orderly, its sheer Gothic lines only slightly weighed down by seventeenth-century fixtures such as the massive pulpit and organ. Of the catalogue of household names from Dutch history represented in the church, Admiral de Ruyter, seventeenth-century Holland's most valiant naval hero, lies in an opulent tomb in the choir, erected in 1681 on what was formerly the high altar; and the poet Vondel is commemorated by a small urn near the entrance.

South to Spui

South of the Royal Palace, Nieuwezijds Voorburgwal broadens out; many of the side streets here are filled with antique and stamp shops – and some of Amsterdam's oldest and most expensive restaurants. Worming its own way south from Dam Square, **Kalverstraat** has been a commercial centre since it hosted a calf market in medieval times; it has now declined into a standard European shopping street, an uninspired strip of monotonous clothes shops differentiated only by the varying strains of disco music they pump out.

A stamp and coin market is held along the south of N.Z. Voorburgwal every Wed & Sat 11am–4pm.

The Amsterdam Historical Museum

Halfway down Kalverstraat, a lopsided and frivolous gateway at no. 92 forms an unexpected entrance to the **Amsterdam Historical**

Museum (Mon–Fri 10am–5pm, Sat & Sun 11am–5pm; ☎523 1822; *f*8, family rate *f*20). Housed in the restored seventeenth-century buildings of the Civic Orphanage, the museum attempts to survey the city's development with artefacts, paintings and documents from the thirteenth century onwards. Much focuses on the Golden Age of the seventeenth century: a large group of paintings portrays the city in its heyday and the art collection shows how the wealthy bourgeoisie decorated their homes. Sadly, though, most of the rest of the museum has poor labelling and lacks continuity. Still, it's worth seeing for the nineteenth-century paintings and photos and, more notably, the play-it-yourself carillon and the Regents' Chamber, unchanged since the Regents dispensed civic charity there three hundred years ago. Directly outside the museum, the glassed-in **Civic Guard Gallery** draws passers-by with free glimpses of the huge company portraits commissioned by Amsterdam worthies, from the 1540s through to the lighter affairs of the seventeenth century.

South to Spui

The Begijnhof

Connected to the Historical Museum is a less obvious attraction, one of the gems of Amsterdam. Perhaps those who run the **Begijnhof** want it this way: enclosed on three sides, this small court of buildings is an enclave of tranquillity that's typically Dutch, and totally removed from the surrounding streets. Most of the houses are seventeenth-century, but one, no. 34, dates from 1475 – the oldest house in Amsterdam, built before the city forbade the construction of houses in wood, an essential precaution against fire.

These kinds of *hofjes* (little courtyards) are found all over the Low Countries. Built by rich individuals or city councils for the poor and elderly, the houses usually face inwards around a small courtyard, their backs to the outside world. This sense of retreat suited the women who would come to lead a religious life here – *hofjes* often had their own chapel – without having to take full vows. The order here was known as *Begijnen*, and such was its standing in the community that it was allowed to quietly continue its tradition of worship even after Catholicism was suppressed in 1587. Mass was inconspicuously celebrated in the concealed **Catholic Church**, a dark Italianate building with a breath-holding silence that seems odd after the natural peace outside. There's none of this sense of mystery about the **English Reformed Church** that takes up one side of the Begijnhof. Plain and unadorned, it was handed over to Amsterdam's English community when the Begijns were deprived of their main place of worship and, like the *hofje* itself, it's almost too charming, a model of prim simplicity. Inside are several old English memorial plaques, and pulpit panels designed by the young Piet Mondrian.

See "The Jordaan and the Western Islands" for details of some of the city's other hofjes.

Spui and around

Back out in the noise and the trams, Spuistraat and Nieuwezijds Voorburgwal culminate in the newly repaved **Spui** (rhymes with "cow"), a chic corner of town with a mixture of bookshops, fashionable restaurants and packed bars and cafés centring on a small, rather cloying statue of a young boy – known as **'t Lieverdje** (Little Darling or Lovable Scamp) – which was a gift to the city from a large cigarette company in 1960.

One of the best of the many bars in the area is Hoppe, the ex-local of Freddie Heineken.

In the mid-1960s, Spui was the scene of a series of demonstrations organized by the **Provos**, an anarchist group devoted to *ludiek* (pranks); though they numbered only a few dozen members, their impact on the city was to last for decades. In 1964, with the alternative subculture then at its most militant, the Provos labelled *'t Lieverdje* an emblem of tomorrow's addicted consumer, and turned up every Saturday evening for *ludiek* with the Spui's assembled drinkers. When the police arrived to break up these small "happenings", they did little to endear themselves to the public – and much to gain sympathy for the Provos (see box).

The Provos and the Kabouters

Amsterdam's reputation as a wacky, offbeat city largely rests on the events of the 1960s, when the social and political discontent that was fermenting all over Western Europe began to coalesce into direct opposition to many of the city council's redevelopment plans. In contrast to similar movements in Paris and London, in Amsterdam this opposition had a uniquely playful aspect, and, possibly as a consequence, gathered substantial public support. In the early 1960s, much governmental faith was pinned on a programme of large-scale public works as a means to benefit society as a whole: the tunnel under the IJ was constructed, opening up Amsterdam North to the rest of the city, and massive new housing projects, such as the Bijlmermeer out to the southeast of the city, seemed emblems of a new future.

Yet discontent began to rise, directed against not only the urban expansionism driving the new development, but large-scale industrialization in general, as well as more widespread trends in consumerism and Cold War nuclear policy. Popular movements began to grow and one such grouping, led by a philosophy student at the University of Amsterdam, **Roel van Duyn**, took to holding small "happenings" around the *'t Lieverdje* statue in central Amsterdam to bring their feelings to public attention. Their reception was, on the whole, positive and enthusiastic, and support grew for the **Provos**, as they were now known (from "provocation"). In 1965, by which time Provo gatherings had grown in size, the police moved in to try and forcefully break one up, causing a small-scale riot to break out. Rioting occurred again a few months later at the wedding of Princess (now Queen) Beatrix, when the Provos, at the head of a by now substantial counter-cultural movement, raised objections to the massive cost of the

---

A short way to the south, in the university library at Singel 425, the **Script Museum** (Mon–Fri 9.30am–1pm & 2–4.30pm; free) is an off-beat collection of different alphabets from around the world. Thankfully, the medium is often more interesting than the message, with stones, snakeskins, and tree bark providing note pads for some weird hieroglyphs.

Heiligeweg, or "Holy Way", which runs between the Singel and Kalverstraat, was so named for its position on the route pilgrims took to Amsterdam (see pp.78–79); nowadays it is an uninspired shopping extension of Kalverstraat. On the right, close by the corner with Kalverstraat, at Heiligeweg 19, is the gateway of the old **Rasphuis** or "House of Correction", topped with a sculpture of a woman punishing two delinquents chained at her sides. Underneath is the single word *Castigatio* (punishment), beneath which is a carving by Hendrik de Keyser showing wolves and lions cringing before the whip, and an inscription that reads "It is a virtue to subdue those before whom all go in dread".

From here, you can turn right on Kalverstraat to reach Muntplein and the edge of the Grachtengordel, or turn round and walk back down Heiligeweg to cross the Singel at Koningsplein, where Leidsestraat stretches ahead of you to the south.

---

event. While the wedding procession was passing through the city, rioters clashed with police amidst smoke bombs and tear gas. After further expressions of discontent in the summer of 1966, Amsterdam's police chief resigned, to be followed a short while later by the mayor.

That same year, the Provos won over two percent of the vote in municipal elections, and gained a seat on the city council. The ideas the Provos brought to city politics – the **White Plans** – were perhaps their most substantial legacy. Under the most famous of these, cars were to be banned from the centre of Amsterdam, and 20,000 white bicycles were to be distributed for people to use free of charge, leaving them at their journey's end for someone else to use. Despite a couple of trials, the plan was never implemented, although recently it has been resurrected for a pilot project.

By 1967, the Provos' plans for the rejuvenation of Amsterdam had become overidealistic and unmanageable, and the group broke apart. Van Duyn then founded a group called the **Kabouters**, after a helpful gnome in Dutch folklore, with a manifesto describing their form of socialism as "not of the clenched fist, but of the intertwined fingers, the erect penis, the escaping butterfly . . ." In the local elections of 1970, capitalizing on the degree of popular support for the Provos, the Kabouters took over the Provos' single council seat, and managed to win four more, on a ticket to implement a number of the White Plans. The Kabouters modified the White Bicycle Plan into a similar idea involving small, economical white cars, but initial trials in 1974 received poor public support and the plan was abandoned. In 1981, after ten or so years of varying degrees of success on the margins of Amsterdam politics, the Kabouters finally disintegrated; Van Duyn, though, continued his involvement in local politics, and today holds the single Green Party seat on the city council.

The Old Centre: eating and drinking

BARS *Belgique, De Buurvrouw, Carel's Café, Cul de Sac, Van Daele, De Drie Fleschjes, Flying Dutchman, 't Gasthuis, Gollem, Hard Rock Café, Harry's American Bar, De Hoogte, Hoppe, Kabul, Het Kantoor, De Koningshut, Luxembourg, Mono Ontbijt & Alcohol, 't Pakhuys, Het Paleis, De Pilsener Club, De Pilserij, De Pool, Scheltema, De Schutter, Tapvreugd, Twin Pigs, Vrankrijk, De Zwart.* **Brown cafés** *Bern, De Engelbewaarder, Ter Kuile, Lokaal 't Loosje.* **Designer bars and grand cafés** *Blincker, De Brakke Grond, Café Dante, Dantzig, Droesem, Frascati, De Jaren, Oibibio.* **Gay bars** *Anco, Argos, Casa Maria, Club Jaecques, Cuckoo's Nest, Dirty Dick's, The Eagle, Shako's, Stablemaster, The Web, Why Not.* **Irish pubs** *Blarney Stone, Durty Nelly's, Fiddlers, O'Reilly's, Tara.* **Sex bars** *G-Force.*

COFFEESHOPS *The Bulldog, Extase, Grasshopper, Homegrown Fantasy, Josephine Baker, Kadinsky, Rusland, De Tweede Kamer.*

TEAROOMS *Café Esprit, Lindsay's Teashop, Puccini, Tatsun, Villa Zeezicht.*

RESTAURANTS Budget *Mensa Atrium, La Place.* **African** *Marrakech.* **American/Latin American** *Café Pacifico.* **Chinese, Thai and Filipino** *Hoi Tin, De Klaas Compaen, Lana Thai, New King, Road to Manila, Tom Yam.* **Dutch** *Het Beeren, Haesje Claes, Keuken van 1870, Oud Holland, De Silveren Spiegel.* **Fish** *Lucius.* **French** *1e Klas Grand Café Restaurant, Hemelse Modder, Luden.* **Indonesian** *Kantjil en de Tijger.* **Pancakes** *Bredero, Pannekoekhuis Upstairs.* **Spanish** *Centra.* **Surinamese** *Kam Yin.* **Vegetarian** *Sisters.*

See *Eating and Drinking*, p.185 for exact locations and reviews.

Chapter 3

The Grachtengordel

The central part of Amsterdam was originally enclosed within the Singel, part of the city's protective moat, but this is now just the first of the five canals that reach right around the city centre in a "girdle of canals" or **GRACHTENGORDEL**. These were dug in the seventeenth century as part of a comprehensive plan to extend the boundaries of a city no longer able to accommodate its burgeoning population. The idea was that the council would buy up the land around the city, dig the canals, and lease plots back to developers on strict conditions. The plan was passed in 1607 and work began six years later, against a backdrop of corruption – Amsterdammers in the know buying up the land they thought the city would subsequently have to purchase.

Increasing the area of the city from 450 to 1800 acres was a monumental task, and the conditions imposed by the burghers were tough. The three main waterways, Herengracht, Keizersgracht and Prinsengracht, were set aside for the residences and offices of the richer and more influential Amsterdam merchants, while the radial canals were reserved for more modest artisans' homes; immigrants newly arrived to cash in on Amsterdam's booming economy were housed in less extravagant quarters in the Jordaan. Even the richest burgher had to comply with a set of stylistic rules when building his house, and taxes were levied according to the width of the property. This resulted in the loose conformity you can see today: tall, narrow residences, whose individualism is restricted to heavy decorative gables and sometimes a gablestone to denote name and occupation. Even the colour of the front doors was regulated, with choice restricted to a shade that has since become known as "Amsterdam Green" – even now, difficult to find outside Holland. It was almost the end of the century before the scheme was finished – a time when, ironically, the decline of Amsterdam's Golden Age had already begun – but it remains to the burghers' credit that it was executed with such success.

See Contexts, p.339, for a history of Amsterdam.

Of the three main canals, **Herengracht** – "Gentlemen's Canal" – was the first to be dug, and the burghers who held economic sway over Amsterdam soon lined it with big, ostentatious houses. The nam-

> This chapter covers the full sweep of the *grachtengordel*, from the Brouwersgracht in the northwest to the River Amstel in the southeast. However, for ease of reference, we've considered it as two areas – **Grachtengordel West** and **Grachtengordel South** – divided at roughly the halfway point by the Leidsegracht. The *Accommodation* and *Eating and Drinking* listings chapters later in the book follow this division.

ing of the canals reflects very clearly the pecking order in the city at that time: Herengracht was closest in, followed by the **Keizersgracht**, or "Emperor's Canal" (after Holy Roman Emperor Maximilian I), and, further out still, the **Prinsengracht**, or "Princes' Canal" (after the princes of the House of Orange). These last two ended up with noticeably smaller houses – though today they're among the city's most sought-after properties. Herengracht remains the city's grandest stretch of water, especially the "Golden Curve" between Leidsestraat and Vijzelstraat (see p.109), but you may find the less pretentious homes and warehouses of Prinsengracht more appealing.

It's hard to pick out any particular points to head for along the three main canals. Though some of the houses are still lived in, many have been turned into offices or hotels, and there's little of specific interest apart from a few museums. Rather, the appeal lies in wandering along selected stretches and admiring the gables, while taking in the calm of the tree-lined waterways, unique features for the centre of a modern European capital. For shops, bars, restaurants and the like, you're better off exploring the streets that connect the canals.

AMSTERDAM

Brouwersgracht to Raadhuisstraat

In the northwest of the centre, running west to east along the top edge of all three main canals is **Brouwersgracht**, one of the most picturesque waterways in the city. In the seventeenth century, Brouwersgracht lay at the edge of Amsterdam's great harbour. It was where many of the ships just returned from the East unloaded their booties of silks and spices, and as one of the major arteries linking the open sea with the city centre, it was lined with storage depots, warehouses and breweries, which capitalized on the shipments of fresh water that had to be brought into the city along this canal – sanitation being what it was then, beer was a far healthier drink than water. Today, the harbour bustle has moved elsewhere, and the warehouses have been converted into apartments, their functional architecture contrasting with the facades lining the major canals. Brouwersgracht has become a quiet, residential canal, filled with trees and birdsong, and offering spectacular views down the lengths of the Herengracht, Keizersgracht and Prinsengracht. From here, to pick any of the three main canals to head down is to miss the other two; this is one of the

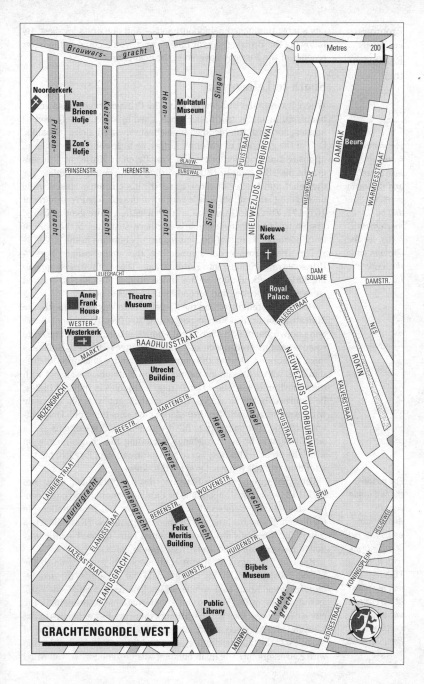

city's most untouched neighbourhoods – and one of its loveliest. By following the Brouwersgracht further west, you'll come to the outer reaches of the Jordaan, covered in the next chapter.

South to Leliegracht

Where it meets the Brouwersgracht, the **Prinsengracht** has a gentle beauty quite unlike its grander rivals, lined by small, closely packed houses, and with tumbledown houseboats moored along its banks. One of the grandest of the city's *hofjes*, or little courtyards, is here, opposite the Noorderkerk – the **Van Brienen Hofje**, at Prinsengracht 89–133. Built in 1804, according to the entrance tablet, "for the relief and shelter of those in need", it's currently closed while undergoing restoration. A little way down the canal at Prinsengracht 157–171, **Zon's Hofje** is smaller, with a leafier, more gentle beauty. Visible from the Prinsengracht's northern stretches is the bulk of the Noorderkerk, one of the less inspiring churches in the city.

For more on the Noorderkerk and its nearby markets, and on Amsterdam's hofjes, see The Jordaan and the Western Islands

The first cross-street connecting the main canals here – **Prinsenstraat**, running into **Herenstraat** – is one of the most appealing little streets in Amsterdam, filled with flower shops, relaxed cafés, greengroceries and second-hand clothes shops.

Between Herengracht and the Singel, a little way to the north, the **Multatuli Museum** at Korsjespoortsteeg 20 (Tues 10am–5pm, Sat & Sun noon–5pm; ☎638 1938; free) – which is basically just one large room – was the birthplace of **Eduard Douwes Dekker**, Holland's most celebrated nineteenth-century writer and a champion of free thinking, who wrote under the pen name Multatuli. Disgusted with the behaviour of his fellow Dutch in their colonies in the East Indies, he returned home to enrage the establishment with his elegantly written satirical novel *Max Havelaar*, now something of a Dutch literary classic. The museum is filled with letters, first editions and a small selection of his furnishings, including the chaise longue on which he breathed his last. There's no information in English, but the attendant can tell you what you need to know.

For possibly the best apple cake in Amsterdam, and a fine cup of coffee to go with it, try Villa Zeezicht, on the Singel at Torensteeg, one bridge north of Raadhuisstraat.

Continue through on to Singel to the red-brick building at **no. 140–142**, which was once home of Captain Banning Cocq, the central character of Rembrandt's *Night Watch*. But more noticeable (and audible) is the quaintly named **Poezenboot** (Kitty Boat), a refuge for the city's stray and unwanted cats, moored a little way down. It's open for visits daily from 1pm to 3pm.

Back on Herengracht, if you continue south you'll come to the **Leliegracht**, one of the tiny radial canals that cut across the *gracht-engordel*, and home to a number of bookshops and canal-side bars, as well as one of the most exclusive international restaurants in the city – *Christophe* (see p.216). Though there are few examples of Art Nouveau and Art Deco architecture to be seen in Amsterdam, one of the finest is the tall, strikingly elegant building at the canal's junction with Keizersgracht. The main building was designed by G. van Arkel in 1905, and added to in the late 1960s; it is now Greenpeace International's world headquarters.

The Anne Frank House

In 1957, the Anne Frank Foundation set up the **Anne Frank House** (June–Aug Mon–Sat 9am–7pm, Sun 10am–7pm; Sept–May Mon–Sat 9am–5pm, Sun 10am–5pm; closed Yom Kippur; ☎556 7100; ƒ10, no museumcards) in the house at Prinsengracht 263, close to the Leliegracht, where the young diarist used to listen to the Westertoren bells until they were taken away to be melted down for the Nazi war effort. The site is now one of the most deservedly popular tourist attractions in town; bearing this in mind, the best time to visit is early morning before the crowds arrive.

Since her name became widely known after World War II, **Anne Frank** has come to stand as both a symbol of the Holocaust and an inspiration to prisoners of conscience of all kinds. Her diary – one teenager's record of life hiding from the Nazis – was a source of inspiration for Nelson Mandela in prison in South Africa, and is still on many school syllabuses around the world today.

The story of Anne, her family and friends, is well known. Anne's father, **Otto Frank**, was a well-to-do Jewish businessman who ran a successful spice-trading business and lived in the southern part of the city. By 1942 the Nazi occupation was taking its toll: all Jews had been forced to wear a yellow star, and were not allowed to use public transport, go to the theatre or cinema, or to stray into certain areas of the city; roundups, too, were becoming increasingly common. As conditions became more difficult, and it looked as if the Franks themselves might be taken away, Otto Frank decided – on the advice of two Dutch friends and colleagues, Mr Koophuis and Mr Kraler – to move the family into their warehouse on the Prinsengracht, the back half of which was unused at the time. The Franks went into hiding in July 1942, along with a Jewish business partner and his family, the Van Daans, separated from the eyes of the outside world by a bookcase that doubled as a door. As far as everyone else was concerned, they had fled to Switzerland.

Yom Kippur, the Jewish Day of Atonement, falls on a different date each year; forthcoming dates are: Oct 11, 1997 Sept 30, 1998 Sept 20, 1999.

So began the two-year occupation of the *achterhuis*, or back annexe. The two families were joined in November 1942 by a Mr Dussel, a dentist friend. Koophuis and Kraler, who continued working in the front office, regularly brought supplies and news of the outside world – which, for the Jews, was becoming daily more perilous. In her diary Anne Frank describes the day-to-day lives of the inhabitants of the annexe: the quarrels, frequent in such a claustrophobic environment; celebrations of birthdays, or of a piece of good news from the Allied Front; and her own, slightly unreal, growing up (much of which, it's been claimed, was deleted by her father).

Two years later, the atmosphere was optimistic: the Allies were clearly winning the war, and it was thought that it wouldn't be long before the fugitives could emerge. It wasn't to be. One day in the summer of 1944 the Franks were betrayed by a Dutch collaborator; the Gestapo arrived and forced Mr Kraler to open up the bookcase, whereupon the occupants of the annexe were all arrested and quickly sent to Westerbork – the transit camp in the north of the country where all Dutch Jews were processed before being moved to Belsen or Auschwitz. Of the eight from the annexe, only Otto Frank survived; Anne and her sister died of typhus within a short time of each other in Belsen, just one week before the German surrender.

Anne Frank's **diary** was among the few things left behind in the annexe. It was retrieved by one of the people who had helped the Franks and handed to Anne's father on his return from Auschwitz; he later decided to publish it. Since its appearance in 1947, it has been constantly in print, translated into 54 languages, and has sold thirteen million copies worldwide.The rooms the Franks lived in for two years are left much the same as they were during the war, even down to the movie star pin-ups in Anne's bedroom and the marks on the wall recording the children's heights. A number of other rooms offer background detail on the war and occupation: one presents a video biography of Anne, from her frustrated hopes in hiding up until to her death in 1945; another details the gruesome atrocities of Nazism, and gives some up-to-date examples of fascism and anti-Semitism in Europe, drawing pertinent parallels with the war years. Anne Frank was only one of 100,000 Dutch Jews who died during that time, but this, her final home, provides one of the most enduring testaments to the horrors of Nazism.

*Related
museums
include the
Verzets-
museum, the
Hollandsche
Schouwburg
and the Jewish
Historical
Museum; for
details, see
Museums and
Galleries,
p.237.*

Westermarkt and around

Starting from the Royal Palace, **Raadhuisstraat** runs west past the elegant curve of the nineteenth-century Art Nouveau **Utrecht Building** towards **Westermarkt**, in the shadow of the Westerkerk. The seventeenth-century French philosopher René Descartes lived at Westermarkt 6 for a short time, happy that the business-oriented character of the city left him able to work and think without being disturbed. As he wrote at the time, "Everybody except me is in business and so absorbed by profit-making I could spend my entire life here without being noticed by a soul."

The Westerkerk

The **Westerkerk** (Mon–Fri 10am–4pm, Sat 10am–1pm) utterly dominates the area, its 85-metre **tower** (April–Sept Mon–Sat 10am–4pm; $f3$) – without question Amsterdam's finest – soaring graciously above the gables of Prinsengracht. On its top perches the crown of Emperor Maximilian, a constantly recurring symbol of Amsterdam and an appropriate finishing touch to what was only the city's second place of worship built expressly for Protestants. The church was designed by Hendrik de Keyser (architect also of the Zuiderkerk and

Noorderkerk) as part of the general seventeenth-century enlarge-
ment of the city, and completed in 1631. But while from the outside
this is probably Amsterdam's most visually appealing church, there's
little of special note within.

Rembrandt, who was living nearby when he died, is commemorated by a small memorial in the north aisle. His pauper's grave can
no longer be located; indeed, there's a possibility that he's not here
at all, since many of the bodies were transferred to a cemetery when
underground heating was installed. The memorial is, however, close
to where Rembrandt's son Titus is buried. Rembrandt worshipped
his son – as evidenced by numerous portraits – and the boy's death
dealt a final crushing blow to the ageing and embittered artist, who
died just over a year later. During renovation of the church in
1990–91, bones were unearthed that could have been those of Titus
or even of Rembrandt himself – a possibility whose tourism potential
excited the church authorities. The only way to prove it one way or
the other was through a chemical analysis of the bones' lead content,
expected to be unusually high in an artist as lead was a major ingre-
dient of paint. The bones were duly taken to the University of
Groningen for analysis, but, due to lack of public funds, the testing
was never begun, and the bones – whoever they belonged to – remain
there still.

Just outside the church, on the Prinsengracht side, you can find a
small, simple **statue** of Anne Frank by the Dutch sculptor Mari
Andriessen – a careful and evocative site, recalling the long years
Anne Frank spent in the *achterhuis* just a few steps away up the
canal.

The Homo-Monument and Theatre Museum

Behind the church, on the corner of Keizersgracht and Westermarkt,
are the pink granite triangles of the **Homo-Monument**, the world's
first memorial to persecuted gays and lesbians. A resonant design by
Karin Daan – during the Nazi occupation all homosexuals were
forced to wear pink triangles sewn into their clothes – the monument
commemorates not only those homosexuals who died in Nazi concentration camps, but also known homosexuals who fought with the
Allies and whose names were omitted from other remembrance monuments. As well as a historical memorial, though, the Homo-monument is a continuing focus for the gay community in general, and the
site of ceremonies and wreath-laying throughout the year, most
notably on Queen's Day (April 30), Coming-Out Day (Sept 5) and
World AIDS Day (Dec 1). The monument's inscription, by the gay
Dutch writer Jacob Israel de Haan, translates as "Such an infinite
desire for friendship".

*The world's
first memorial
to gypsies per-
secuted by the
Nazis – Heleen
Levano's Hel
van Vuur (Hell
of Fire) sculp-
ture – can be
found on
Museumplein.*

The **Theatre Museum**, round the corner at Herengracht 168 (museum closed for rebuilding until June 1997, but previously Tues–Sun
11am–5pm; ☎623 5104; resource centre still accessible Tues–Fri

11am–5pm; free), is also worth a look, both for the house it's installed in – a fine old place with eighteenth-century murals by Jacob de Wit – and for its bold exhibition space, which displays re-creations of contemporary stage-sets, alongside models tracing the earlier days of the theatre in the Netherlands. The resource centre has a library, bookshop and historical collections both on paper and video.

South to Leidsegracht

Below Raadhuisstraat, the main canals retain their appeal for wandering, but it is the small **cross-streets** between them that hold the best possibilities for exploration. Many of these streets are named after animals whose pelts were used in the Jordaan's seventeenth-century tanning industry: Reestraat (Deer's Street), Hartenstraat (Hart's Street), Beren- (Bear's), Wolven- (Wolve's), Elands- (Elk's) and Hazenstraat (Hare's Street), as well as Runstraat (a "run" is a bark used in tanning) and Huidenstraat (Street of Hides). Looiersgracht, just nearby, means "Tanner's Canal".

One of Amsterdam's best bakeries, specializing in sourdoughs and wholegrain breads, is Paul Année, at Runstraat 25.

Though the tanners have (maybe thankfully) gone, they've been replaced by some of the most pleasant shopping streets in the city. Typical of Amsterdam, they're filled with little nooks and crannies to explore, the shops here selling everything from carpets to handmade chocolates, toothbrushes to beeswax candles.

One building you'll notice in your wanderings is the **Felix Meritis** mansion at Keizersgracht 324, near the corner with Berenstraat, a heavy Neoclassical monolith built in the late eighteenth century to house the artistic and scientific activities of the society of the same name. For most of the nineteenth century this was very much the cultural focus of the city, at least for the very wealthy, and it aped the refined manners of the rest of "cultured" Europe in a way only the Dutch could: badly. It's said that when Napoleon visited the city the entire building was redecorated for his reception, only to have him stalk out in disgust, claiming that the place stank of tobacco. Despite the fact that the building's concert hall was notorious among musicians for its appalling acoustics, it was used as a model for the later Concertgebouw. The building used to be the headquarters of the Dutch Communist Party, but they sold it to the council who now lease it to the Felix Meritis Foundation, a centre for experimental and avant-garde arts.

Cross the Keizersgracht from here and you'll come across two of Amsterdam's smallest museums, both tucked away on Herengracht but concerned with very different subject matter. At Herengracht 266, one of the buildings of the Hogeschool van Amsterdam (a vocational university) contains the **Ferdinand Domela Nieuwenhuis Museum**, dedicated to the man who has been called "the father of Dutch socialism", and who was instrumental in persuading turn-of-the-century employers to institute policies of social change. As well as the writings of Domela Nieuwenhuis himself, manuscripts by

---

Grachtengordel West: Eating and drinking

BARS *Aas van Bokalen, De Admiraal, De Beiaard, Belhamel, De Doffer, De Pels, De Prins, P96, Van Puffelen, Sjaalman, Spanjer & Van Twist, Twee Prinsen, De Twee Zwaantjes, De Vergulde Gaper, Wheels.* **Brown cafés** *Hegeraad, Kalkhoven, De Klepel, Het Molenpad, 't Smackzeyl.* **Grand cafés** *Du Lac.*

COFFEESHOPS *Grey Area, Siberië, So Fine, La Tertulia.*

TEAROOMS *Baton Espresso Corner, Cocky's Coffeebar,* *Dialoog, Greenwood's, Lunchcafé Winkel.*

RESTAURANTS American/Latin American *Mexico.* **Dutch** *Zemmel, 't Zwaantje.* **French and Belgian** *Bistro de Vlier, Chez Georges, Intermezzo, De Lieve, D'Theeboom.* **Indian** *Koh-I-Noor, Poorna.* **Italian** *Prego.* **Pancakes** *The Pancake Bakery.* **Surinamese and Caribbean** *Rum Runners.* **Vegetarian** *Bolhoed.*

See Eating and Drinking, p.185, for exact locations and reviews.

Marx, Engels, Proudhon and Kropotkin are on display. To visit the museum you need to call the Hogeschool reception on ☎555 2300 – Carla van Velzen has the key; you could also try Bert Altena (the volunteer curator) on ☎010/408 2477; entrance is free.

On the corner with Huidenstraat, at Herengracht 366, is a four-gabled, seventeenth-century stone house frilled with tendrils, carved fruit and scrollwork. It contains an elaborate eighteenth-century ceiling painted by Jacob de Wit, which you can see if you visit the **Bijbels Museum** (Tues–Sat 10am–5pm, Sun 1–5pm; ☎624 7949; *f*3). This small but imaginative collection has engaging displays relating to Jewish daily life, religious ritual and the history of the Bible in Dutch, including archeological finds from Egypt and the Middle East – and it's all refreshingly ecumenical.

It's a short walk from the museum down to the bend in the Herengracht, and one of the most beautiful views in Amsterdam. From the bridge here you can look down the length of **Leidsegracht**, another of the peaceful radial canals that cut across the *grachtengordel*. It is mostly residential, with houses ranging from ramshackle old cottages to luxurious nouveau-riche town houses. Its atmosphere, though, is often shattered by the flat-topped tourist boats that use the Leidsegracht as a short cut, sounding their horns at the intersections and revving their engines to make the tight turn into Prinsengracht.

Leidseplein and around

Continuing east from Leidsegracht, the three main canals are crossed by one of Amsterdam's principal shopping streets, **Leidsestraat**, a long, slender passage of airline offices, moderately

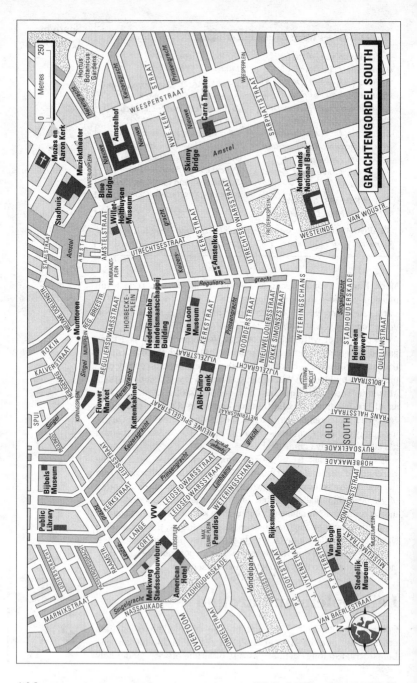

Hortus
Botanicus
Gardens

Herengracht
Keizersgracht
Prinsengracht

WEESPERPLEIN

Mozes en
Aaron Kerk

Muziektheater

WEESPERSTRAAT

Amstelhof

Carré Theater

Stadhuis

Blue
Bridge

WATERLOOPLEIN

Willet-
Holthuysen
Museum

Nieuwe

Nieuwe

N.WE. KERK

Nieuwe

SARPHATISTRAAT

Amstel

Skinny
Bridge

Netherlands
National Bank

STAALSTRAAT

AMSTELSTRAAT

REMBRANDT-
PLEIN

UTRECHTSESTRAAT

KERKSTRAAT

Amstelkerk

Keizers-

gracht

UTRECHTSED WARSSTRAAT

FREDERIKSPLEIN

WESTEINDE

VAN WOUSTR

Reguliers-

gracht

NIEUWE DOELENSTR

Munttoren

ROKIN

MUNTPLEIN REG BREESTR

REGULIERSDWARSSTRAAT

THORBECKE-
PLEIN

Nederlandsche
Handelsmaatschappij
Building

Van Loon
Museum

KERKSTRAAT

Prinsengracht

NOORDERSTRAAT

NIEUWELOOIERSSTRAAT

FOKKE SIMONSZSTRAAT

WETERINGSCHANS

STADHOUDERSKADE

Singelgracht

Heineken
Brewery

QUELLIJNSTRAAT

F.BOLSTRAAT

KALVERSTRAAT

HEILIGEWEG

KONINGSPLEIN

Singel

Herengracht

Flower
Market

Kattenkabinet

Keizersgracht

VIJZELSTRAAT

ABN-Amro
Bank

NIEUWE SPIEGELSTRAAT

Prinsengracht

VIJZELGRACHT

gracht

WETERINGSCHANS

WETERING
CIRCUIT

WETERINGSTRAAT

FRANS HALSSTRAAT

SPUI

Singel

KERKSTRAAT

LANGE

LEIDSE

Bijbels
Museum

Public
Library

RAAMSTR

VOETBOOGSTR

PASSEERDERSGRACHT

KORTE

LEIDSEPLEIN

VVV

Prinsengracht

LEIDSEDWARSSTRAAT

LEIDSEDWARSSTRAAT

Lijnbaans

gracht

Paradiso

MAX
EUWE PLEIN

WETERINGSTRAAT

gracht

Rijksmuseum

HOBBEMAKADE

RUYSDAELKADE

OLD
SOUTH

MARNIXSTRAAT

Melkweg

Stadsschouwburg

American
Hotel

NASSAUKADE

Singelgracht

OVERTOOM

STADHOUDERSKADE

VONDELSTRAAT

Vondelpark

VOSSIUSSTR

P.C. HOOFTSTRAAT

J. LUYKENSTRAAT

P. POTTERSTRAAT

Van Gogh
Museum

Stedelijk
Museum

HONTHORSTSTRAAT

MUSEUMPLEIN

MUSEUMSTRAAT

VAN BAERLESTRAAT

N

upmarket fashion and shoe shops, and uninspired restaurants. On summer afternoons, Leidsestraat can be choked full of promenading window-shoppers, who make way only for the trams that crash dangerously through in both directions; many of these shops now open on Sundays, giving no respite from the crowds. To the north, Leidsestraat crosses the Singel canal at Koningsplein, where the Flower Market leads east to Muntplein and Heiligeweg heads into the Old Centre (see pp.74–92).

At its southern end Leidsestraat broadens out into **Leidseplein**, the cosmopolitan hub of Amsterdam's nightlife, but by day a rather cluttered and disorderly open space, littered with rubbish from the surrounding American burger joints. The square's name reflects current concerns about city-centre traffic reduction: in medieval times, horse-drawn traffic was banned from the centre of Amsterdam, and the *pleinen* (squares) around the fringes were where people left their wagons while visiting the city. Leidseplein, at the end of the road from Leiden, is such a "cart-park". Today, the amount of tram, bike, car and pedestrian traffic constantly moving in every direction across the cobbles, together with the trees dotted around and hiding the sky, combine to give the square a closed-in and frenetic feel.

As for **entertainment**, there's probably a greater concentration of bars, restaurants and clubs around Leidseplein than anywhere else in the city, the surrounding streets extending off in a bright jumble of jutting signs and neon lights; within metres, you can eat Dutch, French, Indonesian, Mexican, Argentinian, Turkish, Greek, Indian or Israeli. Cinemas, theatres and discos abound, too: around the corner, in a converted dairy, lurks the famous **Melkweg** venue, and just nearby is the **Boom Chicago** café-theatre. However, one of the best reasons to come here is for the people-watching. On summer nights especially, the square can ignite with an almost carnival-like vibrancy, drinkers spilling out of cafés to see sword-swallowers and fire-eaters do their tricks, while the restaurants set up tables outside so you can eat without missing the fun. On a good night Leidseplein is Amsterdam at its carefree, exuberant best.

Dominating the square, the **Stadsschouwburg** is one of the city's prime performance spaces, while alongside, and architecturally much more impressive, is the fairy-castle **American Hotel** – the traditional meeting place of Amsterdam media folk, although these days its renowned *Café Americain* is a more mainstream location for high tea. Even if you're not thirsty it's worth a peek inside, the leaded stained glass, shallow brick arches, chandeliers and carefully coordinated furnishings as fine an example of Art Nouveau as you'll find.

A few steps southeast of Leidseplein, just past the *Balie* café, **Max Euweplein** was part of Amsterdam's attempt to spruce itself up in the 1980s, recently fallen somewhat flat. When it was built, the small

Leidseplein and around

On the corner of Leidsestraat and Keizersgracht, the designer department store Metz & Co, with its corner dome by Gerrit Rietveld, has a top-floor restaurant and tearoom with one of the best views of the city.

For reviews of the restaurants and nightlife venues around Leidseplein, see pp.221–222 and pp.199–204.

Amsterdam's main park, the Vondelpark, is minutes away from Leidseplein across the Singelgracht bridge – see p.149–151.

*For full details
on how to go
about joining
the lounge
lizards in the
Holland
Casino, see
Sports and
Activities.*

Italian-style piazza – complete with pillars and bubbling fountain – was packed with extremely chic retail outlets and classy cafés, but most have been forced out by high rents and low returns, and the square is now home to some distinctly tacky postcard and souvenir shops. The **Holland Casino** has survived, though, housed in a former jail – Amsterdam's only legal venue for roulette, blackjack and other such decadent pursuits. Max Euwe was Holland's most famous chess player and only world champion to date, and the **Max Euwe Centre** on the square (Tues–Fri 10.30am–4pm; ☎625 7017; free) contains an interesting exhibition on the history and development of competitive chess, along with a review of Euwe's career. Chess sets are available should you feel inspired, both the real thing and the computer variety.

Spiegelgracht to Vijzelstraat

Weteringschans, home of the famous *Paradiso* music venue, is the most direct route east from Max Euweplein, but the narrow **Lijnbaansgracht** (Tightrope-walk Canal), which runs parallel to the north, makes a far more appealing walk. Reaching right around the modern city centre, here it is lined with tumbledown houses on one side and mirrored-glass apartments and offices on the other. At the first bridge you come to, the Rijksmuseum (see pp.139–147), the twin of Centraal Station, looms across the canal to the right; to the left is tiny Spiegelgracht, an appealing mixture of bookshops and corner cafés that leads into Nieuwe Spiegelstraat and the **Spiegelkwartier**, home to Amsterdam's antiques trade. There are around fifty dealers here, packed into a relatively small area – as you might expect, none of them is particularly inexpensive. *De Appel*, at Nieuwe Spiegelstraat 10 (Tues–Sun noon–5pm; ☎625 5651; ƒ2.50), a lively centre for contemporary art, is a recent, colourful addition to this rather sober-looking street.

*In the web of
tiny streets
east of
Spiegelgracht,
Café de
Wetering, at
Weteringstraat
37, is a won-
derfully atmos-
pheric local
brown café,
complete with
wood beams
and sleeping
cat.*

Cutting across Nieuwe Spiegelstraat, **Kerkstraat** is a narrow street with an eclectic mix of magic mushroom shops, gay bars and art galleries. To the left (west) it leads back to Leidsestraat; to the right (east), it connects with **Vijzelstraat** at the head offices of the **ABN-AMRO bank**, below which the street runs. The building, bland and plastic-looking on the whole, doesn't merit a second glance today, but its construction in the 1950s was the subject of one of Amsterdam's biggest property controversies. During that decade many canals had been filled in and large parts of the city torn down to make way for increased traffic. The tension between the conservationists and developers had been mounting for some time, and when the collapse of a building between Keizersgracht and Prinsengracht left this plot vacant, the scene was set for confrontation. There was immediate protest when it turned out that the *Algemene Bank Nederland* was to buy up the land for office use, and diverse groups of

Amsterdammers joined together to keep the bank out. The architect had already defaced part of the city with the overbearing State Bank building on Frederiksplein, and many people felt he shouldn't be given the opportunity again – particularly not in one of the city's most beautiful areas. That the bank's offices stand today is proof enough that the conservationists lost, but it was an important early skirmish in the city's continuing struggles to keep property barons at bay.

A little way north on Vijzelstraat, the oversized **Nederlandsche Handelsmaatschappij Building** (now also owned by *ABN-AMRO*) is another bank building totally untuned to its surroundings. Though architecturally much more worthwhile than the later building, it would look more at home in downtown Manhattan than on the banks of a Dutch canal.

South to the Heineken Brewery

Below Prinsengracht, Vijzelstraat becomes the filled-in **Vijzelgracht**, culminating at the **Weteringcircuit** roundabout with its two low-key memorials to the horrors of World War II. On the southwestern corner of the roundabout is a small gravelled area with a sculpture of a man shot, holding a bugle: it was here, on March 12, 1945, that 35 people were shot by the Nazis in the last few weeks of the occupation. Opposite there's a memorial to H.M. van Randwijk, a notable figure in the Dutch resistance. The restrained wording on the monument translates as:

> *When to the will of tyrants,*
> *A nation's head is bowed,*
> *It loses more than life and goods –*
> *Its very light goes out.*

Looming on the other side of the canal, strictly speaking on the northern edge of the "Pijp" district, is the bulk of the **Heineken Brewery** – one of the city's best-known attractions (tours Mon–Fri 9.30am & 11am; June–Sept additional tours at 1pm & 2.30pm; July & Aug also tours on Sat noon & 2pm; over-18s only; ƒ2). The site had been devoted to brewing for almost 300 years before it was bought by Adriaan Heineken in 1864 as his company's headquarters. However, after increasing difficulties in transporting the vast quantities of beer demanded by thirsty Amsterdammers along the cramped central city streets, Heineken decided to close down the old brewery in 1986 and move their operations out to more efficient regional centres. Although the brewing facilities have now mostly been taken apart, it's still interesting to explore the old plant and view aspects of the beer-making process. However, the main draw is that afterwards you are given snacks and **free beer** – the atmosphere is highly convivial, as you'd imagine when there are 200 people downing as much free beer as they can drink. Whether you have just one, or drink yourself into a stupor, it's a diverting way to get a lunchtime aperitif.

At Kerkstraat 148, Shizen is a superb Japanese restaurant, with a choice of very affordable macrobiotic fish, vegetarian and vegan dishes.

Just behind the Heineken Brewery, O'Donnells, on the corner of Ferdinand Bolstraat and Quellijnstraat, serves the best pint of Guinness in Amsterdam.

Vijzelstraat to Frederiksplein

Between Vijzelstraat and the Amstel, the southern stretches of the *grachtengordel* become more residential than remarkable, although the little cobbled streets below Prinsengracht, with their faded, ramshackle houses, are samples as representative as you can find of Amsterdam's unique version of inner-city living; faded or not, though, these days such intimate little dwellings come with prices to match their location.

The Van Loon Museum

Standing in stark contrast to its surroundings, the **Van Loon Museum** at Keizersgracht 672, between Vijzelstraat and Reguliersgracht (Mon 10am–5pm, Sun 1–5pm; ☎624 5255; ƒ5), holds perhaps the finest accessible canal house interior in Amsterdam: a less grand and more likeable alternative to its rival, the nearby Willet-Holthuysen Museum (see p.108), with a pleasantly down-at-heel interior of peeling stucco and shabby paintwork. Built in 1672, the house's first tenant was the artist Ferdinand Bol; fortunately, he didn't suffer the fate of many subsequent owners, who seem to have been cursed with a series of bankruptcies and scandals for over two hundred years. The Van Loon family bought the house in 1884. The last family member to occupy the whole house, one Thora van Loon-Egidius, was *dame du paleis* to Queen Wilhelmina, the highest-ranking female position in the land. Of German extraction, she was proud of her roots and apparently used to entertain high-ranking Nazi officials here during the occupation – which later led to her being shunned by the royal family. The current Van Loons still live upstairs in the attic rooms, but the rest of the house is filled with homely bits and pieces that date from 1580 to 1949; there are lots of family portraits, and various upstairs rooms are sumptuously decorated with eighteenth-century wall paintings. Notice, too, the ornate copper balustrade on the staircase, into which are worked the names "Trip" and "Van Hagen", former owners of the house; the Van Loons later filled the spaces between the letters with fresh iron curlicues to prevent their children falling through.

For an always friendly, and occasionally wacky, cup of coffee, drop in on the twins Greg and Gary Christmas from Boston, who run the Backstage café at Utrechtsedwarsstraat 67.

Reguliersgracht to Frederiksplein

Reguliersgracht, the most easterly of the three surviving radial canals cutting across the *grachtengordel*, is perhaps the prettiest of all, with elegant greenery decorating its banks and distinctively steep bridges. It was to have been filled in at the beginning of the century, but was saved by public outcry at the destruction of one of the city's more alluring stretches of water. From a point at the very top of the canal at Thorbeckeplein (and only on a clear day), there's the beautiful view of seven parallel canal bridges, a unique sight even in this city of 1281 bridges.

South along the canal, sandwiched in between Kerkstraat and Prinsengracht, the small open space of the **Amstelveld** is an oasis of village-like calm that few visitors happen upon. The **Amstelkerk**, a seventeenth-century white wooden church with a nineteenth-century Gothic interior, marks the corner, and on Mondays the **flower market** here adds a splash of colour.

Running parallel with Reguliersgracht, **Utrechtsestraat** is probably Amsterdam's most up-and-coming strip, containing most of the area's commercial activity; there are many pleasant mid- to upper-bracket restaurants along the tram-lined street, along with a lively mix of bars and bookshops. Utrechtsestraat ends in the concrete wasteland of **Frederiksplein** – a rambling, rather forbidding area, presided over by the massive glass box of the *Nederlandse Bank*.

North along the Amstel

Leading off Frederiksplein, **Sarphatistraat** crosses the wide and windy reaches of the **River Amstel**, whose eastern side is stacked with highly visible chunky buildings such as the **Carré Theatre**, built as a circus in the early 1900s, but now more often a space for music and drama. Walking north up the western bank of the river, you pass by the **Amstelsluizen**, or Amstel Locks; every night, the City Water Office closes these locks to begin the process of sluicing out the canals. A huge pumping station on Zeeburg island out to the east of the city then starts to pump fresh water from the IJsselmeer into the canal system; similar locks on the west side of the city are left open for the surplus to flow into the IJ and, from there, out to sea via the North Sea Canal. The entire water content of the canals is thus refreshed every three nights – though, what with three centuries of algae and a few hundred rusty bikes, the water is appealing just as long as you're not in it.

Beyond the locks, the **Magere Brug** (Skinny Bridge) is (inexplicably) the focus of much attention in the tourist brochures, and hence the most famous of the city's swinging bridges. Legend has it that the current, admittedly skinny, bridge, which is more than 300 years old, was the replacement for an even older and skinnier one, originally built by two sisters who lived on either side of the river and were fed up of having to walk so far to see each other.

The Six Collection

A fine example of a seventeenth-century patrician canal house, the **Six Collection**, close by at Amstel 218 (guided tours on Mon, Wed & Fri at 10am & 11am; free, but you must have a ticket), comprises an easily absorbed group of paintings in a remarkably unspoiled mansion – though the current Baron Six, who still lives there, has a policy of actively discouraging visitors: you must pick up your **ticket** at the Rijksmuseum information desk (see p.139) *before* you go to the house – and they need your passport as ID. Rembrandt was a friend of the burgomaster and his *Portrait of Jan Six* is the collection's greatest treasure. Painted in 1654, it's a brilliant work, the impressionistic treatment of the hands subtly focusing attention on the subject's face. Also here are Rembrandt's *Portrait of Anna Wijmer*, Six's mother, and Hals's portrait of another figure prominent in Rembrandt's oeuvre, *Dr Tulp*, a great patron of the arts whose daughter married Jan Six. Further connections between the Six family and their works of art are well explained by the staff, and the whole group of paintings is a must if you have any interest in seventeenth-century painting – or indeed in the period at all.

The Willet-Holthuysen Museum

The three great *grachten* hereabouts don't contain houses quite as grand as those to the west, but the **Willet-Holthuysen House**, at Herengracht 605 (Mon–Fri 10am–5pm, Sat & Sun 11am–5pm; ƒ5), is an exception, recently refurbished and with a fine collection of period *objets d'art*. Splendidly decorated in Rococo style, the house was opened to the public as a museum in 1895, after the last owner, Sandra Willet-Holthuysen, died childless. In those days it was a lot less remarkable as a patrician period piece than it is now, and was so little visited that people used to joke that it was the best place for a man to meet his mistress without being noticed. Nowadays it is more a museum than a home, and very much look-don't-touch territory, with displays of Abraham Willet's large collection of glass and ceramics, a well-equipped replica of a seventeenth-century kitchen in the basement, and, out the back, an immaculate eighteenth-century garden – worth the price of admission alone.

Rembrandtplein and the Golden Curve

The area cornered by the Herengracht's eastern reaches is dominated by **Rembrandtplein**, a dishevelled bit of greenery fringed with cafés and their terraces. Formerly Amsterdam's butter market, it was renamed after the great artist in 1876, and today claims to be one of the city's nightlife centres, though the square's crowded restaurants are firmly tourist-targeted: expect to pay inflated prices. Rembrandt's pigeon-spattered statue stands in the middle, his back wisely turned against the square's worst excesses, which include live (but deadly) outdoor music. Of the cafés, only the bar of the **Schiller Hotel** at no. 26 stands out, with an original Art Deco interior reminiscent of a great ocean liner.

The streets leading north from Rembrandtplein to the Amstel are more exciting, containing many of the city's mainstream **gay bars** –

accessible to all, and less costly than their upstart neighbours. **Amstelstraat** is the main thoroughfare east, crossing the river at the **Blauwbrug** (Blue Bridge), and affording wonderful views across the Stadhuis complex (see pp.127–128); the Waterlooplein flea market is steps away. Heading west, the supremely tacky **Reguliersbreestraat** links Rembrandtplein to Muntplein; tucked in among slot-machine arcades and sex shops, though, is the **Tuschinski**, the city's most famous cinema, with an expertly preserved interior that's a wonderful example of the Art Deco excesses of the 1920s. Opened in 1921 by a Polish Jew, Abram Tuschinski, the cinema boasts Expressionist paintings, coloured marbles, and a wonderfully colourful carpet handwoven in Marrakesh in 1984 by sixty women to an original design. Tuschinski himself died in Auschwitz in 1942, and there is a plaque in the cinema's foyer to his memory. Obviously you can see all this if you're here to watch a film (the *Tuschinski* shows all the biggest general releases); if you're not, guided tours are laid on during July and August on Sunday and Monday mornings at 10.30am (ƒ5). The network of alleys behind the *Tuschinski* was once known as **Duivelshoek** (Devil's Corner), and, although it's been tidied up and sanitized, enough backstreet seediness remains to make it a spot most people avoid at night.

Reguliersdwarsstraat also begins at Rembrandtplein, leading west to Koningsplein, although its initial stretches are run-down and unappealing; but if the *Tuschinski* whetted your appetite for films, the *Riksbioscoop* cinema here shows last year's blockbusters for an unbeatable ƒ2.50. To the south of Rembrandtplein, **Thorbeckeplein** scores points for having a thinner concentration of clog and card shops, but is hardly a fitting memorial to Rudolf Thorbecke, a politician whose liberal reforms of the late nineteenth century furthered the city tradition of open-minded tolerance, and whose statue stands in the midst of the topless bars and fast-food joints. An occasional art market brightens the square on Sundays.

The best-value street food in the city is to be had at Maoz on Reguliersbrees-traat, where ƒ5 buys you a high-quality falafel sand-wich and all the salad you can eat.

Shiva, at Reguliersdwar-sstraat 72, near Vijzelstraat, is an outstanding Indian restau-rant, and far from expen-sive; see p.218.

The Golden Curve

From Thorbeckeplein, Herengracht leads west in an elegant sweep to Leidsestraat; the section from Vijzelstraat onwards is perhaps its most touted but least memorable stretch. This is the "**Golden Curve**", where the double-fronted merchant residences of the sixteenth and seventeenth centuries – principally nos. 441–513 and 426–480 – try to outdo each other in size if not in beauty. Most of the houses here date from the eighteenth century, with double stairways (the door underneath was the servants' entrance) and the slightly ornamented cornices that were fashionable at the time. The two-columned portal at Herengracht 502 indicates that this is the mayor's official residence; and there are a couple of neat facades at no. 539 and nos. 504–510, the second bearing carved figures of dolphins on its crest. A little further west, **Herengracht 380** is an exact

Rembrandtplein and the Golden Curve

copy of a Loire chateau – stone again, with a main gable embellished with reclining figures, and a bay window with cherubs, mythical characters, and an abundance of acanthus leaves. But otherwise the houses in this part of town are mainly corporate offices, and markedly less fascinating than the tourist authorities claim. One exception, for its contents at least, is the **Kattenkabinet** (Cats Cabinet) at Herengracht 468 (Tues–Sun 1–5pm; ☎626 5378; ƒ7.50). This is an enormous collection of art and artefacts relating to cats, housed in a seventeenth-century canal house with some original decor and paintings by Jacob de Wit; feline fanatics will be delighted.

From the Kattenkabinet it's a few steps further west to Koningsplein, and the rattle and clatter of the Leidsestraat trams heading down to Leidseplein and up into the Old Centre.

Grachtengordel South: Eating and drinking

BARS *'t Balkje, De Geus, Het Hok, Huyschkaemer, Café Klein Wiener Wad, L & B, Mulliners Wijnlokaal, Oosterling, Reynders, De Tap, Terzijde, Vive la Vie, De Zotte Proeflokaal.* **Brown cafés** *Café de Wetering.* **Designer bars and grand cafés** *Café Americain, De Balie, Françoise, Het Land van Walem, Morlang, Café Schiller.* **Gay bars (Rembrandtplein area)** *Amstel Taveerne, April, Chez Manfred, Company, Cupido, Downtown, Entre Nous, Favourite Tavern, Fellows, Gaiety, Havana, Krokodil, Milord, Monopole Taveerne, Montmartre de Paris.* **Gay bars (Kerkstraat area)** *Camp Café, Cosmo Bar, Mankind, Meia Meia "66", De Spijker.* **Hip-hop bars** *De Duivel.* **Irish pubs** *Mulligan's.*

COFFEESHOPS *Borderline, The Bulldog, Free I, Global Chillage, Grasshopper, Lucky Mothers, Mellow Yellow, The Otherside.*

TEAROOMS *Backstage, Errol Trumpie, Gary's Muffins, Metz, Café Panini, Pompadour*

Patisserie, Café de Stoep, Studio 2, De Utrechtsepoort.

RESTAURANTS African and Middle Eastern *Axum.* **American/Latin American** *Alfonso's, Iguazu, Mister Coco's, Rose's Cantina.* **Budget** *Maoz Falafel, Mr Hot Potato.* **Chinese, Thai and Filipino** *Dynasty.* **Dutch** *De Blauwe Hollander, Hollands Glorie.* **Fish** *De Oesterbar, Sluizer.* **French** *Bonjour, 't Fornuis, Jardin Parisien, Orient Express, Quartier Latin, Sluizer, Le Zinc . . . et les Dames.* **Greek, Balkan and Turkish** *Aphrodite, Izmir.* **Indian** *Akbar, Shiva, Tandoor.* **Indonesian** *Bojo, Puri Mas, Tempo Doeloe, Toko Sari.* **Italian** *Casa di David, Mascagni, Rimini, Tartufo.* **Japanese** *An, Shizen, Tokio Sushi, Yoichi.* **Spanish** *La Cacerola.* **Vegetarian** *Deshima, Golden Temple, De Vrolijke Abrikoos.*

See *Eating and Drinking*, p.185, for exact locations and reviews.

Chapter 4

The Jordaan and the Western Islands

L ying to the west of the city centre, bordered by Prinsengracht on one side and Lijnbaansgracht on the other, **THE JOR-DAAN** (pronounced "yor-dahn") is a likeable and easily explored area of narrow canals, narrower streets and simple, architecturally varied houses. Long home to Amsterdam's working classes, it has seen a twentieth-century transformation into one of the city's most attractive and sought-after residential neighbourhoods. In the seventeenth century many of the Jordaan's inhabitants were merchants or workers based at the nearby docks. The massive boom in sea trade at the time led to the creation of the **WESTERN ISLANDS** to the north, which were dredged out of the river to provide further warehousing and dock space. Today, however, the bustle of commerce has long since departed, and this atmospheric, down-at-heel part of the city is finding new life as a residential quarter. Between the two districts lies an area known as the **SHIPPING QUARTER**, once the administrative heart of maritime trade, housing the headquarters of the pre-eminent Dutch West Indies Company, but nowadays home to some interesting shops and eating places.

The Jordaan

The **Jordaan**'s name is said to come from the French word *jardin* (garden), which was the language of the area's earliest settlers – French Protestant Huguenots, escaping persecution in their Catholic homeland. At that time, the Jordaan was still largely open country, and even today many of the streets and canals are named after flowers and plants. The area fell outside the boundaries of the seventeenth-century *grachtengordel* plan, and was therefore not subject to municipal controls, a fact that led to its becoming a centre for property speculation, developing as a mazy grid of streets following the original polder drainage ditches.

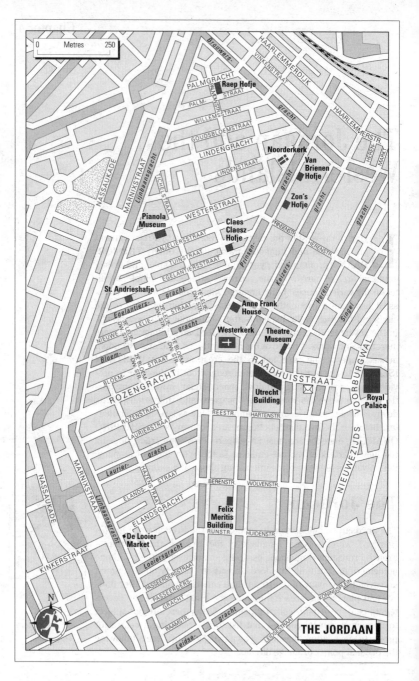

THE JORDAAN

The Jordaan's hofjes

As with much of the city, there are few specific sights to see in the Jordaan; however, it's a wonderful neighbourhood for an extended wander, and its low-key pleasures – all centring on local, residential life – are often hidden away behind anonymous doors and gateways. Most notable among these are the Jordaan's **hofjes** – seventeenth-century almshouses for the city's elderly and needy. There were – and are – *hofjes* all over the city (most famously the Begijnhof – see p.89), but there's a concentration in the Jordaan, and it is worth looking in on a courtyard or two as you come across them: many have real charm. Bear in mind, though, that most are still lived in, so be discreet. For more on *hofjes* – and an account of one of the country's most famous, the Frans Hals Museum in Haarlem – see Part Four, *Out of the City*.

In contrast to the splendour of the three main *grachten*, the Jordaan – looking on the map exactly like a sock drying on a line – became Amsterdam's slum quarter, home to artisans, tradespeople, and Jewish and Huguenot **refugees** from all over Europe (another theory as to the origin of the name is that it's a corruption of *joden*, meaning "Jews"). Though tolerated, the immigrants remained distinct minorities and were treated as such, living in what were often cramped and insanitary quarters. Later, as the city expanded beyond its original frontiers, the Jordaan became the inner-city enclave of Amsterdam's growing industrial **working class**. The area developed a reputation for toughness, and was the scene of many riots – some fuelled by genuine social injustice, others seemingly no more than high spirits running out of control – right up until World War II; in the general mood of post-1945 redevelopment, the city authorities finally got around to renovating the slums and laying on essential services, and the old rebelliousness mostly faded.

The last thirty years have seen increasing gentrification, though the area's traditionally tight-knit communities at first fiercely resisted the influx of middle-class professionals. The Jordaan is nowadays home to many young and affluent "alternative" Amsterdammers, but there remains a core of residents with long-standing roots in the district, and today these working-class, family-oriented Jordaaners live shoulder-to-shoulder with the educated, mostly single newcomers. As you wander through the long, narrow streets, you're just as likely to come across crowded pubs full of locals enjoying a beery knees-up as you are bohemian cafés serving espresso to local artists.

Leidsegracht to Rozengracht

The southern stretches of the Jordaan – which is held to begin somewhere around the **Leidsegracht** – are more pedestrian than the streets above the Rozengracht, and, according to dyed-in-the-wool Jordaaners, this area isn't even strictly the Jordaan. Jordaaners have

The Jordaan (or had) a community spirit much as Cockneys do in London; the tradition goes that any true Jordaaner was born within the sound of the Westerkerk bells – even if the Nazis hadn't melted them down in 1940, you'd still be hard pushed to hear the chimes down near the Leidseplein. These streets – most notably the alleys leading off the **Passeerdersgracht** – have seen a great deal of modern residential development, although tiny areas around Raamstraat and the **Looiersgracht** (pronounced "lawyers-gracht") are still lined with tumbledown cottages, looking for all the world like they belong in some remote village rather than the centre of a capital city.

The Looiersgracht is also home to one of the Jordaan's two **indoor markets**: this one, at Looiersgracht 38, known as the **Rommelmarkt** (daily except Fri 11am–5pm), is basically a vast, permanent flea market and jumble sale, with goods turning up here that were left unsold at the city's other street markets. You can pick up all sorts of stuff, but if you're on the lookout for something specific, Monday is coins and stamps day, Tuesday is records and books, and Thursday is clothes; on other days, and in any spare space at any time, there's masses of general junk.

Amsterdam has numerous markets, selling everything from tulips to flared trousers; you'll find them all listed in Shops and Markets, p.247.

Just round the corner, at Elandsgracht 109, is the more refined **De Looier** market (Mon–Thurs 11am–5pm, Sat 9am–5pm), which comprises a whole variety of dealers selling moderately priced antiques. If you can manage to find your way in (the market takes up a whole row of shopfronts and the entrance isn't obvious), you're forced to pick a path between stacks of this and that, display cases full of china and glass, and forgotten corners of miscellaneous junk that seems to have filtered in by mistake. Some stalls deal in particular objects or styles – silver trinkets, delftware – while others have no qualms about trying to get rid of anything that looks pre-1950s. However, if you know what you're looking at – and for – there are some genuine bargains to be had; there's even a bar and café to help you recover from any impulsive purchases. Incidentally, soccer fans might be interested to know that **Johann Cruyff** – star of Ajax and the national team in the glory days of the mid-70s – bought his first pair of boots from the shop just nearby at Elandsgracht 96.

1001 Kralen, at Rozengracht 54, is something of an Amsterdam institution – kralen means "beads", but . there are a lot more than 1001 in this floor-to-ceiling collection.

The streets from Elandsstraat to the main road at Rozengracht are unremarkable, and while you might like to wander through them to get a sense of ordinary Jordaan life, the **Lijnbaansgracht** (literally Tightrope-walk Canal), which loops around the entire city centre, is a more pleasant walk – quiet, cobbled and leafy, lined with old brick buildings and full of charm. Not far along, at Rozenstraat 59, there's an annexe of the Stedelijk Museum (see p.148) – the **Stedelijk Museum Bureau** (Tues–Sun 11am–5pm; ☎ 422 0471; free) – which provides space for up-and-coming Amsterdam artists, with exhibitions, multimedia installations and occasional lectures and readings.

Rozengracht itself, once a canal, had the misfortune to be filled in to become one of the main traffic routes in and out of the city centre;

it is now a nondescript road, busy with trams (#13, #14 and #17), launderettes, supermarkets and fast-food joints. The house at no. 184, where Rembrandt spent the last ten years of his life, has long since disappeared, and today only a plaque marks the spot ("Here Stood Rembrandt's House, 1410–1669"). From here the Westerkerk (minus its bells) is just steps away.

Rozengracht to the Noorderkerk

The streets and canals extending north from Rozengracht as far as the Brouwersgracht are what old-style Jordaaners consider to be the Jordaan proper. Beyond Rozengracht, the first canal you come to is the **Bloemgracht** (Flower Canal); like the Lauriergracht (Bay-Tree Canal) to the south and the Egelantiersgracht (Rose-Hip Canal) to the north, it's a small and attractive leafy channel, lined with houseboats. With the maze of cross-streets that weaves around it, Bloemgracht exemplifies the new-found charm of the Jordaan. Tiny streets filled with cafés, bars and odd little shops generate a warm, relaxed community atmosphere; murals and slogans have been graffitied onto blank walls with care; and even the bikes have had a special paint job. Remnants of history remain, though: the houses at nos. 87–91 each have striking gablestones, depicting a *steeman* (city-dweller), *landman* (farmer) and *seeman* (sailor) living side by side.

Pick your way down an alley to find one of the Jordaan's hidden *hofjes*, tucked away on Egelantiersgracht between nos. 107 and 114: the **St Andrieshofje** is a small, quiet courtyard surrounded by houses, its entranceway lined with Delft tiles. Not far away, at Egelantiersgracht 12, **Café 't Smalle** is one of Amsterdam's oldest cafés, opened in 1786 as a *proeflokaal*, the tasting house for an adjacent distillery. In the eighteenth century, with no common standard of distilling to follow, each case of *jenever* (Dutch gin) could turn out differently – customers consequently came to expect free samples from each case before they committed themselves to buying. Needless to say, quality control is more certain these days, and free samples much harder to come by, although one recompense for having to pay for your tipple is that it buys you the right to sit on *'t Smalle's* waterside terrace – one of the most pleasant spots in the city. The **Claes Claeszoon Hofje**, a haven of peace even in this quiet area, has its entrance nearby on 1e Egelantiersdwarsstraat; originally built as an almshouse for poor widows in 1616, the *hofje* is now occupied by students of the adjacent Amsterdam Conservatory of Music.

It is around the Egelantiersgracht that the Jordaan's **street naming** system gets extremely convoluted. The main streets of the Jordaan run in pairs all the way up – Elandsgracht (now filled in) next to Elandsstraat, Lauriergracht next to Laurierstraat, and so on. The tiny streets that cross them, though, aren't given their own

One of the most characterful cheap restaurants in the city, De Vliegende Schotel ("The Flying Saucer"), at Nieuwe Leliestraat 162, serves great food in huge portions from around f12.

names but are named instead after the main streets, with the addition of the word *dwars*, meaning "crossing": **Palmdwarsstraat**, for example, is a tiny alley crossing **Palmstraat**. Most of these cross-streets also have the prefixes "1e" (*eerste*), "2e" (*tweede*) or "3e" (*derde*) – first, second or third – thus **1e Bloemdwarsstraat** and **2e Bloemdwarsstraat** both cross Bloemstraat. The problem comes in that the same, dead-straight cross-street can often change its name several times: for instance, in the space of about 300m, the street that starts out as 1e Bloemdwarsstraat becomes first 2e Leliedwarsstraat, then 3e Egelantiersdwarsstraat, and finally, for no apparent reason, Madelievenstraat, before ending at **Anjeliersstraat** (Carnation Street). It's very easy – but fun, all the same – to get lost in the Jordaan.

Café Nol, at Westerstraat 109, is a traditional old Jordaan bar, complete with oom-pah-pah music and much heartiness. For more of the same, nip round the corner to the Twee Zwaantjes, at Prinsengracht 114, or the quieter De Tuin, on 2e Tuindwarsstraat.

The canal running parallel to Anjeliersstraat, which used to be called Anjeliersgracht, was another victim of the need to gain access to the city by cart; it was filled in in 1861 and renamed **Westerstraat**, and is now the main street of the district, with a diverse selection of local shops and a Monday market of clothes, textiles and general bits and pieces. The nearby **2e Anjeliersdwarsstraat** and **2e Tuindwarsstraat** together hold the bulk of the Jordaan's ever-increasing number of trendy stores and clothing shops, and some of its liveliest bars and cafés for restorative sipping.

At Westerstraat 106, the small but fascinating **Pianola Museum** (Sun 1–5pm; other times by appointment; ☎627 9624; ƒ5) has a collection of pianolas and automatic music-machines dating from the beginning of the century, fifteen of which have been restored to working order. These machines, which work on rolls of perforated paper, were the jukeboxes of their day, and the museum has a vast collection of 14,000 rolls of music, some of which were "recorded" by famous pianists and composers – Gershwin, Debussy, Scott Joplin, Art Tatum and others. The museum runs a regular programme of pianola music concerts, where the rolls are played back on restored machines – something like listening to Fats Waller or Paderewski perform live.

The Noorderkerk and around

Westerstraat runs east to join Prinsengracht at Hendrik de Keyser's **Noorderkerk** (rarely open to the public). This church, finished in 1623, was the architect's last creation, and probably his least successful. A bulky, overbearing building of brown and grey, it represented a radical departure from conventional church designs of the time, having a symmetrical Greek cross floor plan, with four equally proportioned arms radiating out from a steepled centre. In many ways, it's hard to believe that this uncompromisingly dour, squat building is the work of the same architect who created the elegant and fanciful Westerkerk nearby.

The square outside the church, the **Noordermarkt**, is desolate and empty most of the week. At one end, the **statue** of three figures clinging to each other commemorates the Riots of 1934, which prevented a proposed reduction in government benefit payments during the Depression – the inscription reads: "The strongest chains are those of unity". At its other end, the Noordermarkt hosts two of Amsterdam's best open-air markets: an antiques and general household goods market on Monday mornings, and the popular Saturday **Boerenmarkt** (farmers' market) – a lively affair full of avuncular characters selling organic fruit and vegetables of all kinds, as well as fresh-baked breads, pestos and mustards for sampling, olive oils, exotic fungi, plus handicrafts. Cross an unmarked border in the market, though, and you'll find a different set of people selling birds and rabbits in distressingly small cages – perhaps a leftover from the Boerenmarkt's origins as a cattle market: look at the gables of Noordermarkt nos. 17, 18 and 19 and you'll see a cow, a chicken and a sheep, a reminder of the old days. Though unremarkable to look at, *Lunchcafé Winkel*, on the edge of the market at the corner with Westerstraat, sells huge wedges of perhaps the best **apple cake** in the entire city (and consequently does a cracking trade among the locals) – for people-watching, it's hard to beat this corner on a summer Saturday.

Just across the Prinsengracht, within the Grachtengordel, are a couple of the loveliest hofjes in the city – see p.96.

Behind the Noorderkerk, **Lindengracht** (Canal of Limes) is another filled-in waterway, which hosts its own Saturday market, though it's less interesting than the Boerenmarkt. The Lindengracht has held a place in the Jordaan's folk history since one day in 1886, when a policeman tried to intervene in a traditional eel-pulling contest (something like a normal tug-o'-war, except the "rope" is a live eel smeared with soap). The locals objected strongly to the policeman's intervention, bundled him away, and proceeded to pelt police reinforcements with whatever came to hand; the high spirits got increasingly out of control, the army was eventually called in to restore order, and, at the end of three days of rioting, 26 people had been killed and hundreds injured.

Wind your way through the alleys north of Lindengracht up into the furthest corner of the Jordaan, and you'll come to **Palmgracht**, the smallest of the district's seven filled-in canals. At Palmgracht 26–38 you can see the buildings of the **Raep Hofje**, funded by the Raep family and sporting a carved *raep* (turnip) above the entrance.

The Shipping Quarter

Brouwersgracht is one of Amsterdam's most picturesque and most photographed canals, marking what is in effect the northern boundary of the Jordaan and the beginning of a district loosely known as the **Scheepvaartsbuurt** or Shipping Quarter, which centres on the long **Haarlemmerdijk**. In the seventeenth century this district was at the cutting edge of Amsterdam's trade, sited between the docks and the city: the **West Indies House**, a little way further east at Herenmarkt, was the home of the Dutch West Indies Company, who

The Shipping Quarter

administered much of the business. Today this is a good area for cheap restaurants and offbeat shops. The warehouses have been largely taken over and converted into spacious apartments, while West Indies House itself has a courtyard containing an overstated statue of Peter Stuyvesant, governor of New Amsterdam (later renamed New York), and a swanky restaurant named after the seventeenth-century Dutch naval hero Piet Hein.

Before World War II, Haarlemmerdijk was a bustling main street, but the trams that used to run here were rerouted after the war, and the bustle has largely faded these days. At the western end of the street, at no. 161, is the small revival **cinema** *The Movies* (box office Mon–Sat 4.30–10.15pm, Sun 2.30–10.15pm; late shows Fri & Sat midnight; ☎624 5790; tickets from *f*12), dating from 1928 and thoroughly and lovingly restored during the 1970s. Even if you don't fancy watching a movie (and there's a wide selection to choose from, changing daily – check the usual listings sources), the restaurant/café/bar is a joy, dripping in period atmosphere, and with a fine blues jukebox.

Padi, at Haarlemmer-dijk 50, is a small, relaxing Indonesian "eethuis", with a good selection of dishes and reasonable prices.

Haarlemmerdijk ends just twenty metres away in the busy Haarlemmerplein traffic junction; off to one side is the oversized and grandiose arch of the **Haarlemmerpoort**, a former gateway to the city that was built for William II's arrival in 1840 and nowadays looks very out of place. Behind it, barely five minutes' walk away, is an entrance to the **Westerpark**, one of the city's smaller and more enticing parks. At the far end of the park you get a good view of the set of vast old buildings at Haarlemmerweg 8–10, which date from 1884 and used to house a gas factory. Following a period in the early 1990s when this was the city's prime venue for underground Acid House parties, the **Westergasfabriek** (☎581 0425) has transformed itself into an up-and-coming centre for performance art, exhibitions, music and culture, in 1996 hosting, among other events, both the annual Drum Rhythm Festival and Art Amsterdam. The *Panorama of the West* is the title of a permanent installation on the site, clearly signposted near the Ketelhuis no. 2: devised by artist Siebe Swart, the intention to show all stages of the Westergasfabriek's history simultaneously is achieved by manipulating images from old and new photographs of the area. It's basically just a huge slide inside a viewing box, but it works remarkably well. Even if nothing else is going on, the *Café West Pacific* just opposite the Ketelhuis, with its open fireplace and warm ambience, attracts a young, impossibly trendy crowd of Amsterdammers; it serves good food before mutating into a disco around 11pm.

The Western Islands

Duck under the railway lines that run right by the Haarlemmerpoort, and you enter the **Western Islands** district. Amsterdam's docks used

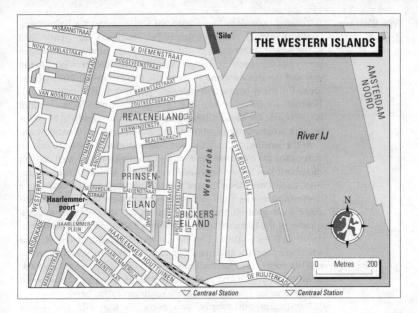

to spread from here along the full frontage of the IJ; the entire Western Islands district was dredged out of the cold waters of the western docks in the seventeenth century to allow more warehouses to be constructed, and so that returning ships could easily moor alongside to unload. However, the construction of Centraal Station in the 1880s slap in the middle of the quayside cast a shadow over the presence of the shipbuilding and mercantile industries in what was rapidly becoming the city centre. Industry and commerce were concentrated onto the artificial Eastern and Western Islands – but the death knell had already sounded. All through the mid-twentieth century, the Western Islands in particular went into terminal industrial decline, although the last oil company only left KNSM Island to the east in the early 1980s. These days major marine-based industry has moved even further westwards, although it remains central to the city's economy – Nissan uses Amsterdam's port as its major European car distribution point. The Western Islands today have a rough-and-ready atmosphere of faded grittiness and the area's residents still retain their connections to boats and the water. Many small boatyards remain in operation, and there are dozens of houseboats moored alongside the tiny streets. However, in an ongoing process of gentrification, the old forgotten warehouses of this district – within walking distance of the inner city and yet utterly ignored by most visitors (and consequently unusually calm) – have mostly been transformed into modern studios, eagerly sought after by artists and musicians.

Turning right onto Sloterdijkstraat and crossing the Galgenbrug (Gallows Bridge), you come first to **Prinseneiland**, named after one of the largest warehouses on the island, which commemorates three princes of the House of Orange. Along with the **Bickerseiland** to the east and the **Realeneiland** to the north, this is a deeply atmospheric area, for many years only sparsely populated. The painter G.H. Breitner – a friend of Van Gogh's – had his studio in the modern house beside the **Sloterdijkbrug**, and the area continues to be popular with artists, many of whom have moved into the old warehouses.

At the junction of Zandhoek and Zoutkeetsgracht is a small restaurant called *De Goudene Real*, easily identifiable by the gold coin on its gablestone. Before Napoleon introduced a system of house numbers, gables were the principal way that visitors could recognize one house from another, and many homeowners went to some lengths to make their gablestones unique. This house up in the merchants' quarter of the city used to be owned by a Catholic tradesman named Jacob Real – a *real* was also the name of a Spanish gold coin. Real used the image of a golden *real* on his gablestone to discreetly advertise his sympathies for the Catholic Spanish cause in a time of war between the Dutch and the Spanish, without being so blatant about things as to lay himself open to accusations of treachery.

Continuing northwards, you come to the wild and windy Barentszsplein housing estate, leading into the even windier **Van Diemenstraat**, overlooking the River IJ. Van Diemen was a Governor General of the Dutch East Indies at the height of the Golden Age, and sponsored the voyage of one Abel Tasman to the South Seas in 1642. Tasman proved for the first time that Australia was a vast island, rather than merely an outcrop of an unknown southern continent; he was modest enough to name the island he discovered on his travels off the southern coast of Australia in honour of his patron. However, after two centuries of deporting all their worst criminals to the penal colony on Van Diemen's Land, the British decided to spruce up the island's image for respectable colonization, and renamed it Tasmania.

The Silo

Within view of Van Diemenstraat, out on a limb of the Westerdoksdijk overlooking the IJ, the vast brick bulk of an old grain silo is the unlikely focus for one of Amsterdam's last remaining **community squats**. Since the 1960s, forty or more people have called the **Silo** (in Dutch pronounced "see-low") home, and have converted many parts of the old building into habitable areas; as well as living quarters, the Silo has space for a large and convivial restaurant, a small shop selling all kinds of organic produce, and even a highly popular nightclub. With the decline in the squatting movement in Amsterdam after its peak in 1980 – when Queen's Day (*Koninginnedag*) was renamed Housing Day (*Woninginnedag*) in protest at the high cost to the supposedly impoverished city council of Queen Beatrix's crowning ceremony –

the occupants of the Silo have fought an increasingly ill-fated rear-guard action against purchase and redevelopment of this unique and tranquil site. Finally, after many delays and much bad feeling, the building was bought in 1996 by a property developer with plans to convert it into a complex of luxury apartments. At the time of writing, though, the squatters were still there: still serving some of the finest vegetarian food to be had in Amsterdam, and still presenting cutting-edge live bands and club nights for all. If you visit, you'll be welcomed, but remember what these people have had to go through, and don't take free access throughout the building for granted.

From here, it's a short walk along the quayside back to Centraal Station, or you can walk down Barentszstraat to catch tram #3 at its terminus on Zoutkeetsgracht. If you head south down Houtmankade, though, and then follow the train tracks west along Zaanstraat, after about fifteen minutes you'll come to Spaarndammerplantsoen and the **Eigen Haard** housing project – one of the most central examples of the Amsterdam School of architecture. Designed by Michael de Klerk, this was one of a number of new schemes that went up in Amsterdam in the 1910s and 1920s, a result of legislation passed to alleviate the previously appalling housing conditions of the city's poor. Architects such as De Klerk and Piet Kramer reacted strongly against the influence of H.P. Berlage, whose style – exemplified in his Beurs stock exchange on Damrak – emphasized clean lines and functionality. Their style was more playful, and Eigen Haard, along with other examples dotted around Amsterdam, features rounded corners to buildings, turrets, and bulging windows and balconies, fanciful decoration that lends individuality to what would otherwise be very plain brick residences.

The Western Islands

At the time of writing, the Silo café opens at 6pm, taking orders for meals served about an hour later on a limited quantity, first-come first-served basis. The restaurant is at the end of the building (last door).

Many more examples of the Amsterdam School of architecture are to be seen in the New South district (The Outer Districts, p.154), for example on Roelof Hartplein and in the De Dageraad housing estate around P.L. Takstraat near Churchill-laan.

The Jordaan and Western Islands: Eating and drinking

BARS *Chris, Daalder, Duende, Gambit, De Kat in de Wijngaert, Koophandel, 't Monumentje, Nol, De Reiger, Café SAS, 't Smalle, Soundgarden, De Tuin, Café West Pacific.* **Gay bars** *Van den Berg, Doll's Place.* **Women-only bars** *Saarein.*

COFFEESHOPS *Barney's Breakfast Bar, Free City, Paradox, Pie in the Sky.*

TEAROOMS *Arnold Cornelis, J.G. Beune, Gary's Muffins, Café Toto.*

RESTAURANTS American/Latin American *Lafitte Cajun, Caramba.* **Chinese, Thai and**

Filipino *Mango Bay, Pathum.* **Dutch** *Claes Claesz, De Eenhoorn, De Eettuin, Koevoet, Moeder's Pot.* **Fish** *Albatros.* **French** *Café Cox, Christophe, De Gouden Reael, Jean Jean, De Kikker.* **Greek** *Plaka.* **Indian** *Himalaya.* **Indonesian** *Padi, Speciaal.* **Italian** *Burger's Patio, Mamma Mia, Toscana di Romana, Toscanini Caffè.* **Spanish** *Casa Tobio, Duende.* **Vegetarian** *Silo, De Vliegende Schotel.*

See *Eating and Drinking*, p.185 for exact locations and reviews.

Chapter 5

The Jodenbuurt and the Eastern Islands

Although there's little evidence nowadays, from the sixteenth century onwards Amsterdam was the refuge of Jews escaping persecution throughout Europe. Under the terms of the Union of Utrecht, Jews enjoyed a tolerance and freedom here that was unknown elsewhere, and they arrived in the city to practise diamond processing, sugar refining and tobacco production – effectively the only trades open to them, since Jews were excluded by the city's guilds and thus prevented from following traditional occupations. This largely impoverished Jewish community lived in one of the city's least desirable areas, the marshland around what is now Waterlooplein, which became known as the **Jodenhoek** (pronounced "yo-den-hook"), or "Jews' Corner". In time, Jews began to occupy houses nearby in St Antoniesbreestraat and Oude Schans and, later, on the canals of Nieuwe Herengracht, Nieuwe Keizersgracht and Nieuwe Prinsengracht to the south: the whole area became known as the **JODENBUURT**, or Jewish Quarter, of Amsterdam.

The rapidly increasing Jewish population in what was still essentially a docklands area, coupled with the huge expansion in sea trade that Amsterdam experienced in the seventeenth century, led to the areas around Oude Schans and Uilenburgergracht becoming overcrowded with both people and ships; as with the Western Islands, a solution was found by dredging land out of the River IJ to accommodate warehouses, docks and living space, thus relieving pressure on the densely populated areas of the Jodenbuurt. The new **EASTERN ISLANDS** of Kattenburg, Wittenburg and Oostenburg soon developed a distinct character – removed from the rest of the city and intimately linked with the sea – that they retain even today. By the end of the last century, the open parkland of Plantage Middenlaan, to the east of Jodenbreestraat, was beginning to be developed and settled by more affluent Jews, and the area became something of an extension to the Jewish Quarter, although here, as elsewhere in the city, only a handful of places still stand as evidence of the long history of

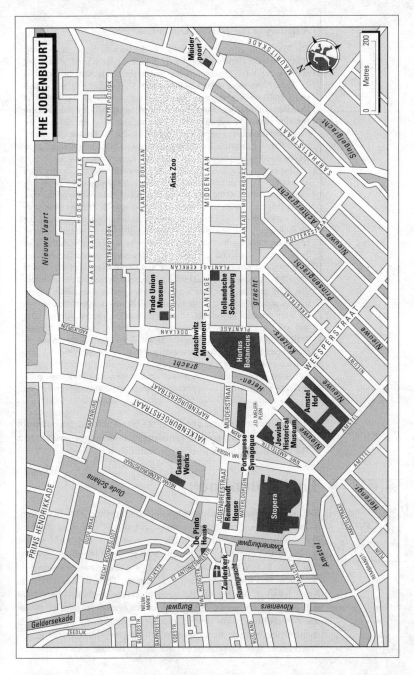

THE JODENBUURT

Muider poort

Mauritskade

N

200

Metres

0

THE JODENBUURT

Entrepotdok

Nieuwe Vaart

Hoogte Kadijk

Laagte Kadijk

Entrepotdok

Kadijksplein

Artis Zoo

Plantage Doklaan

Middenlaan

Plantage Kerklaan

Plantage Muidergracht

Sarphatistraat

Singelgracht

Nieuwe Achtergracht

Roetersstr.

Prinsengracht

Trade Union Museum

H. Polaklaan

Plantage Kerklaan

Hollandsche Schouwburg

Nieuwe Keizersgracht

Kerkstraat

Nieuwe Prinsengracht

Weesperstraat

Nieuwe

Plantage

Dok laan

Auschwitz Monument

gracht

Hortus Botanicus

Plantage

Heren- gracht

Keizers-

Amstel Hof

Amstel

Kattenburgergracht

Rapenburgerstraat

Valkenburgerstraat

Muiderstraat

Mr. Vissersplein

J.D. Meijerplein

Nwe. Amstelstr.

Jewish Historical Museum

Nieuwe Amstel

Amstel

Herengr.

Amstelstraat

Rembrandtplein

Hapenburg

Gassan Works

Nieuwe Uilenburgerstraat

Jodenbreestraat

Rembrandt House

Portuguese Synagogue

Waterlooplein

Stopera

Rapenburg

Prins Hendrikkade

Oude Schans

Oude Waal

Recht Boomssloot

Dijkstr.

St. Antoniesbreestr.

De Pinto House

Zwanenburgwal

Amstel

Gelderskade

Zeedijk

Bloedstr.

Barndesteeg

Koestr.

Nieuwmarkt

Nwe. Hoogstr.

Burgwal

Zuiderkerk

Raamgracht

Kloveniers

Russland

Staalstr.

Rembrandt

Pein

A History of the Jews in Amsterdam

The first major influx of Jews into the Netherlands began in the early 1600s – initially these were Sephardic Jews from Spain and Portugal, but after two or three generations the pattern began to shift in favour of Ashkenazi Jews from Poland and Germany. The country's climate of religious freedom was unparalleled in Europe, thanks to the **Union of Utrecht**, a mutual assistance treaty drawn up in 1579 by the northern Dutch provinces in response to the invading Spanish army. Although the treaty was designed to prevent any suppression of the Protestant majority by the Catholic invaders, its universal principle of religious tolerance guaranteed freedom of religion for the country's Protestants and Jews alike.

Despite these freedoms, though, Jews were still subject – as they were all over Europe – to crippling restrictions. A 1598 proclamation by the city authorities permitted the new immigrants to buy **citizenship**, on the condition that they didn't practise their religion openly. Another proclamation, dating from 1632, forbade Jews from becoming members of the **trade guilds** operating in the city: since the guilds controlled practically all of Amsterdam's commercial activity, this was a de facto withdrawal of Jews' rights to own and run businesses. However, individual Jews found their own way around the restrictions, and began to conduct business in those few trades not governed by the guilds, such as banking and retailing. The 1632 proclamation thus led to an expansion of Amsterdam's commercial base, as it forced the Jews to introduce new, non-guild trades into the city: diamond processing, tobacco production, the refining of sugar and silk, and printing. Despite these commercial successes, though, Amsterdam continued to strengthen its anti-Jewish laws, forbidding Jews from owning shops and from consorting with Christian women.

Even in the oasis of tolerance Amsterdam undoubtedly was at the time, with such stringent measures passed against them, the Jews were compelled by circumstance and public pressure to settle in those areas of the

Jewish life in Amsterdam, a result of the Nazis' mass deportations in the 1940s and the city council's subsequent complete redevelopment of the area in an attempt to improve traffic flow.

AMSTERDAM

The Jodenhoek

By the early years of this century the Jewish people were both commercially and culturally an integral part of the city. The growing demand for diamonds made Jewish expertise invaluable and brought wealth to the community, concentrated in the **Jodenhoek**, for the first time. In the 1930s the community's numbers were swelled by Jews who had fled persecution in Germany. Then in May 1940 the Nazis invaded, sealing off the area to create a ghetto: they took advantage of Amsterdam's network of waterways to restrict movement in and out of the Jewish quarter, raising many of the area's swing bridges, such as those over the Nieuwe Herengracht at the Amstel and the Kloveniersburgwal at Staalstraat. Jews were not city least favoured by its other residents. The area now called Waterlooplein lay at the centre of the first Jewish quarter of Amsterdam: in the mid-seventeenth century, the **Vlooyenburg**, as it was known, was a virtual marshland regularly flooded by the Amstel. Bordered by the Zwanenburgwal to the west and the Amstel to the south, along with the Leprozengracht and Houtgracht, the Vlooyenburg effectively became an island of Jewish poverty in the middle of the thriving, Golden Age city.

In 1796, laws were passed that significantly improved the status of Jews in Amsterdam. The guilds were abolished, opening up all trades; Jews were free to settle wherever they pleased; and, in an act of unprecedented liberalism, Amsterdam granted them the rights both to vote and to stand for government. It was as a direct result of these laws that Amsterdam's Jewish community began to grow and thrive in the nineteenth century, expanding into the area known today as the Jodenhoek: St Antoniesbreestraat, Jodenbreestraat and the area around the Uilenburgergracht, as well as Waterlooplein and Zwanenburgwal. Later, as the Jewish community grew more affluent, they also began to settle in many of the canal houses on the unfashionable eastern bank of the Amstel, and along the Nieuwe Herengracht, Nieuwe Keizersgracht and Nieuwe Prinsengracht.

In 1882, the old ghetto of the Vlooyenburg was razed: Leprozengracht and Houtgracht were filled in, and the Waterlooplein square was created. The mainly Jewish street markets that had previously operated on St Antoniesbreestraat and Jodenbreestraat were transferred to the new square, and this marketplace became the focus for Jewish life in the city. Around 60,000 Jews lived in Amsterdam at the time, a figure that had grown to 120,000 by the time Nazi Germany invaded in 1940. However, a mere five years later, as a result of mass killings and deportations, the number had dropped to 5000. At present, there are about 15,000 Jews resident in the city; but while Jewish life in Amsterdam may have recovered to some extent, the old Jodenhoek is gone for ever.

allowed to use public transport or to own a telephone, and were placed under a curfew. Roundups and deportations continued until the last days of the war: out of a total of 120,000 Jews in the city, 115,000 were murdered in concentration camps.

After the war the Jodenhoek lay deserted: those who used to live here were dead or had been deported, and their few possessions were quickly looted. As the need for wood and raw materials grew during postwar shortages, many houses were slowly dismantled, their final destruction coming in the 1970s with the completion of the metro beneath Waterlooplein. Today few people refer to the Jodenhoek by that name, and many Amsterdammers are unaware of its history.

St Antoniesbreestraat

Nieuwmarkt lies at the edge of what was the Jodenhoek, and from here **St Antoniesbreestraat** leads to its heart, an uncomfortably modernized street whose original houses were demolished in the

*Two very dif-
ferent bars are
within steps of
each other
here: the
trendy, split-
level Tisfris,
at St
Antoniebree-
straat 142,
and Café 't
Sluyswacht,
an old brown
café in the
tiny, brick
building on
the waterside
opposite.*

early 1980s to widen the road for the heavy traffic that the proposed redevelopment of Nieuwmarkt was expected to bring – though the plan was subsequently quashed by public protest. Only the **De Pinto House** at no. 69 survives, easily spotted by its creamy Italianate facade. Isaac De Pinto, a Jew who had fled Portugal to escape the Inquisition, was a founder of the East India Company and used some of the wealth he had accrued to decorate his house; today it's a branch of the public library (Mon & Wed 2–8pm, Fri 2–5pm, Sat 11am–2pm), and worth dropping into for a glimpse of the elaborately painted ceiling.

Nearby, Hendrik de Keyser's landmark **Zuiderkerk** (Mon–Wed & Fri noon–5pm, Thurs noon–8pm; free; tower mid-June to Sept Wed–Sat 2–4pm; *f*3) was the first church built in Amsterdam specifically for Protestant worship; now deconsecrated, it is today a Municipal Information Centre for Housing, with an exhibition on the city that illustrates its growth from the Middle Ages and displays plans for future development. The adjacent new apartment buildings were constructed after the metro line had been laid beneath the area; with their water sculptures and awkward lines, they sit rather uneasily next to the bulk of the church building. As you leave the churchyard to enter St Antoniesbreestraat, notice the ghoulish skull motif above the entrance, the only sign left that this used to be the Zuiderkerk's cemetery.

Jodenbreestraat

*Near Gassan
Diamonds
lurks
Amsterdam's
finest jazz
club, the
Bimhuis, at
Oude Schans
73; see
Entertainment
and Nightlife
for full details.*

St Antoniesbreestraat runs into **Jodenbreestraat** (pronounced "yo-den-bray-straat"), the "Broad Street of the Jews", at one time the Jodenhoek's principal market and centre of Jewish activity. After the shipbuilding industry had moved out to the east, this area, made up of the small islands of Uilenburg and Marken, became the site of the worst living conditions in the city: cramped, dirty streets housing the very poorest Jews, those who weren't able to find employment in the diamond factories – one of the largest of which, the **Gassan Works** (daily 9am–5pm; free), still stands nearby on the southwest corner of Uilenburgergracht. It wasn't until 1911 that the area was declared a health hazard and redevelopment began.

Jodenbreestraat itself was modernized and widened in the 1970s and lost much of its character as a result. The concrete building that was erected along the street's northern side met with such vociferous public scorn that it was pulled down soon after. Its glass and steel replacement, partly occupied by a School for the Arts, was positioned further forward, limiting car access and making Jodenbreestraat as narrow today as it was in the 1930s. There is no evidence, though, of any attempt to preserve the area's heritage – the concerns of the redevelopers seem to have been purely commercial. Reinforcing this impression is the brand-new building opposite, which houses the multimedia **Holland Experience** (open from Nov

1996, daily 9am–10pm; ƒ17.50, under-12s ƒ15; ☎422 2233) – a kind of sensory-bombardment movie about Holland and Amsterdam, with synchronized smells, a moving floor and 80,000 litres of water crashing towards you in a simulated dike-burst.

It's only at the **Rembrandt House**, next door at no. 6 (Mon–Sat 10am–5pm, Sun 1–5pm; ☎638 4668; ƒ7.50), that there's any sense of continuity with the past. Rembrandt bought this house at the height of his fame and popularity, living here for over twenty years and spending a fortune on furnishings – an expense that contributed to his bankruptcy. An inventory made at the time details a huge collection of paintings, sculptures and art treasures he'd amassed, almost all of which went in the bankruptcy hearings, and in 1660 he was forced to move to a more modest house on Rozengracht in the Jordaan. The house itself is mostly a reconstruction and there are no belongings of Rembrandt's on show, the reason to visit being an impressively varied collection of the artist's **etchings**. The biblical illustrations attract the most attention, though the studies of tramps and vagabonds are more accessible; an informative accompanying exhibit explains Rembrandt's engraving techniques.

*The
Jodenhoek*

There's an unrivalled collection of Rembrandt's works in the Rijksmuseum, covered on pp.139–147.

Waterlooplein

Jodenbreestraat runs parallel to its sibling development, the **Muziektheater** and **Town Hall** on **Waterlooplein**, whose building occasioned the biggest public dispute the city had seen since the Nieuwmarkt was dug up in the 1970s to make way for the metro. The Waterlooplein, originally a marshy, insanitary area known as the Vlooyenburg (see box on p.125), was the first neighbourhood to be settled by the Jews, but by the latter part of the nineteenth century the slums had become so horrendous that the area's canals were filled in and its shanty houses razed. The open square that resulted quickly became the largest and liveliest marketplace in the city, and a link between the Jewish community on the eastern side of the Amstel and the predominantly Gentile population to the west. During World War II the area gained a new notoriety as a site for Nazi roundups; arrests were so random that even non-Jews were reluctant to be seen around here. In the 1950s Waterlooplein regained some of its vibrancy with the establishment of the city's **flea market**, although it was at this time that the council took advantage of the depopulation of the Jodenhoek to expand and widen many of the nearby streets to accommodate increasing motor traffic: Jodenbreestraat, Rapenburgerstraat and Muiderstraat were all left with only one side of houses, and Mr Visserplein became little more than a large intersection for traffic heading north to the IJ tunnel.

For full details of the famous flea market, see p.263.

In the late 1970s, when the council announced the building of a massive new opera-and-city-hall complex that would all but fill Waterlooplein, opposition was widespread. People believed that the site, which had been open space for centuries, should, if anything, be turned into a residential area, or at the very least a popular performance space should be built – anything but an elitist opera house. Attempts to prevent the building failed, and the Muziektheater opened in 1986, but since then it has successfully established itself with visitors and performers alike. One of the story's abiding ironies is that the title of the protest campaign – "**Stopera**" – has passed into common usage to describe the Stadhuis-Opera complex. If you'd like to explore backstage and get an idea of the workings of the Muziektheater, you can reserve a place on a guided tour (Wed & Sat 3pm; ☎551 8054; ƒ8.50). To find out what the city is currently up to in terms of planning and building, drop into the **Architecture Centre Amsterdam** (*ARCAM*; Tues–Sat 1–5pm; ☎620 4878; free) at Waterlooplein 213, where there are changing exhibitions on the city's architecture.

In the public **passageway** between the theatre and town hall a series of glass columns give a salutary lesson on the fragility of the Netherlands: two contain water indicating the sea levels in the Dutch towns of Vlissingen and IJmuiden (below knee-level), while another records the levels experienced during the 1953 flood disaster (way above head-height). Downstairs (and so below sea level) a plaque shows what is known as "Normal Amsterdam Level" (NAP), originally calculated in 1684 as the average water level in the river IJ and still the basis for measuring altitude above sea level across Europe.

Outside the Muziektheater, the outline of a house has been marked on the ground, in remembrance of a Jewish boys' orphanage that once stood here. During the Nazi era, its occupants were all sent to the Sobibor concentration camp, from where none returned. Just a few steps round the corner, at the very tip of where Zwanenburgwal and the Amstel meet, there is a black stone memorial to the dead of the Jewish Resistance; the passage from the Bible translates as:

Located right beside the Stopera, on the corner of Zwanenburgwal and the Amstel, Dantzig is a popular and lavish grand café, with stunning river views.

Mr Visserplein

Just behind the Muziektheater, on the corner of Mr Visserplein, is the **Mozes en Aaron Kerk**, originally a small, clandestine Catholic church that was rebuilt in rather glum, Neoclassical style in the mid-nineteenth century. The philosopher Spinoza was born in a house on this site in 1632, a Jewish man whose radical views quickly brought him into conflict with the elders of the Jewish community. When he was 23 the religious authorities excommunicated him, and he was forced to move to The Hague and take up a trade instead.

The area around **Mr Visserplein**, today a busy and dangerous junction for traffic speeding towards the IJ tunnel, contains the most tangible reminders of the Jewish community. Mr Visser himself was President of the Supreme Court of the Netherlands in 1939. He was dismissed the following year when the Nazis occupied the city, and became a highly active member of the Jewish resistance, working for the illegal underground newspaper *Het Parool* ("The Password") and refusing to wear the obligatory yellow Star of David. In 1942, a few days after publicly denouncing Jewish collaboration with the occupying Nazis, he died of natural causes.

The brown and bulky **Portuguese Synagogue** (Mon–Fri & Sun 10am–3pm; closed Yom Kippur; ☎ 624 5351; ƒ2.50), unmissable on the corner of Mr Visserplein, was completed in 1675 by Sephardic Jews who had moved to Amsterdam from Spain and Portugal to escape the Inquisition, and who prospered here in the seventeenth and eighteenth centuries. During the war Amsterdammers kept the building under constant surveillance to ensure no harm came to it. A glance inside gives you an idea of just how wealthy the community was, the high barrel vault emphasizing the synagogue's size, the oak and jacaranda wood its riches. When it was completed the Portuguese Synagogue was the largest in the world; today, its Sephardic community has dwindled to just 600 members, all of whom live outside the city centre.

Across from the Portuguese Synagogue, the **Jewish Historical Museum** (daily 11am–5pm; closed Yom Kippur; ☎ 626 9945; ƒ7) is cleverly housed in a complex of High German synagogues dating from the late seventeenth century. For years after the war these buildings lay in ruins; the museum's collection was only transferred here from the Waag (on the Nieuwmarkt) in 1987. The award-winning museum is one of the most modern and impressive in Europe, presenting an introduction to Jewish life and beliefs, along with displays of photos and artefacts from the Holocaust. The Nieuwe Synagogue of 1752 is the starting point of the exhibition and includes memorabilia from the long history of Jews in the Netherlands. Inevitably, the section concentrating on the war years is the most poignant, but the museum's main focus is the religious tradition of the Dutch Jewish community. As a lesson in how to combine ancient and modern, spiritual and historical, it's hard to beat. In addition, the museum has on permanent display a sequence of endearing and lively autobiographical paintings by Charlotte Salomon, who was killed in the Auschwitz concentration camp at the age of 26; she paints a fascinating and highly articulate picture of her life in art, and the exhibition is well worth making time for.

Between the museum and the Portuguese Synagogue is **J.D. Meijerplein**, named after the lawyer Jonas Daniel Meijer, who in 1796, at the remarkable age of 16, was the first Jew to be admitted to the Amsterdam Bar. It was here that, in February 1941, around four hundred young Jewish men were rounded up, arrested, loaded on trucks, and taken to their eventual execution at Mauthausen concentration camp, in reprisal for the killing of a Nazi sympathizer during a street fight between members of the Jewish Resistance and the

Dutch Nazi Party. The arrests sparked off the **"February Strike"**, a general strike in protest against the deportations and treatment of the Jews, which was organized by the outlawed Communist Party and led by Amsterdam's transport workers and dockers. Although broken after only two days by mass arrests and displays of violence, it was a demonstration of solidarity with the Jews that was unique in occupied Europe and unusual in the Netherlands, where the majority of people had done little to prevent or protest against the actions of the Nazi SS. Mari Andriessen's statue of **The Dockworker** here on the square commemorates the event, but a better memorial, tinged with Amsterdam humour, is the legendary slogan – "Keep your filthy hands off our filthy Jews". The strike is still commemorated annually by a wreath-laying ceremony on February 25.

The Dutch Resistance is documented in the excellent Verzets- museum, in the New South district; see p.157.

AMSTERDAM

South of Nieuwe Herengracht

With the second phase of the digging of the *grachtengordel*, the three main canals that ringed the city centre – and housed Amsterdam's merchants and nobility – were extended across the Amstel towards the new harbour and shipbuilding quarter. The **Amstel Hof**, alongside the Amstel between Nieuwe Herengracht and Nieuwe Keizersgracht, is a large and forbidding former *hofje* that was one of a number of charitable institutions built here: the area was deeply unfashionable, takers for the new land were few, and the city had no option but to offer it to charities at discount prices.

With the success and assimilation of the Jews into mainstream commercial life throughout the seventeenth and eighteenth centuries, the community began to disperse away from its old centre around what is now Waterlooplein. One of the first areas of new settlement for those Jews who had made enough money to move out was the new canal system east of the Amstel, and for 150 years there was a large Jewish community living and working around the Nieuwe Keizersgracht and Nieuwe Prinsengracht. However, following World War II and the depopulation of the area, the council took the opportunity to redevelop: **Weesperstraat**, which cuts through the area due south from Mr Visserplein, was widened to take heavy traffic, and in the 1970s the city's new metro was also built here.

These large-scale construction works removed most of what little remained of the Jewish community that had thrived here, but one painful reminder of the war years still stands at **Nieuwe Keizersgracht 58**. From 1940, this house was the headquarters of the *Judenrat* (Jewish Council), an organization that the Nazis used to cover up the fact that Jews were being deported from the city to their deaths. The Council helped implement the day-to-day running of the deportations, thereby furthering the belief among Jews that they were being taken to new employment in Germany. Just how much the council leaders knew isn't clear, but a good many workers within the organization complied with Nazi orders, believing their own skins would thereby be saved. After the war the surviving leaders of the Jewish Council successfully defended themselves against charges of collaboration, claiming that they had effectively prevented far worse deportation schemes. But the presence of the council office had already given this stretch of Keizersgracht a new name – Nieuwe Martelaarsgracht, the "Canal of the New Martyrs".

Along Plantage Middenlaan

Muiderstraat runs alongside J.D. Meijerplein before crossing the Nieuwe Herengracht, where it broadens out and becomes **Plantage Middenlaan**. On the corner of Muiderstraat and the Nieuwe Herengracht is the lush **Hortus Botanicus** (April–Oct Mon–Fri 9am–5pm, Sat & Sun 11am–5pm; Nov–March Sat & Sun 9am–4pm; ☎625 8411; ƒ7.50; call for details of guided tours), a pocket-sized botanical garden that has been on this site since 1682, and whose six thousand plant species make for a wonderfully relaxing break from the rest of central Amsterdam. It's worth visiting for the sticky pleasures of the hothouses alone, and for the chance to gaze into the jaws of a carnivorous plant, although other attractions include terrapins and the oldest (and probably largest) potted plant in the world. Stop off for coffee and cakes in the orangery.

Across Muiderstraat from the Hortus is Wertheimplantsoen, a small park containing the **Auschwitz monument**, moved here in 1993 from the Nieuwe Oosterbegraafplaats in the east of the city. Designed by the Dutch writer Jan Wolkers, it's a simple affair with symbolically broken mirrors and a cracked urn containing the ashes of some of the Jews who died in Buchenwald: the inscription reads *Nooit meer Auschwitz* (Auschwitz – Never Again).

Continue down the right-hand side of Plantage Middenlaan to reach another sad relic of the war at no. 24, the **Hollandsche Schouwburg**, a predominantly Jewish theatre that after 1940 became the main assembly point for Dutch Jews prior to their deportation. Inside, there was no daylight and families were packed in for days in conditions that foreshadowed those of the camps they would soon be taken to. The house across the street, now a teacher training college, was used as a day nursery. Some – possibly hundreds – managed to escape through here and a plaque outside extols the memory of those "who saved the children". Inside, on the second floor of the adjacent building, there's a small but impressive **exhibition** (daily 11am–4pm; info ☎626 9945; ƒ7) on World War II and the Holocaust, aimed specifically at children. There's also a display on the history of the Hollandsche Schouwburg as a theatre: this area was once the centre of Amsterdam's theatreland.

The building itself is today little more than a shell. Its facade is still intact, but the roof has gone, and what used to be the auditorium is now a quiet, grassy courtyard. A memorial – a column of basalt on a

base in the form of a Star of David – stands where the stage once was.
It seems understated, a failure to grasp the enormity of the crime. Off
the beaten track and with few visitors, it is a temptation to the local
kids, whose shouts usually bring an attendant from his office; a battered vending machine churns out a leaflet and photographs. It's
almost impossible now to imagine the scenes that occurred here, but
the sense of emptiness and loss is strong. If sometimes there seems
to be a hollow ring to fun-loving Amsterdam, this place sums up why.

Cross the road and turn left into Plantage Kerklaan, then left again
to reach Henri Polaklaan, where the **Trade Union Museum** at no. 9

*For a full
account of the
Zoo, see p.265.*

(Tues–Fri 11am–5pm, Sun 1–5pm; ☎624 1166; ƒ5) contains a small
exhibition of documents, cuttings and photos relating to the Dutch
labour movement. Inevitably, this is of fairly esoteric interest, but the
building itself is worth a look. Built by Berlage in 1900 for the mainly Jewish Diamond Workers' Union, it soon became known as the
Rode Burgt (Red Stronghold), and features Berlage's trademark
arches and clever use of light and space. Inside, take a look at the
main hall and committee room, and the murals by the Dutch
Impressionist painter R.N. Roland Holst.

*Next to the
Muider
poort, at
Sarphatistraat
126, De Groene
Olifant is a
characterful
old wood-pan-
elled brown
café, with floor
to ceiling win-
dows and an
excellent, var-
ied menu.*

Stretching along the left-hand side of Plantage Middenlaan from
the corner with Plantage Kerklaan is the **Artis Zoo** (daily 9am–5pm;
☎523 3400; ƒ19, children ƒ12.50), **Planetarium** and **Zoological
Museum**, where you can easily spend a (pricey) few hours. Beyond,
at the end of road, stands the sturdy **Muiderpoort** (pronounced
"mao-der-port"), one of the surviving gates into the city; over the
canal lies the multicultural Oost (East) district, with the Tropenmuseum and the pretty Oosterpark just steps away (see The Outer
Districts).

The Docks and the Eastern Islands

With the expansion of Amsterdam during the seventeenth century,
the old dock areas around Jodenbreestraat were unable to cope with
either the huge increase in maritime trade, or the equally huge
increase in population. As a consequence, large areas along the
banks of the River IJ were dredged to form artificial islands that
could be used for dockland and warehouse space. The broad boulevard that fronts the grey waters of what became the Oosterdok is
Prins Hendrikkade, which runs all the way from the Western Islands
(see pp.118–121) through Stationsplein and on into the **Eastern
Islands**. When the city emerged as a maritime power in the sixteenth
century, this strip served as a harbour front to the ships that carried
its riches: merchant vessels brought grain from the Baltic and took
diamonds, fabric and wines to the north, vastly increasing the city's
importance as a market and bringing about the prosperity of the
Golden Age. Today Prins Hendrikkade is a major artery for cars
heading north via the IJ tunnel, and the only ships docked here

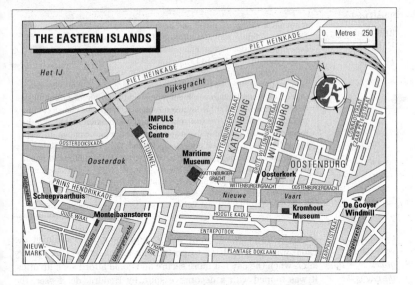

belong to the police or navy. But the road is lined with buildings that point to a more interesting nautical past.

The first of these, about 100m east of Centraal Station at the top of Geldersekade, is the squat **Schreierstoren**, traditionally the place where, in the Middle Ages, tearful women saw their husbands off to sea (a possible translation of the name is Weepers' Tower), though this is probably more romantic invention than fact. A sixteenth-century inlaid stone records the emotional leave-takings, while another much more recent tablet recalls the departure of Henry Hudson from here in 1609 – the voyage on which he inadvertently came across a river, which he named after himself, and an island that the locals called Manhattan; Hudson founded a colony on this island and called it New Amsterdam – some time later, when the English took over, its name was changed to New York.

A little further along Prins Hendrikkade, on the right, the **Scheepvaarthuis** (Shipping Building) at no. 108 is covered inside and out with bas-reliefs and other decoration recalling the city's maritime history; it's also embellished with slender turrets and expressionistic masonry characteristic of the Amsterdam School of architecture that flourished early in this century. Several of the houses along Prins Hendrikkade and the nearby streets boast similarly impressive facades: **Kromme Waal**, opposite the Scheepvaarthuis, has a fussy collection of gables, and the building at Prins Hendrikkade 131 was once the home of Amsterdam's greatest naval hero, Admiral de Ruyter, who is depicted in a stern frieze above the door. A little further along, you come to the wide **Oude Schans** canal, the main entrance to the old shipbuilding quarter. The

A complete change of mood and pace is provided by the spanking new **IMPULS Science and Technology Centre** (open from May 1997; July–Aug daily 10am–9pm; Sept–June Mon–Thurs & Sun 10am–6pm, Fri & Sat 10am–9pm; ☎570 8111), positioned near the entrance to the IJ tunnel in a sleek, all-white building designed by Renzo Piano, who worked on, among other things, the Centre Pompidou in Paris. Funded by a combination of state and local government money and contributions from major Dutch companies, IMPULS describes itself as a "centre for human creativity", and will feature five interrelated themed exhibition areas, with the focus very much on interactive displays and visitor participation. In keeping with the thrust of such projects in Holland, IMPULS also has a national mandate to devote part of its activity to promoting informed public debate of cultural and scientific issues. One of its stated intentions is to "augment the existing vehicles for public understanding of science and technology, such as radio, television and the printed media". Find out more from IMPULS's World Wide Web site at <http://www.park.org>.

One of the least-known brown cafés in the city is the friendly De Druif ("The Grape"), at Rapenburgerplein 83, on the water.

Montelbaanstoren, a tower that stands about halfway down the canal, was built in 1512 to protect the merchant fleet. A century later, when the city felt more secure and could afford such luxuries, it was topped with a decorative spire by Hendrik de Keyser, the architect who did much to create Amsterdam's prickly skyline.

The Maritime Museum

The chief pillar of Amsterdam's wealth in the sixteenth century was the **Dutch East India Company**. Its expeditions established links with India, Sri Lanka, the Indonesian islands and, later, China and Japan, using the Dutch Republic's large fleet of vessels to rob the Portuguese and Spanish of their trade and the undefended islanders of their wood and spices. Dutch expansionism wasn't purely mercantile: not only had the East India Company been given a trading monopoly in all the lands east of the Cape of Good Hope, but also unlimited military, judicial and political powers in the countries it administered. Behind the satisfied smiles of the comfortable burghers of the Golden Age lay a nightmare of slavery and exploitation.

The twin warehouses where the East India Company began its operations still stand at Prins Hendrikkade 176, but a better picture of the might of Dutch naval power can be found just five minutes' walk away in the **Maritime Museum** on Kattenburgerplein (Tues–Sat 10am–5pm, Sun noon–5pm; summer also Mon 10am–5pm; ☎523 2222; ƒ12.50), a well-presented display of the country's maritime past housed in a fortress-like former arsenal of the seventeenth century. Much of it seems to be an endless collection of maps, navigational equipment and weapons, though the large and intricate models of sailing ships and men-of-war – dating from the same period as the original ships – are impressive. A detailed English guidebook is available (and necessary, as all the labelling is in Dutch), and if ships and sailing are your passion you'll doubtless find the place fascinating; for the non-nautical it can be a little tedious. Best head directly for the highlights: a cutaway outrigger of 1840, the glitteringly ostentatious royal barge, and the museum's periscope for a seagull's-eye view of the city. Be sure, also, to check out the eighteenth-century East India Company trading ship moored outside.

The Eastern Islands

As the wealth from the colonies poured in, the old dock area to the southeast around Uilenburg was no longer able to cope, and the East India Company financed a major expansion into the marshland to the east of the existing waterfront, reclaiming land to form the three **Eastern Islands** – **Kattenburg**, **Wittenburg** and **Oostenburg**, cut through by wide canals. The company's shipbuilding industry was transplanted here and, with the construction of houses, bars and even a church, the Eastern Islands became the home of a large community working in the shipfitting and dockyard trades. The nineteenth century brought the construction of iron ships, and on a wharf at Hoogte Kadijk 147 an old shipyard has been converted into the **Kromhout Museum** (Mon–Fri 10am–4pm; ☎627 6777; ƒ3.50, no museumcards), a working museum that patches up ancient boats and presents a slide show that's a useful introduction to the area's history. The Kromhout was one of the few yards to survive the decline of the shipbuilding industry during the nineteenth century. It struggled along producing engines and iron ships until closure in 1969, when it was saved from demolition by being turned into this combination of industrial monument, operating shipyard and museum. Money is still tight, which means that little shipbuilding or restoration is going on at the moment, but the enthusiastic staff and good explanatory background material make this an up-and-coming place, and a useful adjunct to the nearby Maritime Museum.

In time, as the shipyards of the Eastern Islands went out of business, the working-class neighbourhood shrank, and today there's not much to see of a once lively community. The **Oosterkerk**, across the water from the Kromhout, was, like the East India Company building and the Maritime Museum, designed by Daniel Stalpaert; nowadays it functions as a social and exhibition centre, part of an attempt to return to the area some of its former identity. You'll see a local newspaper on sale, and the people here still refer to themselves as "Islanders".

On the other side of the Kromhout, it's worth wandering through to the **Entrepotdok**, a line of old warehouses, each bearing the name of a destination above its door. Recreated as hi-tech offices and apartments, and with weird animal sounds coming from the **Artis Zoo** across the way, it seems an odd sort of end for the Eastern Islands' rich maritime tradition.

Entredok, at Entrepotdok 64, is a friendly local bar, with sunny seating on the waterside.

The Docks and the Eastern Islands

Continue along the waterfront from the Kromhout or Oosterkerk and you'll reach "De Gooyer", a windmill that dates from 1814. There were once mills like this all over Amsterdam, pumping water and grinding grain; today this old corn mill is one of the few that remains, now converted into a brewery called 't IJ, though its sails still turn on the first Saturday of the month – wind permitting.

The Jodenbuurt and Eastern Islands: Eating and Drinking

BARS Docksider, East of Eden, Entredok, 't IJ. **Brown cafés** De Druif, De Groene Olifant, Café 't Sluyswacht. **Designer bars** Tisfris.

RESTAURANTS African Kilimanjaro. **Budget** Mensa

Agora. **Dutch** Koffiehuis van de Volksbond. **Spanish and Portuguese** Iberia, Saudade.

See Eating and Drinking, p.185, for exact locations and reviews.

Chapter 6

Museumplein and the Vondelpark

During the nineteenth century, unable to contain its mushrooming population within the limits of its canals, Amsterdam began to expand, spreading into the neighbourhoods beyond the Singelgracht that now make up the district known as the **Old South** – a large and disparate area that includes the leafy residential quarters immediately south of Leidseplein, as well as the working-class enclaves further east (see the following chapter). However, the sole reason most visitors cross the Singelgracht is to get to Amsterdam's major **museums**, which are packed into a relatively small area around the grassy wedge of **MUSEUMPLEIN**. Thanks to a particularly rich cultural heritage and an enlightened government policy of supporting the arts, the city boasts far more than its fair share of world-class museums: indeed, the immense collections of the three main ones – the **Rijksmuseum**, **Van Gogh** museum and **Stedelijk** – are often the reason people come to Amsterdam. Contributing to the neighbourhood's cultural theme, the country's principal **orchestra**, one of the world's best, performs close by in a grand and dramatic hundred-year-old concert hall. And when you've had enough of museums, a five-minute walk will bring you to the **VONDELPARK**, the city's loveliest green space.

Museumplein itself, which extends south from Stadhouderskade to Van Baerlestraat, is the city centre's largest open space, and, despite being rather bare and windswept, it hosts a variety of outdoor activities, from visiting circuses to political demonstrations; when the Rolling Stones played Amsterdam's *Paradiso* club as a warm-up to their 1995 European tour, tens of thousands of Amsterdammers partied and picnicked in Museumplein, in front of huge video screens relaying the gig live. About halfway down, you'll see a group of slim steel blocks that commemorate the women of the wartime concentration camps, particularly Ravensbruck, where some 92,000 died through starvation, disease or extermination. A "Vrouwen van Ravensbruck" committee organizes annual anti-fascist events, and the text on the right reads: "For those women who defied fascism until the bitter end".

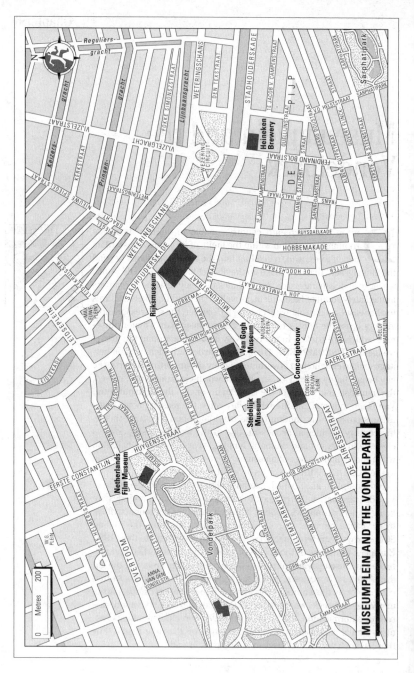

MUSEUMPLEIN AND THE VONDELPARK

The redevelopment of Museumplein

In late 1996, plans were put into action for the entire redevelopment of Museumplein. Both the Van Gogh and the Stedelijk museums are to have new wings added and the oval Van Gogh extension – funded by a private donation – is to be three-quarters buried below ground level. An underground car park is to be built beneath the southern half of Museumplein, with underground parking space for tour buses near the Rijksmuseum. There will even be a subterranean *Albert Heijn* supermarket in the complex. Museumstraat, which currently runs down the middle of the square, will disappear, and a children's playground and a large shallow pond (which will no doubt become a public ice-skating rink in winter) are to occupy Museumplein's northern half; the plans even take account of the popularity of the old skateboarding ramps in the area, which are due to stay. Once all the dust has settled, which might not be until 1998, the whole area is to be re-landscaped. With the uniquely enlightened Dutch version of "major redevelopment", Museumplein might yet be able to survive such an onslaught and still remain a pleasant open space in the city centre.

The Rijksmuseum

At the head of Museumplein, facing onto Stadhouderskade and the Singelgracht, the **Rijksmuseum** (daily 10am–5pm; ☎673 2121; *f*12.50) is a whimsical neo-Gothic structure, built in 1885 by P.J.H. Cuypers, the architect of Centraal Station. It is the one museum you shouldn't leave Amsterdam without visiting, even if only briefly. Its seventeenth-century **Dutch paintings** constitute far and away the best collection to be found anywhere, with twenty or so Rembrandts alone, as well as copious arrays of works by Steen, Hals, Vermeer and many other Dutch artists of the era – all engagingly displayed with the layperson in mind. There are, too, representative displays of every other pre-twentieth-century period of Dutch and Flemish painting, along with treasures in the medieval art and Asiatic sections that are not to be missed. To do justice to the place demands more than one visit; if time is limited, it's best to be content with the core paintings and a few selective forays into other sections. For help in navigating through the museum, the museum shop stocks the comprehensive *Treasures of the Rijksmuseum* at *f*25, as well as a fold-out floor plan.

Fifteenth- and sixteenth-century paintings

Starting from the first-floor shop, the Rijksmuseum's collection of Low Countries paintings runs chronologically through the eastern wing. First off are works from the early **Netherlandish Period**, when divisions between present-day Holland and the Flemish south weren't as sharp as they are today. The canvases here are stylized, commissioned either by the church or by rich patrons who wanted to ensure a good deal come the Day of Judgement, and thus tend to focus on religious themes. This means they're usually full of

THE RIJKSMUSEUM

TOP FLOOR

Foreign Collection

Night Watch

Gallery

of

Honour

15th-17th Century Dutch Paintings

Sculpture and

Applied Art

1. Toilets
2. Information
3. Museum Shop
4. Auditorium / Film Theatre
5. Restaurant
6. Reading Room
7. Educational Services
8. Cloakroom

18th-19th Century Paintings

Islamic Art

SOUTH WING

GROUND FLOOR

Dutch History

Sculpture and

Applied

Art

Prints and Drawings

East Entrance

West Entrance

STADHOUDERSKADE

BASEMENT

Study Collection

South Wing

Entrance

1 (Hobbemastraat)

Asiatic Collection

symbols and allusions, and set against a suitably ecclesiastical back-drop – as with the *Madonna Surrounded by Female Saints*, paint-ed by an unknown artist referred to thereafter as the **Master of the Virgin Among Virgins**. Of the artists here, though, the work of **Geertgen tot Sint Jans** is the most striking: his *Holy Kindred*, painted around 1485, is a skilfully structured portrait of the family of Anna, Mary's mother, which illustrates the symbolism of the peri-od. The Romanesque nave represents the Old Testament, the Gothic choir the New; Mary and Joseph in the foreground parallel the fig-ures of Adam and Eve in the altarpiece; lit candles on the choir screen bring illumination; and Joseph holds a lily, emblem of puri-ty, over Mary's head. Alongside are Geertgen's *Adoration of the Magi*, full of humility and with an engaging fifteenth-century back-drop of processions, castles and mountains, and Jan Mostaert's *Tree of Jesse*, crammed with tumbling, dreamlike, medieval char-acters. An even clearer picture of the Low Countries in the Middle Ages comes across in *The Seven Works of Charity* by the **Master of Alkmaar**. Originally hung in St Laurenskerk in Alkmaar, each panel shows the charitable acts expected of those with sufficient piety (and cash): alms are doled out to the poor against a toytown landscape of medieval Alkmaar.

The rooms move into the sixteenth century with the work of **Jan van Scorel**, represented here by a voluptuous *Mary Magdalen*, next to which is his pupil **Maerten van Heemskerck**'s portrait of the mas-ter of the Mint *Pieter Bicker*, shiftily counting out the cash. Further on, the gallery opens out to reveal soft, delicate compositions, most notably **Cornelis Cornelisz van Haarlem**'s *Bathsheba* and *Fall of Man*, in which the artist (typically) seems more concerned with the elegant and faintly erotic arrangement of his nudes than with the bib-lical stories that inspired them.

Paintings of the Dutch Golden Age

After this begin the classic paintings of the **Dutch Golden Age**: por-traits by Hals and Rembrandt, landscapes by Jan van Goyen and Jacob van Ruisdael, the riotous scenes of Jan Steen and the peaceful interiors of Vermeer and Pieter de Hooch.

See Contexts for a full run-down on the major artists of the Dutch Golden Age.

First, though, are some early seventeenth-century works, includ-ing **Frans Hals**'s expansive *Isaac Massa and His Wife*, and more sensational paintings such as **Dirck van Baburen**'s *Prometheus in Chains* – a work from the Utrecht School, which used the paintings of Caravaggio as its model. Through a small circular gallery devoted to the miniatures of Hendrik Avercamp (skating scenes mostly) and Adriaen van Ostade (grotesque peasants) are a number of thorough-ly Dutch works, among them the soft, tonal river scenes of **Salomon van Ruisdael** and the cool church interiors of **Pieter Saenredam**. Search out especially Saenredam's *Old Town Hall of Amsterdam*, in which the tumbledown predecessor of the current building (now the

Royal Palace) is surrounded by black-hatted townsmen in a set piece of seventeenth-century daily life.

Beyond this is a mixed selection of canvases by **Jacob van Ruisdael** – Salomon's nephew and another landscapist, though quite different in style – and by **Rembrandt** and some of his better-known pupils. Perhaps the most striking is the *Portrait of Maria Trip*, but also look out for Ferdinand Bol's *Portrait of Elizabeth Bas*, Govert Flinck's *Rembrandt as a Shepherd* – interesting if only for its subject – and the *Portrait of Abraham Potter* by **Carel Fabritius**, this last a restrained, skilful work painted by one of Rembrandt's most talented (and shortest-lived) students.

The next rooms take you into the latter half of the seventeenth century, and include works ranging from **Gerrit Berckheyde**'s crisp depictions of Amsterdam and Haarlem to the carousing peasants of **Jan Steen**. Steen's *Morning Toilet* is full of associations, referring either to pleasures just had or about to be taken, while his *Feast of St Nicholas*, with its squabbling children, makes the festival a celebration of pure greed – much like the drunken gluttony of the *Merry Family* nearby. The out-of-control ugliness of *After the Drinking Bout* leaves no room for doubt about what Steen thought of all this ribaldry.

It's in the last few rooms, though, that the Dutch interior really comes into its own, with a gentle moralizing that grows ever more subtle. **Vermeer**'s *The Letter* reveals a tension between servant and mistress – the lute on the woman's lap was a well-known sexual symbol of the time – and the map behind the *Young Woman Reading a Letter* hints at the far-flung places her loved one is writing from. **Gerard ter Borch**, too, depicts apparently innocent scenes, both in subject and title, but his *Lady with a Mirror* glances in a meaningfully anxious manner at her servants, who look on with delicate irony from behind dutiful exteriors, and the blandly named *Interior Scene* is clearly taking place in a brothel. The paintings of **Pieter de Hooch** are less symbolic, more exercises in lighting, but they're as good a visual guide to the everyday life and habits of the seventeenth-century Dutch bourgeoisie as you'll find. So, too, with **Nicholas Maes**, whose *Woman Saying Grace* is not so much a moral tableau as a simple celebration of experience.

Mingling with these interior scenes are more paintings by **Hals** and **Rembrandt** – later works, for the most part, from the painters' mature periods. Hals weighs in with a handful of portraits, including the boisterous *Merry Toper*, while Rembrandt – at his most private and expressive best here – is represented by a portrait of his first wife *Saskia*, a couple of his mother, and a touching depiction of his cowled son, *Titus*. All are in marked contrast to studio-mate **Jan Lievens**' stiff though perceptive *Constantijn Huygens* on the opposite wall, a commissioned work if ever there was one. There was some criticism of this painting among Huygens' high-ranking friends, though Huygens himself seemed pleased enough with it, claiming that the portrait's thoughtful expression accurately "reflected the cares of my heart".

The Gallery of Honour

A small room off to the side of the last one offers an introduction to the **Gallery of Honour** and one of the Rijksmuseum's great treasures: Rembrandt's **The Night Watch**, the most famous and most valuable of all the artist's pictures, restored after being slashed in 1975, and recently cleaned. The painting is a so-called Civil Guard portrait, named after the bands of militia that got together in the sixteenth century to defend the home front during the wars with the Spanish. They later grew into social clubs for local dignitaries – most of whom would commission a group portrait as a mark of prestige. This painting, of the Guards of the Kloveniersdoelen in Amsterdam, was erroneously tagged *The Night Watch* in the nineteenth century – a result both of the romanticism of the age and the fact that for years the painting was covered in soot. There are other misconceptions about the painting, most notably that it was this work that led to the downward shift in Rembrandt's standing with the Amsterdam elite. In fact, there's no evidence that the militia group weren't pleased with the picture, or that Rembrandt's commissions flowed in any more slowly after he had completed it. Though not as subtle as much of the artist's later work, it's an adept piece, full of movement and carefully arranged – these paintings were collections of individual portraits as much as group pictures, and for the artist their difficulty lay in including each individual face while simultaneously producing a coherent group scene. The sponsors would pay for a prominent position in the painting, and the artist had to reflect this too.

The surrounding paintings also depict various companies of the Kloveniersdoelen, and they make for interesting comparison. Two are by **Bartholomeus van der Helst**: the one on the left of *The Night Watch* is probably the best of the lot – it's lively and colourful, but, like the others, its arrangement and lighting are static. Van der Helst's painting to the right includes, as was usual, a self-portrait (on the far left) – as does the one by **Govert Flinck** (on the top far right of his picture). It seems that Rembrandt didn't bother with his, though art historians have been speculating for centuries as to whether the pudgy face peering out from the back of *The Night Watch*, between the soldier and the gesticulating militiaman, could be the artist making a rare Hitchcockian appearance.

Elsewhere, the Gallery of Honour houses the large-scale works from the museum's collection of Dutch paintings. Some of these are notable only for their size – the selection of naval battles particularly – but a number do stand out, as they would in any museum. Two of Rembrandt's better-known pupils crop up here: **Nicholas Maes**, with one of his typically intimate scenes in *Dreaming*, and

An extensive collection of Rembrandt's drawings and etchings is on display in the artist's house, now a museum – see p.127.

The
Rijksmuseum

Ferdinand Bol, with his *Regents of the Nieuwe Zijds Workhouse*
and the elegantly composed *Venus and Adonis*. The dashing *Self-
Portrait* is his too, a rich and successful character leaning on a
sleeping cupid. By way of contrast, **Rembrandt** himself follows with
a late *Self-Portrait*, caught in mid-shrug as the Apostle Paul, a self-
aware and defeated old man. Opposite, *The Staalmeesters* is an
example of one of his later commissions and, like so many of
Rembrandt's works of that time, it demonstrates his ability to capture a staggering range of subtle expressions. Nearby is *The Jewish
Bride*, one of his very last pictures, finished in 1665. No one knows
who the people are, nor whether they are actually married (the title
came later), but the painting is one of Rembrandt's most telling, the
paint dashed on freely and the hands joined lovingly, as Kenneth
Clark wrote, in a "marvellous amalgam of richness, tenderness and
trust".

The Foreign Collection

Tucked away in a small gallery behind *The Night Watch*, the
Rijksmuseum's collection of **Foreign Paintings** is undoubtedly overshadowed by the quality of the surrounding homegrown works. Aside
from a scattering of **Belgian** artists – the lusty scenes of Jordaens
and the bloated pink subjects of Rubens and Van Dyck – **Italian**
works are the collection's mainstay. These include a beautiful
embossed *Mary Magdalen* by Crivelli, a dignified *Portrait of a
Nobleman* by Paolo Veronese, and a couple of *Portraits* by Pietro di
Cosimo. A tiny collection, and one that is often overlooked.

Dutch History

The **Dutch history** section starts promisingly with exhibitions
depicting aspects of life in the Golden Age, focusing, not surprisingly, on the naval might that brought Holland its wealth. Fearsome
model ships impress, but more revealing of everyday life are the
maritime odds and ends from the *Witte Leeuw* (White Lion), an East
Indian vessel, laden with a cargo of pepper and Chinese porcelain,
which sank in 1613. The galleries off this room, however, are for the
most part uninspired, filled with relics from Holland's naval and

colonial past. The prize for the most conspicuous exhibit goes to **Willem Pieneman** for his painting of the *Battle of Waterloo*, a vast canvas that took six years to complete. All the big names of the battle are there (the artist spent two years on the portrait studies alone), but it's a laboured and rather arid piece nonetheless.

Sculpture and Applied Art

The Rijksmuseum owns a huge amount of **applied art**, and unless your tastes are eclectic it's wise to restrict yourself to a single period: easily the most impressive is the top-floor **Medieval and Renaissance** collection. Beginning with a handful of Byzantine trinkets and Limoges enamels, the collection leads off the main hall with the magnificent *Ten Mourners*, sensitive fifteenth-century figures taken from the tomb of Isabelle de Brabant in Antwerp. Contemporaneous with these is the fifteenth-century **carving**, especially the work of **Adriaen van Wesel** of Utrecht, whose scenes (for example, the *Meeting of the Magi*) are packed with vigour and expression. Look out, too, for the *Anna te Drieën*, carvings of the infant Jesus with Mary and her mother Anna – a popular subject in the Low Countries at the time.

Other galleries here are stuffed from floor to ceiling with **delft-ware**, the blue-and-white ceramics to which Delft gave its name in the seventeenth century. The original designs were stylized copies of Chinese ceramics imported by the Dutch East India Company, but the patterns soon changed to depict more traditional Dutch landscapes, animals and comic figures. By the early years of the eighteenth century, Delft's craftspeople had become confident enough to create vases, jars and even musical instruments, in polychrome as well as the traditional blue and white. Examples of each and every period are here, but you'll need an inexhaustible interest to cope with so large a collection.

The South Wing

In 1996, the **South Wing** of the Rijksmuseum reopened after three years of renovation and restoration work, funded to the tune of ƒ23 million by the PTT phone company and the Ministries of Environment and Culture. Originally cobbled together by the architect of the main building, P.J.H. Cuypers, from fragments of walls and buildings sent in to Amsterdam from all over the country – including the city gates of the towns of Groningen and Deventer – the South Wing had remained largely as it was since it opened in 1898; the recent reconstruction has seen climate control (for both visitors and paintings) and a lift installed, among other things. The South Wing can be reached through a passageway from the main building, but it also has its own separate **entrance** at Hobbemastraat 19, round the back of the main building.

Eighteenth- and nineteenth-century paintings

The South Wing's collection of eighteenth- and nineteenth-century Dutch paintings picks up chronologically where the Gallery of Honour leaves off, beginning with the work of **Cornelis Troost**, whose eighteenth-century comic scenes earned him the dubiously deserved title of the "Dutch Hogarth". More enduring are the later pictures, notably the pastels of Pierre-Paul Prud'hon and **Jan Ekels'** *The Writer* – small and simple, its lighting and attention to detail reminiscent of Vermeer.

After this, rooms follow each other in haphazard fashion, containing sundry landscapes and portraiture from the lesser nineteenth-century artists. **Jongkind** is the best of the bunch, his murky *River Landscape in France* typical of the Impressionist style that was developing in the nineteenth century. The chief proponents of Dutch Impressionism originated from or worked in The Hague, and the **Hague School** label covers a variety of styles and painters who shared a clarity and sensitivity in their depiction of the Dutch landscape. Of the major Hague School painters, the Rijksmuseum collection is strongest on the work of **Jan Weissenbruch**, whose land- and seascapes, such as *View near the Geestbrug*, hark back to the compositional techniques of Van Ruisdael and the Maris Brothers. **Jacob Maris's** sultry landscapes are the most representative of the School, while the works of the younger **Willem Maris** are more direct and approachable – his *Ducks* is a good example. **Anton Mauve's** work is similar, his *Morning Ride on the Beach* filled with shimmering gradations of tone that belie the initial simplicity of the scene.

While members of the Hague School were creating gentle landscapes, a younger generation of Impressionist painters working in Amsterdam – the **Amsterdam School** – was using a darker palette to capture city scenes. By far the most important work from this turn-of-the-century group is **G.H. Breitner's** *Singelbrug near Paleisstraat in Amsterdam*, a random moment in the street recorded and framed with photographic dispassion. Breitner worked best when turning his attention to rough, shadowy depictions of the city, as in *Rokin* and *Damrak*. **Isaac Israëls'** work is lighter in tone and mood, with canvases like *Donkey Rides on the Beach* showing his affinities with the French Impressionists of the period.

Asiatic Art

Holland's colonial links with the East mean that Asian art can be found in other collections, but the **Asiatic collection** proper holds the museum's most prized treasures. Of the different cultures, **China** and **Japan** are best represented: the striking twelfth-century *Statue of Avalokiteshvara* and graceful *Paintings* by Kao Ch'i-p'ei, drawn with his fingernails, are the highlights of the Chinese works, while the seventeenth-century **ceramics** and **lacquerwork** are the best of the Japanese. If you're interested, you'll find much more here, from twelfth-century Indonesian gold jewellery to Cambodian carving. This is an excellent collection, and one to linger over.

The
Rijksmuseum

The Rijksmuseum Vincent van Gogh

Vincent van Gogh is arguably the most popular, most reproduced and most talked about of all modern artists, so it's not surprising that the **Rijksmuseum Vincent van Gogh** (open daily 10am–5pm; ☎570 5200; ƒ12.50), comprising the extensive collection of the artist's art-dealer brother Theo, is one of Amsterdam's top tourist attractions. Housed in an angular building designed by the aged Gerritt Rietveld and opened to the public in 1973, it's a gentle and unassuming introduction to the man and his art – and one which, due to the quality of both the collection and the building, succeeds superbly well.

The museum starts with a group of works by Van Gogh's better-known friends and contemporaries, many of whom influenced his work – Gauguin, Emile Bernard, Adolph Monticelli and others. It then moves on to the works of the man himself, presented for the most part chronologically. The first go back to the artist's **early years** in Nuenen, southern Holland, where he was born: dark, sombre works in the main, ranging from an assortment of drab grey and brown still-lifes to the gnarled faces and haunting, flickering light of *The Potato Eaters* – one of Van Gogh's best-known paintings, and the culmination of hundreds of studies of the local peasantry.

Across the hall, the sobriety of these early works is easily transposed onto the **Parisian** urban landscape, particularly in the *View of Paris*, where the city's domes and rooftops hover below Montmartre under a glowering, blustery sky. But before long, under the sway of fellow painters and, after the bleak countryside of North Brabant and the sheer colour of the city itself, his approach began to change. This is most noticeable in the views of Montmartre windmills, a couple of self-portraits, and the pictures from Asnières just outside Paris, where the artist used to travel regularly to paint. Look out also for *A Pair of Shoes*, a painting that used to hang in the house Van Gogh shared with Gauguin in Arles, *Woman in the Café Tambourin* (actually a portrait of the owner, with whom the artist was friendly), and the dazzling movement of *Edge of a Wheatfield*.

In February 1888, Van Gogh moved to **Arles**, inviting Gauguin to join him a little later. With the change of scenery came a heightened interest in colour, and the predominance of yellow as a recurring motif: it's represented best in such paintings as *Van Gogh's Bedroom* and the *Harvest at La Crau*, and most vividly in *The Yellow House*. A canvas from the artist's *Sunflowers* series is justly one of his most lauded works, intensely, almost obsessively, rendered in the deepest oranges, golds and ochres he could find.

Gauguin told of Van Gogh painting these flowers in a near trance; there were usually sunflowers in jars all over their house.

At the asylum in **St Rémy**, where Van Gogh committed himself after snipping off part of his ear and offering it to a local prostitute, nature took on a more abstract form in his work: trees bent into cruel, sinister shapes, skies coloured purple and yellow, as in the *Garden of St Paul's Hospital*. Van Gogh is at his most expressionistic here, the paint applied thickly – often with a palette knife, especially in the final, tortured paintings done at **Auvers**, including *Undergrowth, The Reaper*, or *Wheatfield with Crows*, in which the fields swirl and writhe under black, moving skies. It was a few weeks after completing this last painting that Van Gogh shot and fatally wounded himself.

On the second floor, the museum shows a changing selection from its vast stock of Van Gogh's **drawings**, notebooks and letters, and also affords space to relevant temporary exhibitions. The top floor is used as a **temporary exhibition space** year-round, usually showing works loaned from other galleries that illustrate Van Gogh's artistic influences, or his own influence on other artists. As well as the usual postcards, the museum **shop** sells large prints of the more famous paintings for around ƒ8; ask for a strong triangular box (ƒ3) to protect your purchase. The museum also has a small **library**, crammed with books and a vast collection of clippings on the artist and his work.

Thanks to a donation of several million guilders from a Japanese insurance company (who paid US$35 million for one of the *Sunflowers* canvases in 1987), the Van Gogh Museum is due to expand into a new wing, which will be partly submerged beneath the redeveloped Museumplein; the plans are scheduled for completion around 1998.

The Stedelijk Museum

Amsterdam's number one venue for modern art, the **Stedelijk Museum** (April–Oct daily 11am–7pm; Nov–March daily 11am–5pm; ☎573 2737; ƒ7.50) is still at the cutting edge after a hundred years or more; its permanent collection is unrivalled and its temporary exhibitions – based both on its own acquisitions and on loaned pieces, and regularly extending to photography or video installations – are often of world renown.

The Stedelijk (pronounced "staid-a-lik") is the city's most important contemporary art space, and its **ground floor** is usually given over to at least a couple of **temporary exhibitions**, often by living European artists, as is the bright two-storey 1950s extension at the back. Justifiably, current Dutch art often gets a thorough showing, so keep an eye out for the work of such painters as Jan Dibbets, Rob Scholte and Marlene Dumas.

Also on the ground floor are a couple of permanent **large-scale attractions** – Karel Appel's *Bar* in the foyer, installed for the museum's opening in the 1950s, and the same artist's wild daubings in the restaurant. But perhaps the most interesting permanent exhibit is Ed Kienholz's *Beanery* (1965), in the basement: modelled on his local bar in Los Angeles, the tableau's clock-faced figures, the music and hum of conversation create a nervous, claustrophobic background to the horror of the newspaper headline in the vending machine – "Children Kill Children in Vietnam Riots". For Kienholz, this is *real* time, and time inside the bar is "surrealist time . . . where people waste time, lose time, escape time, ignore time".

Upstairs, the **first floor** is given over to a changing selection of the museum's **permanent collection**. Briefly, and broadly, this starts off with drawings by Picasso, Matisse and their contemporaries, and moves on to paintings by major Impressionists (Manet, Monet, Bonnard) and Post-Impressionists (Ensor, Van Gogh, Cézanne). Further on, Mondriaan holds sway among the *De Stijl* group, from his early, muddy-coloured abstractions to the cool, boldly coloured rectangular blocks for which he's most famous. Kasimir Malevich is similarly well represented, his dense attempts at Cubism leading to the dynamism and bold, primary tones of his "Suprematist" paintings – slices, blocks and bolts of colour that shift around as if about to resolve themselves into some complex computer graphic. Elsewhere, depending on what's on show, you may come across some of the Stedelijk's wide collection of Marc Chagall paintings, and a number of pictures by American Abstract Expressionists Mark Rothko, Ellsworth Kelly and Barnett Newman, in addition to the odd work by Lichtenstein or Warhol. Jean Dubuffet, too, with his swipes at the art establishment, may well have a profile, and you might catch Matisse's large cutout, *The Parakeet and the Mermaid*.

As part of the Museumplein redevelopment, the Stedelijk has been allocated funds from the city council and the state to build a new wing; at the time of writing this was still at the design stage, with the project expected to be completed in 1998.

The Stedelijk Museum

You can see many more works by Appel and other exponents of the CoBrA School at the new CoBrA museum – see p.243 & p.356.

The Vondelpark

Five minutes' walk west of Museumplein, the **Vondelpark** is the city's most enticing park. In 1864 the Association for a Riding and Walking Park in Amsterdam was given permission to transform the soggy meadow outside the Leidsepoort into a city park open to all. Named after the seventeenth-century poet Joost van der Vondel, and funded by local residents, it was beautifully landscaped in the latter part of the last century in the English style, with a bandstand and emphasis on natural growth rather than formal gardens. Today it's a regular forum for drama and other performances in the summer, and

The Vondelpark

Amsterdam's parks and gardens

Finding a patch of green space in the centre of Amsterdam is not as easy as you might think: while the Vondelpark is within easy reach of the museums and Leidseplein, the city's other parks are all inconveniently sited outside the immediate centre. Tucked away in the old Pijp district is the small but delightful **Sarphatipark** (tram #3), with wide lawns for sunbathing and ducks and geese floating on little ponds set among the trees; to the east is the lusher and more rambling **Oosterpark** (tram #3, #6, #9, #10 or #14) and, out to the west, there's the better-kept and more sedate **Westerpark** (tram #3 or #10). Further afield, the large **Amstelpark** (bus #69 or #169 from Amstel station), beyond the ring road to the south, is well worth a visit for its rose garden and carefully tended floral displays, as well as Amsterdam's best preserved windmill, on the park's southern edge, built in 1636 and now a private home. Also in the south, right next to the RAI conference centre, is the rarely visited **Beatrixpark** (tram #5), whose magical walled garden makes a wonderful summer retreat. The **Amsterdamse Bos**, a large woodland area to the south of the city, riddled with paths and trails, is covered on pp.157–158. All the parks listed above are open daily from dawn to dusk.

While in Amsterdam, you shouldn't miss the wonderful 300-year-old **Hortus Botanicus** in the old Jodenbuurt area (see p.131). Other gardens that are open to the public include those of the Golden Age canal house museums: both the **Willet-Holthuysen Museum** (p.108) and the **Van Loon Museum** (p.106) boast exemplary eighteenth-century formal gardens.

For more ideas on what to do with kids in Amsterdam, see p.264.

at weekends young Amsterdam flocks here in force to meet friends, laze by the lake, buy trinkets from the flea markets that spring up in the area, or listen to music – in June, July and August bands give **free concerts** in a specially designed theatre in the middle of the park. There are also several different **children's play areas** dotted around inside. Criss-crossing throughout there's a network of dreamy canals spanned by tiny, elaborate bridges, and if you wander far enough into the interior you might come across the cows, sheep and even llamas that call the park home. Perhaps the highlight of a visit, though, is the extravagantly lush (and well-kept) **rose garden**, where dozens of varieties of all colours and sizes compete for your attention, their fragrances filling the air.

Around the park

Attached to the Film Museum, Café Vertigo is a wonderful place to while away a sunny afternoon (or take refuge from the rain) with a spacious interior and a large terrace overlooking the park.

Just outside the park, on Vondelstraat, the fine neo-Gothic Vondelkerk, designed (again) by Cuypers, is now occupied by offices. Very close to the church, housed in a grand pavilion just inside the park, is the **Netherlands Film Museum** (box office Mon–Fri 9am–10pm, Sat & Sun 1–10pm; nightly screenings, plus matinees on Wed; ☎589 1400; tickets *f*10). Not so much a museum as an art-house cinema, this is a showcase for obscure films on a variety of subjects – most are shown in their original language, with subtitles in Dutch (and occasionally English). Look out for news of the free open-air screenings of classic movies on Saturday nights in summer. The museum's nearby film **library** at Vondelstraat 69 (Tues–Fri 10am–5pm, Sat 11am–5pm; ☎589 1435 afternoons) has a well-catalogued collection of books, magazines and journals, some in English, but you can't borrow any of them. Look out for the Sunday market outside the museum – a dozen or so stalls selling books and posters connected with films past and present.

The Vondelpark

The area around the Vondelpark is one of Amsterdam's better-heeled residential districts, with designer shops and delicatessens along chic **P.C. Hooftstraat** and **Van Baerlestraat**, and some of the city's fancier hotels (and plenty of its cheaper ones, too) on their connecting streets. On Van Baerlestraat, at the bottom end of Museumplein, is the **Concertgebouw** (Concert Hall), home of the famed – and much recorded – Royal Concertgebouw Orchestra. When the German composer Brahms visited Amsterdam in the 1870s he was scathing about the Dutch lack of culture and, in particular, their lack of an even halfway suitable venue for his music. In the face of such ridicule, a consortium of Amsterdam businessmen got together to fund the construction of a brand-new concert hall, in an attempt to bring high culture to a city better known for high finance. The Concertgebouw was completed in 1888, and has since become renowned among musicians and concert-goers for its marvellous acoustics. The building was given a major £12 million facelift a few years ago, after it was discovered that the wooden piles on which it rested were rotting, causing subsidence; the foyer is now around the side, housed in a new, largely glass wing that contrasts nicely with the red brick and stone of the rest of the building. While it is able to draw the world's best orchestras and musicians to Amsterdam, the management of the Concertgebouw operates a policy of accessibility for all: tickets for major events can cost *f*200 or more, but you can get into a minor week-night concert for no more than *f*20 or *f*25, and from September to May there are free walk-in concerts at lunchtime.

Keyser, at Van Baerlestraat 96, is a long-established and elegant place for a quick drink or a full meal.

For Concertgebouw box office details, see p.228.

Museumplein and the Vondelpark: Eating and drinking

BARS *Café Ebeling, Helfensteyn, Kasbah, Welling, Wildschut*. Designer bars and grand cafés *Keyser, Café Vertigo*. Sex cafés *Hellen's Place*.

RESTAURANTS African and Middle Eastern *Hamilcar, Lalibela*. Chinese, Thai and Filipino *New San Kong*. French

Beddington's, Brasserie van Baerle, Le Garage. Greek, Balkan and Turkish *Dionysos, Opatija*. Indian *Maharaja*. Indonesian *Orient, Sama Sebo*. Italian *Mirafiori*.

See *Eating and Drinking*, p.185, for exact locations and reviews.

Chapter 7

The Outer Districts

A msterdam is a small city, and most of its residential **OUTER DISTRICTS** can be easily reached from the city centre. Of these, the **South** holds most interest, with the raucous "De Pijp" quarter and the 1930s architecture of the New South more than justifying the walk or tram ride. As for the other districts, you'll find a good deal less reason to make the effort. The **West** is nothing special, aside from the occasional park and one lively immigrant quarter; nor is the **East**, although a multicultural influence gives the area an interesting diversity, and the Tropenmuseum is a definite draw. Amsterdam **North**, across the IJ, is entirely residential; peaceful for bike-riding through on the way to open country beyond, but unless you're unlucky enough to end up in a hotel here, the highlight of a visit is likely to be the short (free) ferry ride from behind Centraal Station.

The Old South: De Pijp

Across the water to the east of Museumplein, away from the wealth and high culture, lies the busy heart of the Old South: the district known as "**De Pijp**" (The Pipe). This was Amsterdam's first suburb. New development beyond the Singelgracht began around 1870, but after laying down street plans, the city council left the actual house-building to private developers, which resulted in streets of the cheap-to-build but featureless five- and six-storey buildings visible today. The district's name comes from the characteristically narrow terraced streets running between long, sombre canyons of brick tenements; the apartments here were said to resemble pipe-drawers, since each had a tiny street frontage but extended back a long way into the building. De Pijp remains densely populated, with a large proportion of immigrants – Surinamese, Moroccan, Turkish and Indian. It's still one of the city's closest-knit communities, and one of its liveliest.

Ferdinand Bolstraat, running north–south, is the district's main street, but the long, slim east–west thoroughfare of **Albert**

Bagels & Beans, at Ferdinand Bolstraat 70, is a perfect place to sip a good cup of coffee before heading into the Albert Cuyp market.

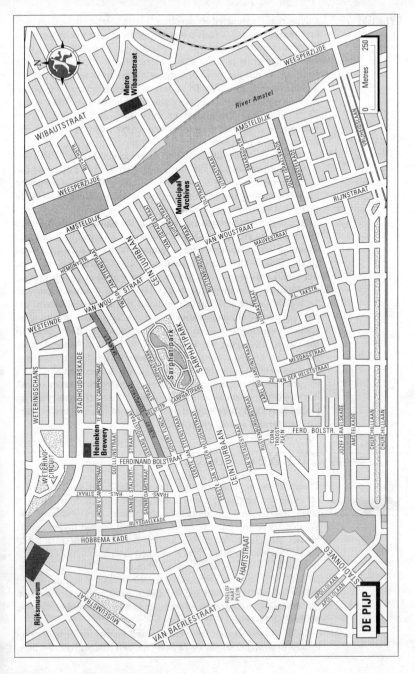

N

Metro
Wibautstraat

WIBAUTSTRAAT

River Amstel

AMSTELDIJK

WEESPERZIJDE

WEESPERZIJDE

AMSTELDIJK

Municipal
Archives

RIJNSTRAAT

VAN WOUSTRAAT

MAUVESTRAAT

VRIJHEIDSLAAN

Metres 250

P.L. TAKSTR.

WESTEINDE

VAN WOU

Sarphatipark
SARPHATIPARK

MESDAGSTRAAT

2E VAN DER HELSTSTRAAT

WETERINGSCHANS

STADHOUDERSKADE

Heineken
Brewery

FERD. BOLSTR.

JOZEF ISRAELSKADE

CHURCHILLLAAN

CHURCHILLLAAN

WETERING
CIRCUIT

Ferdinand Bolstraat

CORN.
TROOST
PLEIN

CENTUURBAAN

RUYSDAELKADE

HOBBEMA KADE

R. HARTSTRAAT

STADIONWEG

APOLLOLAAN

APOLLOLAAN

Rijksmuseum

MUSEUMSTRAAT

ROELOF
HART
PLEIN

VAN BAERLESTRAAT

DE PIJP

The Old South: De Pijp

Cuypstraat (pronouced "cowp-straat") is its heart, and the daily general **market** here – which stretches for over a kilometre between Ferdinand Bolstraat and Van Woustraat – is the largest in the city, with a huge array of stalls selling everything from cut-price carrots to exotic toadstools, raw-herring sandwiches to saucepans, day-glo T-shirts to garlicky olives. This is where working Amsterdammers do their shopping. Check out, too, the bargain-basement and ethnic shops that flank the market on each side, and the Indian and Surinamese restaurants down the side streets – they're often cheaper than their equivalents in the city centre.

A few blocks south of the Albert Cuyp market is the small but pretty **Sarphatipark**, where the surrounding streets offer some of the best general wandering in Amsterdam – there's nothing of particular note, but walking through the area can reveal elements of local life that you'd never see in the centre.

As it heads east towards the river from the Sarphatipark, the main **Ceintuurbaan** artery crosses **Van Woustraat** – a long, unremarkable shopping street, though with a number of speciality ethnic food shops. Follow Ceintuurbaan and turn right along the riverside Amsteldijk, where at no. 67, on the corner with Rustenburgerstraat, the **Municipal Archives** (Sept–May Mon–Fri 8.45am–4.45pm, Sat 9am–12.15pm; ☎572 0202; free) holds regular exhibitions on the city's history – although extensive research facilities are its chief concern. Starting with Count Floris V's granting of toll privileges to the city in 1275 (the oldest document to mention Amsterdam by name), the Archives have a mass of material on the city; perhaps most interesting is the photo collection, which documents changes to each of Amsterdam's streets from the nineteenth century on. All births, marriages and deaths from the early sixteenth century are on record here, and there's an extensive array of newspapers, posters and Amsterdam-related ephemera.

The New South

There's little else to detain you in the Old South, and you'd be better off either walking or catching a tram down into the **New South**, a large district that encompasses the whole area south of the Vondelpark to the railway tracks, along with the old Rivierenbuurt district stretching east to the Amstel. A real contrast to the Old South, this was the first properly planned extension to the city since the concentric canals of the seventeenth century. The Dutch architect H.P. Berlage was responsible for the overall plan, but he died before it could be started and the design was largely carried out in the 1930s by two prominent architects of the Amsterdam School, Michael de Klerk and Piet Kramer.

De Klerk and Kramer were already well known for their housing estates in west and southeast Amsterdam, and Kramer had also been

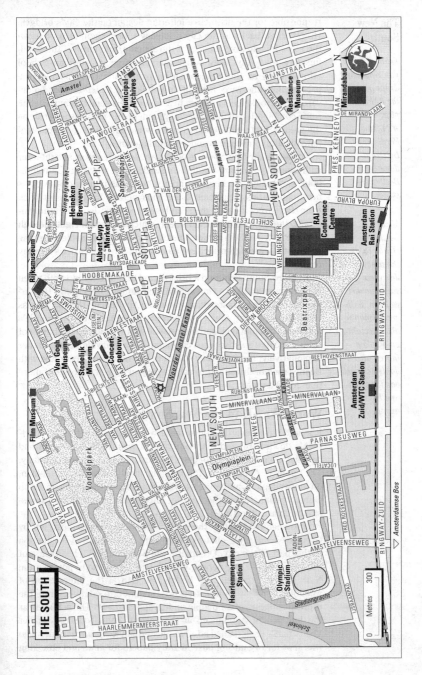

THE SOUTH

*Tram #4 from
Van Woustraat
drops you at
the RAI com-
plex; tram
#24 from
Ferdinand
Bolstraat runs
down
Beethoven-
straat.*

*Meidi-Ya,
Beethoven-
straat 18, is
the premier
Japanese
supermarket
in town, with
every imagin-
able speciality
on display;
there's also a
daytime snack
bar for sushi
and hot take-
aways.*

responsible for the distinctive lettering design on the city's bridges. However, cutbacks in the city's subsidy forced them to tone down the more imaginative aspects of the scheme, and most of the buildings are markedly more sober than previous Amsterdam School efforts, such as the Scheepvaarthuis on Prins Hendrikkade (see p.133). But otherwise they faithfully followed a plan of wide boulevards and crooked side streets in a deliberate attempt to achieve the same combination of monumental grandeur and picturesque scale as the great seventeenth-century canals, while adding the odd splash of individuality to corners, windows and balconies.

Nowadays the New South is one of Amsterdam's most sought-after addresses. **Apollolaan**, **Stadionweg** and, a little way east, **Churchill-laan**, especially, are home to luxury hotels and some of the city's most sumptuous properties, huge idiosyncratic mansions set back from the street behind trees and generous gardens. **Beethoven-straat**, the New South's main street, which run south right through the district from the Noorder Amstel canal, is a fashionable shopping boulevard, with high-priced stores catering for the district's wealthy residents.

The New South achieved a brief period of notoriety in 1969, when John Lennon and Yoko Ono staged their famous week-long "Bed-In" for peace in the **Amsterdam Hilton** at Apollolaan 138. The press came from all over; fans crowded outside, hanging on the couple's antiwar proclamations, and the episode was seen as the beginning of John and Yoko's subsequent campaign for worldwide peace. Rather exploitatively, the suite they stayed in has now been decorated with Beatles memorabilia, and to stay there you'll need to fork out more than £500 a night.

World War II in the New South

It's hard to believe that once there were few takers for the apartments down here, and that soon after it was finished the area had become a second ghetto for Jews fleeing the terror in Nazi Germany. The family of Anne Frank, for example, lived just off Churchill-laan, on Merwedeplein, and there's a whimsical brick **synagogue** on Jacob Obrechtplein, close to the Noorder Amstel canal, built in the Expressionist style of the 1930s.

If you can read Dutch, the novel *Tramhalte Beethovenstraat* by Grete Weil will give you a candid picture of the years of occupation in this part of the city. Otherwise, the New South still has plenty of reminders of the war period, when it was the scene of some of the Nazis' worst excesses. The bedraggled **trio** at the intersection of Apollolaan and Beethovenstraat was sculpted to commemorate the reprisal shooting of 29 people on this spot in 1944. The **school** near the junction of Apollolaan, at the eastern end of Gerrit van der Veenstraat – itself named after an Amsterdam Resistance fighter who was shot for organizing false identity papers for Jews and attacking

Nazi strongholds in the city – was once the headquarters of the Gestapo, where the Frank family were brought after their capture.

The former synagogue at Lekstraat 63 – some twenty minutes' walk away in the Rivierenbuurt district, south of Rooseveltlaan – houses the excellent **Verzetsmuseum** (Museum of the Dutch Resistance; Tues–Fri 10am–5pm, Sat & Sun 1–5pm; ☎644 9797; *f*4.50), charting the rise of the Dutch Resistance from the German invasion of the Netherlands in May 1940 to the country's liberation in 1945. This fascinating collection includes photos, illegal newsletters, anti-Jewish propaganda and deportation orders, and also generates interest by being interactive: slide shows and radio broadcasts start at the touch of a button, while mock-up hiding places and prison cells complete with piped-in prison sounds recreate some of the horrors faced by Dutch Resistance fighters. The museum is primarily designed for those too young to have first-hand knowledge of the period, and though purists may balk at the gimmickry, its aim of revealing the brutality and thoroughness with which the Wehrmacht forces routed Resistance members is forcefully achieved. The English exhibition guide (*f*2.50) is essential. In August and September, the Verzetsmuseum also organizes an interesting **walking tour** of the neighbourhood (*f*12.50).

The southern reaches

At the far end of Beethovenstraat, the dense trees and shrubs of the **Beatrixpark** flank the antiseptic surroundings of the adjacent **RAI exhibition centre**: a complex of trade and conference centres that was built as part of the city's plan to attract more businesspeople (and their expense accounts) to Amsterdam. It's of little general appeal, although one hall very sporadically hosts concerts and there's some good skateboarding to be had in and around the car park; if you're at a loose end, you may want to check out one of the centre's many exhibitions.

At the opposite end of the east–west Stadionweg, the **Olympic Stadium**, built for the 1928 games, is a useful landmark, although construction of the new "Amsterdam ArenA" stadium in Duivendrecht to the southeast has thrown something of a shadow over its future. A few hundred metres to the north is Haarlemmermeer Station, now operating only as the terminus of the **Museum Tramline**, on which old trams brought here from as far away as Vienna and Prague run to and from the Amsterdamse Bos further south – a more appealing, if time-consuming, option than taking the bus (see p.36 for details).

You can reach Haarlemmer-meer Station on tram #6 from Leidseplein or #16 from Centraal Station.

The Amsterdamse Bos

The **Amsterdamse Bos** (Amsterdam Forest) is the overly grand title of the city's largest open space, a 2000-acre woodland park planted during the 1930s in a mammoth project to utilize the energies of the city's unemployed. Originally a bleak area of flat, marshy fields, it combines a rural feel with that of a well-tended city park – there's very little that could be described as "forest". In the north of the park, the Bosbaan, a kilometre-long dead-straight canal, is used for boating and swimming, and there are children's playgrounds and spaces for various sports, including ice skating; there's also a reserve in the south containing bison and buffalo; or you can simply walk or jog your way around a choice of fourteen planned trails.

If you're visiting out of season, or you're not into old trams (see above), you can get here either by tram #5 from the city centre (nearest stop Van Boshuizenstraat, which entails a twenty-minute walk to the park gates), or by catching one of the yellow *NZH* buses (#170, #171 or #172) that run into Amstelveen (pronounced "amstel-fayn") – they leave from just outside the *Victoria Hotel*, opposite Centraal Station, and also stop near the Westerkerk and on Marnixstraat, near Leidsegracht. The buses follow Amstelveenseweg south, and drop you off right near the main entrance to the Bos at the junction with Van Nijenrodeweg. Once here, the best way to get around is to **rent a bicycle** (March–Oct) and follow the 27 miles of paths. It's also possible to rent canoes, canal bikes and motorboats. The **Bosmuseum**, near the southern end of the Bosbaan at Koenenkade 56 (daily 10am–5pm; ☎643 1414; free), provides maps and basic information on the park's facilities, as well as an exhibition on its history and its contemporary role.

The East

A cupolated box topped with a crudely carved pediment, the sturdy **Muiderpoort** (pronounced "mao-der-port") was the scene of Napoleon's triumphant entry into the city in 1811, and today marks the boundary between the centre of Amsterdam and the beginning of **Amsterdam East** (Oost).

The Tropenmuseum

Across the Singelgracht canal on Mauritskade, the gabled and turreted **Royal Tropen Institute** – a more respectable label for what was once the Royal Colonial Institute – has a marble and stucco entrance hall that you can peek into, but the only part that's open to visitors is the excellent **Tropenmuseum**, just around the corner at Linnaeusstraat 2 (Mon & Wed–Fri 10am–5pm, Tues 10am–9.30pm, Sat & Sun noon–5pm; ☎568 8215; ƒ10). As part of the Institute, this only used to display artefacts from the Dutch colonies, but since the 1950s, when Indonesia was granted independence, it has collected applied arts from all over and its holdings now cover the world. Most of the collection is on permanent display and is imaginatively pre-

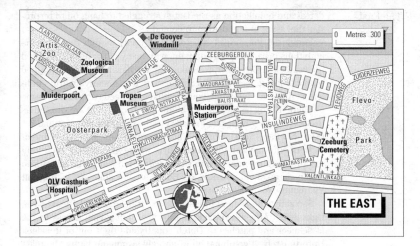

sented through a variety of media – slides, videos and sound record-
ings. All of this makes for an impressively unstuffy and honest expo-
sition of contemporary Third World life and problems, both urban –
the ever-expanding slum dwellings of cities like Bombay – and rural,
examining such issues as the wholesale destruction of the world's
tropical rainforests. As well as traditional museum fare, there are
creative and engaging displays devoted to music-making and pup-
petry, videos on traditional storytelling, and even reconstructions,
down to sounds and smells, of typical streets in India, China or Africa
– really all well worth seeing, even if you have little interest in
ethnography.

While you're here, be sure to have a look in on the **bookshop**,
which has a good selection of titles on Third World subjects. There's
also a popular **restaurant**, which serves dishes from many countries
at reasonable prices (phone to book a table, ☎568 8200); and the
Soeterijn Theatre downstairs, which specializes in cinema, music
and dance from the developing world (see p.233). Another impressive innovation is the attached **Kindermuseum** (Children's Museum;
open by reservation only; ☎568 8233; ƒ10), which deals with the
same themes as the main museum but refuses entry to anyone over
the age of twelve – see *Kids' Amsterdam* for more details.

The Oosterpark and beyond

Behind the Tropen Institute, the **Oosterpark** is a peaceful oblong of
green, and a gentle introduction to the area that extends south and
east – a solidly working-class district for the most part, particularly
on the far side of Linnaeusstraat. There's a high immigrant presence
here, and the street names – Javastraat, Balistraat, Borneostraat –
recall Holland's colonial past, an era which, after the war, ended in

defeat and humiliation as the Dutch struggled to hang on to territories they were in no position to defend.

Today the housing is still relatively poor, though there's some ambitious urban renewal going on, with many of the ageing terraced houses being torn down to make way for new and better-equipped public housing. As in the Old South, there's an underlying drug problem in this area, but while you're unlikely to need (or want) to come out here, it's by no means a forbidding district. There are two things that may make you decide to visit. Firstly, the **Dapperstraat market** (Mon–Sat 9am–5pm), close to the Tropenmuseum, which is a kind of Eastern equivalent to the Albert Cuyp, where Arab men in their long *jalabiyya* robes mingle with Dutch women in jeans, and where you can pick up a quarter-kilo of Edam at one stall and a fragrant Vietnamese *loempia* at the next.

Secondly, the second-to-last stop on tram route #14 leaves you right next to the **Flevopark**, dull in itself but giving access to the IJsselmeer and patches of Dutch countryside right out of Ruisdael. Unfortunately, a combination of an ugly swimming baths, the main Zuiderzeeweg road and the nearby A10 orbital motorway means you'll need some imagination to shut out the twentieth century. To one side of the park, the drab **Zeeburg Jewish cemetery** was once the city's major burial place for impoverished Jews, but few graves remain today.

A museum in this part of town you might want to look in on is the **Nederlands Persmuseum** (Dutch Press Museum), housed in the International Institute for Social History at Cruquiusweg 31 (Mon–Fri 9am–5pm, Sat 9.30am–1pm; ☎668 5866; free), although its displays on the history of the Dutch press since 1903, as revealed in newspapers, leaflets, posters and political cartoons, are of pretty specialized interest. The collection of the Institute itself might appeal to students of the working-class movement and international socialism, with its original letters and writings from the likes of Marx, Lenin, Bakunin and other left-wing (and anarchist) luminaries. To reach the museum, take tram #6 or #10 to Javaplein and follow Molukkenstraat north about 100m past the Zeeburgerdijk.

The West

Of all Amsterdam's outer central districts, Amsterdam West is probably the least interesting for the visitor, as it's primarily a residential area with only a couple of nondescript parks as possible attractions. The **Old West**, beyond the Singelgracht and above the Vondelpark, has a busy Turkish and North African immigrant-based street life that can be worth checking out if you find yourself in the vicinity: trams #7 and #17 run down **Kinkerstraat**, which is a good place to bargain-hunt if you're not after anything fancy, and there's also the vigorous **ten Katestraat market**, about halfway down Kinkerstraat on the right. Outside of this zone, in the New West districts of Bos en Lommer, De Baarsjes and Overtoomse Veld, there's little other than the large but run-of-the-mill **Rembrandtpark** to draw you out this far.

The North

Amsterdam **North**, on the far side of the River IJ, is probably the least visited part of Amsterdam. Cut off from the rest of the city until the construction of the IJ tunnel in the 1960s, it is entirely residential; this is where Amsterdam ends and the rest of Holland begins. Although there are patches of interest in long-inhabited districts such as the **Oud Noord**, to the west of the pretty Florapark, and **Nieuwendam**, around the Vliegenbos park and campground, much of the area reflects the worst of 1960s planning and architecture and feels very removed from the rest of Amsterdam. However, if you have some free time, the rural, village-like atmosphere of remoteness in certain parts can be something of a relief. By far the best way to see the North is to go by **bike** – the built-up area is relentlessly suburban, the streets are long, and there are no trams over here, only a limited bus service. Before you cross the river (see box), visit the VVV and pick up their leaflet (in English) detailing a bike tour of **Waterland**, an area of marshy countryside to the northeast; the leaflet includes a route to follow through Amsterdam North. The most picturesque street to ride along is the **Nieuwendammerdijk**, a long thin lane lined with tiny one-room cottages that look almost comical under their huge and elaborate gables. Follow the Meeuwenlaan from the dropping-off point of the *Adelaarswegveer* ferry (see below) and, at the big roundabout at the end, look to the right for the Nieuwendammerdijk, which runs east to join up with the long dike tracing the edge of the coast past the old fishing villages of Schellingwoude and Durgerdam.

Ferries to Amsterdam North

The *GVB* municipal transport department operates three **ferry** (*veer*) lines between central Amsterdam and the North, all of which carry foot passengers, bicycles and motorbikes – for free. The westernmost, and the only one to take cars, is the *Distelwegveer*, which leaves from the docks north of Houtmankade for Distelweg in the North (Mon–Fri 6.30am–7.30pm). The other two ferries both leave from Pier 8, behind Centraal Station: the *Buiksloterwegveer* – like a huge mobile air-traffic control tower – shuttles back and forth every ten minutes or so, 24 hours a day; the smaller *Adelaarswegveer* leaves from just beside it to the right and connects with the southern end of Meeuwenlaan (Mon–Sat 6.20am–8.50pm). Of the three, the *Adelaarswegveer* gives the best views of Centraal Station and the KNSM island, and has the advantage of parts of the deck being open to the sky and wind.

The Outer Districts: Eating and drinking

BARS IN THE SOUTH *Duvel, Hesp, Café Krull.* **Irish pubs** *O'Donnells.*

COFFEESHOPS IN THE SOUTH *Greenhouse, Katsu, Yo-Yo.*

TEAROOMS IN THE SOUTH *Granny.*

RESTAURANTS IN THE SOUTH African and Middle Eastern *Artist, Eufraat.* **American** *Cajun Louisiana Kitchen.* **Dutch** *Witteveen.* **Greek, Balkan and Turkish** *Lokanta Ceren, Saray*

Lokantasi. **Japanese** *Hotel Okura, Umeno.* **Spanish and Portuguese** *Girassol.* **Surinamese** *Warung Marlon, Warung Swietie.* **Vegetarian** *De Graal, De Waaghals.*

RESTAURANTS IN THE WEST African and Middle Eastern *Beyrouth.* **Budget** *Suzy Creamcheese.* **Greek** *Ouzeri.* **Surinamese** *Riaz.*

See *Eating and Drinking*, p.185, for exact locations and reviews.

Amsterdam: Listings

Amsterdam Listings

Chapter 8

Accommodation

Accommodation in Amsterdam is extremely difficult to find, and can be a major expense: even hostels are pricey for what you get, and the hotels are among the most expensive in Europe. The city's compactness means that you'll inevitably end up somewhere central, but if you arrive without a reservation you'll still need to search hard to find a decent place to stay. At peak times of the year – July and August, Easter and Christmas – it's extremely advisable to book ahead; hotel rooms and even hostel beds can be swallowed up remarkably quickly, and if you leave finding a room to chance, you may well be disappointed (and/or out of pocket). Most of the places we've listed – even the larger hostels – will accept bookings from abroad by fax or e-mail, although the cheaper ones may require some guarantee of payment (such as a credit card number). You can also reserve rooms in advance at no extra charge by contacting the **National Booking Centre**, PO Box 404, 2260 AK Leidschendam, The Netherlands (☎070/320 2500, fax 070/320 2611) – although they don't deal with rooms cheaper than ƒ150 per night. Once you've arrived, VVs all over the country will make advance hotel reservations for a ƒ5 fee (see *Basics*, p.25, for locations and opening times of the Amsterdam VVs); they will also book accommodation on the spot for the same fee, or simply sell you a booklet on hotels in Amsterdam (ƒ4).

To help you choose a place to stay, we've divided our listings by **area**, using the same headings as in the guide chapters – "The Old Centre", "Grachtengordel", etc. This gives a rough pointer as to what you can expect in terms of surroundings. However, bear in mind that while some of the hotels in the Old Centre are on quiet canals, many are on or close to busy traffic or pedestrian streets; you'll be right in the middle of things, but if you're looking for peace and quiet you're probably better off scanning the Grachtengordel West or South listings for a canalside location. Similarly, hotels ideally situated for the major museums (in the "Museumplein" section) might be a tram ride or a half-hour's walk from the city-centre restaurants and bars. All the hostels and hotels we describe are marked on a **map** of the relevant area. We've also pinpointed specifically **gay** or gay-friendly hotels in the listings, although it's illegal for a hotel or hostel to refuse entry to anyone on the grounds of sexual orientation.

Something to bear in mind when choosing a hotel is the fact that many of Amsterdam's buildings have narrow, very steep **staircases**, and not all hotels have installed lifts: in the older houses, construction of lifts is actually illegal. If this is a consideration for you, check before you book.

Note that all directions given are from Centraal Station (abbreviated as "CS"). For information on **camping**, see p.183.

Accommodation

Hostels

The bottom line for most travellers is tak- ing a dormitory bed in a **hostel**, and there are plenty to choose from: official Hostelling International places, unofficial private hostels, even Christian hostels; in fact, you'll probably be accosted outside the train station with numerous offers of beds. Most hostels will either provide (relatively) clean bed linen or charge a few guilders for it; your own sleeping bag might be a better option. Many hos- tels also lock guests out for a short peri- od each day, both for security reasons and to clean the place; some set a nightly curfew, though these are usually late enough not to cause too much of a problem.

The cheapest deal you'll find is around ƒ20 per person per night; at bet- ter-furnished and/or more central hostels the average is closer to ƒ30. Much more and you might as well be in a hotel room. A few otherwise friendly, good- value places have a policy of charging more at the weekends than during the week: the price hike on Friday and Saturday nights can be as much as ƒ5. Despite their protestations, there seems little excuse for this, and if you're plan- ning a weekend stay it might be worth- while moving somewhere else on Friday morning, just to bring the point home. Note that you can pay the same for a bed in a 16-person dorm as you'd pay to be in a 4-person dorm elsewhere: any place that won't allow you to see the dorm before you pay is worth avoid- ing. If you want a little extra privacy, many hostels also offer triples, doubles and singles for much less than you'd pay in a regular hotel, though the quality and size of rooms can leave a lot to be desired.

Hotels

Apart from a couple of ultra-cheap places, most of Amsterdam's **hotels** start at around ƒ80 for a double, and although some form of breakfast – "Dutch" (bread and jam) or "English" (bacon and eggs) – is normally included in the price at all but the cheapest and the most expensive hotels, some places

---

Accommodation prices

Throughout these listings we've used a code system to denote the price of the **cheap- est double room** available in high season, including breakfast. For **hostel** accommo- dation (①), the price is per person. Note that low-season prices can drop by as much as two categories and that larger hotels especially often have rooms at various prices.

① Under ƒ30 (per person)   ③ ƒ100–170   ⑥ ƒ350–450
② ƒ60–100   ④ ƒ170–250   ⑦ over ƒ450
                           ⑤ ƒ250–350

can give the barest value for money. Amsterdam has a huge number of what might be called comfortable family hotels, with basic double rooms with private bathroom hovering more or less around the ƒ175 mark (£70/$110): the ones listed here have something particular to recommend them – location, value for money or ambience. Don't be afraid to ask to see the room first, and to refuse it if you don't like it.

B&Bs, apartments and houseboats

There are very few **bed and breakfasts** in Amsterdam, although *Holiday Link*, PO Box 70160, 9704 AD Groningen (☎050/ 313 4545, fax 050/313 3177), can send you a book for ƒ7.50 that lists reputable B&Bs throughout the country. *Simon's Euroservice* (Bors van Waverenstraat 26, 1181 AM Amstelveen ☎647 5550, fax 645 5319), a small company based to the south of the city, has a list of B&Bs in and around Amsterdam, as well as the rest of Holland. Contact Simon Schetz for a copy of his B&B guide and bear in mind that you'll need to make reservations at least a month before you arrive. He can also help with hotel bookings and apartment rentals nationwide. One well-known, central B&B is run by Marcel van Woerkom (☎622 9834, fax 622 9834), an English-speaking graphic designer and artist, in a restored house on Leidsestraat with four en suite double rooms available for two, three or four people sharing, at around ƒ60 per person. The B&B is extremely popular, with regulars returning year after year, and you need to contact Marcel well in advance to stand any chance of getting a room. Another small B&B is run by Karen McCusker (☎679 2753), who moved to Amsterdam from England in 1979. Cosy and clean, Laura Ashley-style double rooms in her home, close to the Vondelpark, cost around ƒ75; again, call well in advance.

For groups or families especially, short-term **apartment** rentals can work out cheaper than staying in a hotel, with the further advantages of privacy and the convenience of self-catering. Apartments sleeping four or five can often be found for the same price as a double room in a hotel. Many places dotted all the way down the main tourist strip of Damrak advertise short- and long-term apartment rentals – although their prices can seem reasonable, check what's included (and what isn't), and insist on seeing the place yourself before you hand over any money. **Houseboat** rentals are often organized by the same people and tend to be significantly more luxurious and expensive. Apartment and houseboat rental agencies recommended by the VVV include the following:

Amsterdam House, Amstel 176a, 1017 AE Amsterdam ☎626 2577, fax 626 2987.

Gasthuismolen Apartments, Gasthuismolensteeg 10, 1016 AM Amsterdam ☎624 0736, fax 420 9991.

Leidseplein Apartments, Korte Leidsedwarsstraat 79, 1017 PW Amsterdam ☎627 2505, fax 623 0065.

The Old Centre

If you choose to stay in the Old Centre, you'll never have to search for nightlife. Cheap hotels abound in the Red Light District, as you might expect – and this is the first place to start looking if money is tight – but there's also a good selection of quiet, reasonably priced places on and off the canals, close to restaurants and shopping areas. The number in brackets after each hotel's name refers to the map on p.168.

Hostels

Bob's Youth Hostel (18), Nieuwezijds Voorburgwal 92 ☎623 0063, no fax; 10min from CS. An old favourite of backpackers, lively and smoky, *Bob's* has small, clean dorms at ƒ22 per person including breakfast in the coffeeshop on the ground floor (which also does cheap dinners). 3am curfew. ①

Budget Youth Hostel (25), Warmoesstraat 87 ☎625 5974, fax 422 0885; 5min from CS. Unremarkable scruffy hostel

Accommodation

To call Amsterdam from abroad, dial your international access code, followed by ☎31 for Holland, then ☎20 (the area code for Amsterdam, minus its initial 0), followed by the number.

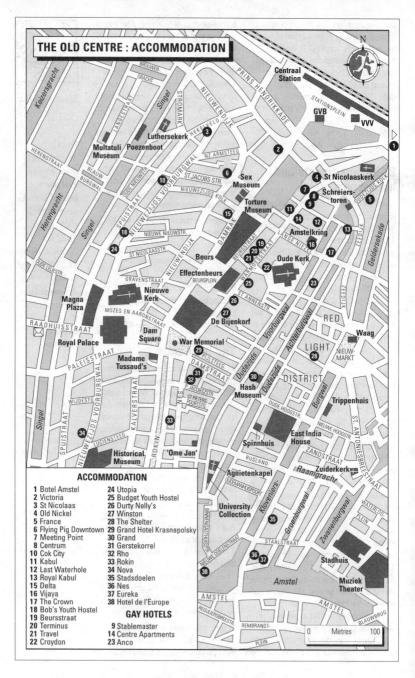

THE OLD CENTRE : ACCOMMODATION

ACCOMMODATION

1 Botel Amstel
2 Victoria
3 St Nicolaas
4 Old Nickel
5 France
6 Flying Pig Downtown
7 Meeting Point
8 Centrum
10 Cok City
11 Kabul
12 Last Waterhole
13 Royal Kabul
15 Delta
16 Vijaya
17 The Crown
18 Bob's Youth Hostel
19 Beursstraat
20 Terminus
21 Travel
22 Croydon

24 Utopia
25 Budget Youth Hostel
26 Durty Nelly's
27 Winston
28 The Shelter
29 Grand Hotel Krasnapolsky
30 Grand
31 Gerstekorrel
32 Rho
33 Rokin
34 Nova
35 Stadsdoelen
36 Nes
37 Eureka
38 Hotel de l'Europe

GAY HOTELS

9 Stablemaster
14 Centre Apartments
23 Anco

amidst the porn merchants. One-armed bandits and cheeseburgers downstairs; sheets cleaned weekly upstairs. Rock-bottom prices on dorms, doubles, triples and quads. No curfew. ①

The Crown (17), Oudezijds Voorburgwal 21 ☎626 9664, no fax; 3min from CS. Friendly hostel-cum-hotel overlooking a canal. Recently revamped small, clean dorms, plus rooms for up to four people from around ƒ40 per person – ask for the choice "honeymoon suite" in the attic. Very safe, despite the location. Late bar until 5am; breakfast extra; weekend price rise. ①–②

Croydon (22), Warmoesstraat 75 ☎627 6065, no fax; 5min from CS. Tatty dorms above a cheap restaurant; breakfast extra. No curfew. ①

Durty Nelly's (26), Warmoesstraat 115 ☎638 0125, no fax; 5min from CS. Good quality partitioned dorms above a packed Irish pub, with a cooked breakfast, sheets and lockers included. Streetside dorms are lighter and airier. ①

Flying Pig Downtown (6), Nieuwendijk 100 ☎420 6822, fax 624 9516; 5min from CS. Clean, large and well-run by ex-travellers familiar with the needs of backpackers. Free use of kitchen facilities, no curfew, and there's a late-night coffeeshop, *Twin Pigs*, next door. Hostel bar open all night. Justifiably popular, and a very good deal. See also the *Flying Pig Vondelpark*, p.180. ①

Kabul (11), Warmoesstraat 38 ☎623 7158, fax 620 0869; 3min from CS. Huge, famous and bustling, with an international clientele and multilingual staff. Rooms sleep between one and sixteen people. Higher than usual dorm rates, and higher than usual breakfast prices on top. However, it's immaculately clean, very safe, there's no lockout or curfew, and there's a late bar next door. Groups are no problem, and you can book in advance. ①

Last Waterhole (12), Oudezijds Armsteeg 12 ☎624 4814, fax 023/542 4789; 3min from CS. Long-established friendly Amsterdam dosshouse. Large dorms;

sheets and towels cost extra. Live bands most nights. Watch out for the weekend price hike. ①

Meeting Point (7), Warmoesstraat 14 ☎627 7499, fax 627 7499; 2min from CS. Warm and cosy central hostel with space in ten-bed dorms going for ƒ25 per person. Check-out 10am. ①

The Shelter (28), Barndesteeg 21 ☎625 3230, fax 623 2282; metro Nieuwmarkt. A non-evangelical Christian youth hostel smack in the middle of the Red Light District. These are the cheapest beds in Amsterdam, with a sizeable breakfast included. Dorms are single-sex, lockers cost ƒ1 and there's a midnight curfew (1am at weekends). You might be handed a booklet on Jesus when you check in, but you'll get a quiet night's sleep and the sheets are clean. ①

Stadsdoelen (35), Kloveniersburgwal 97 ☎624 6832, fax 639 1035; metro Nieuwmarkt, or tram #4, #9, #16, #24 or #25 to Muntplein. The closest to the station of the two official hostels, with clean, semi-private dorms. Sheets cost a steep ƒ6.25. HI members have priority in high season, and non-members pay a ƒ5 supplement. Guests get a range of discounts on activities in the city; you can also book *Eurolines* bus tickets here. The bar serves good-value if basic food, and there's a 2am curfew. The other HI hostel is the *Vondelpark*, see p.180. ①

Hotels

Beursstraat (19), Beursstraat 7 ☎626 3701, no fax; 5min from CS. Basic but very cheap hotel, nestling behind Berlage's Stock Exchange. However, there have been some complaints about surly management, and the raising of room prices after bookings are confirmed. ②

Botel Amstel (1), moored at Oosterdokskade 2 ☎626 4247, fax 639 1952; 2min from CS. Despite the seeming romance of a floating hotel, the rooms are all identically poky, connected by claustrophobic corridors. In-house movies or not, staying here is like

Accommodation

Accommodation

spending your holiday on the cross-Channel ferry. ③

Centrum (8), Warmoesstraat 15 ☎624 3535, fax 420 1666; 3min from CS. Under new management since 1995, and completely revamped. Considering the location, some rooms (high up and at the back) are very quiet and light. Choice of large and small rooms, with or without bath/shower. Friendly and accommodating. ②

Cok City (10), Nieuwezijds Voorburgwal 50 ☎422 0011, fax 420 0357; 10min from CS. Brand new, completely renovated hotel, which makes for a sparkling clean but rather soulless place to stay. There are three more *Cok* hotels down near the Vondelpark. Has a no-smoking floor. ④–⑤

Delta (15), Damrak 42 ☎620 2626, fax 620 3513; 10min from CS. If you really want to stay on Damrak, try this place first – uninspired, plain and characterless, but comfortable enough, it's one of the better options on a bad street. ④

Eureka (37), 's-Gravelandseveer 3 ☎624 6607, fax 624 1346; tram #4, #9, #16, #24 or #25 to Muntplein. Considering it's just across the Amstel from Rembrandtplein, this is a surprisingly quiet part of town. Rooms are small but clean and pleasant, the staff are friendly, and you're perfectly positioned for the nightlife. ④

France (5), Oudezijds Kolk 11 ☎422 3311, fax 422 3925; 2min from CS. New hotel on a tiny, very beautiful and little-used canal in the heart of the medieval centre. Small, comfortable rooms, if a little characterless. ③   250 160 loc.

Gerstekorrel (31), Damstraat 22 ☎624 1367, fax 623 2640; tram #4, #9, #16, #24 or #25 to Dam Square. Small, simple hotel, steps away from the Dam. Newly redecorated in bright colours, making the large rooms even lighter than before. On a noisy, bustling street (ask for a back room). Visit their web page at <http://www.hi.nl/klant/gersteko.htm>. ③

Grand (30), Oudezijds Voorburgwal 197 ☎555 3111, fax 555 3222; tram #4, #9, #16, #24 or #25 to Dam Square. Originally a Royal Inn dating from 1578, and after that the Amsterdam Town Hall, this extraordinary building is a centrepiece of the city's medieval district. It claims to offer "a sublime combination of luxury, warm hospitality and unrivalled grandeur". ƒ650 or so for a double. ⑦

Grand Hotel Krasnapolsky (29), Dam 9 ☎554 9111, fax 622 8607; tram #4, #9, #16, #24 or #25 to Dam Square. A huge mid-nineteenth-century building occupying an entire side of Dam Square, this is a luxuriously grand place to stay. If you can't afford the ƒ500 or more a double room costs, scrape together enough to have a coffee in the fabulous Winter Garden, occupying a spectacular atrium space in the centre of the hotel. ⑦

Hotel de l'Europe (38), Nieuwe Doelenstraat 2 ☎623 4836, fax 624 2962; tram #4, #9, #16, #24 or #25 to Muntplein. Completely redecorated in the last few years, this very central hotel retains a wonderful *fin-de-siècle* charm, with large, well-furnished rooms and a very attractive riverside terrace. A liveried flunkey and red carpet on the pavement outside complete the picture. ⑦

Nes (36), Kloveniersburgwal 137 ☎624 4773, fax 620 9842; tram #4, #9, #16, #24 or #25 to Muntplein. Extremely pleasant and quiet, with a lift; well-positioned away from noise but close to shops and nightlife. Helpful staff. Prices vary, depending on the view. ④

Nova (34), Nieuwezijds Voorburgwal 276 ☎623 0066, fax 627 2026, e-mail <novahtl@pi.net>; tram #1, #2, #5 or #11 to Spui. Under new management since 1995 and now by far the best option at the lower end of this price bracket. Spotless rooms, all en suite and with fridge and TV; friendly staff, a lift and secure access. Perfect, quiet location. Winter discounts. Check out their web site at <http://www.grand.nl/nova>. ④

Old Nickel (4), Nieuwe Brugsteeg 11 ☎624 1912, fax 620 7683, USA contact ☎510/524-6767; 2min from CS. Homely pub with simple rooms above, run by the same family for 20 years. ②

Rho (32), Nes 5 ☎620 7371, fax 620 7826; tram #4, #9, #16, #24 or #25 to Dam Square. A very comfortable hotel in a quiet alley off Dam Square, with an extraordinary high-ceilinged lounge, originally built as a theatre in 1908. The staff let the place down a little, but it's still a fine city-centre option. ④

Rokin (33), Rokin 73 ☎626 7456, fax 625 6453; tram #4, #9, #16, #24 or #25 to Dam or Spui. Something of a bargain considering the location, with doubles from ƒ120, including breakfast. ③

Royal Kabul (13), Oudezijds Voorburgwal 3 ☎638 1461, fax 638 1046; 5min from CS. Beyond the psychedelic hallway, the rooms – some dorms, some doubles and triples – are all a little musty and dusty, but the canalside location is wonderful. Free entry to the *Amnesia* disco downstairs. ③

St Nicolaas (3), Spuistraat 1a ☎626 1384, fax 623 0979; 3min from CS. Very pleasant, well-run little hotel housed in a former mattress factory (with a king-size lift to prove it). All-wood decor throughout, all rooms are en suite and scrupulously clean; the only minus is the traffic noise. Recommended. ③

Terminus (20), Beursstraat 11 ☎622 0535, fax 627 2216; 10min from CS. Small rooms in a rather gloomy hotel on seedy Beursstraat. There's a lift, but you still need to climb the stairs to get to some rooms. ④

Travel (21), Beursstraat 23 ☎626 6532, no fax; 10min from CS. Small, simple hotel on a dingy street; very clean and comfortable inside, with a quiet 24-hr bar and no curfew. Light years away from the backpacker style of nearby places. ③

Utopia (24), Nieuwezijds Voorburgwal 132 ☎626 1295, fax 622 7060; 10min from CS. Self-confessed "smokers' hotel" above a coffeeshop – tiny, musty rooms over the street, reached by a near-vertical staircase. Basic but welcoming. ②

Victoria (2), Damrak 1 ☎623 4255, fax 625 2997; opposite CS. Completely refurbished, this is one of the landmarks of the city, a tall, elegant building, tastefully decorated throughout. Chet Baker, the legendary jazz trumpeter, jumped to his death from one of the upper rooms, but the current management aren't letting on which one. ⑥

Vijaya (16), Oudezijds Voorburgwal 44 ☎626 9406, fax 620 5277; 10min from CS. Stately old canal house in the heart of the Red Light District, with accommodating management and plain rooms. Clean, but no lift. 10 percent discount in winter. ③

Winston (27), Warmoesstraat 123 ☎623 1380, fax 639 2308, e-mail <winston@xs4all.nl>; 10min from CS. Completely refurbished, this is now an ultramodern, very safe and affordable hotel, with light and airy rooms (sleeping from 1 to 8) on 6 floors, some en suite, some with a communal balcony. The management has a two-year plan to get major companies to redecorate all 67 rooms: the Durex Room is already complete, with the Heineken Room and the Chesterfield Room to follow. Lift and full disabled access. Highly recommended. Visit their web site at: <http://www.lostcity.nl/winston>. ③

Gay hotels

Anco (23), Oudezijds Voorburgwal 55 ☎624 1126, fax 620 5275; 10min from CS. Small and friendly hotel, catering exclusively to leather-wearing gay men, in the Red Light District. ③

Centre Apartments (14), Heintje Hoeksteeg 27 ☎627 2503, fax 625 1108; 5min from CS. Studios and apartments for rent in the middle of the Old Centre. The same people also run a small, less expensive guesthouse out in the Jordaan, with singles and doubles. ③

Stablemaster (9), Warmoesstraat 23 ☎625 0148, fax 624 8747; 5min from CS. Small, exclusively male gay hotel above a popular leather bar in the heart of the Red Light action; English-speaking staff. ③

Accommodation

Accommodation

Grachtengordel West

The western section of the canal ring, while only a few minutes' walk from the bustle of Dam Square, has a number of quiet canalside hotels; the Anne Frank House and some of the smaller museums are also close by. There are cheaper options to be found in the strip of hotels on Raadhuisstraat, one of the city's busiest traffic streets. The numbers in brackets in the following listings refer to the map below.

Hotels

Aspen (10), Raadhuisstraat 31 ☎626 6714, fax 620 0866; tram #13, #14 or #17 to Westermarkt. One of a number of inexpensive hotels situated in the Art Nouveau crescent of the Utrecht Building. ③

Brian (3), Singel 69 ☎624 4661, no fax; 10min from CS. Good value at ƒ90 for a double, including breakfast; equally inexpensive triple and quadruple rooms available. But if you're looking for somewhere peaceful, this isn't it. ②

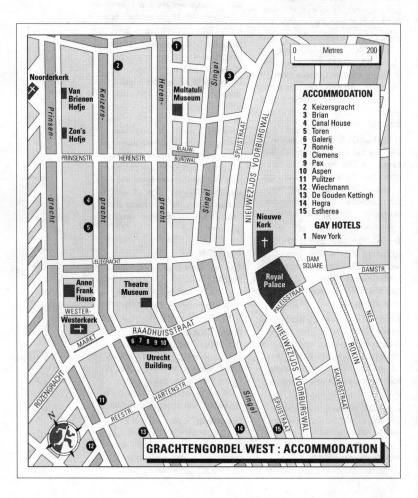

ACCOMMODATION

2 Keizersgracht
3 Brian
4 Canal House
5 Toren
6 Galerij
7 Ronnie
8 Clemens
9 Pax
10 Aspen
11 Pulitzer
12 Wiechmann
13 De Gouden Kettingh
14 Hegra
15 Estherea

GAY HOTELS

1 New York

GRACHTENGORDEL WEST : ACCOMMODATION

Canal House (4), Keizersgracht 148 ☎622 5182, fax 624 1317; tram #13, #14 or #17 to Westermarkt. Magnificently restored seventeenth-century building, centrally located on one of the principal canals. American family-run hotel with a friendly bar and cosy rooms, towards the top of this price bracket. ④ 235

Clemens (8), Raadhuisstraat 39 ☎624 6089, fax 626 9658; tram #13, #14 or #17 to Westermarkt. Just one of the options on this hotel strip. Clean, neat and good value for money. This is one of the city's busiest streets, so ask for a room at the back. ③

Estherea (15), Singel 303 ☎624 5146, fax 623 9001; tram #1, #2, #5 or #11 to Spui. Pleasant middle-of-the-road hotel converted from a row of canal houses; the rooms vary in quality but all are comfortable. ⑤

Galerij (6), Raadhuisstraat 43 ☎624 8851, fax 622 6975; tram #13, #14 or #17 to Westermarkt. One of the Raadhuisstraat budget options. Breakfast not included. ③

De Gouden Kettingh (13), Keizersgracht 268 ☎624 8287, fax 623 9958; tram #13, #14 or #17 to Westermarkt. Rambling old canal house popular with a British and business clientele. The fanciest and best rooms overlook the canal, though all are spacious and pleasant. ④

Hegra (14), Herengracht 269 ☎623 7877, fax 623 8159; tram #1, #2, #5 or #11 to Spui. Welcoming atmosphere and relatively cheap for the location, on a beautiful stretch of the canal. ③

Keizersgracht (2), Keizersgracht 15 ☎625 1364, fax 620 7347; 5min from CS. Terrific location on a major canal close to the station, with a good mixture of small dorms, singles and doubles, all spotless, from ƒ40 per person; breakfast is extra. ②

Pax (9), Raadhuisstraat 37 ☎624 9735, no fax; tram #13, #14 or #17 to Westermarkt. Basic city-centre cheapie with fair-sized rooms – breakfast is extra.

As with most of the hotels along here, ask for a room at the back. ③

Pulitzer (11), Prinsengracht 315 ☎523 5235, fax 627 6753; tram #13, #14 or #17 to Westermarkt. An entire row of seventeenth-century canal houses converted into a determinedly luxurious hotel that's often rated the best in Amsterdam. Subsidence over the centuries means that the inside of the hotel is a warren of steep stairs and crooked corridors, which only adds to its character. Individually decorated rooms are delightful and some have lift access; you're also spoiled for choice between canal views and windows overlooking the sumptuous internal courtyard. Around ƒ500 for a double. ⑦

Ronnie (7), Raadhuisstraat 41 ☎624 2821, fax 661 3639; tram #13, #14 or #17 to Westermarkt. Owned by the American cousins of the *Clemens*'s owners, and with equally good prices and facilities. Friendly and helpful; three-, four- and five-person rooms available. ③

Toren (5), Keizersgracht 164 ☎622 6352, fax 626 9705; tram #13, #14 or #17 to Westermarkt. Fine example of a seventeenth-century canal house, once the home of a Dutch prime minister. Retains a good deal of grace. No lift. ④

Wiechmann (12), Prinsengracht 328 ☎626 3321, fax 626 8962; tram #13, #14 or #17 to Westermarkt. Another canal-house restoration project, family-run for 50 years, with dark wood beams and restrained style throughout. Rooms kept in perfect condition. Close to the Anne Frank House. ④

Gay hotels

New York (1), Herengracht 13 ☎624 3066, fax 620 3230; 5min from CS. Exceptionally popular, exclusively gay hotel, consisting of three modernized seventeenth-century houses. Noted for its high standards. ④

Accommodation

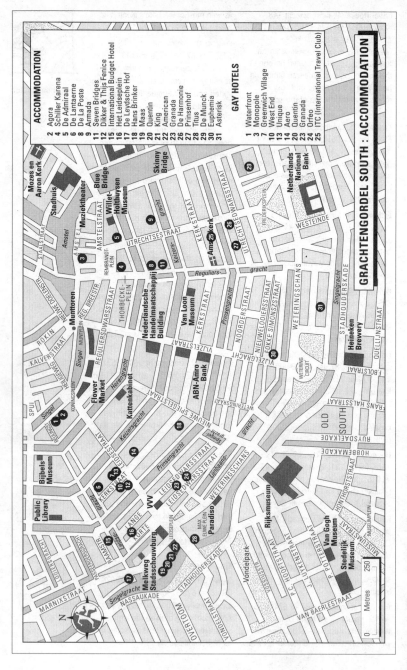

ACCOMMODATION

2 Agora
4 Schiller Karena
5 De Admiral
6 De Lantaerne
8 De La Poste
9 Armada
11 Seven Bridges
12 Dikker & Thijs Fenice
15 International Budget Hotel
16 Het Leidseplein
17 De Leydsche Hof
18 Hans Brinker
19 Maas
20 Quentin
21 King
22 American
23 Granada
26 De Harmonie
27 Prinsenhof
28 Titus
29 De Munck
30 Euphemia
31 Asterisk

GAY HOTELS

1 Waterfront
3 Monopole
7 Greenwich Village
10 West End
13 Unique
14 Aero
20 Quentin
23 Granada
24 Orfeo
25 ITC (International Travel Club)

GRACHTENGORDEL SOUTH : ACCOMMODATION

Grachtengordel South

The southern section of the canal circle is an appealing area to stay, whether you're looking for bustling nightlife or peace and quiet. There are plenty of hotels for all budgets close to the bars and restaurants of Leidseplein and Rembrandtplein, plus a number of very pleasant options along the surrounding canals. The number in brackets in each listing refers to the map on p.174.

Hostels

Euphemia (30), Fokke Simonszstraat 1 ☎622 9045, fax 622 9045, e-mail <euphjm@pi.net>; tram #16, #24 or #25 to Weteringcircuit. Situated a shortish walk from Leidseplein and the major museums, with a likeable laid-back atmosphere: basic rooms are big and have TVs, showers are free, and prices are very reasonable, which means it's usually full. Doubles from ƒ100, three- and four-bed rooms for ƒ30–40 per person. Breakfast is extra. ②

Hans Brinker (18), Kerkstraat 136 ☎622 0687, fax 638 2060; tram #1, #2, #5 or #11 to Prinsengracht. Well-established and raucously popular Amsterdam cheapie, though a little more upmarket than some, with dorm beds going for around ƒ40. Singles and doubles also available at hotel-like prices. The facilities are good, basic and clean, and it's very close to the Leidseplein buzz, but there's little to recommend this place over a normal hotel. ②

International Budget Hotel (15), Leidsegracht 76 ☎624 2784, no fax; email <euphjm@pi.net>; tram #1, #2, #5 or #11 to Prinsengracht. An excellent budget option on a peaceful little canal in the heart of the city, with the same owners as the *Euphemia*. Small, simple rooms for up to four (ƒ40 per person), with singles and doubles available. Friendly young staff. ②

Hotels

Agora (2), Singel 462 ☎627 2200; fax 627 2202; tram #1, #2, #5 or #11 to Koningsplein. Nicely located, small and amiable hotel right near the flower market; doubles cost upwards of ƒ135, three- and four-bed rooms proportionately less. Many rooms have canal views, and the wood-beam decor is delightful. ③

De Admiraal (5), Herengracht 563 ☎626 2150, fax 623 4625; tram #4, #9 or #14 to Rembrandtplein. Friendly hotel close to the nightlife, with wonderful canal views. ③

American (22), Leidsekade 97 ☎624 5322, fax 625 3236; tram #1, #2, #5 or #11 to Leidseplein. Landmark Art Deco hotel dating from 1902 (and in pristine, renovated condition), right on Leidseplein and the water. Large, double-glazed, modern doubles from around ƒ500. If you can't afford to stay, don't leave Amsterdam without soaking up some of the atmosphere at the popular and superbly decorated *Café Americain* overlooking the square. ⑦

Armada (9), Keizersgracht 713 ☎623 2980, fax 623 5829; tram #4 to Keizersgracht. Large if slightly tatty rooms close by the Amstel; at the low end of the price band. ④

Asterisk (31), Den Texstraat 16 ☎624 1768, fax 638 2790; tram #16, #24 or #25 to Weteringcircuit. Good-value budget hotel on the edge of the city centre, just across the canal from the Heineken Brewery. ③

Dikker & Thijs Fenice (12), Prinsengracht 444 ☎626 7721, fax 625 8986; tram #1, #2, #5 or #11 to Prinsengracht. Small and stylish hotel, recently lavishly redecorated, on a beautiful canal close to all the shops. Breakfast not included. ⑤

Granada (23), Leidsekruisstraat 13 ☎623 6711, fax 622 8143; tram #1, #2, #5 or #11 to Leidseplein. Small, unremarkable rooms near Leidseplein in this gay- and lesbian-friendly hotel. ③

De Harmonie (26), Prinsengracht 816 ☎625 0174, fax 622 8021; tram #4 to Prinsengracht. Thoroughly renovated, some rooms are rather small, but it's

Accommodation

Accommodation

nice and central, not far from Rembrandtplein. The Irish manager is the height of politeness. ③

Het Leidseplein (16), Korte Leidsedwarsstraat 79 ☎627 2505, fax 623 0065; tram #1, #2, #5 or #11 to Leidseplein. Smart, mid-sized hotel sandwiched between the calm of Leidsegracht and frenetic Leidseplein. ④

King (21), Leidsekade 85 ☎624 9603, fax 620 7277; tram #1, #2, #5 or #11 to Leidseplein. Nicely situated hotel on the water next to the *American Hotel*; unremarkable doubles from ƒ120. ③

De Lantaerne (6), Leidsegracht 111 ☎623 2221, fax 623 2683; tram #1, #2, #5 or #11 to Leidseplein. Well located for the *Melkweg* and all the nightlife, but rather seedy, despite the elegant building. It can get noisy too, and the management aren't overly friendly. ③

 De Leydsche Hof (17), Leidsegracht 14 ☎623 2148, no fax; tram #1, #2, #5 or #11 to Keizersgracht. Stately canal house on one of the smaller and quieter waterways. ③

Maas (19), Leidsekade 91 ☎623 3868, fax 622 2613; tram #1, #2, #5 or #11 to Leidseplein. Recently renovated hotel on a quiet stretch of water; clean and nicely decorated rooms – ask for the waterbed! ④

De Munck (29), Achtergracht 3 ☎623 6283, fax 620 6647; tram #4 to Frederiksplein. Quiet, clean and recently renovated old hotel steps from the Amstel; the friendly, laid-back proprietor has been known to give off-season discounts. The breakfast room sports a period jukebox with a good collection of 1960s hits. ③

De La Poste (8), Reguliersgracht 3 ☎623 7105, no fax; tram #4 to Herengracht. Slightly shabby rooms (from around ƒ170) in an otherwise friendly enough hotel, steps from Rembrandtplein. ④

Prinsenhof (27), Prinsengracht 810 ☎623 1772, fax 638 3368; tram #4 to Prinsengracht. Tastefully decorated, this is one of the city's top budget options; the

best rooms are at the back. ③

Quentin (20), Leidsekade 89 ☎626 2187, fax 622 0121; tram #1, #2, #5 or #11 to Leidseplein. Very friendly small hotel, often a stopover for artists performing at the *Melkweg*. Welcoming to all, and especially well-regarded among gay and lesbian visitors, but families with children might feel out of place. ③

Schiller Karena (4), Rembrandtplein 26 ☎623 1660, fax 624 0098; tram #4, #9 or #14 to Rembrandtplein. Once something of an artists' hangout, and still has one of the city's best-known and most atmospheric bars on its ground floor. Named after the painter and architect Schiller, whose works are liberally sprinkled throughout the hotel. Wonderful Art Deco furnishings in all the public areas. The drawback is its location on tacky Rembrandtplein. ⑤

★ **Seven Bridges** (11), Reguliersgracht 31 ☎623 1329; tram #4 to Prinsengracht. Perhaps the city's most charming hotel – and certainly one of its better-value ones – with a lovely (and convenient) canalside location and beautifully decorated, spotless rooms. Small and popular, so often booked solid. Breakfast is served in your room. ③

Titus (28), Leidsekade 74 ☎626 5758, fax 638 5870; tram #1, #2, #5 or #11 to Leidseplein. Variable rooms from ƒ120. One of several similarly priced hotels along this stretch of the Leidsekade. ③

Gay hotels

Aero (14), Kerkstraat 49 ☎622 7728, fax 638 8531; tram #1, #2, #5 or #11 to Prinsengracht. Sixteen clean enough rooms, many with shower and/or toilet. Off-season discounts a possibility. No single rooms. ③

Granada (23), Leidsekruisstraat 13 ☎623 6711, fax 622 8143. See main listings above. ③

Greenwich Village (7), Kerkstraat 25 ☎626 9746, fax 625 4081; tram #1, #2, #5 or #11 to Prinsengracht. A well-kept, if slightly down-at-heel hotel surrounded by gay bars and clubs on Amsterdam's main gay street. Helpful and friendly staff. ②–③

ITC (International Travel Club) (25), Prinsengracht 1051 ☎623 0230, fax 624 5846; tram #4 to Prinsengracht. A little way away from the major gay areas, close to the Amstelveld on a tranquil section of canal, and perhaps the least expensive gay hotel of this quality. Off-season discounts. ③

Monopole (3), Amstel 60 ☎624 6271, no fax; tram #4, #9 or #14 to Rembrandtplein. Overlooking the Amstel, very close to the Muziektheater, and right next door to the *Monopole Taverne* and all the Rembrandtplein nightlife. Singles, doubles, triples and quadruples. ②–③

Orfeo (24), Leidsekruisstraat 14 ☎623 1347, no fax; tram #1, #2, #5 or #11 to Prinsengracht. Very pleasant hotel round the back of Leidseplein, with a small Finnish sauna for guests and decent breakfasts served until midday. ③

Quentin (20), Leidsekade 89 ☎626 2187, fax 622 0121. See main listings above. ③

Unique (13), Kerkstraat 37 ☎624 4785, fax 627 0164; tram #1, #2, #5 or #11 to Prinsengracht. Solid budget option on Kerkstraat. ③

Waterfront (1), Singel 458 ☎623 9775, fax 620 7491; tram #1, #2, #5 or #11 to Koningsplein. Smart hotel on a major canal, close to the shopping and nightlife, but a little on the pricey side. ④

West End (10), Kerkstraat 42 ☎624 8074, fax 622 9997. Another conveniently located hotel for the Kerkstraat area, if a little musty, with the late-night *Cosmo* bar downstairs as its main attraction; breakfast not included. ②–③

Jordaan

Staying in the Jordaan puts you in among the locals and well away from the hustle and bustle of the tourist centres. There's no shortage of bars and restaurants in this up-and-coming area – and some of the most beautiful of the city's canals – but you'll be at least fif-teen minutes' walk from the bright lights. Beware that Marnixstraat and Rozengracht are busy traffic streets. The numbers in brackets in the listings refer to the map on p.178.

Hostels

Arrivé (3), Haarlemmerstraat 65 ☎622 1439, fax 622 1983; 10min from CS. A spruced-up hostel with small dorms, singles and doubles for what are in essence hotel prices. Friendly enough, but nothing to write home about. Breakfast included. ②

Eben Haezer (7), Bloemstraat 179 ☎624 4717, fax 627 6137; tram #13, #14 or #17 to Marnixstraat. One of Amsterdam's two Christian youth hostels (the other is the *Shelter*), though neither is evangelical. Lowest bed prices in the city, with breakfast and bedlinen included. Dorms are single-sex, lockers cost ƒ1 and there's a 1am curfew. Sited in a particularly beautiful part of the Jordaan, close to the Lijnbaansgracht canal. ①

Hotels

Acacia (5), Lindengracht 251 ☎622 1460, fax 638 0748; 15min from CS. Amicable hotel run by a young married couple. They let self-catering apartments too. ③

De Bloeiende Ramenas (1), Haarlemmerdijk 61 ☎624 6030, fax 420 2261; 15min from CS. A cross between hostel and hotel, friendly and welcoming, with comfortable rooms at sensible prices. Only disadvantage is the location, to the northwest of the centre and away from any action. ②

La Bohème (8), Marnixstraat 415 ☎624 2828, fax 627 2897; tram #1, #2, #5 or #11 to Leidseplein. One of the best of the many, many hotels spreading up the Marnixstraat from Leidseplein, this small hotel with super-friendly staff has en suite doubles for ƒ105. ③

Schröder (2), Haarlemmerdijk 48b ☎626 6272, fax 620 7683; 15min from CS. Tiny little hotel out on the western edge of the city centre; breakfast not included. ②

Accommodation

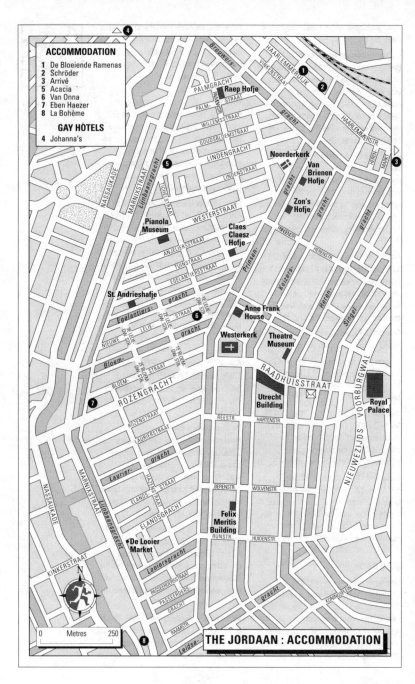

ACCOMMODATION

1 De Bloeiende Ramenas
2 Schröder
3 Arrivé
5 Acacia
6 Van Onna
7 Eben Haezer
8 La Bohème

GAY HOTELS

4 Johanna's

THE JORDAAN : ACCOMMODATION

Van Onna (6) Bloemgracht 102 ☎626 5801, no fax; tram #13, #14 or #17 to Westermarkt. A quiet, comfortable little family-run place on a tranquil canal. ③

Gay hotels

Johanna's (4), Van Hogendorpplein 62 ☎684 8596, fax 684 8596; tram #10 from Leidseplein to Van Limburg Stirumplein. A privately run B&B for gay women; gay men are also welcome. Very friendly and helpful to newcomers. A little difficult to get to, situated out near the Westergasfabriek, but with excellent prices. Johanna also rents out a five-person apartment. Call before you arrive. ②

Jodenbuurt

Very few tourists venture out this way: the streets and canals off the main traffic arteries of Weesperstraat and Plantage Middenlaan are purely residential, with very few bars or restaurants. While

you're pretty much guaranteed a quiet night's sleep here, you'll be a tram ride away from any of the main sights. The number in brackets in each listing refers to the map below.

Hostels

Adam and Eve (4), Sarphatistraat 105 ☎624 6206, fax 638 7200; metro Weesperplein, or tram #6, #7 or #10 from Leidseplein. Good quality, low-budget accommodation; not too far outside the centre and well served by public transport. Mixed and single-sex dorms for around f22 per person (including breakfast). No curfew. ①

Arena (2), 's-Gravensandestraat 51 ☎694 7444, no fax; metro Weesperplein, then walk, or tram #6 from Leidseplein to Korte 's-Gravensandestraat. A little way out of the centre to the east, in a renovated old convent on the edge of the Oosterpark, this place is reinventing itself as a major centre for youth culture.

Accommodation

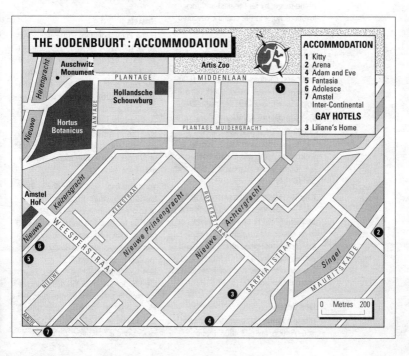

Accommodation

Simply furnished dorms in the attic provide some of the best value accommodation in the city, from ƒ23 per person. Rooms of all sizes are available at good-value prices (en suite doubles from ƒ90), although there is an inescapable (but returnable) ƒ40 deposit. Women-only dorms at peak times. Lockers available. Facilities include an excellent and varied programme of live music, an information centre, bike rental, a great bar and restaurant, the convent gardens, and even parking facilities. Open year-round, but closes 11am–3pm. Wheelchair access. ①

Hotels

Adolesce (6), Nieuwe Keizersgracht 26 ☎626 3959, fax 627 4249; tram #9 or #14 to Waterlooplein. Nicely situated just off the Amstel, on a broad, quiet canal decked with trees. ③

Amstel Inter-Continental (7), Professor Tulpplein 1 ☎622 6060, fax 622 5808; metro Weesperplein. The absolute top-of-the-range; by far the best and most luxurious hotel in the country. Favoured by visiting celebrities and recently renovated in sumptuous style to the tune of ƒ60 million. If you have the money, splash out on a night of ultimate style and class; cheapest doubles from ƒ800. If you're in a regal mood, check out the Royal Suite from ƒ4250 per night. ⑦

Fantasia (5), Nieuwe Keizersgracht 16 ☎623 8259, fax 622 3913; tram #9 or #14 to Waterlooplein. Large, popular and welcoming hotel, with neat if unspectacular rooms and a large dining room and bar. ③

Kitty (1), Plantage Middenlaan 40 ☎622 6819, no fax; tram #9 or #14 to Plantage Badlaan. A little out from the centre, but in an interesting neighbourhood close to the Zoo. Decent-sized rooms for ƒ105 a double, including as much breakfast as you can eat; we've had some complaints about the service. ③

Gay hotels

Liliane's Home (3), Sarphatistraat 119 ☎627 4006, fax 627 4006; metro Weesperplein. A privately run B&B "for women and their gay boyfriends". Liliane runs the place herself, and doesn't have many rooms, so call first. Single ƒ65, double from ƒ110, with triples and quads available. She also rents out two nearby apartments. ③

Museumplein and the Vondelpark

The main reason for staying this far out of the centre is to be within spitting distance of the three main museums – although the nightlife around Leidseplein is also close by. There are no canals in the area, and Overtoom and 1e Constantijn Huygensstraat constantly rumble with traffic, but there are plenty of quiet and comfortable hotels in the smaller side streets, as well as two of the city's best hostels on the edges of the gorgeous Vondelpark. The numbers in brackets in the listings refer to the map opposite.

Hostels

Flying Pig Vondelpark (10), Vossiusstraat 46 ☎400 4187, fax 400 4105; tram #1, #2, #5 or #11 to Leidseplein, then walk. The better of the two *Flying Pig* hostels (the other is on Nieuwendijk, in the centre), immaculately clean and well maintained by a staff of travellers, who well understand their backpacking guests. Free use of kitchen facilities, no curfew and good tourist information. Dorms start at ƒ24 per person, with rooms available too. Great value. ①

Vondelpark (6), Zandpad 5 ☎683 1744, fax 616 6591; tram #1, #2, #5 or #11 to Leidseplein, then walk. Well located and, for facilities, the better of the two HI hostels, with a bar, restaurant, TV lounge and kitchen. As with the *Stadsdoelen* in the centre, sheets cost ƒ6.25 and members have priority in high season. Rates are ƒ26 per person in the dorms, including breakfast, and non-HI members pay ƒ5 extra. Singles, doubles and rooms sleeping up to six are available. Secure lockers and a lift. Curfew 2am. ①

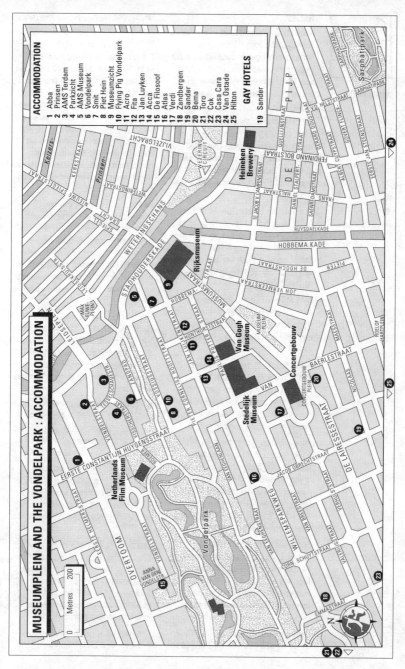

MUSEUMPLEIN AND THE VONDELPARK : ACCOMMODATION

ACCOMMODATION

1 Abba
2 Prinsen
3 AMS Terdam
4 Parkzicht
5 AMS Museum
6 Vondelpark
7 Smit
8 Piet Hein
9 Museumzicht
10 Flying Pig Vondelpark
11 Acro
12 Fita
13 Jan Luyken
14 Acca
15 De Filosoof
16 Atlas
17 Verdi
18 Zandbergen
19 Sander
20 Bema
21 Toro
22 Cok
23 Casa Cara
24 Van Ostade
25 Hilton

GAY HOTELS

19 Sander

Metres 0   200

Heineken Brewery

Rijksmuseum

Van Gogh Museum

Concertgebouw

Stedelijk Museum

Netherlands Film Museum

Vondelpark

Accommodation

Hotels

Abba (1), Overtoom 122 ☎618 3058, fax 685 3477; tram #1 or #11 to 1e Constantijn Huygensstraat. Well-worn but clean rooms awaiting imminent renovation. Friendly, helpful staff; winter discounts. Busy street location, though. ②–③

Acca (14), Van de Veldestraat 3a ☎662 5262, fax 679 9361; tram #2 or #5 to Van Baerlestraat. Intimate little hotel barely a minute from the Stedelijk and Van Gogh museums. Near the top of this price band and beginning to look a little tatty. ③

Acro (11), Jan Luykenstraat 44 ☎662 0526, fax 675 0811; tram #2 or #5 to Van Baerlestraat. Excellent, modern hotel that's been completely refurbished with stylish rooms, a plush bar and self-service restaurant. Well worth the money. ③

AMS Museum (5), P.C. Hooftstraat 2 ☎662 1402, fax 673 3918; tram #2 or #5 to Hobbemastraat. Large and luxurious hotel next door to the Rijksmuseum. ④

AMS Terdam (3), Tesselschadestraat 23 ☎612 6876, fax 683 8313; tram #1, #2, #5 or #11 to Leidseplein, then walk. Large, clean, comfortable hotel close to the museums, with a pleasant enough interior and helpful enough staff. ④

Atlas (16), Van Eeghenstraat 64 ☎676 6336, fax 671 7633; tram #2 to Jacob Obrechtstraat. Situated just to one side of the Vondelpark, this Art Nouveau building houses a personable modern hotel with every convenience and comfort. Small, tranquil and very welcoming. Dinner served on request. ④

Bema (20), Concertgebouwplein 19b ☎679 1396, fax 662 3688; tram #5 to Museumplein. Small but friendly place, kept very clean by the English-speaking manager. The rooms aren't modern, but they're full of character. Handy for concerts and museums. ②

Casa Cara (23), Emmastraat 24 ☎662 3135, fax 676 8119; tram #2 or #16 to Emmastraat. Homely hotel a few minutes from the Concertgebouw and major museums. ②

Cok (22), Koninginneweg 34 ☎664 6111, fax 664 5304; tram #2 to Valeriusplein. Actually three hotels on one site: Tourist Class, Superior Tourist Class and Business Class, with doubles ranging from ƒ200 to ƒ280 depending on which you choose. All are packed with facilities, but make for rather soulless places to stay. The majority of trade comes from package holidaymakers, which means it's crammed during summer months. ④–⑤

De Filosoof (15), Anna van den Vondelstraat 6 ☎683 3013, fax 685 3750; tram #1 or #11 to Jan Pieter Heijestraat. Hospitable small hotel on a charming little street off the Vondelpark, which for some reason names each of its rooms after a different philosopher, with decor to suit. Unique and attractive. ③–④

Fita (12), Jan Luykenstraat 37 ☎679 0976, fax 664 3969; tram #2 or #5 to Van Baerlestraat. Mid-sized, friendly hotel that's been recently revamped – all rooms have bathrooms. In a quiet spot between the Vondelpark and the museums. ④

Jan Luyken (13), Jan Luykenstraat 58 ☎573 0730, fax 676 3841; tram #2 or #5 to Van Baerlestraat. Elegant, privately run hotel in imposing nineteenth-century town houses. Stylish and comfortable. ⑤

Museumzicht (9), Jan Luykenstraat 22 ☎671 5224, fax 671 3597; tram #2 or #5 to Hobbemastraat. Overlooking the Rijksmuseum, with 14 plain-ish rooms on the upper floors of a Victorian house. ②

Parkzicht (4), Roemer Visscherstraat 33 ☎618 1954, fax 618 0897; tram #1 or #11 to 1e Constantijn Huygensstraat. Quiet, unassuming little hotel on a pretty backstreet near the Vondelpark and museums, with an appealingly lived-in look – clean and characterful. ③

Piet Hein (8), Vossiusstraat 53 ☎662 7205, fax 662 1526; tram #2 or #5 to

Hobbemastraat. Calm, low-key and clean, tucked away on a quiet street running past the Vondelpark, midway between Leidseplein and the Concertgebouw. Has had a major revamp recently – ask for the honeymoon suite with waterbed. ③

Prinsen (2), Vondelstraat 38 ☎616 2323, fax 616 6112; tram #1 or #11 to 1e Constantijn Huygensstraat. Affable, refurbished family-style hotel on the edge of the Vondelpark; quiet and with a large, secluded garden at the back. ③

Sander (19), Jacob Obrechtstraat 69 ☎662 7574, fax 679 6067; tram #16 to Jacob Obrechtstraat. Right behind the Concertgebouw, a spacious, pleasant

hotel, welcoming to gay men and women, and everyone else too. ③

Smit (7), P.C. Hooftstraat 24 ☎671 4785, fax 662 9161; tram #2 or #5 to Hobbemastraat. Slightly variable doubles for around ƒ160. ③

Toro (21), Koningslaan 64 ☎673 7223, fax 675 0031; tram #2 to Emmastraat. Lovely hotel in two very comfortably furnished turn-of-the-century town houses on a peaceful residential street by the southern reaches of the Vondelpark. Has its own garden and terrace overlooking a lake in the park. ④

Verdi (17), Wanningstraat 9 ☎676 0073, fax 673 9070; tram #5 to Museumplein.

Accommodation

Campsites

There are several **campsites** in and around Amsterdam, most of them easily accessible by car or public transport. The four listed below are recommended by the VVV, which divides them into "youth campsites", which are self-explanatory, and "family campsites", which are more suitable for those seeking some quiet, or touring with a caravan or camper.

Youth Campsites
Vliegenbos, Meeuwenlaan 138 ☎636 8855, fax 632 2723; bus #32 from CS. (April–Sept). A relaxed and friendly site, just a 10-min bus ride into Amsterdam North from the station. Facilities include a general shop, bar, restaurant and bike rental. Rates are ƒ9.25 a night per person (ƒ10.75 if you're over 30), plus ƒ1 for a tent, ƒ12.50 for a motorbike, ƒ13.50 for a car. Hot showers are included. Also a few huts with bunk beds and basic cooking facilities, for ƒ63 per night for four people; phone ahead to check availability. Pets forbidden.

Zeeburg, Zuiderzeeweg 29 ☎694 4430, fax 694 6238; train from CS (or tram #10 from Leidseplein) to Muiderpoort Station, then bus #37. (March–Dec). Slightly better equipped than the

Vliegenbos, but more difficult to get to. Rates are ƒ6.50 per person, plus ƒ3.50 for a tent, ƒ3.50 for a motorbike, ƒ6 for a car. Hot showers ƒ1.50. Cabins sleeping two (ƒ40) and four (ƒ80) are available.

Family Campsites
Amsterdamse Bos, Kleine Noorddijk 1, Aalsmeer ☎641 6868, fax 640 2378; yellow *NZH* bus #171 from CS. (April–Oct). Facilities include a bar, shop and restaurant, but this is a long way out, on the southern reaches of the lush and well-kept Amsterdam Forest. Rates are ƒ8.25 (ƒ4.25 for under-12s), hot showers included, plus ƒ4.25 for a motorbike or car, camper or caravan. Huts sleeping up to four cost ƒ60 a night.

Gaasper Camping, Loosdrechtdreef 7 ☎696 7326, fax 696 9369; metro Gaasperplas. (March 15–Dec 31). Amsterdam's newest campsite, just the other side of the Bijlmermeer housing complex in Amsterdam Zuidoost (Southeast), and easily reached from Centraal Station by metro. Very close to the wonderful open-air Gaasperplas park, which has facilities for all sorts of outdoor activities. Rates are ƒ6 (ƒ3.50 for under-12s, ƒ3.75 for a dog), plus ƒ7 per tent, ƒ5.50 for a car, ƒ8 for a caravan. Hot showers ƒ1.50.

Accommodation

Small and simple hotel near the Concertgebouw. ③

Zandbergen (18), Willemsparkweg 205 ☎676 9321, fax 676 1860; tram #2 to Jacob Obrechtstraat. Light, airy, family-run hotel on a busy street near the Vondelpark; the rooms are clean and spacious. ④

Gay hotels

Sander (19), Jacob Obrechtstraat 69 ☎662 7574, fax 679 6067. See main listings above. ③

The South

The only reason you'll be staying so far away from the sights is the specific appeal of one of the following places, which are marked off the Museumplein and Vondelpark map on p.181.

Hilton (25), Apollolaan 138 ☎678 0780, fax 662 6688; tram #5 or #24 to Apollolaan. Way outside the centre in the distinctly upmarket New South, with everything you'd expect, including a Yacht Club and a fine Italian restaurant. Doubles hover around the ƒ500 mark, but it's only really worth considering if you can afford to soak up a bit of 1960s nostalgia in its refurbished – and admittedly stunning – Lennon and Ono suite, where the couple held their notorious 1969 "Bed-In" for peace; one night here will set you back ƒ1400. ⑦

Van Ostade (24), Van Ostadestraat 123 ☎679 3452, fax 671 5213; tram #25 to Ceintuurbaan. Friendly, youthful place not far from the Albert Cuyp market in the Pijp; bills itself as a "bicycle hotel", renting bikes (ƒ8 per day) and giving advice on routes and such. Basic but clean rooms. Garage parking for cars. ②–③

Chapter 9

Eating and Drinking

Amsterdam is better known for **drinking** than eating, and with good reason: its selection of bars is one of the real pleasures of the city. As for **eating**, this may not be Europe's culinary capital, but there's a good supply of ethnic restaurants, especially Indonesian and Chinese, and the prices (by big-city standards) are hard to beat. And there are any number of *eetcafés* and bars serving increasingly adventurous food, quite cheaply, in a relaxed and unpretentious setting.

Dutch **mealtimes** are a little idiosyncratic. Breakfast tends to be later than you might expect, and other meals tend to be eaten earlier. If you choose to eat breakfast out of your hotel, you'll find few cafés open before 8 or 8.30am. The standard Dutch lunch hour is from noon to 1pm, and most restaurants are at their busiest between 7 and 8pm (and may stop serving altogether by 10pm).

For such a small city, Amsterdam is filled with places to eat and drink, and you should have no trouble finding somewhere convenient and enjoyable to suit your budget. While the Red Light District area has more than its fair share of tacky, low-quality establishments, there are plenty of good restaurants scattered all over the city, and in much of the centre you can find a bar on almost every corner. With Amsterdam's singular approach to the sale and consumption of marijuana, you might choose to enjoy a joint after your meal rather than a beer: we've included in this chapter a selection of coffeeshops where you can buy and smoke grass.

In this chapter you will find full **listings** and reviews of Amsterdam's bars, cafés, coffeeshops, tearooms and restaurants.; they are also cross-referenced at the end of each chapter in the main guide. We've also given general information about what to expect from Amsterdam's eating, drinking and smoking establishments.

Breakfast, fast food and snacks

In all but the very cheapest hostels and the most expensive hotels, **breakfast** (*ontbijt*) will be included in the price of the room. Though usually nothing fancy, it's always very filling: rolls, cheese, ham, hard-boiled eggs, jam and honey or peanut butter are the principal ingredients. If you're not eating in your hotel, many bars and cafés serve breakfast, and those that don't invariably offer rolls and sandwiches.

For the rest of the day, eating cheaply and well, particularly on your feet, is no

Eating and
Drinking

Dutch cheese

Holland's **cheeses** have an unjustified reputation abroad for being bland and rubbery, possibly because they only export the nastier products and keep the best for themselves. In fact, Dutch cheese can be delicious, although there isn't the variety you get in, say, France or Britain. Most are based on the same soft, creamy *Goudas*, and differences in taste come with the varying stages of maturity – young, mature or old (*jong*, *belegen* or *oud*). *Jong* cheese has a mild flavour, *belegen* is much tastier, while *oud* can be pungent and strong, with a flaky texture

not unlike Italian parmesan. Generally, the older they get, the saltier they are. Among the other cheeses you'll find are the best-known round, red *Edam*, made principally for export and (quite sensibly) not eaten much by the Dutch; *Leidse*, which is simply *Gouda* with cumin seeds; *Maasdammer* and *Leerdammer*, strong, creamy and full of holes; and Dutch-made *Emmentals* and *Gruyères*. The best way to eat cheese here is the way the Dutch do it, in thin slices cut with a special cheese knife (*kaasschaaf*) rather than large hunks.

real problem, although those on the tightest of budgets may find themselves dependent on the dubious delights of **Dutch fast food**. This has its own peculiarities. Chips – *frites* – are the most common standby (*Vlaamse* or "Flemish" are the best), either sprinkled with salt or smothered with huge gobs of mayonnaise (sometimes known as *fritesaus*); some alternative toppings are curry, goulash, peanut or tomato sauce. Chips are often complemented with *kroketten* – spiced minced meat covered with breadcrumbs and deep-fried – or *fricandel*, a frankfurter-like sausage. All these are available over the counter at evil-smelling fast-food places (*FEBO* is the most common chain), or, for a guilder or so, from heated glass compartments outside. As an alternative there are also a number of **Indonesian fast-food** places, serving *saté* and noodle dishes in a *McDonald's*-type atmosphere.

Tastier, and good both as a snack and a full lunch, are the **fish specialities** sold from street kiosks: salted raw herrings, smoked eel, mackerel in a roll, mussels, and various kinds of deep-fried fish; tip your head back and dangle the fish into your mouth, Dutch-style. Other street foods include **pancakes** (*pannekoeken*), sweet or spicy, also widely available at sit-down restaurants; **waffles** (*stroopwafels*) doused with maple syrup; and *poffertjes*, shell-shaped dough balls

served with masses of melted butter and icing sugar – an extremely filling snack. Try also *oliebollen*, greasy doughnuts traditionally eaten at New Year. Dutch **cakes and biscuits** are always good and filling, best eaten in a *banketbakkerij* with a small serving area; or buy a bag and eat them on the go. Apart from the ubiquitous *appelgebak* – a wedge of apple tart flavoured with cinnamon – things to try include *spekulaas*, a cinammon biscuit with a gingerbread texture; *stroopwafels*, butter wafers sandwiched together with syrup; and *amandelkoek*, cakes with a biscuity outside and melt-in-the-mouth almond paste inside.

As for the kind of food you can expect to encounter in bars, there are **sandwiches and rolls** (*boterhammen* and *broodjes*) – often open, and varying from a slice of tired cheese on old bread to something so embellished it's a complete meal – as well as more substantial fare. In the winter, *erwtensoep* (aka *snert*) is available in most bars, and at about ƒ7.50 a shot it makes a great buy for lunch: thick pea soup with smoked sausage, served with a portion of smoked bacon on pumpernickel. Or there's *uitsmijter* (literally, bouncer): one, two or three fried eggs on buttered bread, topped with a choice of ham, cheese or roast beef – at about ƒ10, another good budget lunch.

Restaurant food

Dutch food tends to be higher in protein content than imagination: steak, chicken and fish, along with filling soups and stews, are staple fare. Where possible stick to *dagschotels* (dish of the day, generally available as long as the restaurant is open), a meat and two vegetable combination for which you pay around *f*15, bottom-line, for what tend to be enormous portions. The fish is generally high-quality but not especially cheap (*f*20 and up, on average). Many places advertise "tourist menus", costing an average of *f*15, which are usually extremely dull.

A wide selection of **vegetarian** restaurants offer full-course set meals for around *f*15–17, or hearty dishes for *f*12 or less. Bear in mind that they often close early. Another cheap stand-by is **Italian** food: pizzas and pasta dishes start at a fairly uniform *f*12–14 in all but the ritziest places. **Chinese** restaurants are also common, as are (increasingly) **Spanish** ones, and there are a handful of **Tex-Mex** eateries, all of which serve well-priced, filling food. But Amsterdam's real speciality is its **Indonesian** restaurants, a consequence of the country's imperial adventures and well worth checking out. You can eat à la carte – *Nasi Goreng* and *Bami Goreng* (rice or noodles with meat) are ubiquitous dishes, and chicken or beef in peanut sauce (*saté*) is available everywhere too. Alternatively, order a *rijsttafel*: boiled rice and/or noodles served with a number of spicy side dishes and hot *sambal* sauce on the side. Eaten with the spoon in the right hand, fork in the left, and with dry white or rosé wine or beer, this doesn't come cheap, but it's delicious and is normally more than enough for two.

Drink

Dutch **coffee** is black and strong, and comes in disappointingly small cups. It is often served with *koffiemelk* (evaporated milk); ordinary milk is offered only occasionally. If you want white coffee (*café au lait*), ask for a *koffie verkeerd*. Most bars also serve cappuccino, although bear in mind that many stop serving coffee alto-gether around 11pm. **Tea** generally comes with lemon, if anything; if you want milk you have to ask for it. **Hot chocolate** is also popular, served hot or cold: for a real treat drink it hot with a layer of fresh whipped cream on top.

Alcoholic drinks

The beverage drunk most often in Amsterdam's bars is **beer**. This is usually served in small measures, around half a pint (ask for *een pils*), much of which will be a frothing head – requests to have it poured English-style meet with various responses, but it's always worth trying. **Jenever**, Dutch gin, is not unlike English gin but a bit weaker and a little oilier; it's made from molasses and flavoured with juniper berries. It's served in small glasses and is traditionally drunk straight, often knocked back in one gulp with much hearty back-slapping. There are a number of varieties: *oud* (old) is smooth and mellow, *jong* (young) packs more of a punch – though neither is terribly alcoholic. Ask for a *borreltje* (straight *jenever*), a *bitterje* (with angostura bitters), or, if you've a sweeter tooth, try a *bessenjenever* – blackcurrant-flavoured gin; for a glass of beer with a jenever chaser, ask for a *kopstoot*. Other drinks you'll see include numerous Dutch **liqueurs**, notably *advocaat* (eggnog), and the sweet blue *curacao*; and an assortment of lurid-coloured **fruit brandies**, which are best left for experimentation at the end of an evening. There's also the Dutch-produced brandy, *Vieux*, which tastes as if it's made from prunes but is in fact grape-based.

Beer and *jenever* are both dirt-cheap if bought by the bottle from a shop or supermarket: the commonest beers, all local brews – *Amstel*, *Grolsch* and *Heineken* – cost around *f*1.25 for a half-litre (about a pint), although a small deposit on the bottle will be added (and given back when it's returned). A bottle of *jenever* sells for around *f*18. Imported spirits are considerably more expensive. **Wine**, too, is very reasonable – expect to pay around *f*4–5 for plonk, and *f*7–8 or so for a fairly decent bottle.

Eating and
Drinking

Glossary of Dutch food and drink terms

Although most menus in Amsterdam include full English translations, the list below
will help you to make specific requests.

Basics

Boter	Butter	*Pindakaas*	Peanut
Boterham/broodje	Sandwich/		butter
	roll	*Sla/salade*	Salad
Brood	Bread	*Smeerkaas*	Cheese
Dranken	Drinks		spread
Eieren	Eggs	*Stokbrood*	French
Gerst	Barley		bread
Groenten	Vegetables	*Suiker*	Sugar
Honing	Honey	*Vis*	Fish
Hoofdgerechten	Main	*Vlees*	Meat
	courses	*Voorgerechten*	Starters/
Kaas	Cheese		hors d'oeuvres
Koud	Cold	*Vruchten*	Fruit
Nagerechten	Desserts	*Warm*	Hot
Peper	Pepper	*Zout*	Salt

Starters and snacks

Erwtensoep/snert	Thick pea soup with bacon or sausage
Huzarensalade	Egg salad
Koffietafel	A light midday meal of cold meats, cheese, bread, and perhaps soup
Patates/frites	Chips/French fries
Soep	Soup
Uitsmijter	Ham or cheese with eggs on bread

Meat and poultry

Biefstuk (duitse)	Steak	*Karbonade*	Chop
Biefstuk (hollandse)	Hamburger	*Kip*	Chicken
Eend	Duck	*Kroket*	Spiced minced
Fricandeau	Roast pork		meat in bread
Fricandel	A frankfurter-		crumbs
	like sausage	*Lamsvlees*	Lamb
Gehakt	Minced meat	*Lever*	Liver
Ham	Ham	*Rookvlees*	Smoked beef
Kalfsvlees	Veal	*Spek*	Bacon
Kalkoen	Turkey	*Worst*	Sausages

Fish

Forel	Trout	*Mosselen*	Mussels
Garnalen	Prawns	*Paling*	Eel
Haring	Herring	*Schelvis*	Haddock
Haringsalade	Herring salad	*Schol*	Plaice
Kabeljauw	Cod	*Tong*	Sole
Makreel	Mackerel	*Zalm*	Salmon

Terms

Belegen Filled or topped, as in *belegen broodje* – a small roll topped with cheese, etc

Doorbakken	Well-done	*Gebraden*	Roast
Gebakken	Fried/baked	*Gegrild*	Grilled

Gekookt	Boiled	*Hollandse saus*	Hollandaise (a
Geraspt	Grated		milk and egg
Gerookt	Smoked		sauce)
Gestoofd	Stewed	*Rood*	Rare
Half doorbakken	Medium-done		

Eating and
Drinking

Vegetables

Aardappelen	Potatoes	*Knoflook*	Garlic
Boerenkool	Mashed potato	*Komkommer*	Cucumber
	and cabbage	*Prei*	Leek
Bloemkool	Cauliflower	*Rijst*	Rice
Bonen	Beans	*Sla*	Salad, lettuce
Champignons	Mushrooms	*Uien*	Onions
Erwten	Peas	*Wortelen*	Carrots
Hutspot	Mashed potatoes	*Zuurkool*	Sauerkraut
	and carrots		

Indonesian dishes and terms

Ajam	Chicken	*Nasi Rames*	Rijsttafel on a
Bami	Noodles with		single plate
	meat/chicken	*Pedis*	Hot and spicy
	and vegetables	*Pisang*	Banana
Daging	Beef	*Rijsttafel*	Collection of
Gado gado	Vegetables in		different spicy
	peanut sauce		dishes served
Goreng	Fried		with plain rice
Ikan	Fish	*Sambal*	Hot, chilli-based
Katjang	Peanut		sauce
Kroepoek	Prawn crackers	*Satesaus*	Peanut sauce to
Loempia	Spring rolls		accompany meat
Nasi	Rice		grilled on skewers
Nasi Goreng	Fried rice with	*Seroendeng*	Spicy shredded
	meat/chicken		and fried coconut
	and vegetables	*Tauge*	Bean sprouts

Sweets and desserts

Appelgebak	Apple tart or cake	*Oliebollen*	Doughnuts
Drop	Dutch liquorice,	*Pannekoeken*	Pancakes
	available in *zoet*	*Pepernoten*	Dutch ginger nuts
	(sweet) or *zout* (salted)	*Poffertjes*	Small pancakes, fritters
	varieties – the latter	*(Slag)room*	(Whipped) cream
	being an acquired taste	*Speculaas*	Spice and honey-
Gebak	Pastry		flavoured biscuit
IJs	Ice cream	*Stroopwafels*	Waffles
Koekjes	Biscuits	*Taai-taai*	Dutch honey cake
		Vla	Custard

Fruits and nuts

Aardbei	Strawberry	*Hazelnoot*	Hazelnut
Amandel	Almond	*Kers*	Cherry
Appel	Apple	*Kokosnoot*	Coconut
Appelmoes	Apple purée	*Peer*	Pear
Citroen	Lemon	*Perzik*	Peach
Druiven	Grape	*Pinda*	Peanut
Framboos	Raspberry	*Pruim*	Plum/prune

Eating and Drinking

Drinks			
Bessenjenever	Blackcurrant gin	*Vruchtensap*	Fruit juice
Citroenjenever	Lemon gin	*Wijn*	Wine
Droog	Dry	*(wit/rood/rosé)*	(white/red/rosé)
Frisdranken	Soft drinks	*Vieux*	Dutch brandy
Jenever	Dutch gin	*Zoet*	Sweet
Karnemelk	Buttermilk	*Anijsmelk*	Aniseed-flavoured
Koffie	Coffee		warm milk
Kopstoot	Beer with a *jenev-*	*Appelsap*	Apple juice
	er chaser	*Chocomel*	Chocolate milk
Melk	Milk	*Koffie verkeerd*	Coffee with warm
Met ijs	With ice		milk
Pils	Dutch beer	*Met slagroom*	With whipped cream
Proost!	Cheers!	*Sinaasappelsap*	Orange juice
Thee	Tea	*Tomatensap*	Tomato juice

Bars and Cafés

Amsterdam is well known for its drinking, and with good reason: the selection of **bars** is one of the real pleasures of the city, fuelled by Holland's proximity to two of the premier beer-drinking nations in Europe – Belgium, where monks more or less invented modern beer, and Germany, famous for its beer consumption. The three leading brands of Dutch beer – *Amstel*, *Grolsch* and *Heineken* – are worldwide best-sellers, but are available here in considerably more potent formats than the insipid varieties shunted out for export. Dutch gin, or *jenever*, has a kick all its own, and, in addition, the selection of imported beers and spirits on offer in Amsterdam's bars is exceptionally good, with almost limitless possibilities for experimentation.

There are, in essence, two kinds of Amsterdam bar. The traditional, old-style bar is the **brown café** – a *bruin café* or *bruine kroeg*; these are cosy places so called because of the dingy colour of their walls, stained by years of tobacco smoke. As a backlash, slick, self-consciously modern **designer bars** have sprung up, many of them known as "grand cafés", which tend to be as un-brown as possible and geared towards a largely young crowd. We've included details of the more established ones, although these places come and go –

something like 70 percent are said to close down within a year of opening. Bars, of any kind, open at around 10am or 5pm; both stay open until around 1am during the week, 2am at weekends (sometimes until 3am). Another type of drinking spot – though there are very few of them left – are the **tasting houses** (*proeflokalen*), originally the sampling rooms of small private distillers, now tiny, stand-up places that sell only spirits and close around 8pm.

One growing trend in Amsterdam drinking is **Irish pubs**: at the last count there were seven in and around the city centre, all featuring Guinness and other stouts on tap, Gaelic music of varying quality, and English football live via satellite most weekends. The clue to their success seems to lie much more in the football than the fiddlers – all have rapidly become "locals" for the relatively large numbers of British and Irish living and working in Amsterdam, and although at quiet times the clientele might include a smattering of Amsterdammers, most of the (generally male) drinkers in these places are expats rather than locals.

Prices are fairly standard everywhere, and the only time you'll pay through the nose is when there's music, or if you're foolish (or desperate) enough to step into the obvious tourist traps around

Leidseplein and along Damrak. Reckon on paying roughly *f*2.50 for a standard-measure small beer, called a *pils* (or, if you get it in a straight glass, a *fluitje*). A tiny beer chaser, called a *kleintje pils*, costs the same. Apart from these, different beers come in different glasses – *Oranjeboom*, for instance, is served in a *vasje*; white beer (*witbier*), which is light, cloudy and served with lemon, has its own tumbler, and most of the speciality Belgian beers have special stemmed glasses. Most places should be able to come up with a pint if you really want one (at roughly *f*7), but bear in mind that a quarter of the glass, whether large or small, always comes as foam.

You can also use cafés as a place for **budget eating**. Many – often designated *eetcafés* – offer a complete menu, and most will make you a sandwich or a bowl of soup; at the very least you can snack on hard-boiled eggs from the counter for a guilder or so each. Some bars that specialize in food are listed in the *Restaurants* section.

There are around 1400 bars and cafés in Amsterdam – which works out at roughly one every 50m (or so it seems) – and what follows is inevitably very selective. It does, however, cover a very broad cross-section of places across the city, so wherever you are, and, whatever your tastes, you should be able to find something nearby to suit you.

Coffeeshops

Art, architecture and canals aside, a large proportion of visitors to Amsterdam have come for one thing: the **drugs**. Amsterdam remains just about the only city in the world where you can stand in a public place and announce in a loud, clear voice that you intend to buy and smoke a large, well-packed joint, and then do just that in front of the watching police. In theory, purchases of up to 5g of cannabis, and possession of up to 30g, are tolerated; in practice, most coffeeshops around the city offer discounted bulk purchases of 50g with impunity. Forget about how the law works and take advantage of a unique opportunity – no one will ever call the police on you in Amsterdam for discreet, personal dope-smoking. If in doubt about whether smoking is OK in a given situation, ask somebody – the worst you'll get will be a "no".

Eating and Drinking

For the story of the weed, check out the Hash Marihuana Hemp Museum – see pp.82–83. For more dope on dope, see p.82.

Bar, café, coffeeshop or tearoom?

You might expect a place describing itself as a "café" to be open only during the day, selling simple food, cups of tea and no alcohol. In Amsterdam, though, a "café" – **brown** or **grand** – is just a type of bar. One way to distinguish between brown cafés and grand cafés – apart from the ambience – is in the main activity going on. In a grand café, people might be eating full meals, or drinking coffee, wine or beer; in a brown café, like an English pub, the single main activity is alcohol consumption. Don't worry, though: they both serve more or less the same kind of fare, and if one place doesn't have what you want, somewhere just down the road will.

There is, however, a more fundamental difference between coffeeshops and tearooms. To foreigners, a **coffeeshop** brings to mind a quiet daytime place serving coffee and cakes. Far from it. In Amsterdam, somewhere calling itself a "coffeeshop" is advertising just one thing: cannabis. You might sometimes be able to get coffee and cake, but the main activity in a coffeeshop is smoking. If you want to avoid dope-smoke, there are plenty of places throughout the city where you can sit in the afternoon with a cup of coffee and a sandwich; they tend to shy away from the connotations of "coffeeshop", and have taken to calling themselves **tearooms** instead. Non-smokers should beware that wherever you go it's almost impossible to avoid cigarette smoke.

Eating and Drinking

The first thing you should know about Amsterdam's **coffeeshops** is that locals use them too. The second thing you should know is that the only ones locals use are outside the Red Light District. Practically all the coffeeshops you'll run into in the centre are worth avoiding, either for their decor, their deals or their clientele. Plasticky, neon-lit dives abound, pumping out mainstream varieties of house, rock or reggae at ear-splitting level; the dope on offer is usually limited and of poor quality – and, since they're mostly serving tourists, they can rig the deals without fear of comeback. A short time exploring the city will turn up plenty of more congenial, high-quality outlets for buying and enjoying cannabis, light years away from the tack of the city centre.

When you first walk into a coffeeshop, how you buy the stuff isn't immediately apparent – it's illegal to advertise cannabis in any way, which includes calling attention to the fact that it's available at all. What you have to do is ask to see the **menu**, which is normally kept behind the counter. This will list all the different hashes and grasses on offer, along with (if it's a reputable place) exactly how many grammes you get for your money. Most of the stuff is sold either per gramme, or in bags worth ƒ10 or ƒ25 (the more powerful it is, the less you get). The in-house dealer will be able to help you out with queries.

Hash you may come across originates in various countries and is pretty self-explanatory, apart from *Pollem*, which is compressed resin and stronger than normal. **Marijuana** is a different story, and the old days of imported Colombian, Thai and sensimelia are fading away; taking their place are limitless varieties of *Nederwiet*, Dutch-grown under UV lights and more potent than anything you're likely to have come across. Skunk, Haze and Northern Lights are all popular types of Dutch weed, and should be treated with caution – a smoker of low-grade British draw will be laid low (or high) for hours by a single spliff of Skunk. You would be equally well advised to take care with **space-cakes**, which are widely available: you can never be sure exactly what's in them; they tend to have a delayed reaction (up to two hours before you notice anything strange – don't get impatient and gobble down another one!); and once they kick in, they can bring on an extremely intense, bewildering high – 10–12 hours is common. Some large coffeeshops, such as the *Bulldog*, refuse to sell them, and advise you against buying elsewhere. You may also come across cannabis **seeds** for growing your own. While Amsterdammers are permitted to grow five small marijuana plants for "domestic consumption", the import of cannabis seeds is illegal in any country – don't even think about trying to take some home.

However, for dabblers and committed stone-heads alike, Amsterdam is full of possibilities. The coffeeshops we list are better than average; most of them open around 10am or 11am and close around midnight.

Tearooms

Amsterdam's **tearooms** roughly correspond to the usual concept of a café – places that are generally open all day, might serve alcohol but definitely aren't bars, don't allow dope-smoking, but serve good coffee, sandwiches, light snacks and cakes. Along with *eetcafés* – which are listed in amongst the bars – tearooms make good places to stop off for lunch, or to spend a quiet time reading or writing without distractions.

The Old Centre

All the following places are marked on the map on p.194 – the number in brackets after each name refers to its location.

Bars and cafés

Belgique (37), Gravenstraat 2. Tiny bar behind the Nieuwe Kerk that specializes in brews from Belgium.

Bern (45), Nieuwmarkt 9. Casual and inexpensive brown café patronized by a predominantly arty clientele. Run by a native of Switzerland, its speciality is, not surprisingly, fondue.

Blarney Stone (2), Nieuwendijk 29. Packed and central Irish pub.

Blincker (67), St Barberenstraat 7. Squeezed between the top end of Nes and Oudezijds Voorburgwal, this hi-tech theatre bar, all exposed steel and hanging plants, is more comfortable than it looks.

De Brakke Grond (60), Nes 43. Modern, high-ceilinged bar full of people discussing the performances they've just seen at the adjacent theatre.

De Buurvrouw (54), St Pieterspoortsteeg 29. Dark, noisy bar with a wildly eclectic crowd; a great alternative place to head for in the centre.

Carel's Café (88), Voetboogstraat 6. Large, youth-oriented bar serving slightly overpriced food – though the *dagschotels* are a good buy. Also at Frans Halsstraat 76 and Saenredamstraat 32.

Cul de Sac (43), Oudezijds Achterburgwal 99. Down a long alley in what used to be a seventeenth-century spice warehouse, this is a handy retreat from the Red Light District. Small, quiet and friendly.

Van Daele (48), Paleisstraat 101. Worth mentioning more for what it was than what it is, this used to be the city's most infamous punk bar, called *No Name*; it later became a squatters' bar, then a women's restaurant. Today it's a fairly ordinary bar in a large former squat.

Café Dante (78), Spuistraat 320. Is it a bar? Is it an art gallery? It's both and there are just as many people sitting drinking as there are perusing the walls.

Dantzig (97), Zwanenburgwal 15. Easygoing grand café, right on the water behind Waterlooplein, with comfortable chairs, friendly service and a low-key, chic atmosphere. Food served at lunchtime and in the evenings.

De Drie Fleschjes (35), Gravenstraat 16. Tasting house for spirits and liqueurs, which once would have been made on the premises. No beer, and no seats

either; its clients tend to be well heeled or well soused (often both). Closes 8pm.

Droesem (53), Nes 41. On a thin, theatre-packed alley behind the Dam, this is a highly recommended wine bar. Wine comes in carafes filled from the barrel, along with a high-quality choice of cheeses and other titbits to help it on its way.

Durty Nelly's (41), Warmoesstraat 115. Irish pub in the heart of the Red Light action. With a clean and well-run hostel above, this is one of the better expat Brit/Irish meeting places, packed for the weekend football shown live by satellite.

De Engelbewaarder (85), Kloveniersburgwal 59. Once the meeting place of Amsterdam's bookish types, this is still known as a literary café. It's relaxed and informal, with live jazz on Sunday afternoons.

Fiddlers (22), Warmoesstraat 55. Good enough Irish pub, but you'd do better to walk down the road to *Durty Nelly's*.

Flying Dutchman (3), Martelaarsgracht 13. Principal watering hole of Amsterdam's British expat community, with not a word of Dutch to be heard. Usually packed with stoned regulars crowding in to use the pool table or dartboards, or simply to down the large and reasonably priced beers.

Frascati (61), Nes 59. Theatre bar, elegantly brown with mirrors and a pink marble bar, popular with a young, media-type crowd. Good, too, for both lunchtime and informal evening eating, with full meals for around *f*20, snacks and soups for less. Recommended.

't Gasthuis (82), Grimburgwal 7. Convivial brown café packed during the school year with students from the university across the canal. Good food and seating outside by the water in summer.

G-Force (17), Oudezijds Armsteeg 7. Friendly bar catering for those into S&M, or interested in finding out. A trap-door behind the bar leads down to a fully equipped dungeon – which you can rent privately for *f*100/hr. Hosts regular fetish

Eating and Drinking

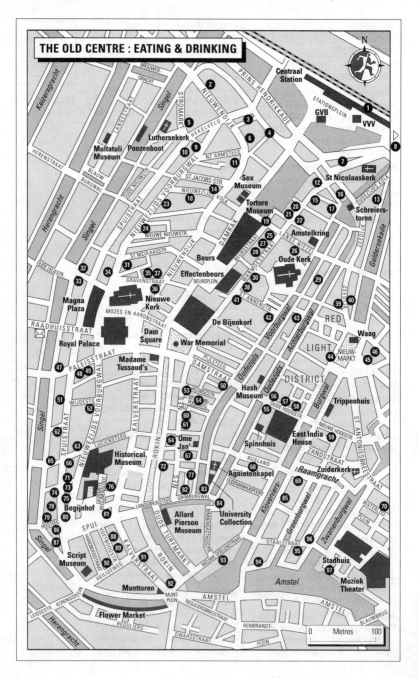

THE OLD CENTRE : EATING & DRINKING

Centraal Station

GVB

VVV

Luthersekerk

Poezenboot

Multatuli Museum

St Nicolaaskerk

Sex Museum

Torture Museum

Schreiers-toren

Amstelkring

Beurs

Oude Kerk

Effectenbeurs

BEURSPLEIN

Magna Plaza

Nieuwe Kerk

MOZES EN AARONSTRAAT

RED

Waag

De Bijenkorf

LIGHT

NIEUW-MARKT

Royal Palace

Dam Square

War Memorial

DISTRICT

Trippenhuis

Madame Tussaud's

Hash Museum

Spinnhuis

East India House

Historical Museum

'Ome Jan'

Agnietenkapel

Zuiderkerk

Raamgracht

Begijnhof

Allard Pierson Museum

University Collection

Script Museum

Stadhuis

Munttoren

Muziek Theater

Flower Market

Amstel

0   Metres   100

Old Centre Map Key

Eating and
Drinking

Eating and
Drinking

parties, and has information on the fetish scene.

Gollem (65), Raamsteeg 4. Small, noisy bar with a huge array of different beers. A genial barman dispenses lists to help you choose.

Hard Rock Café (50), Oudezijds Voorburgwal 246. Not the overblown burger joint found in London, but a small, crowded (smoking) bar serving 1970s-style videos to 1970s-style customers. Patronized mainly by those in Amsterdam for the weed. There's another branch, not a whole lot more appealing, at Korte Leidsedwarsstraat 28.

Harry's American Bar (73), Spuistraat 285. One of a number of would-be sophisticated hangouts at the Spui end of Spuistraat, *Harry's* is primarily a haunt for Amsterdam's more elderly *bons vivants*, with easy-listening jazz and an unhealthily wide selection of cocktails.

De Hoogte (59), Nieuwe Hoogstraat 2a. Small alternative bar on the edge of the Red Light District. Good music, engaging atmosphere, and beers a little cheaper than usual.

Hoppe (86), Spui 18. One of Amsterdam's longest-established and best-known bars, and one of its most likeable, frequented by the city's dark-suited office crowd on their wayward way home. Summer is especially good, when the throngs spill out onto the street.

De Jaren (93), Nieuwe Doelenstraat 20. One of the grandest of the grand cafés, but without a trace of pretentiousness. Overlooking the Amstel next to the university, with three floors, two terraces and as much elegance as you could wish for. There's all kinds of English reading material, too – this is one of the best places to nurse the Sunday paper. Serves reasonably priced food and has a great salad bar. From 10am.

Kabul (21), Warmoesstraat 38. Bar of the adjacent budget hotel, open late.

Het Kantoor (70), Waterlooplein. The best place to run to if the market gets

too much – situated on the first floor, overlooking the mayhem below. Popular with the traders.

De Koningshut (66), Spuistraat 269. In the early evening, at least, it's standing room only in this small, spit-and-sawdust bar, popular with office people on their way home or to dinner. For middle-aged swingers only.

Ter Kuile (32), Torensteeg 8. A new-style brown café and a pleasant place to overlook this stretch of the Singel. Serves food at the usual *eetcafé* prices.

Lokaal 't Loosje (44), Nieuwmarkt 32. Quiet old-style local brown café that's been here for 200 years and looks it. Wonderful for late breakfasts and pensive afternoons.

Luxembourg (87), Spui 22. The prime watering hole of Amsterdam's advertising and media brigade. If you can get past the crowds, it's actually an elegant bar with a good (though pricey) selection of snacks. Overlooks the Singel at the back.

Mono Ontbijt & Alcohol (16), Oudezijds Voorburgwal 2. Open early for greasy breakfasts, with or without alcohol. Suitably heavy sounds accompany your meal.

Oibibio (4), Prins Hendrikkade 20. Airy, relaxed bar attached to a thriving new-age centre – remarkably peaceful for being seconds from Centraal Station.

O'Reilly's (49), Paleisstraat 103. Cavernously vast Irish pub right by Dam Square; light on atmosphere.

't Pakhuys (89), Voetboogstraat 10. An inviting place serving cheapish food; one of a clutch of bars that line this tiny street.

Het Paleis (47), Paleisstraat 16. Bar that's currently in vogue with students from the adjoining university buildings. Laid-back and likeable.

De Pilsener Club (76), Begijnensteeg 4. More like someone's front room than a bar – indeed, all drinks mysteriously appear from a back room. Photographs on the wall record generations of sociable drinking.

De Pilserij (36), Gravenstraat 10. Roomy bar behind the Nieuwe Kerk that has a comfortable back room and plays good jazz. Above all, though, it's the authentic nineteenth-century surroundings that appeal – little has changed, even down to the cash register.

De Pool (55), Oude Hoogstraat 8. Pleasant bar, somewhat quieter than most of the others along this stretch.

Scheltema (52), Nieuwezijds Voorburgwal 242. Journalists' bar, now only frequented by more senior news-hounds and their occasionally famous interviewees, since all the newspaper headquarters along here have now moved to the suburbs. Faded turn-of-the-century feel, with a reading table and meals.

De Schutter (90), Voetboogstraat 13. Former folk music hangout, now simply a spacious upstairs bar, full of people munching on the cheap and basic food.

Tapvreugd (57), Oude Hoogstraat 11. Far and away the most amicable of the loud, crowded music bars on this and surrounding streets.

Tara (72), Rokin 89. Excellent Irish bar with regular live music. The location does it down, but it's worth taking the time to find.

Twin Pigs (11), Nieuwendijk 100. Blues and rock bands blast a semi-stoned crowd in this large, bustling city-centre bar.

Vrankrijk (62), Spuistraat 216. The best and most central of Amsterdam's few remaining squat bars. Cheap drinks, hardcore noise, and almost as many dogs-on-strings as people. Buzz to enter. From 10pm.

De Zwart (80), Spuistraat 334. Less businesslike neighbour of the more famous *Hoppe* across the alley, but similarly crowded.

Gay bars

Anco (29), Oudezijds Voorburgwal 55. Late-night hotel leather bar with a large darkroom.

Argos (38), Warmoesstraat 95. Europe's oldest leather bar, with two bars and a raunchy cellar. Not for the faint-hearted. From 10pm.

Casa Maria (25), Warmoesstraat 60. Mixed gay bar in the heart of the Warmoesstraat scene. Over-25s only.

Club Jaecques (30), Warmoesstraat 93. A meeting place for locals, but appropriate (leather- and denim-clad) visitors are made welcome.

Cuckoo's Nest (18), Nieuwezijds Kolk 6. A cruisey leather bar with a long reputation, this is described as "the best place in town for chance encounters". Vast and infamous darkroom. From 1pm.

Dirty Dick's (27), Warmoesstraat 86. Cruisey leather bar amongst cruisey leather bars. Weekends only from midnight.

The Eagle (28), Warmoesstraat 90. Long-established leather bar popular with men of all ages. Gets very busy after 1am.

Shako's (94), 's Gravelandseveer 2. Friendly, studentish bar in a quiet street on the Amstel.

Stablemaster (15), Warmoesstraat 23. A leather bar with hotel attached; English-speaking staff and a British following.

The Web (14), St Jacobsstraat 6. Strict rubber, leather and denim bar with a dance floor, darkrooms and a pool table. From 2pm.

Why Not (9), Nieuwezijds Voorburgwal 28. Long-standing, intimate bar with a porno cinema above.

Coffeeshops

The Bulldog (42), Oudezijds Voorburgwal 90 and 132 and 218; Singel 12. The biggest and most famous of the coffeeshop chains; see p.205 for details.

Extase (56), Oude Hoogstraat 2. Part of a chain run by the initiator of the Hash Museum. Considerably less chi-chi than the better-known coffeeshops.

Grasshopper, Oudebrugsteeg 16 (19); Nieuwezijds Voorburgwal 57 (23). One of the city's more welcoming coffeeshops,

Eating and Drinking

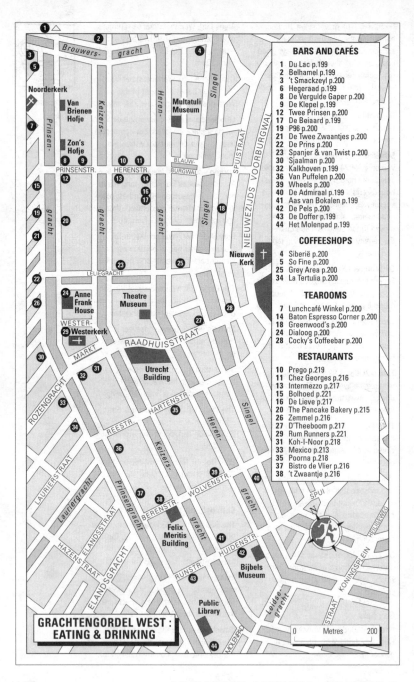

BARS AND CAFÉS

1 Du Lac p.199
2 Belhamel p.199
3 't Smackzeyl p.200
6 Hegeraad p.199
8 De Vergulde Gaper p.200
9 De Klepel p.199
12 Twee Prinsen p.200
17 De Beiaard p.199
19 P96 p.200
21 De Twee Zwaantjes p.200
22 De Prins p.200
23 Spanjer & van Twist p.200
30 Sjaalman p.200
32 Kalkhoven p.199
36 Van Puffelen p.200
39 Wheels p.200
40 De Admiraal p.199
41 Aas van Bokalen p.199
42 De Pels p.200
43 De Doffer p.199
44 Het Molenpad p.199

COFFEESHOPS

4 Siberië p.200
5 So Fine p.200
25 Grey Area p.200
34 La Tertulia p.200

TEAROOMS

7 Lunchcafé Winkel p.200
14 Baton Espresso Corner p.200
18 Greenwood's p.200
24 Dialoog p.200
28 Cocky's Coffeebar p.200

RESTAURANTS

10 Prego p.219
11 Chez Georges p.216
13 Intermezzo p.217
15 Bolhoed p.221
16 De Lieve p.217
20 The Pancake Bakery p.215
26 Zemmel p.216
27 D'Theeboom p.217
29 Rum Runners p.221
31 Koh-I-Noor p.218
33 Mexico p.213
35 Poorna p.218
37 Bistro de Vlier p.216
38 't Zwaantje p.216

GRACHTENGORDEL WEST : EATING & DRINKING

0 — Metres — 200

though at times overwhelmed by tourists.

Homegrown Fantasy (24), Nieuwezijds Voorburgwal 87a. Attached to the Dutch Passion seed company, this sells the widest selection of marijuana in Amsterdam, most of it local.

Josephine Baker (58), Oude Hoogstraat 27. Once known as the *Café de Dood* – "Café of the Dead", after the studiously wasted youth who patronize it – this is the loudest and most squalid hangout in the area.

Kadinsky (63), Rosmarijnsteeg 9. Strictly accurate deals weighed out to a background of jazz dance. Chocolate chip cookies to die for.

Rusland (68), Rusland 16. One of the first Amsterdam coffeeshops, a cramped but vibrant place that's a favourite with both dope fans and tea addicts (it has 43 different kinds). A cut above the rest.

De Tweede Kamer (79), Heisteeg 6. A busy coffeeshop that's more "brown" than most of its rivals. In a tiny alley off Spui.

Tearooms

Café Esprit (81), Spui 10a. Swish modern café, with wonderful sandwiches, rolls and superb salads.

Lindsay's Teashop (91), Kalverstraat 185. An unlikely attempt to recreate a little piece of England in the basement of the American Book Center. The food, though, is fine: real English cream teas, home-made pies and trifles. And it's a refreshing escape from the Kalverstraat shopping mafia.

Puccini (96), Staalstraat 21. Lovely cake and chocolate shop-cum-café, with wonderful handmade pastries and good coffee. Close to Waterlooplein.

Tatsun (6), Nieuwendijk 45. Turkish-style coffee bar with sticky pastries and suchlike.

Villa Zeezicht (33), Torensteeg 3. Small and central, this all-wood café serves excellent rolls and sandwiches, plus some of the best apple cake in the city, fresh-baked every 10min or so.

Grachtengordel West

All the following places are marked on the map opposite – the number in brackets after each name refers to its location.

Bars and cafés

Aas van Bokalen (41), Keizersgracht 335. Unpretentious local bar with good food. Great collection of Motown tapes. Very small, so go either early or late.

De Admiraal (40), Herengracht 319. Large and uniquely comfortable *proeflokaal*, with a vast range of liqueurs and spirits to explore.

De Beiaard (17), Herengracht 90. Light and airy 1950s-style bar for genuine beer aficionados. There's a wide selection of bottled and draught beers, selected with true dedication by the owner, who delights in filling you in on the relative properties of each.

Belhamel (2), Brouwersgracht 60. Kitschy bar/restaurant with an Art Nouveau-style interior and excellent, though costly, French food. The main attraction in summer is one of the most picturesque views in Amsterdam.

De Doffer (43), Runstraat 12. Small, affable bar with food and a billiards table.

Hegeraad (6), Noordermarkt 34. Old-fashioned, lovingly maintained brown café with a fiercely loyal clientele.

Kalkhoven (32), Prinsengracht 283. One of the city's most characteristic brown cafés. Nothing out of the ordinary, but warm and welcoming.

De Klepel (9), Prinsenstraat 22. Quiet bar where people come to play chess. English newspapers.

Du Lac (1), Haarlemmerstraat 118. Very appealing Art Deco grand café, with plenty of foliage; live jazz on Sundays.

Het Molenpad (44), Prinsengracht 653. This is one of the most appealing brown cafés in the city: long, dark and dusty. Also serves remarkably good food. Fills up with a young, professional crowd after 6pm. Recommended.

Eating and Drinking

**Eating and
Drinking**

De Pels (42), Huidenstraat 25. Few surprises in this, one of Amsterdam's quieter but more pleasant bars.

De Prins (22), Prinsengracht 124. Boisterous student bar, with a wide range of drinks and a well-priced menu. A great place to drink in a nice part of town.

P96 (19), Prinsengracht 96. A late-opening bar a little way down the canal from *De Prins*; there's a dartboard, should you feel like a game.

Van Puffelen (36), Prinsengracht 377. More a restaurant than a café, but an appealing place to drink, with a huge choice of international beers and a reading room by day, restaurant by night. Food is French in style and, though not cheap, usually well worth the price.

Sjaalman (30), Prinsengracht 178. Small bar with a pool table and exotic food. Good in summer when the church tower is lit up.

't Smackzeyl (3), Brouwersgracht 101. Uninhibited drinking hole on the fringes of the Jordaan (corner of Prinsengracht). One of the few brown cafés to have Guinness on tap; also an inexpensive menu of light dishes.

Spanjer & Van Twist (23), Leliegracht 60. A gentle place, which comes into its own on summer afternoons, with chairs lining the most peaceful stretch of water in the city centre.

Twee Prinsen (12), Prinsenstraat 27. Cornerside people-watching bar that's a useful starting place for touring the area. Its heated terrace makes it possible to sit outside, even in winter.

De Twee Zwaantjes (21), Prinsengracht 114. Tiny Jordaan bar whose live accordion music and raucous singing you'll either love or hate. Fun, in an oompah-pah sort of way.

De Vergulde Gaper (8), Prinsenstraat 30. Opposite the *Twee Prinsen*, this offers much the same kind of low-key attraction – though it's somewhat larger and there's a wider choice of food. Has a heated terrace should you fancy sitting outside.

Wheels (39), Wolvenstraat 4. Deceptively like any other brown café to look at, but actually the confirmed haunt of a number of British expats. Expect to be served by a friendly north London soul boy.

Coffeeshops

Grey Area (25), Oude Leliestraat 2. High-class coffeeshop with menu (and prices) to match.

Siberië (4), Brouwersgracht 11. Set up by the former staff of *Rusland* and notable for the way it's avoided the over-commercialization of the larger chains. Very relaxed, very friendly, and worth a visit whether you want to smoke or not.

So Fine (5), Prinsengracht 30. Long-established coffeeshop, big on atmosphere at night, with good food and music, a pool table and a video room.

La Tertulia (34), Prinsengracht 312. Tiny corner coffeeshop, complete with indoor rockery and tinkling fountain. Much better outside, though, as it's on a particularly beautiful stretch of the canal.

Tearooms

Baton Espresso Corner (14), Herengracht 82. Convivial tearoom with a huge array of sandwiches. In a central location, handy for cheap lunches.

Cocky's Coffeebar (28), Raadhuisstraat 8. Good no-nonsense place with a wide variety of sandwiches.

Dialoog (24), Prinsengracht 261a. A few doors down from the Anne Frank House, one long room filled with paintings, restrained classical music, and downstairs, a gallery of Latin American art. Good choice of sandwiches and salads, too.

Greenwood's (18), Singel 103. Small, English-style teashop in the basement of a canal house. Pies and sandwiches, pots of tea – and a decent breakfast.

Lunchcafé Winkel (7), Noordermarkt 43. A popular café on the corner with Westerstraat; something of a rendezvous on Saturday mornings, with the Boerenmarkt in full flow, and some of the most delicious apple cake in the city going like, well, hot apple cake.

Grachtengordel South

All the following places are marked on the map on p.202 – the number in brackets after each name refers to its location.

Bars and cafés

Café Americain (72), *American Hotel*, Leidseplein 28. The terrace bar here has been a gathering place for Amsterdam media people for years, and it's worth coming at least once, if only for the decor: Art Nouveau frills coordinated down to the doorknobs. A place to be seen, with prices not surprisingly above average. Good fast lunches, though.

De Balie (92), Kleine Gartmanplantsoen 10. Big high-ceilinged haunt of the city's trendy left, part of the *Balie* cultural centre. Not especially inspiring, but if you're stuck on Leidseplein on a Saturday night, it provides a welcome change of atmosphere.

't Balkje (52), Kerkstraat 46. Snacky meeting place: eggs, eggs and bacon, and eggs, bacon and ham. Beer too.

De Duivel (20), Reguliersdwarsstraat 87. Tucked away on a street of bars and coffeeshops, this is the only hip-hop café in Amsterdam, with continuous beats and a clientele to match. Opposite the hip-hop coffeeshop *Free I*.

Françoise (60), Kerkstraat 176. Quiet and elegant place with a small gallery, serving good breakfasts and lunches. Caters mostly, but not exclusively, for women. Sunday mornings are a delight.

De Geus (76), Korte Leidsedwarsstraat 71. Cheerful place with a limited but tasty menu of Dutch food.

Het Hok (80), Lange Leidsedwarsstraat 134. Games bar, where you can play backgammon, chess or draughts, or just drink against a backdrop of clicking counters. Pleasingly unpretentious after the plastic restaurants of the rest of the street, though women may find the overwhelmingly male atmosphere off-putting.

Huyschkaemer (63), Utrechtsestraat 137. Attractive local bar on an up-and-coming street, and already established as the favourite watering hole of arty students.

Café Klein Wiener Wad (62), Utrechtsestraat 135. Small, self-consciously modern café; trendy and unavoidably intimate.

L & B (70), Korte Leidsedwarsstraat 82. A cosy bar, rather misplaced among the touristy restaurants and clubs of this part of town. Has a selection of 200 different whiskies and bourbons from around the world. Open until 3am.

Het Land van Walem (34), Keizersgracht 449. One of Amsterdam's nouveau-chic cafés: cool, light, and vehemently unbrown. The clientele is stylish, and the food is a kind of hybrid French-Dutch; there's also a wide selection of newspapers and magazines, including some in English. Usually packed.

Morlang (35), Keizersgracht 451. Bar/restaurant of the new wave, yuppie variety (much like the *Walem* next door), serving good food for around ƒ20. Occasional live music.

Mulligan's (11), Amstel 100. By far the best Irish pub in the city, with an authentic atmosphere, superb Gaelic music and good service.

Mulliners Wijnlokaal (93), Lijnsbaansgracht 267. Upmarket wine bar (around ƒ6 a glass, ƒ25 a bottle), serving food as well. Good atmosphere.

Oosterling (64), Utrechtsestraat 140. Stone-floored local bar-cum-off-licence that's been in the same family since the middle of the last century. Very quiet – home to some serious drinkers.

Reynders (73), Leidseplein 6. The last real option if you want to sit out on the Leidseplein. A remnant of days long gone, with aproned waiters and an elegant interior.

Café Schiller (32), Rembrandtplein 26. Art Deco bar of the upstairs hotel, authentic in both feel and decor. Though it's suf-

Eating and Drinking

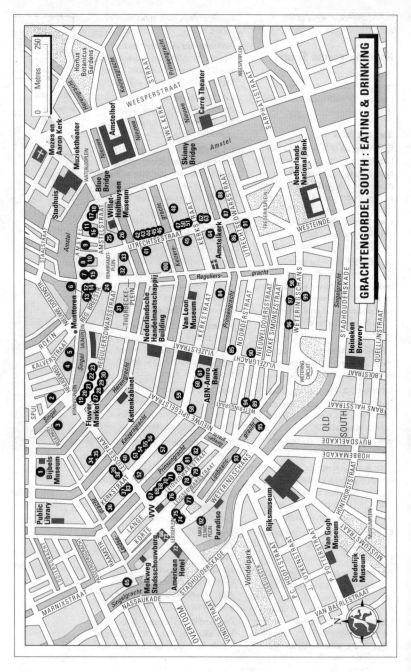

GRACHTENGORDEL SOUTH : EATING & DRINKING

Metres
0   250

Public Library

Bijbels Museum
1

Mozes en Aaron Kerk

Stadhuis

Muziektheater

Amstelhof

WEESPERSTRAAT

Hortus Botanicus Gardens

Blue Bridge

Willet-Holthuysen Museum

Skinny Bridge

Carré Theater

Netherlands National Bank

Amstelkerk

Van Loon Museum

Nederlandsche Handelmaatschappij Building

ABN-Amro Bank

Heineken Brewery

Melkweg Stadsschouwburg

American Hotel

Paradiso

Rijksmuseum

Van Gogh Museum

Stedelijk Museum

Vondelpark

Kattenkabinet

Flower Market

Munttoren

N

Eating and
Drinking

fered something of a decline lately, it still offers a genteel escape from the tackiness of much of Rembrandtplein.

De Tap (68), Prinsengracht 478. Roomy bar with a balcony and more individuality than you'd expect this close to Leidseplein.

Terzijde (55), Kerkstraat 59. Within a stone's throw of Leidsestraat, this is a peaceful little bar used by the locals.

Vive la Vie (16), Amstelstraat 7. Small, campy bar, patronized mostly, but not exclusively, by women and transvestites; steps away from the *iT* disco.

Café de Wetering (94), Weteringstraat 37. Tucked away out of sight off the Spiegelgracht, this is a wonderfully atmospheric local brown café, complete with wood beams and sleeping cat.

De Zotte Proeflokaal (65), Raamstraat 29. Belgian hangout on the edge of the Jordaan. Food, liqueurs and hundreds of different types of beer.

Gay bars (Rembrandtplein)

Amstel Taveerne (8), Amstel 54. Well-established, traditional gay bar with regular singalongs. Always packed, and at its most vivacious in summer when the crowds spill out onto the street.

April (22), Reguliersdwarsstraat 37. On the itinerary of almost every gay visitor to Amsterdam. Lively and cosmopolitan, with a good selection of foreign newspapers, cakes and coffee, as well as booze.

Chez Manfred (12), Halvemaansteeg 10. Camp and often outrageous small bar. Can be packed at peak times, when everyone joins in the singalongs.

Company (17), Amstel 106. Western-style leather bar. Fills up later in the evening.

Cupido (10), Paardenstraat 7. Uninhibited bar in a dodgy alley off Rembrandtplein.

Downtown (21), Reguliersdwarsstraat 31. A favourite with visitors. Relaxed and friendly, with inexpensive meals.

Entre Nous (14), Halvemaansteeg 14. Just down the road from *Chez Manfred*, and with much the same campy ambience.

Favourite Tavern (24), Korte Reguliersdwarsstraat 10. Cosy, traditional brown café with a welcoming atmosphere.

Fellows (7), Amstel 50. Civilized and immaculately clean bar on the river. An ideal location in summer.

Gaiety (6), Amstel 14. Small gay bar with a warm welcome. One of the most popular young gay haunts in Amsterdam.

Havana (19), Reguliersdwarsstraat 17. Stylish and would-be sophisticated hangout patronized by those who like to be seen out on the town.

Krokodil (25), Amstelstraat 34. Amiable, noisy bar in between the discos and clubs.

Milord (18) Amstel 102. Wild bar amongst wild bars.

Monopole Taveerne (9), Amstel 60. Semi-leather bar, popular with both tourists and locals, especially on hot afternoons.

Montmartre de Paris (15), Halvemaansteeg 17. A convivial brown café, with the emphasis on music and entertainment.

Gay bars (Kerkstraat)

Camp Café (53), Kerkstraat 45. Pleasant mix of friendly regulars and foreign visitors. Worth a visit for the ceiling alone, which is covered with a collection of beer mugs from around the world.

Cosmo Bar (37), Kerkstraat 42. Comfortable, quiet bar, part of the *West End Hotel* (see p.177). Daily midnight to 3am.

Mankind (95), Weteringstraat 60. Quiet, non-scene bar with its own terrace and landing stage. Lovely in summer.

Meia Meia "66" (56), Kerkstraat 63. Good if you like Guinness; popular with the clone regulars.

De Spijker (36), Kerkstraat 4. Leather and jeans bar that has made a name for itself with its twice-monthly, safe sex jack-off parties. Open from 1pm.

Coffeeshops

Borderline (26), Amstelstraat 37. Opposite the *iT* disco, with gently bouncing house beats. Open until 2.30am Fri & Sat.

The Bulldog, Leidseplein 15 (75); Korte Leidsedwarsstraat 49. The biggest and most famous of the coffeeshop chains, and a long way from its pokey Red Light District dive origins. The main Leidseplein branch (the Palace), housed in a former police station, has a large cocktail bar, coffeeshop, juice bar and souvenir shop, all with separate entrances. It's big and brash, not at all the place for a quiet smoke, though the dope they sell (packaged up in neat little brand-labelled bags) is reliably good.

Free I (30), Reguliersdwarsstraat 70. Tiny place that looks and feels like an African mud hut, except for the hip-hop beats. Grass specialists.

Global Chillage (54), Kerkstraat 51. Celebrated slice of Amsterdam dope culture, always comfortably filled with tie-dyed stone-heads propped up against the walls, so chilled they're horizontal.

Grasshopper (42), Utrechtsestraat 21. The quietest branch of an Amsterdam institution in dope-smoking; other locations in the Red Light District.

Lucky Mothers (100), Keizersgracht 665. Perhaps the best general coffeeshop in the city – in an old canal house on a quiet stretch of the Keizersgracht near Rembrandtplein, with a welcoming atmosphere, good dope and a wonderful little terrace. Highly recommended.

Mellow Yellow (90), Vijzelgracht 33. Sparse but bright coffeeshop with a small but good-quality dope list. A little out of the way, but makes up for it in friendliness.

The Otherside (27), Reguliersdwarsstraat 6. Gay coffeeshop, (in Dutch, "from the otherside" is a euphemism for gay). Despite stiff competition from its more established neighbours, it's managed to find a niche. Mostly men, but women welcome.

Tearooms

Backstage (86), Utrechtsedwarsstraat 67. Run by former cabaret stars the Christmas Twins (Greg and Gary), this offbeat place also sells knitwear and African jewellery.

Errol Trumpie (38), Leidsestraat 46. The place for pastries and chocolates, with a small tearoom at the back. Try the *koffie complet de patisserie* – a pot of coffee and plate of heavily calorific pastries.

Gary's Muffins, Prinsengracht 454 (67); Reguliersdwarsstraat 53 (23). The best, and most authentic, New York bagels in town, with big, American-style cups of coffee (and half-price refills) and wonderful fresh-baked muffins. Reguliersdwarsstraat branch open until 3am.

Metz (40), Keizersgracht 455. Wonderful café on the top floor of the *Metz* department store, giving panoramic views over the canals of Amsterdam. Pricey, but then in *Metz* you're not supposed to care.

Café Panini (85), Vijzelgracht 3. Tearoom-cum-restaurant with good sandwiches, plus pasta dishes in the evening.

Pompadour Patisserie (1), Huidenstraat 12. A great patisserie specializing in handmade chocolates.

Café de Stoep (2), Singel 415. Peaceful, rather ordinary café that's a good bet for a simple light lunch.

Studio 2 (5), Singel 504. Pleasantly situated, airy tearoom with a delicious selection of rolls and sandwiches. Recommended.

De Utrechtsepoort (87), Utrechtsestraat 113. Small, homely and serving delicious pancakes.

Jordaan

All the following places are marked on the map on p.206 – the number in brackets after each name refers to its location.

Bars and cafés

Chris (44), Bloemstraat 42. Very proud of itself for being the Jordaan's (and

Eating and Drinking

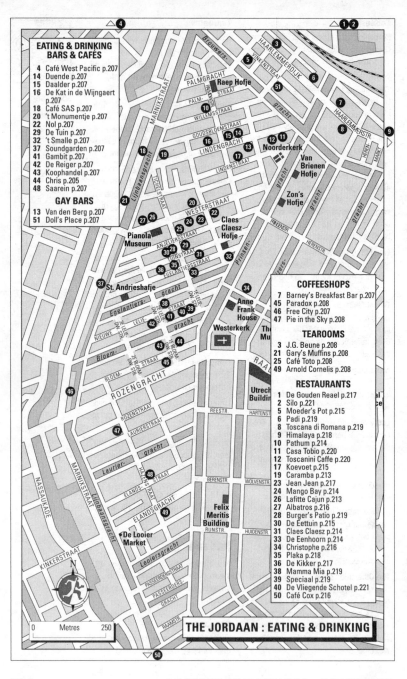

THE JORDAAN : EATING & DRINKING

Amsterdam's) oldest bar, dating from 1624. Comfortable, homely atmosphere.

Daalder (15), Lindengracht 90. A relatively new Jordaan drinking place, normally filled with locals, which makes a good alternative to *De Tuin*.

Duende (14), Lindengracht 62. Wonderful little tapas bar tucked away in the Jordaan, with regular flamenco performances.

Gambit (41), Bloemgracht 20. Chess bar, with boards laid out all day until midnight.

De Kat in de Wijngaert (16), Lindengracht 160. Hefty *bessenjenevers* and an enticing name.

Koophandel (43), Bloemgracht 49. Empty before midnight, this is the early-hours bar you've dreamed of, in an old warehouse on one of Amsterdam's most picturesque canals. Open until at least 3am, often later.

't Monumentje (20), Westerstraat 120. Unspectacular Jordaan local haunt that plays good music. Likeable and inexpensive.

Nol (22), Westerstraat 109. Probably the epitome of the jolly Jordaan singing bar, a luridly lit dive, popular with Jordaan gangsters and ordinary Amsterdammers alike. Opens and closes late, especially at weekends, when the back-slapping joviality and drunken singalongs keep you here until closing time.

De Reiger (42), Nieuwe Leliestraat 34. The Jordaan's main meeting place, an old-style café filled with modish Amsterdammers. Affordable food.

Saarein (48), Elandsstraat 119. Women only; men refused entry at all times. Though some of the former glory of this café is gone, it's still a relaxing place to take it easy. Also a useful starting point for contacts and information. Closed Mon.

Café SAS (18), Marnixstraat 79. An artists' bar and café backing onto a canal, open all day, with couches, armchairs and all kinds of cosiness, enhanced after dark by candlelight.

't Smalle (32), Egelantiersgracht 12. Candle-lit and comfortable, with a barge out front for relaxed summer afternoons. One of the highlights of the city.

Soundgarden (37), Marnixstraat 164. Alternative grunge bar, packed with people and noise, with a canalside terrace as a retreat.

De Tuin (29), 2e Tuindwarsstraat 13. The Jordaan has some marvellously unpretentious bars, and this is one of the best: agreeably unkempt and always filled with locals.

Café West Pacific (4), Westergasfabriek, Haarlemmerweg 8. Large bar with an open fireplace, which attracts a hip young crowd of Amsterdammers. Mutates into a disco after 11pm.

Gay bars

Van den Berg (13), Lindengracht 95. Likeable local café with good food and a billiard table. Frequented mainly by gays and lesbians.

Doll's Place (51), Vinkenstraat 57. A mixed bar, rather off the beaten track but popular with local gays and lesbians.

Coffeeshops

Barney's Breakfast Bar (7), Haarlemmerstraat 102. Not exactly a coffeeshop, but not exactly a café either, *Barney's* is simply the most civilized place in town to enjoy a big joint with a fine breakfast.

Free City (46), Marnixstraat 233. Crowded coffeeshop done up in Mad Max style that's favoured by Amsterdammers in the know. Good dope.

Paradox (45), 1e Bloemdwarsstraat 2. If you're fed up with coffeeshop food offerings of burgers, cheeseburgers or double cheeseburgers, *Paradox* satisfies the munchies with outstanding natural food, including spectacular fresh fruit concoctions. Live music on Sunday afternoons, when English becomes the *lingua franca*. Closes 7pm.

Eating and Drinking

Eating and
Drinking

Pie in the Sky (47), 2e Laurierdwarsstraat
64. Beautiful canal-corner setting, great
for outside summer lounging.

Tearooms

Arnold Cornelis (49) Elandsgracht 78.
Confectioner with a snug tearoom.

J.G. Beune (3), Haarlemmerdijk 156. Age-
old chocolatier with a tearoom attached.

Gary's Muffins (21), Marnixstraat 121.
Branch of the New York bagel-and-muf-
fin teashop, with the biggest cups of
coffee around. Sunday newspaper heav-
en.

Café Toto (25), 2e Anjeliersdwarsstraat 6.
Small place with very tasty hot chocolate.

Jodenbuurt

All the following places are marked on
the map opposite – the number in
brackets after each name refers to its
location.

Bars and cafés

Docksider (7), Entrepotdok 7. Strange
combination of bar, Japanese restaurant
and snooker hall, out in the booming
Eastern Islands district.

De Druif (4), Rapenburgerplein 83. One
of the city's most beguiling bars, and
one that hardly anyone knows about. Its
popularity with the locals lends it a village pub feel.

East of Eden (11), Linnaeusstraat 11. A
wonderfully relaxed little place right near
the Tropenmuseum. Appealing combination of high-ceilinged splendour and
gently waving palm trees, with James
Dean thrown in on top. Well worth a
sunny afternoon.

Entredok (5), Entrepotdok 64. Perhaps
the best of a growing number of bars in
this up-and-coming area. The clientele
hails from the surrounding hi-tech
offices, though increasingly from the residential blocks in between, too.

De Groene Olifant (10), Sarphatistraat
126. Metres from the Muiderpoort, this is
a characterful old wood-panelled brown

café, with floor to ceiling windows and
an excellent, varied menu.

't IJ, in the De Gooyer windmill (1),
Funenkade 7. The beers (*Natte, Zatte*
and *Struis*) are brewed on the premises
and extremely strong. A fun place to
drink yourself silly. Wed–Sun 3–8pm.

Café 't Sluyswacht (8), Jodenbreestraat 1.
A tiny, leaning hut with water on three
sides, which has somehow survived the
upheavals to hit the Jodenbreestraat.
Opposite the Rembrandthuis.

Tisfris (9), St Antoniesbreestraat 142.
Colourful, split-level café and bar near
the Rembrandthuis, and minutes from
Waterlooplein. Youthful and popular.

Museumplein and the Vondelpark

All the following places are marked on
the map on p.210 – the number in
brackets after each name refers to its
location.

Bars and cafés

Café Ebeling (2), Overtoom 52.
Alternative, but not overly raucous, bar
within a few minutes of Leidseplein,
housed in an old bank – with the toilets
in the vaults.

Helfensteyn (1), Overtoom 28. Popular
and agreeable *eetcafé* about a five-min
walk from Leidseplein. Food is a little
pricey, though.

Hellen's Place (10), Overtoom 497. Bills
itself as a "women-friendly erotic café",
and welcomes those of all sexual persuasions to the bar, or the cellar with its
mixed darkroom and S&M facilities. Entry
ƒ5.

Kasbah (33), Amstelveenseweg 134.
Squat bar, part of the OCCII venue (see
p.226), with candles, atmosphere and
cheap drinks.

Keyser (11), Van Baerlestraat 96 ☎671
1441. In operation since 1905, and right
next door to the Concertgebouw, this
café/restaurant exudes *fin-de-siècle*
charm, with ferns, gliding bow-tied waiters, and a dark, carved-wood interior.

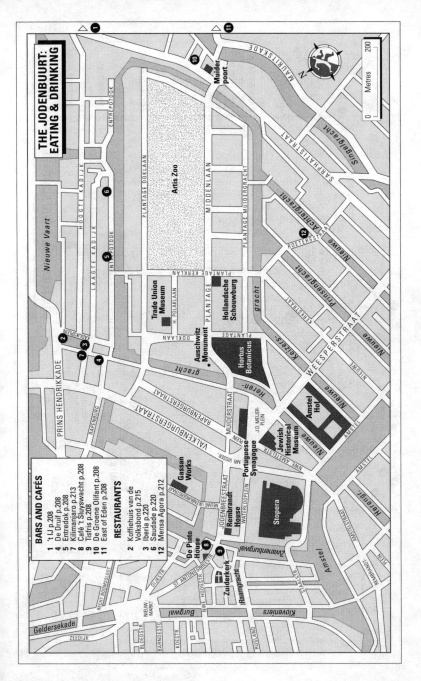

THE JODENBUURT: EATING & DRINKING

BARS AND CAFÉS

1 't IJ p.208
4 De Druif p.208
5 Entredok p.208
8 Kilimanjaro p.213
7 Café 't Sluyswacht p.208
3 Tisfris p.208
10 De Groene Olifant p.208
11 East of Eden p.208

RESTAURANTS

2 Koffiehuis van de
  Volksbond p.215
6 Iberia p.220
3 Saudade p.220
12 Mensa Agora p.212

Nieuwe Vaart

Artis Zoo

Trade Union Museum

Hollandsche Schouwburg

Auschwitz Monument

Hortus Botanicus

Amstel Hof

Jewish Historical Museum

Portuguese Synagogue

Gassan Works

De Pinto House

Zuiderkerk

Rembrandt House

Stopera

Muiderpoort

Geldersekade

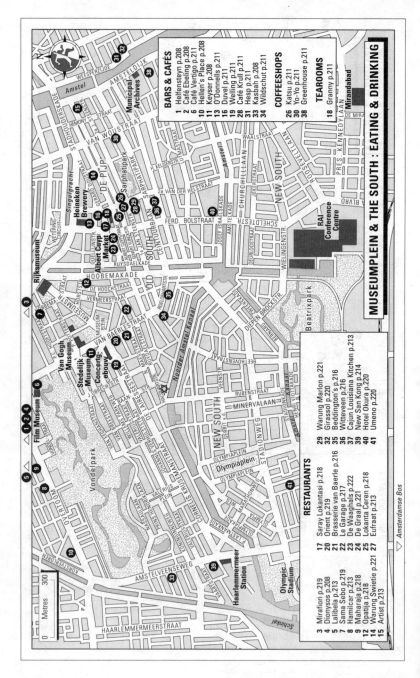

MUSEUMPLEIN & THE SOUTH : EATING & DRINKING

BARS & CAFÉS

1 Helfensteyn p.208
2 Café Ebeling p.208
6 Café Vertigo p.211
10 Hellen's Place p.208
11 Keyser p.208
13 O'Donnells p.211
16 Duvel p.211
19 Welling p.211
28 Café Krull p.211
31 Hesp p.211
33 Kasbah p.208
34 Wildschut p.211

COFFEESHOPS

26 Katsu p.211
30 Yo-Yo p.211
38 Greenhouse p.211

TEAROOMS

18 Granny p.211

RESTAURANTS

3 Mirafiori p.219
4 Dionysos p.208
5 Lalibela p.213
7 Sama Sebo p.219
8 Hamilcar p.213
9 Maharaja p.218
12 Opatija p.218
14 Warung Swietie p.221
15 Artist p.213

17 Saray Lokantasi p.218
20 Orient p.219
21 Brasserie van Baerle p.216
22 Le Garage p.217
23 De Waaghals p.222
24 De Graal p.221
25 Lokanta Ceren p.218
27 Eufraat p.213

29 Warung Marlon p.221
32 Girassol p.220
35 Beddington's p.216
36 Witteveen p.216
37 Cajun Louisiana Kitchen p.213
39 New San Kong p.214
40 Hotel Okura p.220
41 Umeno p.220

Prices are slightly above average, especially for the food, but a wonderful place nonetheless. You'll need to make bookings for the restaurant, and dress accordingly. Closed Sun.

Café Vertigo (6), Vondelpark 3. Attached to the Film Museum, this is a wonderful place to while away a sunny afternoon (or take refuge from the rain), with a spacious interior and a large terrace overlooking the park.

Welling (19), J.W. Brouwersstraat 32. Supposedly the traditional haunt of the gloomy Amsterdam intellectual, *Welling* is usually packed solid with performers and visitors from the Concertgebouw next door.

Wildschut (34), Roelof Hartplein 1. Large and congenial bar famous for its Art Deco trimmings. Not far from the Concertgebouw, with the Amsterdam School architecture all around.

The South

All the following places are marked on the map opposite – the number in brackets after each name refers to its location.

Bars and cafés

Duvel (16), 1e van der Helststraat 59. An *eetcafé* on a pedestrianized street adjacent to Albert Cuypstraat. Handy if you've come to shop in the market.

Hesp (31), Weesperzijde 130. Quite a way out, but with a real old-fashioned atmosphere and rarely any tourists. Frequented by hacks from the nearby *Volkskrant*, *Trouw* and *Parool* newspapers.

Café Krull (28), Sarphatipark 2. On the corner of 1e van der Helststraat, a few metres from the Albert Cuyp, this is an atmospheric place on a lively corner, serving drinks, snacks and jazz all day long from 11am.

O'Donnells (13), Ferdinand Bolstraat 5. The best Guinness in town, in a newly opened but already established Irish pub just behind the Heineken brewery. A

seemingly limitless interior worms its way back into the building.

Coffeeshops

Greenhouse, Tolstraat 4 (38); Waterlooplein 345. Consistently sweeps the boards at the annual Cannabis Cup, with medals for its dope as well as "Best Coffeeshop". Tolstraat is a way down to the south (tram #4), but worth the trek: if you're only buying once, buy here.

Katsu (26), 1e van der Helststraat 70. Tatty, neighbourhood coffeeshop just off the Albert Cuyp market, with excellent weed and a 1970s music collection.

Yo-Yo (30), 2e Jan van der Heijdenstraat 79. About as local as it's possible to get. Down in the Pijp, to the east of the Sarphatipark, a small, airy little place to seek out smoking solitude.

Tearooms

Granny (18), 1e van der Helststraat 45. Just off the Albert Cuyp market, with terrific *appelgebak* and *koffie verkeerd*.

Restaurants

Amsterdam may not be Europe's culinary capital – Dutch cuisine is firmly rooted in the meat, potato and cabbage school of cooking – but as a recompense, the country's colonial adventures have ensured there's a wide range of non-Dutch **restaurants**: Amsterdam is acclaimed for the best Indonesian food outside Indonesia, at prices which – by big-city standards – are hard to beat. Other cuisines from around the world are also well represented: aside from close-at-hand French, Spanish and Italian influences, there are some fine Chinese and Thai restaurants, and a growing number of Moroccan and Middle Eastern places, as well as many covering the range of Indian cuisine. Amsterdam also excels in the quantity and variety of its *eetcafés* and bars, which serve increasingly adventurous food, quite cheaply, in a relaxed and unpretentious setting.

The reviews of restaurants and *eetcafés* that follow are grouped alphabeti-

Eating and
Drinking

Eating and Drinking

Check out the bar and café listings in the previous section for more good-value eating options.

cally by cuisine. We've indicated the average cost for a starter and main course without drinks within each listing, but as a broad guide, very few places charge more than ƒ30 for a main course, and many charge much less than this; you can get a sizeable, quality meal at many *eetcafés* and smaller restaurants for ƒ20 or less. Bars and cafés are also worth checking out: many serve food, and at lunchtime it's possible to fill up cheaply with a bowl of soup or a French bread sandwich.

The majority of *eetcafés* are **open** all day; most restaurants open at 5 or 6pm. The Dutch eat out early – very rarely later than 9pm – and restaurants normally close their doors at 10 or 11pm, though you'll still be served if you're already installed. Times can vary a little according to season or how busy things are that night. Vegetarian restaurants tend to close even earlier than this.

Unless indicated otherwise, all the places we've listed are open seven days a week, from 5 or 6pm until 10 or 11pm. At anywhere we've described as Moderate or Expensive, it's sensible to call ahead and reserve a table. Larger restaurants will probably take major credit cards, but *eetcafés* and smaller restaurants almost certainly won't. All restaurant and café bills include 17.5 percent sales tax as well as a 15 percent service charge. **Tipping** on top of this is completely optional and not expected – if service merits it, the custom is generally to hand some change directly to your server rather than adding it to the bill.

One thing all visitors to the city should be aware of is the practice of several restaurants in and around the tourist centre of Leidseplein of refusing to serve a glass of ordinary water with a meal, insisting that you pay for mineral

---

Budget eating

Listed here are a few places where it's possible to fill up for under ƒ13 per person, which is the least you can expect to pay for a meal in Amsterdam. Check out, too, the pancake places on p.215 and the food delivery box on p.222.

Bojo, reviewed on p.218. Indonesian.

Duende, p.220. Spanish.

Het Beeren, p.215. Dutch.

Keuken van 1870, p.215. Dutch.

Mensa Agora, Roeterstraat 11 ☎525 2699 (12, map p.209). Self-service student cafeteria, with all that that entails. Mon–Fri noon–2pm & 5–7pm.

Mensa Atrium, Oudezijds Achterburgwal 237 ☎525 3999 (84, map p.194). Central self-service cafeteria attached to the University of Amsterdam (but open to all) – full meals for under ƒ10, though the quality leaves a little to be desired. Mon–Fri noon–2pm & 5–7pm.

Maoz Falafel, Reguliersbreestraat 45 ☎624 9290 (13, map p.202). The best street-food in the city – mashed chickpea balls deep-fried and served in

Middle Eastern bread, with as much salad as you can eat, for the grand sum of ƒ5. Mon–Thurs & Sun 11am–2am, Fri & Sat 11am–3am.

Mr Hot Potato, Leidsestraat 44 ☎623 2301 (39, map p.202). The only place in town for baked potatoes – nothing fancy, but cheap at around ƒ5. Daily 10am–8pm.

New King, p.214. Chinese.

La Place, part of *Vroom & Dreesman* department store, Kalverstraat 201 ☎622 0171 (92, map p.194). Self-service buffet-style restaurant, where it's easily possible to fill up for under ƒ10. Daily 10am–9pm.

Rimini, p.219. Italian.

Silo, p.221. Vegetarian/vegan.

Suzy Creamcheese, p.221. Vegetarian.

Toko Sari, p.219. Indonesian takeaway.

water instead. This is a policy of, among others, the famous, and otherwise worthwhile, Indonesian restaurant *Bojo*, the *Good Food Chinese Restaurant* and *Pizza Venezia*. If this is important to you, check with the staff before you sit down: there is absolutely no reason why any restaurant shouldn't give you a glass of water, and ones that refuse to do so don't deserve your money or goodwill.

African and Middle Eastern

Artist, 2e Jan Steenstraat 1 ☎671 4264 (15, map p.210). A small Lebanese restaurant just off Albert Cuypstraat. Inexpensive.

Axum, Utrechtsedwarsstraat 85 ☎622 8389 (88, map p.202). Small Ethiopian *eetcafé*, open from 2pm, with a choice of nine authentic, well-prepared dishes. Budget.

Beyrouth, Kinkerstraat 18 ☎616 0635. Small Lebanese place out in the Old West and well off any beaten tracks; lacking in atmosphere, but the food is highly regarded. Tram #3 or #12 to Kinkerstraat, or #7 or #17 to Bilderdijkstraat. Closed Tues. Inexpensive.

Eufraat, 1e van der Helststraat 72 ☎672 0579 (27, map p.210). Basic *eetcafé* in the midst of the cosmopolitan Pijp district, serving Syrian food which just about translates to the very un-Syrian setting. Daily 11am–midnight. Inexpensive.

Hamilcar, Overtoom 306 ☎683 7981 (8, map p.210). Fine Tunisian and North African cuisine; particularly good for its couscous, usually prepared by the owner-chef. Closed Mon & Tues. Inexpensive.

Kilimanjaro, Rapenburgerplein 6 ☎622 3485 (7, map p.209). Bright African

restaurant in a bedraggled part of town, serving such delicacies as Tanzanian antelope, Moroccan *tajine* and Ethiopian pancakes. Small, simple and super-friendly. Closed Mon. Moderate.

Lalibela, 1e Helmersstraat 249 ☎683 8332 (5, map p.210). Another excellent Ethiopian restaurant, with a well-balanced menu and attentive service. Inexpensive.

Marrakech, Nieuwezijds Voorburgwal 134 ☎623 5003 (34, map p.194). Couscous place with vegetarian options. Inexpensive.

The Americas

Alfonso's, Korte Leidsedwarsstraat 69 ☎627 0580 (79, map p.202). Substantial helpings of relatively bland Mexican food; vegetarian dishes. Good value for Leidseplein, and not too touristy, but avoid the margaritas as they're watery and overpriced. Mon–Fri 5–10.30pm, Sat & Sun noon–10.30pm. Inexpensive.

Cajun Louisiana Kitchen, Ceintuurbaan 260 ☎664 4729 (37, map p.210). Not cheap, but offering authentic Cajun flavours. Moderate.

Caramba, Lindengracht 342 ☎627 1188 (19, map p.206). Steamy, busy Mexican restaurant in the heart of the Jordaan. The margaritas are almost on a par with *Rose's* (see below). Inexpensive.

Iguazu, Prinsengracht 703 ☎420 3910 (83, map p.202). For carnivores only: a superb Argentinian–Brazilian restaurant, with perhaps the best fillet steak in town. Daily noon–midnight. Moderate.

Lafitte Cajun, Westerstraat 200 ☎623 4270 (26, map p.206). More central than the *Louisiana Kitchen*. Closed Tues. Moderate.

Mexico, Prinsengracht 188 ☎624 6538 (33, map p.198). A cheaper and more amiable alternative to the glossier central eateries. Jolly owners, excellent food. Inexpensive.

Mister Coco's, Thorbeckeplein 8 ☎627 2423 (33, map p.202). Bustling, determinedly youthful American restaurant

Eating and Drinking

Eating and Drinking

that lives up to its own slogan of "lousy food and warm beer". Cheap, though (try the all-you-can-eat spare ribs), and very lively. Inexpensive.

Café Pacifico, Warmoesstraat 31 ☎624 2911 (20, map p.194). Quality array of Mexican (and Mexican–Californian) food, in a cramped and crowded little joint only minutes from Centraal Station. Moderate.

Rose's Cantina, Reguliersdwarsstraat 38 ☎625 9797 (29, map p.202). In the heart of trendy Amsterdam, this qualifies as possibly the city's most crowded restaurant. No bookings, and you'll almost certanly have to wait; but it's no hardship to sit at the bar nursing a cocktail and watching the would-be cool bunch. The margaritas should carry a public health warning. Moderate.

Chinese, Thai and Filipino

Dynasty, Reguliersdwarsstraat 30 ☎626 8400 (28, map p.202). Festive choice of Indo-Chinese food, with Vietnamese and Thai options; not for the shoestring traveller. Subdued atmosphere suits the prices (average ƒ75). Closed Tues. Expensive.

Hoi Tin, Zeedijk 122 ☎625 6451 (39, map p.194). One of the best places to choose in Amsterdam's rather dodgy Chinatown, this is a constantly busy place with an enormous menu (in English too) including some vegetarian dishes. Worth a try. Daily noon–midnight. Moderate.

De Klaas Compaen, Raamgracht 9 ☎623 8708 (69, map p.194). Good Thai food at affordable prices. Daily 5–9.45pm. Moderate.

Lana Thai, Warmoesstraat 10 ☎624 2179 (12, map p.194). Among the best Thai restaurants in town, with seating overlooking the water of Damrak. Quality food, chic surroundings but high prices (ƒ40–50). Closed Tues. Expensive.

Mango Bay, Westerstraat 91 ☎638 1039 (24, map p.206). Slow service and high prices (averaging just over ƒ40) for the Filipino food, but the cocktails make up for it. Daily 6pm–midnight. Expensive.

New King, Zeedijk 115 ☎625 2180 (40, map p.194). Extraordinary range of cheap Chinese dishes – don't count on quality, but your wallet will approve. Free limitless jasmine tea. Daily noon–midnight. Budget.

New San Kong, Amstelveenseweg 338 ☎662 9370 (39, map p.210). Don't be put off by the ranch-style decor; the Cantonese food is excellent and not too pricey (try the dim sum). Take tram #24 to the end of the line. Daily noon–10pm. Moderate.

Pathum, Willemsstraat 16 ☎624 4936 (10, map p.206). Cheap and cheerful Thai place, out in the Jordaan. Closed Tues. Inexpensive.

Road to Manila, Geldersekade 23 ☎638 4338 (13, map p.194). Ground-breaking Filipino restaurant renowned for the quality of its food and service. Closed Tues. Moderate.

Tom Yam, Staalstraat 22 ☎622 9533 (95, map p.194). High-quality Thai restaurant in the middle of town. Branches at Prinsengracht 42 and Utrechtsestraat 55 do takeaways. Moderate–Expensive.

Dutch

De Blauwe Hollander, Leidsekruisstraat 28 ☎623 3014 (78, map p.202). Dutch food in generous quantities – something of a boon in an otherwise touristy, unappealing part of town. Expect to share a table. Inexpensive.

Claes Claesz, Egelantiersstraat 24 ☎625 5306 (31, map p.206). Exceptionally friendly Jordaan restaurant that attracts a good mixed crowd and serves excellent Dutch food. Live music most nights. Often has (pricey) special menus to celebrate occasions like Easter or the Queen's Birthday. Closed Mon. Moderate.

De Eenhoorn, 2e Egelantiersdwarsstraat 6 ☎623 8352 (33, map p.206). A less attractive alternative to *De Eettuin* (see below) but just down the road, so handy if it's full. Inexpensive.

De Eettuin, 2e Tuindwarsstraat 10 ☎623 7706 (30, map p.206). Hefty portions of Dutch food, with salad from a serve-yourself bar. Non-meat eaters can content themselves with the large, if dull, vegetarian plate, or the delicious fish casserole. Inexpensive.

Haesje Claes, Spuistraat 275 ☎624 9998 (71, map p.194). Dutch cuisine at its best. Extremely popular – go early to get a table. Daily noon–10pm. Moderate.

Het Beeren, Koningsstraat 15 ☎622 2329 (46, map p.194). Daily 5.30–9.30pm. Huge portions of the simplest Dutch fare – cabbage, mashed potato and steaming stew. Budget.

Hollands Glorie, Kerkstraat 220 ☎624 4764 (61, map p.202). Accessible, welcoming place with a good selection of Dutch dishes and attentive service. Inexpensive.

Keuken van 1870, Spuistraat 4 ☎624 8965 (10, map p.194). Former soup kitchen in the heart of the city, still serving Dutch meat-and-potato staples. Frill-free. Mon–Fri 12.30–8pm, Sat & Sun 4–9pm. Budget.

Koevoet, Lindenstraat 17 ☎624 0846 (17, map p.206). The "Cow's-Foot" – or, alternatively, the "Crowbar" – is a traditional Jordaan *eetcafé* serving unpretentious food at good prices. Closed Mon. Budget.

Koffiehuis van de Volksbond, Kadijksplein 4 ☎622 1209 (2, map p.209). Formerly a Communist Party café (and apparently the place where the local dockworkers used to receive their wages at the end of each week), this is now an Eastern Islands neighbourhood restaurant, with variable food. Inexpensive.

Moeder's Pot, Vinkenstraat 119 ☎623 7643 (5, map p.206). Ultra-cheap Dutch food, usually of fair quality, though recent reports have warned of neglect, under-cooking and watery flavours. Vegetarians should steer clear of the touted vegetarian dish. Mon–Sat 5–9.30pm. Budget.

Oud Holland, Nieuwezijds Voorburgwal 105 ☎624 6848 (31, map p.194). Basic, down-the-line Dutch staples (cabbage-and-potato stew, pea soup, etc) in a seventeenth-century building. Mon–Sat noon–9.30pm. Inexpensive.

De Silveren Spiegel, Kattengat 4 ☎624 6589 (5, map p.194). There's been a

Eating and
Drinking

Pancakes

In the tradition of simple cooking, pancakes are a Dutch speciality – for fillers and light meals, you'd be hard pushed to find better. Although there are plenty of places dotted around town, the three listed below are recommended.

Bredero, Oudezijds Voorburgwal 244 ☎622 9461 (77, map p.194). On the edge of the Red Light District, one of the city's best pancake deals. Daily noon–7pm. Budget.

The Pancake Bakery, Prinsengracht 191 ☎625 1333 (20, map p.198). Open all day, in a beautiful old house on the canal. A large selection of (filled) pancakes from ƒ10, many big enough to count as a meal. Daily noon–9.30pm. Budget.

Pannekoekhuis Upstairs, Grimburgwal 2 ☎626 5603 (83, map p.194). Minuscule place in a tumbledown house opposite the university buildings, with sweet and savoury pancakes at low prices. Student discount. Closes 7pm. Wed–Fri noon–7pm, Sat & Sun noon–6pm. Budget.

Eating and
Drinking

restaurant in this location since 1614, and *The Silver Mirror* is one of the best in the city, with a delicately balanced menu of Dutch cuisine. The proprietor lives on the coast and brings in the fish himself. Spectacular food, with a cellar of 350 wines to complement it. Five-course dinner for two at a table set with silver is a cool ƒ200, though you can get away with around ƒ75 each. Closed Sun. Expensive.

Witteveen, Ceintuurbaan 256 ☎662 4368 (36, map p.210). Held in high regard by locals, this is a thoroughly Dutch, highly atmospheric place for Amsterdam cooking; around ƒ40 and up. Expensive.

Zemmel, Prinsengracht 126 ☎620 6525 (26, map p.198). A good place to eat in summer, with a nice location by the water. Simple food, or you can go there just for a drink. Moderate.

't Zwaantje, Berenstraat 12 ☎623 2373 (38, map p.198). Old-fashioned Dutch restaurant with a nice atmosphere and well-cooked, reasonably priced food. Moderate.

Fish

Albatros, Westerstraat 264 ☎627 9932 (27, map p.206). Family-run restaurant serving some mouth-wateringly imaginative fish dishes. A place to splash out and linger over a meal. Closed Wed. Expensive.

Lucius, Spuistraat 247 ☎624 1831 (51, map p.194). Pricey at around ƒ55 for two courses, but one of the best fish restaurants in town, with wonderful smoked salmon and a vast array of all kinds of fish and seafood, delicately prepared. Very popular. Closed Sun. Expensive.

De Oesterbar, Leidseplein 10 ☎626 3463 (66, map p.202). Veteran restaurant overlooking the Leidseplein action, popular with a largely older crowd. Worth it if everywhere else is full. Daily noon–midnight. Moderate.

Sluizer, Utrechtsestraat 45 ☎626 3557 (46, map p.202). Next door to its trendy meat-based partner (see below), serving

simply prepared, good quality fish. Moderate.

French and Belgian

Beddington's, Roelof Hartstraat 6 ☎676 5201 (35, map p.210). Refined French cuisine blended with Japanese delicacy – always original, never disappointing. The subtlety of flavours is matched by Japanese-inspired presentation (especially for the fish dishes), and a meal here can be memorable, if not cheap at ƒ90 or so for a couple of courses. Closed Sun. Expensive.

Bistro de Vlier, Prinsengracht 422 ☎623 2281 (37, map p.198). Fairly basic cooking in an affable atmosphere. Daily 5.30–11.30pm. Inexpensive.

Bonjour, Keizersgracht 770 ☎626 6040 (48, map p.202). Classy French cuisine in a romantic setting, from about ƒ40. Closed Mon & Tues. Expensive.

Brasserie van Baerle, Van Baerlestraat 158 ☎679 1532 (21, map p.210). Light and airy restaurant serving good food; run by a couple of ex-*KLM* flight attendants. Very popular, especially on Sun. Closed Sat. Moderate.

Café Cox, Marnixstraat 427 ☎620 7222 (50, map p.206). Stylish but amicable bar and restaurant underneath the Stadsschouwburg, serving a wide range of dishes. Inexpensive.

Chez Georges, Herenstraat 3 ☎626 3332 (11, map p.198). A highly rated upmarket Belgian eatery, with all the meat that entails; ƒ45 and up. Closed Wed & Sun. Expensive.

Christophe, Leliegracht 46 ☎625 0807 (34, map p.206). Classic Michelin-starred restaurant on a quiet and beautiful canal, drawing inspiration from the olive-oil-and-basil flavours of southern France and the chef's early years in North Africa. His aubergine terrine with cumin has been dubbed the best vegetarian dish in the world. Reservations far outstrip capacity. Expect to pay ƒ50–60 for two courses. Mon–Sat 6.30–10.30pm. Expensive.

1e Klas Grand Café Restaurant, Platform 2b, Centraal Station ☎625 0131 (1, map p.194). An unlikely setting, but offering good-value (ƒ40 and up) gourmet French cuisine from a well-balanced menu in this deeply atmospheric, restored late nineteenth-century restaurant. Expensive.

't Fornuis, Utrechtsestraat 33 ☎626 9139 (44, map p.202). A slightly cheaper alternative to *Orient Express* (see below), though it's usually very busy. Moderate.

Le Garage, Ruysdaelstraat 54 ☎679 7176 (22, map p.210). This elegant restaurant has quickly become popular with a media crowd and their hangers-on, since it's run by a well-known Dutch TV cook. An eclectic French and Italian menu and sporadic fashion shows. Call to reserve a week ahead, dress to impress and bring at least ƒ60 or so per person. Daily 6–11pm, Mon also noon–2pm. Expensive.

De Gouden Reael, Zandhoek 14 ☎623 3883 (1, map p.206). Fine French food (ƒ40 and up) in a unique setting up in the western harbour. Mon–Fri noon–10pm, Sat 5–10pm. Expensive.

Hemelse Modder, Oude Waal 9 ☎624 3203 (8, map p.194). Tasty meat, fish and vegetarian food in French–Italian style at reasonable prices in an informal atmosphere. Highly popular (especially among the gay community). Closed Mon. Moderate.

Intermezzo, Herenstraat 28 ☎626 0167 (13, map p.198). Good French–Dutch cooking at above-average prices, but worth every penny. Closed Sun. Moderate.

Jardin Parisien, Utrechtsestraat 30a ☎420 4259 (41, map p.202). Cheap and straightforward, with around thirty different menus on offer, most of which seem to start with prawn cocktail. Daily 5pm–midnight. Inexpensive.

Jean Jean, 1e Anjeliersdwarsstraat 12 ☎627 7153 (23, map p.206). Simple, local Jordaan restaurant, with sizeable portions and friendly service. Inexpensive.

De Kikker, Egelantiersstraat 128 ☎627 9198 (36, map p.206). Two-tier, top quality restaurant that has a downstairs *eetcafé*. Upstairs is only really accessible to the well-dressed, wealthy and committed gourmet. Moderate.

De Lieve, Herengracht 88 ☎624 9635 (16, map p.198). Belgian restaurant with a pleasant atmosphere, although reports of the food (from ƒ40 upwards) are mixed. Expensive.

Luden, Spuistraat 304 ☎622 8979 (74, map p.194). Excellent French restaurant that does fine value *prix fixe* menus; expect to pay ƒ40–50. Expensive.

Orient Express, Utrechtsestraat 29 ☎620 5129 (43, map p.202). Not cheap, but very good French food; you can choose from the monthly menu of French-flavoured dishes from each of the countries the Orient Express train passes through. Closed Mon. Moderate.

Quartier Latin, Utrechtsestraat 49 ☎622 7419 (47, map p.202). Small, cosy place, good for a quiet, romantic dinner. Undemanding food and service. Closed Mon. Moderate.

Sluizer, Utrechtsestraat 43 ☎622 6376 (45, map p.202). French-oriented food, in one of Amsterdam's most atmospheric restaurants. There's a fish restaurant of the same name next door – see above. Daily noon–3pm & 5pm–midnight. Moderate.

D'Theeboom, Singel 210 ☎623 8420 (27, map p.198). Classic, ungimmicky French cuisine – around ƒ50 for two courses. Expensive.

Le Zinc . . . et les Dames, Prinsengracht 999 ☎622 9044 (84, map p.202). Wonderfully atmospheric little place

Eating and
Drinking

Eating and
Drinking

serving good quality, simple fare for an average of ƒ45; there's a particularly good wine list. Closed Mon & Sun. Expensive.

Greek, Balkan and Turkish

Aphrodite, Lange Leidsedwarsstraat 91 ☎622 7382 (82, map p.202). Refined Greek cooking in a street where you certainly wouldn't expect it. Fair prices too. Daily 5pm–midnight. Inexpensive.

Dionysos, Overtoom 176 ☎689 4441 (4, map p.210). Fine Greek restaurant a little to the south of Leidseplein, with the distinct added advantage of serving until 1am. Phone ahead if you're going to turn up after midnight. Daily 5pm–1am. Inexpensive.

Izmir, Kerkstraat 66 ☎627 8239 (57, map p.202). Cosy, family-run little Turkish place; welcoming atmosphere and fine kebabs. Daily 5pm–midnight. Inexpensive.

Lokanta Ceren, Albert Cuypstraat 40 ☎673 3524 (25, map p.210). Authentic and well-populated local Turkish place, with a welter of *meze* to suit all tastes and fine kebab dishes. Let the *raki* flow. Daily 2pm–1am. Inexpensive.

Opatija, Hobbemakade 64 ☎671 9495 (12, map p.210). Good range of Croatian specialities, either à la carte or from a choice of set menus. Moderate.

Ouzeri, De Clercqstraat 106 ☎618 1412. Greek *eetcafé* in the Old West where you can compose your own meal and make it as cheap – or as expensive – as you like. Tram #12, #13 or #14 to E. Wolffstraat. Daily 5pm–12.30am.

Plaka, Egelantiersstraat 124 ☎627 9338 (35, map p.206). Enormous plates of greasy Greek grub; vegetarian dishes too. Popular (either book ahead or turn up early) and friendly. Daily 5pm–midnight. Inexpensive.

Saray Lokantasi, Gerard Doustraat 33 ☎671 9216 (17, map p.210). Excellent Turkish eatery down in the Pijp neighbourhood. Popular with students. Inexpensive.

Indian

Akbar, Korte Leidsedwarsstraat 33 ☎624 2211 (77, map p.202). Fabulous South Indian food, especially strong on tandoori, with a fine choice across the board. Plenty for vegetarians. Friendly service. Daily 5–11.30pm. Moderate.

Himalaya, Haarlemmerstraat 11 ☎622 3776 (9, map p.206). Cosy and welcoming atmosphere, with a good selection to choose from. Daily 5–11.30pm. Inexpensive.

Koh-I-Noor, Westermarkt 29 ☎623 3133 (31, map p.198). One of the city's better Indian restaurants, deservedly popular. Inexpensive.

Maharaja, Overtoom 146 ☎616 4838 (9, map p.210). On the far side of the Vondelpark, a small family-run place featuring authentic Northern-style cuisine. Inexpensive.

Poorna, Hartenstraat 29 ☎623 6772 (35, map p.198). The speciality here is spicy tandoori; they also sell Indian silk paintings. Moderate.

Shiva, Reguliersdwarsstraat 72 ☎624 8713 (31, map p.202). The city's outstanding Indian restaurant and far from expensive, with a wide selection of dishes, all expertly prepared. Vegetarians well catered for. Highly recommended. Inexpensive.

Tandoor, Leidseplein 19 ☎623 4415 (74, map p.202). Doesn't live up to its excellent reputation, but pretty good nonetheless. The tandoori dishes are very tasty, and won't break the bank. Inexpensive.

Indonesian

Bojo, Lange Leidsedwarsstraat 51 ☎622 7434 (69, map p.202). Also round the corner at Leidsekruisstraat 12. Possibly the best-value – though certainly not the best – Indonesian place in town. Expect to wait for a table, though – we weren't the first to discover it. Recommended for the quality of the food, but the service can be slow and the atmosphere oppressive. Mon–Wed 4pm–2am, Thurs

& Sun noon–2am, Fri & Sat noon–4am. Budget.

Kantjil en de Tijger, Spuistraat 291 ☎620 0994 (75, map p.194). High-quality food averaging around ƒ55 per person, served in a low-quality environment. Expensive.

Orient, Van Baerlestraat 21 ☎673 4958 (20, map p.210). Excellently prepared dishes, with a wide range to choose from; vegetarians are very well taken care of, and the service is generally good. Expect to pay around ƒ40–50. Daily 5–9pm. Expensive.

Padi, Haarlemmerdijk 50 ☎625 1280 (6, map p.206). Small Indonesian *eetcafé* with a good selection, reasonable prices and a relaxing ambience. Inexpensive.

Puri Mas, Lange Leidsedwarsstraat 37 ☎627 7627 (81, map p.202). Exceptionally good value for money, on a street better known for rip-offs. Friendly and informed service preludes spectacular *rijsttafels*, both meat and vegetarian. Recommended. Moderate.

Sama Sebo, P.C. Hooftstraat 27 ☎662 8146 (7, map p.210). Amsterdam's best-known Indonesian restaurant, especially for its *rijsttafel* – although the prices may initially put you off, it's easy to eat quite reasonably by choosing à la carte dishes, and the food is usually great. Closed Sun. Inexpensive–Moderate.

Speciaal, Nieuwe Leliestraat 142 ☎624 9706 (39, map p.206). Generally agreed to be one of the better Indonesians in this price range. Inexpensive.

Tempo Doeloe, Utrechtsestraat 75 ☎625 6718 (51, map p.202). Reliable, quality place close to Rembrandtplein. As with all Indonesian restaurants, be guid-

ed by the waiter when choosing – some of the dishes are very hot indeed. Daily 6–11.30pm. Moderate.

Toko Sari, Kerkstraat 161 ☎623 2364 (59, map p.202). Tues–Sat 11am–6pm. Fabulous Indonesian takeaway. Budget.

Italian

Burger's Patio, 2e Tuindwarsstraat 12 ☎623 6854 (28, map p.206). Young and convivial Italian restaurant – despite the name, not a burger in sight. Inexpensive.

Casa di David, Singel 426 ☎624 5093 (3, map p.202). Solid-value dark wood Italian restaurant with a long-standing reputation. Pizzas from wood-fired ovens, fresh hand-made pasta, and more substantial fare. Best seats are by the window. Highly recommended. Moderate.

Mamma Mia, 2e Leliedwarsstraat 13 ☎638 7286 (38, map p.206). Good selection of pizzas, in a pleasant, family atmosphere. Budget–Inexpensive.

Mascagni, Utrechtsestraat 65 ☎620 6624 (50, map p.202). Authentic and homely Italian restaurant, family-run, and serving a very large choice of well-cooked dishes. Inexpensive–Moderate.

Mirafiori, Hobbemastraat 2 ☎662 3013 (3, map p.210). Upmarket Italian restaurant with a reputation as one of the city's best. From around ƒ40. Closed Tues. Expensive.

Prego, Herenstraat 25 ☎638 0148 (10, map p.198). Small restaurant serving exceptionally high-quality Mediterranean cuisine from ƒ65 or so for two courses. Daily 7–10.30pm. Expensive.

Rimini, Lange Leidsedwarsstraat 75 ☎622 7014 (71, map p.202). Surprisingly cheap pizza and pasta, most of it well prepared. Daily 4–11.30pm. Budget.

Tartufo, Singel 449 ☎627 7175 (4, map p.202). Two-tiered, two-menu place with a good choice of fair-priced pasta dishes downstairs and more substantial, more expensive fare upstairs. Moderate.

Toscana di Romana, Haarlemmerstraat 130 ☎622 0353 (8, map p.206); also at

Eating and Drinking

Haarlemmerdijk 176. Fairly average food, but the pizzas and pasta dishes are cut from cheap to half-price Mon–Thurs. Inexpensive–Budget.

Toscanini Caffe, Lindengracht 75 ☎623 2813 (12, map p.206). Authentic food prepared in front of your eyes; very popular, so book ahead. At least ƒ55 per person for two courses. Expensive.

Japanese

An, Weteringschans 199 ☎627 0607 (97, map p.202). Excellent cooking in this small, family-run place with an open kitchen. Closed Mon & Tues. Moderate.

Hotel Okura, Ferdinand Bolstraat 333 ☎678 7111 (40, map p.210). Two restaurants in this five-star hotel – *Yamazato* (daily noon–2.30pm & 6–10pm) and *Teppan-Yaki Sazanka* (daily 6.30–10.30pm, plus Mon–Fri noon–2.30pm) – serve the finest Japanese cuisine in the city. Reckon on at least ƒ95 per person. Expensive.

Shizen, Kerkstraat 148 ☎622 8627 (58, map p.202). Superbly prepared, affordable vegetarian and vegan macrobiotic dishes, with fish options. Choice of authentic *tatami* seating (cross-legged at a low table) or a boring table-and-chair. Closed Mon. Moderate.

Tokio Sushi, Utrechtsestraat 98 ☎638 5677 (49, map p.202). Reasonably central outlet for good-quality fresh take-away sushi – box of 6 pieces for ƒ14, or 10 pieces for ƒ23. Larger selections available. Mon–Sat 11–6.30pm. Inexpensive.

Umeno, Agamemnonstraat 27 ☎676 6089 (41, map p.210). Down in the residential New South, but with cooking and prices that are well worth the journey. Closed Mon. Tram #24. Moderate.

Yoichi, Weteringschans 128 ☎622 6829 (98, map p.202). High-class (at least ƒ45 per person) Japanese cuisine in an improbable dark-brown, old Dutch atmosphere. Closed Wed. Expensive.

Spanish and Portuguese

La Cacerola, Weteringstraat 41 ☎626 5397 (89, map p.202). Small and secluded, with likeable if eccentric service – and erratic opening hours. Wed–Fri 6.30–10pm. Moderate.

Casa Tobio, Lindengracht 31 ☎624 8987 (11, map p.206). Small Jordaan restaurant that doles out vast servings of Spanish food; cut costs and risk annoying the management by sharing a paella for two among three – a good general rule for all Spanish places. There have been recent reports of increasing surliness, though. Closed Wed. Inexpensive.

Centra, Lange Niezel 29 ☎622 3050 (26, map p.194). A wonderful selection of Spanish food, masterfully cooked and genially served. In the running for Amsterdam's best Spanish food. Daily 1–11pm. Inexpensive.

Duende, Lindengracht 62 ☎420 6692 (14, map p.206). Wonderful little tapas bar up in the Jordaan, with good, cheap tapas (ƒ3–8 each) to help your drink go down. Mon–Thurs 4pm–1am, Fri 4pm–2am, Sat 2pm–2am, Sun 2pm–1am. Budget.

Girassol, Weesperzijde 135 ☎692 3471 (32, map p.210). Close to Amstel Station, this place is a fair hike out from the centre, but easily merits the journey. A friendly, family-run Portuguese restaurant that Amsterdam foodies have cottoned on to. Inexpensive.

Iberia, Kadijksplein 16 ☎623 6313 (3, map p.209). A little more expensive than some of the others listed here, but good service and great food. Moderate.

Saudade, Entrepotdok 36 ☎625 4845 (6, map p.209). Newly opened Portuguese restaurant out to the east of the centre, with authentic cooking in an appealing canalside setting. Mon & Wed–Sun noon–10pm. Moderate.

Surinamese and Caribbean

Kam Yin, Warmoesstraat 6 ☎625 3115 (7, map p.194). Cheap, if not terribly cheerful, Surinamese–Chinese diner close to Centraal Station. Daily noon–midnight. Budget.

Riaz, Bilderdijkstraat 193 ☎683 6453. Out in the Old West, an excellent

Budget: Under ƒ20

Inexpensive: ƒ20–30

Moderate: ƒ30–40

Expensive: Over ƒ40

Prices are the average cost per person for a starter and main course without drinks.

Eating and Drinking

Surinamese restaurant. Tram #3 or #12 to Kinkerstraat or #7 or #17 to Bilderdijkstraat. Mon–Fri 1–9pm, Sun 2–9pm. Inexpensive.

Rum Runners, Prinsengracht 277 ☎627 4079 (29, map p.198). Caribbean-style bar/restaurant situated in the old Westerkerk hall. Expensive cocktails but well-priced if not always devastatingly tasty food. Moderate.

Warung Marlon, 1e van der Helststraat 55 ☎671 1526 (29, map p.210). Very cheap Surinamese takeaway with a couple of bare tables. There are plenty of other choices in the surrounding streets if this one doesn't appeal. Mon & Wed–Sun 11am–8pm. Budget.

Warung Swietie, 1e Sweelinckstraat 1 ☎671 5833 (14, map p.210). Cheap and cheerful Surinamese–Javanese *eetcafé*. Closed Wed. Daily 11am–9pm. Budget.

Vegetarian and natural

Bolhoed, Prinsengracht 60 ☎626 1803 (15, map p.198). Something of an Amsterdam institution. Familiar vegan and vegetarian options from the daily changing menu, with organic beer to wash it down. More expensive than you might imagine. Daily noon–10pm. Moderate.

Deshima, Weteringschans 65 ☎625 7513 (96, map p.202). A little difficult to spot (it's in the basement), this is actually a macrobiotic food store, with a small restaurant attached. Mon–Fri noon–2pm. Inexpensive.

Golden Temple, Utrechtsestraat 126 ☎626 8560 (91, map p.202). Laid-back place with a little more soul than the average Amsterdam veggie joint. Well-

prepared food and pleasant, attentive service. Walk out satisfied. Daily 5–9.30pm. Inexpensive.

De Graal, Albert Cuypstraat 25 ☎679 3866 (24, map p.210). Smoky, alternative coffeeshop serving macrobiotic food on Mon & Thurs 7–8.30pm. Budget.

Shizen, Kerkstraat 148 ☎622 8627 (58, map p.202). See "Japanese" above. Moderate.

Silo, Westerdoksdijk 51, no phone (2, map p.206). Housed in a huge old grain silo (entry through the last door on your right, at the far end of the building), this is one of the last remaining community squats in Amsterdam, home to 40-odd people. Fantastic food is served in a stone-flagged restaurant overlooking the river five nights a week. Tues, Wed & Sun the food is vegan; on Thurs & Fri it's vegetarian. Limited quantities, so come at 6pm, order and relax. Food is served at 7 or 8. Worth ƒ10 of anyone's money.

Sisters, Nes 102 ☎626 3970 (64, map p.194). A busy and always popular vegetarian restaurant serving delicious, balanced meals, as well as plenty of snack-type dishes. Excellent value. Daily 5–9.30pm. Budget.

Suzy Creamcheese, Cliffordstraat 36 ☎682 0411. You can get a full, three-course meal here for ƒ12.50. The menu changes weekly. Part of a less-than-mainstream community centre near the Westergasfabriek. Tram #10 to Van Hallstraat. Friday only 6–9pm. Budget.

De Vliegende Schotel (Flying Saucer), Nieuwe Leliestraat 162 ☎625 2041 (40, map p.206). Perhaps the best of the city's cheap and wholesome vegetarian restaurants, serving delicious food in large portions. Lots of space, a peaceful ambience and a good noticeboard. Budget.

De Vrolijke Abrikoos, Weteringschans 76 ☎624 4672 (99, map p.202). All ingredients, produce and processes are organic or environmentally friendly in this restaurant that serves fish and meat as well as vegetarian dishes. Mon & Wed–Sun 5.30–9.30pm. Inexpensive.

**Eating and
Drinking**

De Waaghals, Frans Halsstraat 29 ☎679 9609 (23, map p.210). Well-prepared organic dishes in this co-operative-run restaurant near the Albert Cuyp. Tues–Sun 5–9.30pm. Inexpensive.

Food Delivery

Having food **delivered** to your door is just starting to catch on in Amsterdam, and it's still something of a rarity. As well as the places listed below, there are many **pizza lines**, which deliver pizza for free in response to a telephone call. However, the quality of these varies dramatically, and you shouldn't expect anything better than basic. Pizzas usually start at around ƒ14; phone numbers include ☎676 1476, ☎623 5539 and ☎675 0736. All food delivery lines open in the late afternoon, and most close down by 10pm.

Bojo (☎694 2864) will deliver a choice of three *rijsttafels* to your door, from about ƒ30 all-in, good for two people.

Koh-I-Noor (☎623 3133) deliver high-quality, reasonably priced Indian food (see p.218).

Mousaka Express (☎675 7000) are just what you'd expect, with a long delivery menu of Greek speciality dishes; mousaka starts at ƒ15 (vegetarian from ƒ13.50), but they've got everything from ƒ6 tara-masalata to a ƒ55 mixed grill for two.

Ontbijt Service (☎616 1613; orders taken 24hr; daily delivery 6am–1pm) have a range of breakfasts for home or hotel delivery, ranging from ƒ49 for two

people for standard fare (bread, cheese, egg, orange juice, tea/coffee, fruit etc), up to ƒ99 for lots of everything for two, with meat, fish and a bottle of champagne on top.

Porto Ercole (☎624 7654) have a wide range of all kinds of Italian food for delivery, from cold and hot *antipasti* through 20 styles of pizza, fresh home-made pasta and lasagne, to fillet steak and a fine tiramisu. Drop by Vijzelstraat 97 to pick up a menu.

Two in One (☎612 8488) have excellent, reasonably priced Indian and Surinamese food for delivery, at a rough average of ƒ15 per person.

Chapter 10

Entertainment and Nightlife

Although Amsterdam is not generally considered one of the world's major cultural centres, the quality and quantity of music, dance and film on offer here are high – largely thanks to the government's long-term subsidy to the arts. With its uniquely youthful population, the city is at the cutting edge in many ways, though its strengths lie in the graphic arts and new media rather than the performing arts. In fact, there can be a marked lack of daring in Dutch performance, which may have something to do with the stable and homogeneous nature of Dutch society, and its high standard of living. If you spend any time in Amsterdam you're bound to come across plenty of fringe and mainstream events, many of them spontaneous and entertaining, though lacking perhaps the inventiveness or perspective of New York and London. That said, though, Amsterdam buzzes with places offering a wide range of affordable entertainment and you'll never find yourself at a loss for something to do.

Information and Tickets

For information about **what's on**, a good place to start is the **Amsterdam Uitburo**, or **AUB**, the cultural office of the city council, which is housed in a corner of the Stadsschouwburg theatre on Leidseplein (Mon–Sat 9am–6pm, Thurs

until 9pm; ☎621 1211). You can get advice here on anything remotely cultural, as well as tickets and copies of what **listings magazines** there are. Non-Dutch readers have to grapple with the hole left by *Time Out Amsterdam*'s 1996 decision to switch to Internet publication – which has left the city without a single English-language magazine in print. *Time Out*'s weekly updated entertainment pages can now be found at <http://www.timeout.nl>. Critical paper-printed listings of clubs, live music gigs and film screenings are hard to find, and your best bet, until some enterprising publisher fills the obvious gap, is to keep an eye out for posters, billboards, notices, slips of paper stuck on windows, *anything* advertising upcoming events in the city. One possibility is to try and decipher the bare listings in the AUB's own monthly *Uitkrant*, which is comprehensive and free, but in Dutch; or you could settle for the VVV's bland and deadly English-language *What's On In Amsterdam* (f3.50). The newspaper *Het Parool*'s Wednesday entertainment supplement, *Uit en Thuis*, is one of the most up-to-date reference sources. Take a look, too, at the AUB's *Uitlijst* noticeboards, which include a weekly update on pop music events. Any cinema can provide the long, thin, fold-out "Week Agenda", which gives details of all films showing in the city that week (Thursday

**Entertainment
and Nightlife**

to Wednesday) and includes most of the live music events as well. Bars and restaurants often stock similar fortnightly or monthly listings leaflets, most of them sponsored by cigarette companies. *Queer Fish* ("for all normal people") is a photocopied and stapled alternative agenda, available at the *Hair Police*, Kerkstraat 113, and similar outlets for *f*2.

Tickets for most performances can be bought at the Uitburo (for a *f*2 fee) and VVV offices, or reserved by phone through the AUB *Uitlijn* (☎621 1211; *f*5 fee) or, again, the VVV. You can buy tickets for any live music event in the country at the *Nieuwe Muziekhandel* shop, Leidsestraat 50 (☎627 1400; *f*3 fee), up to three weeks in advance. Some major performance venues – the Carré, Muziektheater, Stadsschouwburg and others – sell tickets for each other's productions at no extra cost through the *Kassadienst* plan. You can also book seats at the major venues (such as the Concertgebouw or the Muziektheater) **from abroad** through the *National Bookings Centre* (☎070/320 2500; no booking fee). If you're under 26, the AUB is the place to go for a **Cultureel Jongeren Passport (CJP)**, which costs *f*20 and gets you reductions on entry to theatres, concerts and *filmhuizen*. Generally the only people eligible for **discounts** at cultural events are students, over-65s (though most places will only take Dutch ID) and CJP card-holders.

Rock, Folk and World Music

As far as **live music** goes, Amsterdam is a regular tour stop for many major artists, and something of a testing ground for current rock bands. Until recently, **Dutch rock** was almost uniformly dire, divided fairly evenly between the traditional songs being belted out in cafés in the Jordaan – a brash and sentimental adaptation of French *chansons* – and anaemic Dutch imitations of English and American groups, singing (unconvincingly) in English. The best place to hear the former – if you must – is still

the Jordaan, at cafés such as *Nol* and the *Twee Zwaantjes*, detailed in the *Eating and Drinking* chapter. As for modern pop and rock, times have mercifully changed, and Dutch groups nowadays can lay claim to both quality and originality (2 Unlimited being a notable exception). Look out for the celebrated Urban Dance Squad, the Osdorp Posse and other members of the dance/hip-hop scene, or try to catch rock bands like Bettie Serveert. Mathilde Santing is a popular draw whenever she plays. Bear in mind, too, that Amsterdam is often on the tour circuit of up-and-coming British bands – keep a sharp eye on the listings.

With the construction of the brand-new 50,000-seat *ArenA* out in the southeastern suburbs of the city, Amsterdam has finally gained the stadium **rock venue** it has craved for years. However, the *ArenA* is taking some time to catch on, and, aside from the Tina Turner/Michael Jackson brand of superstar, most major touring acts still choose to play at Rotterdam's *Ahoy* sports hall. The three dedicated music venues in Amsterdam city centre – the *Paradiso*, the *Melkweg* and the *Arena* (not to be confused with the *ArenA*) – are all much smaller, and supply a constantly changing seven-days-a-week programme of music to suit all tastes (and budgets). Alongside the main venues, the city's clubs, bars and multimedia centres sporadically host performances by live bands. As far as **prices** go, for big names you'll pay anything between *f*40 and *f*60 a ticket; ordinary gigs cost *f*10–25, although some places charge a membership (*lidmaatschap*) fee on top. If no price is listed, entrance is usually free.

The Dutch **folk music** tradition is virtually extinct. But there is a still a small and thriving scene in Amsterdam, due mainly to a handful of American and British expatriates and a few sympathetic cafés – as well as a couple of good venues for **world music**. For more information, call the Amsterdam folk organization *Mokum Folk* (☎671 1869). The Utrecht-based *Network for Non-Western*

Music (info ☎030/233 2876) is an organization that regularly brings world music performers to Amsterdam, to play at the Soeterijn Theatre at the Tropenmuseum; music from around the world is also a regular feature of the *Melkweg*'s programme.

Aside from summer Sundays in the Vondelpark, Amsterdam doesn't have any **outdoor music festivals**, although the World Roots Festival and the Drum Rhythm Festival, both in early summer, are multi-venue extravaganzas attracting world-class acts. Of the festivals outside the city, the most famous is the Pink Pop Festival in June, down in the south at the Draf en Renbaan in Landgraaf, near Maastricht. Others include the spring Halfway Festival in Spaarnwoude, halfway between Amsterdam and Haarlem; the May Goffert Pop in Nijmegen; and the June Park Pop, in The Hague. Dates are variable, so check with the VVV before making plans.

Major venues

Melkweg (Milky Way), Lijnbaansgracht 234a ☎624 1777 after 1pm. Probably Amsterdam's most famous entertainment venue, and these days one of the city's prime arts centres, with a young, hip clientele. A former dairy (hence the name) just round the corner from Leidseplein, it was entirely renovated in 1995, and now has two separate halls for live music, putting on a broad range of bands that leans towards African music and lesser-knowns. Late on Friday and Saturday nights, excellent offbeat disco sessions go on well into the small hours. As well as the gigs, there's also a fine monthly film programme, a tearoom selling dope and space-cake, and a bar and restaurant (Marnixstraat entrance) open Mon–Fri 11am–midnight, Sat & Sun 2pm–midnight. Concerts start between 9pm and 11pm, and admission ranges from *f*10 to *f*30, plus compulsory membership (*f*4 for one month, *f*6 for three months; free to CJP card-holders). Closed Mon.

Paradiso, Weteringschans 6–8 ☎623 7348. A converted church near the Leidseplein, with bags of atmosphere, featuring bands ranging from the up-and-coming to the Rolling Stones. Also recently renovated, it has been known to host classical concerts, as well as debates and multimedia events (often in conjunction with the nearby *Balie* centre). Entrance *f*12–30, plus *f*4 membership. Bands usually get started around 9pm.

Arena, 's-Gravensandestraat 51 ☎694 7444. Part of the major reorganization of what used to be the *Sleep-In* hostel, the *Arena* is now a multimedia centre featuring live music and cultural events, and has a bar, coffeeshop and restaurant, while remaining one of the cheapest hostels in the city. Awkwardly located out to the east of the centre (trams #6 and #10), the *Arena*'s intimate hall tends to feature underground bands from around the world. Entrance *f*8–15, with a start time around 9.30pm.

Smaller venues

Akhnaton, Nieuwezijds Kolk 25 ☎624 3396. A "Centre for World Culture", specializing in African and Latin American music and dance parties. On a good night, the place heaves with people.

AMP, KNSM-laan 13 ☎638 0019. Way out in the eastern harbour district, this rehearsal space and recording studio now features live bands at the weekends.

De Buurvrouw, Pietersspoortsteeg 29 ☎625 9654. Eclectic alternative bar featuring loud local bands.

Cruise Inn, Zeeburgerdijk 271 ☎692 7188. Off the beaten track, but with great music from the 1950s and 1960s. Saturday is R&B night.

De Kikker, Egelantiersstraat 130 ☎627 9198. A chic Art Deco place in the middle of the Jordaan, where easy-listening music accompanies the pricey French cuisine. Smooth trios playing bossa nova and French *chansons*; weekends only.

Korsakoff, Lijnbaansgracht 161 ☎625 7854. Late-night performances by some

Entertainment
and Nightlife

Entertainment
and Nightlife

*All the Irish
bars in the
city feature
live Gaelic
music; see
Eating and
Drinking for
details.*

of the better-known local grunge bands, in a lively setting with cheap drinks and a post-punk clientele. Free admission.

Last Waterhole, Oudezijds Armsteeg 12 ☎624 4814. In the depths of the Red Light District, this is the favoured spot for Amsterdam's biker set; however, the Dutch variety lacks bark as well as bite, and travellers from the hostel upstairs are welcome at the pool tables or to join the jam sessions onstage.

Maloe Melo, Lijnbaansgracht 163 ☎420 0232. Next door to the *Korsakoff*, a dark, low-ceilinged bar, with a small back room featuring local bluesy acts.

Meander Café, Voetboogstraat 5 ☎625 8430. Daily live music of the soul, funk and blues variety.

Morlang, Keizersgracht 451 ☎625 2681. Super-trendy café with live music now and again. Soul, jazz and classical.

Mulligans, Amstel 100 ☎622 1330. Irish bar head and shoulders above the rest for atmosphere and authenticity, with Gaelic musicians and storytellers most nights for free.

Naar Boven, Reguliersdwarsstraat 12 ☎623 3981. Uncompromising postmodern interior with an eclectic variety of local talent. Open late.

OCCII, Amstelveenseweg 134 ☎671 7778. Cosy former squat bar at the far end of the Vondelpark, with occasional live alternative music.

Soeterijn, Linnaeusstraat 2 ☎568 8500. Part of the Tropenmuseum, this formal theatre specializes in the drama, dance, film and music of the developing world. A great place for ethnic music and to pick up on acts that you wouldn't normally get to see.

Twin Pigs, Nieuwendijk 100 ☎624 8573. A bar yards from Centraal Station, with free rock and blues acts blasting a semi-stoned crowd.

Winston Kingdom, Warmoesstraat 123 ☎625 3912. Small renovated Red Light District venue, with sporadic R&B and punk/noise nights.

Jazz and Latin

For **jazz** fans, Amsterdam can be a treat. Since the 1940s and 1950s, when American jazz musicians began moving to Europe to escape discrimination back home, the city has had a soft spot for jazz (although Paris stole much of the limelight). Chet Baker lived and died in Amsterdam; he and any number of legendary jazzbos could once be found jamming into the small hours at the *Casablanca* on Zeedijk. Although Zeedijk has been dragged into the 1990s, there's still an excellent range of jazz venues for such a small city, varying from tiny bars staging everything from Dixieland to avant-garde, to the *Bimhuis* – the city's major jazz venue – which plays host to both international names and homegrown talent. Saxophonists Hans Dulfer, Willem Breuker and Theo Loevendie, and percussionist Martin van Duynhoven, are among the **Dutch musicians** you might come across – and they're well worth catching if you get the chance.

It's worth remembering, too, that the Netherlands has one of the best jazz **festivals** in the world, the North Sea Jazz Festival, held in the Congresgebouw in The Hague during July – information from PO Box 87840, 2508 DE The Hague. Comprising three days and nights of continuous jazz on twelve stages, the festival regularly involves over 700 musicians, among them world-class performers from Oscar Peterson to James Brown, Chuck Berry to Guru's Jazzmatazz. Tickets cost from about ƒ100 a day, with supplements for the big names – although, considering the music on offer, this is still a bargain. Special late-night trains are laid on to bring revellers back to Amsterdam after the gigs – hotel rooms in The Hague are booked up months in advance. October is also a good time to catch jazz, with extra concerts and small festivals held all over the country. If your Dutch is up to it, you can get **information** on jazz events all over Holland by phoning *Jazzline* on ☎626 7764.

The Dutch connection with Surinam – a former colony tucked in between

Venezuela and Brazil – means that there is a sizeable **Latin American** community in the city, and, while some of the Andean buskers on the Leidseplein may verge on the yawn-worthy, there is plenty of authentic salsa and other Latin sounds to be discovered.

Venues

Akhnaton, Nieuwezijds Kolk 25 ☎624 3396. A crowded, lively venue that often puts on Latin music.

Café Alto, Korte Leidsedwarsstraat 115 ☎626 3249. It's worth hunting out this legendary little jazz bar just off Leidseplein for the quality modern jazz every night from 10pm until 3am (and often much later). It's big on atmosphere, though slightly cramped, but entry is free, and you don't have to buy a (pricey) beer to hang out and watch the band.

Bamboo Bar, Lange Leidsedwarsstraat 66 ☎624 3993. Legend has it Chet Baker used to live upstairs and jam onstage to pay his rent. These days the *Bamboo* is an unpretentious, friendly bar with blues and jazz, plus occasional salsa nights. Free entry, but you need to buy a drink. Open from 9pm.

Bimhuis, Oude Schans 73–77 ☎623 1361. The city's premier jazz venue for almost 25 years, with an excellent auditorium and ultra-modern bar. Concerts Thurs–Sat, free sessions Mon–Wed. There's also free live music in the bar on Sun at 4pm. Concert tickets are for sale on the day only.

Bourbon Street, Leidsekruisstraat 6 ☎623 3440. Friendly bar with a relaxed atmosphere and quality jazz nightly until 3am.

Canecao, Lange Leidsedwarsstraat 68 ☎638 0611. A wonderful little place filled with the sounds of samba and salsa – not entirely for the tourists.

Casablanca, Zeedijk 26 ☎625 5685. Renovated, and a shadow of its former self, though still hosting live jazz every night.

De Engelbewaarder, Kloveniersburgwal 59 ☎625 3772. Excellent live jazz sessions on Sunday afternoon and evening.

Iboya, Korte Leidsedwarsstraat 29 ☎623 7859. In the slightly less tacky of two ropey tourist streets off the Leidseplein. Theatre, club and restaurant combined; piano bar, Saturday night cabaret and live Latin music late into the night.

IJsbreker, Weesperzijde 23 ☎668 1805. Principally a venue for contemporary music (see below), but with occasional avant-garde and free-jazz evenings.

Joseph Lam Jazz Club, Van Diemenstraat 242 ☎622 8086. Venture into the western harbour district for this trad and Dixieland centre, weekends only from 9pm.

Du Lac, Haarlemmerstraat 118 ☎624 4265. Rather trendified bar with jazz sessions on Sun.

Le Maxim, Leidsekruisstraat 35 ☎624 1920. Intimate piano bar with live music nightly.

Winston Kingdom, Warmoesstraat 123 ☎625 3912. Theatre-café attached to the renovated *Winston Hotel*, with spoken word and jazz-poetry evenings attracting occasional semi-big-name acts from the US.

Entertainment
and Nightlife

Classical Music, Opera and Contemporary Music

There's no shortage of classical music concerts in Amsterdam, with two major orchestras based in the city, plus regular visits by other Dutch orchestras. Under its conductor, Riccardo Chailly, the **Royal Concertgebouw Orchestra** remains one of the most dynamic in the world, and occupies one of the finest concert halls to boot. The other resident orchestra is the **Netherlands Philharmonic**, based at the Beurs van Berlage concert hall, which has a wide symphonic repertoire and also performs with the Netherlands Opera at the Muziektheater. Among visiting orchestras, the Rotterdam Philharmonic (under Valery Gergiev) and the Utrecht Symphony have world-class reputations, as does the Radio

Entertainment and Nightlife

Philharmonic Orchestra, based in Hilversum outside Amsterdam.

As far as **smaller classical ensembles** go, Dutch musicians pioneered the use of period instruments in the 1970s, and Ton Koopman's Amsterdam Baroque Orchestra and Frans Brüggen's Orchestra of the 18th Century are two internationally renowned exponents. Koopman's Amsterdam Baroque Choir and the Amsterdam Bach Soloists are also pre-eminent. As well as the main concert halls, a number of Amsterdam's churches (and former churches) host regular performances of classical and chamber music – both types of venue are listed below.

The most prestigious venue for **opera** is the Muziektheater (otherwise known as the *Stopera*) on Waterlooplein, which is home to the Netherlands Opera company – going from strength to strength under the guidance of Pierre Audi – as well as the National Ballet. Visiting companies sometimes perform here, but more often at the Stadsschouwburg and the Carré theatre.

As far as **contemporary music** goes, the *IJsbreker* centre on the Amstel is a leading showcase for musicians from all over the world. Local talent is headed by the Asko and Schoenberg Ensembles, as well as the Nieuw Ensemble and the Volharding Orchestra. Look out also for Willem Breuker and Maarten Altena, two popular musicians who successfully combine improvised jazz with composed new music.

The most prestigious multi-venue Dutch festival by far is the annual **Holland Festival** every June (info ☎627 6566), which attracts the best domestic mainstream and fringe performers in all areas of the arts, as well as an exciting international line-up. Otherwise, one of the more interesting music-oriented events is the **piano recital** held towards the end of August on a floating stage outside the *Pulitzer Hotel* on the Prinsengracht – with the whole area floodlit and filled with small boats, and every available spot on the banks and bridges taken up, this can be a wonder-

fully atmospheric evening. Also around this time – and from two ends of the musical spectrum – Utrecht plays host to the internationally renowned **Early Music Festival**, and Amsterdam holds the **International Gaudeamus Music Week**, a forum for debate and premier performance of cutting-edge contemporary music.

All the major venues listed below, as well as some of the churches, have wheelchair access, though you should call ahead if you need assistance.

Venues

Beurs van Berlage, Damrak 213 ☎627 0466. The splendid interior of the former stock exchange (see p.75) has been put to use as a venue for theatre and music. The resident Netherlands Philharmonic and Netherlands Chamber Orchestra perform in the huge but comfortable *Yakult Zaal* and the *AGA Zaal*, the latter a very strange, glassed-in room-within-a-room.

Carré Theatre, Amstel 115–125 ☎622 5225. A splendid hundred-year-old structure (originally built for a circus) that now hosts all kinds of top international acts: anything from Russian folk dance to *La Cage aux Folles*, with reputable touring orchestras and opera companies squeezed in between.

Concertgebouw, Concertgebouwplein 2–6 ☎671 8345. After a facelift and the replacement of its crumbling foundations in the early 1990s, the Concertgebouw is now looking – and sounding – better than ever. The acoustics of the *Grote Zaal* (Large Hall) are unparalleled, and a concert here is a wonderful experience. The smaller *Kleine Zaal* regularly hosts chamber concerts, often by the resident Borodin Quartet. Though both halls boast a star-studded international programme, prices are on the whole very reasonable, rarely over ƒ35, and ƒ20 for Sunday morning events. Free Wednesday lunchtime concerts are held from Sept to May (doors open 12.15pm, arrive early), and in July and August there's a heavily subsidized series of summer concerts.

Look out also for occasional swing/jazz nights.

IJsbreker, Weesperzijde 23 ☎668 1805. Out of the town centre by the Amstel, with a delightful terrace on the water. Has a large, varied programme of international modern, chamber and experimental music, as well as featuring obscure, avant-garde local performers. Concerts are occasionally held in the Planetarium of the Artis Zoo.

Marionette Theatre, Nieuwe Jonkerstraat 8 ☎620 8027. A repertoire of Mozart and Offenbach operas performed by marionettes.

Muziektheater, Waterlooplein ☎625 5455. Part of the ƒ306 million complex that includes the city hall. The theatre's resident company, Netherlands Opera, offers the fullest, and most reasonably priced, programme of opera in Amsterdam. Tickets go very quickly. Look out for free lunchtime concerts Sept–May.

Stadsschouwburg, Leidseplein 26 ☎624 2311. These days somewhat overshadowed by the Muziektheater, but still staging significant opera and dance (it's a favourite of the Netherlands Dance Theatre – see below), as well as visiting English-language theatre companies.

The **churches** (and former churches) listed below have regular programmes of chamber and baroque music; others, including the huge **Nieuwe Kerk** on Dam Square, the **Westerkerk**, the **Noorderkerk**, the **Mozes en Aaronkerk** on Waterlooplein, and the tiny **Amstelkerk** on Kerkstraat, as well as numerous small churches out in the residential south and west, occasionally put on one-off concerts, often with very reasonable prices.

Engelse Kerk, Begijnhof 48 ☎624 9665. The church with the biggest programme – three to four performances a week, lunchtime, afternoon and evening, with the emphasis on period instruments.

Oude Kerk, Oudekerksplein 23 ☎625 8284. Hosts organ and carillon recitals, as well as occasional choral events. In summer, in conjunction with the Amstelkring Museum, the church organizes a series of "walking" concert evenings, consisting of three separate concerts at different venues, with time for coffee and a stroll between each.

Waalse Kerk, Oudezijds Achterburgwal 157; information from the Old Music Society on ☎030/236 2236. Weekend afternoon and evening concerts of early music and chamber music.

Theatre and Cabaret

Surprisingly for a city that functions so much in English, there is next to no **English-language drama** to be seen in Amsterdam. The *Stalhouderij* is the only company working in English, performing in a broom-cupboard of a theatre in the Jordaan, although the Theater de Bochel, converted from a bath house, often hosts visiting productions. Apart from these, a tiny handful of part-time companies put on two or three English productions during the summer; there are also performances by touring groups at the theatres listed below and at other venues dotted around town.

English-language **comedy** and **cabaret**, on the other hand, has become a big thing in Amsterdam, spearheaded by the resident and extremely successful Boom Chicago comedy company. During the summer in particular, a number of small venues host mini-seasons of English-language stand-up comedy and cabaret, with touring British performers (Eddie Izzard played the Nieuwe de la Mar in 1996), and material that's generally targeted at visitors to the city.

Most of Amsterdam's larger theatre companies concentrate either on foreign works in translation or Dutch-language theatre, neither of which is likely to be terribly interesting for the non-Dutch speaker. However, there are plenty of **avant-garde** theatre groups in the city, much of whose work relies on visual rather than verbal impact, as well as one or two companies devoted to **mime** (including the famous Griftheater). We've listed the most likely venues below. Look

Entertainment
and Nightlife

**Entertainment
and Nightlife**

Following is a list of the more important venues that put on **avant-garde and mime** productions. Check the usual listings and information sources for details.

Bellevue, Leidsekade 90 ☎ 624 7248.

De Brakke Grond, Nes 45 ☎ 626 6866. Many Flemish productions.

Cosmic Theater, Nes 75 ☎ 622 8858.

De Engelenbak, Nes 71 ☎ 624 0394.

Felix Meritis, Keizersgracht 324 ☎ 623 1311.

Frascati, Nes 63 ☎ 626 6866.

De Nieuw Amsterdam, Spuistraat 2 ☎ 627 8672. Multicultural focus on non-western productions.

Nieuwe de la Mar, Marnixstraat 404 ☎ 623 3462.

Westergasfabriek, Haarlemmerweg 8–10 ☎ 627 9070. Hosts eclectic productions of all kinds.

out also for performances at the Amsterdam Marionette Theatre.

The main **event** to watch out for, apart from the mainstream Holland Festival (see above), is the summer-long **Over Het IJ Festival** (info ☎ 636 1083), a showcase for all kinds of theatre and performance arts at big, often outdoor locations in Amsterdam North (thus "over the IJ"). With a great many interesting fringe companies taking part, including the celebrated Dogtroep, productions are often surprising and exciting. In June, there is also the **International Theatre School Festival** (info ☎ 626 1241), when the four theatres on Nes, a tiny alley running from Dam Square parallel to Rokin, host productions by local and international theatre schools.

Venues

De Balie, Kleine Gartmanplantsoen 10 ☎ 623 2904. A multimedia centre for culture and the arts, located off the Leidseplein, which often plays host to drama, debates, international symposia and the like, sometimes in conjunction with the *Paradiso* next door.

Badhuis-Theater de Bochel, Andreas Bonnstraat 28 ☎ 668 5102. A former bath house out near the Oosterpark, this is now a forum for all kinds of visiting productions and guest directors.

Boom Chicago, Lijnbaansgracht 238 ☎ 639 2707. Something of a phenomenon in Amsterdam in recent years, this rapid-fire improv comedy troupe performs nightly to crowds of both

tourists and locals, and has received rave reviews from *Rough Guide* readers, the Dutch press and *Time* magazine alike. With inexpensive food, the cheapest beer in town (in pitchers, no less!), and a Smoke Boat Cruise following the show at 10.30pm, the comedy need not be funny – but it is. Currently running from May to Oct, but due to move to a permanent location elsewhere in the city by 1998.

Carré Theatre, Amstel 115–125 ☎ 622 5225. A chunky old building on the eastern bank of the Amstel that hosts all kinds of top international acts, with the emphasis on hit musicals.

Comedy Café, Max Euweplein 29 ☎ 620 9164. Small cabaret theatre with a bar that sometimes hosts English-language acts.

Kleine Komedie, Amstel 56 ☎ 624 0534. One of Amsterdam's oldest theatres, established in 1786, with occasional English-language shows, and performances by the odd pop megastar.

Marionette Theatre, Nieuwe Jonkerstraat 8 ☎ 620 8027. Continues an old European tradition with its performances of operas by Mozart and Offenbach. Although they're touring Holland and the rest of Europe for most of the year, the wooden marionettes return to Amsterdam around May, October and Christmas. Call for details of performances, and to find out about their opera dinners.

Melkweg, Lijnbaansgracht 234a ☎ 624 1777 after 1pm. At the centre of the city's cultural scene, this is often the first-choice venue for foreign touring companies.

Stadsschouwburg, Leidseplein 26 ☎624 2311. Often hosts productions on tour from London or New York.

Stalhouderij, 1e Bloemdwarsstraat 4 ☎626 2282. Amsterdam's only non-subsidized English-language theatre company, mounting new productions every six weeks or so in one of the city's smallest, most intimate theatre spaces. Contemporary and modern works, Shakespeare, readings, classes and workshops.

Dance

Of the major **dance companies** based in Amsterdam, the largest and most prestigious is the Muziektheater's National Ballet, under Wayne Eagling – though their critics say they lack verve and imagination. Also working regularly in Amsterdam are the noted Dutch choreographers Toer van Schayk and Rudi van Dantzig, while for **folk dance** fans the excellent Folkloristisch Danstheater is based in the city. However, a constant feature of dance in Holland is the prevalence of non-Dutch choreographers and dancers, and the work of William Forsyth, Lloyd Newson, Saburo Teshigawara and others is regularly on show.

Of the other major Dutch dance companies, which can be seen on tour in Amsterdam – or in nearby Rotterdam and The Hague – the most innovative is The Hague's Netherlands Dance Theatre, with a repertoire of ballet and modern dance featuring inspired choreography by Jiri Kylian and Hans van Manen. The oldest company in the country, the Scapino Ballet (based in Rotterdam), has recently spruced up its image and is gathering a new generation of admirers.

On a smaller scale, Amsterdam is particularly receptive to the latest trends in **modern dance**, and has many experimental dance groups, often incorporating other media into their productions; small productions staged by dance students also abound. Look out for performances by the Dans Werkplaats Amsterdam and often innovative shows from Beppie Blankert's studio, as well as the extraordinary Cloud Chamber company, the mime specialists Griftheater, and Shusaku Takeuchi's vast, open-air water-based extravaganzas. Modern dance and movement theatre companies from outside Amsterdam that often perform in the city include the Rotterdamse Dansgroep, who mainly focus on New York modern dance; Introdans, similar in style to the Netherlands Dance Theatre; and Djazzex, fine exponents of jazz dance.

Dance festivals are a little thin on the ground: **Julidans**, which is held in the Stadsschouwburg every July, is the leading event in the city. Two festivals in The Hague to watch for are the **Holland Dance Festival** (info ☎070/361 6142), which takes place every two years (October 1997 and 1999) and attracts many leading international companies; and **CaDance** (info ☎070/363 7540), next held in November 1998, which premiers contemporary dance works. The Hague is just 45 minutes away from Amsterdam by regular trains from Centraal Station.

Listed below are the theatres that solely host dance productions; dance is sometimes also on the bill at a number of general venues around the city – check the usual listings sources.

Venues

Dans Werkplaats Amsterdam, Arie Biemondstraat 107 ☎689 1789. A dance studio staging occasional productions here and at other locations in the city.

Folkloristisch Danstheater, Kloveniersburgwal 87 ☎623 9112. Original folk dance from around the world, with international choreographers brought in to work with the dancers.

Muziektheater, Waterlooplein ☎625 5455. Home of the National Ballet, but with a third of its dance schedule given over to international companies.

Entertainment
and Nightlife

Entertainment and Nightlife

Two Amsterdam cinemas are worth a visit no matter what's showing: the extravagantly Art Deco Tuschinski (see p.109) and the atmospheric The Movies (see p.118).

For details of gay and lesbian film programmes, see p.57.

Studio Beppie Blankert, Entrepotdok 4 ☎ 638 9398. A veteran Dutch choreographer, Blankert offers freelance Dutch and international dancers a dynamic setting in which to work together.

Het Veem, Van Diemenstraat 410 ☎ 626 0112. Old warehouse converted into dance studios and a small theatre. Good for mime.

Film

Most of Amsterdam's commercial **cinemas** are huge, multiplex picture palaces showing a selection of general releases – and are interesting for just that. There's also a scattering of film houses (*filmhuizen*) showing **revival and art films** and occasional retrospectives; and Amsterdam's multimedia centres often organize film and video programmes, too. Pick up a copy of the "**Week Agenda**" from any cinema for details of all films showing in the city. Weekly programmes change on Thursdays.

All foreign movies playing in Amsterdam (almost no Dutch movies turn up anyway) are shown in their **original language** and subtitled in Dutch – which is fine for British or American fare, but a little frustrating if you fancy Tarkovsky or Pasolini. If you're interested in seeing a non-English-language movie, check with the venue whether it's been **subtitled** in English (*Engels Ondertiteld*) before you go. Films are almost never dubbed into Dutch: if they are, *Nederlands Gesproken* will be printed in the listings. Most major cinemas have four showings a day: two in the afternoon, two in the evening; some also have midnight shows on Fridays and Saturdays. In all the mainstream cinemas, an ancient and deeply irritating policy of sticking a fifteen-minute **interval** (*pauze*) in the middle of the movie persists, although you could use this time to buy yourself a beer – as John Travolta pointed out in *Pulp Fiction*, you can drink while watching the movie without a problem.

As a guide, **tickets** can cost more than ƒ15 for an evening show Friday to Sunday, though it's not hard to find a ticket for ƒ11 during the week. Prices at the *filmhuizen* are slightly lower, and can drop to as little as ƒ6 for a 10am Sunday showing; for a paltry ƒ2.50 you can get in to see last year's blockbusters at the *Riksbioscoop* at Reguliersbreestraat 31 (☎ 624 3639).

Aside from occasional film festivals held by the likes of Amnesty International, Amsterdam's only regular event is the fascinating **International Documentary Film Festival** in December (info ☎ 627 3329). Whereas the Dutch Film Festival, held each September in Utrecht, features only homegrown productions, January's **Rotterdam Film Festival** (info ☎ 010/411 8080) is truly international, with screenings of well over 100 art movies from all parts of the world, as well as the usual accompanying lectures and seminars.

Filmhuizen and Revival Cinemas

Alfa, Hirschpassage, Leidseplein ☎ 627 8806. Interesting, occasionally inspired programming on the edge of the mainstream.

Cavia, Van Hallstraat 52 ☎ 681 1419. Incongruously sited above a martial arts centre, this is one of the best of the small *filmhuizen*, with an eclectic and non-commercial programme of international movies. Tram #10.

Cinecenter, Lijnbaansgracht 236 ☎ 623 6615. Opposite the *Melkweg*, this shows independent and quality commercial films, the majority originating from non-English-speaking countries.

Desmet, Plantage Middenlaan 4a ☎ 627 3434. Often used by directors and actors to promote independent films. Retrospectives change every month. Gay movies at midnight on Saturday and on Sunday afternoon. Tram #7, #9, #14.

Filmmuseum, Vondelpark 3 ☎ 589 1400. Subsidized by the government since the 1940s, the *Filmmuseum* holds literally tens of thousands of prints. Dutch films show regularly, along with all kinds of movies from all corners of the world. Silent movies often have live piano accompaniment, and on summer weekend evenings there are free open-air screenings on the terrace. Also many cheap matinees. Most movies have English subtitles.

Kriterion, Roeterstraat 170 ☎623 1708. Stylish duplex cinema close to Weesperplein metro. Shows arthouse and quality commercial films, with late-night cult favourites. Friendly bar attached. Tram #6, #7, #10.

Melkweg, Lijnbaansgracht 234a ☎624 1777 after 1pm. As well as music, art and dance, the *Melkweg* manages to maintain a consistently good monthly film and video programme, ranging from mainstream fodder through to obscure imports. However, the small cinema is badly insulated from the noise of the concerts below. Closed Mon & Tues.

The Movies, Haarlemmerdijk 161 ☎624 5790. A beautiful Art Deco cinema, and a charming setting for independent films. Worth visiting for the bar and restaurant alone, fully restored to their original sumptuousness. Late shows at the weekend. Tram #3.

Rialto, Ceintuurbaan 338 ☎675 3994. Concentrates on retrospectives and themed series, often with classics slotted in between. On the corner of the Sarphatipark. Tram #24 and #25 from the centre of town.

Soeterijn, Linnaeusstraat 2 ☎568 8500. Attached to the Tropenmuseum, this theatre concentrates mostly on music and dance, but puts on weekly film shows from around the world.

De Uitkijk, Prinsengracht 452 ☎623 7460. The oldest cinema in the city (pronounced "out-kike"), in a converted canal house with no bar, no ice cream and no popcorn – but low prices. Tends to hang on to popular movies for months on end.

Clubs and Discos

Clubbing in Amsterdam is not the exclusive, style-conscious business it is in many other capitals. There is no one really extravagant night spot, and most Amsterdam clubs – even the hip ones – aren't very expensive or difficult to get into, and you go more to dance than to people-watch . . . unless, that is, you try to get into the *iT* or the *RoXY*. As for the music to expect, as in so many other things, Amsterdam is not at the cutting edge of experimentation: **house** is definitely the thing. Hip-hop has its devotees, as do modern and retro funk, jazz and underground trance and trip-hop, but unless you go looking for something special, a random dip into a club will probably turn up mellow, undemanding house beats.

That said, though, there's a recent craze for pumped-up, 200bpm+ **"gabber"** (pronounced the Dutch way, with a throaty "kh" at the beginning), laid on at vast arenas for thousands of shaven-headed speed-freaks. If you can find a gabber event (check for flyers at *Midtown Records*, Nieuwendijk 104 ☎638 4252), expect to pay a hefty ƒ60 or more for entry, although it'll go on until dawn and flyers for after-hours parties will circulate during the rave. Unlike many other places around Europe, there are now practically no **illegal raves** or parties in and around Amsterdam, and although some squat venues still survive in the harbour areas, the old days of acid warehouse parties are well and truly over.

Most clubs have very reasonable **entry prices**, but a singular feature of Amsterdam clubbing is that you tip the bouncer: if you want to get back into the same place next week, ƒ5 in the palm of his hand will do very nicely thank you. As in the rest of the city, toilets cost money (25c or 50c), but drinks prices are not excessively hiked up. **Dress codes** are minimal or nonexistent, except where we've noted in the listings below. As far as **drugs** go, smoking joints is generally fine – though if you can't see or smell the stuff, ask the barman if it's OK. Should you need reminding, Ecstasy, acid and speed are all completely illegal, and you can expect less than favourable

Entertainment and Nightlife

Entertainment and Nightlife

treatment from the bouncers (and the law) if you're spotted with anything.

Although all the places listed below **open** at either 10pm or 11pm, there's not much point turning up anywhere before midnight; unless stated otherwise, everywhere stays open until 5am on Friday and Saturday nights, 4am on other nights.

For **news** and flyers about clubs, upcoming parties and raves, drop in to places like *Clubwear House*, at Herengracht 265 (☎622 8766), and the *Hair Police* and *Conscious Dreams*, next door to each other at Kerkstraat 115 and 117.

Finally, there are a couple of clubs **outside Amsterdam** that you might see advertised around town. *Stalker*, in Haarlem (☎023/531 4652), is a small place with a dedicated following and a consistently adventurous music policy, while the equally popular *De Waakzaamheid*, in Koog aan de Zaan (☎075/628 5829), attracts British and European DJs to its weekend parties.

Mainstream Clubs

Amnesia, Oudezijds Voorburgwal 3 ☎638 1461. Below the *Royal Kabul* hotel, and therefore attracting mainly young tourists. Tends towards the hardcore. Thurs–Sun; ƒ10–15, (free if you're staying in the hotel).

Arena, 's-Gravensandestraat 51 ☎694 7444. Part of a large hostel-cum-multimedia centre, with popular dance parties on Fri and Sat. ƒ5.

Cash, Leidseplein 8 ☎627 8128. Former theatre, and one of the flashiest of the loud and unappealing Leidseplein discos. Plush decor, over-21s only, Top 40 sounds. There's one in every city. Nightly.

Club 114, Herengracht 114 ☎622 7685. One of the longest established club locations in Amsterdam, recently reborn and playing all kinds of non-housey music, from hip-hop to R&B, with heavy trance nights. Nightly; prices vary.

Dansen bij Jansen, Handboogstraat 11 ☎620 1779. Founded by – and for –

students, and very popular. Open nightly; ƒ4, but officially you need student ID to get in.

Escape, Rembrandtplein 11 ☎622 3542. Recently converted from an unexcitingly tacky disco, this is now home to Amsterdam's hottest Saturday night, "Chemistry", every so often featuring Holland's top DJ, Dimitri. A vast hangar, with room for 2000 people (although you may still have to queue). Closed Sun; from ƒ20.

iT, Amstelstraat 24 ☎625 0111. Large disco with a superb sound system. Often features well-known live acts. Has popular and glamorous gay nights (see below), but Thursday and Sunday are mixed gay/straight and attract a dressed-up, uninhibited crowd. ƒ17.50.

Korsakoff, Lijnbaansgracht 161 ☎625 7854. Small, dark grunge club, featuring live bands as well as alternative rock and noise nights. Free.

Mazzo, Rozengracht 114 ☎626 7500. Now back at its original location, one of the city's hippest and most laid-back discos, with a choice of music to appeal to all tastes. Perhaps the easiest-going bouncers in town. Open nightly; around ƒ10.

Melkweg, Lijnbaansgracht 234a ☎624 1777 after 1pm. After the bands have finished, this multimedia centre plays host to some of the most enjoyable theme nights around, everything from African dance parties to experimental jazz-trance. Prices and times vary, but membership (ƒ4 for a month; free with a CJP card) is compulsory. Closed Mon.

Odeon, Singel 460 ☎624 9711. This converted seventeenth-century building is one of the oldest venues in the city – during the 1940s, 50s and 60s it was Amsterdam's premier gay nightspot. Its heady days have passed, though, and now its stylishly elegant interior plays host to an invariably studentish gang. Open nightly; ƒ10.

Paradiso, Weteringschans 6–8 ☎623 7348. One of the principal venues in the city, which on Fridays turns into the unmissable VIP (Vrijdag In Paradiso) Club, from midnight onwards. Also hosts one-off events – check listings.

(36 op de schaal van) Richter, Reguliersdwarsstraat 36 ☎ 626 1573. A small, split-level club supposed to resemble a building after an earthquake (36 on the Richter Scale), with shattered mirrors, broken-down walls and cracked ceilings. Fairly flexible (older) door policy, and its location draws in a few undesirables. Open nightly; ƒ10.

RoXY, Singel 465 ☎ 620 0354. Housed in an old cinema, this has one of the city's best (and loudest) sound systems, and is one of its hippest clubs, a good place to get invited to parties – if you can get in. Wednesday at the RoXY is the most popular gay night in the city. Although they're open at the weekend, the door policy is very strict; if you're going to attempt to get in, try on Thursday night, when DJ Dimitri is in residence. ƒ7.50–12.50.

Seymour Likely Too, Nieuwezijds Voorburgwal 161 ☎ 420 5062. Small club that can be a relief after house, house, house – it's off-limits here, and a slightly older crowd revels instead in hip-hop and jazzy dance tunes. Thurs–Sun; ƒ5–10.

Silo, Westerdoksdijk 51 ☎ 420 5905. Although not actually a club, this huge old place – one of the last surviving community squats – often has all-night dance parties at the weekend. Admission can be high (at least ƒ15, plus "membership"), but the parties go on well past dawn and are part of the dying Amsterdam underground.

Soul Kitchen, Amstelstraat 32a ☎ 620 2333. Relaxed club that's refreshingly oriented towards 1960s and 70s soul and funk rather than the usual housey stuff. Fri & Sat; around ƒ10.

West Pacific, Westergasfabriek, Haarlemmerweg 8–10 ☎ 597 4458. After playing host to many an acid rave in the late 1980s, this converted gas factory is now *the* up-and-coming location in the city. An on-site café with an open fire-

place attracts a trendy crowd of young Amsterdammers, who stay late to party.

Lesbian and Gay Clubs

The places listed below cater either predominantly or exclusively to a gay clientele. Some venues have both gay only and mixed gay/straight nights, as noted. Although there are no regular lesbian-only nights (see "Gay and Lesbian Amsterdam" in *Basics*), many venues run gay nights for both men and women. Gay men should also check out posters and flyers for the monthly *Club Trash* and *Wasteland* events.

COC, Rozenstraat 14 ☎ 626 3087. Very popular women-only disco and café every Sat from 8pm, popular with younger lesbians. Pumping on Friday nights too (mixed men/women). ƒ5.

Cockring, Warmoesstraat 96 ☎ 623 9604. Currently Amsterdam's most popular – and very cruisey – gay men's disco. Light show and bars on two levels. Get there early at the weekend to avoid queuing. Nightly; free.

Exit, Reguliersdwarsstraat 42 ☎ 625 8788. Along with *iT* (see below), the city's most popular gay club, reached through the *April* café. Current sounds play nightly to an upbeat, cruisey crowd. Predominantly male, though women are admitted. Free.

Havana, Reguliersdwarsstraat 17 ☎ 620 6788. Small dance floor above a bar slap in the middle of a buzzing gay area. Very popular with a mixed clientele (gay, yuppie, art crowd); mostly men, but women admitted. Also perhaps the only place in town to cater for people who want to dance but still get up for work the next day. Mon–Thurs & Sun 11pm–1am, Fri & Sat 11pm–2am; free.

iT, Amstelstraat 24 ☎ 625 0111. Saturday night here really is IT, as the city's most glamorous transvestites come out to play and the place gets packed out (men only). Thursday night is free if you're gay, and Sunday is a popular gay/straight night. Around ƒ15.

RoXY, Singel 465 ☎ 620 0354. Wednesday night is "HARD", strictly gay

Entertainment
and Nightlife

Entertainment and Nightlife

only, and very popular with both men and women. ƒ10.

De Trut, Bilderdijkstraat 165 (no phone). Housed in a former factory building, this squat venue holds a Sunday night, gay-only dance party: there's a large dance floor, cheap drinks, and non-commercial music. Very popular with both men and women – the doors are closed at midnight and if you arrive after 11pm you may not get in. Gets very hot as it's in a basement.

Chapter 11

Museums and Galleries

The Netherlands has had a strong and active tradition of government support for the arts since World War II, and the effect on Amsterdam in particular has been dramatic: the city is absolutely full of art. In addition to three world-class **museums**, there are well over 200 private **commercial art galleries**, showcasing art of all kinds. In addition, most bars and cafés have changing exhibitions of photographs or small artworks, many public spaces are decorated with sculptures of one kind or another (some official, but just as many unofficial), and there are schemes to help members of the public hang original works in their own home – through purchase or long-term rental. For active support and mainstream interest in art of all kinds, Amsterdam is unparalleled in Europe.

Galleries

The **contemporary art** scene in Amsterdam is enormous and incredibly diverse. Partly due to a long-standing (but now terminated) system of direct government subsidies to individual artists, and partly due to the Dutch tradition of encouraging individual expression, Amsterdam has long attracted artists from all parts of the world. This active international community has had a marked influence on Amsterdam's galleries, which are eclectic, all-encompassing, and about as unstuffy as it's possible to be.

Galleries are scattered all over the city centre rather than confined to any specific area, though because of the space the older houses offer, you'll often find galleries along the major canals. Your best bet for **information** to supplement

The Dutch tend to use the words "museum" and "gallery" slightly differently from how you might expect. For the Dutch, an art **museum** displays works of art (most often fine art) that are not for sale – they are either national treasures, or they have been purchased directly by the museum for its own collection. Thus the Rijksmuseum, which in Britain or America would be called the National Gallery, here translates as the National Museum. A **galerie** is a much smaller operation, which neither buys nor sells art for itself. Most often rooted in the contemporary art scene, a *galerie* acts as a showcase for changing exhibits by different artists, and also as an agent, selling works on to third parties for a commission. A further complication is that many art-dealers (*kunsthandel*), who buy and sell works of art – generally from better-known artists, while often keeping a stock of prints – have taken to calling themselves galleries, in an attempt to elevate themselves from the purely commercial.

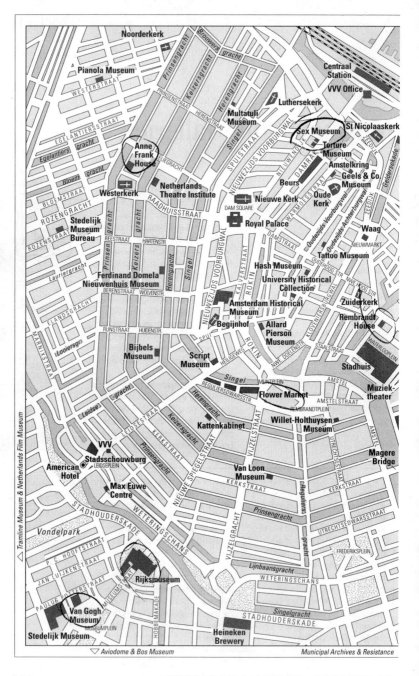

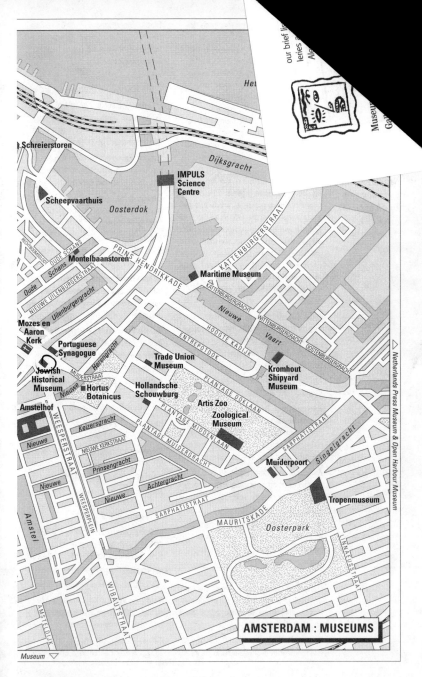

Schreierstoren

Dijksgracht

IMPULS Science Centre

Scheepvaarthuis

Oosterdok

OUDE SCHANS

Montelbaanstoren

PRINS HENDRIKKADE

Oude Schans

NIEUWE UILENBURGERSTRAAT

Uilenburgergracht

Maritime Museum

KATTENBURGERSTRAAT

KATTENBURGERGRACHT

Nieuwe

WITTENBURGERGRACHT

Vaart

OOSTENBURGERGRACHT

Mozes en Aaron Kerk

Portuguese Synagogue

Herengracht

HOOGTE KADIJK

ENTREPOTDOK

Trade Union Museum

Jewish Historical Museum

MUIDERSTRAAT

Nieuwe

Hortus Botanicus

Hollandsche Schouwburg

PLANTAGE DOKLAAN

Kromhout Shipyard Museum

Amstelhof

WEESPERSTRAAT

Keizersgracht

NIEUWE KERKSTRAAT

Artis Zoo

Zoological Museum

PLANTAGE MIDDENLAAN

Nieuwe

PLANTAGE MUIDERGRACHT

SARPHATISTRAAT

Singelgracht

Prinsengracht

WEESPERPLEIN

Achtergracht

Muiderpoort

Nieuwe

Nieuwe

SARPHATISTRAAT

Tropenmuseum

Amstel

MAURITSKADE

Oosterpark

WIBAUTSTRAAT

AMSTELDIJK

LINNAEUSSTRAAT

△ *Netherlands Press Museum & Open Harbour Museum*

AMSTERDAM : MUSEUMS

Museum ▽

...tings (which cover both galleries and art-dealers) is the gallery guide ..rt, which is in Dutch but clearly marks the locations of all the galleries in the city; it's available from some galleries themselves or from larger magazine shops. *What's On In Amsterdam* carries listings of major shows, and more informed entries can be found in *Time Out Amsterdam*, on the Internet at <http://www.timeout.nl>. For dedicated art bookshops, see the *Shops and Markets* chapter.

A distinctive feature of the Amsterdam art scene are **open ateliers**, where neighbourhood groups of artists and galleries throw open their doors to the public for a week or a weekend. These are always worth visiting, but are hard to predict – ask around for details of upcoming events. The mainstream annual art fair, **KunstRai**, is held in early summer at the enormous RAI conference centre.

Galerie Akinci, Lijnbaansgracht 317 ☎638 0480. Eclectic, constantly changing exhibits, often at the cutting edge. Part of a complex of galleries next door to each other.

Amazone, Singel 120 ☎420 5061. Women's art and related exhibitions.

Amsterdamse Beeldhouwers Kollektief, Zeilmakerstraat 15 ☎625 6332. Amsterdam Sculptors' Collective: a permanent exhibit of contemporary Dutch sculptors up in the Western Islands.

Animation Art, Berenstraat 39 ☎627 7600. Comic art specialist, with hand-inked Disney cels for sale.

De Appel, Nieuwe Spiegelstraat 10 ☎625 5651. Centre for the contemporary arts, with regular shows by newcomers.

Arti, Spui 1a ☎623 3367. Impressive nineteenth-century exhibition space showing art by the members of the *Arti et Amicitae* (Arts and Friendship) society. Has another, more internationally slanted space at Rokin 112.

Barbara Farber, Keizersgracht 265; ☎627 6343. American avant-garde and graffiti art.

Bloom, Bloemstraat 150 ☎638 8810. Newly established small gallery, presenting some of the most unconventional exhibitions in the city.

Boomerang, Boomstraat 12 ☎420 3516. Australian and Aboriginal art.

D'Eendt, Spuistraat 272 ☎626 5777. Well-known modern art gallery that critics claim has declined in recent years. Still, it shouldn't be overlooked.

Espace, Keizersgracht 548 ☎624 0802. Paintings and drawings from the 1960s and 1970s; also at Kerkstraat 276.

Galerie Amsterdam, Warmoesstraat 101 ☎624 7408. Paintings and graphic art relating to Amsterdam and environs.

Galerie Binnen, Keizersgracht 82 ☎625 9603. The premier gallery for industrial and interior (*binnen*) design.

Galerie Delaive, Spiegelgracht 23 ☎625 9087. One of the city's best-known galleries, showing the work of established artists.

Galerie Fons Welters, Bloemstraat 140 ☎622 7193. One of the city's best, tending towards sculpture, always of the highest quality.

Galerie Paul Andriesse, Prinsengracht 116 ☎623 6237. Major showcase for the Amsterdam avant-garde.

Jurka, Singel 28 ☎626 6733. Up-to-the-minute paintings and photographs.

Melkweg, Lijnbaansgracht 234a ☎624 1777. Premier multimedia centre, with excellent photographic exhibitions.

Modern African Art Gallery, Kerkstraat 123 ☎620 1958. What it says. Also at Prinsengracht 472.

Mokum, Oudezijds Voorburgwal 334 ☎624 3958. Interesting art from the New Dutch Realism School.

Montevideo, Spuistraat 104 ☎623 7101. Video arts and electronic media.

Nanky de Vreeze, Keizersgracht 22 ☎627 3808. Large, mainstream gallery with very accessible shows.

Reflex, Weteringschans 79a ☎627 2832. Excellent exhibitions of modern

See p.349, for a rundown on Dutch art and artists.

...s and ..leries

art, changing monthly. Also at Weteringschans 83 and Spiegelgracht 8.

Scheltema Holkema Vermeulen, Koningsplein 20 ☎523 1411. The staircase of this large bookshop features changing exhibits of often excellent photography.

Stedelijk Museum Bureau, Rozenstraat 59 ☎422 0471. Recently opened gallery devoted to showing young Amsterdam artists.

Taller, Keizersgracht 607 ☎624 6734. Group of Latin American artists who have been working and exhibiting in this converted coach house for thirty years or more.

Torch, Lauriergracht 94 ☎626 0284. Reliable exhibitions of modern art in this sought-after gallery space.

Fotogalerie 2 1/2 maal 4 1/2, Prinsengracht 356 ☎626 0757. Exceptionally high-quality photographic exhibitions.

W139, Warmoesstraat 139 ☎622 9434. Enormous space right in the heart of the Red Light District, showing work by students and new graduates.

Galerie XY, 2e Laurierdwarsstraat 42 ☎625 0282. Forward-thinking Jordaan gallery, with shows from unknowns cheek-by-jowl with international grandees.

Museums

For a relatively small city, Amsterdam has a vast array of museums catering to all tastes. Although it may be that you find more than enough visual stimulation in the mansions and canals, even the most reluctant museum-goer will be intrigued by the sights and sounds of the world offered by the **Tropenmuseum**, or by the brand-new interactive **IMPULS Science and Technology Centre**, due to open in May 1997 – failing those, the rather less dynamic **Hash Marihuana Hemp Museum** or the newly opened **Tattoo Museum** might appeal. Amsterdam has a superb concentration of art museums, of which three – the **Rijksmuseum**, the

Van Gogh and the **Stedelijk** – rank among the finest in the world. Add to these over thirty small historical museums – including the **Anne Frank House**, an excellent **Jewish Historical Museum**, and the beautiful hidden church of the **Amstelkring** – and you get some idea of just how impressive the range is. The listings below, combined with the map on pp.238–239 and the accounts in the guide chapters, should help you choose.

Museums and Galleries

If you intend to visit more than three or four museums (or the same museum three or four times), you'd be well advised to buy a **museumjaarkaart** (museum year-card), either from the VVV or direct from a museum – take a passport photo and they can issue it on the spot. It costs ƒ45, or ƒ32.50 for under-18s and senior citizens, and gives free (or occasionally reduced) entry to around 400 museums throughout the country for a full year – although it doesn't relieve you of the burden of queuing up to get in every time. Considering it would normally cost you a hefty ƒ25 to visit the essential Rijksmuseum and Van Gogh Museum alone, the *museumjaarkaart* is a real bargain: if you have one, practically all the places listed below let you in for free. Bear in mind, though, that some museums (most notably the Anne Frank House) *don't* give reductions for museumcard-holders; we've indicated this in the listings. An alternative for those under 26 is the **Cultureel Jongeren Passport** or **CJP**, which for ƒ20 gets you reductions on entry to museums, as well as to theatres, concerts and *filmhuizen* (art-house cinemas) – though these reductions can vary, and are sometimes not that substantial. Valid throughout the Netherlands and in Belgium too, the CJP can be bought from the AUB Uitburo in the Stadsschouwburg theatre on Leidseplein. Entry charges for **children** are usually about half the price of adult admission, although the larger museums may offer even better value **family tickets**, usually covering two adults and two children, where one person gets in free. Many museums also offer **group-rate discounts**, although the number of

Museums and Galleries

Page references relate to the relevant guide chapter where the museum is usually described in more detail.

people required for a group varies from eight in some places to twenty or more in others; call ahead for details, and also call the museums direct for information about in-house **guided tours** – although these can be expensive, they're not a bad option if you have limited time, or would like expert information on what you're looking at.

Opening times, particularly for state-run museums, tend to follow a pattern: closed on Monday, open from 10am to 5pm Tuesday to Saturday and from 1 to 5pm on Sunday and public holidays. However, this pattern has recently begun to change, and many larger museums are now open on Monday as well. Bear in mind that Dutch primary schools tend to take Wednesday afternoons off, so this might be a bad time to try and find some peace and quiet in the Zoo (see p.265) or the Tropenmuseum.

Almost all Amsterdam museums offer at least basic **information** in English or a written English guide. Most have temporary special exhibitions or *tentoonstellingen*, and the best way to find out what's on is to pick up a free copy of the English *Museum Magazine* from any museum. "Museum Agenda" in the *Uitkrant* and *What's On In Amsterdam* are also useful for up-to-date listings, as is *Time Out Amsterdam* on the World Wide Web at <http://www.timeout.nl>. However, perhaps your best bet would be to drop into the AUB Uitburo on the Leidseplein and scan the leaflets.

Finally, if you like to take your museums the easy way, the **Museumboot** (museum-boat) runs a regular daily service once every half-hour (45min in winter) from 10am to 5pm, calling at seven jetties located at or near eighteen of the city's major museums; from the jetties it's a short walk to the Anne Frank House, the Amsterdam Historical Museum, Rijksmuseum, Van Gogh and Stedelijk museums, Rembrandt House, Jewish Historical Museum and the Maritime Museum, among others. However, since the larger museums can take some hours to explore (using up valuable time on your day ticket), the

Museumboot is perhaps best used for spending a day cruising between the smaller museums. A hop-on, hop-off day ticket will cost you ƒ22 (ƒ16 if you have a museumcard); a day ticket including a canal cruise and free entrance to Madame Tussaud's waxworks (if you can pack it all in with the museums as well) is ƒ27.50. The office and main boarding point is in front of Centraal Station, although you can also buy tickets from the jetty opposite the Rijksmuseum; for more details call ☎ 625 6464. For gentle canal hops between museums, there's also the **Canal Bus** service, which takes in just the central museums (see "City Transport" in *Basics* for details).

Allard Pierson Museum
Oude Turfmarkt 127 ☎ *525 2556. Tram #4, #9, #14, #16, #24, #25 (stop Spui). Tues–Fri 10am–5pm, Sat, Sun & holidays 1–5pm. ƒ6; over-65s, CJP, students ƒ4.50; under-15s ƒ3; under-12s free. Wheelchair access.*
The city's premier archeological museum. See p.84.

Amstelkring Museum
Oudezijds Voorburgwal 40 ☎ *624 6604. Mon–Sat 10am–5pm, Sun 1–5pm. ƒ7.50; under-19s, over-65s, CJP ƒ5; under-5s free. No wheelchair access.*
A beautiful and well-preserved seventeenth-century clandestine Catholic church and house in the heart of the Red Light District. See p.79.

Amsterdam Historical Museum
Entrances at Kalverstraat 92 and Nieuwezijds Voorburgwal 357 ☎ *523 1822. Tram #1, #2, #4, #5, #9, #11, #14, #16, #24, #25 (stop Spui). Mon–Fri 10am–5pm, Sat & Sun 11am–5pm. ƒ8; under-17s ƒ4. Guided tours Wed 2pm & 3pm. Limited wheelchair access.*
Modern and engaging collection of artefacts relating to the history of the city, with a library, lectures and concerts. See pp.88–89.

Anne Frank House
Prinsengracht 263 ☎ *556 7100. Tram #13, #14, #17 (stop Westermarkt).*

June–Aug Mon–Sat 9am–7pm, Sun 10am–7pm; Sept–May Mon–Sat 9am–5pm, Sun 10am–5pm; closed Yom Kippur. f10; under-17s, over-65s, CJP f5; under-10s free; no museumcards. No wheelchair access.

The secret annexe where Anne Frank and her family hid during the occupation, now a museum. See p.97.

Aviodome
Schiphol Centre ☎ 604 1521. Train to Schiphol Airport, then walk or bus from stop B12. April–Sept daily 10am–5pm; Oct–March Tues–Fri 10am–5pm, Sat & Sun noon–5pm. f8.50; over-65s f7.50; under-12s f6; no museumcards. Wheelchair access.

Huge, hands-on exhibition for buffs and kids alike, with over 30 historic aircraft to examine and clamber onto, including the first motorized plane from 1903 and the latest flight-simulators.

Bijbels Museum
Herengracht 366 ☎ 624 7949. Tram #1, #2, #5, #11 (stop Spui). Mon–Sat 10am–5pm, Sun 1–5pm; over-65s, CJP f3.50; under-16s f2.50. Limited wheelchair access.

Ecumenical museum of life in biblical times, housed in two wonderful canal houses. See p.101.

Bosmuseum
Koenenkade 56, in the Amsterdamse Bos ☎ 643 1414. At the end of the Museum Tramline from Haarlemmermeer Station, or bus #170, #171 or #172. Daily 10am–5pm. Free. Wheelchair access. Information centre for the Amsterdam Forest, in the south of the city. See p.158.

CoBrA Museum of Modern Art
Sandbergplein 1, Amstelveen ☎ 547 5050. Tram #5 (last stop, then walk), or bus #170, #171, #172. Tues–Sun 11am–5pm. f5; over-65s, CJP f3.50; under-16s f2.50. Wheelchair access. Brand-new museum way out in the southern suburbs dedicated to the CoBrA movement of the 1950s and 60s; well worth the journey. For more on the CoBrA movement, see p.356.

Dutch Press Museum
International Institute for Social History, Cruquiusweg 31 ☎ 668 5866. Tram #6, #10 (stop Javaplein), or bus #22. Mon–Fri 9am–5pm, Sat 9.30am–1pm. Free. The history of the Dutch press since 1903, as revealed in newspapers, leaflets, posters and political cartoons. See p.160.

Ferdinand Domela Nieuwenhuis Museum
Herengracht 266 ☎ 555 2300 or ☎ 010/408 2477. Tram #1, #2, #5, #11 (stop Spui). Open by appointment only. Free. Limited wheelchair access. Exhibits covering the life of the man who has been called "the father of Dutch socialism"; manuscripts by Marx and Engels on display. See p.100.

Geels & Co. Museum
Warmoesstraat 67 ☎ 624 0683. Tues 2–4pm, Fri & Sat 2–4.30pm. Free. No wheelchair access. Museum of coffee- and tea-related displays above a shop selling the same. See p.78.

Hash Marihuana Hemp Museum
Oudezijds Achterburgwal 148 ☎ 623 5961. Tram #4, #9, #16, #24, #25 (stop Dam), or metro Nieuwmarkt. Daily 11am–10pm. f6; no museumcards. Limited wheelchair access. The story of the weed, with a growing garden and even a Bible made of hemp. There's a handy head shop next door for hands-on experience. See p.82–83.

Hollandsche Schouwburg
Plantage Middenlaan 24 ☎ 626 9945. Tram #7, #9, #14 (stop Plantage Kerklaan). Daily 11am–4pm. Free. Limited wheelchair access. Sober exhibition on the role of this theatre building during World War II as a holding point for Jews about to be transported to concentration camps. See p.131.

IMPULS Science and Technology Centre
Oosterdok, near entrance to IJ tunnel ☎ 570 8111. Bus #22, #28. Open from May 1997: July & Aug daily 10am–9pm; Sept–June Mon–Thurs & Sun 10am–6pm, Fri & Sat 10am–9pm. Price unconfirmed

Museums and Galleries

Museums and Galleries

– call for details. Wheelchair access. Interactive, sparkling new "centre for human creativity", with bang up-to-date hi-tech displays and exhibits. See p.134.

Jewish Historical Museum

J.D. Meijerplein ☎ 626 9945. Tram #9, #14 (stop Waterlooplein), or metro Waterlooplein. Daily 11am–5pm; closed Yom Kippur. f7; under-16s, over-65s, students f3.50; under-10s free. Wheelchair access.

Innovative and award-winning museum on the history of the Jews in the Netherlands, with many fascinating side exhibits. A cassette tour of the museum is available (f2.50). Also operates walking tours of the district (f50) and visits to the nearby Portuguese Synagogue. See p.129.

Kattenkabinet

Herengracht 468 ☎ 626 5378. Tram #16, #24, #25 (stop Muntplein), or tram #1, #2, #5, #11 (stop Koningsplein). Tues–Sun 1–5pm. f7.50; no museumcards. No wheelchair access.

Hundreds of paintings and art objects related to cats, on display in an old canal house. See p.110.

Kromhout Shipyard Museum

Hoogte Kadijk 147 ☎ 627 6777. Bus #22, #28. Mon–Fri 10am–4pm. f2.50; over-65s f1.75; under-15s f1.50; no museumcards. Limited wheelchair access.

Old shipyard that is part museum, part restorer of old vessels. See p.135.

Maritime Museum (Scheepvaartsmuseum)

Kattenburgerplein 1 ☎ 523 2222. Bus #22, #28. Tues–Sat 10am–5pm, Sun noon–5pm; June–Sept also Mon 10am–5pm. f12.50; under-12s f8; under-6s free. Wheelchair access.

Impressive collection of maritime objects, large and small. See p.134.

Max Euwe Centre

Max Euweplein 30. Tram #1, #2, #5, #6, #7, #10, #11 (stop Leidseplein). Tues–Fri 10.30am–4pm. Free. Limited wheelchair access.

Eponymous museum of the only Dutch

chess champion, full of chess-related bits and pieces. See p.104.

Municipal Archives (Gemeentearchief)

Amsteldijk 67 ☎ 572 0202. Tram #3 (stop Amsteldijk), or tram #4 (stop Lutmastraat). Mon–Fri 8.45am–4.45pm, Sat 9am–12.15pm. Free.

A mass of historical material on the city, though the emphasis is on research rather than exhibitions. See p.154.

Multatuli Museum

Korsjespoortsteeg 20 ☎ 638 1938. Tram #1, #2, #5, #11, #13, #17 (stop Nieuwezijds Kolk). Tues 10am–5pm, Sat & Sun noon–5pm. Free. No wheelchair access.

Museum in the former home of the eighteenth-century Dutch writer. See p.96.

Netherlands Film Museum

Vondelpark 3, next to Roemer Visscherstraat ☎ 589 1400. Tram #1, #6, #11 (stop 1e Constantijn Huygensstraat), or tram #3, #12 (stop Overtoom). Box office open Mon–Fri 9am–10pm, Sat & Sun 1–10pm; films screened nightly, plus Wed matinees; tickets f10. Library and documentation centre at Vondelstraat 69 ☎ 589 1435; Tues–Fri 10am–5pm, Sat 11am–5pm; free. Wheelchair access.

Less a museum than a restored showcase for obscure films on a variety of subjects – not always Dutch and usually organized by theme. See p.150.

Open Harbour Museum

KNSM-laan 311 or Surinamekade 3 ☎ 620 5522. Bus #32, #59. Wed–Fri & Sun 1–5pm. f5; over-65s, CJP, museumcard holders f3.50. Wheelchair access.

History of the harbour of Amsterdam, from a social viewpoint. Interesting and broadly alternative historical analysis.

Pianola Museum

Westerstraat 106 ☎ 627 9624. Tram #3, #10 (stop Marnixplein). Sun 1–5pm; other times by appointment. f5; no museumcards. Limited wheelchair access.

Tiny and fascinating private collection of working pianolas, with occasional weekend concerts. See p.116.

Rembrandt House

Jodenbreestraat 4–6 ☎ 638 4668. Tram #9, #14 (stop Mr Visserplein), or metro Waterlooplein. Mon–Sat 10am–5pm, Sun 1–5pm. f7.50; over-65s f6; under-15s, CJP f5; under-9s free. Limited wheelchair access.

The home of Rembrandt at the height of his fame and popularity, with a wonderful display of his engravings. See p.127.

Resistance Museum *(Verzetsmuseum)*

Lekstraat 63 ☎ 644 9797. Tram #4, #12, #25 (stop Victorieplein). Tues–Fri 10am–5pm, Sat & Sun 1–5pm. f5; under-15s, over-65s, CJP f2.50; under-8s free. Limited wheelchair access.

Excellent display on the rise of the resistance from the invasion in May 1940 to the liberation in 1945, with additional displays on contemporary neo-Nazism. See p.157.

Rijksmuseum

Stadhouderskade 42 ☎ 673 2121. Tram #2, #5 (stop Hobbemastraat), or tram #6, #7, #10 (stop Spiegelgracht). Daily 10am–5pm. South Wing entrance at Hobbemastraat 19 ☎ 573 2911. f12.50; over-65s f7.50; under-18s, CJP f5. Wheelchair access.

The country's national museum, with a marvellous collection of Dutch painting up to 1850, as well as decorative arts, furniture, oriental ceramics and more, spread over 200 rooms. To supplement the brief descriptions, you can take a CD audio tour, which gives instant information on over 550 works in the museum – pick one up at the Front Hall desk or the South Wing entrance for f7.50. See pp.139–147.

Rijksmuseum Vincent van Gogh

Paulus Potterstraat 7 ☎ 570 5200. Tram #2, #3, #5, #12 (stop Van Baerlestraat), or tram #16 (stop Museumplein). Daily 10am–5pm. f12.50; over-65s f7.50; under-18s f5. Wheelchair access.

An extensive and well-presented collection covering all periods and styles of Van Gogh, with a good representative sample of works of contemporaries such as Toulouse-Lautrec and Gauguin. See p.147. For f7 you can take an audio tour

(the machine is shaped like a portable phone – you dial in the number of the painting). Regular lunchtime lectures in English, open symposia and films on relevant art and art-history topics.

Script Museum

University Library, Singel 425. Tram #1, #2, #5, #11 (stop Koningsplein). Mon–Fri 9.30am–1pm & 2–4.30pm. Free. Limited wheelchair access.

Offbeat collection of different writing materials and alphabets from around the world. See p.91.

Sex Museum

Damrak 18 ☎ 627 7431. Daily 10am–11pm. f3.95; no museumcards. Wheelchair access.

Dull and tawdry exhibition of sex-related art and artefacts. See p.76.

Six Collection

Amstel 218. Tram #9, #14 (stop Waterlooplein), or metro Waterlooplein. Apply at the Rijksmuseum information desk beforehand, with your passport, to get a ticket. Guided tours Mon, Wed & Fri 10am & 11am; closed public holidays. Free (but no entry without ticket). Limited wheelchair access.

A private home that displays a handful of the finest paintings of the Dutch Golden Age in a period setting. Be warned, though, that you must follow the procedure outlined above – Baron Six is extremely protective of his privacy. See p.107.

Stedelijk Museum of Modern Art

Paulus Potterstraat 13 ☎ 573 2737. Tram #2, #3, #5, #12 (stop Van Baerlestraat), or tram #16 (stop Museumplein). April–Oct daily 11am–7pm; Nov–March daily 11am–5pm. f8; under-17s, CJP f4; under-7s free. Wheelchair access.

The city's prime venue for modern art. Clear displays from its excellent permanent collection, as well as regular temporary exhibitions. Also has a library and programme of lectures and events. See p.148.

Stedelijk Museum Bureau

Rozenstraat 59 ☎ 422 0471. Tram #13, #14, #17 (stop Marnixstraat). Tues–Sun

Museums and Galleries

Museums and Galleries

For details of museums that specifically appeal to children, see the Kids' Amsterdam chapter.

11am–5pm. Free. Wheelchair access. Annexe of the main museum devoted to cutting-edge exhibitions and multimedia installations by Amsterdam artists. See p.114.

Tattoo Museum
Oudezijds Achterburgwal 130 ☎ 625 1565. Tram #4, #9, #16, #24, #25 (stop Dam), or metro Nieuwmarkt. Tues–Sun noon–5pm. f5; no museumcards. Limited wheelchair access.
The history of the art form, with hundreds of drawings, photos and tools, and even some preserved tattooed skin.

Theatre Museum
Herengracht 168 ☎ 623 5104. Tram #13, #14, #17 (stop Westermarkt). Tues–Sun 11am–5pm. f5; under-9s, over-65s, students, CJP f3. Museum closed for renovation until June 1997. Resource centre open Tues–Fri 11am–5pm; free.
Recreations of contemporary stage sets alongside models that trace the earlier days of the theatre in the Netherlands, fabulously located in a canal house dating from 1638. See p.99.

Torture Museum
Damrak 22 ☎ 639 2027. Daily 10am–11pm. f7.50; students f5.50; under-13s f4; no museumcards. No wheelchair access.
A macabre but well-displayed and informative collection of medieval torture equipment. See p.76.

Trade Union Museum
Henri Polaklaan 9 ☎ 624 1166. Tram #7, #9, #14 (stop Plantage Kerklaan). Tues–Fri 11am–5pm, Sun 1–5pm. f5. Limited wheelchair access.
A small collection of documents, cuttings and photos relating to the Dutch labour movement. See p.132.

Tram Museum
Amstelveenseweg 264 ☎ 673 7538. Tram #6, #16 (stop Haarlemmermeer Station). April–June, Sept & Oct Sun 10am–5.30pm; July & Aug Tues–Sun 10am–5.30pm. f5; over-65s, under-11s,

CJP f2.50; under-4s free; no museumcards. No wheelchair access.
Not so much a museum as a collection of antique trams from all over Europe, which shuttle to and from the Amsterdamse Bos forest every 20min (1hr round trip). See p.157.

Tropenmuseum
Linnaeusstraat 2 ☎ 568 8215. Tram #9, #10, #14 (stop Mauritskade). Mon & Wed–Fri 10am–5pm, Tues 10am–9.30pm, Sat & Sun noon–5pm. f10; under-18s, over-65s, students, CJP f5; museumcard holders f2.50; under-5s free. Wheelchair access. Adjacent "Kindermuseum" open at different times; see Kids' Amsterdam, p.266.
Entertaining exhibits on the realities of life in the developing world, imaginatively displayed through a variety of media. See p.158.

University Historical Collection
Oudezijds Voorburgwal 231 ☎ 525 3341. Tram #4, #9, #14, #16, #24, #25 (stop Spui). Mon–Fri 9am–5pm. Free. No wheelchair access.
Collections of books, prints, letters and suchlike, related to the history of the University of Amsterdam – the buildings beat the exhibits hands-down. See p.83.

Van Loon Museum
Keizersgracht 672 ☎ 624 5255. Tram #16, #24, #25 (stop Keizersgracht). Mon 10am–5pm, Sun 1–5pm; f7.50; over-65s f5; under-12s free; no museumcards. No wheelchair access.
Golden Age canal house with a classically furnished interior; there's also a garden in the eighteenth-century French style. See p.106.

Willet-Holthuysen Museum
Herengracht 605 ☎ 523 1870. Tram #4, #9, #14 (stop Rembrandtplein). Mon–Fri 10am–5pm, Sat & Sun 11am–5pm. f5; under-16s f2.50. No wheelchair access.
Rococo-style, period canal house, somewhat more pristinely restored than the Van Loon. See p.108.

Chapter 12

Shops and Markets

Variety is the essence of **shopping** in Amsterdam. Whereas in other capitals you can spend days trudging around in search of something interesting, here you'll find every kind of store packed into a relatively small area that's nearly always pleasant to wander around. Throw in a handful of great **street markets**, and Amsterdam's shopping possibilities look even better. There are, of course, the obligatory generic malls and pedestrianized shopping streets, where you can find exactly the same stuff you'd see at home (only more expensive), but where Amsterdam scores is in some excellent, unusual **speciality shops** – designer clocks, rubber stamps, Indonesian arts, and condoms, to name just a few.

Shopping in Amsterdam can be divided roughly by **area**, with similar shops often huddled together in neighbouring streets. While exploring, bear in mind that the major canals are mostly given over to homes and offices, and it's along the small radial streets that connect them that many of the most interesting and individual shops are scattered. Broadly, the **Nieuwendijk/Kalverstraat** strip running through Dam Square is where you'll find mostly dull, high-street fashion and mainstream department stores – Saturday afternoon here can be a hellish experience. **Magna Plaza**, just behind the Royal Palace, is a marvellous, striped castle of a building that used to be the main post office, but has now been transformed into a covered mall on

five floors, complete with *Virgin Megastore*, pricey espressos, and teenagers on the escalators. The southern edge of the Red Light District, along **Damstraat** and **Oude Doelenstraat**, although popular, has little to recommend it, and you'd do well to keep one hand on your wallet while window-shopping here. **Koningsplein** and **Leidsestraat** used to be home to the most exclusive of shops; these days many of them have fled south, though there's still a surprisingly good selection of affordable designer shoe and clothes stores. The **Jordaan**, to the west, is where many local artists ply their wares: you can find individual items of genuine interest here, as well as more specialized and adventurous clothes shops and some affordable antiques. Less affordable antiques – the cream of Amsterdam's renowned trade – can be found in the Spiegelkwartier, centred on **Nieuwe Spiegelstraat**, while to the south, **P.C. Hooftstraat**, **Van Baerlestraat** and, further south still, **Beethovenstraat** play host to designer clothiers, upmarket ceramics stores, confectioners and delicatessens.

The consumer revolution is noticeably absent from Amsterdam's cobbled alleys, and the majority of shops you'll come across are individual small businesses rather than chains: in Amsterdam, it's the shopworker, not the consumer, who reigns supreme, as borne out by both the limited **opening hours** of most shops and the relatively

SHOPS AND MARKETS

247

Shops and Markets

high prices. The majority of shops take Monday morning off, not opening up until noon or 1pm and closing again at 6pm. On Tuesday, Wednesday and Friday, hours are the standard 9am to 6pm, while Thursday is late-opening night (*koopavond*), with most places staying open from 9am until 9pm. Saturday hours are normally 8.30 or 9am to 5 or 5.30pm, and all except the larger shops on the main streets are closed on Sunday. A few "night shops" are open between roughly 4pm and 1am; see the box on p.257.

Most small and medium-sized shops – and even some of the larger ones – won't accept **payment** by credit card: don't take it for granted in anywhere but the biggest or most expensive places. Shops that do will accept the range of major cards (*American Express, Visa, Access/Mastercard*, etc), but never travellers' cheques. Practically everywhere, however, takes *Eurocheques*, with the appropriate card as guarantee.

Antiques

By necessity, this is only a sample of what's on offer – you'll find many more antiques shops in every corner of Amsterdam.

Ariëns Kappers/van der Peet, Nieuwe Spiegelstraat 32 ☎623 5336. Original maps and Japanese woodblock prints.

Blitz, Nieuwe Spiegelstraat 37a ☎623 2663. Chinese ceramics.

Couzijn Simon, Prinsengracht 578 ☎624 7691. Antique toys and dolls.

Dick Meijer, Keizersgracht 539 ☎624 9288. Egyptian, Roman and Pre-Columbian antiquities.

Eduard Kramer, Nieuwe Spiegelstraat 64 ☎638 8740. Specialists in fifteenth- to twentieth-century Dutch tiles, with a marvellous selection.

Elisabeth Hendriks, Nieuwe Spiegelstraat 61 ☎623 0085. Snuffbottles.

Gallery de Munt, in the Munttoren, Muntplein 12 ☎623 2271. The best out-let for gifts of antique Delftware, pottery, hand-painted tiles and the like.

Jan Beekhuizen, Nieuwe Spiegelstraat 49 ☎626 3912. European pewter from the fifteenth century onwards.

De Looier, Elandsgracht 109 ☎624 9038. A rambling indoor market selling moderately priced antiques.

Thom & Lenny Nelis, Keizersgracht 541 ☎623 1546. Medical antiques and spectacles.

Tóth Ikonen, Nieuwe Spiegelstraat 68 ☎420 7359. Antique Russian icons.

Van Dreven & Toebosch, Nieuwe Spiegelstraat 33 ☎625 2732. Antique clocks, barometers and music boxes.

Art Supplies, Postcards and Posters

The card and gift shops in the main tourist areas mostly sell items of highly questionable taste, ranging from the tacky to the openly pornographic. In the shops listed below you can get cards that are a cut above the usual dross.

Art Unlimited, Keizersgracht 510 ☎624 8419. Enormous card and poster shop, with excellent stock. All kinds of images: good for communiqués home that don't involve windmills.

De Lach, 1e Bloemdwarsstraat 14 ☎626 6625. Fairy-tale movie poster shop, "from *Casablanca* to *Pulp Fiction*".

Paper Moon, Singel 419 ☎626 1669. Well-stocked card shop.

Quadra, Herengracht 383 ☎626 9472. Original advertising posters from 1900 onwards.

Van Beek, Stadhouderskade 63 ☎662 1670. Long-established outlet for art materials. Graphic arts supplies are sold at the Weteringschans 201 branch.

Van Ginkel, Bilderdijkstraat 99 ☎618 9827. Supplier of art materials, with an emphasis on print-making.

Vlieger, Amstel 52 ☎623 5834. Every kind of paper downstairs, every kind of paint upstairs.

Bikes

Bikes can be **rented** from Centraal Station (and other train stations), or from a number of private outlets all over town – see *Basics*, p.38. When **buying** a bike, don't be tempted by anything you're offered on the street or in a bar – more often than not you'll end up with a stolen bike. Try instead the shops listed below, which rent, sell and repair bikes of all qualities. If you find that no one in the shop speaks English, check out the glossary of basic bike terms on p.37.

Bike City, Bloemgracht 68 ☎626 3721. The best of the sale-and-rental crowd for service and quality – try here first.

De Fietsenmaker, Nieuwe Hoogstraat 23 ☎624 6137. Every bike part you could need. Voted the best bike shop in Amsterdam in a newspaper poll.

Freewheel, Akoleienstraat 7 ☎627 7252. Bike repairs and sales in a shop run by women.

Koenders, Utrechtsedwarsstraat 105 ☎623 4657. Family-run business; second-hand bikes with a guarantee.

Lohman, De Clercqstraat 70 ☎618 3906. New and used racing bikes.

MacBike, Marnixstraat 220 ☎626 6964. Also at Houtkopersburgwal 16 ☎620 0985. Well-respected rental-and-sales firm a little out of the centre.

P. Jonkerk, Lange Leidsedwarsstraat 145 ☎623 2542. Good selection of used bikes.

Ton Kroonenberg, Van Woustraat 59 ☎671 6466. Repairs and sales; service is helpful and courteous.

Zijwind, Ferdinand Bolstraat 168 ☎673 7026. Wide stock of bikes to buy or rent in a shop run by women.

Books and Magazines

Virtually all Amsterdam bookshops stock at least a small selection of **English-language books**, though prices are always inflated (sometimes dramatically). In the city centre it's possible to pick up most English **newspapers** the day they come out, and English-language **magazines** are available, too, from newsstands and bookshops. The **second-hand** and **antiquarian** booksellers listed below are only the most accessible; for a comprehensive list, pick up from any of them the leaflet *Antiquarian & Secondhand Bookshops of Amsterdam*.

General bookstores

Allert de Lange, Damrak 62 ☎624 6744. A fine bookshop, with a great stock of Penguins, a solid travel section and an informed staff.

American Book Center, Kalverstraat 185 ☎625 5537. Vast stock, all in English, with lots of imported US magazines and books. Especially good gay section. Students get ten percent discount.

Athenaeum, Spui 14 ☎623 3933. Excellent all-round bookshop with an adventurous stock. Also the best source of international newspapers and magazines.

The English Bookshop, Lauriergracht 71 ☎626 4230. A small but quirky collection of titles, many of which you won't find elsewhere.

Martyrium, Van Baerlestraat 170 ☎673 2092. Mostly remaindered stock, but none the worse for that – English-language paperbacks and hardbacks galore.

Scheltema Holkema Vermeulen, Koningsplein 20 ☎523 1411. Amsterdam's biggest and best bookshop. Six floors of absolutely everything. Open late and on Sundays.

De Slegte, Kalverstraat 48 ☎622 5933. The Amsterdam branch of a nationwide chain specializing in new and used books at a discount.

W.H. Smith, Kalverstraat 152 ☎638 3821. Dutch branch of the UK high-street chain, with four floors of books and magazines. A predictable selection, but prices are sometimes cheaper here than elsewhere.

Zwart op Wit, Utrechtsestraat 149 ☎622 8174. Small but well-stocked store. Open on Sunday afternoons and until 7pm during the week.

Shops and Markets

For more on cycling in the city, see "City Transport" in Basics.

Shops and
Markets

Second-hand and antiquarian

A. Kok, Oude Hoogstraat 14 ☎623
1191. Antiquarian stock, especially strong
on prints and maps.

Boekenmarkt, Spui. Open-air book market every Friday – see p.262.

The Book Exchange, Kloveniersburgwal
58 ☎626 6266. Rambling old shop with
a crusty proprietor. Huge, dark and dusty.

Book Traffic, Leliegracht 50 ☎620 4690.
An excellent and well-organized selection, run by an American.

Brinkman, Singel 319 ☎623 8353.
Stalwart of the Amsterdam book trade,
Brinkman has occupied the same
premises for forty years. Worldwide mail
order service.

De Kloof, Kloveniersburgwal 44 ☎622
3828. Enormous higgledy-piggledy used
bookshop on four floors. Great for a rum-
mage.

Lorelei, Prinsengracht 495 ☎623 4308.
Second-hand and antiquarian books
with a feminist emphasis. Open Wed–Sat
from noon.

N.C. Berg, Oude Schans 8 ☎624 0848.
Delightfully untidy old bookshop.

Oudemanhuispoort Book Market. See
p.263.

Van Gennep, Nieuwezijds Voorburgwal
330 ☎626 4448. Excellent discount
bookshop with many bargains. Also
good for politics, art and sciences.

Vrouwen In Druk, Westermarkt 5 ☎624
5003. Second-hand books by women.

Art and architecture

Architectura & Natura, Leliegracht 44
☎623 6186. Books on architecture and
interior design.

Art Book, Van Baerlestraat 126 ☎644
0925. The city's best source of high-
gloss art books. Check out also the
shops of the main museums, particularly
the Stedelijk.

Asian Art Bookshop, Nieuwe
Spiegelstraat 18 ☎620 1782. The name
says it all.

Boekie Woekie, Berenstraat 16 ☎639
0507. Books by and on Dutch artists and
graphic designers.

Lankamp & Brinkman, Spiegelgracht 19
☎623 4656. Art and applied arts,
antiques and collectables, plus a good
general stock.

Comics and graphic novels

CIA (Comic Import Amsterdam), Zeedijk
31a ☎620 5078. What it says.

Lambiek, Kerkstraat 78 ☎626 7543. The
city's largest and oldest comic bookshop
and gallery, with an international stock.

Stripwinkel Kapitein Rob, 2e
Egelantiersdwarsstraat 7 ☎622 3869.
Cartoon books old and new.

Vandal Com X, Rozengracht 51a ☎420
2144. US imports.

Computer

Computer Collectief, Amstel 312 ☎638
9003. Vast collection of books, software
and magazines, and an eminently
knowledgeable staff.

Cookery

Kookboekhandel, Runstraat 26 ☎622
4768. Cookery books in a variety of languages, mostly English; also some out-
of-print treasures. The owner is a well-
known Dutch cookery journalist, and can
be grumpy if you don't display enough
knowledge.

Gay, lesbian and women's issues

Intermale, Spuistraat 251 ☎625 0009.
Gay men's bookshop.

Vrolijk, Paleisstraat 135 ☎623 5142.
Self-billed as "the largest gay and lesbian bookstore on the continent".

Xantippe, Prinsengracht 290 ☎623
5854. Wide range of books and
resources by, for and about women.

Language

Intertaal, Van Baerlestraat 76 ☎671
5353. Teach-yourself books and
dictionaries in every language you can
think of.

Politics and society

El Hizjra, Singel 300a ☎ 420 1517. Books on the Middle East and the Arab world.

Fort van Sjakoo, Jodenbreestraat 24 ☎ 625 8979. Anarchist bookshop stocking a wide selection of radical political publications.

Milieuboek, Plantage Middenlaan 2H ☎ 624 4989. Right next to the Hortus Botanicus, and specializing in books on green and environmental issues.

Pantheon, St Antoniesbreestraat 132 ☎ 622 9488. General bookshop with a strong politics and Middle East section.

Tropenmuseum Bookstore, Linnaeusstraat 2 ☎ 568 8295. Books on Third World politics and culture, many in English.

Religion, occult and New Age

Arcanum, Reguliersgracht 54 ☎ 625 0813. Specialists in astrology and the occult.

Au Bout du Monde, Singel 313 ☎ 625 1397. Astrology, philosophy, psychology and mysticism, with classical music playing while you browse.

Himalaya, Warmoesstraat 56 ☎ 626 0899. Cosy New Age bookshop with a marvellous café out the back.

International Evangelist Bookshop, Raadhuisstraat 14 ☎ 620 1859. Bibles and Christian books.

Martyrium, Van Baerlestraat 170 ☎ 673 2092. Enormous selection of books on religious and humanist subjects.

Oibibio, Prins Hendrikkade 20 ☎ 553 9344. Bookshop attached to a large New Age centre.

Psychedelic Bookstore, Lijnsbaansgracht 90 ☎ 638 4334. Everything you'd expect. Daily noon–5pm.

De Roos, Vondelstraat 35 ☎ 689 0436. Delightful New Age centre with a wide selection of esoteric books and the most peaceful café in Amsterdam.

Theatre and film

Cine-Qua-Non, Staalstraat 14 ☎ 625 5588. Mostly English titles on film and cinema history.

International Theatre and Film Books, Leidseplein 26a ☎ 622 6489. Books and magazines on all aspects of the stage and screen.

Travel

A la Carte, Utrechtsestraat 110 ☎ 625 0679. Large and friendly travel bookshop.

Evenaar, Singel 348 ☎ 624 6289. Concentrates more on travel literature than guidebooks. The staff are exceptionally short-tempered – no browsing!

Jacob van Wijngaarden, Overtoom 97 ☎ 612 1901. The city's best travel bookshop, with knowledgeable staff and a huge selection of books and maps.

Pied-à-Terre, Singel 393 ☎ 627 4455. Hiking maps for Holland and beyond, most in English.

Scheltema Holkema Vermeulen, Koningsplein 20 ☎ 523 1411. A multistorey general bookshop with a comprehensive travel section.

Stadsboekwinkel, Waterlooplein 18 ☎ 622 4537. The shop for all books on Amsterdam: architecture, transport, history, urban planning, geography, etc.

Shops and Markets

Clothes and Accessories

When it comes to **clothes**, Amsterdam is in many ways an ideal place to shop: prices aren't through the roof and the city is small enough that a shopping trip doesn't have to destroy your feet. However, don't expect the huge choice of, say, London or New York. The city's department stores (see p.254) tend to be conservative, and the Dutch disapproval of ostentation means that the big international designers stay out of the limelight. What you will find are good-value, if dull, mainstream styles along Kalverstraat and Nieuwendijk, with better stuff along Rokin and Leidsestraat, and the really fancy goods down in the south of the city on P.C. Hooftstraat, Van Baerlestraat and Beethovenstraat. More interestingly, there's a fair array of one-off youth-oriented and second-hand clothing shops dotted around in the

Shops and Markets

For where to buy children's clothes, see Kids' Amsterdam.

Jordaan, on Oude and Nieuwe Hoogstraat, and along the narrow streets that connect the major canals west of the city centre. For **second-hand clothes** the Waterlooplein flea market (see p.263) is a marvellous hunting ground. What follows is a brief rundown of some of the more exciting outlets.

New and designer clothes

Agnès B, Rokin 126 ☎627 1465. Shop of the French designer.

America Today, in Magna Plaza mall ☎638 8447; also at Sarphatistraat 48. Hugely popular outlet for classic US brands, imported direct and sold cheap.

Antonia, Gasthuismolensteeg 12 ☎627 2433. A gathering of adventurous Dutch designers under one roof. Good on shoes and bags too.

Confetti, Prinsenstraat 11 ☎622 3178. Bright, fun, easy to wear and affordable women's clothes.

Cora Kemperman, Leidsestraat 72 ☎625 1284. Well-made designer clothes that won't break the bank.

Diversi, 1e Leliedwarsstraat 6 ☎625 0773. Small but inspired collection of reasonably priced, mainly French clothes for women.

Edgar Vos, P.C. Hooftstraat 134 ☎662 6336. Amsterdam shop of the Dutch *haute couture* designer; power styles for women.

Exota, Nieuwe Leliestraat 32 ☎420 6884; also at Hartenstraat 10. Good, fairly priced selection of simple new and used clothing.

Fever, Prinsengracht 192 ☎623 4500. Elegant, exclusive designs for women. Phone ahead.

G & G, Prinsengracht 514 ☎622 6339. Men's clothing in larger sizes.

Hemp Works, Nieuwendijk 13 ☎421 1762. Not all hemp is like sackcloth – check out these silky hemp shirts and jeans.

Hobbits, Van Baerlestraat 34 and 42 ☎664 0779. High prices but a good and varied selection of women's and men's clothes. Keep an eye out for sales.

Kamikaze, Kalverstraat 158 ☎626 1194. Pretty standard Kalverstraat clothing outlet.

Local Service, Keizersgracht 400 ☎626 6840. Men's and women's fashions. Ultra-trendy and expensive.

Look Out, Utrechtsestraat 91 ☎625 5032. Colourful coats and knits – not cheap.

Mateloos, Bilderdijkstraat 62 ☎683 2384. Clothes for women in larger sizes.

De Mof, Haarlemmerdijk 109 ☎623 1798. Basically an industrial clothier, selling heavy-duty shirts, baggy overalls and the like for rock-bottom prices.

Pauw, Leidsestraat 16 ☎626 5698; also at Heiligeweg 10, and branches all over town. Mainstream and often unexceptional separates for women.

Puck and Hans, Rokin 66 ☎625 5889. Stylish and very popular among the moneyed young; stocks Gaultier.

Raymond Linhard, Van Baerlestraat 50 ☎679 0755. Cheerful, well-priced separates.

Reflections, Stadhouderskade 23a ☎612 6141. The absolute *crème de la crème*, with price tags to match. There's a "casuals" branch at P.C. Hooftstraat 66.

Robin & Rik, Runstraat 30 ☎627 8924. Handmade leather clothes and accessories for men and women.

Robin's Bodywear, Nieuwe Hoogstraat 20 ☎620 1552. Affordable lingerie store with a wide stock.

Sissy Boy, Leidsestraat 15 ☎623 8949; also at Van Baerlestraat 12 and Kalverstraat 210. Pricey but nice enough clothes.

Studio Chazo, Brouwersgracht 270a ☎624 5358. Small, cosy women's clothing shop specializing in wedding and party clothes. Phone first.

Street and clubwear

Clubwear House, Herengracht 265 ☎622 8766. The place for everything to do with clubbing in Amsterdam, from flyers to fabulous clothes. DJs play in-store on Saturdays.

Punch, St Antoniesbreestraat 73 ☎626 6673. Doc Martens and Lonsdale.

Rodolfo's, in Magna Plaza mall ☎623 1214; also at Sarphatistraat 59. Huge collection of in-line skates and skateboards and the latest styles to go with them.

Stilett, Damstraat 14 ☎625 2854. A cut above the regular T-shirt shop, with a jealously protective owner – no pictures!

Vibes, Singel 10 ☎622 3962. Everything for the dedicated skate fiend.

ZX, Kerkstraat 113 ☎620 8567. Eclectic, interesting styles from both sides of the Atlantic. Shares the premises with the *Hair Police*.

Second-hand clothes

Daffodil, Jacob Obrechtstraat 41 ☎679 5634. Designer labels only in this posh second-hand shop down by the Vondelpark.

The End, Nieuwe Hoogstraat 26 ☎625 3162. Unspectacular but inexpensive.

Jojo, Huidenstraat 23 ☎623 3476; also at Runstraat 9. Decent second-hand clothes from all eras. Particularly good for trench coats and 1950s jackets.

Kelere Kelder, Prinsengracht 285 (no phone). Goldmine for used alternative clothing. Fri–Sun 1–6pm.

Lady Day, Hartenstraat 9 ☎623 5820. Good-quality second-hand fashion at reasonable prices.

Laura Dols, Wolvenstraat 7 ☎624 9066. Vintage clothing and lots of hats.

Rose Rood, Kinkerstraat 159 ☎618 2334. Period women's clothing – Victorian undergarments and the like.

Second Best, Wolvenstraat 18 ☎422 0274. Classy cast-offs.

Waterlooplein market – see p.263.

Zipper, Huidenstraat 7 ☎623 7302; also at Nieuwe Hoogstraat 10. Used clothes selected for style and quality – strong on

jeans and flares. Prices are high, but it's very popular, and everything is in good condition.

Shoes and accessories

Abracadabra, Sarphatipark 24 ☎676 6683. Beautiful little shop selling jewellery and bric-a-brac from India.

Big Shoe, Leliegracht 12 ☎622 6645. All designs and styles for larger-sized feet of either sex.

Body Sox, Leidsestraat 35 ☎627 6553. Socks, tights and stockings in every conceivable colour and design.

Bonnier, Haarlemmerstraat 58 ☎622 1641. Very reasonably priced bag and umbrella shop.

Dr Adam's, Oude Doelenstraat 5 ☎622 3734; also at Leidsestraat 25 and P.C. Hooftstraat 90. One of the city's broadest selections of shoes.

The English Hatter, Heiligeweg 40 ☎623 4781. Ties, hats and various other accessories, alongside classic menswear from shirts to cricket sweaters.

Fleco, Westerstraat 189 ☎622 7983. Hats, ties and socks for men.

Freelance Shoes, Rokin 86 ☎420 3205. Attractive designer shoes in all styles.

De Grote Tas D'Zaal, Oude Hoogstraat 6 ☎623 0110. Family-run store now in the third generation, selling a wide selection of serious bags, briefcases and suitcases.

Hoeden M/V, Herengracht 422 ☎626 3038. Designer hats galore, from felt Borsalinos to straw Panamas. Gloves and umbrellas too; intimidating prices, though.

Kenneth Cole, Leidsestraat 20 ☎627 6012. One of the better options on Shoe Street: affordable funky styles and solid, hardwearing boots.

Shoebaloo, Koningsplein 7 ☎626 7993; also at P.C. Hooftstraat 80. Unisex shoes in trendy styles. Check out also *Bagbaloo* around the corner.

Tie Rack, Heiligeweg 7 ☎627 2978; also at Kalverstraat 138 and Centraal

Shops and
Markets

Station. Amsterdam branches of the ubiquitous UK chain.

Tulips, Nieuwe Leliestraat 25 ☎627 5595. Tights and socks – a vast array.

Department Stores

Amsterdam's **department stores**, like many of the city's shops, err on the side of safety. Venture inside only if you have an unfulfilled urge to shop; otherwise save them for specifics. More exciting is **Magna Plaza**, in the old post office building at Nieuwezijds Voorburgwal 182, behind Dam Square, which is not a department store but a covered mall sheltering all kinds of outlets.

De Bijenkorf, Dam 1 ☎621 8080. Dominating the northern corner of Dam Square, this is the city's top shop, a huge bustling place (the name means beehive) that has an indisputably wide range and little snobbishness. Departments to head for include house-hold goods, cosmetics and kidswear; there's also a good range of newspapers and magazines.

HEMA, Nieuwendijk 174 ☎623 4176; also at Reguliersbreestraat 10 and branches out of the centre. A kind of Dutch *Woolworth's*, but of a better quality: good for stocking up on toiletries and other essentials, and occasional designer delights – it's owned by *De Bijenkorf*, and you can sometimes find the same items at knockdown prices. Surprises include wine and salami in the back of the shop.

Maison de Bonneterie, Rokin 140 ☎626 2162. Apart from the building, which rises through balustraded bal-conies to a high central dome, nothing special: very conservative and, on the whole, extremely expensive. By appoint-ment to Her Majesty.

Marks & Spencer, Kalverstraat 66 ☎620 0006. The place to head for if you're feeling homesick; it's got exactly the same stock, only priced with a ƒ not a £.

Metz & Co., Keizersgracht 455 ☎624 8810. By far the city's swishest shop,

with the accent on Liberty prints (it used to be owned by *Liberty's* of London), stylish ceramics and designer furniture of the kind that's exhibited in modern art museums: just the place to pick up a Rietveld chair. If your funds won't stretch quite that far, settle for a cup of coffee in the top-floor Rietveld restaurant, which gives great views over the canals.

Peek & Cloppenberg, Dam 20 ☎623 2837. Less a department store than a multistorey clothes shop with some painfully middle-of-the-road styles. Nonetheless, an Amsterdam institution.

Vroom & Dreesmann, Kalverstraat 203 (entrance also from Rokin) ☎622 0171. The main Amsterdam branch of a mid-dle-ground nationwide chain, just near Muntplein. It's pretty unadventurous, but take comfort from the fact that the restaurant is quite outstanding (for a department store), and they bake fresh bread on the premises as well. Check out also the listening stands in the CD section on the top floor – the best place for a free Mozart recital with a canal view.

Food and Drink

Amsterdam's talent for small specialist outlets extends to food as much as any-thing else. While the city's supermarkets may not impress, there's a whole host of **speciality food** stores where you can buy anything from local fish to imported Heinz beans. We've also listed a selec-tion of **wine and spirits shops**, chosen for their location, specialities or simply because they're good value.

Supermarkets

For home cooking and economical eat-ing and drinking, **supermarkets** are the place to go. Unfortunately, they're rather thin on the ground in the city centre, and most are throwbacks to the 1970s; going supermarket shopping in Amsterdam will probably be the only occasion when you'll long for the imper-sonal efficiency of back home. Aisles are narrow, trolleys are battered (you need a guilder coin to de-chain them), there are too many people and not enough choice. If you're buying fruit or vegetables, you'll need to weigh and price them yourself (unless a price is given per item, *per stuk*) – put them on the scale, press the little picture, then press *BON* to get a sticky barcode. If you're buying beer, juice or water in **bottles** (glass or plastic), a deposit of 15c–ƒ1 will be added on at the checkout; you get it back when you return the empties – to a different store, if you like. Unless you have a bag for all your stuff, you'll have to pay about 35c for an own-brand one. Most supermarkets conform to regular shop hours (see p.48).

Albert Heijn, Koningsplein 4 ☎624 5721. Variable opening hours, currently Mon–Sat 10am–10pm, Sun noon–6pm. Amsterdam's main branch of a nationwide chain but still small, crowded and expensive. There are other central branches at Nieuwmarkt 18 and Waterlooplein 131, but prices are lower in those further out of the centre: Haarlemmerdijk 1, Overtoom 454, Vijzelstraat 117 and Westerstraat 79.

Dirk van den Broek, Heinekenplein 25 ☎611 0812. Beats *Albert Heijn* hands down in everything except image. Cheaper across the board; bigger too. Trams #16, #24 or #25. Mon–Sat roughly 9am–9pm. More branches dotted around the suburbs.

Marks & Spencer, Kalverstraat 66 ☎620 0006. Delectable food section, full of choice goodies, ready to cook or ready to munch. Mon 11am–6pm, Tues, Wed & Fri 10am–6pm, Thurs 10am–9pm, Sat 9.30am–6pm.

De Natuurwinkel, Weteringschans 133 ☎638 4083. Main branch of a chain selling only organic food (thus a little more expensive). Much better tasting fruit and vegetables than anywhere else, also grains, pulses and *Bon Bon Jeanette* chocolates. Superb bread. Smaller branches around town. Mon–Wed & Fri 7am–8pm, Thurs 7am–9pm, Sat 7am–8pm, Sun 11am–6pm.

Beer, wine and spirits

The **legal age** at which you can be sold beer is sixteen; for wines and spirits you need to be eighteen. The Dutch word for an off-licence (liquor store) is *slijterij*.

De Bierkoning, Paleisstraat 125 ☎625 2336. The "Beer King" is aptly named: 850 different beers, with matching glasses to drink them from.

Chabrol, Haarlemmerstraat 7 ☎622 2781. All kinds of alcohol from all parts of the world. A fine selection of wines, and the staff are extremely knowledgeable.

Chateau P.C. Hooft, Honthorststraat 1 ☎664 9371. Extensive but expensive: 50 malt whiskies, 40 champagnes, and Armagnac from 1886.

Cheers, O.Z. Achterburgwal 142 ☎624 2969. Red Light District booze.

Drinkland, Spuistraat 116 ☎638 6573. Largest off-licence in the centre of the city.

Elzinga Wijnen, Frederiksplein 1, corner of Utrechtsestraat ☎623 7270. High-quality wines from around the world.

Gall & Gall, Wolvenstraat 6 ☎623 3836. Most central branch of the largest off-licence chain in Amsterdam. Other outlets at Van Baerlestraat 85, 1e van der Helststraat 82, Rozengracht 72 and Utrechtsestraat 67.

D'Oude Gekroonde, Rosmarijnsteeg 10 ☎623 7711. International beer shop.

Vintner Otterman, Keizersgracht 300 ☎625 5088. Small, exclusive selection of French wines to weep for.

Breads, pastries and sweets

Along with the outlets selling cholesterol- and sugar-packed goodies, we've listed some places where you can buy healthier baked goods. Note that a *warme bakkerij* sells bread and rolls; a *banketbakkerij* sells pastries and cream cakes.

Bonbon Atelier Lawenda, 1e Anjeliersdwarsstraat 17 ☎420 5262. Dreamily wonderful chocolates.

Bon Bon Jeanette, Centraal Station ☎421 5194. Organic, handmade,

Shops and Markets

Shops and Markets

additive-free, preservative-free, low-sugar chocolates – surprisingly delicious.

Errol Trumpie, Leidsestraat 46 ☎624 0233. Not a bandleader but a confectioner – elegant handmade pastries and chocolates, and there's a tearoom too.

Gary's Muffins, Prinsengracht 454 ☎420 1452. The best, most authentic New York bagels in town. Branches at Marnixstraat 121 and at Reguliersdwarsstraat 53, the latter open until 3am.

Hartog's, Ruyschstraat 56 ☎665 1295. Fat-free, 100 percent wholegrain breads, rolls and croissants. From 7am. Metro Wibautstraat.

J.G. Beune, Haarlemmerdijk 156 ☎624 8356. Handmade cakes and chocolates in an old-style interior.

Kwekkeboom, Reguliersbreestraat 36 ☎623 1205. One of the city's most famous pastry shops, showered with awards. Not cheap, but you're paying for the chocolatier's equivalent of Gucci. Also at Ferdinand Bolstraat 119 and Linnaeusstraat 80.

Lanskroon, Singel 385 ☎623 7743. Another famously good pastry shop, with a small area for on-the-spot consumption.

Mediterrané, Haarlemmerdijk 184 ☎620 3550. Famous for their croissants; also North African pastries, French bread, etc.

Paul Année, Runstraat 25 ☎623 5322. The best wholegrain and sourdough breads in town, bar none – all made from organic grains.

Pompadour Chocolaterie, Huidenstraat 12 ☎623 9554. Chocolates and lots of home-made pastries (usually smothered in or filled with chocolate).

Runneboom, 1e van der Helststraat ☎673 5941. Wonderful selection of breads from around the world – fitting, given its location in the multicultural Pijp district. Open from 7am.

Cheese

Arxhoek, Damstraat 19 ☎622 9118. Centrally situated general cheese shop.

Hoving Comestibles, Herenstraat 32 ☎638 0053. Excellent selection of cheeses and other goodies.

Robert & Abraham Kef, Marnixstraat 192 ☎626 2210. A wide range of French cheeses – and facilities for tasting.

Wegewijs, Rozengracht 32 ☎624 4093. Majestic selection and expert advice, with sampling possibilities.

Coffee and tea

The Coffee Company, Leidsestraat 60 ☎622 1519. More of an espresso bar, but with some whole and ground beans for sale as well.

Geels & Co., Warmoesstraat 67 ☎624 0683. Oddly situated among Warmoesstraat's porn shops, this is one of the city's oldest and best-equipped specialists, with low prices on beans and utensils.

Levelt, Prinsengracht 180 ☎624 0823. A specialist tea and coffee company has occupied this shop for over 150 years, and much of the original decor remains. Sound advice and friendly service.

Delis and imported foods

Eichholtz, Leidsestraat 48 ☎622 0305. Specialists in imported foods from Britain and the US. The only place to find Oreo cookies, Pop Tarts, Velveeta and Heinz beans.

Ithaka, 1e Bloemdwarsstraat 18 ☎638 4665. Greek deli with snacks and takeaway meals, in the heart of the Jordaan. Open daily.

La Tienda, 1e Sweelinckstraat 21 ☎671 2519. Musty old Spanish deli, with chorizos, hams and cheeses galore. Also all kinds of Latin American spices.

Meidi-Ya, Beethovenstraat 20 ☎673 7410. Comprehensively stocked Japanese supermarket, with a takeaway section and sushi bar.

Olivaria, Hazenstraat 2a ☎638 3552. Olive oil, and nothing but. Incredible range of oils, all self-imported from small- and medium-sized concerns around the world. Expert advice and a well-stocked tasting table.

Oriental Commodities, Nieuwmarkt 27 ☎626 2797. Warren-like Chinese supermarket. All sorts of stuff squirrelled away in corners – seaweed, water-chestnuts, spicy prawn crackers. Get there early for the handmade tofu.

Renzo, Van Baerlestraat 67 ☎673 1673. Everything freshly made on the premises – from pastas to sandwiches and some exquisite desserts.

Taste of Ireland, Herengracht 228 ☎625 6704. Irish sausages, draught Guinness and freshly baked soda bread, to name just the most obvious items.

Tjin's Toko, 1e van der Helststraat 64 ☎671 7708. Small Asian–American supermarket and deli counter.

Fish and seafood

Although there are lots of fresh herring and seafood stalls dotted around the city at strategic locations, including one or two excellent ones in the Albert Cuyp market, perhaps the best is the award-winning **Bloemberg**, on Van Baerlestraat, more or less opposite the Concertgebouw. To eat your herring the Dutch way, tilt back your head and dangle the fish head-first into your mouth whole. The following are a couple of good fish shops.

Viscenter Volendam, Kinkerstraat 181 ☎618 7062. Out of the centre, but with consistently high-quality fresh and cured fish. Owned and run by a family from Volendam, a fishing village north of Amsterdam.

Volendammer Vishandel, Nieuwe Spiegelstraat 54, on the corner with

Shops and Markets

Night shops (avondwinkels)

Most of these places open when everyone else is starting to think about closing up, and they stay open until well into the night – which sounds great, but you have to pay for the privilege: essentials can cost a barefaced three times the regular price – and at 1am there's nowhere else to go. Most of them, too, are not immediately accessible from the centre of town, and may take a little looking for. Once you're there, though, and if you can suspend your money worries, night shops are like heaven. There are more in the outskirts, too – look in the *Gouden Gids* (Yellow Pages) under "*avondverkoop*"

Avondmarkt, De Wittenkade 94 ☎686 4919. The biggest, best and cheapest of the night shops, just west of the city centre. Tram #10. Daily 4pm–midnight.

Big Bananas, Leidsestraat 73 ☎627 7040. Well stocked, convenient and absurdly expensive. Mon–Fri & Sun 11am–1am, Sat 11am–2am.

Dolf's, Willemsstraat 79 ☎625 9503. One of the better night shops: expensive, but reasonably central, tucked in a corner of the Jordaan. Mon–Sat 3pm–1am, Sun 10am–1am.

Heuft's, Rijnstraat 62 ☎642 4048. Way down in the south, and too expensive to bother about – unless, that is, you fancy a late-night champagne blow-out at home: this is the only night shop to

deliver. Accepts major credit cards (they need to). Mon–Sat 5pm–1am, Sun 3pm–1am.

Mignon, Vijzelstraat 127 ☎420 2687. Unremarkable, expensive, but does the job. Handy if you're in the area. Mon–Fri 5pm–1am, Sat & Sun 11am–1am.

Sterk, Waterlooplein 241 ☎626 5097. Less a night shop than a city centre institution, with all kinds of fresh breads and pastries baked on the premises, a large fresh produce section, friendly staff – this place pulls something over on regular supermarkets. Smaller, lower-key branch out west at De Clercqstraat 3 ☎618 1727. Daily 9am–2am.

Shops and
Markets

Kerkstraat ☎623 2962. Volendam is
obviously a name that sells. A good,
central fish shop with friendly service.

Organic and natural food

De Aanzet, Frans Halsstraat 27 ☎673
3415. Organic supermarket co-operative,
next to *De Waaghals* restaurant (see
p.222) in the Pijp.

De Belly, Nieuwe Leliestraat 174 ☎624
5281. Small and very friendly shop
stocking all things organic.

Boerenmarkt. Weekly organic farmers'
market – see p.262.

Deshima, Weteringschans 65 ☎625
7513. A little difficult to spot (it's in the
basement), this is a macrobiotic food
store with a small restaurant attached.

Gimsel, Huidenstraat 19 ☎624 8087.
Very central, with a good selection of
fruit and vegetables and excellent bread.

De Groene Weg, Huidenstraat 11 ☎627
9132. Organic butcher.

De Natuurwinkel. See "Supermarkets",
above. By far the best selection.

De Weegschaal, Jodenbreestraat 20
☎624 1765. Small, friendly shop near
the Waterlooplein flea market.

Music

The price of CDs in Amsterdam is higher
than in Britain – and outrageous compared to the US. Where the city scores
is in the selection available: there are
lots of small, low-key shops specializing
in one type of music, where you can
turn up classic items unavailable elsewhere. If it's vinyl you're after, you've
come to the wrong country. Some
places still sell records, but it's very
much taken for granted that music
comes on CDs. However, the
Waterlooplein flea market has stacks of
old records (and CDs) on offer, and
some shops – particularly jazz and reggae outlets – do maintain sections
devoted to used vinyl.

Backbeat Records, Egelantiersstraat 19
☎627 1657. Small specialist in soul,

blues, jazz, funk, etc, with a helpful and
enthusiastic owner.

Blues Record Centre, Hendrik
Jacobszstraat 12 ☎679 4503. What it
says. Tram #2. Opens at 1pm.

Boudisque, Haringpakkersteeg 10, in an
alley off the top end of Damrak ☎623
2603. Well known for its wide selection
of rock, house and world music.

Charles, Weteringschans 193 ☎626
5538. Concentrates on classical and folk.

Concerto, Utrechtsestraat 54 ☎623
5228. New and used records and CDs in
all categories; equally good on baroque
as on grunge. The best all-round selection in the city, with the option to listen
before you buy.

Dance Tracks, Nieuwe Nieuwestraat 69
☎639 0853. Imported dance music, hip-
hop, jazz dance, soul and house.

Distortion Records, Westerstraat 72
☎627 0004. Second-hand independent
vinyl.

Fame, Kalverstraat 2 ☎638 2525. Large
and predictable selection of CDs and
tapes.

Forever Changes, Bilderdijkstraat 148
☎612 6378. New wave and collectors'
items, second-hand and new.

Free Record Shop, Kalverstraat 32 & 230
☎626 5808. One of the better pop/rock
chains. Also at Centraal Station,
Leidsestraat 24 and Nieuwendijk 229. No
records.

Get Records, Utrechtsestraat 105 ☎622
3441. Sizeable selection of independent
and alternative CDs, plus some vinyl.
Check out also the deceptively small
R&B section in the back of the shop.

Jazz Inn, Vijzelstraat 7 ☎623 5662. Just
jazz, but all of it.

Midtown, Nieuwendijk 104 ☎638 4252.
House of all kinds from ambient to
200bpm. Also tickets and flyers.

Musiques du Monde, Singel 281 ☎624
1354. As the name suggests, world
music, both new and used. Listen before
you buy.

Outland, Zeedijk 22 ☎ 638 7576. Another good house selection, in a bright and breezily decorated environment.

Record Palace, Weteringschans 33 ☎ 622 3904. Opposite the *Paradiso*, a small shop specializing in records from the 1950s and 60s.

The Sound of the Fifties, Prinsengracht 669 ☎ 623 9745. Small place near the Leidsegracht with stacks of 50s and 60s pop and jazz.

Staalplaat, Jodenbreestraat 24 ☎ 625 4176. Noise, avant-garde and obscure music. Good range of cassettes.

Virgin Megastore, in the Magna Plaza mall ☎ 622 8929. The widest range of everything in the worst buying environment.

New Age and Natural Remedies

The Body Shop, Kalverstraat 157 ☎ 623 9789. The same the world over.

Dela Rosa, Staalstraat 10 ☎ 421 1201. One of the better shops for vitamins and dietary supplements, with friendly, expert advice.

Ego-Soft, Nieuwe Kerkstraat 67 ☎ 626 8069. Approaches New Age from a hi-tech standpoint, with brain machines (including free demonstration), self-awareness programmes on cassette and video, and a selection of natural stimulants.

Erica, Centraal Station ☎ 626 1842. Located in the unlikeliest of surroundings, this little shop is part of a chain selling a sizeable array of herbal remedies, teas, cosmetics and vitamins.

Himalaya, Warmoesstraat 56 ☎ 626 0899. Something of an oasis of calm in the midst of Warmoesstraat's porn shops, this cosy shop has a wide selection of books and magazines from around the world, with New Age music, tarot cards and bric-a-brac, as well as readings, a changing photo/art exhibit, and a marvellous café with a terrace and canal view out the back.

Jacob Hooij, Kloveniersburgwal 10 ☎ 624 3041. In business at this address since 1778, and the shop and its stock are the same now as then. Homeopathic chemist with any amount of herbs and natural cosmetics, as well as a huge stock of *drop* (Dutch liquorice).

Shops and Markets

Smart Shops

Riding on the coat-tails of Amsterdam's liberal policy towards cannabis are a number of what have become known as "smart shops", ostensibly established as outlets for "smart" drugs (memory enhancers, concentration aids, and so on), while doing most of their business selling natural alternatives to hard drugs such as LSD, speed or Ecstasy. These substitutes often have many or all of the effects of the real thing, but with greatly reduced health risks – and the added bonus of legality. A consistently popular alternative to LSD are psychotropic or "magic" mushrooms, which grow wild all over northern Europe, but when processed or dried are classified as hard drugs and thus illegal. *Conscious Dreams* was recently forced to fight a court case over its sale of magic mushrooms; by reclassifying its business as a greengrocery, it was permitted to continue its sale of fresh magic mushrooms (dried ones remain illegal), and retains its role at the centre of a knowledgeable Amsterdam underground devoted to exploring the ramifications of altered states of consciousness.

Conscious Dreams, Kerkstraat 117 ☎ 626 6907. The oldest and best smart shop in Amsterdam.

Dr Paddo, Kerkstraat 93 ☎ 620 5974. Newly opened Amsterdam branch of a nationwide chain.

The Magic Mushroom Gallery, Spuistraat 249 ☎ 427 5765. Most central of the three, with an art exhibit as an added draw.

Shops and
Markets

Kruiderij De Munt, Vijzelstraat 1 ☎ 624
4533. A very wide range of herbal remedies, essential oils, teas and dietary supplements.

Oibibio, Prins Hendrikkade 20 ☎ 553
9355. A remarkably peaceful place,
given the scale of the building. This
multi-floored centre has a huge modern
bar with a vegetarian restaurant
attached, a large shop selling all kinds
of ecological clothes, vitamins and cosmetics, a bookshop, and a sauna on the
roof.

De Roos, Vondelstraat 35 ☎ 689 0081.
Delightful New Age centre, with a warm,
intimate atmosphere. The bookshop has
a wide selection of esoteric books, and
the ground-floor café, with its own rambling garden, is the most peaceful in
Amsterdam. A wide range of courses and
workshops are available, including daily
open sessions in yoga, meditation and
so on.

Miscellaneous Shops

Perhaps more than any other place in
Europe, Amsterdam is a great source of
odd little shops devoted to one particular
product or interest. What follows is a
selection of favourites.

Absolute Danny, Stromarkt 13 ☎ 421
0915. Bills itself as an "erotic lifestyle
store", with everything that implies.

Akkerman, Kalverstraat 149 ☎ 623 1649.
Vast array of pens, inks and writing
implements.

Baobab, Elandsgracht 128 ☎ 626 8398.
Textiles, jewellery and ceramics from
Indonesia and the Far East.

Compendium, Hartenstraat 14 ☎ 638
1579. The place to go if you're into
games. All kinds from tin soldiers to
computer games, mainly for adults.

Condomerie Het Gulden Vlies,
Warmoesstraat 141 ☎ 627 4174.
Condoms of every shape, size and
flavour imaginable. All in the best possible taste.

*For general
toy shops, see
Kids'
Amsterdam,
p.264.*

D. Eberhardt, Damstraat 16 ☎ 420 6408.
Chinese and southeast Asian crafts,
ceramics, clothes and jewellery.

Demmenie Sports, Marnixstraat 2 ☎ 624
3652. Sports shop selling everything you
might need for hiking, camping and sur-
vival.

Donald E. Jongejans, Noorderkerkstraat
18 ☎ 624 6888. Hundreds of spectacle
frames, none of them new, some of
them very ancient. Supplied the specs
for Bertolucci's *The Last Emperor.*

Fair Trade, Huidenstraat 16 ☎ 625 2245.
Crafts from – and books about – the
developing world.

Gerda's, Runstraat 16 ☎ 624 2912.
Amsterdam is full of flower shops, but
this one is the most imaginative and
sensual. An aesthetic experience.

Harrie van Gennip, Govert Flinckstraat
402 ☎ 679 3025. A huge collection of
old and antique stoves from all parts of
Europe, lovingly restored and all in working order.

The Head Shop, Kloveniersburgwal 39
☎ 624 9061. Every dope-smoking acces-
sory you could possibly need, along with
assorted marijuana memorabilia.

Heimwee & Nu, Haarlemmerstraat 85
☎ 622 5295. Antiques, but painted in
colourful "punkish" style. Inexpensive.

Hera Candles, Overtoom 402 ☎ 616
2886. A wonderful little all-wood shop
selling nothing but handmade candles of
all shapes, sizes and scents.

Jan Best, Keizersgracht 357 ☎ 623 2736.
Famed antique lamp shop, with some
wonderfully kitsch examples.

't Japanse Winkeltje, Nieuwezijds
Voorburgwal 177 ☎ 627 9523. Japanese
arts and crafts.

Joe's Vliegerwinkel, Nieuwe Hoogstraat
19 ☎ 625 0139. Kites, frisbees,
boomerangs, diabolos, yoyos, juggling
balls and clubs.

Kitsch Kitchen, 1e Bloemdwarsstraat 21
☎ 622 8261. Crammed full of bowls,

spoons and other kitchen stuff in Day-Glo colours.

't Klompenhuisje, Nieuwe Hoogstraat 9a ☎622 8100. Amsterdam's best and brightest array of clogs.

Knopenwinkel, Wolvenstraat 14 ☎624 0479. Buttons in every conceivable shape and size.

Kramer and **Pontifex**, Reestraat 20 ☎626 5274. On one side of the shop, Mr Kramer repairs old broken dolls and teddies; on the other, Pontifex sell all kinds of candles, oils and incense.

Nieuws Innoventions, Prinsengracht 297 ☎627 9540. Specialists in modern designer items for the home – projector clocks, remote control lamps, Philippe Starck vases, etc. Also round dice, chocolate body-paint and shark laundry pegs.

Olivaria, Hazenstraat 2a ☎638 3552. Olive oil and nothing but. Expert advice, with free samples.

1001 Kralen, Rozengracht 54 ☎624 3681. "Kralen" means beads, and 1001 would seem a conservative estimate in this place, which sells nothing but.

Out of Africa, Herengracht 215 ☎623 4677. African arts and crafts.

P.G.C. Hajenius, Rokin 92 ☎623 7494. Old, established tobacconist selling its own and other brands of cigars, tobacco, smoking accessories, and every make of cigarette you can think of.

Pakhuis Amerika, Prinsengracht 541 ☎639 2583. Second-hand Americana – take home a US mailbox on a pole, crates for Coke bottles, or a real American trashcan.

Partyhouse, Rozengracht 93b ☎624 7851. Every conceivable funny item – masks, rentable costumes and wigs, talking clocks, crazy feet, streamers and hats. You name it.

Peter Doeswijk, Vijzelgracht 11 ☎420 3133. Phones – hundreds of identical, old rotary-dial phones, each painted with

a different design (and they all work). It's chutzpah, if nothing else.

Posthumus, Sint Luciensteeg 23 ☎625 5812. Posh stationery, cards and, best of all, a choice of hundreds of rubber stamps. By appointment to Her Majesty.

Schaak en Go Het Paard, Haarlemmerdijk 147 ☎624 1171. Many different – and very beautiful – types of chessboards and figures; also the Japanese game "Go". Books too.

Shalimar, Utrechtsestraat 25 ☎639 2037. Tiny shop with a wonderful array of antique and modern Indian jewellery.

Taste of Ireland, Herengracht 228 ☎625 6704. Imported food and drink for the homesick.

3-D Holograms, Grimburgwal 2 ☎624 7225. All kinds of holographic art, big and small.

Tibet Shop, Spuistraat 185a ☎420 5438. Books, music, jewellery and more, all made by Tibetan refugees in Nepal and India. The Tibet Support Group (☎623 7699) can give travel advice, information on Tibetan restaurants in Holland, and on anything else concerned with Tibet.

Tikal, Hartenstraat 2a ☎623 2147. Colourful textiles and jewellery from Mexico and Guatemala.

Waterwinkel, Roelof Hartstraat 10 ☎675 5932. The only thing on offer here is water – over 100 different bottled mineral waters from all over the world. Try the wonderful German *Statl Fasching*.

't Winkeltje, Prinsengracht 228 ☎625 1352. Jumble of cheap glassware and crockery, candlesticks, antique tin toys, kitsch souvenirs, old apothecaries' jars and flasks. Perfect for browsing.

Witte Tandenwinkel, Runstraat 5 ☎623 3443. The White Teeth Shop sells wacky toothbrushes and just about every dental hygiene accoutrement you could ever need.

Shops and Markets

Shops and
Markets

Markets

Albert Cuypmarkt

Albert Cuypstraat, between F. Bolstraat and Van Woustraat   Mon–Sat 9am–5pm
The city's principal general goods and food market, with some great bargains to be had – check out Hilten's stall partway down on the right for the best deals on vegetables. Amsterdammers in their natural habitat.

Amstelveld

Prinsengracht, near Utrechtsestraat   Mon 10am–3pm
Flowers and plants, but much less of a scrum than the Bloemenmarkt. Friendly advice on what to buy, and the location is a perfect spot to enjoy the canal.

Bloemenmarkt

Singel, between Koningsplein and Muntplein   Mon–Sat 9am–5pm
Flowers and plants, ostensibly for tourists, but regularly frequented by locals. Bulbs for export (with health certificate). Some stalls open on Sunday as well.

Boekenmarkt

Spui Fri   10am–3pm
Wonderful rambling collection of second-hand books, with many a priceless gem lurking in the unsorted boxes.

Boerenmarkt

Noordermarkt, next to the Noorderkerk   Sat 9am–5pm
Organic farmers' market selling all kinds of organically grown produce, plus amazing fresh breads, exotic fungi, fresh herbs and home-made mustards.

Dapperstraat

Dapperstraat, south of Mauritskade   Mon–Sat 9am–5pm
Covers about the same ground as the Albert Cuyp, but with not a tourist in sight. Bags of atmosphere, exotic snacks on offer, and generally better prices.

Kunstmarkt

Spui   Sun 10am–3pm
Thorbeckeplein, south of Rembrandtplein   Sun 10am–3pm
Low-key but high-quality art market in two locations, with much lower prices than you'll find in the galleries; prints and occasional books as well. Neither operates during the winter.

Lindengracht

Lindengracht, south of Brouwersgracht   Sat 8am–4pm
Rowdy, raucous general household supplies market, a complete switch from the jollity of the neighbouring Boerenmarkt.

De Looier
Elandsgracht 109   Mon–Thurs 11am–5pm, Sat 9am–5pm
*Indoor antiques market, with a whole variety of dealers selling everything from
1950s radios to sixteenth-century Delftware. Generally good quality.*

Nieuwmarkt
Nieuwmarkt   Sat 9am–5pm
*One of the last remnants of the Nieuwmarkt's ancient market history, and a rival
to the more popular and better-stocked Boerenmarkt, with organic produce,
breads, cheeses, and arts and crafts.*

                                                                 Sun 9am–5pm
A low-key antiques market, with some good-quality books, furniture and objets
d'art *dotted in amongst the tat. May–Sept only.*

Noordermarkt
Noordermarkt, next to the Noorderkerk   7.30am–1pm
*Junk-lover's goldmine. Full of all kinds of bargains, tucked away beneath piles of
useless rubbish. Get there early.*

Oudemanhuispoort
Oudemanhuispoort, off O.Z. Achterburgwal   Mon–Sat 10am–4pm
*Very long-standing book market next to the university, with new and used books
of all kinds, many in Dutch but some in English.*

Rommelmarkt
Looiersgracht 38   Mon–Thurs, Sat & Sun 11am–5pm
*A vast, permanent indoor flea market and jumble sale, with things turning up
here that were left unsold at the city's other street markets.*

Stamp and Coin Market
N.Z. Voorburgwal, south of Dam Square   Wed & Sat 11am–4pm
*For collectors of stamps, coins and related memorabilia, organized by the special-
ist shops crowded in the nearby alleys.*

Waterlooplein
Waterlooplein, behind the Stadhuis   Mon–Sat 9am–5pm
*A real Amsterdam institution, and the city's best flea market by far. Sprawling
and chaotic, it's the final resting place for many a pair of yellow corduroy flares;
but there are more wearable clothes to be found, and some wonderful
antique/junk stalls to root through. Second-hand vinyl too.*

Westermarkt
Westerstraat, from the Noorderkerk onwards   Mon–Sat 9am–5pm
Another general goods market, very popular with the Jordaan locals.

Chapter 13

Kids' Amsterdam

With its unique canals, tiny cobbled alleys and – above all – trams, Amsterdam in itself can be entertaining enough for some kids. Still, the Dutch take their children seriously and provide plenty of opportunities for them to satisfy their curiosities through play – practically all the city's parks and most patches of green have some form of playground, and the play area in the Vondelpark is heaven for kids and parents alike. There's also a multitude of attractions specifically aimed at children, ranging from circuses, puppet theatres, urban farms and rides on old trams to one of the best zoos in Europe, with a planetarium attached.

The Dutch attitude towards children is as understanding as you'd expect. If museums don't allow prams then they provide snugglies to carry small children in; most restaurants provide high chairs and special children's menus (though they're not always that great); and bars don't seem to mind accompanied kids, as long as they're reasonably under control. In short, it's very

rare that having a small child in your care will close doors to you. Teenagers, while less welcome in bars, should have enough to gawk at in the city streets to keep them amused.

Babyminding

It's worth noting that not all hotels welcome young children (they'll make this clear when you book), but many of those that do provide a **babyminding service**. If yours doesn't, try contacting **Oppascentrale Kriterion**, Roeterstraat 170 (☎624 5848 5–7pm), a long-established agency with a high reputation, which uses students at least eighteen years old, all of whom are vetted. Between 7pm and midnight rates run at ƒ6 per hour; from midnight to 3am it's ƒ7 per hour, then ƒ10 per hour from 3am to 7pm. Add to this a ƒ5 administration charge, plus a supplement of ƒ5 on Friday and Saturday evenings. The minimum charge is ƒ20.

One area where Amsterdammers fall flat on their face is in keeping **dog-shit** off the streets. They just don't seem able to do it, and the stuff is a major hazard, especially for kids. Although there are teams of street-cleaners armed with high-power hoses to regularly blast the stuff off the pavement, wait another hour or two and there's fresh to replace it. Any patch of green space is obviously susceptible to contamination, too, despite poop-scoop technology, and unless an area is marked as being dog-free, you'd do well to keep one eye on your offspring and the other on your next step.

Parks, playgrounds and farms

The city's most central green spot, the **Vondelpark** (info ☎570 5411), has an excellent playground with all sorts of stuff to do, as well as sandpits, paddling pools, ducks to feed, and even a café where you can take a break. During the summer there's always some free entertainment put on for kids – mime, puppets, acrobats and the like.

Most other city parks offer something to keep children entertained, and the best is the **Gaasperpark**, outside the centre (metro stop Gaasperplas; buses #60, #61, #157, #158, #174), which has terrific play facilities and paddling pools. In the **Amsterdamse Bos** (see p.157) you'll find playgrounds, lakes, and herds of wild deer; you can also rent canoes to explore the waterways, or visit the worthwhile Bosmuseum (see p.158) and the Geitenhouderij Ridammerhoeve (☎645 5034), a very entertaining little farm with hundreds of goats and kids kept for their milk – check for opening times.

There are also plenty of **urban farms** dotted around the city itself – look in the phone book under *Kinderboerderij* for a full list, but worthwhile ones include the **Artis Zoo Children's Farm** (which could easily be visited as part of an Artis day out; see below for details of the zoo itself) and **De Dierenpijp** (Lizzy Ansinghstraat 82 ☎664 8303; afternoons only, closed Tues), in the south of the Pijp district.

City trips and activities

For older children, a good introduction to Amsterdam might be one of the **canal trips** that start from Centraal Station or Damrak. Much more fun, though, is a ride on a **canal bike**. This can get tiring, but jetties where boats can be picked up and dropped off are numerous, and it's quite safe; see p.40 for details. If your kids enjoy being on the water, you could also take them on a **free ferry ride** to Amsterdam North

(only 5–10min away). The best ferry to take is the *Adelaarswegveer*, a small tug-like craft with a partly exposed deck, which leaves every ten-min or so from Pier 8 behind Centraal Station (Mon–Sat 6.20am–8.50pm); once there, you could either come straight back, or walk a few hundred metres west along the riverfront and take the larger, closed-in *Buiksloterwegveer* back to Centraal Station. For details of inexpensive **ferry and tram tours** of Amsterdam, see p.41.

For a great view of the city, try a trek up the **towers** of the Oude Kerk or the Westerkerk (open summer only; see p.78 and p.98).

It's possible to take the kids along when you're **cycling** around the city, by renting either a bike with a child-seat attached, or a tandem, depending on the size of the child. *Bike City* at Bloemgracht 70 (☎626 3721) rents both kinds and gives friendly advice.

In the winter, there's **ice-skating** at the Sporthal Jaap Eden (see p.271), which has indoor and outdoor rinks, open at different times. If the canals are frozen and you don't have any skates, just skeeter along on the ice with everybody else.

The best **swimming pool** for kids is the indoor, tropical-style Mirandabad (De Mirandalaan 9 ☎644 6637), which has all sorts of gimmicks like wave machines, slides and whirlpools; there's also a separate toddlers' pool. In summer, the most popular outdoor pool is in the Flevopark; for details of this and other outdoor pools, see p.273.

Museums and the Zoo

Artis Zoo, Plantage Kerklaan 40 ☎523 3400. Tram #7, #9 or #14. April–Sept daily 9am–6pm; Oct–March daily 9am–5pm; adults ƒ21, children aged 4–11 ƒ13.50; during September admission is reduced to ƒ13/ƒ8.50. No other discounts and no dogs. The ticket includes entry to the zoo and its gardens, the Zoological Museum, the Geological Museum and the Planetarium.

Kids'
Amsterdam

Kids' Amsterdam

Pushchairs can be rented for ƒ2.50, and an English guidebook to the whole complex costs ƒ7.50. The café and restaurant are handily situated between the flamingo pool and the kids' playground.

Opened in 1838, this is the oldest **zoo** in the country, and it's now one of the city's top tourist attractions, though thankfully its layout and refreshing lack of bars and cages mean that it never feels overcrowded. The huge aquariums are currently being renovated (due to be completed in April 1997), and are one of the main features of the zoo. On top of the usual creatures and creepy-crawlies, there is also a Children's Farm where kids can come nose-to-nose with sheep, calves, goats, etc. Feeding times – always popular – are as follows: 11am birds of prey; 11.30am and 3.45pm seals and sea-lions; 2pm pelicans; 2.30pm crocodiles (Sun only); 3pm lions and tigers (not Fri); 3.30pm penguins. The on-site **Planetarium** (same hours, except Mon when it opens at 1pm) has five or six shows daily, all in Dutch – you can pick up a leaflet with an English translation from the desk. All in all, this is one of the best days out in the city. You can also combine an Artis day out with a canal cruise: the *Artis Express* runs daily 10am–5pm every 30min between Centraal Station and the zoo (return ƒ12.50, children 4–11 ƒ8; information on ☎622 2181).

Aviodome, Schiphol Centre ☎604 1521. Train to Schiphol Airport, then walk or take a bus from stop B12. April–Sept daily 10am–5pm; Oct–March Tues–Fri 10am–5pm, Sat & Sun noon–5pm; ƒ8.50, under-12s ƒ6. A huge, hands-on exhibition for buffs and kids alike, with over thirty historic aircraft to examine and clamber onto, including the first motorized plane from 1903 and the latest flight-simulators. Ask for an all-in ticket from Centraal Station, which includes the train fare, entry to the museum, and a coffee and apple cake at Schiphol train station.

IMPULS Science and Technology Centre, Oosterdok, near entrance to IJ tunnel ☎570 8111. Bus #22 or #28. Open from May 1997: July & Aug daily 10am–9pm; Sept–June Mon–Thurs & Sun 10am–6pm, Fri & Sat 10am–9pm; price unconfirmed as yet – call for details. Interactive, sparkling new "centre for human creativity", with bang up-to-date hi-tech displays and exhibits; perfect for hands-on exploration.

Kindermuseum, in the Tropenmuseum, Linnaeusstraat 2 ☎568 8233. Tram #9, #10 or #14. Open Wed afternoon during the school year, plus weekends; phone for exact hours. Adults ƒ7.50 (though you're only allowed in after the "show" has finished), children ƒ4. Designed especially for children between the ages of six and twelve, the aim is to promote international understanding through exhibitions on other cultures. It's far from as dry as it sounds, since the lively exhibits are presented expertly, incorporating art and music and dance performances, and it's all designed to fascinate children (which it does). There are lots of things for kids to get their hands on, but it's best to go on Sunday, when school groups aren't visiting. Exhibits tend to run and run for months; an interactive performance and presentation focusing on the indigenous cultures of Bolivia is planned to start in September 1997.

Madame Tussaud's, Dam 20 ☎622 9239. Daily 10am–5.30pm; adults ƒ17.50, under-15s ƒ15, Family Ticket 1 (2 adults, 2 children and a guidebook) ƒ57.50, Family Ticket 2 (2 adults, 3 children and a guidebook) ƒ63.50. Very large waxwork collection that's similar to the one in London, with the usual smattering of famous people and rock stars, plus some Amsterdam peasants and merchants thrown in for local colour. Hardly the high point of anyone's trip to the city, but there are parts that might excite the kids.

Tram Museum, Amstelveenseweg 264 ☎673 7538. Tram #6 or #16 to Haarlemmermeer Station. April–June, Sept & Oct Sun 10am–5.30pm; July & Aug Tues–Sun 10am–5.30pm. Adults ƒ5, under-11s ƒ2.50, under-4s free. Not so much a museum as a set of working antique trams that run along adapted railway tracks down to the Amsterdamse Bos. Can be fun for kids, and it's a good way to get to the Bos.

Theatres, circuses and funfairs

A number of **theatres** put on inexpensive (around ƒ5) entertainment for children in the afternoon, a fair proportion of which gets around the language problem by being **mime**- or **puppet**-based: check the children's section ("Jeugdagenda") of the monthly *Uitkrant* (see p.51), and look for the words *mimegroep* and *poppentheater*. For general information on children's theatre in Amsterdam, call ☎622 2999. Public holidays and the summer season bring touring **circuses** and the occasional mobile **funfair** (*kermis*) to the city, the latter usually setting up on Dam Square and thus hard to miss. Lastly, check out the **festivals** listings on p.49: many of them, such as the Queen's Birthday celebrations, can be enjoyable for kids.

Carré Theatre, Amstel 115–125 ☎622 5225. Occasionally books internationally famous circuses.

Deridas, Hobbemakade 68 ☎662 1588. Excellent weekly puppet theatre, wonderful for the under-6s. The shows are every Sunday at 11am, but the doors open at 10.15am so that the tots can play first. Booking essential.

Circustheater Elleboog, Passeerdersgracht 32 ☎626 9370. For around ƒ15 or so, kids from ten to seventeen can spend the day learning how to juggle and unicycle, do conjuring tricks, be a clown, and practise face-painting. At the end of the day they put on a little show for the parents. Phone for full details of times and prices – some days are members-only sessions.

De Krakeling, Nieuwe Passeerdersstraat 1 ☎624 5123. Permanent children's theatre, with shows for over- and under-12s. The emphasis is often on full-scale audience participation. Phone for a schedule.

Melkweg, Lijnbaansgracht 234a ☎624 1777. Sunday afternoon activities for children from mid-Oct to early April.

Restaurants

Enfant Terrible, De Genestetstraat 1 ☎612 2032. Near *De Geboortewinkel* (see "Shops", below), this is the only Amsterdam café intended for families. Its wooden interior is surprisingly calm; there is a supervised play area (ƒ2.50 per hour), so you can relax for a few minutes yourself if you need to. They will also mind your child for you for up to three hours (ƒ25), while you take off. Aside from anything else, the food is remarkably good. Open from morning until after dinner, this is a wonderful idea, and it works very well.

KinderKookKafé, Oudezijds Achterburgwal 193 ☎625 3257. Another fabulous idea – a whole restaurant entirely run by children, from cooking to waitering to dishwashing (though there are adult staff on hand). The food is simple but well done, and the whole experience is worth it just for the novelty. Booking is essential, as the café is only open to the public for weekend dinners. Children aged 2–5 pay ƒ5, those aged 5–12 ƒ10, and adults pay ƒ15.

Shops

Azzurro Kids, P.C. Hooftstraat 122 ☎673 0457. Perhaps the city's chicest kids' clothes store.

De Beestenwinkel, Staalstraat 11 ☎623 1805. Stuffed toy animals, priced from 50c to ƒ100.

Bell Tree, Spiegelgracht 10 ☎625 8830. A beautiful shop full of old-fashioned toys, mobiles, models and kids' books.

Berend Botje, Zocherstraat 87 ☎618 3349. Second-hand clothes for children, near the Vondelpark.

Kids'
Amsterdam

Kids' Amsterdam

De Bijenkorf, Dam 1 ☎621 8080. This department store has one of the best (and most reasonable) toy sections in town.

Boon, Gravenstraat 11 ☎620 8438. One of the flashiest clothes stores for kids you'll ever see, with their own designer label, *Boontje*.

De Geboortewinkel, Bosboom Toussaintstraat 22 ☎683 1806. Specialists in all kinds of stuff for new or expectant parents.

Intertoys, Heiligeweg 26 ☎622 1122. Amsterdam's largest toy shop, with branches throughout the city.

De Kinderboekwinkel, Nieuwezijds Voorburgwal 344 ☎622 7741. Also at Rozengracht 34. Children's books, arranged by age, some of them in English.

De Kinderbrillenwinkel, Nieuwezijds Voorburgwal 129 ☎626 4091. Shop specializing in spectacles for children.

Kleine Nicolaas, Cornelis Schuytstraat 19 ☎676 9661. Handmade toys.

Chapter 14

Sports and Activities

Most visitors to laid-back Amsterdam tend to confine their exercise to walking around the major sights. But if you get the urge to stretch your muscles, there's a range of **participatory sports** to get into. In winter, skating on the frozen waterways is the most popular and enjoyable activity; other sports are generally based in private, health or sports clubs, to which you can usually get a day pass, though many are outside the centre of town. There are also a number of less energetic activities you can get involved in, whether your tastes run to chess, blackjack, or relaxing in a flotation tank.

As a **spectator**, you're limited mainly to cheering on the talented and successful local football (soccer) team Ajax (pronounced "eye-axe") in their spanking new ArenA stadium out in the suburbs – though their Rotterdam rivals Feyenoord, and the currently struggling PSV team from Eindhoven, are just a train ride away. Less mainstream offerings include Holland's own *korfbal* and the weird spectacle of pole sitting. For up-to-the-minute details on all the sports listed here, or to find out where you can partake in your own favourite sporting activity, call the City Hall sports information service on ☎ 552 2490.

Baseball (Honkbal)

The local team is the **Amsterdam Pirates**, based at Sportpark Jan van Galenstraat (tram #13) ☎616 2151.

Matches take place on Saturday afternoons in the summer, and are free while the Pirates languish in a lower division. To **play**, you need only wander into the Vondelpark on any summer afternoon – impromptu baseball games spring up all over.

Beaches

The Netherlands has some great **beaches**, although the weather is unreliable and the infamous North Sea water is often murky and full of jellyfish. For swimming or sunbathing, the nearest resort is **Zandvoort**, a short train-ride from Amsterdam – though be warned that it attracts large crowds in season. Otherwise, there are low-key resorts and long sandy beaches all the way up the dune-filled western coastline: Katwijk and Noordwijk can be reached by bus from Leiden, Castricum-aan-Zee, Bergen-aan-Zee and Egmond-aan-Zee by bus from Alkmaar. With your own vehicle, or a willingness to hike, it's possible to find any number of deserted spots in between. See the *Out of the City* section for more details.

Bowling

Knijn Bowling Centre, Scheldeplein 3, opposite the RAI complex ☎664 2211. The closest bowling alley to the city centre, with eighteen lanes, a bar and a pool. Lanes cost between ƒ27.50 and ƒ42.50 per hour, with a maximum of six people per lane. Reservations

**Sports and
Activities**

recommended. Mon–Sat 10am–1am,
Sun noon–midnight.

Bungee Jumping

For one of the most unlikely bungee
jumps imaginable, a new permanent
jump site opened in 1996 behind
Centraal Station. Here you can throw
yourself from a height of 75m into the
Amsterdam skies, and even request a
masochistic dip in the River IJ. The site is
thoroughly legal and operated by
Bungee Jump Holland (☎070/310
6242), part of the Dutch Federation of
Bungee Jumping. The first jump costs
ƒ100, the second ƒ75; you can also buy
a ten-jump season ticket for a mere
ƒ400. Aug–Oct Mon–Fri 2–10pm, Sat &
Sun noon–10pm.

Chess and Draughts

There are three **cafés** in Amsterdam
where chess and draughts are played to
the exclusion of (almost) everything else:
Gambit at Bloemgracht 20, *Het Hok* at
Lange Leidsedwarsstraat 134, and
Domino, Leidsekruisstraat 19. There's a
small charge for a board. See *Eating and
Drinking* for more details.

Floating

Koan Float, at Prinsengracht 662 (☎625
4970), is the only place in Amsterdam
currently offering floating as a relaxation
technique. The idea is to float in a large
bath of warm water, to which magne-
sium and sodium salt have been added
to aid muscular relaxation and provide
buoyancy. Because the water is the
same temperature as your body, the
sensation is of floating freely, and you
don't have to move to stay afloat, allowing your mind and body to release pent-
up stress. There are two lockable individual floating cabins, each with its own
shower, so you don't even need to bring
a swimming costume; once you're
inside, lights, music and clothing are
optional. Advance reservations are
essential. Current charges are ƒ30 per
30-min though you can float as long as

you like, and there are discounts for
return visits. Towels are provided. Tues
5.30–9.30pm, Wed–Fri 11.30am–9.30pm,
Sat & Sun 2–9pm.

Football

It's a mark of the local dominance of
Ajax, **Feyenoord** and **PSV** that most foreigners would be hard pushed to name
any other Dutch teams – indeed, in
recent years Ajax have been Dutch
champions three years running. After
their 1995 European Cup and World
Club Championship victories, Ajax also
remain at or near the top of the
European game, and the Dutch style of
play – based on secure passing with
sudden, decisive breaks – has made
Dutch players highly sought after all
over Europe. Despite all this, with the
building of the extraordinary new all-
seater ArenA stadium in the suburbs, it's
become more than a little difficult to
get to see Ajax play. You can't buy a
ticket without a "clipcard", and although
these only cost ƒ10 for two years, you
must apply in advance (fax 311 1480)
and wait six weeks for your application
to be processed. Having done all that,
ticket prices are around ƒ35 (and more
or less the same for Feyenoord and
PSV). The season runs from September
to May, and matches are generally on
Sunday at 2.30pm, with occasional
games at 8pm on Wednesday. For a full
list of all league matches, consult the
VVV.

Ajax Amsterdam, ArenA stadium, Bijlmer;
metro Bijlmer ☎311 1450. A talented
and entertaining team currently at the
peak of its power, although as far as
crowd trouble goes Ajax's "F-side" mob
are every bit as bad as anything British
fans can come up with.

Feyenoord Rotterdam, Olympiaweg 50,
Rotterdam ☎010/492 9499. One of the
country's major teams. Trains stop near
the ground.

PSV Eindhoven, Frederiklaan 10a,
Eindhoven ☎040/250 5505.
Experiencing tough times recently,

though always in the running for major honours.

Gambling

If you're itching to strike it rich with your last few guilders, Amsterdam will prove a disappointment. There's no horse racing to speak of and there's just one legal casino in the city. You can, however, place bets on British horse races at **Hippo Toto**, at Leidsestraat 101 (☎623 8583) and 1e Constantijn Huygensstraat 43 (☎683 6758). The only legal place to play the tables in Amsterdam is the **Holland Casino**, Max Euweplein 62 (daily 1.30pm–2am; over-18s only; cover charge ƒ6; ☎620 1006). Men need to wear a jacket, and you should be prepared to show some sort of ID. For the really desperate, there's another Holland Casino inside Schiphol Airport (☎023/571 8044), but since it's beyond passport control you've got to show a boarding card to get in.

Gyms and Saunas

Deco, Herengracht 115 ☎623 8215. In the running for Amsterdam's most stylish sauna and steam bath, with a magnificent Art Deco interior and a nice café. A great place to hang out for the day without a stitch on. Highly recommended. Entry costs ƒ16.50 Mon–Fri before 2pm, at other times it's ƒ24 for 5hr. Mon–Sat 11am–11pm, Sun 1–6pm.

Garden Gym, Jodenbreestraat 158 ☎626 8772. Weight-training and dance-workout studio, with saunas, solarium, massage and self-defence classes. Mainly, but not exclusively, for women. A sauna costs ƒ17.50; a day pass for all activities ƒ22.50 (including a sauna). Mon, Wed & Fri 9am–11pm, Tues & Thurs noon–11pm, Sat 11am–6.30pm, Sun 10am–7pm.

Oibibio, Prins Hendrikkade 20 ☎553 9311. Sauna attached to a large New Age centre – one of the best places to sink into a bath of hot mud. ƒ22 before 5pm, ƒ26 thereafter. Daily 11am–midnight.

Sauna Damrak, Damrak 54 ☎622 6012. Centrally located sauna. ƒ27, including towels. Mon–Fri 10am–11pm, Sat & Sun noon–8pm.

Splash, Looiersgracht 26 ☎624 8404. Very popular hi-tech fitness centre with sauna, tanning salon and Turkish bath. Daily aerobic classes and single-sex training rooms. Day pass ƒ35, week pass ƒ65, two weeks ƒ95. Daily 7am–midnight.

De Stokerij, 1e Rozendwarsstraat 8 ☎625 9417. Council fitness centre with facilities for football, tennis, volleyball, etc, plus a gym. ƒ3.50 for a lesson, otherwise you must buy a month's pass for ƒ60. Daily 8am–11pm.

Hockey

Amsterdam, Wagener Stadium, Nieuwe Kalfjeslaan, Amstelveen ☎640 1141; bus #170, #171 or #172. The major club in the area; its stadium, set in the Amsterdamse Bos, also plays host to international matches. The season runs September to May, with matches on Sunday afternoon; tickets to domestic games are free.

Horse Riding

Amsterdamse Manege, Nieuwe Kalfjeslaan, Amstelveen ☎643 1342. The place for a ride in the Amsterdamse Bos – but only with supervision. You need your own boots and riding hat, and you must reserve ahead. ƒ27.50 per hour.

Ice-skating

When it's really cold, skaters can get spoiled in Amsterdam: almost every drop of available water is utilized, and the **canals** provide an exhilarating way to whizz round the city – much more fun than going round a rink. Surprisingly, the canal cruises continue even when the ice is solid, with the boats crunching their way up and down the Prinsengracht; happily, though, they leave the Keizersgracht alone, and the

Sports and Activities

full sweep of it becomes a fairy-tale scene, with whole families of bundled-up Amsterdammers taking to the ice. Before you venture out, however, take note of a few **safety points**:

• If no one's on the ice, don't try skating – locals have a better idea of its thickness.

• To gain confidence, start off on the smaller ponds in the Vondelpark.

• Be careful under bridges, where the ice takes longest to freeze.

• If the ice gives way and you find yourself in the water, head for the darkest spot you can see in the ice above – that's the hole.

It's also possible to skate out of Amsterdam and into surrounding towns – through the Waterland or to Muiderslot and Naarden, for example. One of the great events in Holland's sporting calendar is the annual **Elfstedentocht**, a race across eleven towns and 200km of frozen waterways in Friesland. Though the race had to be suspended for twenty years, a recent spate of cold winters has meant a number of competitions and an increasing number of participants – over 16,000 at the last count. For more details, call the organizers, *De Friese Elfsteden*, in the town of Leeuwarden (☎058/215 5020 1–2pm). If you're around in January and the ice is good, you'll hear talk of little else.

Rinks and skate rental

Most Amsterdammers have their own skates, and there are surprisingly few places where you can **rent** a pair. If Dutch friends can't help, you can rent some at a rink or sports hall, but they won't allow you to take them away. **Buying** a pair from a department store or sports shop will cost close to *f*100; the best way to find a second-hand pair is to keep an eye on noticeboards in bars and suchlike.

Sporthal Jaap Eden, Radioweg 64 ☎694 9652. Tram #9. Large complex with an indoor and outdoor rink. *f*7, *f*4.50 for under-15s. You can rent skates for *f*9 from *Waterman Sport* next door

(☎694 9884), but you can only use them at Jaap Eden, and you must leave your passport or driving licence as deposit. Oct–March only: outdoor rink Mon–Wed & Fri 8.30am–4.30pm & 8–10pm, Thurs 8.30am–4.30pm, Sat 2–4pm, Sun 11am–4pm; indoor rink Mon–Wed & Fri 2–4pm & 8–10pm, Thurs 2–4pm.

In-line skating

If you're equipped with skates, or a skateboard, there are several free public ramps at the northeastern edge of Museumplein, scheduled to remain in place despite the major development work going on there. Check out also the car park of the huge RAI conference centre. Three places to **rent** skates, gear and boards are: *The Old Man*, Damstraat 16 ☎627 0043; *Rodolfo's*, in the Magna Plaza mall on Nieuwezijds Voorburgwal ☎623 1214, and also at Sarphatistraat 59 ☎622 5488; and *Vibes*, Singel 10 ☎622 3962. If you're renting to skate around town – and many do – take care not to get stuck in the tram-tracks. The **Vrieshuis Amerika** squat venue occasionally hosts indoor skating events with live music – look for flyers.

Korfbal

This is a home-grown sport, cobbled together from netball, basketball and volleyball, and played with mixed teams and a high basket. **Blauw Wit** play at the Sportpark J. Banckersweg, off Jan van Galenstraat (☎618 3616), on Sunday at 2pm from September to June (free).

Pole Sitting

Every year in July or early August, there's the chance to witness the offbeat spectator sport of pole sitting. In Noorderwijkerhout, just north of Scheveningen on the coast near The Hague, there's a **pole sitting marathon** that lasts about five days. Although not exactly a dynamic sport, it generates a fair amount of excitement as some fifteen braves sit it out on poles perched in the North Sea. The last one left is the winner.

Running and Jogging

The main circuits are in the **Vondelpark** and **Amsterdamse Bos**, the latter with routes of varying distances signposted throughout. The **Amsterdam Marathon**, should you be up for it (a little over 42km – info on ☎663 0781), takes place in late September – 1997 will see the 22nd running of the event; the start and finish lines are in front of the RAI building. A week beforehand, there is the easier-going **Dam to Dam Race**, covering the 16km between Amsterdam and Zaandam.

Snooker and Carambole

There are plenty of bars and cafés across the city where you can find a game of **pool**, although you may have to go to a hall to play **snooker**. A popular local variation on billiards (*biljart*) is **carambole**, played on a table without pockets. You score by making cannons, and the skill of some of the locals, often spinning the ball through impossible angles, is unbelievable. You'll find tables in many cafés, and get plenty of advice on how to play if you so much as look at a ball.

Snooker and pool halls

Snooker and Pool Centre Bavaria, Van Ostadestraat 97. The first, third and fourth floors comprise the **pool centre** (Mon–Thurs & Sun 2pm–1am, Fri & Sat 2pm–2am; ☎676 7903), with 26 tables costing a flat rate of ƒ13.50 per hour plus drinks. The second floor is the **snooker centre** (Mon–Thurs & Sun 11am–1am, Fri & Sat 11am–2am; ☎676 4059), which has seven tables at ƒ10 per hour before 2pm, ƒ15 after 2pm. There's also one carambole table, charged at ƒ10 per hour.

Snooker Centre, Rokin 28 ☎620 4974. Twelve tables at ƒ15.50 per hour. Mon–Thurs & Sun 11am–2am, Fri & Sat 11am–3am.

Snooker Centre de Keizer, Keizersgracht 256 ☎623 1586. Eight high-quality tables in a seventeenth-century canal house. Charges are ƒ8.50 per hour before 7pm, ƒ15 after 7pm; members pay a little less. Mon–Thurs noon–1am, Fri & Sat noon–2am, Sun 1pm–1am.

Snooker Centre de Munt, Reguliersbreestraat 16 ☎620 2040. Twelve tables costing ƒ15 per hour. Mon–Thurs & Sun 11am–1am, Fri & Sat 11am–1.30am.

Swimming pools (Zwembaden)

Flevoparkbad, Zeeburgerdijk 630 ☎692 5030. Tram #3 or #10. The best outdoor pool in the city; gets very busy on sunny days. Mid-May to mid-Sept daily 10am–5pm, until 9pm on warm days.

Jan van Galenbad, Jan van Galenstraat 315 ☎612 8001. Outdoor pool in the west of the city. May–Sept.

Marnixbad, Marnixplein 9 ☎625 4843. Central 25m indoor pool complete with slides and whirlpools. ƒ4.25, with discounts for repeat visits.

De Mirandabad, De Mirandalaan 9 ☎644 6637. Superbly equipped swimming centre (outdoor and indoor pools), with wave machine, whirlpools and slides. Adults ƒ5.75, kids ƒ4.50. As with all the pools, you should call before you set out, since certain times are set aside for small children, family groups etc.

Zuiderbad, Hobbemastraat 26 ☎679 2217. Lovely old pool that's been around for close on 100 years and is thus refreshingly free of the gimmicks that clutter up the others. That said, they have a naturist hour on Sunday from 2.30 to 3.30pm. ƒ4.50.

Table Tennis (Tafeltennis)

Table Tennis Centre, Keizersgracht 209 ☎624 5780. Very central table tennis hall, with a bar. ƒ12.50 per table per hour. Reservations essential after 6pm. Mon–Sat 2.30pm–1am, Sun 1–11pm.

Sports and Activities

Sports and Activities

Tennis and Squash

Most outdoor tennis courts are for members only, and those that aren't need to be reserved well in advance. Your best bets for getting a game at short notice are either at the open-air tennis courts in the Vondelpark, or at one of the following.

Frans Otten Stadion, Stadionstraat 10 ☎662 8767. Five indoor tennis courts and twenty squash courts. Tennis courts are charged at ƒ25 per hour before 5pm, ƒ30 after 5pm; squash courts are ƒ30 then ƒ37.50 per hour. Racket rental ƒ5. Call ahead to reserve a court in the evenings. Mon–Fri 9am–midnight, Sat & Sun 9am–8pm.

Gold Star Tennis, K. Lotsylaan 20, near Vrije Universiteit (next to Station Zuid) ☎644 5483. Tram #5. Twelve indoor and 24 outdoor tennis courts, for ƒ35–45 per hour. Racket rental ƒ5. Daily 9am–10pm, with longer hours in summer.

Squash City, Ketelmakerstraat 6 ☎626 7883. Fifteen squash courts at ƒ13.50 per person for 45min, rising to ƒ17.50 after 5.15pm; all prices include use of the sauna and fitness area. Racket rental ƒ5. Call ahead to reserve courts. Mon–Fri 8.45am–midnight, Sat & Sun 8.45am–10pm.

Out of the City

Chapter 15

Introduction and Practicalities

A lthough Amsterdammers may try to persuade you that there's nothing remotely worth seeing outside their own city, the Netherlands is a compact country, its rail services are fast and frequent, and day trips can be made easily from the capital to a number of extremely worthwhile destinations.

The options really split into two groups: the cities of the **Randstad** conurbation, which stretches south of Amsterdam, and the comparatively rural area to the **north**, where your journeys are more likely to focus on the old ports of the IJsselmeer. The quickest and most convenient method of getting anywhere is by *Nederlandse Spoorwegen* or *NS*, the Dutch **rail network** – all the Randstad cities and most of the other places we cover in this chapter are accessible by direct trains from Centraal Station. *NS* offers day return (*dagretour*) tickets that give substantial savings on the normal return fare; alternatively, if you're heading for one specific attraction, or taking kids along, it might be worth buying a day excursion fare (*dagtochten*), which combines travel and reduced admission on the same ticket. There's also the Railrunner pass, which allows 4- to 11-year-olds to pay a fixed fare of *f*2.50 to any destination, so long as they're accompanied by a fare-paying adult. Those intending to take a longer tour of the country should consider Rail Rover tickets (currently *f*313 for five consecutive days), which allow travel throughout the Dutch rail network, or Euro Domino tickets, which can be bought abroad or in the Netherlands (see p.6 in *Basics*). You can get answers to all enquiries on anything to do with **public transport** in the whole country – trains, buses, trams, fares and schedules – by calling ☎06/9292 (Mon–Fri 6am–midnight, Sat & Sun 7am–midnight; 50c/min). In addition, *NS* publishes copious literature outlining all these offers, available from most Dutch train stations, and, in Britain, from the *Holland Rail* office at Chase House, Gilbert Street, Ropley, Hants SO24 0BY (☎01962/773646, fax 01962/773625).

See Basics, p.39, for details of car rental companies in Amsterdam, and the main rules of the road in the Netherlands.

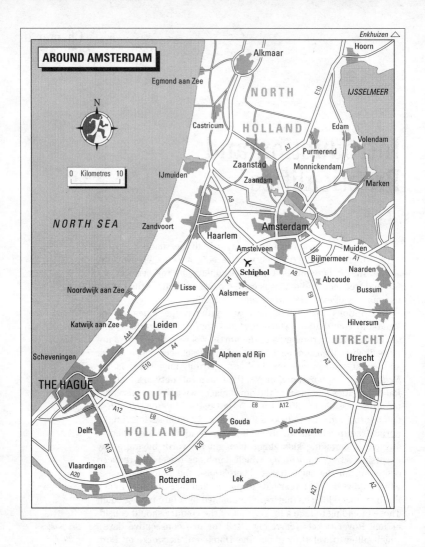

N

NORTH SEA

Enkhuizen △

Hoorn

Alkmaar

Egmond aan Zee

NORTH

HOLLAND

IJSSELMEER

Castricum

Edam

0 Kilometres 10

IJmuiden

Zaanstad

Purmerend

Volendam

Zaandam

Monnickendam

Marken

Zandvoort

Haarlem

Amsterdam

Amstelveen

Muiden

Schiphol

Bijlmermeer

Naarden

Noordwijk aan Zee

Lisse

Aalsmeer

Abcoude

Bussum

Katwijk aan Zee

Leiden

Hilversum

Scheveningen

Alphen a/d Rijn

UTRECHT

THE HAGUE

SOUTH

Utrecht

HOLLAND

Delft

Gouda

Oudewater

Vlaardingen

Rotterdam

Lek

The Dutch **road network** is similarly comprehensive and efficient. **Car rental** costs are fairly standard for Europe: prices for the smallest vehicle (inclusive of collision damage waiver and insurance) start at about ƒ75 a day. The international rental companies all have offices in Amsterdam, although you may be able to make some savings by going to local operators.

If you're not pressed for time, **cycling** is an ideal way of seeing the countryside: the landscape is gentle and there's an extensive system of bike paths, often away from the main roads. Bikes can be rented from almost all train stations (see *Basics*, p.38, for details). Cycling maps (scale 1:100,000) are available from the VVV (around *f*9 each) or from the ANWB (*f*12 each).

A good starting point wherever you go is the local VVV office, which can help with detailed maps, restaurant listings and accommodation – usually costing around *f*40 per person per night in a lower-grade hotel, a little less in private rooms. The opening times listed in the following chapters are for summer (April–Sept); expect hours to be slightly reduced at other times of the year.

The VVV offices in Amsterdam (see p.25) can advise on travel in any part of the country.

Chapter 16

The Randstad Cities

A msterdam forms the northeasternmost point of the dense urban conglomeration known as the Randstad, made up primarily of the cities that were the principal power bases of the Dutch trading empire during the seventeenth century. Despite their close proximity to each other, most of these cities retain surprisingly distinct characters, and they're also well connected by a major train line, making it possible to visit more than one in a day out from the capital.

Haarlem is the closest to Amsterdam, just a quarter of an hour away by train but with a character all of its own, and with enticing attractions like the Frans Hals Museum. Further down the line, **Leiden** has a highly respected university and a number of excellent museums; **The Hague** is the rather pompous political capital of the country, although there's plenty to see there, most notably a fine collection of pictures in its Mauritshuis gallery; and **Utrecht**, to the east, exudes a pleasant provincialism that offers a refreshing change from the capital. Bear in mind, too, that in between most of the Randstad cities lie the best of the Dutch **bulbfields**, a blaze of colour if you're here between March and June; and all along the nearby coast are some of the country's finest **beaches** – long sandy strands fringed by endless expanses of dunes.

ACCOMMODATION PRICE CODES

The following codes are used in this chapter to denote the price of the cheapest double room available in high season, including breakfast. For hostel accommodation (①), the price is per person. Note that low-season prices can drop by as much as two categories and that larger hotels especially often have rooms at various prices.

①	Under ƒ30 per person	⑤	ƒ250–350
②	ƒ60–100	⑥	ƒ350–450
③	ƒ100–170	⑦	over ƒ450
④	ƒ170–250		

For more general accommodation information, see p.165.

Haarlem

Just fifteen minutes from Amsterdam by train, **HAARLEM** has quite a different pace and feel from the capital, an easily absorbed city of around 150,000 people that sees itself as a step above its neighbours. The Frans Hals Museum, in the almshouse where the artist spent his last – and for some, his most brilliant – years, is worth an afternoon in itself; there are also numerous beaches within easy reach, as well as some of the best of the bulbfields; and the city's young and vigorous nightlife may well keep you here until the last train back – which is, conveniently, after midnight.

Arrival, information and accommodation

The **train station**, connected to Amsterdam and Leiden by four trains an hour, is located on the north side of the city, about ten minutes' walk from the centre; **buses** stop right outside. The VVV, attached to the station (April–Sept Mon–Sat 9am–5.30pm; Oct–March Mon–Fri 9am–5.30pm, Sat 9am–4pm; ☎06/320 24043 – ƒ1/min), has maps of the town (ƒ1) and can book **private rooms** for a ƒ7 fee, though you'll find more choice in Zandvoort, about twenty minutes away by half-hourly bus #80 (from Tempelierstraat) or #81 (from the train station). The same goes for **hotels**, though Haarlem has a few reasonably priced and central places worth considering, like the *Carillon* at Grote Markt 27 (☎023/531 0591, fax 531 4909; ③) and the *Amadeus* at Grote Markt 10 (☎023/532 4530, fax 532 2328; ③). The slightly less expensive *Fehres* is about fifteen minutes' walk from the centre (or take bus #7 from the station, or the train one stop to Overveen) at Zijlweg 299 (☎023/527 7368, no fax; ②). There's also a **youth hostel** at Jan Gijzenpad 3 (March–Oct; ☎023/537 3793; ①); buses #2 and #6 run there frequently from the station – a ten-minute journey. **Campers** could try the campsites among the dunes out at Bloemendaal-aan-Zee – either *De Lakens* at Zeeweg 60 (☎023/525 1902) or *Bloemendaal* at Zeeweg 72 (☎023/ 526 3453) – or alternatively *De Branding* at Boulevard Barnaart 30 near Zandvoort (☎023/571 3055). Bus #81 from the train station runs to all of them, though they're only open from April to October. Haarlem's own site, *De Liede* at Lieoever 68 (☎023/533 2360), is open all year – to get there take bus #80 from Tempelierstraat.

The Town

For a long time the residence of the Counts of Holland, Haarlem was sacked by the Spanish under Frederick of Toledo in 1572. There are reminders of this all over the town, since, after a seven-month siege, the revenge exacted by the inconvenienced Frederick was terrible: nearly the whole population was massacred, including the entire Protestant

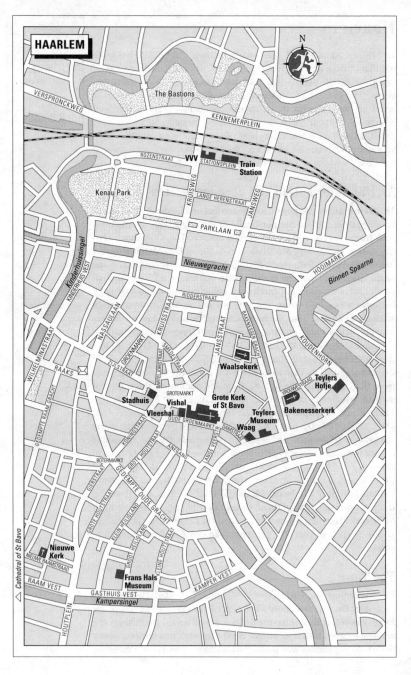

HAARLEM

VERSPRONCKWEG

The Bastions

KENNEMERPLEIN

ROZENSTRAAT **VVV** STATIONSPLEIN **Train Station**

Kenau Park

KRUISWEG

LANGE HERENSTRAAT

JANSWEG

PARKLAAN

Nieuwegracht

HOOIMARKT

Binnen Spaarne

KINDERHUISSINGEL

KINDERHUIS VEST

NASSAULAAN

RIDDERSTRAAT

KRUISSTRAAT

JANSSTRAAT

BAKENESSER GRACHT

KOUDENHORN

WILHELMINASTRAAT

GEDEMPTE RAAM GRACHT

RAAKS

GROENMARKT

ZIJLSTRAAT

BARTELJORISSTRAAT

SMEDESTRAAT

GROTEMARKT

Waalsekerk

Stadhuis

Vishal

Vleeshal

OUDE GROENMARKT

Grote Kerk of St Bavo

LANGE VEERST

Teylers Museum

VROUWESTRAAT

Teylers Hofje

Bakenesserkerk

Waag

DAMSTRAT

KONINGSTRAAT

BOTERMARKT

GIERSTRAAT

ANEGANG

GROTE HOUTSTRAAT

GEDEMPTE OUDE GRACHT

△ *Cathedral of St Bavo*

Nieuwe Kerk

NIEUWE RAAMSTRAAT

KLEIN HEILIGLAND

GROOT HEILIGLAND

KLENE HOUTSTRAAT

KAMPER VEST

RAAM VEST

Frans Hals Museum

GASTHUIS VEST

Kampersingel

HOUTPLEIN

clergy. Recaptured in 1577 by William the Silent, Haarlem went on to enjoy its greatest prosperity in the seventeenth century, becoming a centre for the arts and home to a flourishing school of painters.

Nowadays, the place retains an air of quiet affluence, with all the picturesque qualities of Amsterdam but little of the sleaze. The core of the city is **Grote Markt**, an open space flanked by a concentration of Gothic and Renaissance architecture, most notably the gabled and balconied **Stadhuis** at one end. This dates from the fourteenth century, though it has been much rebuilt over the years, the last time in 1630 – a date recorded on the facade. Inside, the main hall is normally open to visitors during office hours; it's decorated with a few fifteenth-century paintings. At the other end of Grote Markt there's a statue of one **Laurens Coster**, who, Haarlemmers insist, was the true inventor of printing. Legend tells of him cutting a letter "A" from the bark of a tree and dropping it into the sand by accident. Plausible enough, but most authorities seem to agree that Gutenberg was the more likely source of the printed word.

Coster stands in the shadow of the **Grote Kerk of St Bavo** (Mon–Sat 10am–4pm; Oct–Jan closes at 3.30pm; ƒ3.50), where he is believed to be buried. If you've been to the Rijksmuseum in Amsterdam, the church may seem familiar, at least from the outside, since it was the principal focus of the seventeenth-century painter Berckheyde's many views of this square – only the black-coated burghers are missing. Dating originally from the early fourteenth century, the church suffered severe fire damage soon after its construction, which took the best part of 200 years to put right. It now dwarfs the surrounding clutter of streets and houses, and serves as a landmark from almost anywhere in the city. Inside, it is breathtakingly high, its beauty enhanced by the bare, white-painted power of the Gothic vaulting. The mighty Christian Müller organ of 1738 is said to have been played by Handel and Mozart and is one of the biggest in the world, with 5000 pipes and snazzy Baroque embellishment. You can hear it played on Tuesday evenings between mid-May and mid-September. Beneath the organ, Xaverij's lovely group of draped marble figures represents Poetry and Music offering thanks to the town, represented as patroness of the arts, for her generosity, while in the choir there's a late fifteenth-century painting that the church traditionally (though dubiously) attributes to Geertgen tot Sint Jans, along with memorials to painters Pieter Saenredam and Frans Hals – both of whom are buried here. Outside, at the church's western end, the **Vishal** and, opposite it, Lieven de Key's profusely decorated **Vleeshal** (the former fish and meat markets), hold regular art exhibitions that are usually free of charge (Mon–Sat 11am–5pm, Sun 1–5pm).

The Frans Hals Museum

Haarlem's chief attraction, the **Frans Hals Museum** at Groot Heiligland 62 (Mon–Sat 11am–5pm, Sun 1–5pm; ☎023/516 4200;

ƒ6.50), is just a five-minute stroll from Grote Markt, housed in the Oudemannenhuis almshouse where the aged Hals is supposed to have lived out his last destitute years on public funds. Little is known about Frans Hals. Born in Antwerp, the son of Flemish refugees who settled in Haarlem in the late 1580s, his extant oeuvre is relatively small: some two hundred paintings and nothing like the number of sketches and studies left behind by Rembrandt – partly because Hals wasn't fashionable until the nineteenth century, and a lot of his work was lost before it became collectable. His outstanding gift was as a portraitist, showing a sympathy with his subjects and an ability to capture fleeting expression that some say even Rembrandt lacked. Seemingly quick and careless flashes of colour form a coherent whole, leaving us a set of seventeenth-century figures that are curiously alive.

The museum begins with the work of other artists: first, a small group of **sixteenth-century works**, the most prominent a triptych by Gerard David, and an early anti-imperialist painting – *West Indian Scene* by Jan Mostaert – in which the naked natives try fruitlessly to defend themselves against the cannon and sword of their invaders. Van Scorel's *Baptism of Christ* and *Knights of Jerusalem* follow, along with works by Van Goyen, Brouwer and Van Ostade, and a good group of paintings by the **Haarlem Mannerists**, including works by Carel van Mander, leading light of the Haarlem School and mentor of many of the other painters represented here. Cornelis Cornelisz van Haarlem most closely follows Van Mander's guidelines: *The Marriage of Peleus and Thetis* was a popular subject, probably because it was interpreted as a warning against discord, appropriate during the long war with Spain – though Cornelisz gives as much attention to the arrangement of elegant nudes as to his subject. The same is true of his *Massacre of the Innocents*, which could refer to the siege of Haarlem just twenty years earlier.

Hals himself was a pupil of Van Mander, too, though he seems to have learned little more than the barest rudiments from him. His paintings in the west wing – a set of "Civic Guard" portraits of the companies initially formed to defend the country from the Spanish, later becoming just local social clubs – established his reputation as a portraitist, and earned him a regular income. There was a special skill involved in painting these: for the first time Hals made the group portrait a unified whole instead of a static collection of individual portraits; his figures are carefully arranged, but so cleverly as not to appear contrived. For a time, Hals himself was a member of the Company of St George, and in the *Officers of the Militia Company of St George* he appears in the top left-hand corner – one of his few self-portraits.

After this, there are numberless scenes of Haarlem by Berckheyde and Saenredam, among others; landscapes by the Ruisdaels and Berchem; and some group portraits by Veerspronck and the elderly Frans Hals. Hals's later paintings are darker, more contemplative works, closer to Rembrandt in their lighting. The *Governors of the St Elizabeth Gasthuis*, painted in 1641, is a good example, as are the portraits of the *Regents* and *Regentesses of the Oudemannhuis* itself – perhaps the museum's finest treasures. These were commissioned when Hals was in his eighties, a poor man despite a successful painting career, hounded for money by the town's tradesmen and by the mothers of his illegitimate children, and dependent on the charity of the people depicted here. Their cold, hard faces stare out of the gloom, the women reproachful, the men only slightly more affable – except for the character just right of centre, who has been labelled (and indeed looks) completely drunk. There are those who claim Hals had lost his touch by the time he painted these, yet the sinister, almost ghostly power of the paintings, facing each other across the room, suggests quite the opposite. Van Gogh's remark that "Frans Hals had no fewer than twenty-seven blacks" suddenly makes perfect sense.

Other galleries hold lesser works by lesser artists. There's a new wing, which houses temporary exhibitions, usually of modern and contemporary artists, and permanent paintings by Israëls, Appel and Jan Sluyters – though lamentably few of the last. More interesting is the Oudemannhuis itself, a fairly typical *hofje* whose style of low buildings and peaceful courtyards you'll see repeated with slight variations all over town – and indeed the country. Classical concerts are held here regularly from September to May, usually in the afternoon on the third Sunday of each month. For detailed information, call ☎023/531 9180.

The hofjes and Haarlem's other sights
As for the rest of town, Haarlem has a greater number of **hofjes** than most Dutch cities – over twenty, in fact – proof of the town's prosperity in the seventeenth century. The VVV has information on where to find them in their "Hofjestocht" brochure, and they run guided tours every Saturday at 10am, in July and August also on Wednesday at 10am. Most are still inhabited, so you're confined to looking around the courtyard, but the women who sit outside seem used to the occasional visitor and won't throw you out.

Second in the pecking order of Haarlem sights, the **Teylers Museum**, at Spaarne 16 (Tues–Sat 10am–5pm, Sun 1–5pm; *f*7), is Holland's oldest museum, founded in 1778 by wealthy local philanthropist Pieter Teyler van der Hulst. This should appeal to scientific and artistic tastes alike, as it contains everything from fossils, bones and crystals, to weird, H.G. Wells-type technology (including an enormous eighteenth-century electrostatic generator), and sketches and line drawings by Michelangelo, Raphael, Rembrandt and Claude, among others. The drawings are covered to protect them from the light, but don't be afraid to pull back the curtains and peek. Look in, too, on the rooms beyond, filled with work by eighteenth- and nine-teenth-century Dutch painters, principally Breitner, Israëls, Weissen-bruch and, not least, Wijbrand Hendriks, who was the keeper of the art collection here.

Teyler also lent his charity to the **Teyler's Hofje**, a little way east around the bend of the Spaarne at Koudenhorn 64, a solid late eight-eenth-century building that is more monumental in style than the town's other *hofjes*. Nearby, the elegant tower of the late fifteenth-century **Bakenesser Kerk** forms the other main protrusion on the Haarlem skyline, though the church is usually kept closed. Two other sights that may help structure your wanderings are on the opposite side of town. Van Campen's **Nieuwe Kerk** was built – rather unsuc-cessfully – on to Lieven de Key's bulbed, typically Dutch tower in 1649; the interior is symmetrical with a soberness that's quite chill-ing after the soaring heights of the Grote Kerk. Just beyond, and much less self-effacing, the Roman Catholic **Cathedral of St Bavo** (April–Oct Mon–Sat 10am–noon & 2–4.30pm) is one of the largest ecclesiastical structures in Holland, designed by Joseph Cuijpers and built between 1895 and 1906. It's broad and spacious inside, cupo-las and turrets crowding around an apse reminiscent of Byzantine churches or mosques, the whole surmounted by a distinctive copper dome.

Eating and drinking

For **lunches and snacks**, try *Mephisto*, Grote Markt 29, which is open all day Wednesday to Sunday and serves very reasonable Dutch food. *Café 1900*, Barteljorisstraat 10, is also good for lunch, a trendy locals' hangout serving drinks and light meals in an impressive turn-of-the-century interior (it also has live music on Sundays); *H. Ferd. Kuipers* is an excellent patisserie and tearoom at Barteljorisstraat 22. In the evening, there's *Alfonso's* Tex-Mex restaurant just behind the Grote Kerk at Oude Groenmarkt 8; the *Piccolo* restaurant, at Riviervischmarkt 1, which serves pasta and decent pizzas; or try the Indonesian *rijstaffels* at *De Lachende Javaen*, on Frankestraat. *Pamukkale* is a lively Turkish restaurant at Gedempte Oudegracht 29, with music at the weekends.

Once you've eaten, visit *Ze Crack*, at the junction of Lange Veerstraat and Kleine Houtstraat, a dim, smoky bar with good music and lots of English people drinking beer by the pint. On the same street, closer to Grote Markt at Lange Veerstraat 9, *'t Ouwe Proef* is more typically Dutch, a *proeflokaal* that also sells beer – it's at its liveliest early evening.

Around Haarlem: Bloemendaal and Zandvoort

West of Haarlem, the town's moneyed outskirts give way to the thick woodland and rugged dune landscape of the **Kennemerduinen**

National Park, which stretches down to the sea. Accessible by train from both Amsterdam and Haarlem (to Bloemendaal station, then walk – there's a map outside the station), this is an easy way to leave the city behind for a day: it's about a three-hour hike through the dunes from station to sea. Bus #81 from Haarlem train station ignores the park and runs straight to the coast at **BLOEMENDAAL-AAN-ZEE**, which is the rather grandiose name for a group of beach-side shacks housing a thriving ice-cream trade. A little further south, and reachable direct from Amsterdam (Marnixstraat) on bus #80, or from Haarlem train station on bus #81, **ZANDVOORT** is a major Dutch seaside resort, an agglomeration of modern and faceless apartment complexes that rise out of the dunes. As resorts go it's pretty standard – packed and oppressive in summer, depressingly dead in winter. The best reason to visit is the championship motor racing circuit, which provides background noise to everyone's sunbathing. If you come for the beach, and manage to fight your way through the crush to the water, watch out – the sea here is murky and ominously close to the smoky chimneys of **IJmuiden** to the north.

You can visit the Keukenhof Gardens (see p.292) directly from Haarlem; special express buses run every 30min Mon–Sat in season – contact the VVV for details.

Leiden

The home of Holland's most prestigious university, **LEIDEN** has a definite academic air. Like Haarlem to the north, you get the feeling it regards itself as separate from, and independent of, Amsterdam – which is fair enough. There's enough here to justify at least a day trip – regular trains from Amsterdam take just over thirty minutes – and the town's energy, derived largely from its students, strongly counters the myth that there's nothing worth experiencing outside the capital. Leiden's museums, too, are varied and comprehensive enough to merit a visit in themselves – though you need to be selective. The town's real charm, though, lies in the peace and prettiness of its gabled streets and canals.

The university was a gift from William the Silent, a reward for Leiden's enduring (like Haarlem and Alkmaar) a year-long siege by the Spanish. The town emerged victorious on October 3, 1574, when William cut through the dykes around the city and sailed in with his fleet for a dramatic eleventh-hour rescue. This event is still commemorated with an annual fair, fireworks, and the consumption of two traditional dishes: herring and white bread, which the fleet was supposed to have brought with them, and *hutspot*, a vegetable and potato stew, a cauldron of which was apparently found simmering in the abandoned Spanish camp.

Arrival, information and accommodation

Leiden's ultra-modern **train station** is next to the bus station on the northwest edge of town, about ten minutes' walk from the centre.

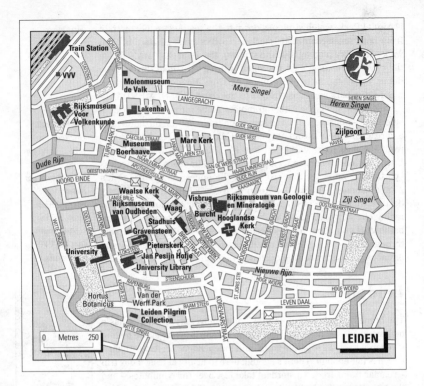

The VVV, opposite at Stationsplein 210 (Mon–Fri 9am–5.30pm, Sat 9am–4pm; ☎071/514 6846), have useful maps and brochures detailing walking tours of the town, and can advise on accommodation and make **room bookings** in private homes for about ƒ40 a person. However, Leiden is fairly short on **hotel** space for a town of its size, and there are no special bargains. *The Rose* (☎071/514 6630, fax 514 5127; ③) is attractive and well located at Beestenmarkt 14; to get there, follow Stationsweg from the station until you reach the first square, where it's on your left. An alternative is *De Ceder* (☎071/517 5903, fax 515 7098; ③), out at Rijnsburgerweg 80: turn left outside the station and left again under the train tracks. Closer to the centre of town, the *Nieuw Minerva* (☎071/512 6358, fax 514 2674; ④) is a pleasant place at Boommarkt 23. Reasonably priced accommodation is more plentiful in the nearby seaside resorts of Katwijk and Noordwijk (see p.294). Of the two, **Katwijk** is the more pleasant place to stay, with several hotels and pensions along its seafront Boulevard; try *Perk*, at Boulevard 60 (☎071/401 2369, no fax; ③), or *Het Anker*, Boulevard 129 (☎071/401 3890, fax 407 3907; ③). There is a **youth hostel** in Leiden at Lange Scheistraat 9, behind the Lakenhal museum on a small alley joining Langegracht and Oude Veste. If you're **camping**, the closest large site is the Leiden *Koningshof*, fifteen minutes away in Rijnsburg, 5km north of Leiden – take bus #40 from the train station; otherwise, **Noordwijk** has several campsites, Katwijk one. All are open from April to October.

The Town

Leiden's most appealing quarter is bordered by Witte Singel and Breestraat, focusing on Rapenburg, a peaceful area of narrow pedestrian streets and canals. Here, at Rapenburg 28, is perhaps the city's best-known attraction, the **Rijksmuseum Van Oudheden** (Tues–Sat 10am–5pm, Sun noon–5pm; *f*5), Holland's principal archeological museum, with a huge collection. You can see one of its major exhibits, the *Temple of Taffeh*, for free. Situated in a courtyard in front of the museum entrance, this was a gift from the Egyptian government in gratitude for the Dutch part in the 1960s UNESCO excavations in Abyssinia (Ethiopia), which succeeded in uncovering submerged Nubian monuments. Dating back to the first century AD, the temple was adapted in the fourth century to the worship of Isis, eventually being sanctified as a Christian church four hundred years later. The Egyptians placed very firm conditions on their legacy: no one should have to pay to see it, and the temperature and humidity must be carefully regulated, with the lights overhead simulating the passage of the sun.

Inside the museum proper, the first exhibit is the remains of a temple to Nehellania – a goddess of sailors – which was uncovered in Zeeland. Next comes classical Greek and Roman sculpture, leading chronologically through Hellenistic works to busts, statues and friezes from Imperial Rome. The best collection, though, is the Egyptian one, beginning with wall reliefs, statues and sarcophagi from tombs and temples, and continuing in the rooms immediately above with a set of mummies and sarcophagi as complete as you're likely to see outside Egypt. The *Three Figures of Maya*, to name just one exhibit, are exceptionally well preserved. The third floor is devoted to the Netherlands: an archeological history of the country from prehistoric, Roman and medieval times, which is, perhaps inevitably, less interesting than the rest of the museum.

Further along Rapenburg, at no. 73, the original home of the **university** still stands, part of it open as a **museum** (Wed–Fri 1–5pm; free) detailing the university's history. Through the courtyard, the **Hortus Botanicus** (Mon–Fri 9am–5pm, Sun 10am–5pm; April–Sept also Sat 9am–5pm; *f*5) is a lovely spot, lushly planted and subtly landscaped across to the Witte Singel canal. Planted in 1587, this is one of the oldest botanical gardens in Europe, a mixture of carefully tended beds of shrubs and hothouses full of tropical foliage. Leave by the exit off to the left, across the canal, where a red door hides a reconstruction of the original garden, the **Clusiustuin** (same hours), named after the botanist who first brought tulips to Holland.

Leiden

Cross Rapenburg from the university museum, and you're in the network of narrow streets that constitutes the medieval town, converging on a central square and the **Pieterskerk** (daily 1.30–4pm), Leiden's principal church. Deconsecrated now, and used occasionally for a Saturday antique market, it has an empty warehouse-like feel. But among the fixtures that remain are a simple and beautiful Renaissance rood screen in the choir, and a host of memorials to the sundry notables buried here – among them **John Robinson**, leader of the Pilgrim Fathers.

Robinson lived in a house on the site of what is now the **Jan Pesijn Hofje** on Kloksteeg, right by the church. A curate in England at the turn of the seventeenth century, he was suspended from preaching in 1604, later fleeing with his congregation to pursue his Puritan form of worship in the more amenable atmosphere of Calvinist Holland. Settling in Leiden, Robinson acted as pastor to growing numbers, but still found himself at odds with the establishment. In 1620, a hundred of his followers – "The Pilgrim Fathers" – sailed via Plymouth for the freedom and abundance of America, though Robinson died before he could join them; he's buried in the church.

If you want to find out more, stroll down to the **Leiden Pilgrim Collection** at Vliet 45 (Mon–Fri 9.30am–4.30pm; free), part of the city archives and a mine of information on Robinson's group during their stay in Leiden. Otherwise, continue east onto **Breestraat**, which marks the edge of Leiden's commercial centre, flanked by the long, ornate Renaissance front of the late sixteenth-century **Stadhuis**, the only part of the building to survive a fire in 1929. Behind, the rivers that cut Leiden into islands converge at the busiest point in town, the site of a vigorous Wednesday and Saturday general **market** that sprawls right over the sequence of bridges into the blandly pedestrian **Haarlemmerstraat**, the town's main shopping street.

The junction of the Oude and Nieuwe Rijn is marked by the mid-seventeenth-century **Waag**, a replacement for a previous Gothic structure, built to a design by Pieter Post and fronted with a naturalistic frieze by Rombout Verhulst. Across the water from here, on an island formed by the fork in the two sections of river, the **Burcht** (daily 10am–9pm; free) is the shell of a twelfth-century fort perched on an ancient mound; it's worth climbing up on the battlements for a panoramic view of Leiden's roofs and towers. The nearby **Hoogland-sekerk** (April–Oct Mon 1–3.30pm, Tues–Sat 11am–4pm; free) is a light, lofty church with a central pillar that features an epitaph to Pieter van der Werff, the burgomaster at the time of the 1574 siege, who became a hero during its final days. When the situation became so desperate that most people were all for giving up, the burgomaster, no doubt remembering the massacre of Haarlem, offered his own body to them as food. His invitation was rejected, but – the story goes – it succeeded in instilling new determination in the flagging citizens.

Across the Oude Rijn from here is the **Museum Boerhaave** at Lange Agnietenstraat 10 (Tues–Sat 10am–5pm, Sun noon–5pm; ƒ5), named after the seventeenth-century Leiden surgeon and giving a brief but absorbing overview of scientific and medical developments over the last three centuries, with particular reference to Dutch achievements, and including some gruesome surgical implements, pickled brains and suchlike. Five minutes' walk from here, Leiden's municipal museum, housed in the old **Lakenhal** (cloth-hall) at Oude Singel 28–32 (Tues–Sat 10am–5pm, Sun noon–5pm; ƒ5), has a similarly engaging exhibition, with a picture gallery devoted to natives of the town as well as mixed rooms of furniture, tiles, glass and ceramics. It's also the only museum in Leiden regularly to exhibit modern Dutch art. Upstairs, the rooms look much as they would have when Leiden's cloth trade was at its height – though most have since been decorated with paintings or now house temporary exhibitions. Downstairs there's a series of sixteenth-century paintings centring on Lucas van Leyden's *Last Judgement* triptych, plus canvases by Rembrandt, Jacob van Swanenburgh (first teacher of the young Rembrandt) and associated Leiden painters – among them Jan Lievens (with whom Rembrandt shared a studio), Gerrit Dou (who initiated the Leiden tradition of small, minutely detailed pictures), and the Van Mieris brothers. There's also a painting depicting the sixteenth-century siege that shows the heroic Van der Werff in full flow.

Around the corner on Molenwerf, the **Molenmuseum de Valk**, 2e Binnenvestgracht 1 (Tues–Sat 10am–5pm, Sun 1–5pm; ƒ5), is a restored grain mill, one of twenty that used to surround Leiden. The downstairs rooms are furnished in simple, period style; upstairs, a slide show recounts the history of windmills in Holland, while displays detail their development and showcase their tools and grinding apparatus, all immaculately preserved. An absorbing way to spend an hour, it's only five minutes' stroll from the station.

There's one other museum between here and the station, the **Rijksmuseum voor Volkenkunde** at Steenstraat 1 (Tues–Fri 10am–5pm, Sat & Sun noon–5pm; ƒ7). The national ethnological museum, this has comprehensive sections on Indonesia and the Dutch colonies, along with reasonable ones on the South Pacific and Far East. However, it gives most other parts of the world a less than thorough showing and is not an essential stop by any means.

Thanks to its university, Leiden is a good place to buy **books**. *Kooyker*, Breestraat 93, has a decent selection of titles in English; there's also a branch of *De Slegte* at Breestraat 73. Consider also taking a **canal trip** around the city centre. These run from Beestenmarkt during summer and cost ƒ10 per person for a forty-minute tour.

Eating and drinking

It's easy to eat and drink cheaply in Leiden. The streets around the Pieterskerk and the Hoogslandeskerk both hold concentrations of bars and restaurants. For lunch, *M'n Broer*, by the Pieterskerk at Kloksteeg 7, has a reasonable menu, while *Barrera*, opposite the old university building on Rapenburg, is a cosy bar that serves sandwiches. In the evening, *De Brasserie*, Lange Mare 38, is popular, with Dutch meals starting at ƒ20; *Koetshuis de Burcht*, off Burgsteeg beside the Burcht, is a trendy French/Dutch bistro. The studenty pub/restaurant *La Bota*, at Herensteeg 9 by the Pieterskerk, has some of the best value local food in town, and an excellent array of beers. *Cojico*, at Breestraat 33, is an amiable Mexican place with main dishes for ƒ12–25. *Jazzcafé The Duke*, on the corner of Oude Singel and Nieuwe Beestenmarkt, near the Lakenhal, has a friendly bar and live jazz several nights of the week; around the corner, *Café Jazzmatazz*, next to the youth hostel, also features live music and attracts an expat crowd.

Around Leiden: the bulbfields and the coast

Along with Haarlem to the north, Leiden is the best base for seeing something of the Dutch **bulbfields** that have flourished here since the late sixteenth century, when one Carolus Clusius, a Dutch botanist, brought the first tulip bulb over from Asia Minor and watched it prosper on Holland's sandy soil. Although bulbs are grown in North Holland too, the centre of the Dutch bulb-growing industry is the area around Leiden and up towards Haarlem. The flowers are inevitably a major tourist pull, and one of Holland's most lucrative businesses, supporting some ten thousand growers in what is these days a billion-guilder industry. Obviously spring is the best time to see something of the blooms, when the view from the train – which cuts directly through the main growing areas – can be sufficient in itself, the fields divided into stark geometric blocks of pure colour. With your own transport you can take in the full beauty of the bulbfields by way of special routes marked by hexagonal signposts – local VVVs sell pamphlets listing the best vantage points.

Lisse: the Keukenhof Gardens

If you'd like a closer look at the best of the Dutch flower industry, head for **LISSE**, halfway between Leiden and Haarlem, which is home to the **Keukenhof Gardens** (late March to end of May; daily 8am–7.30pm; ƒ16), the largest flower gardens in the world. The Keukenhof was set up in 1949, designed by a group of prominent bulb growers to convert people to the joys of growing flowers from bulbs in their own gardens. Literally the "kitchen garden", its site is the former estate of a fifteenth-century countess, who used to grow herbs and vegetables for her dining table here – hence the name.

Some seven million flowers are on show for their full flowering period, complemented, in case of especially harsh winters, by 5000 square metres of glasshouses holding indoor displays. You could easily spend a whole day here, swooning among the sheer abundance of it all, but to get the best of it you need to come early, before the tour buses pack the place. There are three restaurants in the 28 hectares of grounds, and well-marked paths take you all the way through the gardens, which hold daffodils, narcissi and hyacinths in April, and tulips from mid-April until the end of May. Special Express bus #54 (ƒ22, including admission to the gardens) runs to the Keukenhof from Leiden bus station twice an hour from Monday to Saturday.

You can also visit the Keukenhof Gardens from Haarlem – see p.287.

Aalsmeer – and more flowers
You can see the industry in action in **AALSMEER**, 23km north of Leiden, towards Amsterdam, whose **flower auction**, again the largest in the world, is held daily in a building approximately the size of 75 football fields (Mon–Fri 7.30–11am; ƒ5). The dealing is fast and furious, and the turnover staggering. In an average year around ƒ1.5 billion (about £500m/$800m) worth of plants and flowers are traded here, many of them arriving in florists' shops throughout Europe on the same day. In case it all seems a mystery, there are headphones with recorded information in English placed strategically around. Be sure to arrive well before 10am or you won't see a single flower.

There are other places, too, with bulbs and flowers, though none as spectacular as the Keukenhof, nor as vibrant as the Aalsmeer auction. The **Frans Roozen nurseries** at Vogelenzangseweg 49 in **VOGELENZANG**, about 8km south of Haarlem (April & May daily 8am–6pm; July–Sept Mon–Fri 9am–5pm; ƒ2), have a show glasshouse displaying blooms; get there on the hourly #90 bus from Haarlem train station. **RIJNSBURG**, 5km north of Leiden by bus #31, #40 or #41, is the starting point of an annual flower parade in early August, which continues on to Leiden and Noordwijk. There's a similar parade from Haarlem to Noordwijk (see below) at the end of April, culminating in a display of the floats in the town.

The coast: Katwijk and Noordwijk
Like all of the towns in this part of Holland, Leiden has easy access to some fine beaches, though the coastal resorts themselves aren't much to write home about; unless you're keen to swim, the only reason for visiting is for their larger – and cheaper – supply of accommodation and campsites. **KATWIJK-AAN-ZEE**, accessible by a number of buses from the stop opposite Leiden's bus station (every 20min; journey time 25min), is the stock Dutch seaside town, less crowded than Zandvoort and without the pretensions of Scheveningen, but pretty dreary nonetheless – although it does preserve some of the features of an old coastal village in the lines of

terraced houses that spread out around the seventeenth-century lighthouse. Its expanse of undeveloped sand dunes, though, which stretch along the shore south towards The Hague, makes an ideal area for secluded sunbathing. Otherwise its main attraction is the **Katwijk Sluices**, just north of the resort area, alongside the main bus route. Completed in 1807, these are a series of gates that regulate the flow of the Oude Rijn as it approaches the sea: around high tide, the gates are closed; when they are opened, the pressure of the accumulated water washes aside the sand deposited at the mouth of the river by the sea – a simple system that finally determined the course of the Oude Rijn, which for centuries had been continually diverted by the sand deposits, turning the surrounding fields into a giant swamp. The VVV (April–June Mon–Sat 9am–6pm; July & Aug Mon–Sat 9am–6pm, Sun 11am–3pm; Sept–March Mon–Fri 9am–5pm, Sat 9am–1pm; ☎071/407 5444), a stone's throw from the beach at Vuurbaakplein 11, is useful for finding accommodation when the town gets busy with Dutch and German tourists in summer. They can also give you information on the herring gutting competition, one of Katwijk's big annual events.

NOORDWIJK-AAN-ZEE, some 3km up the coast and accessible by buses from the same stop in Leiden, is of even less appeal, not much more than a string of grandiose hotel developments built across the undulating sand dunes behind the coast. However, it again offers some excellent stretches of beach. The one time it's worth coming to see the town itself is on the penultimate weekend in April, when the **flower parade** arrives from Haarlem and makes an illuminated tour of night-time Noordwijk. The floats are displayed in the village the next morning.

The Hague and Scheveningen

With its urbane atmosphere, **THE HAGUE** (in Dutch, *Den Haag*) is different from any other Dutch city. Since the sixteenth century it's been the political capital and the home of national institutions, in a country built on civic independence and munificence. Frequently disregarded until the development of central government in the nineteenth century, The Hague's older buildings are a rather subdued and modest collection, with little of Amsterdam's flamboyance. Most of the city's canal houses are demurely classical, with an overpowering sense of sedate prosperity. In 1859, English poet Matthew Arnold wrote: "I never saw a city where the well-to-do classes seemed to have given the whole place so much of their own air of wealth, finished cleanliness, and comfort; but I never saw one, either, in which my heart would so have sunk at the thought of living." Things haven't changed much: the "well-to-do classes" – mostly multinational executives and diplomats in dark Mercedes – ensure that many of the hotels and restaurants are firmly in the expense account category,

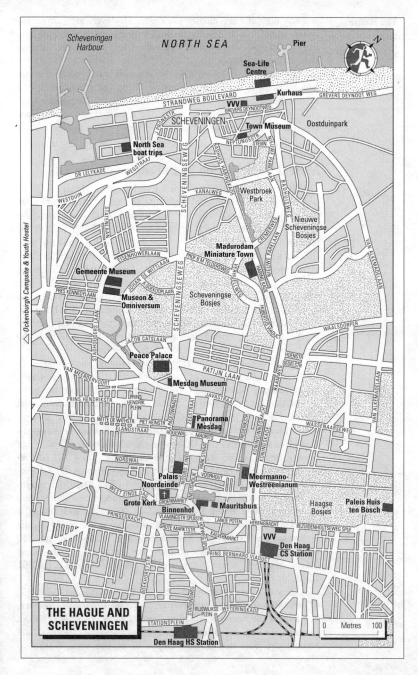

Scheveningen Harbour

NORTH SEA

Pier

Sea-Life
Centre

Kurhaus

STRANDWEG BOULEVARD

GREVERS DEYNOOT WEG

VVV

GREVERS DEYNOOTWEG

SCHEVENINGEN

Oostduinpark

Town Museum

NEPTUNUSSTR

STEVIN

NIEUWE PARKLAAN

North Sea
boat trips

DR LELYKADE

WEGSTRAAT

KANALWEG

Westbroek
Park

WESTDUIN

STATENLAAN

EISENHOWERLAAN

Nieuwe
Scheveningse
Bosjes

BADHUISWEG

CREMERWEG

Gemeente Museum

JULIAN DE WITTLAAN

J BOECKOOPLAAN

Madurodam
Miniature Town

PROF B M TELDERSWEG

TEHELENWEG

Museon &
Omniversum

PRES KENNEDYLAAN

Scheveningse
Bosjes

NIEUWE PARKLAAN

KONINGINNEGRACHT

HUBERTUS VIADUCT

VAN ALKEMADELAAN

WAALSDORPER

JACOB CATSLAAN

Peace Palace

PATIJN LAAN

HOENSTR
DEDELSTR

VAN MEERDERVOORT

Mesdag Museum

JAVASTRAAT

RAAMWEG

Mesdag Museum

PRINS HENDRIKSTR

PRINS
HENDRIK
PLEIN

WITTE DE WITHSTR

PIET HEINSTR

PALUWKASTR

ZEESTRAAT

Panorama
Mesdag

FREDERIKSTR

KONINGINNEGRACHT

WASSENAARSEWEG

VAN ALKEMADELAAN

ELANDSTRAAT

HOGEWAL

MAURITS

NORDWAL

NOORD EINDE

PARK STRAAT

VOORHOUT

Meermanno-
Westreenianum

WEST EINDE DAG

Palais
Noordeinde

GROENMARKT

Grote Kerk

Binnenhof

Mauritshuis

Paleis Huis
ten Bosch

Haagse
Bosjes

PRINSEGRACHT

VLAMINGSTR SPUISTR

GROTE MARKTSTR

LANGE POTEN

HERENGRACHT

BEZUIDENHOUTSEWEG SPUI

BOEKHORSTSTR

KALVERMART

JS DENNAR

PRINS BERNHARD VIADUCT

VVV

Den Haag
CS Station

STATIONSWEG

RIJSWIJKSE
PLEIN

WETERINGKADE

THE HAGUE AND
SCHEVENINGEN

STATIONSPLEIN

0   Metres   100

Den Haag HS Station

The Hague
and
Scheveningen

and the nightlife is similarly packaged. However, away from the mediocrity of wealth, The Hague does have cheaper and livelier bars and restaurants – and even its share of restless adolescents hanging around the pizza joints.

The town may be rather drab, but it boasts some excellent museums, principally the famed collection of old Dutch masters at the **Mauritshuis**, and more modern works of art at the **Gemeente Museum**. And when you're tired of art, the satellite town of **Scheveningen** is the country's largest resort, with wide sandy beaches to laze on.

Arrival, information and accommodation

The Hague has two **train stations** – **Den Haag HS** (Hollands Spoor) and **Den Haag CS** (Centraal Station) – and trains from Amsterdam (45min) stop at one or the other, but not both. Of the two, Den Haag CS is the more convenient, situated five minutes' walk east of the town centre, and next door to the complex housing the bus and tram stations and the VVV (Mon–Sat 9am–5.30pm, July & Aug also Sun 10am–5pm; ☎06/340 35051 – 75c/min). Den Haag HS is 1km to the south, near the budget hotels, and frequent trains connect the two. The Hague may be the country's third largest city, but almost everything worth seeing is within easy walking distance of Den Haag CS; if you intend to use the city's buses and trams, the VVV and counters at the train station sell the standard *strippenkaart*, plus the *dagkaart* – the best bet if you're only here for the day.

Accommodation in The Hague is hard to find and often expensive – you might be better off basing yourself in Scheveningen (see below), twenty minutes' ride away by tram, where rooms are more plentiful and slightly cheaper. If you do want to stay in town, then you may as well pay the extra guilders and let the VVV arrange somewhere for you to stay – especially as the cheaper pensions are spread out all over the city. Otherwise, there's a cluster of **hotels** just outside Den Haag HS station: the *Aristo*, Stationsweg 164 (☎389 0847; ③), which is clean and tidy but slightly cramped; the *Astoria*, Stationsweg 139 (☎070/384 0401, fax 354 1653; ④), which is a little smarter and more comfortable than its budget neighbours; and the *Bristol*, Stationsweg 130 (☎070/384 0073; ③), which has the cheapest singles in town. Of the city's more upmarket hotels, the best value are *'t Centrum*, Veenkade 6 (☎070/346 3657, fax 310 6460; ④), a small, friendly place by the canal west of the Royal Palace, and the *Paleis*, Molenstraat 26 (☎070/362 2461, fax 361 4533; ⑤).

The **youth hostel** *Ockenburgh* (☎070/397 0011, fax 397 2251; ②) is at Monsterseweg 4, some 10km to the west of the town centre, just behind the beach at Kijkduin (bus #122, #123 or #124 from Centraal Station). It's attached to a hotel of the same name (④), and adjoins the best and largest **campsite** in the area, *Camping*

Ockenburgh, Wijndaelerweg 25 (March–Oct; ☎070/325 2364). All can be reached by bus #4 from the station, though they're about ten minutes' walk from the nearest bus stop – ask the driver to let you off.

The City Centre

Right in the centre and the oldest part of the city, the **Binnenhof** (inner court) is the home of Holland's bicameral parliament. Count William II built a castle here in the thirteenth century, and the settlement that grew up around it became known as the Count's Domain or *'s Gravenhage* (literally "Count's Hedge") – the city's official name right up until the 1990s. As the embodiment of central rather than municipal power, the Binnenhof had a chequered history – empty or occupied, feted or ignored – until the nineteenth century, when The Hague shared political capital status with Brussels during the uneasy times of the United Kingdom of the Netherlands. Thereafter it became the seat of government, home to an effective legislature. The present rectangular complex is a rather mundane affair, a confusing mixture of shape and style that irritated nineteenth-century Dutch parliamentarians with its obvious lack of prestige; their modern equivalents, the members of the Tweedekamer (Second Chamber), moved into a new extension in 1992.

The best view of the Binnenhof is from the front, where a small lake – the **Hof Vijver** (Court Pond) – mirrors the attractive symmetry of the facade. Though the Binnenhof is a major tourist attraction, there's precious little to see except the **Ridderzaal** (Hall of the Knights), a slender-turreted structure used for state occasions. It's been a courtroom, market and stable, and so repeatedly replaced and renovated that little of the thirteenth-century original remains. An undramatic guided tour of the Ridderzaal and the chambers of parliament (often closed Mon & Tues) starts regularly from the information office at Binnenhof 8a (Mon–Sat 10am–4pm; last tour 3.45pm; ƒ5).

The Mauritshuis Collection

To the immediate east of the Binnenhof, the **Royal Picture Gallery Mauritshuis** is located in a magnificent seventeenth-century mansion at Korte Vijverberg 8 (Tues–Sat 10am–5pm, Sun 11am–5pm; ƒ10 paid as you leave the gallery). Generally considered to be one of the best galleries in Europe, it's famous for its extensive range of Flemish and Dutch paintings from the fifteenth to the eighteenth centuries, based on the collection accumulated by Prince William V of Orange (1748–1806). All the major Dutch artists are represented, and there are multilingual cards in each room providing background notes on all the major canvases. At present the rooms are not numbered, and the policy of the museum is (rather awkwardly) to spread the works of many of the key artists through several rooms, rather than keeping them together. For further information, there's a free brochure available at the entrance, while the museum shop sells an excellent guidebook for ƒ25. Alternatively, you can join one of the irregular and expensive conducted tours – prices depend on length of tour; ask at reception for times. During major exhibitions, expect the paintings to be moved around or removed from show.

The entrance and museum shop are in the **basement** on the east side of the building, together with **Andy Warhol**'s *Queen Beatrix*, a twentieth-century aperitif to the collection above. Up the stairs on the **first floor**, walk back towards the old front doors and into the room on the left, where **Hans Memling**'s *Portrait of a Man* is a typically observant work, right down to the scar on the nose. Close by, **Rogier van der Weyden**'s *The Lamentation of Christ* is a harrowing picture of death and sorrow, with Christ's head hanging down toward the earth, surrounded by the faces of the mourners, each with a particular expression of anguish and pain. **Quinten Metsys** was the first major artist to work in Antwerp, where he was made a Master of the Guild in 1519. An influential figure, he attempted to imbue his religious pictures with spiritual sensitivity, and his *Descent from the Cross* is a fine example – Christ's suffering face under the weight of the Cross contrasted with the grinning, taunting onlookers behind.

Proceeding in a counterclockwise direction, through a series of rooms on either side of the Italianate dining room, exhibits include two giant allegorical canvases by Jan Sanders van Hemessen; Lucas Cranach the Younger's spirited *Man with a Red Beard*; and two works by **Hans Holbein the Younger**, a striking *Portrait of Robert Cheeseman*, where all the materials – the fur collar, the falcon's feathers and the cape – seem to take on the appropriate texture, and his *Portrait of Jane Seymour*, one of several pictures commissioned by Henry VIII, who sent him abroad to paint matrimonial candidates. Holbein's vibrant technique was later to land him in hot water: an over-flattering portrait of Anne of Cleves swayed Henry into an unhappy marriage with his "Flanders' Mare" that was to last only six months.

Of a number of paintings by **Adriaen Brouwer**, *Quarrel at a Card Table* and *Inn with Drunken Peasants* are two of the better known, with thick, rough brush strokes recording contemporary Flemish lowlife. Brouwer could approach this subject with some authority, as he spent most of his brief life either in taverns or in prison. **Peter Paul Rubens**, the acclaimed painter and diplomat, was a contemporary of Brouwer, though the two could hardly be more dissimilar: Rubens's *Portrait of Isabella Brant*, his first wife, is a typically grand, rather statuesque work, not perhaps as intriguing as *Adam and Eve in Paradise*, a collaboration between Rubens, who painted the figures, and **Jan Bruegel the Elder**, who filled in the dreamlike animals and landscape behind. In the same room are two examples of the work of Rubens's chief assistant, **Anthony van**

Dyck, a portrait specialist who found fame at the court of King Charles I. His *Pieter Stevens of Antwerp* and *Quinton Simons of Antwerp* are good, early examples of the tendency to flatter and ennoble his subjects that no doubt helped him into the job. Nearby, and again showing the influence of Rubens, is the robust *Adoration of the Shepherds* by Jacob Jordaens.

On the **second-floor** landing, the broad brush strokes of **Frans Hals**'s *Laughing Boy* are far removed from the restrained style he was forced to adopt in his more familiar paintings of the burghers of Haarlem. **Carel Fabritius**, pupil of Rembrandt and (possibly) the teacher of Vermeer, was killed in a gunpowder explosion at Delft when he was only 22. Few of his canvases have survived, but an exquisite example is *The Goldfinch*, a curious, almost impressionistic work, with the bird reduced to a blur of colour. One of his Delft contemporaries was **Gerard Houckgeest**, who specialized in church interiors, as in *The Tomb of William of Orange*, a minutely observed study of exact architectural lines lightened by expanses of white marble.

Off the second-floor landing, on the left at the front of the museum, is the Mauritshuis's most famous painting, **Jan Vermeer**'s *View of Delft*, a superb townscape of 1658, with the fine lines of the city drawn beneath a cloudy sky, a patchwork of varying light and shade – though the dispassionate, photographic quality the painting has in reproduction is oddly lacking in the large canvas. In the same room, Gerard Ter Borch's *Lice Hunt*, a vignette of seventeenth-century domestic life, makes a striking contrast to Vermeer's detachment.

Heading in a counterclockwise direction, other highlights include the busy stick-like figures of the *Winter Scene* by Hendrik Avercamp, the deaf and dumb artist from Kampen, and Paulus Potter's lifelike *Young Bull*, a massive canvas complete with dung and rather frightening testicles. Best known of the **Rembrandts** is the *Anatomy Lesson of Dr Tulp* from 1632, the artist's first commission in Amsterdam. The peering pose of the "students" who lean over the corpse solved the problem of emphasis falling on the body rather than on the subjects of the portrait, who were in fact members of the surgeons' guild. It's to be hoped that Tulp's skills as an anatomist were better than his medical advice, which included the recommendation that his patients drink fifty cups of tea a day.

Dotted throughout the museum are no fewer than thirteen paintings by **Jan Steen**, including a wonderfully riotous picture carrying the legend "The way you hear it, is the way you sing it" – a parable on the young learning bad habits from the old – and a typically salacious *Girl Eating Oysters*.

The rest of the city centre
A few metres to the west of the Binnenhof, the **Gevangenpoort** or "Prisoner's Gate Museum", at Buitenhof 33 (hourly guided tours

Mon–Fri 10am–4pm, Sun 1–5pm; last tour 4pm; ƒ5), was originally part of the city's fortifications. Used as a prison until the nineteenth century, it now contains an array of instruments of torture and punishment, centred around its Chamber of Horrors. As well as the guillotine blades, racks and gallows, the old cells are in a good state of repair – including the *ridderkamer* for the more privileged captive. Here Cornelius de Witt, Burgomaster of Dordrecht, was imprisoned before he and his brother Johan, another staunch Republican and leader of the States of Holland, were dragged out and murdered by an Orangist mob in 1672. The brothers were shot, beheaded and cut into pieces that were then auctioned to the crowd; Johan's tongue is preserved for macabre posterity in the storerooms of the Gemeente Museum. The Gevangenpoort is understandably popular; join the line about fifteen minutes before each hourly tour to guarantee a place.

Down the street at Buitenhof 35, the **Prince William V Gallery** (Tues–Sun 11am–4pm; ƒ2.50, free with Mauritshuis ticket) has paintings by Rembrandt, Jordaens and Paulus Potter among others, but it's more interesting as a reconstruction of a typical eighteenth-century gallery – or "cabinet", as they were known. The fashion then was to sandwich paintings together in a cramped patchwork from floor to ceiling: though it's faithful to the period, this makes viewing difficult for eyes accustomed to spacious modern museums.

A five-minute walk away to the west, and easily the best of The Hague's old churches, St Jacobskerk or the **Grote Kerk** (July & Aug Mon 11am–4pm; otherwise closed to the public except for exhibitions, usually Mon–Fri 11am–4pm, Sun 1–5pm; free) is a hall church with an exhilarating sense of breadth and warmly decorated vaulting. The one thing you can't miss, as it's placed where the high altar should be, is the memorial to the unmemorable Admiral Opdam, who was blown up with his ship during the little-remembered naval battle of Lowestoft in 1665. Keep an eye open for the Renaissance pulpit: similar to the one in Delft's Oude Kerk, it has carved panels framing the apostles in false perspective. For the energetic, the **church tower** (open Wed at noon for groups of 8–10 people; ☎070/365 8665) provides blustery views over the town.

Just fifty metres north of the Grote Kerk, the sixteenth-century **Paleis Noordeinde** (closed to visitors; gardens open daily dawn to dusk, free) is one of several royal buildings that lure tourists to this part of town. In 1980, Queen Juliana abdicated in favour of her daughter Beatrix, who proceeded to return the royal residence from the province of Utrecht to The Hague. Despite the queen's attempts to demystify the monarchy, there's no deterring the enthusiasts who sign on for expensive royal tours around the peripheries of the palace and Beatrix's other residence just outside town, the seventeenth-century **Huis ten Bosch** (House in the Woods; closed to the public). Just east of the palace, the brand new **Games of Chance**

Museum (Mon–Fri 9am–4pm; free) is worth a glance for its small displays on the popular Dutch lotteries dating back to 1496, though, as yet, nothing is labelled in English.

The street running east from the palace, **Lange Voorhout**, is fringed by an impressive spread of diplomatic mansions and the *Hotel des Indes*, where the ballerina Anna Pavlova died in 1931 and where today you stand the best chance of being flattened by a chauffeur-driven limousine. Just to the east, the **Meermanno-Westreenianum Museum**, Prinsessegracht 30 (Mon–Sat 1–5pm; ƒ3.50), has a small collection of remarkably well-preserved medieval illuminated manuscripts and bibles; and nearby, the **Hague Historical Museum**, Korte Vijverberg 7 (Tues–Fri 11am–5pm, Sat & Sun noon–5pm; ƒ7.50), mixes local history with temporary exhibitions on topical issues.

Much of the rest of the centre is drab and dreary, an apparently random mixture of the stately old and the brashly new (the giant *Babylon* shopping complex by the Centraal Station wins the ugliness award). During the war the occupying German forces built a V2 launching site just outside the city: as a result it was almost as thoroughly bombed by the Allies as its neighbour Rotterdam had been by the Luftwaffe.

North of the city centre

Ten minutes' walk north of the centre along Noordeinde, also accessible by trams #7 and #8, the **Panorama Mesdag**, Zeestraat 65b (Mon–Sat 10am–5pm, Sun noon–5pm; ƒ6), was designed in the late nineteenth century by Hendrik Mesdag, banker turned painter and local citizen become Hague School luminary. His unremarkable seascapes are tinged with an unappealing bourgeois sentimentality, but there's no denying the achievement of his panorama, a depiction of Scheveningen as it would have appeared in 1881. Completed in four months with help from his wife and the young G.H. Breitner, the painting is so naturalistic that it takes a few moments for the tricks of lighting and perspective to become apparent. Five minutes' walk from the Panorama at Laan van Meerdervoort 7f is the house Mesdag bought as a home and gallery. At the time it overlooked one of his favourite subjects, the dunes, the inspiration for much of his work, and today contains the **Mesdag Museum** (under renovation at the time of writing, but normally Tues–Sat 10am–5pm, Sun 1–5pm). His collection includes a number of Hague School paintings which, like his own work, take the seascapes of the nearby coast as their subject. There are also paintings by Corot, Rousseau, Delacroix and Millet, though none of them represents the artists' best achievements. Perhaps the most interesting exhibits are the florid and distinctive paintings of Antonio Mancini, whose oddly disquieting subjects are reminiscent of Klimt.

The Hague
and
Scheveningen

The Peace Palace

Round the corner from the Mesdag Museum, framing Carnegieplein, the **Peace Palace** (occasionally closed for court sittings; otherwise hourly guided tours Mon–Fri at 10am, 11am, 2pm & 3pm; June–Sept also at 4pm; ƒ5; check with the VVV for times of tours in English) is home to the Court of International Justice and, for all the wrong reasons, serves as a monument to the futility of war. Towards the end of the nineteenth century, Tsar Nicholas II called an international conference for the peaceful reconciliation of national problems. The result was the First Hague Peace Conference of 1899, whose purpose was to "help find a lasting peace and, above all, a way of limiting the progressive development of existing arms". This in turn led to the formation of a Permanent Court of Arbitration housed in a nondescript building in the city until the American industrialist Andrew Carnegie donated $1.5 million for the construction of a new home – the Peace Palace. These honourable aims came to nothing with the mass slaughter of World War I: just as the donations of tapestries, urns, marble and stained glass were arriving from all over the world, so Europe's military commanders were preparing their offensives. Backed by a massive law library, fifteen judges are still in action today, conducting trade matters in English and diplomatic affairs in French. Widely respected and generally considered neutral, their judgements are nevertheless not binding.

The Gemeentemuseum, Museon and Omniversum

North of the Peace Palace, the **Gemeentemuseum**, Stadhouderslaan 41 (Tues–Sun 11am–5pm; ƒ8; bus #4 from Centraal Station), is arguably the best and certainly the most diverse of The Hague's many museums. Designed by H.P. Berlage in the 1930s, it's generally considered to be his masterpiece, although its layout can be confusing, and the labelling is erratic. However, the museum's stock of musical instruments is outstanding – especially the harpsichords and early pianos – and the Islamic ceramics are extraordinary. The manageable Delft collection is among the world's best and, while the collection of modern art is frustrating, it does attempt to outline the development of Dutch painting through the Romantic, Hague and Expressionist schools to the De Stijl movement. **Mondrian**, the De Stijl group's most famous member, dominates this part of the gallery: the museum has the world's largest collection of his paintings, though much of it consists of (deservedly) unfamiliar early works painted before he evolved the abstraction of form into the geometry and pure colour for which he's best known.

Adjoining the Gemeentemuseum is a modern building that houses the **Museon** (Tues–Fri 10am–5pm, Sat & Sun noon–5pm; ƒ7), a sequence of nonspecialist exhibitions on human activities related to the history of the earth. Self-consciously internationalist, it's aimed at school parties, as is the adjoining **Omniversum** or "Space Theatre" (shows on the hour Tues & Wed 10am–5pm, Thurs–Sun 10am–9pm; *f*17.50). A planetarium in all but name, it possesses all the technical gadgetry you'd expect.

Madurodam Miniature Town

Halfway between The Hague and Scheveningen, the **Madurodam Miniature Town** (daily April–Sept 9am–10pm; Oct–March 9am–5pm; *f*19.50, children *f*14; tram #1 or #9) , a copy of a Dutch town on a 1:25 scale, is heavily plugged by the tourist authorities, though its origins are of more interest than the place itself. The original money was put up by J.M.L. Maduro, who wished to establish a memorial to his son who had distinguished himself during the German invasion of 1940, and died in Dachau concentration camp five years later. There's a memorial to him just by the entrance, and profits from the miniature town are used for general Dutch social and cultural activities. Madurodam is very popular with children, but the attached **Sand World**, a recently added collection of sand sculptures, is rather more engaging.

Eating and drinking

There are plenty of cheap places to eat around the town centre: *Greve*, at Torenstraat 138, north of Grote Kerk, serves up snacks and sizeable Dutch meals, while for pizzas try *Pinelli*, on the way to the Grote Kerk at Dagelijkse Groenmarkt 31. *De Apendans* at Herenstraat 113 is a popular, no-frills restaurant serving simple Dutch food for *f*15 and up. You can get Indonesian snacks at *Eethuis Nirwana*, Prinsestraat 65, and large portions of local dishes at *Eethuis Neighbours*, Papestraat 28. For more variety, the streets around Denneweg and Frederikstraat, just north of Lange Voorhout, have some interesting restaurants. The popular vegetarian *De Dageraad* is at Hooikade 4; *Pannekoekhuys Maliehuys* at Maliestraat 8 offers pancakes and steaks; and *Plato*, Frederikstraat 32, has an excellent French/Dutch menu.

There are plenty of good **bars** scattered around town, too. South of the Grote Kerk, *Zwarte Ruiter* and the cavernous *De Boterwaag* face each other across the busy Grote Markt square, both with a wide range of beers and a studenty clientele. Along Papestraat, *Café de Paap*, at no. 32, has occasional live music, while the *Old-Timer*, at no. 23a, is a more peaceful option. On Plein, just east of the Binnenhof, *Berger* at no. 18 and *Plein 19* both attract a young, professional crowd, while a few blocks north, on Denneweg, there are some mellow bars among the antique shops – try *De Pompernickel* at no. 27, *De Landeman* at no. 48, or *2005*, opposite. A little south of town, *De Paas* has a lovely spot by the canal on Dunne Bierkade, just west of Wagenstraat. There are several **gay bars** in town: try *Boko* at Nieuwe Schoolstraat 2, *Stairs*, Nieuwe Schoolstraat 11, or the mixed *De Landeman*, Denneweg 48.

The **North Sea Jazz Festival**, held every year in mid-July at the
Nederlands Congresgebouw, Churchillplein 10, is The Hague's most prestigious event, attracting international media coverage and many of the
world's most famous musicians. Details of performances are available
from the VVV, which will also reserve accommodation, virtually impossible to find after the festival has begun. Various kinds of tickets can be purchased: a *dagkaart*, for example, valid for an entire day, costs around
ƒ100. See also *Entertainment and Nightlife*, p.223.

To find out **what's on**, pick up a copy of the VVV's free monthly
magazine, which gives details of concerts, theatre performances,
special events and other entertainments in and around The Hague.

Listings

Bike rental At either of The Hague's train stations for ƒ8 a day (ƒ6 with a valid
train ticket), plus a ƒ100 deposit.

Car rental *Achilles*, Prinses Marijkestraat 5 ☎070/381 1811; *Avis*, Theresia-
straat 216 ☎070/385 0698; *Budget*, Mercuriusweg 9 ☎070/382 0609;
Europcar, Hotel Sofitel, Koningin Julianaplein 35 ☎070/385 1708.

Embassies *Australia*, Carnegielaan 12 ☎070/310 8200; *Canada*, Sophia-
laan 7 ☎070/361 4111; *Ireland*, Dr Kuyperstraat 9 ☎070/363 0993; *UK*,
Lange Voorhout 10 ☎070/364 5800; *USA*, Lange Voorhout 102 ☎070/310
9209.

Markets General: Herman Costerstraat (Mon, Wed, Fri & Sat 8am–5pm).
Food: Markthof, Gedempte Gracht/Spui (Mon 11am–6pm, Tues–Sat
9am–6pm). Antiques, books and curios: Lange Voorhout (mid-May to Sept
Thurs & Sun 10am–6pm); Plein (Oct to mid-May Thurs 10am–6pm).

Medical In an emergency call ☎112 for an ambulance. The most central 24-
hr casualty department is at Hospital Westeinde, Lijnbaan 32 ☎070/330 2000.

Pharmacies Night services listed in newspapers and at the VVV.

Police Emergency ☎112 or ☎070/310 4911; tourist assistance ☎070/310
3274.

Post office On Nobelstraat, Prinsenstraat and Kerkplein.

Taxis HTMC ☎070/390 7722; HCT ☎070/364 2828.

Scheveningen

Situated on the coast about 4km from the centre of The Hague, the
old fishing port of **SCHEVENINGEN** has none of its neighbour's
businesslike air, enjoying instead its status as Holland's top coastal
resort, drawing more than nine million visitors a year to its beach,
pier and casino. It's not a particularly attractive place, but it can
make a good alternative base if you're keen to see something of The
Hague, as its hotels are cheaper and more plentiful. At certain times
of year it's worth a special visit – in mid-June for example, when the
town hosts a massive international **kite festival** that takes over the
beach and much of the town.

Scheveningen was a fashionable resort in the nineteenth century, but faded after the 1920s; it's currently being redeveloped as an all-year resort. The centre of town is called **Scheveningen Bad**, grouped around the massive **Kurhaus** hotel that's the most potent symbol of the town's bygone era. Sadly, it's the only reminder, the rest of the town centre being a rather tacky mix of shops, guesthouses and amusement arcades, both around the hotel and along the busy seafront. Inside, the *Kurhaus* has recently been refurbished and is worth a peek into for its main central hall, which looks much as it would have done in the town's heyday – richly frescoed, with mermaids and semi-clad maidens cavorting high above the gathered diners. You can enjoy the atmosphere for the price of a cup of coffee, or attend one of the classical concerts occasionally held here.

The town **museum** at Neptunusstraat 92 (Tues–Sat 10am–5pm; April–Oct also Mon 10am–5pm; ƒ3.50) recaptures some of the atmosphere of old Scheveningen, with a collection of figures in nineteenth-century costume, dioramas showing the cramped conditions on board the primitive fishing boats, and items such as nets and compasses from the boats themselves. Walk 100m towards the beach for the brand new **Statues on the Sea Museum** (*Beelden aan Zee*) at Harteveltstraat 1 (Tues–Sun 11am–5pm; ƒ6), which comprises a thoughtfully arranged collection of modern sculpture, some of it outdoors on a patio overlooking the sea. Nearby at Strandweg 13, the environment-conscious **Sea-Life Centre** (daily July & Aug 10am–9pm; Sept–June 10am–6pm; ƒ14) should appeal to children, with its aquarium featuring sharks and rays, plus exhibits on North Sea fish and crustaceans.

Most people come here for the **beach** – a marvellous stretch, though very crowded in summer, and it's hard to be sure about the condition of the water. The **pier** isn't especially impressive either, its appendages packed with the rods of fishermen and various amusements, and you're better off strolling a little way north to the emptier stretches of beach and dunes in the **Oostduinpark**. Otherwise, a kilometre or so in the opposite direction, Scheveningen's harbour and fishing port still flourish in the more workaday environs of **Scheveningen Haven**, the site of a large container depot and an early morning **fish auction**, by the more northerly of the two docks at Visafslagweg 1 (Mon–Sat 7–10am), though this is very much a technical, computerized affair. **Boat trips** on the North Sea

---

One of the difficulties involved in getting to Scheveningen is pronouncing the name. During World War II, resistance groups tested suspected Nazi infiltrators by getting them to say "Scheveningen" – an impossible feat for a German-speaker apparently, and not much easier for English-speakers. To get somewhere close to the Dutch pronunciation, try the following: "s-KHAY-ve-ning-uh". The "kh" is pronounced as in the Scottish "loch", the last "n" is dropped, and there's no "sh" sound at all.

(June–Sept daily at 4pm) start from Dr Lelykade, beside the southern dock (tram #8 from The Hague), and fishing trips can be arranged at the same place.

Practicalities

Trams #1, #7 and #9 run from Den Haag CS to Scheveningen, stopping by the *Kurhaus*; from Den Haag HS, take tram #8. Tram #1 also connects with Delft (see below). If you decide to stay in Scheveningen, head for the VVV, just east of the *Kurhaus* in the Palace Promenade at Gevers Deynootweg 1134 (April–June & Sept Mon–Sat 10am–6.30pm, Sun 10am–5pm; July & Aug Mon–Sat 10am–8pm, Sun 10am–5pm; Oct–April Mon–Sat 9am–5.30pm, Sun 10am–5pm; ☎06/340 35051 – 75c/min). They can find you a **room** in a private home; or you can call to make reservations on ☎070/363 5676. Failing that, there are plenty of reasonable **hotels**, such as *Bali*, Badhuisweg 1 (☎070/350 2434, fax 354 0363; ③), or the *Albion*, Gevers Deynootweg 118 (☎070/355 7987, fax 355 5970; ③); there's also a cluster along the seafront Zeekant, on the other side of the *Kurhaus*, including the comfortable *Aquarius* at Zeekant 107 (☎070/354 3684, fax 354 3684; ③) and the *Strandhotel* at no. 111 (☎070/354 0193, fax 354 3558; ③). Scheveningen has two **youth hostels**, the *Scheveningen*, Gevers Deynootweg 2 (☎070/354 7003, ②), and *Marion*, Havenkade 3a (☎070/354 3501; ②).

When it comes to **eating**, the seafront hosts a string of cheap if unexciting places, or there's good Italian food at *La Galleria*, behind the *Kurhaus* at Gevers Deynootplein 120. In Scheveningen Haven, as you'd expect, there are some excellent waterside restaurants with guaranteed fresh fish: try the simple and inexpensive *Haven Restaurant* at Treilerdwarsweg 2 or, round the corner at Dr Lelykade 5, the more upmarket *Ducdalf* (☎070/355 7692). For evening **drinking**, head for the *Kings Arms*, a mock-English pub outside the *Kurhaus* on Gevers Deynootplein. Evening entertainment is limited to an eight-screen **cinema** behind the *Kurhaus*.

Delft

DELFT has considerable charm: gabled red-roofed houses stand beside tree-lined canals, and the pastel colours of the brickwork and bridges give the town a faded, placid tranquillity – a tranquillity that from spring onwards is systematically destroyed by droves of tourists. They arrive in their air-conditioned busloads and descend to congest the narrow streets, buy an overpriced piece of gift pottery, and photograph the spire of the Nieuwe Kerk. And beneath all the tourists, the gift shops and the tearooms, old Delft itself gets increasingly difficult to find.

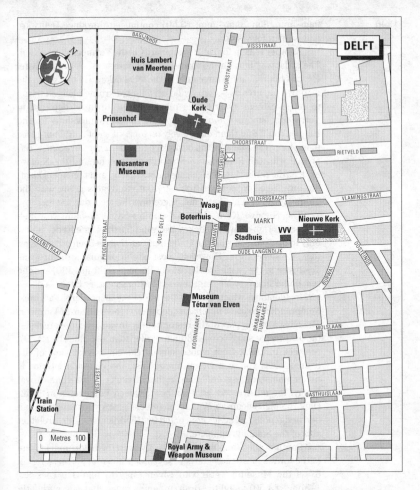

(Map labels)

BAGIJNHOF

VISSSTRAAT

VOORSTRAAT

Huis Lambert
van Meerten

Oude
Kerk

Prinsenhof

CHOORSTRAAT

RIETVELD

Nusantara
Museum

HIPPOLYTUSBUURT

VOLDERSGRACHT

VLAMINGSTRAAT

Waag

OUDE DELFT

Boterhuis

MARKT

Nieuwe Kerk

WIJNHAVEN

Stadhuis

VVV

HAVENSTRAAT

OUDE LANGENDIJK

OOSTEINDE

PHOENIXSTRAAT

Museum
Tétar van Elven

BURWAL

KOORNMARKT

BRABANTSE
TURFMARKT

MOLSLAAN

WESTVEST

GASTHUISLAAN

Train
Station

0   Metres 100

Royal Army &
Weapon Museum

The Town

Why is Delft so popular? Apart from its prettiness, the obvious
answer is **Delftware**, the clunky blue-and-white ceramics to which
the town gave its name in the seventeenth century. If you've already
experienced the vast collection in Amsterdam's Rijksmuseum, it
needs no introduction; and though production of the "real" Delftware
is down to a trickle, cheap mass-produced copies have found a profitable niche in today's shops. For those sufficiently interested, the
Huis Lambert van Meerten Museum at Oude Delft 199 (Tues–Sat
10am–5pm, Sun 1–5pm; ƒ3.50) has the town's best collection of
Delft, and a splendid array of tiles from around the world, while the
factory *De Porceleyne Fles* at Rotterdamsweg 196 (Mon–Sat

Delft

9am–5pm, Sun 10am–5pm; ƒ3.50) continues to produce Delftware and is open for visits.

Another reason for Delft's popularity is the **Vermeer** connection. The artist was born in the town and died here, too – leaving a wife, eleven children, and a huge debt to the local baker. He had given the man two pictures as security, and his wife bankrupted herself trying to retrieve them. Only traces remain of the town as depicted in Vermeer's famous *View of Delft*, now in the Mauritshuis in The Hague. You'll find them most easily on foot – it's not a difficult place to explore. The **Markt** is the best place to start, a central point of reference with the Renaissance Stadhuis at one end and the Nieuwe Kerk at the other. Lined with cafés, restaurants, and teenagers blasting out disco on their ghettoblasters, it really gets going with the Thursday general market – not, therefore, the ideal day to visit.

The **Nieuwe Kerk** (March–Oct Mon–Sat 9am–6pm; Nov–Feb Mon–Sat 11am–4pm; ƒ4, ticket also valid for the Oude Kerk) is new only in comparison with the Oude Kerk, as there's been a church on this site since 1381. However, most of the original structure was destroyed in the great fire that swept through Delft in 1536, and the remainder in a powder magazine explosion a century later – a disaster, incidentally, which claimed the life of the artist Carel Fabritius, Rembrandt's greatest pupil and (debatably) the teacher of Vermeer. The most striking part of the restoration is, in fact, the most recent – the 100-metre spire (closes 30min earlier than the church; ƒ2.50), replaced in 1872, from whose summit there's a great view of the town. Unless you're a Dutch monarchist, the church's interior is rather uninspiring: it contains the burial vaults of the Dutch royal family, the most recent addition being Queen Wilhelmina in 1962. Only the Mausoleum of William the Silent grabs your attention, an odd hodgepodge of styles concocted by Hendrik de Keyser, architect also of the Stadhuis opposite.

South of the Stadhuis, signs direct you to the **Koornmarkt**, one of the town's most characteristic seventeenth-century streets. At no. 67 is the **Museum Tétar van Elven** (May to mid-Oct Tues–Sat 1–5pm; ƒ3.50), slightly drab in appearance but an authentic restoration of the eighteenth-century patrician house that was the studio and home of Paul Tétar van Elven, a provincial and somewhat forgettable artist/collector. From the museum, follow **Wijnhaven**, an old canal, north to reach the stretch of water known as Hippolytusbuurt, at the far end of which is the Gothic **Oude Kerk** (March–Oct Mon–Sat 9am–6pm; Nov–Feb Mon–Sat 11am–4pm; ƒ4, ticket also valid for the Nieuwe Kerk), arguably the town's finest building. Simple and unbuttressed, with an unhealthily leaning tower, it's the result of a succession of churches here from the thirteenth to the seventeenth centuries; the strong and unornamented vaulting proves interiors don't have to be elaborate to avoid being sombre. The pride of the church is its pulpit of 1548, intricately carved with figures emphasized in false perspective, but also notable is the modern stained glass representing the history of the Netherlands – particularly the 1945 liberation – in the north transept. If you're curious about the tombs – including that of Admiral Maarten van Tromp, famed for hoisting a broom at his masthead to "sweep the seas clear of the English" as he sailed up the Medway – take a look at the *Striking Points* pamphlet available at the entrance.

Opposite the Oude Kerk is the former Convent of St Agatha, or the **Prinsenhof** as it came to be known (Tues–Sat 10am–5pm, Sun 1–5pm; June–Aug also Mon 1–5pm; ƒ5). Housing Delft's municipal art collection (a good group of works, including paintings by Aertsen and Honthorst), it has been restored in the style of the late sixteenth century – an era when the building served as the base of **William the Silent** in his Protestant revolt against the Spanish invaders. From here William planned sorties against the Imperial Catholic troops of Phillip II, achieving considerable success with his *Watergeuzen* or sea-beggars, a kind of commando-guerrilla unit that initially operated from England. He met his death here at the hands of a French assassin: the bullets that passed through him, made of three pellets welded into one, left their mark on the Prinsenhof walls and can still be seen. If you have the time, the **Royal Army and Weapon Museum** (Tues–Sat 10am–5pm, Sun 1–5pm; ƒ4.50), near the station at Korte Geer 1, is worth a visit. It has a good display of weaponry, uniforms and military accoutrements – which sounds dull, but isn't, even if you're not an enthusiast. The museum attempts to trace the military history of the Netherlands from the Spanish wars up to the imperialist adventures of the 1950s – which are dealt with in surprisingly candid detail.

Finally, particularly when the crowds are around, bear in mind that the best way to get a feel for old Delft is to get out from the centre a little. Follow the canal east down Oosteinde to the **Oostpoort**, the only surviving city gate, dating from around 1400, and head north from there along the main canal, Rijn Schiekanaal, where the crowds thin out a little.

Practicalities

From the train station it's a short walk into town and the **VVV** at Markt 85 (April–Oct Mon–Fri 9am–6pm, Sat 9am–5pm, Sun 10am–3pm; Nov–March Mon–Fri 9am–5.30pm, Sat 9am–5pm; ☎015/212 6100). The cheapest **accommodation** is in the pensions around the station or the Markt; the VVV have full details. Try *Les Compagnons*, Markt 61 (☎015/214 0102; ③); *'t Raedthuys*, Markt 38 (☎015/212 5115; ③); or *Monopole*, Markt 48 (☎015/212 3059; ③). More upmarket are the canalside *Leeuwenbrug*, Koornmarkt 16 (☎015/214 7741, fax 215 9759; ④), and the very comfortable *De Ark*, Koornmarkt 65 (☎015/215 7999; ⑤). There's a **campsite**, *De*

Delftse Hout, at Kortftlaan 5 (bus #60 from the station), which is open from April to October.

For **eating**, most places around the Markt are a little over-priced, although *Sunrise Pub*, at Markt 66a, is okay for a quick snack. *Grand Café Central*, Wijnhaven 4, is also popular for snacks and fuller meals, and the day-menus at *'t Walletje*, just south of Markt at Burgwal 7, are usually good value. *La Fontanella*, Voldersgracht 8, has decent Italian food from around *f*15, while *V*, at Voorstraat 9, pulls a big student crowd to its large bar and restaurant. *Locus Publicus*, Brabantse Turfmarkt 67, is another popular local hangout, serving a staggering array of beers as well as snacks.

Gouda

A pretty little place some 25km northeast of Rotterdam, **GOUDA** is almost everything you'd expect of a Dutch country town: a ring of quiet canals that encircle ancient buildings and old docks. More surprisingly, its **Markt**, a ten-minute walk from the train station, is the largest in Holland – a reminder of the town's prominence as a centre of the medieval cloth trade, and of its later success in the manufacture of cheeses and clay pipes.

Holland's other major cheese market is held in Alkmaar, detailed in the following chapter.

Gouda's main claim to fame is its **cheese market**, held in the Markt every Thursday morning from June to August. Traditionally, some thousand local farmers brought their home-produced cheeses here to be weighed, tested, and graded for moisture, smell and taste. These details were marked on the cheeses and formed the basis for negotiation between buyer and seller, the exact price set by an elaborate hand-clapping system, which itself was based on trust and memory, for deals were never written down. Today, the cheese market is a shadow of its former self, a couple of locals in traditional dress standing outside the Waag, surrounded by modern open-air stands. The promised mixture of food and tradition is mercilessly milked by tour operators, who herd their victims into this rather dreary scene every week – but don't let this put you off a visit, since Gouda's charms are to be found elsewhere.

There's a **jazz festival** in the town in early September, and if you happen to be in the area in mid-December, it's worth phoning the Gouda VVV to find out exactly when the town will be holding its splendid candlelit pre-Christmas festival. All electric lights are extinguished on the main square, and it's lit by thousands of candles, creating a magical, picture-book atmosphere.

The Town

Slap-bang in the middle of the Markt is the elegant Gothic **Stadhuis**, dating from 1450, its facade fringed by statues of counts and countesses of Burgundy above a tinkling carillon that plays every half-hour. Nearby, on the north side of the square, the **Waag** is a tidy seventeenth-century building, decorated with a detailed relief of cheese weighing; the place has been converted into a cheese museum (April–Oct Tues–Sat 10am–5pm, Sun noon–5pm; free).

To the south, just off the Markt, **St Janskerk** (March–Oct Mon–Sat 9am–5pm; Nov–Feb Mon–Sat 10am–4pm; ƒ3) was built in the sixteenth century and is famous for its magnificent **stained-glass windows**. As well as their intrinsic beauty, the windows show the way religious art changed as Holland switched from being a Catholic-dominated society to a Calvinist one. The biblical-themed windows executed by Dirk and Wouter Crabeth between 1555 and 1571, when Holland was still Catholic, show an amazing clarity of detail and richness of colour. Their last work, *Judith Slaying Holofernes* (window no. 6), is perhaps the finest, the story unfolding in intricate perspective. By comparison, the post-Reformation windows, which date from 1572 to 1603, adopt an allegorical and heraldic style characteristic of more secular art. *The Relief of Leiden* (window no. 25) shows William the Silent retaking the town from the Spanish, though Delft and its burgomasters take prominence – no doubt because they paid the bill for its construction. All the windows are numbered and a detailed guide is available at the entrance for ƒ3.

By the side of the church, the flamboyant **Lazarus Gate** of 1609 was once part of the town's leper hospital, until it was moved here to form the back entrance to the **Catharina Gasthuis**, a hospice until 1910. A likeable conglomeration of sixteenth-century rooms and halls, including an old isolation cell for the insane, the interior of the Gasthuis has been turned into the municipal **Stedelijk Museum** (Mon–Sat 10am–5pm, Sun noon–5pm; ƒ4). The collection incorporates a fine sample of early religious art, notably a large triptych by Dirk Barendsz, *Life of Mary*, and a characteristically austere *Annunciation* by the Bruges artist Pieter Pourbus. Other highlights include a spacious hall, *Het Ruim*, that was once a sort of medieval hostel, but is now dominated by paintings of the civic guard, principally two group portraits by Ferdinand Bol; the intricate silver-gilt *Chalice and Eucharist Dish* was presented to the guard in the early fifteenth century. Two later rooms have a modest selection of Hague and Barbizon School canvases, notably work by Anton Mauve and Charles Daubigny. Downstairs, beside the isolation cell, there is a delightful collection of torture instruments from the old city jail.

Gouda's other museum, **De Moriaan** (Mon–Sat 10am–5pm, Sun noon–5pm; entry with Stedelijk Museum ticket), in a cosy old merchant's house at Westhaven 29, displays a mixed bag of exhibits, from clay pipes to ceramics and tiles. Westhaven itself is a charming jumble of old buildings that head off towards the old tollhouse and a dilapidated mill beside the Hollandse IJssel river, on the southern edge of the town centre. There's a restored, fully operational **grain**

Gouda

mill five minutes' walk west of the Markt, at Vest 65 (Mon–Sat 9am–5pm; *f*1.50).

Practicalities

Gouda's **train** and **bus stations** are to the immediate north of the town centre, ten minutes from the VVV at Markt 27 (Mon–Fri 9am–5pm, Sat 10am–4pm; ☎0182/513666), which has a limited supply of private **rooms**, and will call ahead to make bookings for a small charge. The most reasonably priced **hotel** is the *De Utrechtse Dom*, at Geuzenstraat 6 (☎0182/527984; ②), five minutes' walk to the east of St Janskerk. There are three other, more agreeable hotels in the centre: the *Het Blauwe Kruis*, Westhaven 4 (☎0182/512677; ③); the *De Keizerskroon*, at Keizerstraat 11 (☎0182/528096; ④), to the west of Westhaven; and the *Het Trefpunt*, at Westhaven 46 (☎0182/512879; ④).

For **food**, Gouda has literally dozens of cafés and snack bars catering to the hundreds of tourists who day-trip here throughout the season. *'t Groot Stedelijk*, Markt 44, has a variety of cheap dishes, as does *Café Central*, Markt 26; there are pancakes at *'t Goudse Winkeltje*, Achter de Kerk 9a; pizzas at the *Rimini*, Markt 28; and decent Indonesian food at *Warung Srikandi*, Lange Groenendaal 108. The most popular spot for beer and Dutch food is the excellent *Eetcafé Vidocq*, Koster Gijzensteeg 8 (turn left out of the market past *Café Central*, and take the first turning on the right).

Utrecht

"I groaned with the idea of living all winter in so shocking a place", wrote Boswell in 1763, and UTRECHT still promises little as you approach: surrounded by shopping centres and industrial developments, the town only begins to reveal itself in the old area around the Dom Kerk, roughly enclosed by the Oude and Nieuwe Grachten. These distinctive sunken canals date from the fourteenth century, and their brick cellars, used as warehouses when Utrecht was a river port, have been converted to chic cafés and restaurants. Although the liveliest places in town, they don't disguise Utrecht's provincialism: just half an hour from Amsterdam, all the brashness and vitality of the capital is absent, and it's the museums and churches rather than the nightlife that make the town enjoyable.

Founded by the Romans in the first century AD, the city of Utrecht became the site of a wealthy and powerful medieval bishopric, which controlled the surrounding region under the auspices of the German emperors. In 1527 the bishop sold off his secular rights and shortly afterwards the town council enthusiastically joined the revolt against Spain. Indeed, the agreement that formalized the opposition to the Habsburgs, the **Union of Utrecht**, was signed here

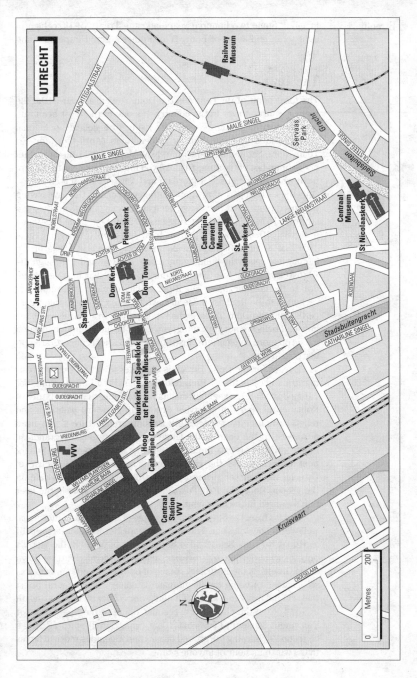

UTRECHT

Railway Museum

MALIE SINGEL

MALIE SINGEL

Servaas Park

LEPELENBURG

NACHTEGAALSTRAAT

NOBELSTRAAT

KORTE DWARSSTRAAT

NIEUWEGRACHT

LANGE NIEUWSTRAAT

St Pieterskerk

DRIFT

ACHTER STR.

ACHTER DE DOM

Catharijne Convent Museum

St Catharijnekerk

JANSKERKHOF

Janskerk

Don Kerk

Dom Tower

Centraal Museum

Stadhuis

OUDEGRACHT

OUDEGRACHT

St Nicolaaskerk

Stadsbuitengracht

CATHARIJNE SINGEL

SPRINGWEG

GEERTEBOL WERK

Buurkerk and Speelklok tot Pierement Museum

Hoog Catharijne Centre

CATHARIJNE BAAN

VREDENBURG

VVV

WILLEMS PLANTSOEN

CATHARIJNE BAAN

CATHARIJNE SINGEL

Centraal Station VVV

Kruisvaart

CROESELAAN

N

0   200
Metres

in 1579. Some two hundred years later the **Treaty of Utrecht** brought to an end some of Louis IV of France's grand imperial ambitions.

The Town

The focal point of the centre is the **Dom Tower**, at over 110m the highest church tower in the country. It's one of the most beautiful, too, its soaring, unbuttressed lines rising to a delicate octagonal lantern added in 1380. Hourly guided tours (April–Oct Mon–Fri 10am–5pm, Sat & Sun noon–5pm; Nov–March Sat 11am–5pm, Sun noon–5pm; last entry 4pm; ƒ4) take you unnervingly near to the top, from where you can see Rotterdam and Amsterdam on a clear day. Only the eastern part of the great cathedral remains, the nave having collapsed (with what must have been an apocalyptic crash) during a storm in 1674. It's worth peering inside (May–Sept Mon–Fri 10am–5pm, Sat 10am–3.30pm, Sun 2–4pm; Oct–April Mon–Fri 11am–4pm, Sat 10am–3.30pm, Sun 2–4pm; free) to get a sense of the hangar-like space the building once had, and to wander through the **Kloostergang**, the fourteenth-century cloisters that link the cathedral to the chapterhouse. The Kloostertuin, or cloister gardens, are reckoned to be the best place in town to listen to the carillon concerts from the Dom Tower, which you can do from a pleasant tea house. If bells are not your thing, you might be lucky enough to catch music on more conventional instruments – classical concerts are regularly held here.

Except for the Dom, Utrecht's churches aren't all that interesting: the oldest is the **St Pieterskerk** (Tues–Fri 11am–4.30pm, Sat 11am–3pm; free), a shabbily maintained building that's a mixture of Romanesque and Gothic styles with twelfth-century paintings and reliefs. You'll come across more striking architecture if you head northwest to the bend in the Oude Gracht, between the grandiose nineteenth-century **Stadhuis** and the huge brick Amsterdam School **post office**. Across the canal from here is the oldest house in Utrecht, the fourteenth-century **Huis Oudaen**, which has a café on the ground floor, the *Proeflokaal*, where you can sample the beer that's brewed in the basement.

Not far from the Stadhuis are a couple of unusual little museums, well worth checking out. The **Museum voor het Kruideniersbedrijf** at Hoogt 8 (Tues–Sat 12.30–4.30pm; free) is possibly the world's only museum devoted to groceries. Also in the vicinity, further down Oude Gracht, is the **Buurkerk**, home of one sister Bertken, who was so ashamed of being the illegitimate daughter of a cathedral priest that she hid away in a small cell here – for 57 years, until her death in 1514. Now the church is a peculiar home to the **Speelklok tot Pierement Museum** (Tues–Sat 10am–5pm, Sun 1–5pm; ƒ7.50), a collection of burping fairground organs and ingenious musical boxes that's worth an hour of anyone's time.

The city's other museums are a little way from the centre. The national collection of ecclesiastical art, the **Catharijne Convent Museum** (Tues–Fri 10am–5pm, Sat & Sun 11am–5pm; ƒ7), ten minutes' walk south of the Dom Kerk at Nieuwe Gracht 63, has a mass of paintings, manuscripts and church ornaments from the ninth century on, brilliantly exhibited in a complex built around the old convent. The excellent collection of paintings includes work by Geertgen tot Sint Jans, Rembrandt, Hals and, best of all, a luminously beautiful *Virgin and Child* by Van Cleve. Part of the convent is the late Gothic St Catherine's church, its radiant white interior enhanced by floral decoration.

Keep walking down along Nieuwe Gracht and you reach Utrecht's other important museum, the **Centraal Museum**, at Agnietenstraat 1 (Tues–Sat 10am–5pm, Sun noon–5pm; ƒ6). Its claim to hold "25,000 curiosities" seems a bit exaggerated, but it does have a good collection of paintings by Utrecht artists of the sixteenth and seventeenth centuries. **Van Scorel** lived in Utrecht in between visits to Rome, and brought north with him the influence of Italian humanism. His paintings, like the vividly individual portraits of the *Jerusalem Brotherhood*, combine High Renaissance style with native Dutch observation. The central figure in white is Van Scorel himself: he made a trip to Jerusalem around 1520, which accounts for his unusually accurate depiction of the city in *Christ's Entry into Jerusalem*. A group of painters influenced by another Italian, Caravaggio, became known as the **Utrecht School**. Paintings such as Honthorst's *The Procuress* adapt his chiaroscuro technique to genre subjects, and develop an erotic content that would itself influence later genre painters like Jan Steen and Gerrit Dou. Even more skilled and realistic is Terbrugghen's *The Calling of St Matthew*, a beautiful balance of gestures dramatizing the tax collector's summoning by Christ to become one of the apostles.

Gerrit Rietveld, the De Stijl designer, was most famous for both his brightly coloured zigzag and geometrical chairs, displayed in the applied art section. Part of the De Stijl philosophy was that the approach could be used in any area of design, though Rietveld's angular furniture is probably better to look at than to sit on. There are more pieces of his furniture outside the town centre in the **Schröderhuis**, Prins Hendriklaan 50 (bus #4 from the train station), which he designed and built in 1924 for one Truus Schröder and her three children (organized tours Wed–Sat 11am–5pm; ƒ9; call first: ☎030/236 2310). This is hailed as one of the most influential pieces of modern architecture in Europe, demonstrating the organic union of lines and rectangles that was the hallmark of the De Stijl movement. The design of the ground floor had to meet the rigours of the building licence, and Rietveld got around the planning restrictions by letting his imagination rip only on the upper floor, the actual living space, designing a completely flexible environment where only the

For more on the De Stijl movement, see "Dutch Art" in Contexts, p.349.

Boat trips

Perhaps the easiest and most pleasant way of seeing Utrecht's museums is by the **Museumboot**. This leaves from the Viebrug (daily on the hour 11am–3pm; ƒ7 one-way, ƒ13 return; tickets give fifty percent discount at the museums), and follows a route spanning Oude Gracht near the main post office, and chugging along to Gaardbrug (for the Speelklok tot Pierement Museum and Dom Tower), to the Centraal Museum, the Railway Museum and the Catharijne Convent Museum. There are also regular **canal trips** through the town, departing hourly from Oude Gracht at the corner of Lange Viestraat and Potterstraat, near the Viebrug (June–Sept Mon, Wed & Fri–Sun 11am–5pm, Tues & Thurs 11am–5pm & 6–9pm; Oct–May daily 11am–5pm; ƒ10; ☎030/272 0111).

---

outer walls are solid – indeed the entire top floor can be subdivided in any way you want by simply sliding the temporary walls.

Back in Utrecht itself, there are two final museums that might detain you. The **Spoorweg (Railway) Museum** at Maliebaanstation (Tues–Sat 10am–5pm, Sun 1–5pm; ƒ11; bus #3 from the station) consists of trains, buses and trams sitting in Utrecht's disused train station: there's not much information, but the attendants are enthusiastic. The **Moluks Historisch Museum**, at Kruisstraat 313 (Tues–Sun 1–5pm; ƒ4.50; bus #11 from the station), has displays on the Moluccans and their integration into Dutch society, as well as exhibitions of Moluccan art.

Practicalities

Utrecht's **train and bus stations** both lead into the Hoog Catharijne shopping centre, on the edge of the city centre; the main VVV office is at Vredenburg 90 (Mon–Fri 9am–6pm, Sat 9am–4pm; ☎06/340 34085 – 50c/min), a seven-minute walk away. Though the city is compact enough to explore on foot, touring the canals, either by boat (see box) or by cycling along the towpaths, adds another dimension to a visit. **Bikes** can be rented from the train station.

The VVV offers the usual help with **accommodation**. Among the cheaper hotels, there's the tiny *Parkhotel*, near the Centraal Museum at Tolsteegsingel 34 (☎030/251 6712, fax 254 0401; ③), and the *Hotel Ouwi*, fifteen minutes' walk northeast of the centre at FC Donderstraat 12 (☎030/271 6303, fax 271 4619; ③). *Hotel Smits*, at Vredenburg 14 (☎030/233 1232, fax 232 8451; ⑦), is the most central place to stay; the small and attractive *Malie* (☎030/231 6424, fax 234 0661; ⑤), east of the centre at Maliestraat 2, is better value if you can afford it. The nearest **youth hostel** is at Rhijnauwenselaan 14 in the town of **Bunnik**, linked to the train station by bus #40 or #41; though a little far out, it's beautifully sited in an old country manor house. You can reach the well-equipped **campsite** at Arienslaan 5 on the #57 bus from the train station.

There are masses of decent places to **eat** along Oude Gracht, both on the street and down by the canal, including the cheap canalside pancake bakery *De Oude Muntkelder* at no. 112, the Italian *Le Connaisseur* at no. 59, the vegetarian *De Werfkring* at no. 123, and the pricier but popular *Tantes Bistro* at no. 61. A little way north from here, near the Janskerk, *Café Zeezicht* at Nobelstraat 2 serves reasonably priced breakfasts, lunches and dinners, with live music on Tuesday nights. And check out the nearby *Grand Café Polman's Huis*, on the corner of Jansdam and Keistraat, if only for its turn-of-the-century interior. Utrecht's media folk hang out at *Café Orloff*, just off Wed, a good place for breakfast or a coffee.

There are several good **bars** around the junction of Oude Gracht and Wed, near the Dom. The noisy *Kafe Belgie* at Oude Gracht 196 serves lots of different beers, or try the friendly *De Witte Ballons* at Lijnmarkt 10. Other good places to drink include *Winkel van Sinkel*, Oude Gracht 158, a large and often crowded bar fronted by caryatids, and *Stadkasteel Oudaen*, Oude Gracht 99, where they brew their own beer and serve good Dutch food. Utrecht's **gay** crowd hangs out at *De Wolkenkrabber*, Oude Gracht 47, which has a disco, *De Roze Wolk*, right underneath. For more sedate entertainment, there are a number of *filmhuizen* showing **alternative movies**, such as *'t Hoogt*, at Hoogt 4.

Chapter 17

North and East of Amsterdam

N orth of Amsterdam, there are more beaches and bulbfields, and in general a more rural atmosphere prevails. Among the towns, **Alkmaar** is perhaps the most renowned, primarily for its cheese market, although its consequent popularity with visitors can be offputting during the busy summer months, when it's often besieged by tour groups. The same goes for the villages on the edge of the IJsselmeer, a short way northeast of the city, where places like **Marken**, **Volendam** and **Edam** sport a self-consciously packaged prettiness that is the epitome of the rather bogus image of Holland manufactured for the tourist. A couple of places southeast of the capital, **Muiden** and **Naarden**, are a fair antidote, each with highly individual – and enjoyable – historical centres, easily combined for a day out. Consider, too, travelling a little further afield, to either **Hoorn** or **Enkhuizen**. Two old Zuider Zee trading ports, both can be reached on a day trip from Amsterdam (they're respectively 40min and 1hr away by train, on the same line); they preserve lovely old centres and quiet, mast-spiked harbours, and Enkhuizen is the home of the impressive **Zuider Zee Museum**, which attempts (fairly successfully)

ACCOMMODATION PRICE CODES

The following codes are used in this chapter to denote the price of the **cheapest double room** available in high season, including breakfast. For **hostel** accommodation (①), the price is per person. Note that low-season prices can drop by as much as two categories and that larger hotels especially often have rooms at various prices.

①	Under ƒ30 per person	⑤	ƒ250–350
②	ƒ60–100	⑥	ƒ350–450
③	ƒ100–170	⑦	over ƒ450
④	ƒ170–250		

For more general accommodation information, see p.165.

to recreate life as it was before the sea was closed off by the barrier dam and the IJsselmeer was created.

Zaandam and Zaanse Schans

Most of the trains heading north out of Amsterdam pass through the build-up of settlements that spreads north from the banks of the IJ and is known as **Zaanstad**. Looking out of the train window, it's arguable that there's no real reason to get off, and you really would not be missing all that much if you didn't. The core of Zaanstad is **ZAANDAM**, a small, largely modern town that was a popular tourist hangout in the nineteenth century, when it was known as "La Chine d'Hollande" for the faintly oriental appearance of its windmills, canals, masts, and row upon row of brightly painted houses. Claude Monet spent some time here in the 1870s, and, despite being suspected of spying and under constant police surveillance, immortalized the place in a series of paintings.

Follow the main street, Gedempte Gracht, from the train station for five minutes (the VVV is at no. 76; Mon–Fri 9am–5.30pm, Sat 9am–4pm; ☎075/616 2221), turn right down Damstraat, right again, and left down Krimp, and you can see something of Monet's Zaandam, the harbour spiked with masts beyond a little grouping of wooden houses. On Krimp itself is the town's main claim to fame, the **Czaar Petershuisje** (Tues–Fri 10am–1pm & 2–5pm, Sat & Sun 1–5pm; ƒ2.50), a house in which the Russian Tsar Peter the Great stayed when he came to study shipbuilding here. In those days Zaandam was an important shipbuilding centre, and the tsar made four visits to the town, the first in 1697 when he arrived incognito and stayed in the simple home of one Gerrit Kist, who had formerly served with him. A tottering wooden structure enclosed within a brick shelter, the house is no more than two rooms really, decorated with a handful of portraits of the benign-looking emperor and the graffiti of tourists going back to the mid-nineteenth century. Among the few things to see is the cupboard bed in which Peter is supposed to have slept, together with the calling cards and pennants of various visiting Russian delegations; around the outside of the house is an exhibition on the shipbuilding industry in Zaandam. As Napoleon is said to have remarked on visiting the house, "Nothing is too small for great men."

Most visitors to Zaanstad are, however, here to visit the recreated Dutch village of **Zaanse Schans** (you can walk round the village at any time, but the mills and exhibitions are open March–Oct Tues–Sun 10am–5pm, Nov–Feb Sat & Sun 10am–5pm; each one ƒ1.50–3.50). The village is made up of houses, windmills and workshops assembled from all over the country, and is an energetic, but ultimately rather phoney attempt to reproduce a Dutch village as it would have looked at the end of the seventeenth century. It's a pret-

**Zaandam
and Zaanse
Schans**

ty enough place, but it gets crammed in summer, and is frankly not worth the effort for its clog-making displays and pseudo-artisans' premises. However, this is the closest place to Amsterdam that you'll get to see windmills, if that's what you're after, some of them still in operation, grinding mustard and producing oil. Among other specific attractions are a clock museum and period room, and you can also take **boat trips** on the Zaan River from just nearby (March–Oct Tues–Sun hourly 10am–5pm; ƒ8). **To get here** from Zaandam, take bus #88; to get to Zaandam from Amsterdam, take bus #92 or #94, or a train to Koog Zaandijk station, from where it's a five- to ten-minute walk – ask at Amsterdam Centraal Station for the all-in *Rail Idee* ticket, which covers the train, a boat cruise, entrance to the museums and refreshments at Zaanse Schans.

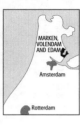

Marken, Volendam and Edam

The majority of visitors heading out of Amsterdam make for the settlements on the banks of the **IJsselmeer** – which is a compelling reason to avoid these places during the high season from June to September, when they can be positively swamped with tourists here to see the locals in their traditional costume. Most of them are dressing up for show, of course, and if you visit at other times of year you're likely to get a much more genuine impression of these long-standing communities, which were founded on fishing but have had to turn to clog-selling to survive.

You can get to the villages directly from Amsterdam by bus. Bus #111 leaves every half-hour from opposite the St Nicolaaskerk for the thirty-minute journey to Marken, passing through **MONNICK-ENDAM** on the way. Monnickendam is a picturesque little village that has retained some sense of its past by way of preserving a large number of old buildings, and it's worth stopping off briefly to stroll around its centre and visit the VVV in the tower of the Grote Kerk (July & Aug Mon–Sat 10am–6pm, Sun 2–5pm; Sept–June Mon–Fri 9.30am–12.30pm & 1.30–5pm, Sat 9.30am–5pm; ☎0299/651998), which has maps and information on both Monnickendam and Marken.

The bus then continues on to **MARKEN**, a popular place that was once an island in the Zuider Zee; until its road connection to the mainland was constructed in 1957, it was largely a closed community, supported by a small fishing industry. At one time its biggest problem was the genetic defects caused by constant intermarrying; now it's how to contain the tourists, whose numbers increase yearly. Marken's distinctness has in many ways been its downfall; its character – or what remains of it – has been artificially preserved: the harbour is still brightly painted in the local colours, and traditional costumes and clogs are worn. Recently a series of eel-smoking houses have been converted into the **Marken Museum** at

Kerkbuurt 44 (April–Oct Mon–Sat 10am–5pm, Sun 1–4pm), devoted to the history of the former island and its fishing industry. Although visitors now supply the income lost when the Zuider Zee was closed off, it turns out to have been a desperate remedy. From Marken, a **ferry** runs to nearby Volendam in summer (April–Oct daily every 30min 10am–5pm; journey time 20min; *f*4.50; information ☎0299/363331); otherwise, you'll have to take bus #111 back to the Bernardbrug on the outskirts of Monnickendam in order to catch bus #110, which runs between Amsterdam and Volendam to the north.

Volendam

VOLENDAM – accessible direct from Amsterdam on bus #110, or by ferry from Marken (see above) – is a larger village than Marken, worth visiting for the scraps of local culture that remain, and for some great views over the uniquely flat and silvery IJsselmeer. For a time, Volendam was something of an artists' retreat: Picasso and Renoir both stayed for a while at the *Hotel Spaander* on the harbourfront, whose bar is suitably crammed with paintings and drawings. These days the harbour serves ferries rather than fishing boats, while the main street, Haven, is lined with tawdry knick-knack stores, but it's still relatively easy to find a quiet spot. One street back from the harbour, follow narrow Meerzijde right to its western end, where there's a nineteenth-century church in the midst of a maze of tiny alleys; look out for the plaque at the corner of Berend Demmerstraat and Josefstraat that marks the height of the floodwaters of 1916. The Volendam VVV (see below) sells a leaflet describing a walk through the old section of the village (*f*1.50). Needless to say, **fish** is the dish of the day here, and you can snack your way along the waterfront fish stands fairly inexpensively. The **Volendam Museum**, next door to the VVV at Zeestraat 37 (daily 10am–5pm; *f*3.50), is eminently missable, its highlight being a local character's collection of eleven million cigar-bands.

Practicalities

Bus #111 from Amsterdam leaves half-hourly from opposite the St Nicolaaskerk near Centraal Station, passing through the outskirts of Monnickendam before reaching Volendam (30min). It drops you on Zeestraat, close to the Volendam Museum and VVV at Zeestraat 37 (April–Sept daily 10am–5pm; Oct–March Mon–Sat 10am–3pm; ☎0299/363747). Walk straight down the road from the bus stop for about 100m and you'll come to the harbour. Should you want to stay, Volendam's three **accommodation** options are all within five minutes' walk along the harbourfront: *Hotel Spaander*, Haven 15 (☎0299/363595, fax 369615; ③), is the most atmospheric by far, and it's worth stopping off for a drink in the bar, even if you don't stay. The two other hotels – the *Lutine*, Haven 80 (☎0299/363234,

**Marken,
Voldendam
and Edam**

fax 362254; ③), and *Van de Hogen*, Haven 106 (☎0299/363775, fax 3369498; ②) – are nothing special. You can rent **bikes** at *Konig*, Edammerweg 26, or *Bien*, Plutostraat 40b, to get to nearby Edam; it's also possible to take the ferry to Marken and then cycle the 14km back to Volendam in time to drop off your bike. All the VVVs in the area sell **cycling maps**.

Edam

Further on down the #110 bus route from Amsterdam, just 3km from Volendam, you might expect **EDAM** to be a nightmare, especially considering its reputation for the red balls of cheese that the Dutch produce for export. In fact, Edam is in many ways one of the most pleasant day trips you can make from Amsterdam, though in high season you'd be advised to suspend any illusions of authenticity. The main draw is the enormous **Grote Kerk** (April–Oct daily 2–4.30pm) on the edge of the fields to the north of the village. This is the largest three-ridged church in Europe, with a huge organ built in 1663, some spectacular stained glass, and a vaulted ceiling constructed in wood in an attempt to limit the subsidence caused by the building's massive weight. Following lightning strikes on the church tower in 1602 and 1699, both of which started extensive town fires, the spire was purposely shortened and now looks almost comically stubby; the elegant tower you can see from all over the village belongs instead to the even older **Speeltoren** of 1561, 100m to the south.

Edam's nominal centre is the tiny square of **Damplein**, with its humpbacked bridge over the Keizersgracht and the village's grandest building, the eighteenth-century **Stadhuis**, which is rather plain from the outside but contains a superabundance of luxuriant stuccowork within. Grote Kerkstraat leads north from Damplein, and the step-gabled brick house near the corner here is Edam's oldest, dating from 1530 and housing the **Captain's House Museum** (April–Oct Mon–Sat 10am–4pm, Sun 2–4pm; *f*10), famous for its floating cellar, allegedly built by a retired captain who could not bear the thought of sleeping on dry land.

Turn left onto Spui and right along Prinsenstraat to reach Kaasmarkt and the sixteenth-century **Kaaswaag**, or cheese-weighing house (April–Oct daily 10am–5pm); it's here that Edam sold its cheese up until 1922, although these days there's just a heavily touristed and utterly phoney **cheese market** every Wednesday in July and August (10am–12.30pm). If this is not your kind of thing, then a short wander down the canals and cobbled lanes will take you out of the crush. Aim for the impossibly skinny Kwakelbrug, due south of the Speeltoren tower, and follow Schepenmakersdijk west along the canal; there are some quaint summerhouse follies constructed in the gardens of former mayors' residences along the canal banks. Edam's VVV, in the Stadhuis (see below), sells a **walking-tour** booklet for *f*3.50.

Practicalities

The half-hourly bus #110 from Amsterdam's St Nicolaaskerk stops
after forty minutes at Edam's nominal bus station, a collection of battered bus shelters to the southwest of the village. Cross the distinctive swing-bridge, turn right and follow Lingerzijde as it jinks left and
right around the base of the Speeltoren, and you'll arrive in Damplein, where the VVV (April–Sept Mon–Sat 10am–5pm; Oct–March
Mon–Sat 10am–12.30pm; ☎0299/371727) can supply you with
information on the town and surrounding area. They also sell lists
(ƒ1) of hotels and **rooms** in private homes; the latter start at around
ƒ30 per person. There are only two **hotels** in Edam itself: the over-
luxurious *Fortuna* at Spuistraat 7 (☎0299/371671, fax 371469;
③), and the much more appealing *Damhotel*, opposite the VVV at
Keizersgracht 1 (☎0299/371766, fax 374031; ③). The nearest
campsite is at Zeevangszeedijk 7 (☎0299/371994): follow the long
canal east from Damplein for about twenty minutes. **Eating and
drinking** opportunities in Edam are surprisingly limited for such a
popular village: the hotels named above are probably your best bet
for either a beer or a full meal, although the *Hof van Holland* and
the *Café Suisse*, both next to the bus station, are possible alternatives. You can rent **bikes** at *Ronald Schot*, very close to the
Speeltoren at Kleine Kerkstraat 9, or from *Tweewielers*, Schepenmakersdijk 6.

Hoorn

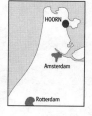

HOORN, the ancient capital of an area known as West Friesland,
"rises from the sea like an enchanted city of the east, with its spires
and its harbour tower beautifully unreal". So wrote the English travel writer E.V. Lucas in 1905, and the town is still very much a place
you should either arrive at or leave by sea – though you probably
won't get the chance to do either. During the seventeenth century
this was one of the richest of the Dutch ports, referred to by the poet
Vondel as the trumpet and capital of the Zuider Zee, handling the
important Baltic trade and that of the Dutch colonies. The Dutch
East India Company was run from here, Tasman left here to "discover" Tasmania and New Zealand, and in 1616 William Schouten sailed
out to navigate a passage around South America, calling its south-
ernmost point "Cape Hoorn" after his native town. The harbour silt-
ed up in the eighteenth century, however, stemming trade and grad-
ually turning Hoorn into one of the so-called "dead cities" of the
Zuider Zee – a process completed with the creation of the IJsselmeer.

The Town

Not surprisingly, Hoorn's former glories are hard to detect in what is
today a quiet provincial backwater: the harbour is a yacht marina,

Hoorn

and the elegant streets and houses, almost entirely surrounded by water, provide only the faintest echoes of the town's balmy seventeenth-century prosperity. At the town centre is **Rode Steen**, literally "Red Stone", an unassuming square that used to hold the town scaffold and now focuses on the swashbuckling statue of **J.P. Coen**, founder of the Dutch East Indies empire and one of the bright lights of the seventeenth century. Coen was a headstrong and determined leader of the Dutch imperial effort, under whom the Far East colonies were consolidated, and rivals like the English fought off. His settling of places such as Molucca and Batavia was something of a personal crusade, and his austere, almost puritanical way of life was in sharp contrast to the wild and unprincipled behaviour of many of his compatriots on the islands.

On one side of Rode Steen stands the early seventeenth-century **Waag**, designed by Hendrik de Keyser and now a smart restaurant. On the other side, and dominating the square, the **Westfries Museum** (Mon–Fri 11am–5pm, Sat & Sun 2–5pm; *f*5) is Hoorn's most prominent sight, housed in the elaborately gabled former West Friesland government building, and decorated with the coats of arms of the house of Orange-Nassau, West Friesland, and the seven major towns of the region. Inside, the museum recreates – convincingly – interiors from the time when Hoorn's power was at its height. Standing out among the various portraits, furniture and ceramics, the walls of the council chamber (room 7) are covered with militia portraits by Jan Rotius, who portrays himself in the painting by the window – he's the figure by the flag on the left – and employs some crafty effects in the other canvases. Walk past the figure in the far right of the central painting and watch his foot change position from left to right as you pass. Upstairs, in room 16, there's a painting from 1632 by Jan van Goyen (*Landscape with a Peasant Cart*) and a wooden fireplace carved with tiny scenes showing a whaling expedition – Hoorn was once a whaling port of some importance. Other items of interest include a view of Hoorn painted in 1622, a room containing portraits of various East India Company dignitaries, including one of the severe Coen, while on the top floor there are mock-ups of workshops and stores of the time, even a prison cell.

Close to the harbour at Bierkade 4, two former cheese warehouses have been converted into the **Museum of the Twentieth Century** (Tues–Sun 10am–5pm; *f*4.50), which houses permanent displays on daily life in this century – not exactly gripping, the main exhibition is supplemented by changing exhibits with titles such as "Travel Posters – A Nostalgic Journey" and "100 Years of Blokker" (*Blokker* is the Dutch equivalent of *Woolworth's*). A six-by five-metre scale model of Hoorn in 1650, and an audiovisual display relating the role of the town in the Dutch Golden Age, are more interesting, though they'll cost you an extra *f*2.50 (there's a combined ticket for *f*6).

There's not all that much of special interest in the rest of Hoorn, but it's a good place to drift around aimlessly, and the old **harbour** and the canals that lead down to it (follow G. Havensteeg from Rode Steen) are very pretty, the waterfront lined with gabled houses looking out to the stolid **Hoofdtoren**, a defensive gateway from 1532. On the other side of Rode Steen, on Kerkstraat, the **Boterhal**, formerly the St Jans Gasthuis, exhibits works by Hoorn artists. It's a delightful building with a trap gable, tapering to a single window and built at an angle to the main body; this too holds a small exhibition of work by local artists.

Practicalities

From Amsterdam, the easiest way to reach Hoorn is by half-hourly train (journey time 40min); coming from Edam, take bus #114 from the bus station (30min). Both leave you at Hoorn's **train station** on the northern edge of town, about ten minutes' walk from the centre. Follow Veemarkt from outside the station to get to the VVV at no. 4, on the left almost at the end of the road (Mon 1–6pm, Tues–Fri 9.30am–6pm, Sat 9.30am–5pm; July & Aug also Thurs 7–9pm; ☎06/340 31055 – 50c/min). There's a **youth hostel** about 2km out from the centre at Schellinkhouterdijk 1a (July & Aug only; ☎0229/214256; ①) – take bus #132, #137 or #147 from the station and get off at the home for stray animals; otherwise, the cheapest **hotels** are *De Posthoorn*, close to the VVV at Breed 27 ((☎0229/214057, fax 270167; ②), *De Magneet*, close to the harbour at Kleine Oost 5 (☎0229/215021, fax 237044; ③), and *Bastion* at Lepelaar 1 (☎0229/249844, fax 249540; ③).

As for **eating**, *Sweet Dreams*, Kerkstraat 1, is a good cheap place for a lunch of Mexican food or omelettes, and couldn't be more central; it stays open until midnight (closed Sun). *Het Witte Paard*, by the Grote Kerk at Lange Kerkstraat 27, serves Dutch and vegetarian dishes daily until 11pm. *De Eethoorn*, at Kerkplein 7, is an inexpensive *eetcafé*, close by a number of reasonable drinking places; it's open daily from 5pm. Other options include the pizza and pasta restaurant *Isola Bella* at Grote Oost 65, five minutes from Rode Steen (closed Mon) and any of a number of bars and restaurants grouped around the harbour.

Medemblik

Hoorn is the starting point of **steam train services** (information ☎0229/214862) to **MEDEMBLIK**, which can make a wonderful day out, especially if you have kids. (Trains run March–June, Sept & Oct Tues–Sun 11.05am; July & Aug Mon & Fri–Sun 11.05am & 2.20pm, Tues–Thurs 11.05am, 12.20pm & 2.20pm; mid-July to mid-Aug also Wed 1.20pm; journey time 1hr; ƒ12.75 one-way, ƒ20.75 return, under-11s ƒ9.50/15.50). Once in Medemblik, take some time to wander around – the town dates from the fourth century, and has a mar-

Hoorn

vellous Gothic church and thirteenth-century **castle** (April–Sept Mon–Sat 10am–5pm, Sun 2–5pm; Oct–March Sun 2–5pm; ƒ3.50), complete with dungeons, dining halls and cellars (information from the Medemblik VVV on ☎0227/542852). From Medemblik, a **ferry** runs to Enkhuizen (March–June, Sept & Oct Tues–Sun 12.30pm; July & Aug Tues–Sun 12.30pm & 4.30pm; journey time 1hr 30min). You can buy a **combination round-trip ticket** in Hoorn that gets you to Medemblik by steam train, then to Enkhuizen by ferry, and back to Hoorn by a regular train (ƒ25, under-11s ƒ18).

Enkhuizen

Another "dead city", though much smaller than Hoorn, **ENKH-UIZEN**, twenty minutes further east by train, was also an important seventeenth-century port, with the largest herring fleet in the country. However, it too declined at the end of the seventeenth century, and the town now offers much the same sort of attractions as Hoorn, retaining its broad mast-spattered harbours and peaceful canals. It also has a genuinely major attraction in the **Zuider Zee Museum**, which brings busloads of tourists up here during the summer to experience what is a very deliberate attempt to capture the lifestyle that existed here when the town was still a flourishing port – and which was destroyed once and for all with the building of the Afsluitdijk. Enkhuizen is also a good place to visit for its summer ferry connections to Stavoren and Urk across the IJsselmeer.

The Town and the Zuider Zee Museum

A few hundred metres from the two main harbours, **Westerstraat** is Enkhuizen's main spine, a busy pedestrianized street that is home to most of the town's shops and restaurants. At one end is the **Westerkerk**, an early fifteenth-century Gothic church with an odd wooden belfry, added in 1519. A right turn from here leads into a residential part of town: very pretty, with its canals crossed by white-painted footbridges. The other end of Westerstraat is marginally more monumental, zeroing in on the mid-sixteenth-century **Waag** on Kaasmarkt, which houses the **Stedelijk Waagmuseum** of local odds and ends (currently being renovated, but previously open April–Oct Tues–Fri 11am–5pm, Sat & Sun 2–5pm). Nearby is the solid, classically styled mid-seventeenth-century **Stadhuis** – behind which the dangerously leaning **Gevangenis** was once the town prison. This is closed to the public, but a peek through its barred windows gives some idea of the bleakness of conditions for the average prisoner 300 years ago, most of the main furnishings still being in place.

Close by here, along the waterfront at Wierdijk 18, the indoor section of the Zuider Zee Museum, the **Binnenmuseum** (closed until May 1998, but previously open daily 10am–5pm; ƒ5, under-12s ƒ4 –

see Buitenmuseum, below, for combined tickets), has a collection of fishing vessels and equipment, and Zuider Zee arts and crafts, recently spruced up and displayed in bright new surroundings. Exhibits include regional costumes and painted furniture from Hindeloopen, an ice-cutting boat from Urk that was once charged with the responsibility of keeping the shipping lanes open between the island and the port of Kampen, displays of sail- and rope-making implements, and much else besides.

Most people, however, give the Binnenmuseum a miss and instead make straight for the **Buitenmuseum** on the far side of the harbour (April–Oct daily 10am–5pm; ƒ15, under-12s ƒ10; tickets, which cover the compulsory boat ride and entry to both Zuider Zee museums, are sold at the VVV and the free museum car park at the end of the Lelystad road). Buildings from 39 different locations have been transplanted here, recreating various towns and villages in a period portrayal of the vanished way of life around the Zuider Zee. The only way to **get there** is by the museum's own dedicated boat service, either from the train station or, if you're driving, from the museum parking area. Once there, you can either tour the museum by way of the free hourly guided tours, or – rather nicer – simply wander around taking it all in at your own pace.

Close by the ferry wharf there's a series of lime kilns, conspicuous by their tall chimneys, from where a path takes you through the best of the museum's many intriguing corners, beginning with a row of cottages from Monnickendam, close to the information centre. A number of streets lined with cottages lead off from here in a mock-up of a typical Zuider Zee fishing village, with examples of buildings from Urk among other places, their modest, precisely furnished interiors open to visitors and sometimes peopled by characters in traditional dress hamming it up for the tourists. Further on, a number of buildings sit along and around a central canal. There's a post office from Den Oever, a grocery from Harderwijk, an old laundry, thick with the smell of washing, a pharmacy and a bakery from Hoorn, the latter selling pastries and chocolate, while a cottage from Hindeloopen doubles up as a restaurant. It all sounds rather kitsch, and in a way it is: there are regular demonstrations of the old ways and crafts, goats and sheep roam the stretches of meadow, and the exhibition is mounted in such an earnest way as almost to beg criticism. But the attention to detail is very impressive, and the whole thing is never overdone, with the result that many parts of the museum are genuinely picturesque. If you see nothing else in Enkhuizen (and many people don't), you really shouldn't miss it.

Practicalities

Trains to Enkhuizen – the end of the line – stop right on the corner of the Buiten Haven harbour, in between the **ferry wharves** and the **bus station**. There's a VVV office just outside the train station at

Tussen Twee Havens 1 (April–June, Sept & Oct daily 9am–5pm; July & Aug Mon–Sat 9am–6pm, Sun 9am–5pm; Nov–March Mon–Fri 9am–5pm, Sat 9am–2pm; ☎0228/313164), which opens at 8.15am in summer to sell ferry tickets (see below). From here, follow the edge of the small harbour round, turn left onto Spoorstraat, go over the bridge and continue to where Spoorstraat crosses the main shopping street of Westerstraat.

For **accommodation**, the wonderful circular dormitory in the Drommedaris Tower (open year-round from 2pm; ☎0228/312076; ①), a student house on Paktuinen in the outer harbour, offers what are probably the cheapest beds in Holland. If you prefer to sleep in privacy, the cheapest hotel is the *Het Wapen* at Breedstraat 59 (☎0228/313434, fax 320020; ②), conveniently close to the Zuider Zee museums and the harbours. Another inexpensive option is *Villa Oud Enkhuizen*, at Westerstraat 217 (☎0228/314266, fax 318171; ③). There are two **campsites** handily located on the northern side of town: closest is the *Enkhuizer Zand* on the far side of the Zuider Zee Museum at Kooizandweg 4 (☎0228/317289); to get to the other, *De Vest* (☎0228/321221), follow Vijzelstraat north off Westerstraat, continue down Noorderweg, and turn left by the old town ramparts. Both sites are open April to September only.

Restaurants in Enkhuizen tend on the whole to be expensive. *Desimir*, at Spoorstraat 12, serves relatively cheap Balkan-style food; *Markerwaard*, Dijk 62, is a good Dutch restaurant; and you can get reasonable pizza and pasta at *Marco Polod*, Melkmarkt 4. The *Café Drommedaris*, in the Drommedaris Tower, serves well-priced food for lunch and dinner.

In summer you can travel on from Enkhuizen **by ferry** to the peaceful village of Medemblik to the north, and to Stavoren and Urk, on the other side of the IJsselmeer; when there was still access to the open sea, all three were fishing ports, but these days they're only worth visiting for a glimpse of provincial Dutch life. Ferries leave from behind the train station, and you can buy tickets from the VVV at the station. Ferries **to Stavoren** run roughly three times daily (information ☎020/626 2466), and there are twice-daily services **to Medemblik** (☎0229/219231); boats only run **to Urk** in July and August (3 daily Mon–Sat; ☎0527/683407). Prices range from ƒ16 to ƒ20 return, plus an extra ƒ9.50 to take a bike.

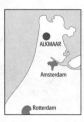

Alkmaar

An hour from Amsterdam by train, **ALKMAAR** is typical of small-town Holland, its pretty, partially canalized centre surrounded by water and offering a low-key, undemanding provincialism that makes a pleasant change after the rigours of the big city. It's also a good base for exploring the nearby dunes and beaches, or even the towns of West Friesland. Alkmaar is probably best known for its **cheese**

market, an ancient affair that these days ranks as one of the most
extravagant tourist spectacles in Holland. Cheese has been sold on
the main square here since the 1300s, and although no serious buying goes on here now, it's an institution that continues to draw
crowds – though nowadays they're primarily tourists. If you do want
to see it (it's held every Friday morning, mid-April to mid-Sept), be
sure to get there early, as by the 10am opening the crowds are
already thick. The ceremony starts with the buyers sniffing, crumbling, and finally tasting each cheese, followed by heated bartering.
Once a deal has been concluded, the cheeses – golden discs of Gouda
mainly, laid out in rows and piles on the square – are borne away on
ornamental carriers by four groups of porters for weighing.
Payment, tradition has it, takes place in the cafés around the square.

The Town

Even if you've only come for the cheese market, it's worth seeing
something of the rest of the town before you leave. On the main
square, the **Waag** was originally a chapel dedicated to the Holy
Spirit, but was converted, and given its magnificent east gable, shortly after the town's famous victory against the Spanish in 1573, when
its citizens withstood a long siege by Frederick of Toledo – a victory
that marked the beginning of the end for the Spaniards. Nowadays
the Waag houses the VVV (see below) and the **Kaasmuseum**
(April–Oct Mon–Thurs & Sat 10am–4pm, Fri 9am–4pm; ƒ3), with
displays on the history of cheese, cheese-making equipment and
suchlike. Across the other side of the square, the **Biermuseum de
Boom**, housed in the old De Boom brewery at Houttil 1 (April–Oct
Tues–Sat 10am–4pm, Sun 1–4pm; Nov–March Tues–Sun 1–4pm;
ƒ3), has displays tracing the brewing process from the malting to
bottling stage, aided by authentic props from this and other breweries the world over. There's lots of technical equipment, enlivened
by mannekins and empty bottles from once innumerable Dutch
brewers – though few, curiously, from De Boom itself. It's an engaging little museum, lovingly put together by enthusiasts, and there's a
shop upstairs where you can buy a huge range of beers and associated merchandise, as well as a downstairs bar serving some eighty
varieties of Dutch beer.

The **Stedelijk Museum**, a couple of minutes west of the Waag on
Doelenstraat (Tues–Fri 10am–5pm, Sat & Sun 1–5pm; ƒ3), displays
pictures and plans of the siege of 1573, along with a *Holy Family* by
Honthorst and portraits by Maerten van Heemskerk and Caesar van
Everdingen, the last a local and very minor seventeenth-century fig-
ure who worked in the Mannerist style of the Haarlem painters. Five
minutes south along Doelenstraat you'll spot the **St Laurenskerk**, a
Gothic church of the later fifteenth century that's worth looking into
for its huge organ, commissioned at the suggestion of Constantijn
Huygens by Maria Tesselschade, local resident and friend of the

Golden Age elite. The case was designed by Jacob van Campen and painted by Caesar van Everdingen. In the apse is the tomb of Count Floris V, penultimate in the line of medieval counts of North Holland, who did much to establish the independence of the towns hereabouts and was murdered by nobles in 1296. Alkmaar's main shopping street, **Langestraat**, leads east from here; partway along is the street's only notable building, the **Stadhuis**, a florid affair, half of which (the eastern side and tower) dates from the early sixteenth century.

Practicalities

Alkmaar's **train station** is on Stationsstraat, about fifteen minutes' walk west of the centre of town; to get to the centre, turn right outside the station, then left at the traffic lights, and follow the road for ten minutes or so, across the water, to the St Laurenskerk. The VVV is five minutes away from here, housed in the Waag on Waagplein (Mon–Wed 9am–5.30pm, Thurs–Sat 9am–6pm; ☎072/511 4284). They have plenty of **private rooms** for about ƒ28 per person, including breakfast; failing that, *De Nachtegaal* is the cheapest and most central hotel, opposite the town hall at Langestraat 100 (☎072/511 2894, no fax; ②); or try *Henry's*, Houttil 34 (☎072/511 3283; no fax; ②). *Motel Stad en Land* is a slightly more expensive option, still in the centre, at Stationsweg 92 (☎072/512 3911, fax 511 8440; ③). If you're **camping**, there are two sites in the area: *Camping Alkmaar* (☎072/511 6924; May–Sept) is ten minutes' bus ride northwest of the town centre at Bergenweg 201 – take bus #168 or #169 from the train station. *Camping Molengroet*, Molengroet 1 (☎0226/393444), is beautifully situated on the edge of a lake outside town, but it's unreachable on public transport – ask the VVV for details.

There are quite a few decent places to **eat** in Alkmaar. *Jelle's Eethuisje*, between Laat and Oude Gracht at Ridderstraat 24, is good for light lunches and cheap evening meals. *Ikan Mas*, one of several restaurants in the old part of town at Fnidsen 101–103, is a decent Indonesian that does a reasonable *rijsttafel*, while *Rose's Cantina*, two doors down, serves Tex-Mex dishes. *Eetcafé Vestibule*, Ritsevoort 12, has cheap and basic dishes, and *'t Gulden Vlies*, Koorstraat 30, is a recommended grand café. *Porto Fino*, close to the Waag at Mient 5, is a small and simple Italian place. **Drinking**, too, is well catered for. There are two groups of bars, one on Waagplein, the other on the nearby canal of Verdronkenoord, by the old Vismarkt. Among the former, *De Kaasbeurs*, Houttil 30, is a lively place during the day but closes in the early evening; *Café Corridor*, virtually next door, plays loud music late into the night and has a small dance floor at the back. *Proeflokaal 't Apothekertje*, a few doors down, is a quieter, old-style bar, open until 2am. On Verdronkenoord, *De Pilaren* is another noisy place, though catering to a slightly older crowd; take refuge in the *Café Stapper*, next door, if the music gets too much. Tucked away in the alleys of the old part of town is the dark and dingy *Odeon* bar, at Hekelstraat 19, which has a pool table in the back.

If you just want to have a quick look around Alkmaar after the cheese market, in summer you can take a 45-minute **boat trip** around the town (information ☎072/511 7750), departing from Mient, near the Waag (during the cheese market on Fri every 20min from 9.30am; otherwise May–Aug daily on the hour 11am–6pm; April, Sept & Oct Mon–Sat only; 45min; ƒ6).

Around Alkmaar – and points north

The seashore close to Alkmaar is the area's best feature and, if the weather is warm, it's a good place to cool off after the crush of the cheese market. Bus #168 leaves Alkmaar station every fifteen minutes for the ten-minute ride to **BERGEN**, a cheerful village that has been something of a retreat for artists since the Expressionist Bergen School worked here early this century. There are a number of galleries around the village, including the **KCB** gallery (Tues–Sat 11am–5pm, Sun 2–5pm; ƒ2.50), next door to the VVV at Plein 7, which holds regular exhibitions of work by contemporary Bergen artists; a small collection of older work is held in the **Sterkenhuis Museum** on Oude Prinsweg (May, June & Sept Tues–Sat 10am–noon & 3–5pm; July & Aug Tues–Sat 10am–noon, 3–5pm & 7–9pm; ƒ3), which also contains documentation on the defeat of the Duke of York here in 1799, along with period rooms and old costumes.

There's a permanent exhibition of Bergen School paintings on display at the **Smithuizen Museum**, Stationsweg 83 (Jan–Oct Fri–Sun 2–6pm; Nov & Dec Fri & Sat 2–6pm; free), in **HEILOO**, just ten minutes south of Alkmaar on bus #166 (hourly) or #176 (every 30min) from the train station. Heiloo is also important for bulbs, and has a summer exhibition of flowers and plants in its **Hortus Bulborum** – fair compensation if you missed the Keukenhof. If you're particularly interested in bulbs, you can visit a museum devoted to their cultivation, south of the town at Dusseldorpweg 64 in **LIMMEN**, which has exhibits on two centuries of bulb-growing in Holland (mid-April to mid-Sept Mon & Tues 9am–noon & 2–5pm, Fri 9am–noon; free). Bus #176 runs every half-hour from Alkmaar through Heiloo (Stationsweg stop) and on to Limmen.

From Alkmaar and Bergen, hourly bus #168 runs on to **BERGEN-AAN-ZEE**, a bleak place in itself but with access to some strikingly untouched dunes and beach. It also has an **aquarium** (daily 10am–6pm) crammed full of marine life, useful if the weather turns or you have kids in tow. About 3km to the south, **EGMOND-AAN-ZEE** (accessible from Alkmaar or Bergen-aan-Zee by hourly bus #165) is a little larger but not much more attractive, though it also boasts huge expanses of sand. A short way inland across the dunes, in **EGMOND-AAN-DE-HOEF**, you can see the remains of the castle of the counts of North Holland, destroyed in 1574. Egmond is also an entry point for the **Noordhollands Duinreservaat**, an area of woods and dunes that stretches south for 15km or more beyond Castricum and holds a couple of campsites and any number of cycle paths, not to mention a superb beach.

The coast north of Bergen, between **Camperduin** and **Petten**, has no dunes, and the sea is kept at bay by means of a four-and-a-half-kilometre-long **dike** – something you can learn more about at the **"de dijk te kijk"** (the dike on show) exhibition at Strandweg 4 just outside Petten (and signposted from the village), where there are old maps, photos and drawings illustrating the building of the defence (April, May & Oct Sat & Sun 2–5pm; June–Sept daily 10am–5pm; free).

Muiden and Naarden

MUIDEN (pronounced "mao-dun"), just 13km east of Amsterdam by bus, is squashed around the Vecht, a river usually crammed with pleasure boats and dinghies sailing out to the IJmeer and the IJsselmeer beyond. It's the most famous sailing harbour in this marshy area known as "Het Gooi", not least because the royal yacht *De Groene Draek* is often moored here. As well as the harbour there are two beaches on the IJmeer here, **Muiderberg** and **Muiderzand**. Although most of the sightseeing that's done here consists of weekend admirals eyeing up each other's boats, the **Rijksmuseum Muiderslot** at Herengracht 1 (April–Oct Mon–Fri 10am–4pm, Sat & Sun 1–4pm; Nov–March Sat & Sun 1–3pm; guided tours only – call ahead to arrange one in English ☎0294/261325; ƒ7.50) provides an extra spark of interest. In the thirteenth century this was the home of Count Floris V, a sort of aristocratic Robin Hood who favoured the common people at the nobles' expense. They responded by kidnapping the count, imprisoning him in his own castle and stabbing him to death. Destroyed and rebuilt in the fourteenth century, Muiderslot's interior these days recreates the period of a more recent occupant, the poet Pieter Hooft. He was chatelain here from 1609 to 1647, a sinecure that allowed him to entertain a group of artistic and literary friends, including Grotius, Vondel, Huygens, and other Amsterdam intellectuals, who became known as the Muiden Circle. The obligatory guided tours centre on this clique, recreating the period in a way that's both believable and likeable.

From the jetty outside the Muiderslot, boats depart regularly for the imposing fortress-island of **Pampus** (April–Oct Tues–Sun 10am–5pm; ☎0294/262326; ƒ17.50, including entry to fortress), a couple of kilometres out to sea. It was built at the end of the nineteenth century as part of Amsterdam's defence system, but has now fallen into ruin.

Naarden

Take a look at a postcard of **NAARDEN**, about 10km east of Muiden, and it seems as if the town was formed by a giant pastry cutter: the double rings of ramparts and moats, unique in northern Europe, were engineered between 1675 and 1685 to defend Naarden and the eastern approach to Amsterdam. They were still in use as recently as the 1920s, and one of the fortified spurs is now the wonderfully explorable **Vestingmuseum** (Fortification Museum) at Westvalstraat 6 (April–Oct Tues–Fri 10am–5pm, Sat & Sun noon–5pm; June–Aug also Mon 10.30am–5pm; Nov–March Sun noon–4pm – phone for Christmas hours ☎035/694 5459; ƒ7.50, under-16s ƒ5). The museum is partly underground and its claustrophobic passages demonstrate how the garrison defended the town for 250 years. For ƒ4 you can take a boat trip around the fortress.

The rest of Naarden's tiny centre is peaceful and attractive. The small, low houses mostly date from after 1572, when the Spanish sacked the town and massacred the inhabitants, an act designed to warn other settlements in the area against insurrection. Fortunately they spared the late Gothic **Grote Kerk** (June to mid-Sept daily 2–4pm) and its superb vault paintings. Based on drawings by Dürer, these twenty wooden panels were painted between 1510 and 1518 and show an Old Testament story on the south side, paralleled by one from the New Testament on the north. To study the paintings without breaking your neck, borrow a mirror at the church's entrance. The church is also noted for its wonderful acoustics and every year hosts several acclaimed performances of Bach's *St Matthew Passion* in the days leading up to Easter (call the VVV for details). A haul up the Grote Kerk's square **tower** (hourly tours May–Aug Wed–Sat 1–4pm; Sept Wed–Sat 2 & 3pm; ƒ5) gives the best view of the fortress island and, less attractively, the TV tower in Hilversum. The elaborately step-gabled building opposite the church is the **Stadhuis**, built in 1601 and still in use today; if the door's open, you're free to wander round inside.

Naarden is best-known, however, for the relatively low-key **Comenius Museum** at Kloosterstraat 33 (April–Oct Tues–Sat 10am–5pm, Sun noon–5pm; Nov–March Tues–Sun 2–5pm; ƒ2.50). Jan Amos Komenski, known as Comenius, was a seventeenth-century philosopher, cartographer and educational reformer. Born in Moravia (today part of the Czech Republic), he spent much of his life travelling across Europe as a religious exile before finally settling in Amsterdam in 1656 – at the time, much of his writing was far too radical to be published anywhere else. After his death in 1670, for some unexplained reason he was buried 25km away in Naarden. Comenius is well known in the Czech and Slovak republics as a groundbreaking educational theorist – he created the first ever picture book for children and Bratislava's university is dedicated to his memory – and today half the visitors to the museum are Czech and Slovak tourists.

The museum itself is interesting enough, with good exhibits relating Comenius's work to the better-known philosophers of the time (such as Descartes), but you may find it all a little overpowering.

Just next door, with access from the museum, is Comenius's **Mausoleum**, the last remnant of a medieval convent dating from 1438. In the 1930s the Dutch authorities refused the Czechoslovak government's request for the repatriation of the philosopher's remains, and instead sold the building and the land it stands on to them for the symbolic price of one guilder; the mausoleum remains a tiny slice of Czech territory in Holland.

Practicalities

The only way to get to Muiden and Naarden is by *Midnet* bus #136 to Hilversum, which leaves Amsterdam (Weesperplein and Amstel Station) every half-hour and passes through Muiden (after 40min), Muiderberg (45min) and Naarden (55min). Be warned, though, that once you break free of the Amsterdam suburbs signposts are few and far between and you can easily sail past Muiden and Muiderberg without noticing – ask the driver to drop you off in the right place. In **Muiden**, the bus stops at the edge of the village, where there are signposts to the Muiderslot castle and the VVV, at Kazernestraat 10 (April–Sept Mon–Fri 10am–5pm, Sat 10am–2pm; ☎0294/261389), which has information on renting watersports equipment. If you fancy pottering around in **boats**, the *Muiden Jachtverhuur Station* (MYCS), Naarderstraat 10 (☎0294/261413), rents out sailboats. As far as eating and drinking goes, there are a couple of obvious places in the village, but you'll find a far better choice in Naarden.

In **Naarden**, the bus drops you within sight of the Grote Kerk's tower. The village is so tiny and signposts so plentiful that you'll have no trouble finding any of the museums, or the VVV, about ten minutes' walk away at Adriaan Dortsmanplein (May–Sept Mon–Fri 9.15am–5pm, Sat 10am–4pm, Sun noon–4pm; Oct–April Mon–Fri 10.30am–2pm, Sat 10am–2pm; in winter you can get information from the post office next door when the VVV is closed; ☎035/694 2836). From the bus stop, follow Cattenhagestraat to the main shopping street of Marktstraat and you'll find plenty of **eating and drinking** opportunities: there's a nice little place for a beer and a snack – *Café Demmers* – at Marktstraat 52, right opposite the more fancy *Salon de Thé Sans Doute*. Next door to the Grote Kerk is the dark-wood *Café Petit Restaurant De Doelen* at Marktstraat 7, perfect for an inexpensive meal, and round the other side of the church you'll find the more upmarket *Gooische Brasserie*, with a tiny terrace overlooking the tower. For a little variety, check out the Chinese-Indonesian *Good Dates* at Cattenhagestraat 34, or, if you feel like a splurge, follow the signs to the *Het Arsenaal*, in the town's old weapons store dating from 1688, where a French-Dutch meal will set you back around *f*70 a head. There's a small **market** outside the VVV on Saturdays from 8am to 2pm.

From Naarden, bus #136 winds through the stockbroker-belt towns of Bussum, Blaricum, Huizen and Laren, where there are more signs of wealth than you'll ever see in understated Amsterdam – but not much reason to get off the bus. Regular trains from both Bussum (15min beyond Naarden) and Hilversum (45min further) take you back to Amsterdam Centraal Station.

Muiden and
Naarden

The Contexts

A History of Amsterdam

To a great extent, a history of Amsterdam is a history of the whole of the Netherlands. The city has been at the centre of national events since its sixteenth-century ascendancy: it was the most glorious cultural and trading centre throughout the Golden Age, and, despite a brief downturn in the eighteenth century, has grown in stature in the last few decades, gaining notoriety for its progressiveness during the 1960s and 70s, and more recently increasing credibility as a centre for commerce and business once more.

The Earliest Years

Amsterdam's earliest history is as murky as the marshes from which it arose. A settlement first appeared here in the eleventh century, founded along with a number of other small towns on the barely populated coast. Previously, this stretch of peat bogs and marshes had been uninhabitable, and it was only when the level of the sea fell and floods became less frequent that colonies sprang up, settling on the higher ground of river banks and dams for protection against the floods.

As its name suggests, Amsterdam was founded on a dam on the River Amstel, and the first mention of the settlement comes in a toll privilege charter granted by Count Floris V in 1275 (a document that can be seen in the city archives). By this time Haarlem, Delft and Leiden were already established; Amsterdam itself began to flourish in 1323, when the Count of Holland designated the small town as a toll port for beer imported from Hamburg. Amsterdam soon became an important transit port for grain and a trading force within the Baltic.

As the city grew, its **market** diversified. English wool was imported, made into cloth in Leiden and Haarlem and exported via Amsterdam; the cloth trade drew workers into the town to work along Warmoesstraat and the Amstel, and ships were able to sail right up to Dam Square to pick up the finished work and drop off imported wood, fish, salt and spices.

Though the city's **population** rose steadily throughout the sixteenth century to around 12,000, Amsterdam was relatively small compared to Antwerp or London: building on the waterlogged soil was difficult and slow, requiring timber piles to be driven into the firmer sand below. And with the extensive use of timber and thatch, fires were a frequent occurrence. A particularly disastrous blaze in 1452 resulted in such destruction that the city council made building with slate and stone obligatory – one of the few wooden houses that survived the fire still stands today at the entrance to the Begijnhof. In the mid-sixteenth century the city underwent its first expansion, as burgeoning trade with the Hanseatic towns of the Baltic made the city second only to Antwerp as a marketplace and warehouse for northern and western Europe. The trade in cloth, grain, gems and wine brought craftspeople to the city, and its merchant fleet grew: by the 1550s three-quarters of all grain cargo out of the Baltic was carried in Amsterdam vessels. The foundations were being laid for the supreme wealth of the Golden Age.

The Rise of Protestantism

At the beginning of the sixteenth century the superstition and elaborate ritual of the established **Church** found itself under attack throughout northern Europe. Erasmus of Rotterdam advanced the concept of an idealized human, seeing man as the crowning of creation rather than the sinful creature of The Fall. In 1517 Martin Luther produced his 95 theses against the church practice of indulgences; his writings and Bible translations were printed in the Netherlands. But it was Calvin (who differed from Luther in his views on the roles of Church and State) who gained the most popularity in Amsterdam. In 1535 the **Anabaptists**, an early Protestant movement, rioted, occupying Amsterdam's town hall and calling on passers-by to repent. Previously the town had accepted the Anabaptists, but it acted swiftly when civic rule was challenged: the town hall was besieged and the surviving Anabaptists executed on Dam Square. Afterwards, an atmosphere of anti-Protestant repression temporarily prevailed.

Around this time, the fanatically Catholic **Philip II** succeeded to the Spanish throne. Through a series of marriages the Spanish monarchy had come to rule over the Low Countries, and Philip was determined to rid the Netherlands of the heresy of Protestantism. He came face to face with a rapidly spreading Calvinist movement, and in 1564 Amsterdam Calvinists voiced complaints about nepotism in the city administration to Margaret of Palma, Philip's sister and regent of the Low Countries. Their protests were acknowledged, thus reinforcing the power of the Protestant movement, which was by now gaining favour among Amsterdam nobles, too. In 1565 a winter crop failure caused a famine among mainly Calvinist workers and roused discontent against Catholic Spain and Philip's anti-Protestant edicts. Later that year, a wave of **iconoclasm** swept the country: in Amsterdam, Calvinist mobs ran riot in the churches, stripping them of their treasures and their rich decoration; only when promised the Franciscan church for worship were they mollified. Many churches, particularly in North Holland, were never restored, leaving them with the plain whitewashed interiors still seen today. The ferocity of the outbreak shocked the nobility into renewed support for Spain; most of the radical Protestant leaders saw what was coming and quietly slipped away abroad.

War with Spain

Philip's answer to the iconoclasm was to send in an army of 10,000 men, led by the **Duke of Alva**, to suppress the heresy absolutely; the duke's first act was to condemn to death 12,000 of those who had taken part in the rebellion the previous

year. **William the Silent**, an apostate prince of the House of Orange-Nassau and the country's largest landowner, organized the Protestant revolt against Spanish rule, taking the cities of Delft, Haarlem and Leiden from Alva's troops. Amsterdam, however, prudently remained on the side of the stronger force until it became clear that William was winning – and his forces had surrounded the town. After the fall of Amsterdam the Catholic clergy was expelled and Catholic churches and monasteries were handed over for Protestant use.

In 1579 the seven Dutch provinces signed the Union of Utrecht, bringing about the formation of the **United Provinces**, an alliance against Spain that was the first consolidation of the northern Low Countries into an identifiable country. The Utrecht agreement stipulated **freedom of religious belief**, ensuring that anti-Spanish sentiment wasn't translated into divisive anti-Catholicism. Though this tolerant measure didn't extend to freedom of worship, a blind eye was turned to the celebration of Mass if it was done privately and inconspicuously – a move that gave rise to "clandestine" Catholic churches like that of the **Amstelkring** on Oudezijds Voorburgwal, today a museum.

With the revolt against Spain concluded, Amsterdam was free to carry on with what it did best – trading and making money.

The Golden Age

The brilliance of Amsterdam's explosion onto the European scene is as difficult to underestimate as it is to detail. The size of its **merchant fleet** carrying Baltic grain into Europe had long been considerable. Even the determined Spaniards had been unable to undermine Dutch **maritime superiority**, and, following the effective removal of Antwerp as a competitor, Amsterdam became the emporium for the products of northern and southern Europe and the new colonies in the West Indies. The city didn't prosper from its market alone, though; Amsterdam ships also carried the produce, a cargo trade that greatly increased the city's wealth.

Dutch **banking and investment** brought further prosperity, and by the mid-seventeenth century Amsterdam's wealth was spectacular. The Calvinist bourgeoisie indulged themselves in fine and whimsically decorated canal houses, and commissioned images of themselves in group portraits. Civic pride knew no bounds as great monuments to self-aggrandizement, such as the new **Town Hall**, were hastily erected, and, if some went hungry, few starved, as the poor were cared for in municipal almshouses.

The arts flourished and **religious tolerance** extended even to the traditional scapegoats, the Jews, and in particular the Sephardic Jews, who had been hounded from Spain by the Inquisition but were guaranteed freedom from religious persecution under the terms of the Union of Utrecht. The Jews brought with them their skills in the gem trade, and by the end of the eighteenth century they accounted for ten percent of the city's population. Guilds and craft associations thrived, and in the first half of the century Amsterdam's population increased fourfold. Agricultural workers were drawn to the city by the better wages offered in Dutch industry, along with Huguenot refugees from France and Protestants escaping persecution in the still-Catholic south.

To accommodate its growing populace, Amsterdam **expanded** several times during the seventeenth century. The grandest and most elaborate plan to enlarge the city was begun in 1613, with the building of the western stretches of the **Herengracht**, **Keizersgracht** and **Prinsengracht**, the three great canals that epitomize the wealth and self-confidence of the Golden Age. In 1663 the sweeping crescent was extended east and north beyond the IJ, but by this time the population had begun to stabilize, and the stretch that would have completed the ring of canals around the city was left only partially developed – an area that would in time become the Jodenbuurt or Jewish Quarter.

One organization that kept the city's coffers brimming throughout the Golden Age was the **East India Company**. Formed by the newly powerful Dutch Republic in 1602, the Amsterdam-controlled enterprise sent ships to Asia, Indonesia and as far away as China to bring back spices, wood and other assorted plunder. Given a trading monopoly in all lands east of the Cape of Good Hope, it had unlimited military powers over the lands it controlled, and was effectively the occupying government in Malaya, Ceylon and Malacca. Twenty years later the **West Indies Company** was inaugurated to protect new Dutch interests in the Americas and Africa. Expending most of its energies in waging war on Spanish and Portuguese colonies from a base in Surinam, it never achieved the success of the East India

Company and was dismantled in 1674, ten years after its small colony of New Amsterdam had been captured by the British – and renamed New York. Elsewhere, Amsterdam held on to its colonies for as long as possible – Java and Sumatra were still under Dutch control after World War II.

Gentle Decline – 1650 to 1800

Part of the reason Amsterdam achieved such economic pre-eminence in the first part of the seventeenth century was that its rivals were expending their energies elsewhere: England was in the turmoil of the Civil War, France was struggling with economic problems brought on by skirmishes with the Spanish, and Germany was ravaged by the Thirty Years' War. By the second half of the century all three countries were back on their feet and fighting: England's navy was attacking the Dutch fleet, Louis XIV of France attempted an invasion of the Low Countries that all but reached Amsterdam, and the troops of the Bishop of Münster occupied the east of the country. While none of these threats came to very much, they signalled the passing of Amsterdam's – and the country's – headiest days.

Though the French had been defeated, Louis retained designs on the United Provinces. When his grandson succeeded to the Spanish throne, which brought with it control of the Spanish Netherlands (Brabant, Flanders and Antwerp), Louis forced him to hand the area over to French control. In response, England, Austria and the United Provinces formed an alliance against the French, and so began the **Wars of the Spanish Succession**, a haphazard conflict that dragged on until 1713. The fighting drained the nation's wealth, tarnishing Amsterdam's dazzling riches. A slow decline in the city's fortunes began, furthered by a mood of conservatism growing in reaction against the lucrative speculation of the previous century. Towards the end of the eighteenth century, Amsterdam and the United Provinces saw a rising tension between Dutch loyalists and the pro-French ruling families (who styled themselves "Patriots"). By the 1780s there was near-civil war, and in 1795, aided by the Patriots, the French invaded, setting up the **Batavian Republic** and administering it from Amsterdam. Effectively under French control, the Dutch were enthusiastically at **war with England**,

and in 1806 Napoleon installed his brother **Louis** as King of The Netherlands in Amsterdam's town hall (giving it, incidentally, its title of **Royal Palace**) in an attempt to create a commercial gulf between the country and England. Amsterdam merchants, with an ever-canny eye to profit, had continued trading with England while the naval battles raged. Once settled, however, Louis was not willing to allow the country to become a simple satellite of France: he ignored Napoleon's directives and after just four years of rule was forced to abdicate. Following Napoleon's disastrous retreat from Moscow, French rule weakened, and eventually the country was returned to **Dutch control** under William I.

The Nineteenth Century

With the **unification of the Netherlands** in 1813 – a process that incorporated parts of the former Spanish Netherlands and brought about the formation of Belgium – the **status of Amsterdam** changed. Previously, the self-governing city, made bold by its economic independence, could (and frequently did) act in its own self-interest, at the expense of the nation. From 1813, however, it was integrated within the country with no more rights than any other city – Amsterdam was the capital in name, but the seat of government (and the centre for all decision-making) was The Hague.

Though the **industrial revolution** arrived late, in the first years of the nineteenth century Amsterdam regained parts of its **colonies** in the West and East Indies. Colonial trade improved but, like all trade, it was hampered by the Zuider Zee, whose shallows and sandbanks prevented new, larger ships from entering the city. The North Holland Canal, completed in 1824 to bypass the Zuider Zee, made little difference, and it was Rotterdam, strategically placed on the Rhine inlets between the industries of the Ruhr and Britain, that prospered at Amsterdam's expense. Even the opening of the **North Sea Canal** in 1876 failed to push Amsterdam's trade ahead of Rotterdam's, though the capital did house the country's **shipbuilding industry**, remnants of which can still be seen at the Kromhout yards in the Eastern Islands.

Between 1850 and the turn of the century, the population of Amsterdam, which had remained static since the 1650s, doubled. Most of the newcomers to the city were poor and the

housing built for them reflected this; the small homes around De Pijp in the Old South remain good examples of the low-cost housing that the more affluent working classes could afford. The Jordaan, one of the city's most impoverished quarters in the early part of the century, was cleared: its polluted canals were filled in and small, inexpensive homes were built. The Jordaan project was one of many put together by philanthropic social organizations, and the council, too, embraced what were at the time forward-looking policies to **alleviate poverty** and increase education for the poor. The political climate was outstandingly liberal, influenced by cabinet leader **J.R. Thorbecke** and an increasingly socialist contingent on the Amsterdam city council.

Until the hard years of the depression the city continued to grow. The rise in the standard of living among working people meant that they could afford better homes, usually under the auspices of housing associations or the city's own building programmes. The most interesting of these were the estates built in what came to be called the **New South**: designed by a group known as the **Amsterdam School** of architects, they combined Modernism with elements of home-grown styles – and were extremely successful.

The War Years

At the outbreak of **World War I**, the Netherlands remained neutral, though it suffered privations as a result of the Allied blockade of Dutch ports through which the Germans might be supplied. Similar attempts to remain neutral in **World War II** soon failed: German troops invaded on May 10, 1940, and the Dutch were quickly overwhelmed; Queen Wilhelmina fled to London, and Arthur Seyss-Inquart was installed as the Nazis' puppet leader. Members of the **NSB**, the Dutch fascist party, which had welcomed the invaders, found themselves rapidly promoted to positions of authority, but, in the early years of the occupation at least, life for ordinary Amsterdammers went on much as usual. Even when the first roundups of the Jews began in 1941, most people pretended they weren't happening, the single popular demonstration against the Nazi actions being the quickly suppressed **February strike**.

The **Dutch Resistance** was instrumental in destroying German supplies and munitions and carrying out harassing attacks in the city, and as the Resistance grew, underground newspapers flourished – today's newspapers *Trouw* (Loyalty) and *Het Parool* (The Password) began life as illegal newsletters. Around 13,000 Resistance fighters and sympathizers lost their lives during the war, and the city's old **Jewish quarter**, swollen by those who had fled Germany during the persecutions of the 1930s, was obliterated, leaving only the deserted Jodenhoek and the diary of a young girl as testaments to the horrors.

After the War

The years immediately after the war were spent patching up the damage of occupation and liberation. It was a period of intense **poverty** in the capital, as food, fuel and building materials were practically nonexistent; a common sight on the streets were handcart burials of those who had died of hunger or hypothermia, black cardboard coffins being trundled to mass graves. As the liberating Canadians had moved nearer to Amsterdam, the Germans had blown up all the dikes and the sluices on the North Sea coast at IJmuiden, and repairing these further slowed the process of rebuilding. The sea itself claimed victims in 1953, when an unusually high tide swept over Zeeland's coastal defences, flooding 40,000 acres of land and drowning more than 1800 people. The subsequent **Delta Project**, which secured the area, also ensured the safety of cities to the south of Amsterdam, although Amsterdam itself had already been deeply affected by the 1932 completion of the **Afsluitdijk**, which closed off the traditional route of ships into the city through the Zuider Zee (later known as the IJsselmeer). The later opening of the **Amsterdam-Rhine canal** did much to boost the city's fortunes, with massive cargo-handling facilities built to accommodate the import of grain and the supply of ore for the Ruhr furnaces. Steadily the rebuilding continued: in Amsterdam all the land projected for use by the year 2000 was used up by the "garden cities". Giant suburbs such as **Bijlmermeer** to the southeast were the last word in 1960s large-scale residential planning, with low-cost modern housing, play areas and traffic-free foot and cycle paths.

The 1960s and 1970s: Radical Movements

The 1960s were above all a period of change and some notoriety for Amsterdam, as the city witnessed the growth of a number of radical causes and protest movements. In 1965, for example, a group of young people made it a weekly ritual to gather round a statue in the centre of Amsterdam to watch a remarkable performer, one-time window cleaner and magician *extraordinaire*, Jasper Grootveld. Grootveld had won notoriety a couple of years earlier by painting "K" – for *kanker* (cancer) – on cigarette billboards throughout the city. Later he set up an "anti-smoking temple" and proclaimed the statue of the Lieverdje (Lovable Rascal) on the Spui the symbol of "tomorrow's addicted consumer", since it had been donated to the city by a cigarette manufacturer.

Grootveld wasn't the only interesting character around town: Roel van Duyn, a philosophy student at Amsterdam University and the initiator of a New Left movement and the **Provos** (short for *provocatie* – "provocation"), started joining in Grootveld's magic happenings, sparking a chain of rebellion that would influence events in the Netherlands for the next twenty years. The number of real Provos never exceeded about 25, but their actions and street "happenings" appealed to a large number of young people. The group had no coherent structure: they emerged into public consciousness through one common aim – to bring points of political or social conflict to public attention by spectacular means. More than anything they were masters of publicity, and pursued their "games" with a spirit of fun rather than grim political fanaticism. They reflected the swinging sixties attitude of young people all over the western world.

In July 1965 the police intervened at a Saturday night "Happening" for the first time, and set a pattern for future confrontations; they had already confiscated the first two issues of the Provos' magazine, in which their initiator, Van Duyn, published the group's manifesto and in which their policies later appeared under the title "The White Plans". These included the famous but unsuccessful **white bicycle plan**, which proposed that the council ban all cars in the city centre and supply 20,000 bicycles (painted white) for general public use – the idea being that you picked up a bike, rode it to your destination, and then left it for someone else to use.

There were regular incidents throughout 1965 and 1966 involving a variety of Provo protests, but it was the action taken on March 10, 1966, the wedding day of Princess Beatrix and Claus von Amsberg, that provoked the most serious unrest: smoke bombs were thrown at the wedding procession and fights with the police broke out across the city. The following month Provo Hans Tuynman was arrested for handing a policeman a leaflet protesting against police actions. Street demonstrations followed, along with further arrests, and when Tuynman was sentenced to three months' imprisonment on May 11, anger spread. Throughout all this conflict, however, the Provos were winning increased public support: in the municipal elections of 1966 they received over 13,000 votes – two and a half percent of the total, and enough for a seat on the council. But this achievement didn't mean the end of the Provos' street actions. Indeed, the next event in which they were involved was one of the most violent of the 1960s. It started with a demonstration by city construction workers on June 13, during which one worker suddenly died. Such was the anti-police feeling that it was assumed he had been killed by police patrolling the protest, and the following day the workers staged a strike and marched through the city with thousands of supporters, including the Provos, who by now were regarded as the champions of the public versus the police. The worker actually died of a heart attack, but the mood had been set and there were clashes between police and rioters for four days. A month later the Hague government ordered the dismissal of Amsterdam's police chief and, a year later, that of the mayor.

But by May 1967 the Provos' inspiration was waning, and at a final gathering in the Vondelpark they announced that they would disband, even though they still had a member on the city council.

The next phase in the Provo phenomenon was the creation of the "Oranje Free State", a so-called alternative society set up by Van Duyn in 1970 in the form of a mock government with its own "ministers" and "policies". The new movement, whose members were named **Kabouters** after a helpful gnome in Dutch folklore, was successful if short-lived. It adopted some of the more reasonable "white policies" of the Provos and went so far as to win seats in six municipalities, including five in Amsterdam, on a vaguely socialist ticket. "No longer the socialism of the clenched fist, but of the intertwined fingers, the erect penis, the escaping butterfly . . . ", their manifesto proclaimed. But before long the

Kabouter movement, too, faded, amid disputes over methodology.

As the Provo and Kabouter movements disappeared, many of their members joined **neighbourhood committees**, set up to oppose certain plans of the city council. By far the most violently attacked scheme was the plan to build a **metro line** through the Nieuwmarkt to the new suburb of Bijlmermeer. The initial idea was conceived in 1968 and consisted of a plan to build a four-line network for an estimated ƒ250 million. By 1973, the cost had risen to ƒ1500 million – for just one line. It was the council's policy of coping with the ever-growing problem of housing by **moving residents** to these suburbs that infuriated Amsterdammers, who felt that their town was being sold off to big businesses and their homes converted to banks and offices, thereby creating a city centre that ordinary people couldn't afford to live in. The opponents of the metro plan objected to the number of houses that would have to be demolished, contending that it was merely an elitist development, of no real use to the public.

Official **clearance of the Nieuwmarkt** area was scheduled for February 1975, but by December 1974 confrontation between police and protesters had already begun. Many residents of the condemned houses refused to move, and further violent clashes were inevitable. The worst came on March 24, 1975, a day that became known as **Blue Monday**: the police began a clearing action early in the morning and their tactics were heavy-handed. Tear-gas grenades were fired through windows smashed by water cannons, armoured cars ripped through front doors, and the police charged in to arrest occupants (residents and supporters), who threw paint cans and powder bombs in retaliation. The fighting went on late into the night with thousands of demonstrators joining in. At the end of the day, 30 people – including 19 policemen – had been wounded, and 47 arrested; 450 complaints were filed against the police. A couple of weeks later came another big clash, but this time the demonstrators used different tactics, forming human barricades in front of the houses to be cleared. The police charged, armed with truncheons; it was an easy eviction. But the protesters had made their point, and afterwards showed their spirit of rebellion by holding parties on the rubble-strewn sites. Despite continuing opposition, the metro eventually opened in 1980.

The 1980s: squatters and protesters

The social consciousness and radicalism of the 1960s had reached Amsterdam early, and word of the psychedelic revolution had been quick to catch on. Dam Square and the Vondelpark became open-air urban campsites, and the pilgrims of alternative culture descended on the easy-going, dope-happy capital. Just as quickly the revolution faded, replaced by the cynicism of the 1970s and the resurgence of the conservative right. The city's housing problems were to continue as a counterculture focus, however, and in the early 1980s the US deployment of **Cruise missiles** in the Netherlands temporarily galvanized opposition. In spite of large-scale protest (over four million people signed an anti-Cruise petition, the *volkspetitonnment*, and there were many demonstrations in the city), the missiles were scheduled to be deployed in 1985; the nearest missile base to Amsterdam, **Woensdrecht**, was seventy miles away and the focus of popular opposition. However, arms negotiations between the US and USSR meant that the missiles never arrived – and that the buildings created to house them were all a waste of time and money.

Meanwhile, the ever-increasing problem of housing had brought about the emergence of a new movement – the **squatters**. At first the squatters' movement was peripheral, consisting mainly of independently operating neighbourhood committees. There was little sense of unity until joint actions to defend a handful of symbolic Amsterdam squats took place. These shaped the development of the squatters' movement, which became something of a political force, with clearly defined rights and the ear of the city council.

Four events help explain how this transformation of the squatters' movement occurred: the actions at the key squats of Vondelstraat, Lucky Luyk and Wyers – and the national day of squatting on April 30, 1980.

The end of the **Vondelstraat** squat in Amsterdam's most prestigious neighbourhood was perhaps the most famous squatting event in the Netherlands. Three days after the empty office premises were occupied in March 1980, police tanks were ordered to remove the squatters. About 500 police took part and the resulting riots spread through the streets and reached the tourist area of Leidseplein. Battles raged the whole day and fifty people were wounded. The squatters were evicted, but it wasn't long before they reoccupied the building. The significance of the Vondelstraat squat was that the attempted eviction and ensuing riots cost the council a considerable amount of money – a fact the squatters used tactically by making future evictions too expensive for the authorities to undertake.

The next major event involved not a specific squat but protest actions on April 30, 1980 – the **coronation day** of Queen Beatrix. Squatters in Amsterdam and throughout the Netherlands staged protests against the huge amounts of money being spent on the festivities, in addition to the reputed ƒ84 million spent on the rebuilding of her residence in The Hague. Two hundred buildings in 27 cities were squatted; half of these squats were cleared the same day, and it was one of these clearances that sparked off the first battle in Amsterdam. Then, in the afternoon, a protest demonstration set off to march through the city to Dam Square, where the crowning ceremony was taking place. Confrontation with the police began almost immediately on Waterlooplein, and from then on the city centre turned into complete chaos. The squatters' ranks were swelled by other protesters angered by the coronation expenditure at a time when the city council claimed it could not afford to build homes. Public festivities came to an abrupt halt as fighting broke out in the streets and continued until the early hours. Tear gas enveloped the city, while Special Squad Police made repeated charges, and many revellers were caught up with the rebels as the police cordoned off the most militant areas.

The squatting movement was reaching its peak. After the success of the Vondelstraat squat in 1980, an estimated 10,000 squatters took over buildings across Amsterdam. The eviction of those who had occupied **Lucky Luyk**, a villa on Jan Luykenstraat, was the most violent and most expensive the city had known to date, with damage running into millions of guilders.

Lucky Luyk was originally squatted in July 1980 after standing empty for a few years. In October squatters were forcibly evicted by the *knokploegen* – groups of heavies rented by property owners to protect their investments. Two months later the owners of the villa won a court order for the evacuation of the building. At this stage, the city council stepped in to pre-empt the violence that was certain to accompany such an action: they bought the villa for ƒ350,000 – giving the owners an easy ƒ73,000 profit. The squatters weren't happy, but agreed to leave the building if it were used for young people's housing. On October 11, 1982, two days before a meeting between the council and the squatters, twelve policemen from the Special Squad broke into Lucky Luyk through the roof and arrested the five occupants – a surprise attack that enraged squatters across the country and resulted in sympathy actions in many other cities.

In Amsterdam, riots soon started and lasted for three days. Supporters of the Lucky Luyk, who included many non-squatters, built barricades, wrecked cars, destroyed property and set fire to a tram, while police retaliated with tear gas and water cannons. The mayor declared unprecedented emergency measures, permitting the police to arrest anyone suspected of disrupting public order.

The squatters had learned a lesson: the authorities had had enough and were learning new and easier methods of eviction – and were prepared to evict at any cost. Squatters needed to develop a new defence tactic. They hit on politics, and found a new case to fight – **Wyers**. This building, a former distribution centre for a textile firm, had been occupied in October 1981 by about a hundred squatters from all over the city. They were soon informed that *Hollandse Beton Maatschappij*, one of the country's largest building companies, had just obtained permission to build luxury apartments and shops on the site. Trouble was postponed temporarily when *HBM* decided the time was not right for their financial investment and scrapped their plans. But in the spring of 1982 they reapplied for building rights, this time to put up a hotel on behalf of *Holiday Inn*. The initial application was turned down, but an amended plan was approved by the council in June 1983. An eviction order was presented to the Wyers inhabitants, but the squatters found legal loopholes in it and the clearance was delayed.

The squatters were meanwhile busy preparing an alternative plan to present to the council, in which the building would be used as a combined cultural-residential complex with space for small businesses and studios. This constructive alternative won the support of many people, and even the council considered it a viable idea. Dialogue between the council and the squatters

continued, but then Wyers was cleared in February 1984, with the usual pictures of water cannons and tear gas spread across the front pages of Europe's newspapers. The eviction itself was relatively peaceful: the squatters had decided not to resist and instead linked arms around the site and waited for the police onslaught. Today the *Holiday Inn Crowne Plaza* stands on Nieuwezijds Voorburgwal as a testament to the fact that the squatters failed here: but as banners proclaimed after the eviction, "You can demolish Wyers but you will never destroy the ideas behind Wyers".

In the later 1980s, under the socialist mayor, Ed van Thijn, new construction in the city firmly targeted Amsterdam's luxury hotel market rather than addressing its residential needs, and the city's former radicalism seemed suspended. One of the most controversial issues of the late 1980s was the building of the **Muziektheater/Stadhuis** on Waterlooplein. Historically the site chosen for the new opera building was sensitive, as it was part of the old Jodenhoek and had been a public space for centuries; politically, the building of a highbrow cultural centre was attacked as elitist; and architecturally the plans were a clumsy hybrid, with different designers responsible for each section.

The Muziektheater was bound to come in for flak, and got it from the **Stopera** campaign, whose name was a convenient contraction of "Stop the Opera". No doubt the fact that Amsterdam was angling for the 1992 Olympics was the reason the council railroaded the plans through, yet, compared to episodes from the past, protest was surprisingly slight. Though the building is today an ugly intruder on the Amstel, it seems to have won over many of its erstwhile opponents – perhaps because Amsterdammers can accommodate any public building more easily than a private one. On the other hand, it's a sign of the times that there was little fuss made over the new casino that opened just off the Leidseplein in 1994, along with a neighbouring private residential and shopping development, all of massive and unappealing proportions.

Amsterdam in the 1990s

For a while at the end of the 1980s, some of the ideas (and idealism) of decades past seemed to be reappearing on a national level, although they were often thwarted by entrenched interests. In the elections of 1989 **Groen Links**, the Green-Left coalition of mainly small left and ecology parties, had a strong showing, and the previous year the Netherlands had become the first European country to officially adopt a **National Environment Plan**, a radical agenda of Green policies: as yet, however, the Plan has still to be implemented. In Amsterdam, the city council adopted a plan for a **traffic-free centre** after a narrow majority voted for the policy in an admittedly low turnout referendum; implementation of the plan, however, has likewise been stalled for years. Meanwhile, the far-right **Centrum Democratische** party had also won enough votes in 1989, and again in 1994, to gain unheard-of representation in the Lower House of the Dutch parliament, events which occasioned multiple demonstrations. As the most powerful group in the Social Democratic Party put it, the *Nieuw Links* (New Left) has largely given way to the era of the *Nieuw Flinks* (New Firm).

However, at the heart of the Dutch body politic lies **consensus**: in the **1994 elections**, although the Labour Party won the largest share of the vote, it took three months of high-level politicking to thrash out a deal forming an unprecedented "left-right" **coalition government** under Prime Minister Wim Kok, with the Labour Party sharing power with both the left-of-centre "66 Democrats" and the right-wing Liberal Party. This coalition excluded the previously influential Christian Democrats – but then it proceeded to embark on a largely Christian Democrat programme, keeping everybody happy. Another force in Dutch politics also emerged from the 1994 elections: **pensioners' parties** won eight seats in the Lower House, highlighting public dismay over government plans to freeze state old-age pensions, and raising the possibility that pensioners could be included in the government formation process.

For all parties, **Schiphol Airport** remains a problem. Essential to the national economy (it's Europe's most important airport, after Heathrow), it will need to grow still more in the next few years, which means the area around it will suffer further. Some doubts still exist about the airport's safety after the incident in October 1992, when an *El Al* Boeing 747 cargo plane **crashed** into the Bijlmermeer housing estate, narrowly missing a block scheduled for demolition and destroying the showpiece of the redesigned estate. Around fifty people were killed, though the exact total

will never be known: the estate was densely filled with people from Surinam and the Dutch Antilles, some of whom were probably in the country illegally. The plane's cargo of kerosene and secret unspecified "military chemicals" destroyed a vast swathe of the estate, and it's fortunate that casualties were relatively low.

One consequence of the disaster was that the government ordered an amnesty on Surinamese and Antillean **immigrants** who had entered the country illegally, in order to allow a full death toll to be established. The resulting racist backlash fuelled the attacks on foreign immigrants that were already occurring throughout western Europe at the time, although the situation in Holland was not nearly as bad as in Germany. Of all the immigrant communities in the Netherlands, the South Moluccans have shown the least desire to integrate fully, and the Dutch government has consistently made concerted efforts – with little gain – to establish communications with them and other fringe groups. The tradition – and reality – of Dutch liberalism means that up to 50,000 or more people each year seek **asylum** in the Netherlands, where they generally get a much more positive reception than in almost any other country.

Towards the year 2000

On the brink of the new millennium, Amsterdam is increasingly **thinking big**; the days of "happenings" and helpful gnomes seem long gone. Tourism throughout the country generates a turnover of ƒ36 billion annually – in 1995, over two million people took canal trips in Amsterdam alone – and massive public and private works projects are an ongoing response to both the burgeoning tourism industry and a shift in locals' self-perception. The brand-new multimedia "Holland Experience" complex opened in Amsterdam in 1996, its aim to present to the world "a literally sensational view" of the country and its capital, in a vast, multimillion-guilder attempt to replace the parochial image of tulips and windmills with that of a modern, technology-driven society. The hard-headedly pragmatic city council under Mayor Schelto Patijn has embarked on a series of measures intended to bury Amsterdam's docile, freewheeling image and replace it with one more suited to a dynamic European capital: the notoriously liberal **drug laws** have been tightened up, crackdowns have begun on the more extreme forms of **pornography** being shipped in and out of Amsterdam, **squats** are now no more evident or significant in Amsterdam than in any other European city, and **redevelopment** of empty areas of land in and around the city centre is proceeding apace, most notably with the high-income housing complexes shooting up on the long-derelict KNSM island. Throughout the mid-1990s, in Duivendrecht, an otherwise unremarkable southeastern commuter suburb, one of the most modern **stadiums** in Europe was quietly under construction, and in 1996 the 51,000-capacity Amsterdam ArenA finally opened. The new home of Ajax Amsterdam, one of Europe's most successful football teams, the ArenA is also destined to become the large-scale venue for rock concerts and mass entertainments that the city has so sorely lacked.

And yet, throughout the turmoil, the country is somehow managing to retain the idiosyncratic mix of single-minded commercialism and cosy domesticity that has characterized it for centuries. On the one hand, there are bodies such as the **Netherlands Foreign Investment Agency**, which has managed the remarkable feat of attracting over twenty percent of US and Japanese investment in Europe to this one tiny country. And on the other, sitting easily alongside the practical business of making money, the ghosts of Amsterdam's hippie past still survive. 1996 saw the Provos' old **white bicycle** scheme resurrected for a 21st-century Amsterdam, backed by public funding. For just pennies a time, anyone will be able to ride one of up to 1000 bikes scattered around the city; both bikes and payments are to be tracked by a city-wide electronic card system. A pilot project is already underway, and, if all goes well, by 1999 at least one of the dreams of Amsterdam's counterculture, nurtured for thirty years or more, could finally become a reality.

Dutch Art

This is the very briefest of introductions to the subject, designed to serve only as a quick reference on your way round the major galleries. For more in-depth and academic studies, see the recommendations in "Books" on p.370. For a list of where to find the paintings mentioned here, turn to the end of this section.

Beginnings

Until the sixteenth century the area now known as the Low Countries was in effect one country, the most artistically productive part of which was Flanders in modern Belgium, and it was there that the solid realist base of later Dutch painting developed. Today the works of these **early Flemish painters** are pretty sparse in Holland, and even in Belgium few collections are as complete as they might be; indeed, many ended up as the property of the ruling Habsburgs and were removed to Spain. Most Dutch galleries do, however, have a few examples.

Jan van Eyck (1385–1441) is generally regarded as the originator of Low Countries painting, and has even been credited with the invention of oil painting itself – though it seems more likely that he simply perfected a new technique by thinning his paint with the recently discovered turpentine, thus making it more flexible. His most famous work still in the Low Countries is the Ghent altarpiece (debatably painted with the help of his lesser-known brother, Hubert), which was revolutionary in its realism, for the first time using elements of native landscape in depicting biblical themes.

Firmly in the Van Eyck tradition were the **Master of Flemalle** (1387–1444) and **Rogier van der Weyden** (1400–64). The Flemalle master is a shadowy figure: some believe he was the teacher of Van der Weyden, others that the two artists were in fact the same person. There are differences between the two, however: the Flemalle master's paintings are close to Van Eyck's, whereas Van der Weyden shows a more emotional and religious intensity. Van der Weyden influenced such painters as **Dieric Bouts** (1415–75), who was born in Haarlem but worked in Louvain, and is recognizable by his stiff, rather elongated figures. **Hugo van der Goes** (d. 1482) was the next Ghent master after Van Eyck, most famous for the Portinari altarpiece in Florence's Uffizi gallery; after a short painting career, he died insane. Few doubt that **Hans Memling** (1440–94) was a pupil of Van der Weyden: active in Bruges throughout his life, he is best remembered for the pastoral charm of his landscapes and the quality of his portraiture, much of which survives on the rescued side panels of triptychs. More renowned are **Hieronymus Bosch** (1450–1516), whose frequently reprinted and discussed religious allegories are filled with macabre visions of tortured people and grotesque beasts, and **Pieter Bruegel the Elder** (1525–69), whose gruesome allegories and innovative interpretations of religious subjects are firmly placed in Low Countries settings.

Meanwhile, there were movements based to the north of Flanders. **Geertgen tot Sint Jans** ("Little Gerard of the Brotherhood of St John"; d. 1490), a student of Albert van Ouwater, had been working in **Haarlem**, initiating – in a strangely naive style – an artistic tradition in the city that would prevail throughout the seventeenth century. **Jan Mostaert** (1475–1555) took over after Geertgen's death, and continued to develop a style that diverged more and more from that of the southern provinces. **Lucas van Leyden** (1489–1533) was the first painter to effect real changes in northern painting. Born in Leiden, his bright colours and narrative technique were refreshingly new at the time, and he introduced a novel dynamism into what had become a rigidly formal treatment of devotional subjects. There was rivalry, of course. Eager to publicize Haarlem as the artistic capital of the northern Netherlands, Carel van Mander (see below) claimed Haarlem native **Jan van Scorel** (1495–1562) as the better painter, complaining, too, of Van Leyden's dandyish ways.

Certainly Van Scorel's influence should not be underestimated. At this time every painter was expected to travel to Italy to view the works of Renaissance artists. When the Bishop of Utrecht became Pope Hadrian VI, he took Van Scorel with him as court painter, giving him the opportunity to introduce Italian styles into what had been a completely independent tradition. Hadrian died soon after, and Van Scorel returned north, combining the ideas he had picked up in Italy with Haarlem realism and passing them on to **Maerten van Heemskerck** (1498–1574), who went off to Italy himself in 1532, staying there five years before returning to Haarlem.

The Golden Age

The seventeenth century begins with **Carel van Mander**, Haarlem painter, art impresario and one of the few chroniclers of the art of the Low Countries. His *Schilderboek* of 1604 put Flemish and Dutch traditions into context for the first time, and in addition specified the rules of fine painting. Examples of his own work are rare, but his followers were many, among them **Cornelius Cornelisz van Haarlem** (1562–1638), who produced elegant renditions of biblical and mythical themes; and **Hendrik Goltzius** (1558–1616), who was a skilled engraver and an integral member of Van Mander's Haarlem academy. These painters' enthusiasm for Italian art, combined with the influence of a late revival of Gothicism, resulted in works that combined Mannerist and Classical elements. An interest in realism was also felt, and, for them, the subject became less important than the way in which it was depicted: biblical stories became merely a vehicle whereby artists could apply their skills in painting the human body, landscapes, or copious displays of food – all of which served to break religion's stranglehold on art, and make legitimate a whole range of everyday subjects for the painter.

In Holland (and this was where the north and the south finally diverged) this break with tradition was compounded by the **Reformation**: the austere Calvinism that had replaced the Catholic faith in the northern provinces had no use for images or symbols of devotion in its churches. Instead, painters catered to the public, and no longer visited Italy to learn their craft; the real giants of the seventeenth century – Hals, Rembrandt, Vermeer – stayed in the Netherlands all their lives. Another innovation was that painting split into more distinct categories – genre, portrait, landscape – and artists tended (with notable exceptions) to confine themselves to one field throughout their careers. So began the greatest age of Dutch art.

Historical and Religious Painting

If Italy continued to hold sway in the Netherlands it was not through the Renaissance painters but rather via the fashionable new realism of Caravaggio. Many artists – Rembrandt for one – continued to portray classical subjects, but in a way that was totally at odds with the Mannerists' stylish flights of imagination. The Utrecht artist **Abraham Bloemaert** (1564–1651), though a solid Mannerist throughout his career, encouraged these new ideas, and his students – **Gerard van Honthorst** (1590–1656), **Hendrik Terbrugghen** (1588–1629) and **Dirck van Baburen** (1590–1624) – formed the nucleus of the influential **Utrecht School**, which followed Caravaggio almost to the point of slavishness. Honthorst was perhaps the leading figure, learning his craft from Bloemaert and travelling to Rome, where he was nicknamed "Gerardo delle Notti" for his ingenious handling of light and shade. In his later paintings, however, this was to become more routine technique than inspired invention, and though a supremely competent artist, Honthorst remains somewhat discredited among critics today. Terbrugghen's reputation seems to have aged rather better: he soon forgot Caravaggio and developed a more individual style, his later, lighter work having a great influence on the young Vermeer. After the obligatory jaunt to Rome, Baburen shared a studio with Terbrugghen and produced some fairly original work – work which also had some influence on Vermeer – but today he is the least studied member of the group and few of his paintings survive.

But it's **Rembrandt** who was considered the most original historical artist of the seventeenth century, painting religious scenes throughout his life. In the 1630s, the poet and statesman Constantijn Huygens procured for him his greatest commission – a series of five paintings of the Passion, beautifully composed and uncompromisingly realistic. Later, however, Rembrandt received fewer and fewer commissions, since his treatment of biblical and historical subjects was far less dramatic than that of his contemporaries. It's significant that while the more conventional Jordaens, Honthorst and Van Everdingen were busy decorating the Huis ten Bosch near The Hague for patron Stadholder Frederick Henry, Rembrandt was having his monumental *Conspiracy of Claudius Civilis* (painted for the new Amsterdam Town Hall) rejected – probably because it was thought too pagan an interpretation of what was an important symbolic event in Dutch history. **Aert van Gelder** (1645–1727), Rembrandt's last pupil and probably the only one to concentrate on historical painting, followed the style of his master closely, producing shimmering biblical scenes well into the eighteenth century.

Genre Painting

Genre refers to scenes from everyday life, a subject that, with the decline of the church as patron, had become popular in Holland by the mid-seventeenth century. Many painters devoted themselves solely to such work. Some genre paintings were simply non-idealized portrayals of common scenes, while others, by means of symbols or carefully disguised details, made moral entreaties to the viewer.

Among early seventeenth-century painters, **Hendrik Terbrugghen** and **Gerard Honthorst** spent much of their time on religious subjects, but also adapted the realism and strong chiaroscuro learned from Caravaggio to a number of tableaux of everyday life. **Frans Hals**, too, is better known as a portraitist, but his early genre paintings no doubt influenced his pupil, **Adriaen Brouwer** (1605–38), whose riotous tavern scenes were well received in their day and collected by, among others, Rubens and Rembrandt. Brouwer spent only a couple of years in Haarlem under Hals before returning to his native Flanders, where he influenced the younger **David Teniers**. **Adriaen van Ostade** (1610–85), on the other hand, stayed in Haarlem most of his life,

skilfully painting groups of peasants and tavern brawls – though his later acceptance by the establishment led him to water down the realism he had learnt from Brouwer. He was teacher to his brother **Isaak** (1621–49), who produced a large number of open-air peasant scenes, subtle combinations of genre and landscape work.

The English critic E.V. Lucas dubbed Teniers, Brouwer and Ostade "coarse and boorish" compared with **Jan Steen** (1625–79), who, along with Vermeer, is probably the most admired Dutch genre painter. You can see what he had in mind: Steen's paintings offer the same Rabelaisian peasantry in full fling, but they go their debauched ways in broad daylight, and nowhere do you see the filthy rogues in shadowy hovels favoured by Brouwer and Ostade. Steen offers more humour, too, as well as more moralizing, identifying with the hedonistic mob and reproaching them at the same time. Indeed, many of his pictures are illustrations of well-known proverbs of the time – popular epithets on the evils of drink or the transience of human existence that were supposed to teach as well as entertain.

Gerrit Dou (1613–75) was Rembrandt's Leiden contemporary and one of his first pupils. It's difficult to detect any trace of the master's influence in his work, however; Dou initiated a style of his own: tiny, minutely realized and beautifully finished views of a kind of ordinary life that was decidedly more genteel than Brouwer's – or even Steen's for that matter. He was admired, above all, for his painstaking attention to detail: and he would, it's said, sit in his studio for hours waiting for the dust to settle before starting work. Among his students, **Frans van Mieris** (1635–81) continued the highly finished portrayals of the Dutch bourgeoisie, as did **Gabriel Metsu** (1629–67) – perhaps Dou's greatest pupil – whose pictures often convey an overtly moral message. Another pupil of Rembrandt's, though a much later one, was **Nicholaes Maes** (1629–93), whose early works were almost entirely genre paintings, sensitively executed and again with a moralizing message. His later paintings show the influence of a more refined style of portrait, which he had picked up in France.

As a native of Zwolle, **Gerard ter Borch** (1619–81) found himself far from all these Leiden/Rembrandt connections; despite trips abroad to most of the artistic capitals of Europe, he remained very much a provincial painter all his life, depicting Holland's merchant class at play and becoming renowned for his curious doll-like figures and his enormous ability to capture the textures of different cloths. His domestic scenes were not unlike those of **Pieter de Hooch** (1629–after 1684), whose simple depictions of everyday life are deliberately unsentimental, and, for the first time, have little or no moral commentary. De Hooch's favourite trick was to paint darkened rooms with an open door leading through to a sunlit courtyard, a practice that, along with his trademark rusty red colour, makes his work easy to identify and, at its best, exquisite. That said, his later pictures reflect the encroaching decadence of the Dutch Republic: the rooms are more richly decorated, the arrangements more contrived and the subjects far less homely.

It was, however, **Jan Vermeer** (1632–75) who brought the most sophisticated methods to painting interiors, depicting the play of natural light on indoor surfaces with superlative skill. And it's for this and the curious peace and intimacy of his pictures that he's best known. Another recorder of the better-heeled Dutch households and, like De Hooch, without a moral tone, he is regarded (with Hals and Rembrandt) as one of the big three Dutch painters – though he was, it seems, a slow worker, and only about forty small paintings can be attributed to him with any certainty. Living all his life in Delft, Vermeer is perhaps the epitome of the seventeenth-century Dutch painter – rejecting the pomp and ostentation of the High Renaissance to record quietly his contemporaries at home, painting for a public that demanded no more than that.

Portraits

Naturally, the ruling bourgeoisie of Holland's flourishing mercantile society wanted to put their success on record, and it's little wonder that portraiture was the best way for a young painter to make a living. **Michiel Jansz Miereveld** (1567–1641), court painter to Frederick Henry in The Hague, was the first real portraitist of the Dutch Republic, but it wasn't long before his stiff and rather conservative figures were superseded by the more spontaneous renderings of **Frans Hals** (1585–1666). Hals is perhaps best known for his "corporation pictures" – portraits of the members of the Dutch civil guard regiments that had been formed in most of the larger towns

while the threat of invasion by the Spanish was still imminent. These large group pieces demanded superlative technique, since the painter had to create a collection of individual portraits while retaining a sense of the group, and accord prominence based on the importance of the sitter and the size of the payment each had made. Hals was particularly good at this, using innovative lighting effects, arranging his sitters subtly, and putting all the elements together in a fluid and dynamic composition. He also painted many individual portraits, making the ability to capture fleeting and telling expressions his trademark; his pictures of children are particularly sensitive. Later in life, his work became darker and more akin to Rembrandt's.

Jan Cornelisz Verspronck (1597–1662) and **Bartholomeus van der Helst** (1613–70) were the other great Haarlem portraitists after Frans Hals – Verspronck recognizable by the smooth, shiny glow he always gave to his sitters' faces, Van der Helst by a competent but unadventurous style. Of the two, Van der Helst was the more popular, influencing a number of later painters and leaving Haarlem while still young to begin a solidly successful career as portrait painter to Amsterdam's burghers.

The reputation of **Rembrandt van Rijn** (1606–69) is still relatively recent – nineteenth-century connoisseurs preferred Gerard Dou – but he is now justly regarded as one of the greatest and most versatile painters of all time. Born in Leiden, the son of a miller, he was apprenticed at an early age to Jacob van Swanenburgh, a then quite important, though uninventive, local artist. He shared a studio with Jan Lievens, a promising painter and something of a rival for a while (now all but forgotten), before going up to Amsterdam to study under the fashionable Pieter Lastman. Soon he was painting commissions for the city elite and became an accepted member of their circle. The poet and statesman Constantijn Huygens acted as his agent, pulling strings to obtain all of Rembrandt's more lucrative jobs, and in 1634 Rembrandt married Saskia van Ulenborch, daughter of the burgomaster of Leeuwarden and quite a catch for the still relatively humble artist. His self-portraits at the time show the confident face of security – on top of things and quite sure of where he's going.

Rembrandt would not always be the darling of the Amsterdam smart set, but his fall from grace was still some way off when he painted

The Night Watch, a group portrait often associated with the artist's decline in popularity. But, although Rembrandt's fluent arrangement of his subjects was totally original, there's no evidence that the military company who commissioned the painting was anything but pleased with the result. More likely culprits are the artist's later pieces, whose obscure lighting and psychological insight took the conservative Amsterdam burghers by surprise. His patrons were certainly not sufficiently enthusiastic about his work to support his taste for art collecting and his expensive house on Jodenbreestraat, and in 1656 possibly the most brilliant artist the city would ever know was declared bankrupt; he died thirteen years later – as his last self-portraits show, a broken and embittered old man. Throughout his career Rembrandt maintained a large studio, and his influence pervaded the next generation of Dutch painters. Some – Dou and Maes – more famous for their genre work, have already been mentioned. Others turned to portraiture.

Govert Flinck (1615–60) was perhaps Rembrandt's most faithful follower, and he was, ironically, given the job of decorating Amsterdam's new town hall after his teacher had been passed over. He died at a tragically young age before he could execute his designs, and Rembrandt was one of several artists commissioned to paint them – though his contribution was removed shortly afterwards. The work of **Ferdinand Bol** (1616–80) was so heavily influenced by Rembrandt that for a long time art historians couldn't tell the two apart. Most of the pitifully slim extant work of **Carel Fabritius** (1622–54) was portraiture, but he too died young, before he could properly realize his promise as perhaps the most gifted of all Rembrandt's students. Generally regarded as the teacher of Vermeer, he forms a link between the two masters, combining Rembrandt's technique with his own practice of painting figures against a dark background, prefiguring the lighting and colouring of the Delft painter.

Landscapes

Aside from Bruegel, whose depictions of his native surroundings make him the first true Low Countries landscape painter, **Gillis van Coninxloo** (1544–1607) stands out as the earliest Dutch landscapist. He imbued the native scenery with elements of fantasy, painting the richly wooded views he had seen on his travels around Europe as backdrops to biblical scenes. In the early seventeenth century, **Hercules Seghers** (1590–1638), apprenticed to Coninxloo, carried on his mentor's style of depicting forested and mountainous landscapes, some real, others not: his work is scarce but is believed to have had considerable influence on the landscape work of Rembrandt. **Esaias van der Velde**'s (1591–1632) quaint and unpretentious scenes show the first real affinity with the Dutch countryside, but while his influence was likewise great, he was soon overtaken in stature by his pupil **Jan van Goyen** (1596–1656), a remarkable painter who belongs to the so-called "tonal phase" of Dutch landscape painting. Van Goyen's early pictures were highly coloured and close to those of his teacher, but it didn't take him long to develop a marked touch of his own, using tones of green, brown and grey to lend everything a characteristic translucent haze. His paintings are, above all, of nature, and if he included figures it was just for the sake of scale. Neglected until a little over a century ago, his fluid and rapid brushwork became more accepted as the Impressionists rose in stature.

Another "tonal" painter and a native of Haarlem, **Salomon van Ruisdael** (1600–70) was also directly affected by Van der Velde, and his simple and atmospheric, though not terribly adventurous, landscapes were for a long time consistently confused with those of Van Goyen. More esteemed is his nephew, **Jacob van Ruisdael** (1628–82), generally considered the greatest of all Dutch landscapists, whose fastidiously observed views of quiet flatlands dominated by stormy skies were to influence European painters' impressions of nature right up to the nineteenth century. Constable, certainly, acknowledged a debt to him. Ruisdael's foremost pupil was **Meindert Hobbema** (1638–1709), who followed the master faithfully, sometimes even painting the same views (his *Avenue at Middelharnis* may be familiar).

Nicholas Berchem (1620–83) and **Jan Both** (1618–52) were the "Italianizers" of Dutch landscapes. They studied in Rome and were influenced by Claude, taking back to Holland rich, golden views of the world, full of steep gorges and hills, picturesque ruins and wandering shepherds. **Allart van Everdingen** (1621–75) had a similar approach, but his subject matter stemmed from travels in Scandinavia, which, after his return to Holland, he reproduced in all its mountainous glory. **Aelbert Cuyp** (1620–91), on the other hand, stayed in Dordrecht all his life, painting what was probably the favourite city skyline of Dutch landscapists. He inherited the warm tones of the Italianizers, and his pictures are always suffused with a deep, golden glow.

Of a number of specialist seventeenth-century painters who can be included here, **Paulus Potter** (1625–54) is rated as the best painter of **domestic animals**. He produced a fair amount of work in a short life, the most reputed being his lovingly executed pictures of cows and horses. The accurate rendering of **architectural** features also became a specialized field, in which **Pieter Saenredam** (1597–1665), with his finely realized paintings of Dutch church interiors, is the most widely known exponent. **Emanuel de Witte** (1616–92) continued in the same vein, though his churches lack the spartan crispness of Saenredam's. **Gerrit Berckheyde** (1638–98) worked in Haarlem soon after, but he limited his views to the outside of buildings, producing variations on the same scenes around town.

In the seventeenth century another thriving category of painting was the **still life**, in which objects were gathered together to remind the viewer of the transience of human life and the meaninglessness of all worldly pursuits: often a skull would be joined by a book, a pipe or a goblet, and some half-eaten food. Again, two Haarlem painters dominated this field: **Pieter Claesz** (1598–1660) and **Willem Heda** (1594–1680), who confined themselves almost entirely to painting these carefully arranged groups of objects.

The Eighteenth and Nineteenth Centuries

With the demise of Holland's economic boom, the quality – and originality – of Dutch painting began to decline. The delicacy of some of the classical seventeenth-century painters was replaced by finicky still lifes and minute studies of flowers, or finely finished portraiture and religious scenes, as in the work of **Adrian van der Werff** (1659–1722). Of the era's big names, **Gerard de Lairesse** (1640–1711) spent most of his time decorating the splendid civic halls and palaces that were going up all over the place, and, like the buildings he worked on, his style and influences were French. **Jacob de Wit** (1695–1754) continued where Lairesse left off, receiving more

commissions in churches as Catholicism was allowed out of the closet. The period's only painter of any true renown was **Cornelis Troost** (1697–1750) who, although he didn't produce anything really new, painted competent portraits and some neat, faintly satirical pieces that have since earned him the title of "The Dutch Hogarth". Cosy interiors also continued to prove popular and the Haarlem painter **Wybrand Hendriks** (1744–1831) satisfied demand with numerous proficient examples.

Johann Barthold Jongkind (1819–91) was the first great artist to emerge in the nineteenth century, painting landscapes and seascapes that were to influence Monet and the early Impressionists: he spent most of his life in France and his work was exhibited in Paris with the Barbizon painters, though he owed less to them than to the landscapes of Van Goyen and the seventeenth-century "tonal" artists.

Jongkind's work was a logical precursor to the art of the **Hague School**, a group of painters based in and around that city between 1870 and 1900 who tried to re-establish a characteristically Dutch national school of painting. They produced atmospheric studies of the dunes and polderlands around The Hague, nature pictures that are characterized by grey, rain-filled skies, windswept seas, and silvery, flat beaches – pictures that, for some, verge on the sentimental. **J.H. Weissenbruch** (1824–1903) was a founding member, a specialist in low, flat beach scenes dotted with stranded boats. The banker-turned-artist **H.W. Mesdag** (1831–1915) did the same but with more skill than imagination, while **Jacob Maris** (1837–99), one of three artist brothers, was perhaps the most typical of the Hague School, with his rural and sea scenes heavily covered by grey chasing skies. His brother **Matthijs Maris** (1839–1917) was less predictable, ultimately tiring of his colleagues' interest in straight observation and going to London to design windows, while **Willem Maris** (1844–1910), the youngest, is best known for his small, unpretentious studies of nature.

Anton Mauve (1838–88) is more famous, an exponent of soft, pastel landscapes and an early teacher of Van Gogh. Profoundly influenced by the French Barbizon painters – Corot, Millet et al – he went to Hilversum in 1885 to set up his own group, which became known as the "Dutch Barbizon". **Jozef Israëls** (1826–1911) has often been likened to Millet, though it's generally agreed that he had more in common with the Impressionists, and his best pictures are his melancholy portraits and interiors. Lastly, **Johan Bosboom**'s (1817–91) church interiors may be said to sum up the nostalgia of the Hague School: shadowy and populated by figures in seventeenth-century dress, they seem to yearn for Holland's Golden Age.

Vincent van Gogh (1853–90), on the other hand, was one of the least "Dutch" of Dutch artists, and he lived out most of his relatively short painting career in France. After countless studies of peasant life in his native North Brabant – studies which culminated in the sombre *Potato Eaters* – he went to live in Paris with his art-dealer brother Theo. There, under the influence of the Impressionists, he lightened his palette, following the pointillist work of Seurat and "trying to render intense colour and not a grey harmony". Two years later he went south to Arles, the "land of blue tones and gay colours", and, struck by the harsh Mediterranean light, his characteristic style began to develop. A disastrous attempt to live with Gauguin, and the much-publicized episode when he cut off part of his ear and presented it to a woman in a nearby brothel, led eventually to his committal in an asylum at St-Rémy, where he produced some of his most famous, and most expressionistic, canvases – strongly coloured and with the paint thickly, almost frantically, applied.

Like Van Gogh, **Jan Toorop** (1858–1928) went through multiple artistic changes, though he did not need to travel the world to do so; he radically adapted his technique from a fairly conventional pointillism through a tired Expressionism to Symbolism with an Art-Nouveau feel. Roughly contemporary, **G.H. Breitner** (1857–1923) was a better painter, and one who refined his style rather than changed it. His snapshot-like impressions of his beloved Amsterdam figure among his best work and offered a promising start to the new century.

The Twentieth Century

Most of the trends in the visual arts of the early twentieth century found their way to the Netherlands at one time or another: of many minor names, **Jan Sluyters** (1881–1957) was the Dutch pioneer of Cubism. But only one movement was specifically Dutch – **De Stijl** literally "the Style".

Piet Mondrian (1872–1944) was De Stijl's leading figure, developing the realism he had learned from the Hague School painters – via Cubism, which he criticized for being too cowardly to depart totally from representation – into a complete abstraction of form which he called **Neo-Plasticism**. He was something of a mystic, and this was to some extent responsible for the direction that De Stijl – and his paintings – took: canvases painted with grids of lines and blocks made up of the three primary colours and white, black and grey. Mondrian believed this freed the work of art from the vagaries of personal perception, making it possible to obtain what he called "a true vision of reality".

De Stijl took other forms too: there was a magazine of the same name, and the movement introduced new concepts into every aspect of design, from painting to interior design to architecture. But in all these media, lines were kept simple, colours bold and clear. **Theo van Doesburg** (1883–1931) was a De Stijl co-founder and major theorist: his work is similar to Mondrian's except for the noticeable absence of thick, black borders and the diagonals that he introduced into his work, calling his paintings "contra-compositions" – which, he said, were both more dynamic and more in touch with twentieth-century life. **Bart van der Leck** (1876–1958) was the third member of the circle, identifiable by white canvases covered by seemingly randomly placed interlocking coloured triangles.

Mondrian split with De Stijl in 1925, going on to attain new artistic extremes of clarity and soberness before moving to New York in the 1940s and producing atypically exuberant works such as *Victory Boogie Woogie* – named for the artist's love of jazz.

During and after De Stijl, a number of other movements flourished, though their impact was not so great and their influence largely confined to the Netherlands. The Expressionist **Bergen School** was probably the most localized, its best-known exponent **Charley Toorop** (1891–1955), daughter of Jan, who developed a distinctively glaring but strangely sensitive realism. **De Ploeg** (The Plough), centred in Groningen, was headed by **Jan Wiegers** (1893–1959) and influenced by Kirchner and the German Expressionists; the group's artists set out to capture the uninviting landscapes around their native town, and produced violently coloured canvases that hark back to Van Gogh. Another group, known as the **Magic Realists**, surfaced in the 1930s, painting quasi-surrealistic scenes that, according to their leading light, **Carel Willinck** (b. 1900), revealed "a world stranger and more dreadful in its haughty impenetrability than the most terrifying nightmare".

Postwar Dutch art began with **CoBrA**: a loose grouping of like-minded painters from Denmark, Belgium and Holland, whose name derives from the initial letters of their respective capital cities. Their first exhibition at Amsterdam's Stedelijk Museum in 1949 provoked a huge uproar, at the centre of which was **Karel Appel** (b. 1921), whose brutal Abstract Expressionist pieces, plastered with paint inches thick, were, he maintained, necessary for the era – indeed, inevitable reflections of it. "I paint like a barbarian in a bar-barous age", he claimed. In the graphic arts the most famous twentieth-century figure is **M.C. Escher** (1898–1970).

As for today, there's as vibrant an art scene as there ever was, best exemplified in Amsterdam by the rotating exhibitions of the Stedelijk and by the dozens of galleries and exhibition spaces throughout the city. Among contemporary Dutch artists, look out for the abstract work of **Edgar Fernhout** and **Ad Dekkers**, the reliefs of **Jan Schoonhoven**, the multimedia productions of **Jan Dibbets**, the glowering realism of **Marlene Dumas**, the imprecisely coloured geometric designs of **Rob van Koningsbruggen**, the smeary expressionism of **Toon Verhoef**, and the exuberant figures of **Rene Daniels** – to name only the most important figures.

Dutch Galleries: a Hit List

In **Amsterdam** itself, the **Rijksmuseum** gives a complete overview of Dutch art up to the end of the nineteenth century, in particular the work of Rembrandt, Hals and the major artists of the Golden Age; the **Van Gogh Museum** is best for the Impressionists and, of course, Van Gogh; and for twentieth-century and contemporary Dutch art, there's the **Stedelijk**. The **CoBrA Museum of Modern Art** is in **Amstelveen** in the southern suburbs. Within easy reach of the city, the **Frans Hals Museum** in **Haarlem** holds some of the best work of Hals and the Haarlem School; also in Haarlem, the **Teyler's Museum** is strong on eighteenth- and nineteenth-century Dutch works. In **Leiden**, the **Lakenhal** has works by, among others, local artists Dou and Rembrandt, and the **Centraal** in **Utrecht** has paintings by Van Scorel and the Utrecht School. Also in Utrecht, the **Catharijne Convent Museum** boasts an excellent collection of works by Flemish artists and by Hals and Rembrandt.

Further afield, **The Hague**'s **Gemeente Museum** owns the country's largest set of Mondrians, and its **Mauritshuis** collection contains works by Rembrandt, Vermeer and others of the era. The **Boymans van Beuningen Museum** in **Rotterdam** has a weighty stock of works by Flemish primitives and surrealists, as well as works by Rembrandt and other seventeenth-century artists, and nearby **Dordrecht**'s **Municipal Museum** offers an assortment of seventeenth-century paintings that includes work by Aelbert Cuyp, and later canvases by the Hague School and Breitner.

The **Kroller-Muller Museum**, just outside **Arnhem**, is probably the country's finest modern art collection, and has a superb collection of Van Goghs; a little further east, **Enschede**'s **Rijksmuseum Twenthe** displays quality works from the Golden Age to the twentieth century.

The City in Fiction

Amsterdam lives more frantically in fiction than in reality. It's the capital of Dutch literature not only in the sense that most Dutch writers have lived here at some time or are living here now, but it also forms the backdrop to most contemporary Dutch novels. A fair amount of Dutch literature has been translated into English in recent years, notably the work of Cees Nooteboom, Marga Minco, Harry Mulisch and Simon Carmiggelt. There's also, of course, English-language fiction set in Amsterdam or the Netherlands, of which the detective writer Nicolas Freeling is perhaps the best-known exponent.

Simon Carmiggelt

Humour is a frequent theme of Dutch literature, and Simon Carmiggelt was one of the country's best-loved humorous writers – and a true poet of Amsterdam in his own way. He moved to the capital during the war, working as a production manager and journalist on the then illegal newspaper, *Het Parool*. In 1946, he started writing a daily column in the paper, entitled *Kronkel*, meaning "twist" or "kink". It was an almost immediate success, and he continued to write his *Kronkels* for several decades, in the end turning out almost 10,000. They're a unique genre – short, usually humorous anecdotes of everyday life, with a strong undercurrent of melancholy and a seriousness at their heart. They concern ordinary people, poignantly observed with razor-sharp – but never cruel – wit and intelligence. Some of the strongest have been bundled together in anthologies, two of which – *A Dutchman's Slight Adventures* (1966) and *I'm Just Kidding* (1972) – were translated into English. Simon Carmiggelt died in 1989.

Corner

In a café in the Albert Cuypstraat, where the open-air market pulses with sounds and colour, I ran into my friend Ben.

"Did you know Joop Groenteman?" he asked.

"You mean the one who sold fruit?" I replied.

"Yes. You heard about his death?"

I nodded. A fishmonger had told me. "It's a shame," said Ben. "A real loss for the market. He had a nice stall – always polished his fruit. And he had that typical Amsterdam sense of humour that seems to be disappearing. He'd say "Hi" to big people and "Lo" to little ones. If somebody wanted to buy two apples, he'd ask where the party was. No one was allowed to pick and choose his fruit. Joop handed it out from behind the plank. Somebody asked him once if he had a plastic bag, and he said, 'I got false teeth. Ain't that bad enough?' He never lost his touch, not even in the hospital."

"Did you go see him there?" I enquired.

"Yes, several times," Ben said. "Once his bed was empty. On the pillow lay a note: 'Back in two hours. Put whatever you brought on the bed.' He had to go on a diet because he was too fat. They weighed him every day. One morning he tied a portable radio around his waist with a rope, put his bathrobe over it, and got on the scale. To the nurse's alarm he'd suddenly gained eight pounds. That was his idea of fun in the hospital. During one visit I asked him when he'd get out. He said, 'Oh, someday soon, either through the front door or the back.'"

Ben smiled sadly.

"He died rather unexpectedly," he resumed. "There was an enormous crowd at his funeral. I was touched by the sight of all his friends from the market standing round the grave with their hats on and each one of them shovelling three spadesful of earth on to his coffin. Oh well, he at least attained the goal of his life."

"What goal?" I asked.

"The same one every open-air merchant has," Ben answered, "a place on a corner. If you're on a corner, you sell more. But it's awfully hard to get a corner place."

"Joop managed it, though?"

"Yes – but not in the Albert Cuyp," said Ben. "That corner place was a sort of obsession to him. He knew his chance was practically nil. So then he decided that if he couldn't get one while he was alive, he'd make sure of it when he died. Every time the collector for the burial insurance came along, he'd say 'Remember, I want a corner grave.' But when he did die, there wasn't a single corner to be had. Well, that's not quite right. It just happened that there was one corner with a stone to the memory of someone who had died in the furnaces of a concentration camp. Nobody was really buried there. And the cemetery people gave permission to have the stone placed somewhere else and to let Joop have that plot. So he finally got what he wanted. A place on the corner."

Herring-man

It was morning, and I paused to buy a herring at one of those curious legged vending carts that stand along Amsterdam's canals.

"Onions?" asked the white-jacketed herring-man. He was big and broad-shouldered, and his hair was turning grey – a football believer, by the looks of him, who never misses Sunday in the stadium.

"No onions," I answered.

Two other men were standing there eating. They wore overalls and were obviously fellow-workers.

"There's them that take onions, and them that don't," one of the men said tolerantly. The herring-man nodded.

"Take me, now, I never eat pickles with 'em," said the other in the coquettish tone of a girl revealing some little charm that she just happens to possess.

"Give me another, please," I said.

The herring-man cut the fish in three pieces and reached with his glistening hand into the dish of onions.

"No, no onions," I said.

He smiled his apology. "Excuse me. My mind was wandering," he said.

The men in overalls also ordered another round and then began to wrangle about some futility or other on which they disagreed. They were still at it after I had paid and proceeded to a café just across from the herring-cart, where I sat down at a table by the window. For Dutchmen they talked rather strenuously with their hands. A farmer once told me that when the first cock begins to crow early in the morning, all the other roosters in the neighbourhood immediately raise their voices, hoping to drown him out. Most males are cut from the same cloth.

"What'll it be?" asked the elderly waitress in the café.

"Coffee." As she was getting it a fat, slovenly creature came in. Months ago she had had her hair dyed straw yellow, but later had become so nostalgic for her own natural brown that her skull was now dappled with two colours.

"Have you heard?" she asked.

"What?"

"The herring-man's son ran into a streetcar on his motorbike yesterday," she said, "and now he's good and dead. The docs at the hospital couldn't save him. They came to tell his pa about a half an hour ago."

The elderly waitress served my coffee.

"How awful," she said.

I looked across the street. The overalled quarrellers were gone, and the broad, strong herring-man stood cleaning his fish with automatic expertness.

"The kid was just seventeen," said the fat woman. "He was learning to be a pastry cook. Won third prize at the food show with his chocolate castle."

"Those *motorbikes* are rotten things," the waitress said.

"People are mysterious," a friend of mine once wrote, and as I thought of those words I suddenly remembered the onions the herring-man nearly gave me with my second fish, his smiling apology: "My mind was wandering."

Genius

The little café lay on a broad, busy thoroughfare in one of the new sections of Amsterdam. The barkeeper-host had only one guest: an ancient man who sat amiably behind his empty genever glass. I placed my order and added, "Give grandfather something, too."

"You've got one coming," called the barkeeper. The old man smiled and tipped me a left-handed military salute, his fingers at his fragile temple. Then he got up, walked over to me, and asked, "Would you be interested in a chance on a first-class smoked sausage, guaranteed weight two pounds?"

"I certainly would be," I replied.

"It just costs a quarter, and the drawing will take place next Saturday," he said.

I fished out twenty-five cents and put it on the bar, and in return he gave me a piece of cardboard on which the number 79 was written in ink.

"A number with a tail," he said. "Lucky for you."

He picked up the quarter, put on his homburg hat, and left the café with a friendly "Good afternoon, gentlemen." Through the window I saw him unlocking an old bicycle. Then, wheeling his means of transport, he disappeared from view.

"How old is he?" I asked.

"Eighty-six."

"And he still rides a bicycle?"

The barkeeper shook his head.

"No," he replied, "but he has to cross over, and it's a busy street. He's got a theory that traffic can see someone with a bicycle in his hand better than someone without a bicycle. So that's the why and the wherefore. When he gets across, he parks the bike and locks it up, and then the next day he's got it all ready to walk across again."

I thought it over.

"Not a bad idea," I said.

"Oh, he's all there, that one," said the barkeeper. "Take that lottery, now. He made it up himself. I guess he sells about a hundred chances here every week. That's twenty-five guilders. And he only has to fork over one sausage on Saturday evening. Figure it out for yourself."

I did so, cursorily. He really got his money's worth out of that sausage, no doubt of it.

"And he runs the drawing all by himself," the barkeeper went on. "Clever as all get out. Because if a customer says, 'I've bought a lot of chances from you, but I never win,' you can bet your boots he *will* win the very next Saturday. The old man takes care that he does. Gets the customer off his neck for a good long time. Pretty smart, huh?"

I nodded and said, "He must have been a businessman?"

"Well no. He was in the navy. They've paid him a pension for ages and ages. He's costing them a pretty penny."

All of a sudden I saw the old man on the other side of the street. He locked his bicycle against a wall and wandered away.

"He can get home from there without crossing any more streets," said the barkeeper.

I let him fill my glass again.

"I gave him a drink, but I didn't see him take it," I remarked.

The barkeeper nodded.

"He's sharp as tacks about that, too," he said. "Here's what he does. He's old and spry, and nearly everybody buys him something. But he

never drinks more than two a day. So I write all the free ones down for him." He glanced at a notepad that lay beside the cash register. "Let's see. Counting the one from you, he's a hundred and sixty-seven to the good."

Cees Nooteboom

Cees Nooteboom is one of Holland's best-known writers. He published his first novel in 1955, but only really came to public attention after the publication of his third novel, *Rituals*, in 1980. The central theme of all his work is the phenomenon of time: *Rituals* in particular is about the passing of time and the different ways of controlling the process. Inni Wintrop, the main character, is an outsider, a "dilettante" as he describes himself. The book is almost entirely set in Amsterdam, and although it describes the inner life of Inni himself, it also paints a vivid picture of the decaying city. Each section details a decade of Inni's life; the one reprinted below describes an encounter from his forties.

Rituals

There were days, thought Inni Wintrop, when it seemed as if a recurrent, fairly absurd phenomenon were trying to prove that the world is an absurdity that can best be approached with nonchalance, because life would otherwise become unbearable.

There were days, for instance, when you kept meeting cripples, days with too many blind people, days when you saw three times in succession a left shoe lying by the roadside. It seemed as if all these things were trying to mean something but could not. They left only a vague sense of unease, as if somewhere there existed a dark plan for the world that allowed itself to be hinted at only in this clumsy way.

The day on which he was destined to meet Philip Taads, of whose existence he had hitherto been unaware, was the day of the three doves. The dead one, the live one, and the dazed one, which could not possibly have been one and the same, because he had seen the dead one first. These three, he thought later, had made an attempt at annunciation that had succeeded insofar as it had made the encounter with Taads the Younger more mysterious.

It was now 1973, and Inni had turned forty in a decade he did not approve of. One ought not, he felt, to live in the second half of any century, and this particular century was altogether bad. There was something sad and at the same time ridiculous about all these fading years piling on top of one another until at last the millennium arrived. And they contained a contradiction, too: in order to reach the hundred, and in this case the thousand, that had to be completed, one had to add them up; but the feeling that went with the process seemed to have more to do with subtraction. It was as if no one, especially not Time, could wait for those ever dustier, ever higher figures finally to be declared void by a revolution of a row of glittering, perfectly shaped noughts, whereupon they would be relegated to the scrap heap of history. The only people apparently still sure of anything in these days of superstitious expectation were the Pope, the sixth of his name already, a white-robed Italian with an unusually tormented face that faintly resembled Eichmann's, and a number of terrorists of different persuasions, who tried in vain to anticipate the great witches' cauldron. The fact that he was now forty no longer in itself bothered Inni very much.

"Forty," he said, "is the age at which you have to do everything for the third time, or else you'll have to start training to be a cross-tempered old man," and he had decided to do the latter.

After Zita, he had had a long-lasting affair with an actress who had finally, in self-preservation, turned him out of the house like an old chair.

"What I miss most about her," he said to his friend the writer, "is her absence. These people are never at home. You get addicted to that."

He now lived alone and intended to keep it that way. The years passed, but even this was noticeable only in photographs. He bought and sold things, was not addicted to drugs, smoked less than one packet of Egyptian cigarettes a day, and drank neither more nor less than most of his friends.

This was the situation on the radiant June morning when, on the bridge between the Herenstraat and the Prinsenstraat, a dove flew straight at him as if it bore itself into his heart. Instead, it smashed against a car approaching from the Prinsengracht. The car drove on and the dove was left lying in the street, a gray and dusty, suddenly silly-looking little thing. A blonde-haired girl got off her bicycle and went up to the dove at the same time as Inni.

"Is it dead, do you think?" she asked.

He crouched down and turned the bird onto its back. The head did not turn with the rest of the body and continued to stare at the road surface.

"Finito," said Inni.

The girl put her bike away.

"I daren't pick it up," she said, "Will you?"

She used the familiar form of you. As long as they still do that, I am not yet old, thought Inni, picking up the dove. He did not like doves. They were not a bit like the image he used to have of the Holy Ghost, and the fact that all those promises of peace had never come to anything was probably their fault as well. Two white, softly cooing doves in the garden of a Tuscan villa, that was all right, but the gray hordes marching across the Dam Square with spurs on their boots (their heads making those idiotic mechanical pecking movements) could surely have nothing to do with a Spirit which had allegedly chosen that particular shape in which to descend upon Mary.

"What are you going to do with it?" asked the girl.

Inni looked around and saw on the bridge a wooden skip belonging to the Council. He went up to it. It was full of sand. Gently he laid the dove in it. The girl had followed him. An erotic moment. Man with dead dove, girl with bike and blue eyes. She was beautiful.

"Don't put it in there," she said. "The workmen will chuck it straight into the canal."

What does it matter whether it rots away in sand or in water, thought Inni, who often claimed he would prefer to be blown up after his death. But this was not the moment to hold a discourse on transience.

"Are you in a hurry?" he asked.

"No."

"Give me that bag then." From her handlebar hung a plastic bag, one from the Athenaeum Book Store.

"What's in there?"

"A book by Jan Wolkers."

"It can go in there then," said Inni. "There's no blood."

He put the dove in the bag.

"Jump on the back."

He took her bike without looking at her and rode off.

"Hey," she said. He heard her rapid footsteps and felt her jumping on the back of the bike. In the shop windows he caught brief glimpses of something that looked like happiness. Middle-aged gentleman on girl's bicycle, girl in jeans and white sneakers on the back.

He rode down the Prinsengracht to the Haarlemmerdijk and from a distance saw the barriers of the bridge going down. They got off, and as the bridge slowly rose, they saw the second dove. It was sitting inside one of the open metal supports under the bridge, totally unconcerned as it allowed itself to be lifted up like a child on the Ferris wheel.

For a moment Inni felt an impulse to take the dead dove out of the plastic bag and lift it up like a peace offering to its slowly ascending living colleague, but he did not think the girl would like it. And besides, what would be the meaning of such a gesture? He shuddered, as usual not knowing why. The dove came down again and vanished invulnerably under the asphalt. They cycled on, to the Westerpark. With her small, brown hands, the girl dug a grave in the damp, black earth, somewhere in a corner.

"Deep enough?"

"For a dove, yes."

He laid the bird, which was now wearing its head like a hood on its back, into the hole. Together they smoothed the loose earth on top of it.

"Shall we go and have a drink?" he asked.

"All right."

Something in this minimal death, either the death itself or the summary ritual surrounding it, had made them allies. Something now had to happen, and if this something had anything to do with death, it would not be obvious. He cycled along the Nassaukade. She was not heavy. This was what pleased him most about his strange life – that when he had gotten up that morning, he had not known that he would now be cycling here with a girl at his back, but that such a possibility was always there. It gave him, he thought, something invincible. He looked at the faces of the men in the oncoming cars, and he knew that his life, in its absurdity, was right. Emptiness, loneliness, anxiety – these were the drawbacks – but there were also compensations, and this was one of them. She was humming softly and then fell silent. She said suddenly, as if she had taken a decision, "This is where I live."

Translated by Adrienne Dixon;
© Louisiana State University Press, 1983.

Rudi van Dantzig

Rudi van Dantzig is one of Holland's most famous choreographers, and was, until 1991, artistic director of the Dutch National Ballet. *For a Lost Soldier*, published in 1986, is his debut novel, an almost entirely autobiographical account of his experiences as a child during the war years. It's an extremely well-written novel, convincingly portraying the confusion and loneliness of the approximately 50,000 Dutch children evacuated to foster families during the hunger winter. The novel's leading character is Jeroen, an eleven-year-old boy from Amsterdam who is sent away to live with a family in Friesland. During the Liberation celebrations, he meets an American soldier, Walt, with whom he has a brief sexual encounter; Walt disappears a few days later. The extract below details Jeroen's desperate search for Walt shortly after his return to Amsterdam.

For a Lost Soldier

I set out on a series of reconnoitring expeditions through Amsterdam, tours of exploration that will take me to every corner. On a small map I look up the most important streets to see how I can best fan out to criss-cross the town, then make plans on pieces of paper showing exactly how the streets on each of my expeditions join up and what they are called. To make doubly sure I also use abbreviations: H.W. for Hoofdweg, H.S. for Haarlemmerstraat. The pieces of paper are carefully stored away inside the dust-jacket of a book, but I am satisfied that even if somebody found the notes, they wouldn't be able to make head or tail of them. It is a well-hidden secret.

For my first expedition I get up in good time. I yawn a great deal and act as cheerfully as I can to disguise the paralysing uncertainty that is governing my every move.

"We're going straight to the field, Mum, we're going to build a hut," but she is very busy and scarcely listens.

"Take care and don't be back too late."

The street smells fresh as if the air has been scrubbed with soap. I feel dizzy with excitement and as soon as I have rounded the corner I start to run towards the bridge. Now it's beginning, and everything is sure to be all right, all my waiting and searching is about to come to an end; the solution lies hidden over there, somewhere in the clear light filling the streets.

The bright air I inhale makes me feel that I am about to burst. I want to sing, shout, cheer myself hoarse.

I have marked my piece of paper, among a tangle of crossing and twisting lines, with H.W, O.T, W.S, Hoofdweg, Overtoom, Weteringschans.

The Hoofdweg is close by, just over the bridge. It is the broad street we have to cross when we go to the swimming baths. I know the gloomy houses and the narrow, flowerless gardens from the many times I've walked by in other summers, towel and swimming trunks rolled under my arm. But beyond that, and past Mercatorplein, Amsterdam is unknown territory to me, ominous virgin land.

The unfamiliar streets make me hesitate, my excitement seeps away and suddenly I feel unsure and tired. The town bewilders me: shops with queues outside, people on bicycles carrying bags, beflagged streets in the early morning sun, squares where wooden platforms have been put up for neighbourhood celebrations, whole districts with music pouring out of loudspeakers all day. An unsolvable jigsaw puzzle. Now and then I stop in sheer desperation, study my hopelessly inadequate piece of paper, and wonder if it would not be much better to give up the attempt altogether.

But whenever I see an army vehicle, or catch a glimpse of a uniform, I revive and walk a little faster, sometimes trotting after a moving car in the hope that it will come to a stop and he will jump out.

Time after time I lose my way and have to walk back quite far, and sometimes, if I can summon up enough courage, I ask for directions.

"Please, Mevrouw, could you tell me how to get to the Overtoom?"

"Dear me, child, you're going the wrong way. Over there, right at the end, turn left, that'll take you straight there."

The Overtoom, when I finally reach it, seems to be a street without beginning or end. I walk, stop, cross the road, search: not a trace of W.S. Does my plan bear any resemblance to the real thing?

I take off my shoes and look at the dark impression of my sweaty foot on the pavement. Do I have to go on, search any more? What time is it, how long have I been walking the streets?

Off we sail to Overtoom,
We drink milk and cream at home,
Milk and cream with apple pie,
Little children must not lie.

Over and over again, automatically, the jingle runs through my mind, driving me mad.

As I walk back home, slowly, keeping to the shady side of the street as much as I can, I think of the other expeditions hidden away in the dust-jacket of my book. The routes I picked out and wrote down with so much eagerness and trust seem pointless and unworkable now. I scold myself: I must not give up, only a coward would do that. Walt is waiting for me, he has no one, and he'll be so happy to see me again.

At home I sit down in a chair by the window, too tired to talk, and when I do give an answer to my mother my voice sounds thin and weak, as if it were finding it difficult to escape from my chest. She sits down next to me on the arm of the chair, lifts my chin up and asks where we have been playing such tiring games, she hasn't seen me down in the street all morning, though the other boys were there.

"Were you really out in the field?"

"Ask them if you don't believe me!" I run onto the balcony, tear my first route map up into pieces and watch the shreds fluttering down into the garden like snowflakes.

When my father gets back home he says, "So, my boy, you and I had best go into town straightway, you still haven't seen the illuminations."

With me on the back, he cycles as far as the Concertgebouw, where he leans the bike against a wall and walks with me past a large green space with badly worn grass. Here, too, there are soldiers, tents, trucks. Why don't I look this time, why do I go and walk on the other side of my father and cling – "Don't hang on so tight!" – to his arm?

"Now you'll see something," he says, "something you've never even dreamed of, just you wait and see."

Walt moving his quivering leg to and fro, his warm, yielding skin, the smell of the thick hair in his armpits . . .

I trudge along beside my father, my soles burning, too tired to look at anything.

We walk through the gateway of a large building, a sluice that echoes to the sound of voices, and through which the people have to squeeze before fanning out again on the other side. There are hundreds of them now, all moving in the same direction towards a buzzing hive of activity, a surging mass of bodies.

There is a sweet smell of food coming from a small tent in the middle of the street in front of which people are crowding so thickly that I can't see what is being sold.

I stop in my tracks, suddenly dying for food, dying just to stay where I am and to yield myself up to that wonderful sweet smell. But my father has already walked on and I have to wriggle through the crowds to catch up with him.

Beside a bridge he pushes me forward between the packed bodies so that I can see the canal, a long stretch of softly shimmering water bordered by overhanging trees. At one end brilliantly twinkling arches of light have been suspended that blaze in the darkness and are reflected in the still water. Speechless and enchanted I stare at the crystal-clear world full of dotted lines, a vision of luminous radiation that traces a winking and sparkling route leading from bridge to bridge, from arch to arch, from me to my lost soldier.

I grip my father's hand. "Come on," I say, "let's have a look. Come on!"

Festoons of light bulbs are hanging wherever we go, like stars stretched across the water, and the people walk past them in silent, admiring rows. The banks of the canal feel as cosy as candle-lit sitting-rooms.

"Well?" my father breaks the spell. "It's quite something, isn't it? In Friesland, you'd never have dreamed that anything like that existed, would you now?"

We take a short cut through dark narrow streets. I can hear dull cracks, sounds that come as a surprise in the dark, as if a sniper were firing at us.

My father starts to run.

"Hurry, or we'll be too late."

An explosion of light spurts up against the black horizon and whirls apart, pink and pale green fountains of confetti that shower down over a brilliant sign standing etched in the sky.

And another shower of stars rains down to the sound of muffled explosions and cheers from the crowd, the sky trembling with the shattering of triumphal arches.

I look at the luminous sign in the sky as if it is a mirage.

"Daddy, that letter, what's it for? Why is it there?" Why did I have to ask, why didn't I just add my own letters, fulfil my own wishful thinking?

"That W? You know what that's for. The W, the W's for Queen Wilhelmina . . ." I can hear a scornful note in his voice as if he is mocking me.

"Willy here, Willy there," he says, "but the whole crew took off to England and left us properly in the lurch."

I'm not listening, I don't want to hear what he has to say.

W isn't Wilhelmina: it stands for Walt! It's a sign specially for me . . .

Reprinted by permission of The Bodley Head.

Marga Minco

Marga Minco's *Empty House*, first published in 1966, is another wartime novel. During the German occupation her entire family, being Jewish, was deported and killed in concentration camps. Minco herself managed to escape this fate and spent much of the war in hiding in Amsterdam. In 1944 she moved to Kloveniersburgwal 49, which served as a safe house for various Dutch artists during the ensuing hunger winter; it's this house – or, rather, the house next door – that is the model for the various empty houses in the novel. In the following extract, the main character, Sepha, meets Yona, another Jewish survivor and later to become a great friend, when travelling back from Friesland to the safe house.

An Empty House

As soon as we were in the centre Yona put on her rucksack and tapped on the window of the cab. We'd been delayed a lot because the lorry which had picked us up at our spot beyond Zwolle had to go to all kinds of small villages and made one detour after another. We sat in the back on crates. Yona had grazed her knee heaving herself up over the tail-gate. I'd not seen it because I'd been making a place for us to sit.

"What have you done?" I asked.

"Damn it," she cried, "I'm not as agile as you. I told you. I spent all my time holed up in a kind of loft." She tied a hanky round her knee. "One step from the door to the bed. Do you think I did keep-fit exercises or something?"

I thought of the fire-escape which I'd gone up and down practically every day. In the end I could do it one-handed.

"Have you somewhere to go to in Amsterdam?"

I expected her to say it was none of my business, but she seemed not to hear me. The lorry thundered along a road where they'd just cleared away barricades.

"Do you know," she said, "at first I didn't know where I was?" Suddenly her voice was much less sharp. "All I knew was that it was a low house with an attic window above the back door. "You don't live here," said the woman of the house. She always wore a blue striped apron. "But I am here though," I said. "No," she said, "you must remember that you're not here, you're nowhere." She didn't say it unpleasantly, she wished me no harm. But I couldn't get it out of my mind – you're nowhere. It's as if, by degrees, you start believing it yourself, as if you begin to doubt yourself. I sometimes sat staring at my hands for ages. There was no mirror and they'd white-washed the attic window. It was only by looking at my hand that I recognized myself, proved to myself that I was there."

"Didn't anybody ever come to see you?"

"Yes. In the beginning. But I didn't feel like talking. They soon got the message. They let me come downstairs in the evenings occasionally, the windows were blacked out and the front and back doors bolted. It didn't impress me as being anything special. Later on, I even began to dislike it. I saw that they were scared stiff when I was sitting in the room. They listened to every noise from outside. I told them that I'd rather stay upstairs, that I didn't want to run any risks. You can even get used to a loft. At least it was mine, my loft."

While talking, she had turned round; she sat with her back half turned towards me. I had to bend forward to catch her last words. Her scarf had slipped off. Her hair kept brushing my face. Once we were near Amsterdam, she started talking about her father who went with her to the Concertgebouw every week, accompanied her on long walks and ate cakes with her in small tea-rooms. She talked about him as if he were a friend. And again I had to hear details of the house. She walked me through rooms and corridors, showed me the court-yard, the cellar with wine-racks, the attic with the old-fashioned pulley. I knew it as if I had lived there myself. Where would she sleep tonight?

"If you want to, you can come home with me," I said. "I shan't have any time. I've so much to do. There's a case of mine somewhere as well. I can't remember what I put in it."

We drove across Berlage Bridge. It was still light. She'd fallen silent during the last few kilo-metres and sat with her chin in her hands. "The south district," I heard her say. "Nothing has changed here, of course."

I wrote my address on a little piece of paper and gave it to her. She put it in the pocket of her khaki shirt without looking at it.

"You must come," I shouted after her when she had got out at Ceintuurbaan. She walked away without a backward glance, hands on the straps of her rucksack, hunched forward as if there were stones in it. I lost sight of her because I was looking at a tram coming from Ferdinand Bolstraat. The trams were running again. There were tiny flags on the front. Flags were hanging everywhere. And portraits of the Queen. And orange hangings. Everyone seemed to be in the streets. It was the last evening of the Liberation celebrations. The driver dropped me off at Rokin. I'd not far to go. If I walked quickly, I could be there in five minutes. The door was usually open, the lock was broken – less than half a minute for the three flights of stairs. I could leave my case downstairs.

People were walking in rows right across the full width of the street. The majority had orange buttonholes or red, white and blue ribbons. There were a lot of children with paper hats, flags and tooters. Two mouth-organ players and a saxophonist in a traditional *Volendammer* costume drifted with the mass, though far apart. I tried to get through as quickly as possible. I bumped into a child who dropped his flag, which was about to be trodden underfoot. I made room with my case, grabbed the flag from the ground and thrust it into his hand. Jazz music resounded from a bar in Damstraat. The door was open. Men and women were sitting at the bar with their arms around each other. Their bodies shook. All that was left in the baker's window were bread-crumbs. Here it was even busier. Groups of Canadians stood at the corners, besieged by whores, black-market traders and dog-end collectors.

I'd not seen much of the Liberation in the Frisian village. The woman I'd stayed with baked her own bread; she had done so throughout the war and she just went on doing it. When I was alone in the kitchen with her she asked with avid interest about my experiences in the hunger winter. She wanted to know everything about the church with corpses, the men with rattles, the people suffering from beriberi on the steps of the Palace, the emaciated children who went to the soup-kitchen with their pans. I spared her no details. About the recycled fat which gave us diarrhoea, the rotten fen potatoes, the wet, clay-like bread, about the ulcers and legs full of sores. I saw it as a way of giving something back.

At last I was at the bridge. I looked at the house with the large expanses of window and the grimy door. At the house next door, the raised pavement and the neck gable. The windows were bricked up. The debris was piled high behind. All that was left were bare walls. I put down my case to change hands. It was as if, only then, that I felt how hungry I was, how stiff my knees were from sitting for hours on the crate. There was something strange about the houses, as if I'd been away for years. But it could have been that I'd never stopped on the bridge before, never looked at them from that angle. The barge was still there. An oil-lamp was burning behind the portholes.

Our front door was closed. The lock had been mended in the meantime. I ought to have had a key somewhere. I didn't want to ring. I'd never realized that the staircase was so dark when the front door was shut. Without thinking, I groped for the banister and banged my hand against the rough wall. "It's nice, soft wood," Mark had said as he sawed the banister into logs. "You can cut it nicely into pieces with a sharp knife." The steps on the upper flight grated as if there were sand on them. I pushed the door open with my case.

There was a black lady's handbag on the bed. A leather bag with a brass clasp. Who had a bag like that? The leather was supple and smooth, except for some creases on the underside. I walked to the table which was full of bottles and glasses. I saw a long dog-end lying in one of the ashtrays. The cigarette must have been carefully put out. Afterwards the burnt tobacco had been nipped off. I found the empty packet on the floor, Sweet Caporal. The divan was strewn with newspapers. Eisenhower standing in a car. Montgomery standing in a car. A new Bailey bridge built in record time.

I had to look among the piled-up crockery in the kitchen for a cup. I rinsed it a long time before I drank from it. I felt the water sink into my stomach; it gurgled as if it was falling into a smooth, cold hollow. The tower clock sounded the half-hour. The house became even quieter. There appeared to be nobody home on the other floors either. Half nine? It got dark quickly now. It was already dark under the few trees left along the canal. I opened one of the windows and leant outside. A man and a woman tottered along the pavement on the other side. They held each other firmly under the arm. They would suddenly lurch forward a few metres, slowly right

themselves and start up again. The nine o'clock man always walked there too. I'd not heard him since the Liberation.

Reprinted by permission of Peter Owen Publishers, London.

Nicolas Freeling

Creator of the Dutch detective Van der Valk, Nicolas Freeling was born in England but has lived all his life in Europe, where most of his novels are set. He actually left Amsterdam over twenty years ago and nowadays rarely returns to the city. But in the Van der Valk novels he evokes Amsterdam (and Amsterdammers) as well as any writer ever has, subtly and unsentimentally using the city and its people as a vivid backdrop to his fast-moving action. The following extract is from A *Long Silence*, first published in 1972.

A Long Silence

Arlette came out into the open air and saw that spring had come to Amsterdam. The pale, acid sun of late afternoon lay on the inner harbour beyond the Prins Hendrik Kade: the wind off the water was sharp. It gave her a shock. A succession of quick rhythmic taps, as at the start of a violin concerto of Beethoven. That she noticed this means, I think, that from that moment she was sane again. But it is possible that I am mistaken. Even if insane one can have, surely, the same perceptions as other people, and this "click" is a familiar thing. Exactly the same happens when one takes a night train down from Paris to the Coast, and one wakes somewhere between Saint Raphael and Cannes and looks out, and there is the Mediterranean. Or was.

The pungent salt smell, the northern, maritime keynotes of seagull and herring, the pointed brick buildings, tall and narrow like herons, with their mosaic of parti-coloured shutters, eaves, sills, that gives the landscapes their stiff, heraldic look (one is back beyond Brueghel, beyond Van Eyck, to the primitives whose artists we do not know, so that they have names like the Master of the Saint Ursula Legend). The lavish use of paint in flat bright primary colours which typifies these Baltic, Hanseatic quay-sides is startling to the visitor from central Europe. Even the Dutch flags waving everywhere (there are no more determined flagwavers) upset and worried Arlette: she had not realised how in a short time her eye had accustomed itself to the subtle and faded colourings of France, so that it was as though she had never left home. The sharp flat brightness of Holland! The painters' light which hurts the unaccustomed eye . . . Arlette never wore sunglasses in France, except on the sea, or on the snow, yet here, she remembered suddenly, she had practically gone to bed in them. It was all so familiar. She had lived here, she had to keep reminding herself, for twenty years.

She had no notion of where she wanted to go, but she knew that now she was here, a small pause would bring the spinning, whirling patterns of the kaleidoscope to rest. She crossed the road and down the steps to the little wooden terrace – a drink, and get her breath back! Everything was new – the pale heavy squatness of the Dutch café's cup-and-saucer, left on her table by the last occupant; the delightful rhythmic skyline across the harbour of the Saint Nicolaas church and the corner of the Zeedijk! Tourists were flocking into waterbuses, and now she was a tourist too. An old waiter was wiping the table while holding a tray full of empty bottles, which wavered in front of her eye.

"Mevrouw?"

"Give me a chocomilk, if at least you've got one that's good and cold."

Another click! She was talking Dutch, and as fluently as ever she had! He was back before she had got over it.

"Nou, mevrouwtje – cold as Finnegan's feet." His voice had the real Amsterdam caw to it. "You aren't Dutch though, are you now?"

"Only a tourist," smiling.

"Well now, by-your-leave: proper-sounding Dutch you talk there," chattily, bumping the glass down and pouring in the clawky chocomilk.

"Thank you very much."

"Tot Uw dienst. Ja ja ja, kom er aan" to a fussy man, waving and banging his saucer with a coin.

Neem mij niet kwa-a-lijk; een be-hoor-lijk Nederlands spreekt U daar. Like a flock of rooks. Yah, yah ya-ah, kom er a-an. And she was blinded by tears again, hearing her husband's exact intonation – when with her he spoke a Dutch whose accent sometimes unconsciously – ludicrously – copied hers, but when with the real thing, the rasecht like himself his accent would begin to caw too as though in self-parody.

Next door to her were sitting two American girls, earnest, quiet, dusty-haired, looking quite clean though their jeans were as darkly greasy as the mud the dredger over there was turning up off the harbour bottom. Scraps of conversation floated across.

"She's a lovely person, ever so quiet but really mature, you know what I mean, yes, from Toledo." Arlette knew that Van der Valk would have guffawed and her eyes cleared.

I see her there, at the start of her absurd and terrifying mission. She has the characteristic feminine memory for detail, the naively earnest certainty that she has to get everything right. Had I asked what those two girls were drinking she would have known for sure, and been delighted at my asking.

I have not seen Amsterdam for four or five years, and it might be as long again before I shall. This is just as well. I do not want my imagination to get in the way of Arlette's senses. Piet, whose imagination worked like mine, saw things in an entirely different way to her. We were sitting once together on that same terrace.

"Look at that dam building," pointing at the Central Station, a construction I am fond of, built with loving attention to every useless detail by an architect of the last century whose name I have forgotten (a Dutch equivalent of Sir Giles Gilbert Scott). "Isn't it lovely?" Lovely is not the word I would have chosen but it is oddly right.

"The Railway Age," he went on. "Make a wonderful museum – old wooden carriages, tuff-tuff locos with long funnels, Madame Tussaud figures of station-masters with beards, policemen wearing helmets, huge great soup-strainer moustaches, women with bustle and reticules . . ." Yes, indeed, and children in sailor suits. Arlette's mind does not behave like this.

I am changed, thought Arlette, and unchanged. I am the same housewife, familiar with these streets, these people. I am not pricked or tickled by anything here, like a tourist. I see all this with the coolness and objectivity of experience. I am not going to rush into anything stupid or imprudent. This is a town I know, and I am going to find myself perfectly able to cope with the problem. I am not alone or helpless; I have here many friends, and there are many more who were Piet's friends and who will help me for his sake. But I am no longer the thoughtless and innocent little wife of a little man in a little job, standing on the corner with shopping bag wondering whether to have a cabbage or a cauli. I am a liberated woman, and that is going to make a difference.

A tout was circling around the cluster of tables, sizing up likely suckers. A year or so ago he would have been handing out cards for a restaurant or hotel, looking for a quickie trip around the sights, with waterbus, Anne Frank and the Rembrandthuis all thrown in for only ten guilders. Now – he had closed in on the two American girls and she could hear his pidgin-German patois that is the international language of the European tout – selling live sex-shows. The two girls glanced up for a second with polite indifference, and went back to their earnest, careful, intense conversation, paying no further attention to him at all. He broke off the patter, circled backwards like a boxer and gave Arlette a careful glance: Frenchwomen, generally fascinated by the immoralities and debaucheries of these English and these Scandinavians – a likely buyer, as long as they have first done their duty with a really good orgy at Marks and Spencer's. Arlette met his eye with such a chill and knowing look that he shuffled back into the ropes and made off sideways: cow has been to the sex-show and has no money left. Amsterdam too has changed and not changed, she thought.

"Raffishness" was always the first cliché tourists used, the Amsterdammers were always intensely, idiotically proud of their red-light district and since time immemorial a stroll to look at "the ladies behind the windows" was proposed to every eager tourist the very first night.

They have taken now with such relish to the new role of exhibitionist shop-window that it is hard not to laugh – the visitor's first reaction generally is roars of laughter. The Dutch have a belief that sex has made them less provincial somehow – for few attitudes are more provincial than the anxious striving to be modern-and-progressive. Paris doesn't exist any more, and London is slipping, they will tell one with a boastful pathos, and Holland-is-where-it's-at. A bit immature, really, as the two nineteen-year-olds from Dubuque were probably at that moment saying. Arlette was a humble woman. She saw herself as snobbish, narrow, rigid, French provincial bourgeois. Piet, born and bred in Amsterdam, used to describe himself as a peasant. This humility gave them both an unusual breadth, stability, balance. I remember his telling me once how to his mind his career if not his life had been an abject failure.

"But there," drinking brandy reflectively, being indeed a real soak and loving it, "what else could I have done?"

Arlette, walking through the lazy, dirty sunshine of late afternoon in Amsterdam, was thinking too, "What else could I have done?" She had come to lay a ghost. Not that she – hardheaded woman – believed in ghosts, but she had lived long enough to know they were there. Piet was a believer in ghosts. "I have known malign influences outside the bathroom door," he used to say. He was delighted when I gave him to read the finely-made old thriller of Mr A.E.W. Mason which is called The Prisoner in the Opal: he saw the point at once, and when he brought it back he said that he too, with the most sordid, materialistic, bourgeois of enquiries, always made the effort "to pierce the opal crust". Poor old Piet.

Once we were having dinner together in a Japanese restaurant. We had had three pernods, big ones, the ones Piet with his horrible Dutch ideas of wit which he took for esprit described as "Des Grand Pers". We were watching the cook slicing raw fish into fine transparent slices.

"There is poetry," said Piet suddenly, "in those fingers." I turned around suspiciously, because this is a paraphrase from a good writer, whom Piet had certainly not read. I used the phrase as an epigraph to a book I once wrote about cooks – which Piet had not read either. "Poetry in the fat fingers of cooks" – I looked at Piet suspiciously.

"So," with tactful calm, "is that a quotation?"

"No," innocent, "Just a phrase. Thought it would please you, haw." That crude guffaw; completely Piet. The stinker; to this day I don't know whether he was kidding me. A skilful user of flattery, but damn it, a friend.

The Damrak, the Dam, the Rokin. Squalid remnants of food, flung upon the pavements. The young were unable or unwilling to spend much on food, she thought, and what they got for their money probably deserved to be flung: one could not blame them too much, just because one felt revolted. But one did blame them: beastly children.

The Utrechtsestraat. The Frederincksplein. And once out of the tourist stamping-ground, Arlette knew suddenly where she was going. She was heading unerringly and as though she had never been away straight towards the flat where she had lived for twenty years. It was a longish way to walk, all the way from the Central Station and carrying a suitcase too. Why had she done it? She would have said, "What else could I have done?" crossly, for when she got there she was very tired and slightly footsore, dishevelled, her hair full of dust, smelling of sweat and ready to cry.

"Arlette! My dear girl! What are you doing? – but come in! I'm so happy to see you – and at the same time, my poor child, I'm so sad! Not that we know anything – what one reads in the paper nowadays – Pah! And again Pah! come in, my dear girl, come in – you don't mean to say you walked . . . from the station? You didn't! You couldn't! Sit down child, do. The lavy? But of course you know where it is, that's not something you'll have forgotten. I'll make some coffee. My dear girl, marvellous to see you, and the dear boys? – no no, I must be patient, go and have a pee child, and a wash, do you good." The old biddy who had always had a ground floor flat, and still did . . . She taught the piano. It had been the most familiar background noise to Arlette's life throughout the boys' childhood; her voice carried tremendously.

"One, Two, not so hasty. Pedal there, you're not giving those notes their value, that's a sharp, can't you hear it?" And coming back from shopping an hour later another one was being put through its hoops. "Watch your tempo, not so much espressivo, you're sentimentalising, this is the Ruysdaelskade, not the Wiener Wald or something."

"Lumpenpack," she would mutter, coming out on the landing for a breather and finding Arlette emptying the dustbin.

Old Mother Counterpoint, Piet always called her, and sometimes in deference to Jane Austen "Bates" ("Mother hears perfectly well; you only have to shout a little and say it two or at the most three times"). A wonderful person really. A mine of information on the quarter, possessor of efficient intelligence networks in every shop, an endless gabble on the telephone, forever fixing things for someone else. She could find anything for you; a furnished room, a second-hand pram scarcely used, a boy's bike, a shop where they were having a sale of materials ever so cheap – even if she didn't have her finger on it she knew a man who would let you have it wholesale. Warm-hearted old girl. Gushing, but wonderfully kind, and gentle, and sometimes even tactful.

"You take yours black, dear, oh yes, I hadn't forgotten – you think I'd forget a thing like that? Not gaga yet, thank God. Good heavens, it must be seven years. But you haven't aged dear, a few lines yes – badges of honour my pet, that's what I call them. Tell me – can you bear to talk about

it? Where are you staying? By the look of you you could do with a square meal."

"I don't know, I was wondering . . ."

"But my poor pet of course, how can you ask, you know I'd be more than pleased and I've plenty of room, it's just can you bear all the little fussinesses of a frightened old maid – oh nonsense child, now don't be tiresome. Now I'll tell you what, no don't interrupt, I'm going to the butcher, yes still the same awful fellow, all those terrible people, how they'll be thrilled, just wait till he hears, I'll frighten him, he gave me an escalope last week and tough . . . my poor girl, since you left he thinks everything is permitted him. I'll get a couple of nice veal cutlets and we'll have dinner, just you wait and I'll get something to drink too, I love the excuse and what's more I'll make pancakes. I never bother by myself, you take your shoes off and put your feet up and read the paper, nonsense you'll do no such thing, I want to and anyway I'll enjoy it: would you perhaps love a bath, my pet?" The voice floated off into the hallway.

"Where's my goloshes, oh dear, oh here they are now how did they get that way, oh wait till I tell the wretch the cutlets are for you, he'll jump out of his skin . . ." The front door slammed. Arlette was home.

It was a nice evening. Bates brought Beaujolais – Beaujolais! "I remember you used to buy it, child, I hope you still like it. Cutlets."

"He practically went on his knees when he heard, with the tears in his eyes he swore on his mother's grave you'd be able to cut them with a fork and I just looked and said 'She'd better', that's all."

"Bananas – I've got some rum somewhere, hasn't been touched in five years I'd say, pah, all dusty, do you think it'll still be all right dear, not gone poisonous or anything, one never knows now, they put chemicals in to make things smell better, awful man in the supermarket and I swear he squirts the oranges with an aerosol thing to make them smell like oranges, forlorn hope is all I can say."

The rum was tasted, and pronounced fit for pancakes.

"And how's Amsterdam?" asked Arlette, laughing.

It wasn't what it was; it wasn't what it had been. Arlette had been prepared to be bored with old-maidish gush about how we don't sleep safe in our beds of nights, not like when we had a policeman in the house, which did give someone a sense of security somehow. She ought to have known better really, because old mother

Counterpoint had the tough dryness, the voluble energy, the inconsequent loquacity she expected – and indeed remembered, but the warm-hearted kindness was illuminated by a shrewd observation she had never given the old biddy credit for.

"Well, my dear, it would ill become me to complain. I'll have this flat for as long as I live and they can't put my rent up, I have to spread my butter thinner but I'm getting old and I need less of it. I have the sunshine still and the plants and my birds and they'll all last my time. I think it comes much harder on a girl your age, who can remember what things used to be, and who still has to move with the changes and accept them, whereas people expect me to be eccentric and silly. And I'm sorrier still for the young ones. They don't have any patterns to move by: it must give a terrible sense of insecurity and I think that's what makes them so unhappy. Everyone kowtows to them and it must be horrid really. Look at the word young, I mean it used to mean what it said and no more, young cheese or a young woman and that was that – and now they talk about a young chair or a young frock and it's supposed to mean good, and when you keep ascribing virtue to people, and implying all the time that they should be admired and imitated, well dear, it makes their life very difficult and wearisome; I used to know a holy nun and she said sometimes that everybody being convinced one was good made a heavy cross to carry. When the young do wicked things I can't help feeling that it's because they're dreadfully unhappy. Of course there's progress, lots and lots of progress, and it makes me very happy. I don't have many pupils now, but I'm always struck when they come, so tall and healthy and active, so unlike the pale little tots when I was a young woman, and I remember very hard times, my dear, all the men drunk always because their lives were so hard, but they don't seem to me any happier or more contented and they complain more because they expect much more. I can't really see what they mean talking about progress because that seems to me that people are good and get better and the fact is, my pet, as you and I know, people are born bad and tend to get worse and putting good before evil is always a dreadful struggle dear, whatever they say. One is so vain and so selfish."

And Arlette, who had had a good rest, a delicious bath, and a good supper, found herself pouring out her whole tale and most of her heart.

"Well," said Bates at the end with great commonsense, "that has done you a great deal of good my dear, and that's a fact, just like taking off one's stays, girls don't wear stays any more and they don't know what they miss."

Arlette felt inclined to argue that it was a good thing to be no longer obliged to wear stays.

"Of course dear, don't think I don't agree with you, healthy girls with good stomach muscles playing tennis, and no more of that fainting and vapouring. But I maintain that it was a good thing for a girl to know constraint. Sex education and women's lib, all dreadful cant. Girls who married without knowing the meaning of the word sex were sometimes very happy and sometimes very unhappy, and I don't believe they are any happier now. I married a sailor, dear, and learned how to go without."

"It doesn't make me any happier now," said Arlette dryly.

"No dear, and that's just what I felt in 1940 when my ship got torpedoed. So now let's be very sensible. You've come here very confused and embittered, and you don't want anything to do with the police, and you're probably quite right because really poor dears they've simply no notion, but at the present you've no notion either. You'd never of thought about asking my advice because I'm a silly old bag but I'll give it you, and it is that you probably can find out who killed your husband, because it's surprising what you can do when you try, but it's as well to have friends you can count on, and you can count on me for a start, and with that my dear we'll go to bed, your eyes are dropping out."

"Did you join the resistance, in 1940 I mean?" asked Arlette.

"Yes I did, and what's more once I threw a bomb at a bad man in the Euterpestraat, and that was a dreadful place, the Gestapo headquarters here in Amsterdam and it was very hard because I was horribly frightened of the bomb, and even more frightened of the bad man who had soldiers with him and most of all because I knew they would take hostages and execute them, but it had to be done, you see."

"I do see," said Arlette seriously, "it wasn't the moment to take off one's stays and feel comfortable."

"Right, my pet, right," said old mother Counterpoint.

Books

History and Society

Dedalo Carasso, *A Short History of Amsterdam*. Brief, socialist-slanted account, well illustrated with artefacts from the Historical Museum.

Geoffrey Cotterell, *Amsterdam*. Popularized, off-beat history giving a highly readable account of the city up to the late 1960s.

Pieter Geyl, *The Revolt of The Netherlands 1555–1609; The Netherlands in the Seventeenth Century 1609–1648*. Geyl's history of the Dutch-speaking peoples is the definitive account of Holland's history during its formative years, chronicling the uprising against the Spanish and the formation of the United Provinces. Quite the best thing you can read on the period.

Mark Girouard, *Cities and People: A Social and Architectural History*. Has an informed and well-illustrated chapter on the city's social history.

Christopher Hibbert, *Cities and Civilisation*. Includes a chapter on Amsterdam in the age of Rembrandt. Some interesting facts about seventeenth-century daily life.

J.H. Huizinga, *Dutch Civilisation in the 17th Century*. Analysis of life and culture in the Dutch Republic by the country's most widely respected historian.

J.L. Price, *Culture and Society in the Dutch Republic in the 17th Century*. An accurate, intelligent account of the Golden Age.

Simon Schama, *The Embarrassment of Riches: An Interpretation of Dutch Culture in the Golden Age*. The most recent – and one of the most accessible – works on the Golden Age, drawing on a wide variety of archive sources.

Jan Stoutenbeek et al, *A Guide to Jewish Amsterdam*. Fascinating, if perhaps overdetailed, guide to just about every Jewish monument in the city. You can purchase a copy before you leave from the *Netherlands Board of Tourism*, or in better Amsterdam bookshops.

Sir William Temple, *Observations upon the United Provinces of The Netherlands*. Written by a seventeenth-century English diplomat, and a good, evocative account of the country at the time.

Art and Architecture

Pierre Cabanne, *Van Gogh*. Standard mix of art criticism and biography, drawing heavily on the artist's own letters.

Kenneth Clark, *Civilisation*. Includes a warm and scholarly rundown on the Golden Age, with illuminating insights on the way in which the art reflected the period.

Eugene Fromentin, *The Masters of Past Time: Dutch and Flemish Painting from Van Eyck to Rembrandt*. Entertaining essays on the major Dutch and Flemish painters.

R.H. Fuchs, *Dutch Painting*. As complete an introduction to the subject – from Flemish origins to the present day – as you could wish for in just a couple of hundred pages.

Guus Kemme (ed.), *Amsterdam Architecture: A Guide*. Illustrated guide to the architecture of Amsterdam, with potted accounts of the major buildings.

Paul Overy, *De Stijl*. Recently published reassessment of all aspects of the De Stijl movement. Clearly written and comprehensive.

Christian Rheinwald, *Amsterdam Art Guide*. Comprehensive guide to the city's galleries, shops and contact points, for artists and those wanting to investigate the art scene.

Jacob Rosenberg et al, *Dutch Art and Architecture 1600–1800*. Full and erudite anthology of essays on the art and buildings of the Golden Age and after. For dedicated Dutch-art fans only.

Irving Stone, *Lust for Life*. Everything you ever wanted to know about Van Gogh in a pop genius-is-pain biography.

Christopher White, *Rembrandt*. The most widely available – and wide-ranging – study of the painter and his work.

Literature

Simon Carmiggelt, *Kronkels*. Second collection of Carmiggelt's "slight adventures", three of which are reprinted on pp.357–359.

Rudi van Dantzig, *For a Lost Soldier*. Honest and convincing tale, largely autobiographical, that tells of a young boy's sexual awakening against a background of war and liberation. See the extract on pp.361–363.

Anne Frank, *The Diary of a Young Girl*. Lucid and moving, the most revealing thing you can read on the plight of Amsterdam's Jews during the war years.

Nicolas Freeling, *A City Solitary; Love in Amsterdam; Cold Iron; Strike Out Where Not Applicable; A Long Silence*. Freeling writes detective novels, and his most famous creation is the rebel cop, Van der Valk, around whom a successful British TV series was made. Light, carefully crafted tales, with just the right amount of twists to make them classic cops 'n' robbers reading – and with good Amsterdam (and Dutch) locations. There's an extract from *A Long Silence* on pp.365–369.

Etty Hillesum, *Etty: An Interrupted Life*. Diary of an Amsterdam Jewish young woman uprooted from her life in the city and taken to Auschwitz, where she died. As with Anne Frank's more famous journal, penetratingly written – though on the whole much less readable.

Margo Minco, *The Fall; An Empty House; The Glass Bridge*. Prolific author and wartime survivor,

Minco is one of Holland's leading contemporary authors. Her work (especially *The Fall*) focuses on the city's Jewish community, particularly in the war years. See the extract from *An Empty House* on pp.363–365.

Harry Mulisch, *The Assault*. Set part in Haarlem, part in Amsterdam, this traces the story of a young boy who loses his family in a reprisal-raid by the Nazis. A powerful tale, made into an excellent and effective film.

Multatuli, *Max Havelaar: or the Coffee Auctions of the Dutch Trading Company*. Classic nineteenth-century Dutch satire of colonial life in the East Indies. Eloquent and, at times, amusing.

Cees Nooteboom, *Rituals*. An existentialist novel of the 1980s, mapping the empty existence of a rich Amsterdammer who dabbles in antiques. Bleak but absorbing. See the extract on pp359–361.

Jona Oberski, *Childhood*. First published in 1978, this is a Jewish child's eye-witness account of the war years, the camps and executions. Written with feeling and precision.

Janwillem van de Wetering, *Hard Rain*. An offbeat detective tale set in Amsterdam and provincial Holland. Like Van de Wetering's other stories, it's a humane, quirky and humorous story, worth reading for the characters and locations as much as for the inventive narrative.

David Veronese, *Jana*. A hip thriller set in the underworld of Amsterdam and London.

Jan Wolkers, *Turkish Delight*. Wolkers is one of The Netherlands' best-known artists and writers, and this is one of his early novels, a close examination of the relationship between a bitter, working-class sculptor and his young, middle-class wife. A compelling work, at times misogynistic and even offensive, by a writer who seeks reaction above all.

Language

It's unlikely that you'll need to speak anything other than English while you're in Amsterdam: the Dutch have a seemingly natural talent for languages, and your attempts at speaking theirs may be met with some amusement. Outside Amsterdam people aren't quite as cosmopolitan, but even so the following words and phrases of Dutch should be the most you'll need to get by; see also the detailed Food Glossary in *Basics*.

Pronunciation

Dutch is pronounced much the same as English, but with a few differences:

v is like the English f in **f**ar

w like the v in **v**at

j like the initial sound of **y**ellow

ch and **g** are like the Scottish lo**ch**

(the word for canal – *gracht* – has two of these sounds)

ng is as in bri**ng**

nj as in o**nj**on

y is not a consonant, but another way of writing **ij**

Otherwise, double consonants keep their separate sounds – **half**, for example, is pronounced "hul-uf", and **sch** is never like "shoe".

Doubling the letter lengthens the vowel sound:

a is like the English cat

aa like Ma or Pa

e like let

ee like late

ie as in see

o as in pop

oo in pope

oe as in soon

u is like wood

uu the French tu

ui, **au** and **ou** as in out

ei, **ij** and **y** as in fine

eu is like the diphthong in the French l**eu**r

Dutch numbers

When saying a number, the Dutch generally transpose the last two digits: for example, *drie guilden vijf en twintig* is ƒ3.25.

0	*nul*	18	*achttien*
1	*een*	19	*negentien*
2	*twee*	20	*twintig*
3	*drie*	21	*een en twintig*
4	*vier*	22	*twee en twintig*
5	*vijf*	30	*dertig*
6	*zes*	40	*veertig*
7	*zeven*	50	*vijftig*
8	*acht*	60	*zestig*
9	*negen*	70	*zeventig*
10	*tien*	80	*tachtig*
11	*elf*	90	*negentig*
12	*twaalf*	100	*honderd*
13	*dertien*	101	*honderd een*
14	*veertien*	200	*twee honderd*
15	*vijftien*	201	*twee honderd een*
16	*zestien*	500	*vijf honderd*
17	*zeventien*	1000	*duizend*

Dutch words and phrases

Basics and Greetings

Yes	*ja*
No	*nee*
Please	*alstublieft*
(No) Thank you	*(nee) dank u* or *bedankt*
Hello	*hallo* or *dag*
Good morning	*goedemorgen*
Good afternoon	*goedemiddag*
Good evening	*goedenavond*
Goodbye	*tot ziens*
See you later	*tot straks*
Do you speak English?	*spreekt u Engels?*
I don't understand	*Ik begrijp het niet*
Women/men	*vrouwen/mannen*
Children	*kinderen*
Men's/women's toilets	*heren/dames*

Other essentials

I want ...	*Ik wil ...*
I don't want ...	*Ik wil niet ...* (+verb) *Ik wil geen ...* (+noun)
How much is ... ?	*Wat kost ... ?*
Post office	*postkantoor*
Stamp(s)	*postzegel(s)*
Money exchange	*wisselkantoor*
Cash desk	*kassa*
How do I get to ... ?	*Hoe kom ik in ... ?*
Where is ... ?	*Waar is ... ?*
How far is it to ... ?	*Hoe ver is het naar ... ?*
When?	*Wanneer?*
Far/near	*ver/dichtbij*
Left/right	*links/rechts*
Straight ahead	*rechtuit gaan*
Platform	*spoor* or *perron*
Ticket office	*loket*
Here/there	*hier/daar*
Good/bad	*goed/slecht*
Big/small	*groot/klein*
Open/closed	*open/gesloten*

Push/pull	*duwen/trekken*
New/old	*nieuw/oud*
Cheap/expensive	*goedkoop/duur*
Hot/cold	*heet* or *warm/koud*
With/without	*met/zonder*

Days and Times

Sunday	*Zondag*
Monday	*Maandag*
Tuesday	*Dinsdag*
Wednesday	*Woensdag*
Thursday	*Donderdag*
Friday	*Vrijdag*
Saturday	*Zaterdag*
Yesterday	*gisteren*
Today	*vandaag*
Tomorrow	*morgen*
Tomorrow morning	*morgenochtend*
Year	*jaar*
Month	*maand*
Week	*week*
Day	*dag*
Hour	*uur*
Minute	*minuut*
What time is it?	*Hoe laat is het?*
It's ...	*Het is ...*
3.00	*drie uur*
3.05	*vijf over drie*
3.10	*tien over drie*
3.15	*kwart over drie*
3.20	*tien voor half vier*
3.25	*vijf voor half vier*
3.30	*half vier*
3.35	*vijf over half vier*
3.40	*tien over half vier*
3.45	*kwart voor vier*
3.50	*tien voor vier*
3.55	*vijf voor vier*
8am	*acht uur 's-ochtends*
1pm	*ein uur 's-middags*
8pm	*acht uur 's-avonds*
1am	*ein uur 's-nachts*

A Glossary of Dutch and Architectural Terms

AMBULATORY Covered passage around the outer edge of a choir of a church.

AMSTERDAMMERTJE Phallic-shaped objects set alongside Amsterdam streets to keep drivers off the pavements and out of the canals.

APSE Semicircular protrusion, usually at the east end of a church.

A.U.B. *Alstublieft* – "please" (also shown as **S.V.P.** from French).

BAROQUE High Renaissance period of art and architecture, distinguished by extreme ornateness.

BG *Begane grond* – "ground floor" ("basement" is **K** for *kelder*).

BRUG Bridge.

BTW *Belasting Toegevoegde Waarde* – VAT.

BURGHER Member of the upper or mercantile classes of a town, usually with certain civic powers.

CABINET-PIECE Small, finely detailed painting of a domestic scene.

CARILLON A set of tuned church bells, either operated by an automatic mechanism or played by a keyboard.

FIETSPAD Cycle path.

GASTHUIS Hospice for the sick or infirm.

GEEN TOEGANG No entry.

GEMEENTE Municipal; e.g. *Gemeentehuis* – "town hall."

GEZELLIG A hard term to translate – something like "cosy", "comfortable" and "inviting" in one – which is often said to lie at the heart of the Dutch psyche. A long, relaxed meal in a favourite restaurant with friends is *gezellig*; grabbing a quick snack is not. The best brown cafés ooze *gezelligheid*; Kalverstraat on a Saturday afternoon definitely doesn't.

GESLOTEN Closed.

GEVEL Gable. The only decoration practical on the narrow-fronted canal house was on its

gables. Initially fairly simple, they developed into an ostentatious riot of individualism in the late seventeenth century before turning to a more restrained classicism in the eighteenth and nineteenth centuries.

GRACHT Canal.

GRATIS TOEGANG Free admission.

HIJSTBALK Pulley beam, often decorated, affixed to the top of a gable to lift goods, furniture etc. Essential in canal houses whose staircases were narrow and steep, *hijstbalken* are still very much in use today.

HOF Courtyard.

HOFJE Almshouse, usually for elderly women who could look after themselves but needed small charities such as food and fuel; usually a number of buildings centred around a small, peaceful courtyard.

HUIS House.

KERK Church.

KONINKLIJK Royal.

LET OP! Attention!

MARKT Central town square and the heart of most Dutch communities, usually still the site of weekly markets.

MISERICORD Ledge on choir stall on which occupant can be supported while standing; often carved.

MOKUM A Yiddish word meaning "city", originally used by the Jewish community to indicate Amsterdam; now in general usage as a nickname for the city.

NEDERLAND The Netherlands.

NEDERLANDS Dutch.

NEOCLASSICAL Architectural style derived from Greek and Roman elements – pillars, domes, colonnades, etc – popular in the Netherlands during French rule in the early nineteenth century.

NOODUITGANG Emergency exit.

OOST East.

POLDER An area of land reclaimed from the sea.

POSTBUS PO Box.

PLEIN A square or open space.

RAADHUIS Town hall.

RIJK State.

SPIONNETJE Small mirror on a canal house enabling the occupant to see who is at the door without descending the stairs.

STADHUIS Most commonly used word for a town hall.

STEEG Alley.

STICHTING Charitable institute or foundation.

STEDELIJK Civic, municipal.

STRAAT Street.

T/M *Tot en met* – "up to and including".

TOEGANG Entrance.

UITGANG Exit.

V.A. *Vanaf* – "from".

V.S. *Verenigde Staten* – "United States".

WAAG Old public weighing house, a common feature of most towns – usually found on the *Markt.*

WEG Way.

WIJK District (of a city).

Z.O.Z. Please turn over (page, leaflet etc).

ZUID South.

Index

direct orders from

Amsterdam	1-85828-218-7	UK£8.99	US$14.95	CAN$19.99
Andalucia	1-85828-219-5	9.99	16.95	22.99
Australia	1-85828-220-9	13.99	21.95	29.99
Bali	1-85828-134-2	8.99	14.95	19.99
Barcelona	1-85828-221-7	8.99	14.95	19.99
Berlin	1-85828-129-6	8.99	14.95	19.99
Belgium & Luxembourg	1-85828-222-5	10.99	17.95	23.99
Brazil	1-85828-223-3	13.99	21.95	29.99
Britain	1-85828-208-X	12.99	19.95	25.99
Brittany & Normandy	1-85828-224-1	9.99	16.95	22.99
Bulgaria	1-85828-183-0	9.99	16.95	22.99
California	1-85828-181-4	10.99	16.95	22.99
Canada	1-85828-130-X	10.99	14.95	19.99
China	1-85828-225-X	15.99	24.95	32.99
Corfu	1-85828-226-8	8.99	14.95	19.99
Corsica	1-85828-227-6	9.99	16.95	22.99
Costa Rica	1-85828-136-9	9.99	15.95	21.99
Crete	1-85828-132-6	8.99	14.95	18.99
Cyprus	1-85828-182-2	9.99	16.95	22.99
Czech & Slovak Republics	1-85828-121-0	9.99	16.95	22.99
Egypt	1-85828-188-1	10.99	17.95	23.99
Europe	1-85828-289-6	14.99	19.95	25.99
England	1-85828-160-1	10.99	17.95	23.99
First Time Europe	1-85828-270-5	7.99	9.95	12.99
Florida	1-85828-184-4	10.99	16.95	22.99
France	1-85828-228-4	12.99	19.95	25.99
Germany	1-85828-128-8	11.99	17.95	23.99
Goa	1-85828-275-6	8.99	14.95	19.99
Greece	1-85828-300-0	12.99	19.95	25.99
Greek Islands	1-85828-163-6	8.99	14.95	19.99
Guatemala	1-85828-189-X	10.99	16.95	22.99
Hawaii: Big Island	1-85828-158-X	8.99	12.95	16.99
Hawaii	1-85828-206-3	10.99	16.95	22.99
Holland	1-85828-229-2	10.99	17.95	23.99
Hong Kong	1-85828-187-3	8.99	14.95	19.99
Hungary	1-85828-123-7	8.99	14.95	19.99
India	1-85828-200-4	14.99	23.95	31.99
Ireland	1-85828-179-2	10.99	17.95	23.99
Italy	1-85828-167-9	12.99	19.95	25.99
Jamaica	1-85828-230-6	9.99	16.95	22.99
Kenya	1-85828-192-X	11.99	18.95	24.99
London	1-85828-231-4	9.99	15.95	21.99
Mallorca & Menorca	1-85828-165-2	8.99	14.95	19.99
Malaysia, Singapore & Brunei	1-85828-232-2	11.99	18.95	24.99
Mexico	1-85828-044-3	10.99	16.95	22.99
Morocco	1-85828-040-0	9.99	16.95	21.99
Moscow	1-85828-118-0	8.99	14.95	19.99
Nepal	1-85828-190-3	10.99	17.95	23.99
New York	1-85828-296-9	9.99	15.95	21.99
Norway	1-85828-234-9	10.99	17.95	23.99
Pacific Northwest	1-85828-092-3	9.99	14.95	19.99
Paris	1-85828-235-7	8.99	14.95	19.99

In the UK, Rough Guides are available from all good bookstores, but can be obtained from Penguin by contacting: Penguin Direct, Penguin Books Ltd, Bath Road, Harmondsworth, West Drayton, Middlesex UB7 0DA; or telephone the credit line on 0181-899 4036 (9am–5pm) and ask for Penguin Direct. Visa and Access accepted. Delivery will normally be within 14 working days. Penguin Direct ordering facilities are only available in the UK and the USA. The availability and published prices quoted are correct at the time of going to press but are subject to alteration without prior notice.

around the world

Poland	1-85828-168-7	10.99	17.95	23.99
Portugal	1-85828-180-6	9.99	16.95	22.99
Prague	1-85828-122-9	8.99	14.95	19.99
Provence	1-85828-127-X	9.99	16.95	22.99
Pyrenees	1-85828-093-1	8.99	15.95	19.99
Rhodes & the Dodecanese	1-85828-120-2	8.99	14.95	19.99
Romania	1-85828-097-4	9.99	15.95	21.99
San Francisco	1-85828-185-7	8.99	14.95	19.99
Scandinavia	1-85828-236-5	12.99	20.95	27.99
Scotland	1-85828-166-0	9.99	16.95	22.99
Sicily	1-85828-178-4	9.99	16.95	22.99
Singapore	1-85828-237-3	8.99	14.95	19.99
South Africa	1-85828-238-1	12.99	19.95	25.99
Soutwest USA	1-85828-239-X	10.99	16.95	22.99
Spain	1-85828-240-3	11.99	18.95	24.99
St Petersburg	1-85828-133-4	8.99	14.95	19.99
Sweden	1-85828-241-1	10.99	17.95	23.99
Thailand	1-85828-140-7	10.99	17.95	24.99
Tunisia	1-85828-139-3	10.99	17.95	24.99
Turkey	1-85828-242-X	12.99	19.95	25.99
Tuscany & Umbria	1-85828-243-8	10.99	17.95	23.99
USA	1-85828-161-X	14.99	19.95	25.99
Venice	1-85828-170-9	8.99	14.95	19.99
Vietnam	1-85828-191-1	9.99	15.95	21.99
Wales	1-85828-245-4	10.99	17.95	23.99
Washington DC	1-85828-246-2	8.99	14.95	19.99
West Africa	1-85828-101-6	15.99	24.95	34.99
More Women Travel	1-85828-098-2	10.99	16.95	22.99
Zimbabwe & Botswana	1-85828-186-5	11.99	18.95	24.99
Phrasebooks				
Czech	1-85828-148-2	3.50	5.00	7.00
French	1-85828-144-X	3.50	5.00	7.00
German	1-85828-146-6	3.50	5.00	7.00
Greek	1-85828-145-8	3.50	5.00	7.00
Italian	1-85828-143-1	3.50	5.00	7.00
Mexican	1-85828-176-8	3.50	5.00	7.00
Portuguese	1-85828-175-X	3.50	5.00	7.00
Polish	1-85828-174-1	3.50	5.00	7.00
Spanish	1-85828-147-4	3.50	5.00	7.00
Thai	1-85828-177-6	3.50	5.00	7.00
Turkish	1-85828-173-3	3.50	5.00	7.00
Vietnamese	1-85828-172-5	3.50	5.00	7.00
Reference				
Classical Music	1-85828-113-X	12.99	19.95	25.99
European Football	1-85828-256-X	14.99	23.95	31.99
Internet	1-85828-288-8	5.00	8.00	10.00
Jazz	1-85828-137-7	16.99	24.95	34.99
Opera	1-85828-138-5	16.99	24.95	34.99
Reggae	1-85828-247-0	12.99	19.95	25.99
Rock	1-85828-201-2	17.99	26.95	35.00
World Music	1-85828-017-6	16.99	22.95	29.99

the perfect getaway vehicle

low-price holiday car rental.

rent a car from holiday autos and you'll give yourself real freedom to explore your holiday destination. with great-value, fully-inclusive rates in over 4,000 locations worldwide, wherever you're escaping to, we're there to make sure you get excellent prices and superb service.

what's more, you can book now with complete confidence. our £5 undercut* ensures that you are guaranteed the best value for money in holiday destinations right around the globe.

drive away with a great deal, call holiday autos now on **0990 300 400** and quote ref RG.

holiday autos miles ahead

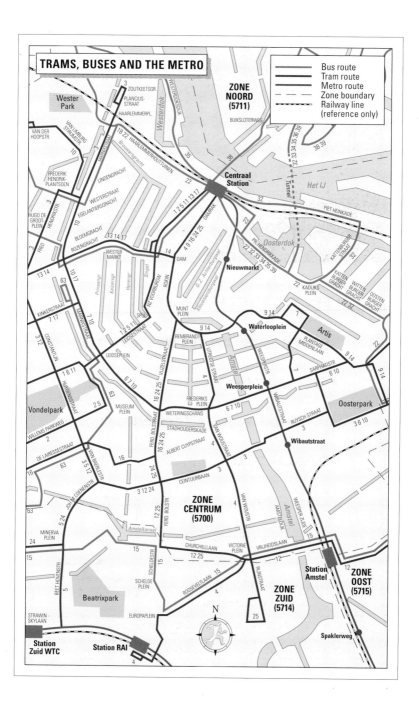

TRAMS, BUSES AND THE METRO

Bus route	
Tram route	
Metro route	
Zone boundary	
Railway line (reference only)	

Wester Park

ZONE NOORD (5711)

ZOUTKEETSGR
PLANCIUS-STRAAT
HAARLEMMERPL.
BUIKSLOTERWEG
Westerdok
Westerdoksdijk

VAN DER HOOPSTR.
VAN LIMBURG STIRUMSTR.
FREDERIK HENDRIK-PLANTSOEN
HUGO DE GROOT-PLEIN
FRED
HENDRIKSTR
LINDENGRACHT
WESTERSTRAAT
EGELANTIERSGRACHT
BLOEMGRACHT
ROZENGRACHT
WESTER MARKT

Brouwersgracht
HAARLEMMERHOUTTUINEN
18 22
35
38
32 33 34 35 36 39
38 39

Centraal Station

Het IJ
Tunnel
PIET HEINKADE

22
Oosterdok
PRL HENDRIKKADE
22 32 33 34 35 39
KADIJKS PLEIN
22
KATTEN BURGER GRACHT
WITTEN BURGER GRACHT
OOSTEN BURGER GRACHT
KATTENBURGER STRAAT
32

KINKERSTRAAT
7 17
3 12
CONSTANTIJN
HUYGENSSTRAAT
MARNIXSTRAAT
13 14
10 17
63
10 17
10
DAM
14
4 3 16 24 25
ROKIN
NZ VOORBURGW
SPUI
MUNT PLEIN
9 14
PN
LEIDSESTRAAT
1 2 5 11
Singel
Herengr
Keizersgr
Prinsengr
Nieuwmarkt
O.Z. Achterburgwal
Kloveniersburgwal

Waterlooplein
9 14
1
Artis
PLANTAGE MIDDENLAAN
9 14
22

REMBRANDT PLEIN
LEIDSEPLEIN
UTRECHTSE-STRAAT
WEESPERSTR
SARPHATISTR
6 10
9 14

Vondelpark
1 6 11
2 5
63
6 7 10
16 24 25
VLZELSTRAAT
FREDERIKS PLEIN
WETERINGSCHANS
MUSEUM PLEIN
FERD BOLSTRAAT
STADHOUDERSKADE
ALBERT CUYPSTRAAT
Weesperplein
6 7 10
WIBAUTSTRAAT
RUYSCH STRAAT
3
Oosterpark
3 6 10
Amstel
VAN WOUSTRAAT

WILLEMS PARKWEG
2
DE LAIRESSESTRAAT
63
3 5 12
16
VAN BAERLESTR
16
24
4
CEINTUURBAAN
3 12 24
12 25
FERD BOLSTR
3
Wibautstraat
4

JOHAN COENENSTR.
63
5 24
Amstelkanaal
ZONE CENTRUM (5700)
CHURCHILLLAAN
12 25
VICTORIE PLEIN
VAN WOUSTR
VRIJHEIDSLAAN
12
15
Amstel
AMSTELDIJK
WEESPER ZIJDE
RIJNSTRAAT

MINERVA PLEIN
24
15
SCHELDESTR
15
ROOSEVELTLAAN
15
SCHELDE PLEIN
4
ZONE ZUID (5714)
25
Station Amstel
ZONE OOST (5715)
12

Beatrixpark
5
STRAWIN-SKYLAAN
EUROPAPLEIN
N
Spaklerweg

Station Zuid WTC
Station RAI
4
BEET HOVENSTR

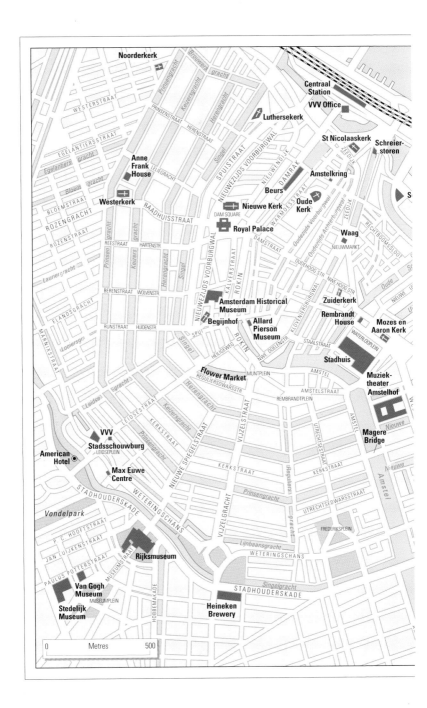

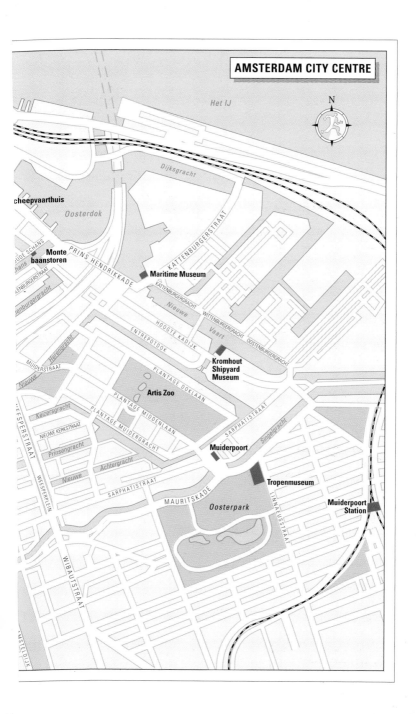

AMSTERDAM CITY CENTRE

N

Het IJ

Dijksgracht

cheepvaarthuis

Oosterdok

OUDE SCHANS

Monte
baanstoren

PRINS HENDRIKKADE

KATTENBURGERSTRAAT

Maritime Museum

KATTENBURGERGRACHT

Nieuwe

WITTENBURGERGRACHT

Vaart

OOSTENBURGERGRACHT

HOOGTE KADIJK

ENTREPOTDOK

Kromhout
Shipyard
Museum

MUIDERSTRAAT

Herengracht

Nieuwe

PLANTAGE DOKLAAN

PLANTAGE MIDDENLAAN

Artis Zoo

Keizersgracht

NIEUWE KERKSTRAAT

PLANTAGE MUIDERGRACHT

SARPHATISTRAAT

Singelgracht

Prinsengracht

WESPERSTRAAT

Achtergracht

Muiderpoort

WESPERPLEIN

Nieuwe

SARPHATISTRAAT

Tropenmuseum

Muiderpoort
Station

MAURITSKADE

Oosterpark

LINNAEUSSTRAAT

WIBAUTSTRAAT

AMSTELDIJK

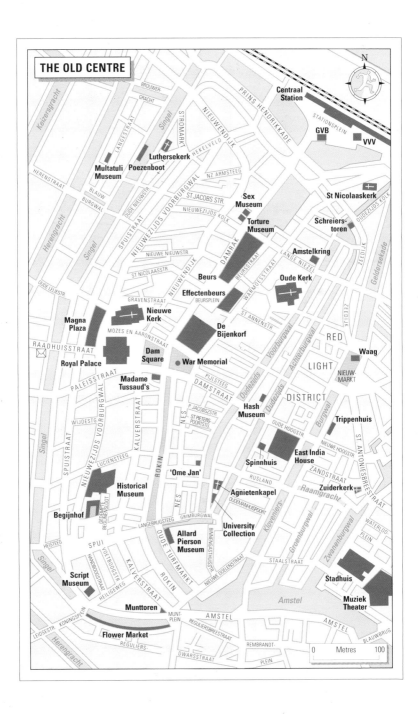

THE OLD CENTRE

N

Centraal Station

GVB
VVV

STATIONSPLEIN

PRINS HENDRIKKADE

Lutherskerk
Poezenboot

Multatuli
Museum

St Nicolaaskerk

Sex
Museum

Schreiers-
toren

Torture
Museum

Amstelkring

Beurs

Oude Kerk

Effectenbeurs
BEURSPLEIN

Magna
Plaza

Nieuwe
Kerk

De Bijenkorf

RED

Dam
Square

Waag

Royal Palace

War Memorial

LIGHT

NIEUW-
MARKT

RAADHUISSTRAAT

Madame
Tussaud's

DISTRICT

Hash
Museum

Trippenhuis

Spinnhuis

East India
House

'Ome Jan'

Historical
Museum

Agnietenkapel

Zuiderkerk

University
Collection

Begijnhof

Allard
Pierson
Museum

Script
Museum

Stadhuis

Munttoren

Muziek
Theater

Flower Market

Amstel

Amstel

0   Metres   100

BLAUWBRUG